Heart & Mind

Heart & Mind

THE PRACTICE OF CARDIAC PSYCHOLOGY

Edited by

Robert Allan, PhD, and Stephen Scheidt, MD

American Psychological Association
Washington, DC

Published by
American Psychological Association
750 First Street, NE
Washington, DC 20002

Copies may be ordered from
APA Order Department
P.O. Box 2710
Hyattsville, MD 20784

In the UK and Europe, copies may be ordered from
American Psychological Association
3 Henrietta Street
Covent Garden, London
WC2E 8LU England

Typeset in Goudy by PRO-Image Corporation, Techna-Type Div., York, PA

Printer: Data Reproductions Corp., Rochester Hills, MI
Cover Designer: Graphic Answers, Arlington, VA
Technical/Production Editor: Molly R. Flickinger

Library of Congress Cataloging-in-Publication Data
Heart and mind : the practice of cardiac psychology / edited by Robert
    Allan and Stephen Scheidt.
        p.   cm.
    Includes bibliographical references and indexes.
    ISBN 1-55798-356-9 (acid-free paper)
    1. Coronary heart disease—Psychological aspects.   2. Type A
behavior.   I. Allan, Robert, 1945–   .   II. Scheidt, Stephen S.
RC685.C6H35   1996
616.1'23'0019—dc20   96-10543
                                                                              CIP

British Library Cataloguing-in-Publication Data
A CIP record is available from the British Library

Printed in the United States of America
First edition

CONTENTS

CONTRIBUTORS

Robert Allan, PhD, Clinical Assistant Professor of Psychology in Medicine and Psychiatry, Cornell University Medical College, and Co-Director, The Coronary Risk Reduction Program, The New York Hospital–Cornell Medical Center

Herbert Benson, MD, Associate Professor of Medicine, Harvard Medical School; President of the Mind/Body Medical Institute; Chief of the Division of Behavorial Medicine, Deaconess Hospital, Harvard Medical School; and Co-Editor in Chief of *Mind/Body Medicine*

James H. Billings, PhD, Senior Vice President and Director of Institute Operations, Preventive Medicine Research Institute, Sausalito, CA

Paul E. Bracke, PhD, Psychologist, Meyer Friedman Institute, University of California, San Francisco–Mount Zion Medical Center

Gunilla Burell, PhD, Assistant Professor of Psychology, Centre for Caring Sciences, Uppsala University, Uppsala, Sweden

Marianne Delon, MSW, Cardiac Care and Surgical Intensive Care Units, The New York Hospital–Cornell Medical Center

Jeffrey Fisher, MD, Clinical Associate Professor of Medicine, Cornell University Medical College, and Associate Attending Physician, The New York Hospital–Cornell Medical Center

Nancy Fleischmann, BA, Type A Interviewer, Meyer Friedman Institute, University of California, San Francisco–Mount Zion Medical Center

Meyer Friedman, MD, Founder and Director, Meyer Friedman Institute, University of California, San Francisco–Mount Zion Medical Center

Richard Friedman, PhD, Professor of Psychiatry, Department of Psychiatry and Behavioral Science, Division of Behavioral Medicine, School of Medicine, State University of New York at Stony Brook, and Co-Editor in Chief, *Mind/Body Medicine*

Jeffrey P. Gold, MD, Professor of Cardiothoracic Surgery, Cornell University Medical College, and Attending Cardiothoracic Surgeon, The New York Hospital–Cornell Medical Center

Peter Halperin, MD, Instructor in Psychiatry, Harvard and Tufts Medical Schools, Boston

Sue C. Jacobs, PhD, Associate Professor, Director of Counseling Psychology Training Program, Department of Counseling, University of North Dakota, Grand Forks

Sharon Krass, Research Associate, Department of Psychiatry and Behavioral Science, Division of Behavioral Medicine, School of Medicine, State University of New York at Stony Brook

Andrew Littman, MD, Associate Psychiatrist, Massachusetts General Hospital; Instructor in Psychiatry, Harvard Medical School; and Director of Behavorial Medicine, Division of Preventive Cardiology, Massachusetts General Hospital

Patricia Myers, Research Associate, Department of Psychiatry and Behavioral Science, Division of Behavioral Medicine, School of Medicine, State University of New York at Stony Brook

Dean M. Ornish, MD, President and Director, Preventive Medicine Research Institute, Sausalito, CA

Thomas G. Pickering, MD, D Phil, Professor of Medicine, Cornell University Medical College, and Attending Physician, The New York Hospital–Cornell Medical Center

Lynda H. Powell, PhD, Associate Professor and Director, Section of Epidemiology, Department of Preventive Medicine, Rush–Presbyterian–St. Luke's Medical Center, Rush University, Chicago

Virginia A. Price, PhD, Psychologist, Meyer Friedman Institute, University of California, San Francisco–Mount Zion Medical Center

William Clifford Roberts, MD, Director, Baylor Cardiovascular Institute, Baylor University Medical College, Dallas, TX, and Editor in Chief, *American Journal of Cardiology*

Stephen Scheidt, MD, Professor of Clinical Medicine and Director of the Cardiology Training Program, Cornell University Medical College; Co-Director, The Coronary Risk Reduction Program, and Attending Physician, The New York Hospital–Cornell Medical Center

Larry W. Scherwitz, PhD, Director of Research, Preventive Medicine Research Institute, Sausalito, CA

Leonard Schwartzburd, PhD, Director of Psychological Services, Clinical Institute of Behavioral Medicine, Berkeley, CA

Jane B. Sherwood, RN, Institute for Prevention of Cardiovascular Disease, Deaconess Hospital, Harvard University, and Coordinator, Determinants of Time of Myocardial Infarction Onset Study

Stephen Sparler, MA, Senior Research Associate, Preventive Medicine Research Institute, Sausalito, CA

Richard A. Stein, MD, Professor of Medicine, State University of New York Health Science Center, Brooklyn, and Director of Prevention and Rehabilitation Cardiology, Lenox Hill Hospital, NY

Rick Sullivan, MS, Psychotherapist and Consultant, Preventive Medicine Research Institute's Retreat Program, Sausalito, CA

Katayoun Tabrizi, MD, Clinical Associate, Psychiatry and Behavorial Sciences, Duke University Medical Center, Durham, NC, and Staff Psychiatrist, Affective Disorder Unit, John Umstead Hospital, Butner, NC

Carl E. Thoresen, PhD, Professor of Psychology, School of Education, Stanford University

Diane K. Ulmer, RN, MS, Managing Partner, Ulmer and Associates, and Clinical Director, Clinical Institute of Behavioral Medicine, Berkeley, CA

Redford B. Williams, Jr., MD, Professor of Psychiatry and Behavorial Sciences, and Director of the Behavioral Medicine Research Center, Duke University Medical Center, Durham, NC

FOREWORD

Heart and Mind: The Practice of Cardiac Psychology is an important volume that introduces a new era in the treatment of heart disease. Although the field is relatively new, the practice of cardiac psychology has the potential to significantly reduce the human and economic costs of heart disease.

Millions of people still believe the myth that cancer is the greatest threat to their health. They are wrong. Heart disease remains the Number 1 killer of Americans, and it threatens more people every day. In 1993, heart and vascular diseases killed nearly one million Americans, almost as many as cancer, accidents, pneumonia, influenza, and all other causes of death combined.[1] The annual American death toll from cardiovascular disease exceeds by nearly two thirds the combined combat death tolls for Americans from both world wars, the Korean War, and the Vietnam War (*Academic American Encyclopedia*, 1990). Every 33 seconds, an American dies because of cardiovascular disease (American Heart Association, 1995).

Heart disease touches the lives of all Americans. Some form of heart disease afflicts more than 1 in 4 people. This year alone, approximately 1.5 million Americans will have a heart attack, the major manifestation of the disease. About one third of heart attack patients will die. In addition, contrary to the misconception that heart disease affects only middle-aged men, half of the deaths from coronary heart disease occur in women. Twice as many women die each year of heart and vascular diseases than die of all forms of cancer.

All statistics (except data on wars) are from the American Heart Association's (1995) *Heart and Stroke Facts: 1996 Statistical Supplement*.

In addition to the effects of heart disease on the health of the population, its economic impact is staggering. For 1996, the cost of heart disease is estimated to reach $151 billion: $129 billion in direct health expenditures and $21 billion in indirect costs of lost output from affected workers.

Although the health and economic impacts of heart disease continue to be discouraging, there is a bright side. Physicians are learning enough about heart disease to make a difference for their patients. However, the power of this information will remain underused unless doctors can convince patients to make the lifestyle changes necessary to promote cardiovascular health. A heart attack is sudden, but the buildup of plaque and scar tissue takes place over many years. As physicians, we are in a position to educate, that is, to dispel some of the myths among patients about their disease.

Often patients have said to me, "Dr. Cooley, thanks for making my heart as good as new." Although such words are gratifying, patients with heart disease need to realize that medical and interventional treatments are not cures. Although their lives may be saved by coronary angioplasty or coronary artery bypass graft surgery, patients must understand that their hearts will never be "as good as new." What we physicians have given them is another chance: We have temporarily "bypassed" their disease. To receive the most benefit from treatment, patients should modify their lifestyles to eliminate or decrease the risk factors that contributed to their disease. For patients to modify risk factors, cardiologists and cardiovascular surgeons need to recognize the importance of treating the entire patient, because heart disease can ravage the mind as well as the body. As Hippocrates admonished, "You ought not to attempt to cure the body without the soul . . . and this . . . is the reason why the cure of many diseases is unknown to physicians . . . because they disregard the whole" (Plato, 1871/1953, p. 103). Psychosocial factors such as stress, Type A behavior pattern, anger and hostility, and social isolation have all been linked to heart disease. Peer or family support can alleviate these factors. Other modifiable risk factors—smoking, a sedentary lifestyle, diet, and hypertension—also have behavioral components. Each of these psychosocial factors is discussed in *Heart and Mind*.

Throughout the 50 years of my practice, I have become increasingly aware that lifestyle intervention is important for my patients. All patients with heart disease can benefit from this approach to treatment. Although most surgeons (and cardiologists) acknowledge the importance of eliminating or decreasing risk factors, they need to become more active and systematic in ensuring that patients receive counseling for enacting a lifestyle intervention. These positive changes in health habits must occur both at home and at work. Patients must be actively encouraged to eat less dietary cholesterol and saturated fats, to stop smoking, to control their blood pressure, and to become more physically fit. Encouraging lifestyle intervention needs to become a therapy as standard as prescribing medications or performing surgery or angioplasty.

We could all begin by reading *Heart and Mind*. The editors are experts in their fields, as are the other contributors; all are respected researchers and clinicians. The editors have divided the book into four parts that encompass the spectrum of cardiac psychology: (a) an introduction to the field, with a wonderful history and an excellent description of the atherosclerotic process; (b) relevant clinical trials, including the Lifestyle Heart Trial and the Recurrent Coronary Prevention Project; (c) useful clinical techniques and interventions (including helpful information for the partners of heart patients); and (d) the practice of cardiac psychology, with an emphasis on the future.

The obvious audience for this book includes cardiac surgeons, cardiologists, psychiatrists, psychologists, social workers, and nurses who care for heart patients. However, the lifestyle interventions proposed are so worthwhile that anyone interested in promoting a heart-healthy lifestyle should be interested in this work. In the new world of managed care, primary care physicians will take more responsibility for such preventive care. Thus, they too should know the lessons that can be learned from this volume.

Never before has the heart revealed so many of its secrets. Cardiovascular disease is not inevitable, even though a few risk factors (mainly gender and heredity) are beyond human control. Moreover, effective methods for treating cardiovascular disease do exist. Still, the dramatic techniques for treating heart disease that are available today will never benefit everyone who has the disease. Thus, preventive measures must become the primary means used to control or forestall this too prevalent disease. The growing emphasis on each individual's active participation in preventing heart disease is an immense sign of hope. Until heart disease is conquered, however, everyone should heed the message of *Heart and Mind* and widely and systematically promote lifestyle intervention. Only by controlling their risk will patients be assured of their best chance for living a long and full life.

DENTON A. COOLEY, MD
President and Surgeon-in-Chief
Texas Heart Institute

REFERENCES

Academic American Encyclopedia (Vols. 12, 19, & 20). (1990). Danbury, CT: Grolier.

American Heart Association. (1995). *Heart and stroke facts: 1996 statistical supplement*. Dallas, TX: Author.

Plato. (1953). *The dialogues of Plato* (B. Jowett, Trans.). Oxford, England: Jowett Copyright Trustee. (Original work published 1871)

PREFACE

This book is a natural outgrowth of a journey that began in 1981 with a visit by Dr. Robert Allan to Dr. Meyer Friedman and his staff. This visit was prompted by an interest in Type A behavior that resulted from Allan's father's first heart attack at the age of 46. At the time, Friedman and Rosenman's *Type-A Behavior and Your Heart* was a best-seller, and the Recurrent Coronary Prevention Project—the first major clinical trial for modification of Type A behavior—was getting underway. Coincidentally, shortly after this visit, Allan was referred his first cardiac patient for psychotherapy.

After considerable study and psychological treatment of a few patients with coronary heart disease (CHD), Allan gave a lecture on Type A behavior to a group of cardiovascular social workers at Columbia University. He was subsequently invited by one of the attendees to lead a Type A behavior modification group at the Nassau County, New York, chapter of the American Heart Association. After some success with this program, Allan invited Dr. Stephen Scheidt to sit in on a stress reduction group. Subsequently, Scheidt invited Allan to study cardiology at the New York Hospital–Cornell Medical Center. So began a collaboration between psychology and cardiology that has resulted in this volume.

At first, at the medical center, it seemed to Allan that the vast majority of patients with cardiac disease were scarcely interested in psychotherapy, and he saw little relationship between psychological factors and many of the patients' illnesses. The cardiologists appeared to have little time to consider psychological issues; however, occasionally, patients who were unusually anxious or tense would be referred to Allan to discuss personal issues and, sometimes, to learn the relaxation response (see chap. 14). Gradually, the cardiology staff began to take more notice of psychological issues, especially as they related to CHD.

A formal Coronary Risk Reduction Program was eventually established at the New York Hospital–Cornell Medical Center, and, shortly thereafter, a satellite program was set up at the Coronary Detection and Intervention Center of the 92nd Street YM–YWHA in New York City. Now, several years later, these programs—and many others like them at hospitals, cardiac rehabilitation centers, and other locales all over the country—provide assistance to patients who have cardiac diseases. Research collaboration has developed between psychologists and cardiologists in several areas, including "triggers" of acute myocardial infarction.

Why did one cardiologist respond to one psychologist, and why should cardiologists (and internists, family practitioners, or primary care physicians) pay attention to this emerging body of knowledge we call *cardiac psychology*? Because, despite the major triumphs of medical research in this century, researchers do not really understand the basic biology of atherosclerosis. Researchers and practitioners have made a good start on reducing death and disability due to CHD, but it remains by far the leading killer of both men and women, and, as every physician senses (even those not familiar with the scientific studies), the extraordinary reductions in CHD in the United States over the past 35 years have resulted less from high-tech medical interventions than from lifestyle changes made by people themselves. Psychological factors are so clearly involved in lifestyle choices that—grudgingly at first, but with increasing enthusiasm—Scheidt and other members of the Division of Cardiology at the New York Hospital–Cornell Medical Center welcomed the chance to learn more about psychological issues and the application of psychological techniques to the care of cardiac patients without the requirement of a diagnosis of psychiatric "disease."

Physicians have long recognized that the standard coronary risk factors (age, gender, hyperlipidemia, smoking, hypertension, and sedentary lifestyle) are not terribly reliable predictors of CHD in any one individual (or of recurrence in those who already have CHD). Psychological factors may provide at least part of the missing link in understanding this disease. Although there is continuing controversy over some psychological factors, the strength of the links between specific factors and CHD is striking.

Every physician knows instinctively of the enormous influence that the psyche has on patients' well-being and functioning. The opportunity presented by collaboration between cardiology and psychology in day-to-day work in a hospital—or by reading this book—must be taken to improve practitioners' ability to heal patients. We hope this volume will increase awareness of the relationship between psychological and physiological factors as they dually influence cardiac health. We hope as well to encourage medical and mental health professionals to work together in their quest to heal.

ROBERT ALLAN
STEPHEN SCHEIDT

ACKNOWLEDGMENTS

Many people have helped along the path in this collaboration between psychology and cardiology. Francoise Richards, RN, referred that first cardiac patient to Robert Allan. The Psychosocial Committee and, particularly, Dr. Emanual Plesent at the Nassau County, New York, chapter of the American Heart Association, were early supporters of perhaps the first Type A behavior modification group in the New York metropolitan area. Also at the Nassau Heart Association at that time and deserving thanks are Alton Blakeslee, Barbara Blaustein, Flora Kletsky, and Joyce Spencer. Donald Farmer, former director of the association, coined the phrase "Heart and Mind" for one of the first conferences on the East Coast in this young field and was immensely helpful in supporting psychosocial intervention for cardiac patients.

Among our colleagues are a number of psychologists, psychiatrists, and physicians who helped during the earlier years of cardiac psychology practice, including Kul Chadda, MD; Martin V. Cohen, PhD; Sidney Finkle, MD; Herbert Friedman, PhD; Michael Jason, MD; Niki Kantrowitz, MD; Shari R. Midoneck, MD; Tana Nilchaikovit, MD; Gary Paluba, PhD; Kathleen Porrego, MD; George Striker, PhD; Drorit Tamari, MS; Allen R. Weiss, PhD; Edward Wolf, MD; and Steven Zeldes, MD.

At the New York Hospital–Cornell Medical Center (NYH-CMC) Cardiovascular Center, cardiologists and other physicians who have been supportive of our work include Drs. Holly Andersen, Dory Altman, Deborah Ascheim, Olivier Ameisen, Phyllis August, Jonathan Bella, Geoffrey Bergman, Jon Blumenfeld, Jeffrey Borer, Norman Brachfeld, Robert Campagna, Jean Cacciabaudo, Bruce Charash, James Christodoulou, Richard Devereux, Howard Eisenstein, Erica Engelstein, Jeffrey Fisher, Jack Flyer, Richard Fuchs, Barbara Gerling, Harvey Goldberg, Gregory Gustafson, Rebecca Hahn, Edmund Herrold, Clare Hochreiter, Donna Ingram, Lawrence Inra, Rajiv Jauhar, Erica Jones, Mazen Kamen, Lawrence Katz, Paul Kligfield, David Lefkowitz, Bruce Lerman, Jerrold Lieberman, Andrew Lituchy, Jennifer Liu, Norman Magid, Samuel Mann, Steven Markowitz, Ellen Mellow, David Miller, Jeffrey Moses, Peter Okin, Manish Parikh, Mark Pecker, Thomas Pickering, Martin Post, Mary Roman, Isadore Rosenfeld, Timothy Sanborn, Robert Savillo, Theodore Schreiber, Charles Smithen, Henry Solomon, Julio Sotelo, Artur Spokojny, Kenneth Stein, Israel Tamari, Theodore Tyberg, Donald Wallerson, Daniel Waxman, Stanley Yormak, Benjamin Zola, Michael Zullo, Michael Zukowsky, and Donna Zwas. We also thank Drs. Bruce Gordon and Stuart Saal of the NYH-CMC Rogosin Lipid Control Center.

The NYH-CMC nursing and social work staff have been essential in identifying patients for risk reduction classes that continue to take place twice weekly on the Coronary Care Step-Down Unit. We express particular thanks to nurses Sandra Andrasko, Cecilia Constantino, Hope Copperstone, Susan Discenza, Siobhan Ferguson, Tracy Gillan, Emily Matera, Kathleen Moran, Denise Salvasi, Suzanne Sherwyn, Badia Rahman, Aliyama Samuel, and Violet Samuels as well as social workers Marianne Delon and Jodi Silverman. Nurses and medical technologists who have been interested and supportive of our work in the NYH-CMC Division of Cardiology Outpatient Department include Ann Du Moulin, Janice Francis, Jennifer Grimes, Geri Helseth, Lena Mara, Catherine McGowan, Rose Marie Merion, Barbara Mulrenin, Marcia Richardson, Carolyn Ryan, Elizabeth Scott-Blanchard, and Virginia Van Slyck.

Debrie Allen, Manny Aquilina, Arlene Botter, Wanda Brown, Anna Christian, Rochelle Katz, Emogene Lawrence, Barbara Maroney, Zavette Smallwood, and Anne Marie Zerafa have been of great help in dealing with patient scheduling and a variety of other matters in a frequently hectic outpatient environment.

The NYH-CMC Public Relations Department has arranged numerous television and radio appearances as we have been asked to comment about new studies in the field over the past several years. We particularly thank Myrna Manners, Kathy Robinson, and Jonathan Weil, PhD.

Lynn Harmonay and Jeanette Lopez-Edell were instrumental in arranging for a number of stress management programs that we have presented through the Corporate Care Division of NYH-CMC, and we acknowledge their help and support for this area of mutual interest.

We particularly wish to thank Dr. John H. Laragh, long-time chief of the Division of Cardiology at NYH-CMC, for allowing a psychologist to tread on traditionally medical "territory" and supporting teaching, research, and patient care activities in cardiac psychology before they were fashionable. Gratitude is also extended to Dr. Bruce Lerman, who recently took over the helm as chief of the Division of Cardiology.

Dr. David Clayson and his able assistant Katie Hicks helped Robert Allan obtain a joint appointment in the Department of Psychiatry. We would also like to thank Drs. Robert Michels and Milton Viederman, from the Department of Psychiatry, for their interest and enthusiasm for cardiac psychology.

The staff at the Coronary Detection and Intervention Center of the "92nd Street Y," New York City, where we established a satellite program in 1988 under the auspices of Richard Stein, MD, Barbara Klein, RN, and exercise physiologists Dan Myers, MS, and Neil Bilboa, MS, have been most helpful.

We recently established a stress reduction–support group program at The New York Hospital of Queens Cardiac Health Center and thank Dr. John Nicholson and Donna Cheslik, RN, for their patience and encouragement, particularly during a difficult start-up period. We also appreciate the enthusiasm for our efforts in Queens from Jennifer Caro, Kathleen Malsch, Janice McCabe, and Dr. Martin Kay.

A stress reduction program is also underway at the recently established NYH-CMC Cardiac Health Center in Manhattan, and we would like to thank Dr. Paul Kligfield, Abby Jacobson, RN, Martha McKittrick, RD, and Barbara Schobel for their support.

Dr. Meyer Friedman, whose brilliance, honesty, and integrity have motivated us and many others to become interested in this field, deserves special thanks. He and the other contributors to this volume have given us a great deal by allowing us to learn from them and their work.

Dr. Dean Ornish, who has shaped the terrain of preventive cardiology, and Dr. Larry Scherwitz—both of the Preventive Medicine Research Institute—also deserve our special thanks for their vision. Dr. Scherwitz made a number of extremely valuable suggestions about organizing this volume.

Dr. Peter Kaufmann, at the National Institute of Health, a reviewer during the book's development phase, made many helpful suggestions, and, at the American Psychological Association (APA), Development Editor Paula Whyman and Production Editor Molly Flickinger have helped to strengthen this book with their insistence on the highest standards of scholarship.

The library staff at Cornell University Medical College has provided invaluable assistance over many years. Rhonda Shafner came through in a pinch with important antiquarian references from the New York Academy of Medicine.

Several people helped us craft our chapter on the empirical basis for cardiac psychology. We are grateful to Drs. Larry Scherwitz and Joseph Schwartz for their helpful reviews; to Drs. John Barefoot, Murray Mittleman, and Paul Landsbergis for their assistance with our sections on hostility, triggers for myocardial infarction, and job strain, respectively; to Drs.

Paul Kligfield and Richard Stiller for valuable insights into the life of John Hunter; and to E. S. C. Weiner, coeditor of the *Oxford English Dictionary*, for assistance with the etymology of the words *stress* and *anger*. Dr. Frank Miller, Director of the Affective Disorders Program at the Payne Whitney Clinic, provided a valuable review and suggestions for the chapter on psychopharmacology. Drs. Samuel Mann and Jeffrey Fisher assisted with their reviews of the glossary.

We also wish to thank Beverly Borg, our charming and dedicated cardiology administrator at NYH-CMC, for help over many months in putting this text on paper.

A great deal of office assistance was required to bring this volume to fruition, and we thank Anna Barquero, Diana Barquero, Jean Liu, Julio Martinez, Vanessa Nayar, and Sheila Wright for their help. Thanks to Willie Perry for computer support.

Cardiac psychology has turned into a business practice over the years that Robert Allan has been working to help develop this new clinical specialty. We are grateful to Carl DeRosa, Lisa Galen, Fran Gillen, Julia Martinez, Lee Anne McClymont, and Sandra Rinaldo for their help with important matters.

We wish to acknowledge a number of well-wishers (who cannot be neatly categorized) at NYH-CMC, including Drs. Linda Gerber, Gary James, Nili Wachtel, and Jean E. Sealy-Laragh.

We thank our patients, who have afforded us the privilege of learning important details about the relationship between heart and mind by sharing their most intimate thoughts and feelings.

We are extraordinarily grateful to the chapter authors of this volume, who labored hard through the numerous revisions required to bring this manuscript to APA form and standards. We are indeed privileged to have their contributions. Their work and dedication comprise the heart of cardiac psychology and the soul of this book.

Finally, we thank our wives and children—Amanda and Sara Allan and Andrea, Vivian, and Leslie Scheidt—and Robert Allan's mother, Lillian Gottfurcht, for their patience and good-natured acceptance of the time taken from them to bring this volume to fruition.

I

INTRODUCTION TO CARDIAC PSYCHOLOGY

1

INTRODUCTION: THE EMERGENCE OF CARDIAC PSYCHOLOGY

ROBERT ALLAN

Coronary heart disease (CHD) is the leading cause of death and disability in the United States (American Heart Association, 1995).[1] CHD is also a major source of death and disability for the rest of the Western world, particularly in industrialized countries (Zevallos, Chiriboga, & Hebert, 1992). The manifestations of CHD—angina pectoris (chest pain due to CHD), myocardial infarction (MI, or heart attack), and sudden cardiac death (SCD)—are almost always the result of atherosclerosis: deposition of fat and cholesterol-laden plaques in the linings of the coronary arteries (Zevallos et al., 1992). In addition, stroke and peripheral vascular disease, two other important diseases of the cardiovascular system, are often the result of the atherosclerotic process in the arteries that nourish the brain and legs, respectively.

MI is the single largest killer of men and women in the United States. This year, approximately 1.5 million people will have an MI, and about one third of them will die. Currently, there are approximately 13,490,000 people in the United States living with CHD. According to data from the Framingham Heart Study,[2] 45% of CHD is "premature," meaning that it occurs in people under the age of 65.

---

[1]All U.S. statistics provided in this chapter are from the American Heart Association's (1995) *Heart and Stroke Facts: 1996 Statistical Supplement.*
[2]Ongoing for nearly a half-century, the Framingham Heart Study has investigated cardiac risk factors for three generations of citizens living in the midsized industrial city of Framingham, Massachusetts.

Atherosclerosis is not caused by a single agent, such as a viral or bacterial infection, but results from a number of risk factors, many of which are determined by a person's lifestyle. Behavioral factors play a key role in the prevalence and severity of several of the well-accepted risk factors for atherosclerosis. Figure 1 shows the standard risk factors as well as the more tentative psychosocial risk factors for CHD. Clearly, cigarette smoking, sedentary living, and dietary intake of cholesterol-rich and high-saturated-fat or high-calorie foods are life choices. Hypertension also has a behavioral

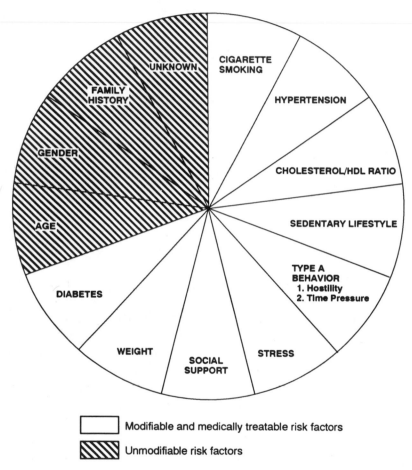

Modifiable and medically treatable risk factors

Unmodifiable risk factors

Figure 1. Risk factors for coronary heart disease (CHD). A number of risk factors have been established. Cigarette smoking, elevated serum cholesterol (and cholesterol–HDL [high-density lipoprotein] ratio), hypertension, and sedentary lifestyle are considered the standard risk factors. Psychosocial risk factors are still tentative and, sometimes, controversial. The degree of risk sometimes depends on the degree to which the risk factor occurs in a person's life (e.g., the risk from cigarette smoking varies with the amount smoked). Similarly, the higher the serum cholesterol or cholesterol–HDL ratio, the greater the risk. Risk factors combine synergistically; that is, their total effect is greater than the sum of the parts.

component for those who are salt-sensitive, overweight, or both. Thus, each of the four major modifiable risk factors for CHD has a behavioral component. Psychological stress, the Type A behavior pattern, anger and hostility, and social isolation or lack of social support are some of the psychosocial variables that have been linked to the development of CHD in otherwise healthy populations. In addition, depression has been shown to increase CHD risk and mortality after MI. Other psychosocial variables that may contribute to CHD risk include job strain, vital exhaustion (lack of energy, demoralization, and increased irritability), anxiety, and cardiac denial (ignoring the significance of cardiac symptoms). In chapter 3, coeditor Stephen Scheidt and I summarize the scientific literature supporting a relationship between psychosocial factors and CHD. We believe that the burgeoning literature of observational, epidemiological, and experimental studies linking psychosocial and behavioral factors to CHD deserves recognition as the new field of "cardiac psychology"—an evolving body of knowledge to help promote and support heart-healthy living.

A significant segment of the population with CHD, as well as the general public, stands to benefit from cardiac psychology. Thus, one goal of this volume is to document the very latest developments in this area, for psychologists, cardiologists, cardiothoracic surgeons, internists, psychiatrists, social workers, nurses, exercise physiologists, and other health professionals who may be involved in the day-to-day care of patients with CHD and their families. The interdisciplinary contributions in the volume were chosen with an eye toward promoting the enhancement of traditional medical care with cardiac psychology. Another important goal is to stimulate further clinical, epidemiological, and laboratory research in this young and rapidly evolving field.

Given the unique interdisciplinary nature of this volume, a glossary is provided at the end of the book to allow easy reference for those who may need explanations of commonly used terms in cardiology. An understanding of these terms is vital for the cardiac psychologist and will facilitate the relationship between medical and psychology professionals.

The importance of coronary risk factor modification has taken a recent quantum leap with the demonstration by several investigators—including Brown et al. (1990), Blankenhorn et al. (1987), Ornish (Gould et al., 1995), and others—that regression of atherosclerosis, long considered the holy grail in clinical cardiology, is achievable. This was first suggested by decreases in the size of visible atherosclerotic plaques on serial coronary angiograms several years apart in patients given powerful diet or drug therapy to lower their serum cholesterol, and some of these groups of investigators now report that clinical events such as acute MI, unstable angina, SCD, or need for coronary artery bypass graft (CABG) surgery decline far more dramatically than would be expected from the relatively small regression in plaque size. Indeed, although the extent of improvement in minimal luminal diameter of stenotic lesions has been small, generally only 1%–2%, as much as a 25%–75% reduction in cardiac events such as nonfatal and fatal MI and the need for invasive procedures has been shown in some studies (Deedwania, 1995). It may be that plaques cannot only become smaller, but in some way may also be "stabilized," so that clinical events are reduced substantially in the short term. In addition, several studies, notably two large trials of antilipid drugs—one in patients with overt CHD (Scandinavian Simvastatin Survival Study Group, 1994) and one in patients with little if any heart disease (Shepherd et al., 1995)—have demonstrated conclusively that total mortality (the "hardest" end result imaginable) can be significantly reduced with medical and diet therapy designed to reduce serum cholesterol. Thus, the case for coronary risk reduction by young and old and those with and without known heart disease in U.S. society, where so many are vulnerable to CHD, is both compelling and encouraging.

ORIGINS OF CARDIAC PSYCHOLOGY

Recognition of the importance of the link between psyche and soma can be traced to the ancient Far East. Huang Ti, the "Yellow Emperor" (2697–2597 B.C.), observed, "when the minds of the people are closed and wisdom is locked out they remain tied to disease" (cited in Strauss, 1968, p. 38). Perhaps the first observation in cardiac psychology can be attributed to William Harvey, discoverer of the circulatory system, who declared in 1628 that "a mental disturbance provoking pain, excessive joy, hope or anxiety extends to the heart, where it affects temper and rate" (Harvey, 1628/1928, p. 107). Just prior to the beginning of the twentieth century, Sir William Osler (1897), often called the father of modern internal medicine, was perhaps the first physician to link atherosclerosis directly with excesses of behavior, which he described as "the Nemesis through which Nature exacts retributive justice for the transgression of her laws" (p. 154). Furthermore, Osler (1910) described the typical atherosclerosis patient as a "keen and ambitious man, the indicator of whose engine is always at 'full speed ahead'" (p. 839). Earlier in this century, important hypotheses linking psychological factors directly with physiological effects were the "fight or flight response," first identified by Cannon (1932), and Selye's "general alarm reaction" (1956). Beginning with the description of the Type A behavior pattern by Friedman and Rosenman (1959), two San Francisco cardiologists, there was a proliferation of research in cardiac psychology.

THE CURRENT STATE OF CLINICAL CARDIOLOGY

Contemporary cardiology excels at managing life-threatening conditions (e.g., acute MI and unstable angina) with high-tech methods for diagnosis and treatment, such as the coronary care unit, thrombolysis (medication to dissolve the thrombus that causes most MIs), cardiac catheterization, percutaneous transluminal coronary angioplasty (PTCA), and CABG surgery. However, cardiologists have generally been far less interested in the day-to-day support that is often needed to help patients maintain a heart-healthy lifestyle and thus reduce the risk of cardiac events. It is here that psychologists and other mental health practitioners may find their expertise of great benefit, particularly for individuals who develop CHD before the age of 65, when the disease is considered premature and often has a substantial lifestyle component.

One valuable insight is that mental health providers need not apologize for "only" improving the quality of life for cardiac patients (although data from the Burell study, chap. 11, this volume, indicate that psychosocial intervention may actually extend life span or delay mortality). Many invasive procedures in cardiology are similarly palliative and may not reduce mortality. For example, except for patients with "left main" and "triple vessel" coronary artery disease with decreased left ventricular function, CABG surgery has not been shown to increase life expectancy (Yusuf et al., 1994), nor has PTCA (Gersh, 1994), the other frequently used invasive procedure in cardiology. These procedures reduce the physical pain of angina pectoris or increase exercise tolerance and, hence, improve quality of life. Psychological intervention with cardiac patients reduces psychological pain—oftentimes severe anxiety, hostility, and depression—and thus improves quality of life as well. In my experience, successful psychological treatment of cardiac patients has resulted in more satisfying lives, not only for patients but also for their families.

The most compelling data in behavioral medicine today are to be found in cardiac psychology. There is a large database linking behavioral and psychological factors with the onset of CHD as well as with secondary cardiac events in individuals who already have CHD (see chap. 3, this volume). Furthermore, a number of clinical trials have demonstrated reduced CHD morbidity and mortality with lifestyle programs that include a psychosocial component. Indeed, if the results of these clinical interventions can be replicated and the methodology transferred to other mental health professionals, then a revolution is possible in cardiac care. This direction seems particularly relevant in light of the current economic climate promoting reduced medical costs through prevention.

Cardiac psychology promises to be an important new specialty in mental health. The coming decade should bring many coronary risk reduction programs, particularly for secondary prevention of CHD, springing up at hospitals and cardiac rehabilitation centers around the world.

Open-minded cardiologists will be pleased with the assistance that mental health practitioners can offer by providing education and by reducing the countless questions that many patients have after a cardiac event. Many of these questions are the result of anxiety, which can often be alleviated by offering information, support, and reassurance.

OVERVIEW OF THE BOOK

This book attempts to establish the empirical and clinical basis for the new specialty of cardiac psychology. The chapters provide a broad overview of the field, particularly for mental health clinicians who have an interest in developing a practice specialty in cardiac psychology. Part 1, an introduction to cardiac psychology, offers a working knowledge of the most important issues that will confront the practitioner. In chapter 2, Scheidt begins with a whirlwind tour of cardiology, to assist readers in understanding the essential medical aspects of the field. Knowledge of cardiac physiology and the standard diagnostic tests and treatments in cardiology are essential.

Scheidt and I continue with the empirical basis for cardiac psychology in chapter 3, offering a review of what we believe are the most important studies in the field, as well as our own conclusions. Although some areas are marked by less than optimal research studies, methodologies have been improving in recent years.

Chapter 4 presents an optimistic view of cardiac psychology from a clinical cardiologist with a strong focus on the psychological well-being of his patients. In this chapter, Fisher provides the sensitive observations of a health provider on the "front lines" of cardiologic care.

In chapter 5, Roberts describes the physiological basis for atherosclerosis, with particular emphasis on cholesterol, lipids, and the coronary-prone American diet. It is critical that the cardiac psychologist have a thorough understanding of the nutritional issues in preventive cardiology, because it is a subject of immense concern to patients with CHD. Roberts offers the controversial view that cholesterol is the only direct risk factor for atherosclerosis. Although some will be taken aback by this assertion, he nonetheless presents a fascinating perspective on eating habits in U.S. society. Although Roberts does not consider psychosocial factors relevant for the development of atherosclerosis if serum cholesterol is under 150 mg/dl, quite interestingly, he nonetheless considers these factors of central importance as triggers when atherosclerotic events do occur.

Perhaps no issue has generated as much controversy in cardiac psychology as the diagnosis of Type A behavior, the subject of chapter 6, by Meyer Friedman, Fleischmann, and Price. Both the clinician and the researcher will find this description important because cardiac patients frequently display many of the manifestations described therein. An insecurity scale, developed recently to assess the presumed "nucleus" of the Type A behavior pattern, is also included in this chapter. This chapter is essential reading because two of the clinical interventions presented in this volume focus on modification of Type A behavior, and readers will want to be knowledgeable about the disorder.

Until recently, little attention has been focused on CHD risk factors that may be unique to women, and even less attention has been given to the possible psychological factors that may predispose women to CHD. In chapter 7, Jacobs and Sherwood review the limited and emerging research in this area and make suggestions for future research.

CABG surgery is one of the two most common invasive procedures in cardiology, PTCA being the other. Of the two, CABG is clearly more invasive and likely to contribute to psychological adjustment reactions. In chapter 8, Gold discusses the psychological issues that often emerge with CABG and results of the still very limited empirical investigations in this area. One surprising revelation is the high prevalence of new onset depression after CABG.

Part 2 of this volume, Clinical Trials, focuses on lifestyle interventions with cardiac patients. A number of studies have shown that such intervention can reduce morbidity and mortality after the diagnosis of CHD. Each of the three studies considered most important for the field is described in detail in its own chapter.

First, in chapter 9, Billings, Scherwitz, Sullivan, Sparler, and Ornish present the pioneering treatment and highly encouraging results of the Lifestyle Heart Trial, developed by Dean Ornish and colleagues. In this approach, a comprehensive lifestyle is prescribed for CHD patients, with the goal of reversing coronary atherosclerosis without drugs or surgery. The program requires an ambitious effort and more than 14 hours per week from the participant. Included are a vegetarian diet with less than 10% fat, moderate exercise 3 times a week, twice weekly group therapy, and 1 hour a day of yoga and meditation. The study's results suggest that nothing short of this great effort is sufficient to achieve regression with lifestyle change alone, and, indeed, results have revealed a dose-response relationship between adherence to the program and degree of regression, with those who did the most achieving the most dramatic results.

Chapter 10, by Bracke and Thoresen, describes the theory and methodology used in the Recurrent Coronary Prevention Project (RCPP), the largest psychological intervention for post-MI patients ($N = 1,013$) and refinements in technique at the Meyer Friedman Institute that have evolved since completion of this trial in 1986. The RCPP demonstrated a 44% reduction in recurrent MI when group counseling was used for reduction of Type A behavior.

Gunilla Burell attempted to replicate and build on the RCPP with Project New Life, using 268 post-CABG patients in Sweden. In chapter

11, she presents the techniques and results of this intervention. Also included in this chapter is a discussion of issues particularly relevant to the women in this trial.

Part 3, Clinical Technique and Intervention, describes in greater detail some of the methods used in the clinical trials described in chapters 9, 10 and 11. Chapter 12 presents the "hook," a metaphor used in the RCPP and Project New Life to help patients reduce unwanted anger. Patients in the RCPP indicated that the hook was the single most helpful technique in their treatment. The metaphor and its rationale are described by its creator, Lynda Powell.

Modification of time pressure, one of the other major symptoms of Type A behavior, is the subject of chapter 13, written by key personnel in the RCPP. Chapters 12 and 13 both offer practical tools for reducing Type A behavior.

All three of the clinical trials described in Part 2 made extensive use of the "relaxation response," which is the subject of chapter 14, written by Richard Friedman and Herbert Benson. Benson not only coined the term but also provided much of the impetus for the current interest in spiritual practices to enhance traditional medicine.

Cardiac rehabilitation programs are often a part of recovery from MI and CABG, and they are particularly valuable to the angina patient, who can generally increase stamina with exercise training. In chapter 15, Stein discusses the rationale and methods of exercise training for the CHD patient. It is widely acknowledged within the cardiology community that one of the major benefits and reasons for the success of cardiac rehabilitation programs is the social support that they informally provide to participants.

Many patients suffer depression and anxiety after a cardiac event. Chapter 16, by Tabrizi, Littman, Williams, and Scheidt, provides a summary of the current state of psychopharmacotherapy for cardiac patients, with an emphasis on treatment for depression and anxiety. The psychological side effects of cardiac medications are discussed as well.

The spouse or partner of a patient in cardiac care is typically neglected, yet this person is often in great distress and of great importance for the patient's successful lifestyle change. In chapter 17, Delon, a social worker with vast experience in this area, provides valuable insight to health professionals about family issues during the patient's stay in the cardiac care unit.

The chapters in Part 4, Cardiac Psychology in Practice, discuss cardiac psychology as a contemporary clinical specialty. In chapter 18, Halperin discusses the development of a practice, with particular emphasis on overcoming the resistance likely to be encountered when dealing with patients as well as health care providers. In chapter 19, Scheidt and I are joined by colleague Thomas G. Pickering, a noted authority on psychosocial factors in hypertension and CHD. We present our conclusions about the current state of cardiac psychology and discuss strengths and weaknesses in the literature, target areas for psychological intervention in light of this literature, and suggest new directions for research and treatment.

The contents of this volume were chosen in an attempt to provide a thorough review of the emerging field of cardiac psychology; however, this review is not exhaustive. Discussion has necessarily been limited to atherosclerotic coronary events, and research related to stroke or peripheral vascular disease has purposely not been cited, so as to avoid the important issue of whether similar risk factors affect all cardiovascular diseases. Also notably absent is discussion of smoking cessation, which is a leading contributing cause of CHD. Interestingly, more than 90% of the 30 million smokers who stopped between 1964 and 1982 did not quit through a formal program, and most smokers state that they would prefer to stop on their own (Ockene, 1992). In addition, both observational studies and randomized trials have indicated that physicians can have a powerful impact (50%–63% quit rates) on their patients' smoking behavior, particularly when they intervene after an acute cardiac event, such as MI (Ockene, 1992). Interested readers can consult Ockene for an expanded review of this subject. Another conspicuous omission is discussion of the distressing fact that the least educated, lower socioeconomic population has a much higher rate of CHD than the general population (American Heart Association, 1995). Clearly, much effort is needed to help this segment of the population reduce the behavioral factors associated with CHD. We have not addressed issues affecting minorities either, because there has been little research in this area.

The leading cause of death and disability in the United States is CHD. The new field of cardiac psychology may help create a revolution in cardiac care, helping individuals, particularly cardiac patients, reduce their risk. It is possible to foresee a time in the not-too-distant future when CHD will be much less common, and this development will be aided by cardiac psychology and its influence in fostering a heart-healthy lifestyle.

REFERENCES

American Heart Association. (1995). *Heart and stroke facts: 1996 statistical supplement*. Dallas, TX: Author.

Blankenhorn, D. H., Nessim, S. A., Johnson, R. L., Johnson, R. L., Sanmarco, M. E., Azen, S. P., & Cashin-Hemphill, L. (1987). Beneficial effects of combined colestipol-niacin therapy in coronary atherosclerosis and coronary venous bypass grafts. *Journal of the American Medical Association, 257*, 3233–3240.

Brown, B. G., Albers, J. J., Fisher, L. D., Schaefer, B. A., Lin, J.-T., Kaplan, C., Zhao, X.-Q., Bisson, B. D., Fitzpatrick, V. F., & Dodge, H. T. (1990). Regression of coronary disease as a result of intensive lipid-lowering therapy in men with high levels of apolipoprotein B. *New England Journal of Medicine*, *323*, 1289–1298.

Cannon, W. B. (1932). *The wisdom of the body*. New York: Norton.

Deedwania, P. C. (1995). Clinical perspectives on primary and secondary prevention of coronary atherosclerosis. *Medical Clinics of North America*, *79*, 973–998.

Friedman, M., & Rosenman, R. H. (1959). Association of specific overt behavior pattern with blood and cardiovascular findings: blood cholesterol level, blood clotting time, incidence of arcus senilis, and clinical coronary artery disease. *Journal of the American Medical Association*, *169*, 1286–1296.

Gersh, B. J. (1994). Efficacy of percutaneous transluminal coronary angioplasty (PTCA) in coronary artery disease: Why we need clinical trials. In E. J. Topol (Ed.), *Textbook of interventional cardiology* (2nd ed., pp. 251–273). Philadelphia: W. B. Saunders.

Gould, K. L., Ornish, D., Scherwitz, L., Brown, S., Edens, R. P., Hess, M. J., Mulani, N., Bolomey, L., Dobbs, F., Armstrong, W. T., Merritt, T., Ports, T., Sparler, S., & Billings, J. (1995). Changes in myocardial perfusion abnormalities by positron emission tomography after long-term, intense risk factor modification. *Journal of the American Medical Association*, *274*, 894–901.

Harvey, W. (1928). *Anatomical studies on the motion of the heart and blood* (C. D. Leake, Trans.). Springfield, IL: Charles C Thomas. (Original work published 1628)

Ockene, J. K. (1992). Smoking intervention: A behavioral, educational, and pharmacologic perspective. In I. S. Ockene & J. K. Ockene (Eds.), *Prevention of coronary heart disease* (pp. 201–230). Boston: Little, Brown.

Osler, W. (1897). *Lectures on angina pectoris and allied states*. New York: Appleton-Century-Crofts.

Osler, W. (1910). The Lumleian Lectures in angina pectoris. *Lancet*, 839–844.

Scandinavian Simvastatin Survival Study Group. (1994). Randomised trial of cholesterol lowering in 4444 patients with coronary heart disease: The Scandinavian Simvastatin Survival Study (4S). *Lancet*, *344*, 1383–1389.

Selye, H. (1956). *The stress of life*. New York: McGraw-Hill.

Shepherd, J., Cobbe, S. M., Ford, I., Isles, C. G., Lorimer, A. R., Macfarlane, P. W., McKillop, J. H., & Packard, C. J., for the West of Scotland Coronary Prevention Study Group. (1995). Prevention of coronary heart disease with pravastatin in men with hypercholesterolemia. *New England Journal of Medicine*, *333*, 1301–1307.

Strauss, M. B. (1968). *Familiar medical quotations*. Boston: Little, Brown.

Yusuf, S., Zucker, H. D., Peduzzi, P., Fisher, L. D., Takaro, T., Kennedy, J. W., Davis, K., Killip, T., Passamani, E., Norris, R., Morris, C., Mathur, V., Varnauskas, E., & Chalmers, T. C. (1994). Effect of coronary artery bypass graft surgery on survival: Overview of 10-year results from randomised trials by the Coronary Artery Bypass Graft Surgery Trialists Collaboration. *Lancet*, *344*, 563–570.

Zevallos, J. C., Chiriboga, D., & Hebert, J. R. (1992). An international perspective on coronary heart disease and related risk factors. In I. S. Ockene & J. K. Ockene (Eds.), *Prevention of coronary heart disease* (pp. 147–170). Boston: Little, Brown.

Aorta

Pulmonary Artery

Left Atrium

Left Circumflex Artery

Left Anterior
Descending Artery

Left Ventricle

Superior Vena Cava

Right Atrium

Right Coronary
Artery

Right Ventricle

© Richard LaRocco

2

A WHIRLWIND TOUR OF CARDIOLOGY FOR THE MENTAL HEALTH PROFESSIONAL

STEPHEN SCHEIDT

Although there are many different kinds of heart disease, the vast majority of patients in the United States have one of three major types. The first is coronary artery disease, or coronary heart disease (CHD),[1] a disease of the arteries that feed the heart itself that is almost always due to atherosclerosis (deposition of fatty and other material that obstructs the coronary arteries). The second type is valvular heart disease, which is narrowing or leakage of one or more of the four heart valves. The third type, cardiomyopathy, is weakening of the heart muscle—caused by prolonged hypertension, genetic defects of muscle, and other known factors, but most often of totally unknown etiology—which can have various consequences, most notably, congestive heart failure (CHF).

In this chapter, I describe the causes, diagnosis, clinical manifestations, and therapy for the three major types of heart disease: CHD, with its major syndromes of acute myocardial infarction (MI), angina pectoris, and sudden cardiac death (SCD); valvular heart disease, with its two broad categories of rheumatic and degenerative valvular disease and the individual valve lesions of aortic stenosis and regurgitation, mitral stenosis and

---

[1]The terms *coronary artery disease* and *coronary heart disease* are often used interchangeably by physicians to discuss cardiovascular conditions caused by disease (almost always atherosclerotic) of the coronary arteries.

regurgitation, tricuspid regurgitation, and mitral valve prolapse; and cardiomyopathy, with its common presentation of CHF.[2]

I also touch briefly on pericardial disease, endocarditis, and arrhythmias and, in the Appendix, provide highlights of cardiac pharmacology. It is hoped that, after reading this chapter, the noncardiologist will understand the terms and acronyms commonly used, the natural history, and the major treatments of most patients with cardiac disease and, thus, will gain a better understanding of what patients who have cardiac disease experience in the course of their diagnosis and treatment.

CHD

CHD is the most important disease of Westernized countries, because it is by far the single largest cause of death in adult men and women, accounting for half a million deaths annually in the United States. It is a disease of the arteries that feed the heart muscle itself and has as its major manifestations acute MI (or heart attack), angina pectoris, and SCD.

In theory, there are a number of potential diseases that might affect the coronary arteries, but in practice CHD is almost exclusively due to atherosclerosis. Very rare nonatherosclerotic causes of CHD can include any of the following: spasm of unknown etiology, termed *Prinzmetal's angina*; spasm due to cocaine use; inflammation of coronary arteries due to lupus erythematosis or other unusual diseases; diseases of the aortic root in and around the ostia (openings) of the coronary arteries, including dissecting aneurysm and endocarditis on the aortic valve; and congenital anomalies of or emboli into the coronary arteries. All of these etiologies together probably account for less than 1% of cases of CHD, however, and the remainder is atherosclerotic.

The Atherosclerotic Process

Atherosclerotic disease is a common disease of Western men (and, after menopause, of women), occurring preferentially at certain sites in the body. These sites are notably (a) the aorta and peripheral arteries, where atherosclerosis is manifested by aortic disease (often asymptomatic bulges called *aortic aneurysms* that can rupture suddenly) and narrowings of arteries in the legs (resulting in "intermittent claudication," or pain in the calves or thighs when walking); (b) the renal arteries (manifested by kidney fail-

---

[2]The information that I provide in this chapter is elementary cardiology; therefore, I do not provide comprehensive references throughout the chapter. Interested readers should consult Hills, Lange, Winniford, and Page's (1995) *Manual of Clinical Problems in Cardiology*, as well as these two standard texts in cardiology: Braunwald's (1992) *Heart Disease: A Textbook of Cardiovascular Medicine* and Schlant and Alexander's (1994) *Hurst's The Heart*.

ure and some cases of hypertension); (c) the carotid and brain arteries (manifested by strokes and transient ischemic attacks); and (d) the coronary arteries. Deposition of fatty material in the walls of arteries over many years eventually results in an obstruction that limits blood flow. In some cases, a blood clot forms at the site of the preexisting atherosclerotic narrowing, causing sudden and sometimes catastrophic total reduction in flow.

Although an immense amount of research has been done on atherosclerosis, scientists still do not understand the basic process. The leading hypothesis posits that a number of interacting factors are involved in the production and growth of atherosclerotic plaques over years and decades:

- Injury of some undetermined sort occurs to blood vessels.
- Functional abnormalities of the cells lining blood vessels (the endothelium) occur.
- Some components of the reparative process—involving the endothelium, platelets, white blood cells, or elements of the blood-clotting system that are meant to migrate to a site of injury, stem any blood loss, and repair any injury—somehow unexpectedly produce adverse effects that result in atherosclerotic plaques.
- Abnormalities occur in circulating white blood cells called *monocytes* as well as in smooth muscle cells within the walls of arteries, such that these cells move through certain barriers and migrate to a position just under the inner lining of the artery (the subendothelial area), change both anatomically and functionally, and begin to accumulate lipid (fat). The changed cells are called *macrophages* and, when full of fat, are called *lipid-laden microphages*.
- Excess lipid, partially genetically determined and partially related to modern human lifestyle (quite different from the ancestral hunter–gatherer existence of only a few thousand years ago, which was mainly vegetarian, involved high physical exercise, and often scarcity of food), enters the walls of blood vessels and is taken up by cells, possibly aided by injury or response to injury of the blood vessel wall. Eventually, the macrophages cannot take up any more lipid, and some of them rupture, releasing lipid into the extracellular space. This lipid, within the blood vessel wall but outside of cells, seems to be able to damage the blood vessel wall.
- Some sort of abnormal oxidative process, perhaps of low-density lipoprotein (LDL; one of the blood fats), occurs that allows this substance to more easily enter blood vessel walls, and once inside the walls, to cause damage to the vessels.
- An ongoing process takes place within the blood vessel wall—possibly reparative, possibly irritative, possibly designed

to wall off abnormal components (particularly extracellular lipids) that are not supposed to be found within the wall—but this process "overreacts" and eventually produces a large plaque that narrows the lumen (channel for blood flow) as well as excess fibrous (scar) tissue and calcium (thus producing the stiffening and hardening of vessels that gives the appelation *sclerosis* to the disease, even though it is the narrowing, not the hardening, that causes clinical problems).[3]

- Rupture of the fibrous cap of the plaque (that portion of the blood vessel wall that isolates the potentially irritating components of the plaque from the remainder of the blood vessel wall and the lumen) exposes substances within the plaque to the flowing blood. It is not understood why some plaques rupture (and others never do) nor whether rupture is a random event or is associated with precipitating factors that, if identified, might lead to better control of the process. Material within the plaque, as well as some components of the injured arterial wall, is intensely thrombogenic (provokes clotting), and a clot forms at or near the site of plaque rupture. It is the sudden formation of the clot that is thought to account for most of the catastrophic clinical events in the course of CHD, including SCD, acute MI, and unstable angina pectoris.

Even though the exact mechanism by which atherosclerosis occurs has not been pinpointed, a great deal of understanding concerning risk factors, and much knowledge about prevention and even regression of atherosclerosis, has been accumulated.

Risk Factors

In population studies, a number of risk factors are undisputed as being associated with a higher incidence of atherosclerosis; several other factors are controversial. Generally accepted risk factors for CHD include

- Increasing age.
- Male sex.
- High blood pressure (which is variously defined; e.g., the Joint National Commission uses >140 mm Hg systolic or >90 diastolic). This risk factor simply involves elevation of the blood

---

[3]*Athero*, the other part of *atherosclerosis*, is derived from the Greek word *atheros*—meaning "gruel" or "porridge"—because the abnormal plaque that lines the walls of blood vessels looks and feels like old breakfast cereal that has sat too long on top of the stove, or at least so thought the pathologists who first described the disease from autopsy specimens many years ago.

pressure: either the systolic pressure (when the heart pumps) or the diastolic pressure (when the heart relaxes).[4]

- High total blood cholesterol or LDL. Blood lipids, including cholesterol, are fats and thus are not soluble in blood, which is an aqueous solution. To be transported in blood, lipids are linked to a protein, thus the term *lipoprotein*. Excess LDL is associated with more atherosclerotic disease.
- Low high-density lipoprotein (HDL; the so-called good cholesterol), which carries cholesterol to the liver for eventual degradation and removal from the body. High HDL is associated with less atherosclerotic disease, whereas low HDL is a risk factor, and quite a powerful one, for CHD.
- Lack of physical exercise.
- Major obesity (being approximately 35% or more above ideal weight).
- Diabetes mellitus.

Controversial risk factors for CHD include Type A behavior; other psychosocial attributes such as stress, social isolation, or depression; and high blood triglycerides.

CLINICAL SYNDROMES OF ATHEROSCLEROTIC CORONARY DISEASE

The main clinical syndromes of atherosclerotic coronary disease are acute MI, angina pectoris, and SCD. Silent ischemia (lack of blood to a portion of heart muscle without chest pain or other symptoms perceived by the patient) and ischemic cardiomyopathy, or heart failure, are much less common presentations. Patients with clinical CHD almost always have one or more significant narrowings of coronary arteries; "significant" is usually defined as narrowing of a major coronary artery by 70% or more. Often there will be several narrowings or even total obstructions in one, two, or all three of the major coronary arteries (so-called single-, double-, or triple-vessel disease). There is no clear difference in the number, severity, or location of anatomic coronary artery narrowings in patients with one or another of the clinical syndromes of CHD, and it is not clear why, for example, one patient may suffer from exertional angina for 20 years, another may develop a large MI, or a third has SCD with no premonitory signs as the first manifestation of CHD.

---

[4]There is an increasing tendency among cardiologists to use the term *high blood pressure* rather than *hypertension*, because the latter word includes *tension*, which has remarkably little to do with the level of blood pressure in most people.

Angina Pectoris

Angina pectoris—literally, "strangling in the chest"—refers to reasonably reproducible exertional symptoms, usually but not always and not exclusively in the chest, in people who have coronary artery narrowings. In the classic form of angina pectoris, patients complain of tightening, or pressure, or a "band" around the chest that comes on with exertion and usually disappears within 1–2 minutes or, at most, 5–10 minutes of stopping exertion. It is also promptly (within 1–2 minutes) relieved by ingestion of sublingual nitroglycerin, a rapidly acting coronary and peripheral vasodilator. In some patients, the discomfort will radiate from the left chest to the left arm or hand; in others, it may occur in the left shoulder, the epigastrium (pit of the stomach up under the rib cage), the right chest or shoulder, the jaw, or even in the back. It is often accompanied by some shortness of breath but not usually by sweating, nausea, vomiting, dizziness, or other associated symptoms (see my discussion of MI, below). The classic and most common precipitating cause of angina is physical exertion, but many patients report experiencing angina with emotional upset. Cold, anger, hurrying, time pressure, and exertion soon after eating or soon after arising are also common precipitating factors.

Diagnosis of Ischemic Heart Disease

A middle-aged American man who has left chest pressure radiating into the left hand occurring regularly with physical exertion and relieved promptly with stopping exertion or with sublingual nitroglycerin almost certainly has angina and, thus, obstructive coronary artery atherosclerotic disease—all of which can be determined from his clinical history. Diagnostic tests that confirm the etiology and suggest modes of therapy include the electrocardiogram (ECG), stress testing, cardiac catheterization, echocardiography, and Holter monitoring.

The Standard ECG

Figure 1 is a schematic of the electrocardiographic complex, which is the sum of many tiny electrical vectors from all the cells of the heart, summed into one set of electrical forces that can be recorded at various points on the surface of the body. A standard ECG comprises 12 separate recordings from 12 different vantage points. The machine switches automatically from one external recording site to another and puts them all together as 12 "leads" on one page. Some leads (recording sites) look at events on the front (anterior) wall of the heart, some at the inferior wall, and some at the left side (lateral wall). One segment of the ECG complex, the ST segment, is particularly important for the diagnosis of ischemia; this

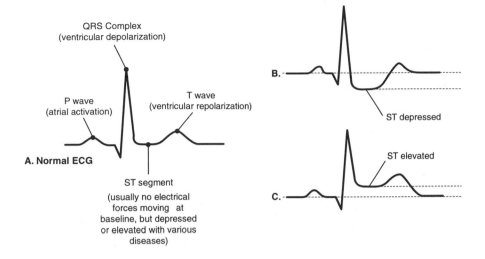

Figure 1. Schematic of the electrocardiographic complex. QRS complex = the total electrical activity of the ventricles; ECG = electrocardiogram.

portion of the complex ordinarily should be at the baseline (which means that no electrical current is flowing either toward or away from the recording electrode; see Part A of Figure 1). In mild or moderate ischemia, however, the ST segment is depressed (Part B), and in severe ischemia—especially if the entire heart muscle wall, through and through from endocardium to epicardium, is ischemic—the ST segment is elevated (Part C). ST-segment elevation is a reasonably specific sign that an acute MI is in progress, and this sign is thus much sought and much feared by physicians in emergency rooms.

Although it is true that ST-segment depression is a sign of ischemia, the standard ECG is actually a very poor test for confirming or denying CHD. If an ECG should happen to be taken while the patient is having angina and then is repeated some time afterward, and there are transient ST-segment depressions that disappear as symptoms are relieved, then this is quite suggestive of the diagnosis of CHD. However, an ECG taken at rest, when there are no symptoms and no ischemia, is unlikely to show anything useful regarding angina. ECGs do show evidence of recent or old myocardial infarcts, which certainly makes possible the diagnosis of CHD as well as hypertrophy of various chambers (which might suggest valvular disease or hypertension) and other diseases.

Stress Testing

Using the ECG and a treadmill or stationary bicycle, a cardiologist can perform a simple stress test by increasing the speed and elevation of the treadmill or workload on the bicycle in increments to gradually increase the work of the heart. The most common exercise protocol is the "Bruce protocol," named after cardiologist Robert Bruce, which usually proceeds as follows: beginning with Stage 1, with the treadmill at a turtlelike 1.7 mph and with no (0%) grade for 3 minutes; proceeding to Stage 2, at 2.5 mph (a bit less than normal strolling speed) with a 10% uphill grade; then to Stage 3, at 3.4 mph (a bit faster than strolling) with 12% grade; and, finally, to Stage 4, at 4.2 mph (just short of a jog) with 14% grade. The endpoint of the test is either symptoms, major changes on the ECG, or reaching at least 85% of the maximum predicted heart rate. (The maximum heart rate varies with age: Young people will be able to raise their heart rates to nearly 200 with maximal exertion, whereas people in their 60s can only reach a peak heart rate of 160 or so.) So long as the heart is pushed sufficiently—and here, "sufficiently" means doing enough exercise so that the peak heart rate during the stress test is at least 85% of what is theoretically attainable for that patient's age group—the stress test is reasonably accurate at diagnosing CHD.

Advantages of this type of stress test are that it is relatively inexpensive (only a few hundred dollars), quick (20 minutes), totally noninvasive, gives reasonable information about presence or absence of CHD, and gives some information about prognosis. (Patients who develop a great deal of ECG change at a very early stage of exercise, prolonged changes after stopping exercise, or major arrhythmias during exercise or those who have to stop early in the test are at much higher risk of MI or SCD than those without such findings on the stress test.) Disadvantages include substantial false negatives (i.e., missing CHD in a patient who has it) and false positives (finding ECG changes in a patient who does not have CHD), perhaps 15%–25% of each; the patient has to be able to exercise to a reasonable degree; and it cannot be used or is much less accurate in people with certain types of abnormalities in the baseline ECG.

Another form of stress testing involves using a tracer dose of radioactivity that is taken up by well-perfused heart muscle and can be imaged with a scintillation camera (a sort of Geiger counter) at rest and with exercise. This might be a thallium stress test (which uses the radioisotope thallium, an analogue of potassium) or a newer version known as the "sestamibi" (or sometimes just "mibi") stress test (which uses a different radioisotope that accomplishes much the same thing). Sometimes the general term *perfusion stress test* is used.

Advantages of perfusion testing are that it can be more accurate than the ECG stress test (in a good lab, perhaps only 10%–15% false negatives and false positives occur) and it is much better at localizing portions of the heart where there has been permanent damage (e.g., a myocardial infarct) or where there is reversible ischemia (heart muscle supplied by narrowed arteries that gets enough blood at rest, but not enough during exercise). Disadvantages are that it is frightfully expensive (often $750–$1,500) and it takes approximately 4–5 hours.

Yet another type of test uses a tracer dose of radioactivity to image the blood within the cavity of the heart—the so-called blood pool that the heart is pumping in and out. By looking at the motion of the various portions of heart muscle squeezing on this blood pool, one can deduce that normally pumping areas are not ischemic and identify areas of muscle that contract poorly or not at all as not being properly supplied with blood. This testing has various names, including "gated blood pool scan," "multiple gated acquisition of images" (MUGA), or "radionuclide ventriculogram."

Blood pool or MUGA scans have several advantages. In a good lab, they are more accurate than the ECG stress test; they are good at localizing portions of the heart muscle with either permanent damage or reversible ischemia; and, finally, they are able to give an estimate of overall pumping function of the heart, which is one of the most powerful prognostic factors in determining outcome in many types of heart disease. Disadvantages are that they are expensive, they do not allow one to see all portions of the heart as well as one can on perfusion scans, and they are probably harder to read than perfusion scans.

Using some form of stress, either physical exercise or a drug (see discussion below of pharmacological stress), and the echocardiogram, rather than the radioactive tracer imaging of the blood pool described above, cardiologists can also directly assess regional and overall wall motion of the heart. The advantages to the echocardiogram are that it is quite sensitive, it is potentially cheaper and simpler (without radioactivity and all its attendant problems) than the radioisotope tests, and it measures the overall pumping function of the heart. Disadvantages are that it depends more on the skill of the individual operator than do the radioisotope methods and it is sometimes difficult to get high-frequency sound waves into the heart, especially if patients breathe hard with physical exercise (which is one reason why drugs are often used to stress the heart). With pharmacologically induced stress, various drugs are injected intravenously that make the heart work harder (e.g., dobutamine or persantine) for a few minutes while one of the radioisotope or echocardiographic tests is done on people who cannot exercise (e.g., because of peripheral vascular or orthopedic disease).

Cardiac Catheterization

The "gold standard" for diagnosis of CHD is cardiac catheterization, in which a small catheter is inserted into an artery (these days almost always a femoral artery in the groin, using only local anesthesia) and passed retrograde up the aorta into the ostia of the right and left coronary arteries. A radioopaque dye is injected, and cine films are taken of the coronary arteries. (This portion of a catheterization is also known as "coronary angiography.") Narrowings or obstructions can be precisely localized and their suitability assessed for angioplasty, other catheterization lab interventional techniques, or coronary artery bypass graft (CABG) surgery. Although the various noninvasive tests described above may be able to indicate presence or absence of coronary disease reasonably well, nothing but angiography can assess suitability for the various types of invasive therapy. A catheter is usually also passed retrograde through the aortic valve and into the left ventricle, a larger dose of radioopaque dye injected, and cine films taken of the left ventricle pumping to show regional and overall left ventricular function. (This is known as a "left heart cath.") If there are questions concerning valvular disease (as in a small minority of cases), pressure measurements may be taken in various chambers of the heart, and other catheters may be inserted through veins into the right side of the heart (a "right heart cath").

Echocardiography

Standard echocardiograms (i.e., those done at rest) are not used to diagnose CHD, but they are extraordinarily useful for diagnosing valvular disease and cardiomyopathy, which can sometimes produce signs or symptoms mimicking CHD. Echocardiograms, or "echos," can show the size, shape, thickness, and function of each of the various heart chambers; using Doppler, flow across valves and its direction can be estimated rather well, and good estimates of valvular stenosis or regurgitation—presence, severity, changes over time, and likely need for intervention based on effects of the valvular lesion on the various portions of the heart—are obtainable from an echo. Given the ability of an echocardiogram to examine the contraction of heart muscle, global decreases in contractility often are highly suggestive of cardiomyopathy. Being totally noninvasive and without any risk whatsoever, these days, the echo is almost always the screening test before cardiac catheterization for valvular disease or cardiomyopathy.

Holter Monitoring

The Holter monitor (named after N. J. Holter, who conceived of and built the first models in the early 1960s) is a small, Walkman-sized device that records 1 or 2 leads of the ECG throughout a 24-hour day while the patient goes about his or her usual activities. The patient generally keeps a diary to record any symptoms, so that the scanner can search the tape for any electrocardiographic events coinciding with and providing an explanation for any symptoms. Although theoretically Holter monitors might be useful for detecting ST-segment changes during out-of-hospital angina, the fact that only 1 or 2 leads, and thus only 1 or 2 areas of heart muscle, are monitored (vs. 12 or more leads or sites with the ECG recorded in the exercise laboratory during the standard exercise stress test) means that the Holter monitor is not frequently used for the diagnosis of angina (although it is indispensable for diagnosing silent ischemia). Rather, Holter monitors are most used for evaluation of arrhythmias and symptoms that might be associated with arrhythmias (e.g., palpitations or syncope [fainting]), which occur in patients with CHD as well as other types of heart disease.

Prognosis and Treatment of Stable Coronary Artery Disease

By the time any clinical symptoms of CHD appear (e.g., angina or acute MI), coronary atherosclerosis is often anatomically far advanced. Nearly all patients with symptomatic CHD will have narrowing of 70% or more of the cross-sectional area of at least one major coronary artery. As a general rule, of 100 patients with chronic stable angina, about 40% will have disease of all three major coronary vessels (triple-vessel disease), 40% will have double-vessel disease, 10%–15% will have single-vessel disease, and a few will have little or no obvious disease. Severity of anginal symptoms does not correlate at all with extent of anatomic disease.

Figure 2 shows a schematic diagram of the coronary arteries. The three major arteries are as follows: (a) the right coronary artery (RCA), supplying the right ventricle (thin-walled, pumping only a short distance to the lungs under relatively low pressure, and thus rarely the cause of problems in CHD) and then, in its final portion, supplying the bottom (inferior) wall of the important left ventricle; (b) the left anterior descending (LAD) artery, which descends and supplies the large front (anterior) wall of the left ventricle and the intraventricular septum; and (c) the left circumflex (LCx) artery, which circles back and around to the left and supplies the far lateral (side) wall and sometimes part of the bottom wall of the left ventricle. Some branches of the major arteries may be quite important (especially if there are obstructions in the main vessels), particularly the diagonal and septal branches originating from the LAD, the obtuse marginal branches (om1, om2, etc.) from the circumflex, and the posterior descending and posterolateral branches from the distal RCA.

Figure 3 shows examples of various typical types of coronary blockages. Three blockages are obviously worse than two or one; a total blockage is worse than a partial one, and a proximal blockage (closer to the origin of the vessel) is worse than a distal one (farther from the vessel's origin) because a larger area of the heart muscle is in jeopardy.

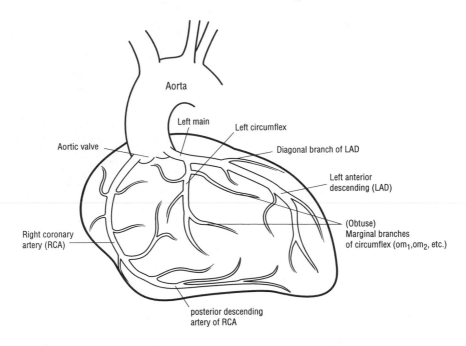

Aorta

Left main

Left circumflex

Aortic valve

Diagonal branch of LAD

Left anterior
descending (LAD)

Right coronary
artery (RCA)

(Obtuse)
Marginal branches
of circumflex (om_1,om_2, etc.)

posterior descending
artery of RCA

Figure 2. Schematic of the coronary arteries.

Prognosis in chronic stable angina is related to several factors. First, narrowing of the left main trunk (the short section between the left coronary ostium and the branching into the two main LAD and LCx arteries) is the most ominous and usually mandates immediate CABG surgery. Second, triple-vessel disease has a worse prognosis than double-vessel disease. Alternatively, single-vessel disease, in most cases, has quite a good prognosis, and surgery is rarely recommended. Third, proximal severe narrowings of the arteries have a worse prognosis; disease of the proximal LAD is particularly dangerous and usually requires intervention (angioplasty or CABG surgery). Fourth, in most people, either the LCx or the RCA is large and supplies the inferior wall of the left ventricle; that vessel is thus termed *dominant*. The nondominant vessel (which is more often the LCx) does not supply much heart muscle; therefore, disease there is not very important and rarely requires interventional therapy.

Prognosis is also better in people who have suffered no damage to heart muscle (i.e., have a normal left ventricle) and worse in those who have had one or more MIs and whose left ventricular function is below normal. Patients with triple-vessel disease and subnormal left ventricular function have a particularly poor prognosis if treated with medications; this group (as well as those with left main disease) definitely benefit from CABG surgery, whereas data are much less clear for other categories of

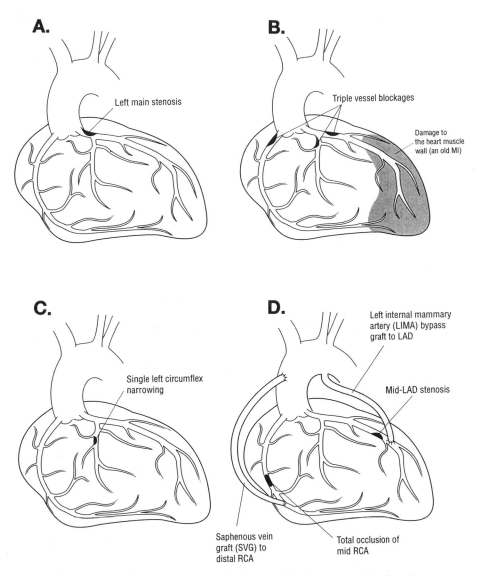

Figure 3. Examples of common types of coronary heart disease. A: Left main stenosis, which is very dangerous. B: Proximal (at the beginning of the vessel) triple-vessel blockages, which are dangerous. C: Single left circumflex narrowing, which is statistically not that dangerous (can be fixed with angioplasty). D: Double-vessel disease (Mid-LAD stenosis and mid-right total occlusion), shown with bypass grafts; of medium importance in comparison with A, B, and C. MI = myocardial infarction; LAD = left anterior descending.

angina patients (those with single- or double-vessel disease and those with normal left ventricular function).

The quantitative measurement used to describe ventricular function is usually the ejection fraction. In a normal heart, there are approximately 100 ml of blood in the left ventricle at the end of diastole, when in-flow (diastolic filling) is complete. During systole, the contraction phase, not all but a little more than half (usually about 55% ± 5%) of this blood is ejected in the normal heart. This ratio of the ejected volume to the filling volume is called the *ejection fraction*. Normal ranges for ejection fraction vary somewhat between the various means of measurement (in the catheterization lab, on an echo, or by nuclear study) and in various hospital laboratories, but in general a normal ejection fraction is greater than 50%, whereas ejection fraction below 45% is suspect, and below 40% is clearly abnormal.

A final factor related to prognosis in chronic stable angina is that prognosis is better in patients with good exercise tolerance and good stress tests and worse in people with poor exercise capacity and those with strongly positive stress tests (e.g., with ECG changes early in the test, at a very low level of exercise).

Low-risk angina patients have mild-to-moderate angina and an inability to exercise (they are able to walk more than two blocks and climb at least one flight of stairs without problems) and no angina at rest. They have good left ventricular function (ejection fraction >40%–45%), and their stress tests are not "alarmingly positive" (i.e., do not suggest large amounts of jeopardized myocardium at low stress levels). If a coronary angiogram is done, such patients will usually have no left main or proximal LAD disease. Low-risk patients have an annual mortality rate of 2%–4% per year or less and an additional yearly rate of MI that is about half that. In other words, no major cardiac problem will occur in 90%–95% of low-risk angina patients in any given year. These rates of serious complications are low enough so that it has not been possible to demonstrate improved outcome with interventional therapy (CABG surgery or angioplasty); thus, patients and their physicians have a choice of medical (drug) or interventional therapy.

High-risk angina patients have more severe angina, with chest pain at minimal activity or at rest, an "alarmingly positive" stress test, or both. They often have proximal triple-vessel or left main coronary artery narrowings and may have subnormal left ventricular function. High-risk patients have an annual mortality rate above 4%–6% and as high as 10% per year when they have left main disease (plus, again, an additional MI rate that is about half the death rate). High-risk patients certainly need further diagnostic tests, usually a cardiac catheterization; interventional therapy according to the individual situation is often recommended.

Therapy of Angina Pectoris

Once diagnosed, angina pectoris can be treated medically with either pharmacologic therapy or interventional therapy. Pharmacologic therapy for angina includes the use of five categories of drugs:

- Beta-blockers
- Calcium blockers
- Nitrates
- Aspirin and other antiplatelet drugs
- Antilipid drugs (depending on the blood lipid abnormalities)

See the Appendix to this chapter for more detailed descriptions of these types of drugs and their usage.

Interventional therapy for angina can include any of the following invasive procedures: percutaneous transluminal coronary angioplasty (PTCA) and recent variations on this procedure, implantation of stents, and CABG surgery.

PTCA

PTCA, or angioplasty, is a procedure done by an interventional cardiologist (not a surgeon) in the cardiac catheterization laboratory, whereby a small balloon, deflated on the end of a catheter, is introduced into an artery (under local anesthesia, usually into the femoral artery in the groin, exactly as in the procedure used for cardiac catheterization), passed retrograde up the aorta through the coronary ostia, and to the site of the blockage to be treated. The blockage must be partial, not total, so that the deflated balloon can be positioned next to the plaque. Once in position, the balloon is inflated at high pressure (6–10 times atmospheric pressure) but at controlled volume (the balloon has a certain size that it cannot exceed), so that the plaque is "squashed" but the artery is not unduly stretched. Sometimes it is necessary to do several inflations, each for 30–90 seconds, before a particularly hard plaque is sufficiently squashed.

Interventional cardiologists pick and choose in advance (from the cine films obtained at coronary angiography) those plaques that they think will give a good result without undue risk. In general, lesions that are amenable to successful, low-risk PTCA are those that are short, not around very sharp bends, not at points where very important vessels branch off from the vessel being treated, not at ostia, and "protected" by some other open vessel (so that if a complication should occur, and the treated vessel should temporarily occlude during or just after PTCA, the tissue supplied by the vessel will have an alternative source of blood supply).

Standard PTCA has an initial ("primary") success rate well over 90% in most laboratories and very low complication rates: The death rate from PTCA is perhaps 0.5%, with MI occurring as a complication of PTCA in about 1% and emergency CABG surgery needed because of acute closure of the vessel post-PTCA in about 1%. Perforation of the treated vessel is very rare, but dissection (tearing of the wall) is not uncommon (although dissection usually causes no problems other than the need to keep the patient on heparin anticoagulation a day or two longer than otherwise would have been the case). Damage to the peripheral vessel where the angioplasty catheter was introduced (usually the femoral artery) occurs occasionally. By far the biggest problem with angioplasty has been the high frequency of what is known as *restenosis*—developing in 30%–35% of patients, usually within 3–6 months of the procedure—with no known way to predict who will develop early restenosis and, so far, no treatment that will prevent it. Restenosis appears to be an exuberant rapidly developing atherosclerosis that may be related to the vessel-wall damage caused by the PTCA procedure; it often returns the vessel to approximately the same degree of stenosis that existed before the procedure, rather than making things worse than if PTCA had never been done. After a patient has one episode of restenosis, many interventional cardiologists will recommend a second try at PTCA. The second time around, the odds of restenosis seem to still be 1 in 3 (i.e., patients again have a 2 in 3 chance of success with this nonsurgical procedure, even after one failure). There would often be a tendency to try one of the newer devices, such as laser, atherectomy, or a stent (vide infra) after one episode of restenosis. After two episodes of restenosis, however, it would appear that there is something biologically different about that patient and that PTCA is not likely to work, no matter how many times one tries. Such patients have to undergo CABG surgery if it is felt that their stenotic coronary artery lesions must be treated.

With regard to this difficult issue of restenosis with PTCA, patients simply have to be informed of the relatively high risk (1 in 3 that the procedure will be for naught) balanced by the exceedingly low mortality and morbidity associated with PTCA and the fact that almost no disability results from the procedure (patients are out of the hospital and back at normal activities within 48–72 hours of PTCA).

Newer Variations on Standard PTCA

There are several devices, approved by the U.S. Food and Drug Administration and tested in several thousand patients, that purport to offer advantages of one sort or another over standard balloon angioplasty. The most important of these include (a) laser angioplasty catheters that transmit laser light through fiber optics in the catheter and vaporize atherosclerotic plaque rather than squash it; (b) atherectomy catheters of several designs, which actually cut away atherosclerotic plaque; and (c) ablation catheters, which remove plaque in ways other than cutting (e.g., the rotablator, which rotates at high speed and shears off tiny fragments of plaque).

In general, these alternative devices are used in a minority of patients in whom standard PTCA is felt unlikely to succeed (e.g., those with a lesion at an ostium). The devices are associated with slightly higher (but still quite low) complication rates than standard balloon PTCA, and they are often used in conjunction with standard PTCA; for example, an atherectomy might be done first, and then the lesion is "finished off" with a standard balloon angioplasty. It was initially hoped that the removal of atherosclerotic tissue and creation of a wider lumen than is often achieved with standard PTCA might lower the restenosis rate, but, in general, the newer devices seem to have the same 30%–35% restenosis rate as standard PTCA.

Stents

Stents are tiny metal devices that are delivered by a catheter in a collapsed state to the site of an obstructing lesion and then expanded (either springing out by their own elastic recoil or being expanded by the delivery catheter) so as to mechanically stent (support) the atherosclerotic lesion and mechanically prevent collapse of the vessel or regrowth of atherosclerosis. Because stents are foreign bodies within the arterial tree, patients used to be vigorously anticoagulated for a time after their placement, and the rate of bleeding and vascular complications was considerable. Recently, many laboratories have reduced the intensity of anticoagulation considerably in stents that appear optimally placed in the coronary artery; many patients now receive only the antiplatelet drugs aspirin and (for a few weeks) ticlopidine. Two European studies (Fischman et al., 1994; Serruys et al., 1994) seem to suggest that stents are indeed associated with lower restenosis rates in comparison with standard PTCA.

CABG

CABG surgery is so effective because of a curious attribute of the atherosclerotic process: It is segmental, usually affecting one or a few short segments of arteries while leaving the remainder of the artery quite untouched. Although there are a few unfortunate patients with diffuse atherosclerosis throughout their arteries (especially those with severe diabetes), the vast majority of angina patients have circumscribed narrowings and then clear sections into which a bypass graft can be inserted to supply the remainder of the artery (and heart muscle) beyond (downstream from) the blockage. It is not necessary to do anything at all to the area of blockage, and, possibly, the damage done to a vessel by trying to clean out areas of atherosclerotic blockage might do more harm than good. New conduits for blood are simply attached to the aorta and then to the blocked artery at a clear spot downstream from the blockage (see Figure 3D). The best replacement for a coronary artery is another artery, but there are few expendable arteries in the body, except for the mammary arteries. These two arteries, which run on the inside of the sternum (breastbone), are hardly needed to supply breast tissue in either men or postmenopausal women (which includes most of those with sufficient coronary atherosclerosis to require bypass surgery). The proximal end of a mammary artery is left connected to the aorta, and the distal end is disconnected from the inner surface of the chest wall and from the breast tissue and plugged into a coronary artery. These days, most patients in whom anatomy is suitable have the left internal mammary artery (LIMA) used to bypass important lesions of the left anterior descending coronary artery (which is located on the front of the heart, close to the sternum); unfortunately, the right internal mammary artery usually is not long enough to reach beyond most lesions in the right or circumflex coronary arteries. Thus, most patients these days receive one LIMA, and for other bypasses saphenous vein grafts (SVGs) are used, whereby portions of vein are removed from the upper or lower leg, which has several extra veins to compensate for anything removed and used as a graft.

More than 350,000 CABG procedures are done yearly in the United States; the operative mortality rate is 1%–2% on average, but this percentage is higher in women (about 1.5 times that of men, even when the slightly higher age and larger number of risk factors in women who need CABG surgery are corrected for), in elderly people (but no major increases until after age 80), in those with subnormal left ventricular function, and in those with various other risk factors. CABG surgery is associated with relief of angina in the vast majority of patients; indeed, patients experience better pain relief and improved exercise tolerance for several years in comparison with those patients treated medically. However, an enormous debate continues to rage 25-plus years after the first CABG surgery about (a) whether surgery patients live longer than medically treated patients (some subgroups do, like those with left main disease and triple-vessel disease with subnormal ejection fraction, but other subgroups may not), (b) whether surgery prevents MIs (uncertain), and (c) whether surgery puts people back to work. With regard to the last controversy, surgery does not seem to have any better result than medical therapy: In spite of less anginal pain and better exercise tolerance, more than half of angina patients retire within 2–5 years of treatment, whether treated with medicines or CABG (some of this, of course, may be because angina tends to occur in people who are nearing retirement age anyway).

The Acute Coronary Syndromes

Although angina pectoris is often quite bothersome to patients and its presence suggests advanced coronary atherosclerosis, chronic stable angina by its very name can continue for years or decades with little change in the patient's status and relatively low rates of catastrophic events. In some patients, something changes, and their coronary disease becomes unstable. The pathogenesis of the unstable coronary syndromes is certainly not settled, but a current hypothesis is that, in many cases, thrombosis is added to atherosclerosis. Often, thrombosis seems related to rupture of the atherosclerotic plaque, which allows material from the inside of the plaque to come in contact with the bloodstream. This apparently sets off many different events, including attraction and activation of platelets, activation of thrombin and the clotting system, changes in the function of the coronary arterial wall itself (particularly the endothelium), and many other physiological events. Three clinical acute coronary syndromes have been recognized: acute MI, unstable angina and non-Q-MI, and ventricular arrhythmia and SCD.

Acute MI

Acute MI is death of heart muscle. There are two types, so-called Q-wave and non-Q-wave infarctions. Q waves are electrocardiographic manifestations of through-and-through damage to the wall of the heart (from the epicardium through to the endocardium, the outside to the inside of the wall) and are usually associated with a total occlusion of the coronary artery that supplies that portion of the heart wall.

Clinically, an MI is usually manifested by severe and prolonged chest pain, classically lasting more than 20–30 minutes, often accompanied by associated symptoms, such as sweating, shortness of breath, nausea or vomiting, and a feeling of impending doom. Many patients have atypical symptoms, including shoulder or arm pains that are confused with arthritis, epigastric pains that are confused with gastrointestinal disease (ironically, often described as "heartburn"), or sometimes no symptoms whatever. (As many as 20% of infarcts in some studies have been discovered accidentally months or even years later when an ECG is routinely done; this percentage of "silent infarcts" is higher still in people with diabetes and elderly people.) It is striking how similar the symptoms of acute MI are to the manifestations of panic attacks. Sometimes the context will provide clues: A young woman with no cardiac risk factors and a plausible emotional trigger for the symptoms is more likely to be having a panic attack, whereas a middle-aged, overweight, hypertensive, diabetic, heavy-smoking man is more likely to be suffering an acute MI. At times, however, it is impossible to be sure, and those practitioners intent on diagnosing either an acute MI or a panic attack should always consider the differential diagnosis and take appropriate diagnostic steps to attempt to clarify what is really going on. In a great many patients, presenting symptoms and signs are compatible with, but not diagnostic of, acute MI, and they will be observed for several hours or a day or two to rule out MI (i.e., appropriate tests are run [see below] to either confirm or deny that the symptoms represent an MI).

The diagnosis of acute MI is made from the clinical history (prolonged chest discomfort, often with associated symptoms); the ECG (some changes, e.g., new ST-segment elevations, are very reliable; other ECG findings are only suggestive; and some patients have no ECG changes whatsoever, so that it is unwise to rely on the ECG alone); and measurement of cardiac enzymes that are normally contained within heart muscle cells and only leak out into the blood if those cells die. The most commonly used enzyme is creatine (phospho) kinase, or CK (formerly known as CPK). It takes about 6 hours from the time heart muscle dies for CK to leak out of the heart into the bloodstream sufficiently to be measurable as an elevation of blood CK. CK is found not only in the heart but also in other tissues, such as skeletal muscle, so a more specific form of CK—the myocardial fraction, or CK-MB—is also measured to differentiate enzyme in the blood of heart muscle origin from enzyme originating from other sites.

There are two very important reasons for beginning therapy for acute MI as soon as possible: (a) the potential for minimizing damage with thrombolytic therapy (administering drugs that dissolve the clot that has acutely obstructed the atherosclerotic vessel), and (b) the considerable risk of life-threatening ventricular arrhythmia that occurs in 5%–10% of patients in the first few hours following acute coronary occlusion. If the patient is hospitalized with continuous ECG monitoring, a computer or nurse detects the life-threatening arrhythmia within seconds of onset; a powerful electrical shock is given with equipment that is always located immediately at hand in coronary care or other monitored units; and, aside from a considerable scare to both patient and medical personnel, no harm usually results and a life is saved. As to thrombolytic therapy, it is now incontrovertible that substantial numbers of lives have been saved with one of the clot-dissolving agents: tPA (tissue plasminogen activator), which is a naturally occurring substance in the body that is available through genetic engineering in large doses to be administered immediately and intravenously to "beef up" the body's own clot-dissolving mechanisms, or streptokinase, a substance derived from streptococcal bacteria that has similar effects to tPA. Both agents open the thrombosed infarct-related artery within 30–90 minutes in at least two thirds of patients. Such rapid restoration of blood flow not only saves lives during the initial hospitalization but also reduces the amount of eventual myocardial damage and so improves long-term survival.

One complication of acute MI is arrhythmia, not only the life-threatening ventricular arrhythmias and cardiac arrest, but also atrial arrhythmias (which are a sign of considerable myocardial damage and also can cause problems in their own right, especially if the ventricular rate associated with atrial fibrillation, atrial flutter, or atrial tachycardia is very high). CHF can also occur when a good deal of heart muscle is infarcted. In the most severe form of heart failure, cardiogenic shock occurs when the heart cannot even maintain the blood pressure >90 mm systolic, and, as a result, perfusion is compromised to the most vital areas of the body: the brain (causing confusion and decreased mental status), the kidneys (causing greatly decreased urine output), and other areas. Shock is associated with damage to >40% of the entire left ventricle. Patients with acute MI also develop blood clots (thrombi) that may occur in the legs (venous thrombosis) and cause emboli to the lungs (pulmonary emboli) or may develop in the cavity of the left ventricle itself (most likely at the site where the MI extends to the inner wall of the heart). These clots, called *mural thrombi* (*mural* is Latin for "wall"), can also embolize, and if clots travel to the brain, they produce embolic strokes, which occur in about 1% of patients in the first few days following acute MI.

The treatment of acute MI encompasses a host of possibilities, most of which have been validated through large randomized clinical trials as reducing early or late mortality. These treatments are outlined briefly below:

- Thrombolytic therapy: Administering tPA is slightly more effective than streptokinase, but both are far better than nothing in patients who have ST-segment elevations (the usual sign of a Q-wave MI and thus of a clot totally obstructing a coronary artery, which can be dissolved by the thrombolytic agent 60%–80% of the time).
- Aspirin: A single aspirin, taken early in the course of MI, has a major beneficial effect, again because of its effect in dissolving clots.
- Heparin: This is an intravenously administered anticoagulant that potentiates the effect of tPA and, in particular, prevents reocclusion of a coronary artery that has been opened by a thrombolytic agent in the first few hours after MI.
- Warfarin (Coumadin): This oral anticoagulant, administered chronically, probably reduces recurrent MI by reducing the chance of recurrent thrombosis for several years after MI.
- Acute and chronic beta-blockers: By decreasing heart rate and contractility, and thus oxygen needs, these agents decrease muscle damage in the critical early hours when the coronary artery is occluded. Beta-blockers are also excellent antiarrhythmic agents (discussed below) and decrease the death rate, especially from SCD, for at least 6 years after MI (and possibly longer; data are only available to 6 years so far).
- Angiotensin converting enzyme (ACE) inhibitors: These vasodilators are thought to effectively reduce the work of the heart and thus decrease the extent of myocardial damage, but they probably have other actions. ACE inhibitors are useful for treating large MIs and especially for patients with heart failure or poor ventricular function in preventing death, recurrent MI, and CHF for several years after MI.

Other treatment of MI involves helping patients deal with the stress of this sudden, usually unexpected, and often emotionally shattering event; assisting in lifestyle changes to reduce risk factors (e.g., smoking, high-fat diet, high serum cholesterol, obesity, or sedentary lifestyle) that probably contributed to the atherosclerosis that caused this MI and may cause future MIs if not controlled; and providing rehabilitation to prevent adverse physical and emotional consequences of inactivity for the 2–3 weeks or so that are generally advised for fibrous healing of the MI.

Unstable Angina and Non-Q MI

These two syndromes, quite different in their emotional implications, have recently been considered together because they appear to have the same pathologic substrate: an atherosclerotic plaque with an overlying thrombus, but rather than a total occlusion (as in Q-wave MI), there is subtotal occlusion by the thrombus. Because there is some flow through the area, damage to heart muscle tends to be less than in the Q-wave type of MI, as well as not full thickness endocardium to epicardium. This results in a different ECG pattern: New ST depressions occur rather than ST elevations, and Q waves do not develop (thus "non-Q infarction," or NQMI). In some cases the flow through the lesion is sufficient so that no tissue dies, cardiac enzymes do not rise, and the condition is called "unstable angina." In both unstable angina and NQMI, there is substantial chest pain, often as long (>20 minutes) and as severe as in other types of MI. Chest pain often occurs at rest and without exertion or other obvious factors that usually precipitate chronic stable angina. Unstable angina usually results in brief hospitalization to rule out MI (if there is no muscle damage, then no healing period is necessary) and often some sort of examination to assess the extent of provokable ischemia. Although the initial death and complication rate of unstable angina and NQMI are quite low, total deaths and recurrent MIs 1 year after NQMI are the same as in patients with the larger Q-wave infarcts. This is because the coronary atherosclerosis is just as bad in NQMI as in Q-wave MI. The patient was lucky once that the clot was not totally occlusive, but a substantial chance remains that another clot will occur, often outside the hospital, and so the recurrent infarct rate is higher and the eventual death rate the same in the non-Q "small" MI group as in the "large infarct" Q-wave group.

The treatment of unstable angina includes any or all of the following:

- Hospitalization and bed rest to reduce myocardial blood and oxygen needs.
- Aspirin (initially) to treat partially occlusive coronary artery thrombi; if at-rest chest pain persists, then intravenous heparin is added as a stronger anticlot agent.

- Nitroglycerin to dilate coronary arteries and reduce myocardial oxygen needs by also dilating peripheral veins and reducing venous return to the heart. It is initially given sublingually, orally, or as a patch or paste on the skin; if at-rest pain persists, however, intravenous nitroglycerin is a powerful treatment for the myocardial ischemia of unstable angina.
- Beta-blockers to reduce heart rate, blood pressure, and contractility.
- Cardiac catheterization (often) to delineate anatomy; if at-rest pain persists, then PTCA if feasible. If at-rest pain stops, then a stress test is often administered to assess the extent of provokable ischemia (if results are alarming, then the same calculations apply as were discussed above for stable angina).

Neither CABG nor thrombolytic therapy has been proven effective as a general rule in patients with unstable angina, so they are used infrequently.

Ventricular Arrhythmia and SCD

Some patients with atherosclerotic CHD and myocardial ischemia have chronic stable angina, with chest discomfort precipitated only by physical exertion. Others, with sudden and total thrombotic occlusions of a major coronary vessel, develop acute MI with severe prolonged pain, death of heart muscle, and sometimes pumping difficulties due to loss of a great deal of functioning muscle. A third group, with partially but not totally occlusive thrombi, develop at-rest pain and transient ECG changes and have unstable angina or a small NQMI, usually without hemodynamic consequences. A final clinical consequence of sudden and severe myocardial ischemia is disturbance of cardiac rhythm, most often the development of ventricular arrhythmias of one sort or another. There is a continuum of such arrhythmias:

1. Single ventricular premature contractions (VPCs), often seen in the context of acute or chronic CHD and not considered terribly dangerous;
2. Couplets or triplets (two or three VPCs in a row), with these repetitive ventricular beats considered more ominous and sometimes presaging;
3. Self-limited bursts of many VPCs in a row, termed "nonsustained ventricular tachycardia";
4. Sustained ventricular tachycardia, which is a very rapid (usually 160–280 beats/minute) rhythm originating in the ventricle, often associated with major symptoms (dizziness, fainting, chest pain, palpitations, and weakness) and signs of

hemodynamic compromise (very low blood pressure). This frequently degenerates to

5. Ventricular fibrillation, a chaotic movement of electrical impulses through the myocardium in such an uncoordinated way that effective heart pumping stops, forward cardiac output and blood pressure fall to near nothing, and cardiac arrest ensues within seconds. With circulatory collapse, brain death occurs within 4–6 minutes unless effective cardiopulmonary resuscitation (CPR) is begun immediately.

Unfortunately, ventricular fibrillation is not infrequently the first and last symptom of acute cardiac disease in large numbers of patients; there are 200,000–300,000 SCDs every year in the United States. The definition of SCD is usually death within 1 hour of onset of symptoms in a person not expected to die; this excludes hospitalized patients with terminal diseases whose final event may be stopping of the heart but whose basic problem is not SCD. Note also that the definition of SCD does not exclude prior cardiac disease, and, indeed, many people who drop dead suddenly in the street did have known heart disease—perhaps a heart attack a year or two before—but were not expected to die that day.

When the hearts of people who die suddenly are examined at autopsy, the same pathology is found as occurs in patients who have died of acute MI: atherosclerotic plaques, a plaque rupture, and a totally occlusive thrombus on top of the plaque, but no necrosis (cell death) of the heart wall (no MI) because death occurred so quickly. Intriguingly, in patients who have been resuscitated and then hospitalized, about half do develop signs of MI (i.e., the ventricular fibrillation was a manifestation of the earliest stages of acute MI), but half never do (i.e., myocardial ischemia can cause life-threatening ventricular arrhythmia without necessarily causing muscle death).

Although the treatment of angina has improved greatly and the mortality and morbidity of acute MI are much reduced in comparison with 20 years ago, there has been relatively little progress in reducing the toll of SCD because the vast majority of events occur on the street or in the home, outside of the medical care system. Improved paramedic services and better public education have helped only a bit. A few cities have trained large numbers of citizens in CPR so that, in theory, help should be close at hand in many instances when cardiac arrest occurs. However, in most places in the United States, paramedics cannot reach cardiac arrest victims within the 4–6 minute window before brain death occurs, and that time frame does not even take into account the necessity for someone to witness the event, recognize that a cardiac arrest has occurred, and take the proper actions immediately, including calling for paramedics.

Although little progress has been made in reducing the toll of SCD in people without previously known CHD, there have been many new developments in the burgeoning field of electrophysiology if a patient has been identified as being at high risk for life-threatening arrhythmia. Patients at highest risk include those with major past myocardial damage (one large or several smaller infarcts); those who have had heart failure; those with ventricular arrhythmia and poor left ventricular function, particularly if they have had fainting spells (syncopal episodes); those with documented sustained ventricular arrhythmias; and those who have had a prior cardiac arrest (patients surviving one cardiac arrest have a 20%–40% chance of having another within a year or two).

Once a major ventricular arrhythmia is suspected, a screening test called the "signal-averaged ECG" can be done to search for very low amplitude electrical currents within the heart at a time when such currents should not be detectable. If the test is positive or if other events lead to a very high suspicion of serious ventricular arrhythmia, then patients can be referred for an electrophysiologic study (EPS), which is a type of cardiac catheterization in which catheters are introduced into the heart to stimulate the heart electrically and attempt to reproduce the life-threatening arrhythmia under controlled circumstances in the laboratory (if the arrhythmia occurs, emergency equipment is instantly available, and the arrhythmia is terminated within seconds).

If a serious arrhythmia cannot be provoked in the EP laboratory (a "negative EPS"), then it is highly unlikely that serious arrhythmia will occur spontaneously outside the hospital. Thus, patient and referring physician can be reassured, and neither antiarrhythmic drugs nor other antiarrhythmic therapy need be given. If a serious arrhythmia can be provoked in the EP laboratory, then intravenous doses of one or more standard antiarrhythmic drugs are tried to see whether they suppress the dangerous arrhythmia. If they do, then the effective antiarrhythmic drug or drugs are prescribed after discharge from the hospital. Experience has shown that if an arrhythmia is controlled by a certain drug in the EP laboratory, then the drug will provide good control after hospital discharge. If a serious arrhythmia can be provoked in the EP laboratory and it cannot be suppressed or prevented by standard antiarrhythmic medications, then two choices exist: (a) administration of the unusual but often effective drug amiodarone (not amenable to laboratory testing for effectiveness because results in the laboratory do not seem to correlate with effectiveness in everyday life after hospital discharge) or (b) implantation of an automatic implantable cardioverter defibrillator (AICD), an automated miniaturized defibrillator that continuously monitors the heart rhythm and automatically administers an electrical shock to the heart within a few seconds after it detects a life-threatening arrhythmia. Although it is invasive, expensive, complicated, and often more than a bit scary for the patient and the uninitiated physician to realize that prevention of a possible cardiac arrest and death is in the hands of a small internally implanted, battery-powered box, the AICD has proven exceptionally reliable, and very few SCDs occur in patients who have received AICDs.

VALVULAR HEART DISEASE

Etiology and Anatomy of Valvular Disease

Many years ago, valvular disease was synonymous with rheumatic heart disease, but because infectious diseases have declined in developed countries, acute rheumatic fever and thus, the late sequela of rheumatic heart disease, is presently responsible for less than half of valvular disease in the United States.

Acute rheumatic fever is an autoimmune disease and occurs about 3 weeks after an untreated or unrecognized streptococcal infection, very often a "strep throat" in children or adolescents. Although doctors do not fully understand the pathogenesis of rheumatic heart disease, it appears that some antigens in the heart are similar to antigens in certain species of streptococcus bacteria, and as the body fights off the streptococcal infection, it generates antibodies that attack certain portions of the heart as well as the bacteria. Acute rheumatic fever usually occurs in children or adolescents and can be a serious illness, but it can also be so benign that much of the time adults with evidence of unequivocal rheumatic valvular disease can recall no history of childhood acute rheumatic fever. More important than the initial illness, though, is the insidious development over years and even decades of fibrous (scar) tissue that primarily affects one or more of the cardiac valves.

The late sequelae of rheumatic heart disease almost always affect the mitral valve, with or without involvement of other valves as well. The valve between the left atrium (the reservoir or holding chamber for blood returning from the lungs) and the left ventricle (the main pumping chamber to the body) is called the *mitral valve*, so named because, from some angles, it supposedly resembles a bishop's mitre. To most people, this valve looks more like a parachute, with two valve leaflets tethered to the wall of the left ventricle by fibrous strands called *chordae* that are the equivalent of cords (shrouds) holding the canopy of a parachute to the harness and preventing the main body of the device from billowing upward. In late rheumatic disease, the mitral valve is usually affected by a scarring process that leads to shortening and fusion of the chordae and also fusion of the commissures, the "seams" where the two valve leaflets are joined. Eventually, calcium is deposited in the scar tissue. The end result is a valve that is far less mobile than normal, most often considerably narrowed and unable to allow sufficient blood to flow through it during exercise, when blood flow must increase to meet the needs of the body. Obstruction to flow at the mitral valve, termed *mitral stenosis*, has exactly the same consequences as construction lane closures on a major freeway. First, there is backup of blood (or traffic) before the obstruction, which in the cardiovascular system produces dilation and increased pressures in the left atrium and the lungs and may result in movement of fluid from the bloodstream into the interstitial tissue or, in extreme cases, even into the alveoli of the lungs themselves, where gas exchange occurs. The increased lung fluid makes the lungs heavier and stiffer, and the patient has increased difficulty breathing (shortness of breath, or dyspnea). The second consequence of obstruction at the mitral valve is the body's inability to increase blood flow through the valve when needed, so that patients often are tired and must reduce their levels of activity. A stiff, immobile, possibly calcified rheumatic mitral valve may not only fail to open properly (stenosis) but may also not close properly, producing a leak backward into the left atrium when the left ventricle contracts forcefully in systole. This condition, known as *mitral regurgitation* or *mitral insufficiency*, similarly raises pressures in the left atrium and pulmonary circulation (causing dyspnea and other consequences). However, it also puts a strain on the left ventricle because the pumping chamber now must pump much more blood than normal: It must pump forward (out the aorta) to meet the needs of the body in addition to any blood leaking backward through the mitral valve into the left atrium.

The other valve often affected by rheumatic valvular disease is the aortic valve, located at the exit of the left ventricle where the aorta begins. Similar to the pathologic process that affects the mitral valve, rheumatic aortic disease can cause aortic stenosis, in which the valve leaflets or cusps are thickened, scarred, fibrotic, and often calcified and the commissures are fused, and thus the valve does not open properly. Because of their deformities and immobility, the valve leaflets also may not close properly, producing a leak from the aorta backward into the left ventricle when the ventricle relaxes in diastole, termed *aortic regurgitation* or *aortic insufficiency*.

On the other, right side of the heart, the valve between the right atrium and right ventricle is the tricuspid valve. Quite similar to the mitral valve, the tricuspid valve also is parachutelike, with large leaflets or cusps tethered to the ventricular wall by chords. However, the tricuspid has three rather than two cusps (hence its name). The tricuspid valve is rarely affected directly by the rheumatic autoimmune process, but it is commonly involved secondarily from the high pressures that are transmitted backward through the left atrium and the lungs to the right side of the heart and, thus, the tricuspid valve, in patients with either mitral stenosis or regurgitation. Eventually, the tricuspid valve is so stretched or dilated that it does not close completely, and tricuspid insufficiency or regurgitation occurs.

The fourth heart valve, the pulmonic valve, is anatomically and functionally nearly identical to the aortic valve and located just next to it at the exit to the right ventricle, which is the beginning of the pulmonary artery. Primary disease of the pulmonic valve is almost unheard of in adults; there are congenital anomalies of the pulmonic valve, but these are usually discovered and treated early in life.

Apart from rheumatic disease, the other major cause of valvular disease is degenerative disease. As the U.S. population ages, degenerative valvular disease is increasingly important; presently, among native-born Americans who have valvular disease, the etiology is more likely degenerative than rheumatic.

In many cases, degenerative disease is actually some inborn propensity that is exacerbated with the passage of time. For example, in mitral valve prolapse (MVP), a person is born with a tendency for the mitral valve to be more easily stretched and to develop larger, thinner leaflets with extra "folded over" or so-called redundant tissue. Then, after 20 or 30 years of wear and tear, the stretchable and redundant mitral valve apparatus is stretched to the point where it prolapses backward into the left atrium or leaks (see Figure 4).

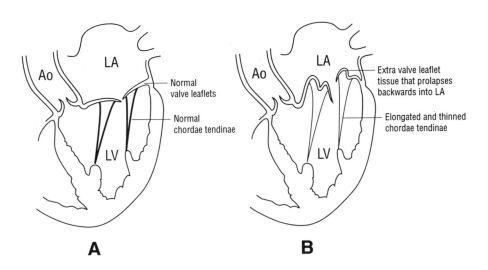

Figure 4. Schematic of a heart with a normal mitral valve (A) and one with mitral valve prolapse (B). LA = left atrium; LV = left ventricle; Ao = aorta.

MVP—also known as "floppy mitral valve"—is astonishingly prevalent in the U.S. population, occurring in as many as 6%–10% of females and about 4% of males. The tendency to develop MVP is inherited, so that the disease runs in families, but by no means will all people with the genetic condition actually develop clinical disease. The clinical manifestations of MVP are described below.

Clinical Syndromes of Valvular Disease

Valvular disease may come to medical attention because of a patient's complaints, but more often it is first discovered when a physician hears a heart murmur during a physical examination. What causes heart murmurs? Basically, it is turbulent blood flow. The situation is quite akin to water flowing down a smooth streambed. As long as the stream is straight and wide, with a smooth bottom, there is little turbulence and little sound. However, add sharp turns, sudden narrowing of the banks, or large boulders in the streambed, and the water no longer flows smoothly: ripples, eddies, or rapids develop, and the stream is no longer silent but, rather, becomes a "babbling brook." The situation of flowing blood within the heart is quite analogous: As long as there is a normal valve with a sufficiently wide opening (orifice) the blood flows through smoothly and there is neither turbulence nor sound, whereas with a thickened, stiffened, calcified, or narrowed valve, turbulence results and produces audible vibrations that the physician hears through the stethoscope as a heart murmur.

It should be noted that not all heart murmurs indicate significant anatomic disease. A smooth-bottomed, wide, and straight river may flow quietly during the summer, but the same river may generate turbulence and, thus, sound with vastly increased flow during the spring runoff of melting snow. Similarly, in some people—especially those young or thin or with high blood flow (e.g., during pregnancy, after exercise, or with anemia)—a murmur may be heard in the absence of any anatomic disease. This is usually termed a *physiologic*, or *innocent*, murmur.

Aortic Stenosis

Aortic stenosis is narrowing of the valve leading out of the left ventricle to the aorta and supplying the entire body aside from the lungs. Aortic stenosis causes a systolic murmur heard at the base of the heart.[5]

---

[5]The anatomic descriptions of the heart are a bit counterintuitive. The free tip of the heart, which indeed looks like an apex, is called the "apex" but is actually situated closest to the feet (a bit below the left nipple in most people). The heart is tethered by its connections to the great vessels, the aorta and pulmonary artery, both of which leave the heart at the end nearer the head, just slightly below the Adam's apple, which is called the "base" of the heart. Thus the base, which for a bookcase or pyramid usually means "down," is actually that part of the heart that is uppermost, near the throat, whereas the apex, in most figures of speech usually taken to mean the top, is, in the human heart, nearest the feet.

There are frequently no symptoms associated with aortic stenosis until rather late in the course of the disease. When symptoms do develop, the three major ones are exertional chest pain (similar to angina pectoris, the chest pain caused by narrowing of coronary arteries), heart failure, and syncope (sudden loss of consciousness). Any of these three symptoms in a patient with significant aortic stenosis is grounds for major concern: It has been estimated that the median survival period (if no corrective action is taken) in patients with angina and aortic stenosis is only 2 years; after syncope and aortic stenosis, only 1 year; and after heart failure and aortic stenosis, less than a year.

If the physical examination and noninvasive tests (notably, the echocardiogram) are compatible with significant aortic stenosis, then the standard for definitive diagnosis is cardiac catheterization. A normal aortic valve is approximately 4 cm^2 in area. Important aortic stenosis begins when the valve is narrowed to about half of its normal size, a valve area somewhat less than 2 cm^2. Severe aortic stenosis is generally diagnosed for those with aortic valve areas below 1 cm^2, and critical aortic stenosis (where serious consideration is given to early valve replacement) is indicated by valve areas of approximately 0.8 cm^2 or less.

The treatment for significant aortic stenosis is usually surgical replacement. These days, aortic valve replacement carries an average operative mortality of 3%–5%. There is a procedure called *aortic balloon valvotomy* that is done in the cardiac catheterization laboratory and involves passing a balloon to the aortic valve and forcefully inflating it to break up some of the scar tissue that narrows the valve. Although not requiring surgery and its attendant risks, balloon valvotomy has been less successful than initially hoped, with substantial complications during the procedure itself and a high incidence of redevelopment of substantial stenosis within a year or less after the procedure. Thus balloon aortic valvotomy is used only occasionally, for the very old or prohibitively high-risk surgical candidate.

Aortic Regurgitation

In addition to rheumatic or degenerative etiologies, there are other causes of aortic insufficiency or regurgitation. One group of etiologies involves the aorta, rather than the valve. In fact, several degenerative diseases attack the aortic root and, in weakening the attachments of the valve, produce aortic regurgitation. These include idiopathic dilation of the aortic root, a disease of unknown etiology wherein the wall of the early portion of the aorta weakens with time; dissecting aneurysm of the aorta, where there is weakening and tearing within the several layers of the wall of the aorta; bacterial endocarditis, where an infection on or near the valve destroys valve tissue or attachments to the aortic wall; and, rarely, inflammatory or autoimmune diseases that attack the aortic root or valve. There are also other, genetic causes such as Marfan's syndrome. In past generations, syphilis in its late phase could attack the ascending (initial portion of the) aorta, and as dilation of the ascending aorta developed, so did aortic regurgitation.

Symptoms of aortic insufficiency, as with aortic stenosis, are often delayed for years or even decades, so significant valvular leaks (and sometimes, unfortunately, significant and even irreversible myocardial damage) may occur before the patient is aware that anything is wrong. The physician may hear a diastolic murmur over the aortic area at the base of the heart or find abnormally low diastolic blood pressure. The patient may complain of shortness of breath or may develop CHF as the first manifestation of aortic insufficiency. The echocardiogram can give a fair estimate of the amount of regurgitation, and, as with aortic stenosis, cardiac catheterization is done when it seems likely that valve replacement is needed. The standard treatment for significant aortic regurgitation is valve replacement, which carries an operative mortality rate of 5%–10%. Vasodilating drugs that reduce "afterload"—that is, the pressure faced by the heart after cardiac contraction begins and the left ventricle begins to eject blood—reduce the amount of regurgitation and may delay the need for valve replacement.

Mitral Stenosis

The third major valvular lesion is mitral stenosis, which is essentially always of rheumatic etiology. Obstruction to flow between the left atrium and the left ventricle develops over long periods of time, often decades, with two major consequences: (a) shortness of breath (dyspnea), caused by increased pressures within the lungs, and (b) fatigue, caused by too little blood getting through the stenotic mitral valve. Long-standing mitral stenosis also frequently causes an irregular rhythm called *atrial fibrillation*, which greatly increases the risk of embolic stroke. The severity of mitral stenosis can be estimated from echocardiograms and is diagnosed definitively by cardiac catheterization when the patient's symptoms of dyspnea or fatigue seriously interfere with a normal lifestyle. Treatment is sometimes a surgical repair of the valve called a *mitral commisurotomy* but, more often, mitral valve replacement.

Mitral Regurgitation

Mitral regurgitation can be of rheumatic origin but there are two other important causes. One is CHD, related to dysfunction of the portion of the left ventricle that acts as a strut to hold the mitral valve in place as the left ventricle contracts. As the ventricle contracts and ejects blood, the cavity gets smaller; the mitral supporting apparatus must also shorten to keep the valve from ballooning backward into the left atrium. The muscular struts that hold the valve leaflets tight as the ventricle contracts are called *papillary muscles*. In some MIs, the papillary muscles themselves are damaged, and dysfunction (or sometimes, frank rupture of these small muscles) can produce mitral regurgitation; in other cases, dilation or bulging of the wall of the left ventricle at or near the papillary muscles interferes enough with normal papillary muscle function to produce mitral regurgitation.

Another important reason for mitral regurgitation, these days certainly the most common etiology, is MVP. As noted above, MVP is a congenital connective tissue disorder wherein the valve structures stretch with the passage of time. In the United States, approximately 6%–10% of females and about 4% of males are born with this tendency, which works out to tens of millions of people in the United States.

The vast majority of patients with MVP have either no symptoms or very minor problems that fall in the category of "nuisance" rather than true danger. Some patients develop a small leak through the floppy valve, (minor mitral regurgitation) and, thus, have heart murmurs. An even smaller number develop substantial mitral regurgitation and may need a valve replacement. A certain proportion of patients with MVP have arrhythmias, some of which cause palpitations (and there are many people who complain of palpitations without there being much or anything in the way of arrhythmia). However, serious or life-threatening arrhythmia is extremely rare. There is a slightly increased risk of subacute bacterial endocarditis, a dangerous infection of the heart valve. In addition, chest pains of various sorts are not uncommon in patients who have MVP. All in all, serious complications requiring substantial medical intervention occur in only a small minority of patients with MVP—perhaps 5%–10% of patients with MVP over a lifetime—yet most cardiologists are constantly bedeviled by various and sundry complaints and anxieties from those who have MVP.

There is ongoing debate about the frequency, pathogenesis, nature, and even the existence of psychological manifestations of MVP. There clearly is an association between classic panic attacks and MVP, although the proportion of patients with MVP who actually have true panic attacks is quite small. More important and less certain is what may be an association between MVP and various other symptoms, including palpitations, chest pains, shortness of breath, and anxiety. Although some well-done scientific studies in referral centers have shown little or no association between MVP and anxiety or various symptoms that appear related to anxiety, atypical, hard-to-diagnose and hard-to-treat symptoms are so commonly encountered in everyday practice that it is hard to believe that there is not some association between MVP and various psychosomatic-sounding complaints. Therapeutically, it is important for both physicians and patients to know that the vast majority of people with MVP have what is truly a trivial condition; that most will never have any substantial disability referable to MVP; and that, for the vast majority, the only change in their lives will be the need to take prophylactic antibiotics for dental work. (For the large number of people with MVP who have a click only without murmur,[6] even this is not needed.) The average patient with MVP will require only a physical examination and perhaps an occasional echocardiogram once every year or two to be sure that substantial regurgitation is not developing; for everyone else, an enormous amount of reassurance is in order.

CARDIOMYOPATHY

The third major type of heart disease is cardiomyopathy: disease of the heart muscle itself. The word itself stems from the Greek words *cardio* for "heart"; *myo* for "muscle"; and *pathos,* meaning "pain" or "unhappiness." Somewhat less literally, the disease is one in which the heart muscle is unable to pump required amounts of blood while maintaining the expected pressures and volumes within the chambers of the heart.

Etiology

There are a large number of possible etiologies for cardiomyopathy, but in the United States the vast majority of cases are due to one of five causes: atherosclerotic disease (ischemic cardiomyopathy); hypertension; alcohol; an unusual genetic condition in which the heart muscle is initially hypertrophied but eventually weakened (hypertrophic cardiomyopathy); or unknown causes (idiopathic cardiomyopathy).

Ischemic cardiomyopathy refers to the situation wherein the amount of functioning cardiac muscle is greatly reduced because of one or more MIs. In some patients, the MIs are recognized as they occur; in others, the loss of sufficient muscle to produce heart failure is due to the cumulative effect of several smaller infarcts, sometimes even silent infarcts. It is entirely possible, then—and indeed, by no means rare—for a person to present with cardiomyopathy that eventually turns out to be of ischemic etiology despite never having suffered a clinically diagnosed acute MI.

A second major cause of cardiomyopathy is hypertension. After many years of pumping against increased resistance, heart muscle hypertrophies, eventually may dilate, and in some patients function is lost permanently, even if high blood pressure is subsequently controlled. Because hypertension can be completely silent, it is not uncommon for the first manifesta-

---

[6]This is an abnormal sound heard through the stethoscope in some patients with MVP, caused by the valve leaflets' prolapse suddenly being checked when the chordae become taut at the limit of their ability to stretch.

tion of long-standing undiagnosed hypertension to be hypertensive cardiomyopathy, and the damage to the heart muscle may already be irreversible.

Various agents are toxic to heart muscle and can produce irreversible damage under certain conditions. Alcohol (more than 4–6 drinks per day over a prolonged period) and certain chemotherapeutic agents (e.g., adriamycin, when used in high doses or for a long time) are the only common toxic etiologies. Some highly unusual causes do exist, however, including beri-beri, a few infectious diseases (notably, HIV), and dozens of other rare specific etiologies that, altogether, account for only a few cases in the United States.

One specific type of cardiomyopathy is genetic and not uncommon: hypertrophic cardiomyopathy. In the early stages of this unusual disease, there is thickening of the walls of the left ventricle and an increase in the strength of contraction of the muscle. However, the wall thickening is not uniform and is most prominent in the septum dividing the left and right ventricles, resulting in so-called asymmetric septal hypertrophy. The septum, especially its upper part, forms one wall of the outflow tract of the left ventricle, and substantial hypertrophy in this area can literally obstruct the ventricle's own outflow. The characteristic location of this obstruction to outflow, just below the aortic valve, explains the more common name of the disease: idiopathic hypertrophic subaortic stenosis, or IHSS. For reasons that are not understood, perhaps related to the long-standing obstruction to its own outflow (but perhaps not), eventually the supernormal heart muscle function deteriorates to subnormal, and the situation resembles other cardiomyopathies. Major cardiac arrhythmias, including a substantial risk of SCD, are part of the clinical picture of IHSS (as they are with other cardiomyopathies); many of the often highly publicized sudden and unexpected deaths of young people during athletic events turn out at autopsy to be associated with undiagnosed cardiomyopathy, either hypertrophic or idiopathic.

Each newly discovered patient with cardiomyopathy or heart failure should undergo an echocardiogram to rule out valvular disease and IHSS, a stress test and often cardiac catheterization to rule out CHD or ischemic cardiomyopathy, and a selective search for other potential etiologies as indicated by individual circumstances. If no cause is found, the diagnosis becomes unknown—or idiopathic—cardiomyopathy, which may be responsible for as many as half the cases of cardiomyopathy in the United States.

CHF

The clinical presentation of cardiomyopathy is most often CHF, so termed because one of the more obvious manifestations is the buildup of excess fluid; heart failure can also result from coronary disease (one or more episodes of MI, in which substantial portions of heart muscle have died) or from valvular disease. The responses of the heart to a decrease in its pumping ability are, first, to dilate the pumping chambers and start contraction with higher volumes and pressures that develop during diastole, the filling phase; second, the use of adrenergic (adrenalinlike) stimulation to increase the force of contraction; and third, thickening of the heart muscle wall (hypertrophy). Unfortunately, each of these compensatory mechanisms causes problems of its own. Reliance on increased adrenergic drive often causes tachycardia (increased heart rate), sometimes increased blood pressure, and sometimes cardiac arrhythmias. Increasing diastolic filling volumes and pressures results in increased pressures transmitted backward through the cardiovascular system, and often these increased back pressures cause leakage of fluid out of blood vessels into the tissues. Hypertrophy is associated with a tendency to sometimes dangerous arrhythmias.

The symptoms of CHF include shortness of breath, particularly with exertion (dyspnea on exertion); orthopnea (the inability to lie flat); paroxysmal nocturnal dyspnea (awakening some time after lying down, and having to sit up or stand to breathe); leg edema; and, in the most severe cases, pain in the right upper quadrant of the abdomen (from liver engorgement with excess fluid); increased abdominal girth (ascites, or fluid within the peritoneal cavity); cyanosis (blue color of the mucous membranes or nail beds due to diminished oxygen in the blood); and greatly diminished exercise capacity or fatigue (low cardiac output).

There are three generally accepted therapies for heart failure: diuretics, digoxin, and ACE inhibitors. Diuretics are given to get rid of any excess fluid; some salt restriction is frequently requested, although compliance with very low sodium diets is difficult and can remove pleasure from eating. Most physicians request that patients remove the salt shaker from the table, add no extra salt in cooking, and use prudence in eating out and in not eating obviously salt-laden foods. Most of people's daily salt consumption (about three fourths) comes from salt that is commercially added in food processing, so that careful shopping, constant reading of food labels, and efforts to use more fresh and less processed foods are important for those with CHF (Mattes & Donnelly, 1991). Diuretics, especially the powerful "loop" diuretics (e.g., furosemide [Lasix], ethacrynic acid [Edecrin], or bumetanide [Bumex]; so termed because of their action in that part of the kidney called the "loop of Henle") cause not only loss of water and sodium but also loss of potassium and magnesium. These last two elements are important for muscle strength and for protection against cardiac arrhythmia, so potassium supplements are usually administered together with powerful diuretics.

Digitalis has been in use for well over 200 years, yet there has been recent argument over its efficacy. Although there are still some dissenters, most cardiologists do believe that digitalis drugs (today almost exclusively digoxin [Lanoxin]) are modestly effective in increasing the strength of contraction of the heart, and they are usually given to patients with substantial heart failure. Digoxin in excess has a number of side effects, including anorexia, nausea, and cardiac arrhythmia, so reasonably close monitoring is advised.

ACE inhibitors (captopril [Capoten], enalapril [Vasotec], lisinopril [Prinivil or Zestril], and many others) were developed as antihypertensive drugs but have proved to be extraordinarily useful in therapy for heart failure. By vasodilating peripheral vessels, they reduce afterload, an effect akin to opening several new lanes on an overcrowded freeway. Although nothing has been done to the engines of individual automobiles, the new lanes allow everyone to move faster. In the same way, although ACE inhibitors have no direct effect on myocardial contractility, the decrease in peripheral resistance that they provide usually allows the heart to improve its pumping efficiency. It is now incontrovertible that ACE inhibitors prolong survival in patients with major CHF, as well as reduce hospitalizations for CHF and even (by mechanisms that are quite obscure) reduce the incidence of future MI (Pfeffer et al., 1992).

What is highly disappointing is that an ongoing search for better drugs that improve contractility, the basic defect in CHF, has, to date, proved fruitless. This leaves a major dilemma for a substantial number of patients with severe CHF or cardiomyopathy whose symptoms cannot be controlled with the standard therapies of digoxin, diuretics, salt restriction, and ACE inhibitors. There are some short-term temporizing treatments, and then there is cardiac transplantation. Although heart transplantation has good operative results and even fair medium-term survival, it is applicable to only a small number of patients with severe CHF and cardiomyopathy, because of the severe shortage of donor hearts, the enormous cost, the immense physical and psychological burdens on the very sick patient, the need for lifelong immunosuppressive drugs, and a host of other reasons. Currently there is an amazing lack of good therapy for severe ventricular dysfunction, and as deaths from other types of heart disease decline, morbidity and mortality from cardiomyopathy looms as one of the most pressing problems in modern cardiology.

OTHER TYPES OF HEART DISEASE

Pericardial Disease

A membrane surrounding the heart, the pericardium, consists of two layers with a tiny bit of fluid between the layers, thus allowing the heart to expand and contract easily with minimal friction. Occasionally, the pericardium becomes inflamed ("pericarditis"), causing chest pain and certain ECG changes. This is most often a benign, self-limited disease caused by a viral infection, but it rarely can be prolonged, severe, or recurrent or can even cause so much accumulation of fluid or scar tissue between the two layers of pericardium as to interfere with the pumping function of the heart. The major importance of pericarditis in everyday cardiology is that its symptoms of acute chest pain and ECG changes can sometimes mimic acute MI.

Endocarditis

Rarely, bacteria from the bloodstream can lodge on structures of the cardiovascular system, begin to grow, and cause a very serious infection that is lethal if not treated properly, known as *endocarditis*. The most common predisposing factor is a damaged structure within the bloodstream, particularly a diseased (stenotic or regurgitant) valve, together with some situation when bacteria enter the bloodstream (particularly during dental work or manipulation in an area of the body that cannot be sterilized, such as the mouth, gastrointestinal, or genitourinary tract). Endocarditis can be insidious in its onset, with infection present for weeks before fever, anemia, fatigue, or other vague symptoms bring the patient to seek medical attention. The diagnosis is made by finding bacteria circulating in the bloodstream, and the treatment is high-dose intravenous antibiotics, often for many weeks or even months.

Arrhythmias

Ventricular arrhythmias were discussed above in the section on CHD. Although CHD is probably the most common underlying etiology for serious ventricular arrhythmias, other causes are cardiomyopathy, far-advanced valvular disease, and a number of drugs (e.g., excess digoxin; certain antiarrhythmic drugs—a paradox, where a drug meant to treat arrhythmia actually has the opposite effect and provokes it; and tricyclic antidepressants [quite rare, and usually only overdoses, but see the section on bradyarrhythmias, below]).

Atrial arrhythmias are quite common and are caused by a number of etiologies. Atrial fibrillation is the most common, occurring in several million Americans; it is associated with the advanced stages of coronary, valvular, or cardiomyopathic disease; with hyperthyroidism; and in some older patients, occurs as a substitute rhythm when the normal rhythm that drives the heart (the sinoatrial node, or just the "sinus") no longer works properly. Atrial fibrillation is sometimes converted back to normal sinus rhythm with an electrical shock (administered across the chest, rather than the head, as in electroconvulsive therapy, although otherwise the procedures are not dissimilar), but many patients who do convert with the electrical shock unfortunately revert back to atrial fibrillation within a relatively short time. Cardiac function is only mildly affected by atrial fibrillation, and many patients are quite unaware of the arrhythmia so long as the heart rate (the rate at which the ventricles pump) is in the normal range, something that is usually not difficult to achieve with digoxin or other drugs. Atrial fibrillation is associated with a substantial risk of stroke from clots that form in the fibrillating ("quivering," but not properly emptying) atria; thus, an additional therapy is anticoagulation (thinning of the blood) to prevent such clots from forming and breaking loose to cause strokes and other mischief far from the heart.

Other atrial arrhythmias occur as a result of congenital electrical short circuits, which allow the electrical currents of the heart to take unusual pathways and sometimes cause very rapid beating of the heart. The usual patient complaint is palpitations, and this can occur in young people with no other manifestations of heart disease. Thus, a cardiac workup, often including some sort of ambulatory monitoring, is often in order if a patient gives a believable complaint of palpitations not related to psychological stress.

Bradyarrhythmias and some conduction defects are slow rhythms, sometimes so slow that the heart does not pump enough blood to the brain, and so patients become dizzy, faint, or (rarely) even have a cardiac arrest. (Note that although the word *arrest* suggests "stopping," the more common arrhythmia associated with cardiac arrest is the very rapid, chaotic ventricular fibrillation, in which no blood is pumped and so the circulation is "arrested." Slow rhythms, where the heart actually "stops," are quite rare.) Slow heart rhythms and conduction defects[7] have a number of causes: degenerative disease of the electrical system of the heart (quite akin to "fraying" and intermittent malfunction or eventual nonfunction of the electrical wires of an 80-year-old lamp); certain types of MI, as a complication of some heart surgery; and a number of drugs, notably digoxin, beta-blockers, certain calcium blockers, and tricyclic antidepressants. The treatment of symptomatic bradyarrhythmias or conduction defects is implantation of an electrical pacemaker.

CONCLUSION

CHD (also termed *CAD*) has three major clinical syndromes: angina pectoris, acute MI, and SCD. All of these are associated with one or more

---

[7]Conduction defects occur in severe cases where electrical impulses do not move properly from the normal intrinsic pacemaker of the heart (the sinus node), located at the top of the heart in the right atrium, to the pumping chambers (the ventricles) at the bottom of the heart.

atherosclerotic narrowings or total occlusions of coronary arteries. Given the relationships between risk factors and the incidence of CHD, as well as the importance of psychosocial factors in affecting traditional risk factors for atherosclerosis (such as obesity; high calorie, high-fat, or high-saturated-fat diet; and lack of physical exercise), it is clear that more links need to be forged between the cardiologic and psychological aspects of caring for people who already have CHD or at are risk for developing it. Furthermore, certain psychosocial factors appear to have considerable influence on survival after acute MI.

There are fewer patients with valvular heart disease or cardiomyopathy, and their pathogenesis is not clearly related to psychosocial factors, but many of the symptoms—and some of the drugs used in their treatment—do have implications for psychologists.

The Appendix on cardiac drugs at the end of this chapter summarizes both therapeutic and adverse effects, which should alert both psychologists and cardiologists to the potential for good and harm from the drugs that are commonly used with cardiac patients.

Brief as this chapter has been in attempting an overview of so much of cardiac disease, psychologists need to understand the natural history of the major cardiac conditions, and cardiologists need to be sensitive to the psychological nuances of caring for such patients. It is hoped that improved mutual understanding will foster collaboration between practitioners of heart and mind for the benefit of their mutual patients.

REFERENCES

Anticoagulants in the Secondary Prevention of Events in Coronary Thrombosis (ASPECT) Research Group. (1994). Effect of long-term oral anticoagulant treatment on mortality and cardiovascular morbidity after myocardial infarction. *Lancet, 343,* 499–503.

Braunwald, E. (1992). *Heart disease: A textbook of cardiovascular medicine* (Vols. 1–2, 4th ed.). Philadelphia: W. B. Saunders.

Fischman, D. L., Leon, M. B., Baim, D. S., Schatz, R. A., Savage, M. P., Penn, I., Detre, K., Veltri, L., Ricci, D., Nobuyoshi, N., Cleman, M., Heuser, R., Almond, D., Teirstein, P. S., Fish, R. D., Colombo, A., Brinker, J., Moses, J., Shaknovich, A., Hirshfeld, J., Bailey, S., Ellis, S., Rake, R., & Goldberg, S., for the Stent Restenosis Study Investigators. (1994). A randomized comparison of coronary stent placement and balloon angioplasty in the treatment of coronary artery disease. *New England Journal of Medicine, 331,* 496–501.

Hills, L. D., Lange, R. A., Winniford, M. D., & Page, R. L. (1995). *Manual of clinical problems in cardiology* (5th ed.). Boston: Little, Brown.

Mattes, R. D., & Donnelly, D. (1991). Relative contributions of dietary sodium sources. *Journal of the American College of Nutrition, 10,* 383–393.

Pfeffer, M. A., Braunwald, E., Moye, L. A., Basta, L., Brown, E. J., Jr., Cuddy, T. E., Davis, B. R., Geltman, E. M., Goldman, S., Flaker, G. C., Klein, M., Lamas, G. A., Packer, M., Rouleau, J., Rouleau, J. L., Rutherford, J., Wertheimer, J. H., & Hawkins, C. M., on behalf of the SAVE Investigators. (1992). Effect of captopril on mortality and morbidity in patients with left ventricular dysfunction after myocardial infarction: Results of the Survival and Ventricular Enlargement Trial. *New England Journal of Medicine, 327,* 669–677.

Scandinavian Simvastatin Survival Study Group. (1994). Randomised trial of cholesterol lowering in 4444 patients with CHD: The Scandinavian Simvastatin Survival Study (4S). *Lancet, 344,* 1383–1389.

Schlant, R. C., & Alexander, R. W. (1994). *Hurst's The heart* (Vols. 1–2, 8th ed.). New York: McGraw-Hill.

Serruys, P. W., de Jaegere, P., Kiemeneij, F., Macaya, C., Rutsch, W., Heyndrickx, G., Emanuelsson, H., Marco, J., Legrand, V., Materna, P., Belardi, J., Sigwart, U., Colombo, A., Goy, J. J., van den Heuvel, P., Delcan, J., & Morel, M., for the Benestent Study Group. (1994). A comparison of balloon-expandable-stent implantation with balloon angioplasty in patients with coronary artery disease. *New England Journal of Medicine, 331,* 489–495.

Shepherd, J., Cobbe, S. M., Ford, I., Isles, C. G., Lorimer, A. R., Macfarlane, P. W., McKillop, J. H., & Packard, C. J., for the West of Scotland Coronary Prevention Study Group. (1995). Prevention of coronary heart disease with pravastatin in men with hypercholesterolemia. *New England Journal of Medicine, 333,* 1301–1307.

Smith, P., Arnesen, H., & Holme, I. (1990). The effect of warfarin on mortality and reinfarction after myocardial infarction. *New England Journal of Medicine, 323,* 147–152.

Steering Committee of the Physicians' Health Study Research Group. (1989). Final report on the aspirin component of the ongoing Physicians' Health Study. *New England Journal of Medicine, 321,* 129–135.

APPENDIX
CARDIAC PHARMACOLOGY

Beta-Blockers

Class effects: These drugs block the beta-division of the adrenergic (sympathetic) nervous system, reducing heart rate, blood pressure (thus are antihypertensive), and strength of cardiac contraction. All of these effects reduce myocardial oxygen needs; thus, the drugs are anti-ischemic. They are also antiarrhythmic, suppressing premature contractions and often more serious atrial and ventricular arrhythmias. The drugs are also cardioprotective in that they reduce myocardial infarct size if given immediately after acute myocardial infarction (MI). They reduce recurrent MI when given chronically after an initial MI, and slightly increase heart size, and so reduce amount of mitral prolapse.

Patients: Those with MI (acutely and chronically), angina, hypertension, ventricular premature contractions (VPCs) and other arrhythmias, and mitral valve prolapse (MVP).

Side effects: Hypotension, extreme bradycardia, or congestive heart failure (CHF)—all rare; exacerbation of peripheral vascular disease; bronchospasm (do not use in patients with asthma or chronic pulmonary disease); may potentially mask or exacerbate diabetic hypoglycemia (rare); and some central nervous system (CNS) and mental status effects (less pep, diminished sexual desire, disordered sleep patterns, or worsened depression).

Specific Drugs

Propranolol (Inderal):[1] The prototype of beta-blockers, it is not cardioselective (i.e., tends to have more noncardiac side effects, such as bronchospasm in susceptible patients). *Nearly identical:* timolol (Blocadren) and many others.

Metoprolol (Lopressor, Toprol): More cardioselective.

Nadolol (Corgard): Cardioselective, also less lipid soluble than most others, so least likely to penetrate blood–brain barrier; theoretically has somewhat fewer CNS side effects. *Nearly identical:* atenolol (Tenormin).

Acebutolol (Sectral): Has intrinsic sympathomimetic effect, so that at low doses it does not decrease heart rate and blood pressure as much; useful in patients with low resting heart rate or blood pressure in whom one wants only to blunt responses to exercise. *Nearly identical:* pindolol (Visken).

---

[1]Throughout the Appendix, generic drug names are followed by trade names in parentheses.

Calcium Blockers

Class effects: These drugs are vasodilators of both peripheral arteries (are antihypertensive) and coronary arteries (are anti-ischemic). They do not appear universally effective in preventing recurrent MI (only under certain circumstances) and, thus, are not equivalent to beta-blockers for post-MI patients.

Specific Drugs

Diltiazem (Cardizem, Dilacor, others): Few side effects so most widely used. Can cause slow heart rate (bradycardia). Useful in preventing recurrent MI only after non-Q MI and only in those with good ventricular function.

Nifedipine (Procardia, Adalat): Probably the best vasodilator of the first-generation calcium blockers (those first available in the United States), so are often used for hypertension. Greater tendency than other calcium blockers to cause reflex tachycardia, palpitations, headache, and leg edema. Can cause depression of cardiac function and precipitate heart failure in a few patients who have poor ventricular function to begin with. *Nearly identical:* nicardipine (Cardene), nimodipine (Nimotop).

Amlodipine (Norvasc): More "vascular selective," that is, has fewer cardiac side effects such as precipitation of CHF. *Nearly identical:* isradipine (Dynacirc), felodipine (Plendil).

Verapamil (Calan, Isoptin, and Verelan): Probably the most powerful of the calcium blockers for angina because it slows heart rate and decreases contractility. Most likely to depress myocardial function and produce CHF, and also most likely to cause heart block. Intriguing suggestions have been made that verapamil and other calcium blockers may interfere with or delay atherosclerosis in experimental animals, but this has been hard to prove in humans. Often causes constipation.

Nitrates

Class effects: Nitrates induce coronary vasodilation, including dilation at sites of coronary artery stenoses; dilate peripheral veins, so they reduce venous return to the heart and thus heart size, which lowers myocardial oxygen needs; and are metabolized in vascular smooth muscle cells to nitric oxide, which is the local messenger substance that causes vasodilation, prevents platelets and monocytes from affecting the wall, and produces other salutory effects in coronary and other arteries. Nitrates are all subject to "tolerance"; that is, with continuous administration, their effects wane or even disappear. Thus, a "nitrate-free interval" of 8–10 hours is generally recommended to preserve efficacy in long-term administration.

Side effects: Headache, tachycardia, palpitations, hypotension.

Specific Drugs

Note that the differences between nitrate preparations are differences in rapidity of onset or duration of action; all nitrates work in the same manner.

Sublingual nitroglycerin: For the treatment of acute anginal attacks. Taken under the tongue, but not swallowed. Onset occurs within 30–90 seconds, duration of action is less than 30 minutes.

Isosorbide dinitrate (Sorbitrate, Isordil, and others): About 4-hour duration of action when taken orally. Requires 8–10-hour nitrate-free interval to avoid tolerance (usually at night).

Isosorbide mononitrate (Ismo, Imdur): Longer-acting preparations, taken once or twice a day.

Nitroglycerin transdermal patches (Transderm-Nitro, Nitrodur, others): Nitroglycerin absorbed continuously through the skin. Patch needs to be removed for the 8–10-hr nitrate-free interval (usually at night).

ACE Inhibitors

Class effects: These are vasodilators and antiangiotensin II drugs and, thus, excellent antihypertensives, especially in patients with high plasma renin. They are also a mainstay of therapy for CHF (reduce mortality, acute MI, and hospitalizations for CHF in patients with symptomatic CHF, as well as in those with poor ventricular function who have not yet developed symptoms of CHF).

Side effects: Substantial incidence of dry cough, which can become bothersome enough so that the drug has to be stopped. Can cause hyperkalemia and increase serum creatinine (reduce kidney function) in a few patients.

Specific Drugs

Although there are slight differences among the various drugs in this class, there is little evidence to suggest that any one is much different from another. Therefore, I simply list them alphabetically: benazepril (Lotensin), captopril (Capoten), enalapril (Vasotec), fosinopril (Monopril), lisinopril (Zestril, Prinivil), quinapril (Accupril), ramipril (Altace), and others.

Antilipid Agents

These agents are pharmacologically quite different and are listed as a separate class only because their ultimate goal is similar: to improve lipid profiles and thereby reduce atherosclerosis. Some are better at reducing low-density lipoprotein (LDL) and total cholesterol, others at increasing high-density lipoprotein (HDL); both effects are considered desirable.

Specific Drugs

Lovastatin (Mevacor): The prototype of a new class of drugs (the "statins") that interfere with an enzyme called *HMG Co-A reductase* and thereby reduce cholesterol production. Highly effective in reducing LDL and total cholesterol, and modestly raise HDL. Several clinical trials of one of the statins have shown highly favorable results in reducing serum cholesterols over the long term; in reducing clinical CHD events; and, just recently, in reducing the total death rate in a group of 4,444 patients with known heart disease (Scandinavian Simvastatin Survival Study Group, 1994) as well as in 6,595 patients with high serum cholesterol but no heart disease (Shepherd et al., 1995). *Side effects:* Occasionally raise liver enzymes and rarely can cause skeletal muscle damage, so require periodic blood tests. Should not be used together with niacin or gemfibrozil or may increase the risk of muscle damage. *Nearly identical:* pravastatin (Pravachol), simvastatin (Zocor), fluvastatin (Lescol).

Claims have been made that some of these agents (e.g., lovastatin) cause more sleep disturbance and possibly other psychological problems than others, but head-to-head comparisons have not been done and psychological problems are quite rare.

Gemfibrozil (Lopid): Often effective in raising HDL, a bit less effective in lowering LDL and total cholesterol. The net effect on the total cholesterol to HDL ratio—considered perhaps the best predictor of risk of atherosclerotic disease—is favorable in many patients on gemfibrozil. *Side effects:* Raises liver enzymes, occasional gastrointestinal upset.

Niacin: A vitamin, but when used in megadoses is effective in raising HDL and modestly effective in lowering LDL and total cholesterol. Very inexpensive, by far the cheapest of all the (expensive) antilipid agents. *Side effects:* Major flushing, which causes most patients to stop the drug unless it is initiated gradually and with a good deal of physician or nurse support; also elevation of liver enzymes and increase in blood sugar.

Cholestyramine (Questran): A resin that attaches itself to bile acids (a precursor of cholesterol) as they recirculate through the intestinal tract and, by carrying the precursor out in the stools, lowers serum cholesterol. *Problems:* Lots of gastrointestinal difficulties; the medication itself is a powder, and taking it is a bit like eating sand. One of the first drugs used in large-scale clinical trials because it was felt that this drug, which remains in the gastrointestinal tract and is not absorbed into the body, would be entirely safe. However, there has been a curious occurrence in an early large-scale clinical trial, wherein CHD events fell considerably, but the total death rate did not because of a seeming excess of suicides and other violent deaths. Some lingering questions about psychiatric side effects of antilipid drugs in general remain, although the Scandinavian Simvastatin and western Scotland (Shepherd et al., 1995) trials (see above) have made everyone feel a lot better about wider recommendations for drug therapy of hyperlipidemia. *Nearly identical:* colestipol (Colestid).

Probucol (Lorelco): An unusual drug that interferes with oxidation of LDL. Lowers LDL and total cholesterol, but unfortunately lowers HDL too (not considered a good thing). No good clinical trial of efficacy has been done in humans, so this drug is rarely used today.

Digoxin (Lanoxin)

Effects: This drug increases the strength of heart contractions and decreases ventricular rate in atrial fibrillation, flutter, and atrial tachycardia.

Patients: CHF, atrial fibrillation, other atrial arrhythmias.

Side effects (with high doses or overdoses): Nausea, vomiting, or anorexia; yellow or other colored vision; VPCs, heart block, junctional rhythm, or other arrhythmias. *Similar:* digitoxin (rarely used).

Diuretics

Class effects: Diuretics increase urine flow and decrease fluid in the body and vascular system; some are also vasodilators, and the combined effects of decreased body fluid and dilated vessels reduce blood pressure.

Patients: Those with hypertension and CHF.

Side effects: Variable; see specific drugs.

Specific Drugs

Furosemide (Lasix): Powerful, most widely used in the United States; causes hypokalemia (decreased body and serum potassium), so usually given together with potassium supplements; causes increased uric acid and sometimes gout; raises blood glucose and cholesterol slightly. *Nearly identical:* bumetanide (Bumex).

Ethacrynic acid (Edecrin): Similar to furosemide but generally used only in those allergic to furosemide.

Hydrochlorothiazide (Esidrex, Hydrodiuril, and others): Weaker than furosemide, very inexpensive, good for hypertension in many patients, and side effects similar to furosemide. *Nearly identical:* chlorthalidone (Hygroton) and many other thiazide diuretics.

Spironolactone (Aldactone): Medium strength as a diuretic. Potassium sparing (usually does not require supplemental potassium and may even raise potassium unduly). *Nearly identical:* triamterene (Dyrenium).

Metolazone (Zaroxolyn): Not a very powerful diuretic when used alone, but synergistic with furosemide and often used in difficult situations when high-dose furosemide alone does not produce sufficient diuresis.

Antiplatelet and Anticoagulant Agents

Warfarin (Coumadin)

This is the prototype anticoagulant drug (and currently essentially the only one used in the United States). It interferes with Vitamin K, which is necessary to activate several of the clotting factors of the body.

Patients: Those with mechanical valve replacements; most patients with atrial fibrillation; many patients with cardiomyopathy or poor ventricular function; some patients with coronary artery stents; some patients with recent clots in coronary arteries (e.g., after complicated percutaneous transluminal coronary angioplasty or thrombolysis); and possibly to prevent recurrent MI in patients who have recently suffered acute MI. (Two studies [Anticoagulants in the Secondary Prevention of Events in Coronary Thrombosis Research Group, 1994; Smith, Arnesen, & Holme, 1990] have shown warfarin to be effective, but currently most cardiologists are anticoagulating only patients who have large infarcts, especially anterior wall infarcts with a large dead area that is not contracting and where a clot might form.)

Side effects: Excessive anticoagulation can produce bleeding anywhere, including life-threatening bleeding such as into the brain and the gastrointestinal tract. Thus, the level of anticoagulation must be monitored closely, usually with monthly (at least) prothrombin time (PT): a blood test that measures the level of anticoagulation and allows periodic adjustment of the warfarin dose by the physician or nurse.

Aspirin

Aspirin is a very powerful antiplatelet drug that acetylates (and, essentially, paralyzes) platelets for the several-day lifespan of circulating platelets. This provides substantial protection against clots, in coronary arteries and elsewhere.

Patients: In those with acute MI, reduces death rate by 25% when taken immediately in the emergency room together with thrombolytic therapy; after acute MI, is modestly effective in preventing recurrence (about 10%–15% decrease in recurrence rates); in those with unstable angina, decreases rate of development of acute MI in the next 3 months by 50%; possibly reduces the incidence of MI in those who have never had CHD (in a study of 20,000-plus healthy physicians who took one buffered aspirin every other day, there were 100 fewer heart attacks [139 on aspirin vs. 239 on placebo] at a cost of about 21 more strokes and 31 more gastrointestinal ulcers; Steering Committee of the Physicians' Health Study Research Group, 1989).

Dipyridamole (Persantin)

A modestly effective antiplatelet drug that is rarely used, because aspirin is just as effective and much cheaper. Dipyridamole is used when antiplatelet effects are desired in patients who cannot take aspirin for one reason or another.

Ticlopidine (Ticlid)

A new antiplatelet agent whose place in cardiac pharmacology is not yet clear. It is much more expensive than aspirin and has yet to prove itself superior, but it is often used for a brief period (perhaps 1 month) after PTCA with stents to provide maximum antiplatelet effect. It also may be useful after transient ischemic attacks, precursors of stroke, to prevent a stroke.

Side effect: Neutropenia (depression of white blood cell count, which may be so severe as to leave the body unable to fight infections and, thus, be life threatening; white blood cell count must be monitored closely).

Antiarrhythmics

Quinidine: One of the so-called Class I antiarrhythmic drugs that are modestly effective in preventing or suppressing both atrial and ventricular arrhythmia, but also have been incriminated in increasing death rates in patients taking the drugs because of their ability to provoke serious arrhythmia. Usage is thus falling rapidly. *Similar (not structurally, but have pharmacologically similar actions):* procainamide (Procan, Pronestyl, others), flecainide (Tambocor), propafenone (Rhythmol), disopyramide (Norpace), mexilitine (Mexitil), moricizine (Ethmozine).

Amiodarone (Cardarone): A highly unusual drug that has become the antiarrhythmic drug "of last resort" for life-threatening ventricular arrhythmias, either when other drugs are proven ineffective by electrophysiologic study or because of the fears that the Class I antiarrhythmic drugs described above may actually provoke arrhythmia and increase the death rate. Amiodarone has to be given with a loading dose over a 10–14-day period before it is effective, dissolves in body fat, and can take months to be excreted after it is stopped.

Amiodarone is often used together with an implantable defibrillator; the implanted device is the ultimate protection against sudden death, but the drug prevents or reduces the number of serious arrhythmias that cause the device to fire, thus lengthening battery life and minimizing the psychological (and sometimes physical) effects of being defibrillated multiple times. *Similar (although without the pulmonary side effects)*: sotalol (Betapace). *Side effects:* A scary collection of problems, including lung damage (rarely but occasionally irreversible and capable of causing death even after the drug is stopped), interference with thyroid function, slow heart rate, provocation of serious arrhythmia, and others. Side effects are usually dose related.

3

EMPIRICAL BASIS FOR CARDIAC PSYCHOLOGY

ROBERT ALLAN and STEPHEN SCHEIDT

Systematic investigation of the relationship between heart and mind began in the late 1950s with the pioneering work of Meyer Friedman and Ray Rosenman, the two San Francisco cardiologists who coined the term *Type A behavior pattern* (TABP). Since that time there has been a great deal of research on psychosocial factors and coronary heart disease (CHD). The factors that appear most important include (a) TABP, (b) anger and hostility, (c) psychological stress, (d) job strain, (e) vital exhaustion, (f) social isolation and lack of social support, (g) depression, (h) anxiety, and (i) cardiac denial. In this chapter, we present highlights from the scientific literature linking each of these factors with CHD, followed by conclusions about the current validity of these relationships that we have reached as a psychologist–cardiologist team with an active interest in this field for more than a decade. Also included are data on patients with noncardiac chest pain, a sizable segment of the population referred for cardiologic workup and a group worthy of psychological study.

We also review a number of clinical trials for modification of psychosocial factors with patients who have CHD. Each of the three most im-

We have been supported in part by grants from the Pinewood Foundation, the Nathaniel and Josephine Sokolski Foundation, the Horace W. Goldsmith Foundation, and the Terner Foundation. Portions of this chapter have been published previously in *The Prevention of Sudden Cardiac Death* (Kostis & Sanders, 1991), *Prevention of Myocardial Infarction* (Manson & Hennekens, 1996), and *Cardiovascular Reviews & Reports* (Allan & Scheidt, 1992, 1993).

portant interventions—the Lifestyle Heart Trial, the Recurrent Coronary Prevention Project (RCPP), and Project New Life—is presented in detail in its own chapter in Part II of this volume. We conclude with a brief consideration of physiological mechanisms that may link psychosocial factors to CHD and suggestions about the future of cardiac psychology.

PSYCHOSOCIAL RISK FACTORS

TABP

TABP is a complex clinical phenomenon characterized by free-floating hostility, time pressure, and a number of psychomotor signs. It is an "action–emotion complex" that requires both cues from the environment and a predisposition to act in certain ways: a person–environment interaction. The empirical database for cardiac psychology was largely inspired by the Type A hypothesis, which has generated hundreds of studies and suggested numerous refinements. The hypothesis was originally formulated as follows:

> Type A behavior pattern is an action–emotion complex that can be observed in any person who is aggressively involved in a chronic, incessant struggle to achieve more and more in less and less time, and if required to do so, against the opposing efforts of other things or other persons. It is not psychosis or a complex of worries or fears or phobias or obsessions, but a socially acceptable—indeed often praised—form of conflict. Persons possessing this pattern also are quite prone to exhibit a free-floating but extraordinarily well-rationalized hostility. As might be expected, there are degrees in the intensity of this behavior pattern. . . . For Type A behavior pattern to explode into being, the environmental challenge must always serve as the fuse for this explosion. (M. Friedman & Rosenman, 1974, p. 67)

Ten years later, M. Friedman and Ulmer (1984) offered a more psychodynamic formulation of TABP, which is presented in Figure 1. In this model, insecurity and inadequate self-esteem form the nucleus of the behavior pattern. A life-long overemphasis on achievement is thought to be propelled by an unconscious drive for self-esteem. It is theorized that an individual becomes overly identified with personal accomplishment as a symbolic—yet unattainable—quest for self-worth. The two major symptoms of TABP are time urgency and free-floating hostility. In Type A theory, time urgency is thought to develop out of a preoccupation with productivity as the individual becomes driven to accomplish more and more in less and less time. Free-floating hostility is hypothesized to arise from a lack of unconditional love during childhood because of parental overem-

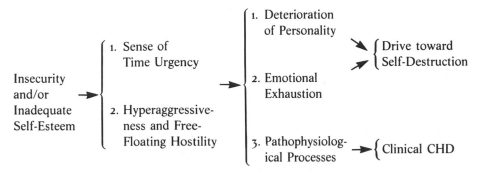

Figure 1. Interrelationships between Type A behavior components and pathophysiological processes. CHD = coronary heart disease. From *Treating Type-A Behavior and Your Heart* (p. 70), by M. Friedman and D. Ulmer, 1984, New York: Knopf. Copyright 1984 by Knopf. Reprinted with permission.

phasis on accomplishment. Free-floating hostility can also be intertwined with time pressure, triggered by a perception of interference with self-defining achievements.

Positive self-esteem and a sense of personal security, however, are unlikely to be attained solely by worldly accomplishment and may be more strongly related to interpersonal connectedness and "feeling loved." Hence, achievement leaves the individual unfulfilled when he or she is motivated by an unconscious, symbolic search for self-worth. Typically, a success cannot be savored for long but leads to a new round of challenges that are "bigger and better." Ultimately, time urgency, hyperaggressiveness, and free-floating hostility become pervasive, leading to a deterioration of personality and exhaustion. It is hypothesized that the pathophysiological processes accompanying the chronic Type A struggle accelerate atherogenesis, leading to premature CHD over the course of several decades.

The Case of John Hunter

The life of eighteenth-century English surgeon John Hunter provides a fascinating illustration of the Type A paradigm. Although it is unusual to observe poor self-esteem directly (particularly at a distance of two centuries), there is good reason to believe that Hunter suffered from this condition. First, Hunter had little formal education and never received a medical degree. Everard Home, Hunter's brother-in-law, disciple, and first biographer, described him as insecure: "[John had] diffidence respecting himself. . . . Giving lectures was always particularly unpleasant . . . so that the desire of submitting his opinion to the world and learning their general estimation were scarcely sufficient to overcome his natural dislike to speaking in public" (Home, 1794, p. xxiv). Before public lectures Hunter would often compose himself with a draught of laudanum (opium), and Home also noted that Hunter sometimes revised his lectures for 20 years before "giving them to press."

Hunter was a driven man, and this no doubt contributed to his vast productivity. When a person is driven by insecurity, however, the desire for achievement can become insatiable and give rise to the symptoms of time urgency and free-floating hostility. Failure to meet temporal expectations would often trigger Hunter's wrath. According to another early biographer (Ottley, 1841), "Hunter was a great economist of time. . . . Any unnecessary discomposure of . . . engagements greatly annoyed him, and caused him to give vent to his feelings in no unmeasured terms" (p. 43). Hunter's personality might be characterized as a bit heartless: "His temper was very warm and impatient, readily provoked, and when irritated, not easily soothed" (Home, 1794, p. lxiv).

Hunter's lifestyle and pace were hyperaggressive, another Type A characteristic, and it might be said that the manner in which he treated his own body was also somewhat heartless:

> Four hours of sleep . . . with an hour after dinner, was all the time he devoted to the refreshment of his body. He had no home amusements . . . for the relaxation of his mind. (Ottley, 1841, p. 43)

> He was generally to be found in his dissecting room before six in the morning and worked there until breakfast at nine. Then he saw patients at his house until twelve, after which he went out on his rounds. . . . He dined at four, slept an hour, and spent the evening working. At twelve the family retired to bed and the butler brought a fresh argand lamp, by the light of which Hunter continued his labors until one or two in the morning, or even later in winter. Of course, all this had the inevitable result: he broke down and had to go to Bath for a long convalescence. But the warning seems only to have made him work harder . . . and the pace grew faster. (Gloyne, 1950, p. 46)

A number of curious incidents in Hunter's life suggest self-destructiveness, another characteristic of TABP. Clearly, Hunter's hyperaggressive work habits negatively affected his health. This hard-driving manner, however, also extended to other spheres. For example, on one occasion he broke his Achilles tendon as a result of strenuous dancing, and on another he was nearly killed by a prize bull with which he was play-wrestling.

Hunter began to manifest angina pectoris when he was approximately 45 years of age:

> The symptoms of Mr. Hunter's complaint, for the last twenty years of his life, may be considered as those of angina pectoris, and form one of the most complete histories of that disease on record. . . . The affections . . . were readily brought on by exercise. . . . affections of the

mind also brought them on; but coolly thinking or reasoning did not appear to have that affect. (Home, 1794, p. xiv)

By the age of 65, Hunter had become the foremost surgeon in London. His contributions to the field of anatomy were prodigious and included the first explorations of the lymph system, important discoveries about the male and female reproductive systems, and, in 1792, the first description of "instantaneous" death from a "violent affection of the mind" (Hunter, 1792). For the last 5 years of his life, Hunter owned city and country homes and employed more than 50 people. He had been appointed Surgeon General to the Army, Inspector General of Hospitals, and Surgeon Extraordinary to George III, King of England. "He was almost adored by the rising generation of medical men, who seemed to quote him as the schools at one time did Aristotle" (Adams, 1817, p. 172).

Hunter was an eminent scientist and surgeon, a person who achieved fame and glory in his day. Yet, despite all this worldly success, things were not right in many of his interpersonal relationships. Beginning in 1788, "there was already war between Hunter and his colleagues" (Paget, 1797, p. 201). Hunter "depressed the merit of others and exalted his own . . . he affected to be too proud to explain. . . . He estranged himself from all intercourse with the corporation of surgeons. . . . He hated his equals in the profession, and who can esteem him who hates them?" (Foot, 1794, p. 276). At around this time, two young Scots without formal training applied to study at St. George's Hospital and appealed to Hunter's influence for their admission. Hunter took up the cause of these men, who surely must have reminded him of his younger self, against "a regulation which, thirty years sooner would have excluded himself from the hospital" (Adams, 1817, p. 196). Furthermore, in attempting to gain more training for students, in an open letter to colleagues, Hunter complained:

I paid more attention to the pupils than . . . was then the practice of the other surgeons. The pupils of course looked up to me . . . and even threatened to recommend their young acquaintances to other hospitals if more general attention was not paid to them. (Kligfield, 1980, p. 368)

In a bold move that generated great antipathy, Hunter unilaterally declared that he would not share students' tuition with the other surgeons at St. George's Hospital: "as the increase of the pupils became very considerable, and the greater number entered with me the only method left was to keep the money I received by the pupils as my own property" (Kligfield, 1980, p. 369). A special court ruled against Hunter in this matter, and his colleagues rearranged hospital responsibilities so that Hunter's already overburdened schedule would become even more unmanageable. Such were the circumstances surrounding the hospital board meeting on October 16, 1793.

Early that morning, Hunter met a baronet along the road and told her "that he was going to the hospital; that he was fearful some unpleasant rencontre might ensue, and if such should be the case, he knew it must be his death" (Adams, 1817, p. 196). The habitually punctual Hunter arrived late. After being contradicted by a colleague,

> not being perfectly the master of the circumstances . . . [he] withheld his sentiments, in which state of restraint he went into the next room, and turning around . . . gave a deep groan, and dropt down dead.
>
> It is a curious circumstance that, the first attack of these complaints was produced by an affection of the mind, and every future return of any consequence arose from the same cause . . . and as his mind was irritated by trifles, these produced the most violent effects on the disease. (Home, 1794, p. lxi)

Some time before that fateful board meeting, in a statement of supreme irony, Hunter had been quoted as saying that his life was "in the hands of any rascal who chooses to annoy or tease me" (*Dictionary of National Biography*, 1908, p. 290; Kobler, 1960). Commenting on Hunter's description of "death from . . . a violent affection of the mind," Adams (1817) wryly noted, "if he had not his own death in view, he has at least described its immediate cause . . . with a perspicuity which could not have been exceeded if he had attended the examination of his own corpse" (p. 91).

Diagnosis of TABP

The diagnosis of TABP has been a major issue almost since its first description. Diagnosis was originally made with a structured interview (SI), first detailed by M. Friedman and Powell (1984). An updated version, the videotaped clinical examination (VCE), was introduced by M. Friedman and Ghandour (1993). (Instructions for administration and scoring of the VCE are provided by M. Friedman, Fleischmann, and Price in chap. 6 of this volume.) Scores for the TABP are obtained not only from content responses to a series of questions but also from how an individual responds. Psychomotor signs are considered as important as free-floating hostility and time pressure, the two major symptoms of TABP. Most recently, Price, Friedman, and Ghandour (1995) published a 10-item insecurity scale, now used as part of the VCE, to tap into the presumed nucleus of TABP (see chap. 6, this volume).

Several questionnaires have been developed for diagnosing TABP. The Jenkins Activity Survey (Jenkins, Rosenman, & Zyzanski, 1974) has been used most extensively, although it does not reflect the hostility component. Both the Framingham Type A scale (Haynes, Levine, Scotch, Feinleib, & Kannel, 1978) and the Bortner scale (Bortner, 1969) have been used for successful prediction of CHD. The VCE and the questionnaires measure different aspects of TABP, and variability in research findings can, in many instances, be traced to this important fact.

Epidemiology of TABP

A number of studies that have attempted to relate the TABP to CHD are summarized in Table 1. Briefly, the Western Collaborative Group Study was the first large-scale prospective investigation of TABP (Rosenman et al., 1975), with men classified as Type A having approximately twice the incidence of CHD as those rated Type B. Type B behavior has generally been defined as the absence of Type A behavior (TAB). Subsequently, positive TABP–CHD relationships were found for both men and women in the Framingham Heart Study in the 1980s (Haynes & Feinleib, 1982; Haynes, Feinleib, & Kannel, 1980). The most recent Framingham data, however, report a Type A association only with angina pectoris and not with either myocardial infarction (MI) or fatal coronary events (Eaker, Abbott, & Kannel, 1989). In one cross-sectional study, R. B. Williams et al. (1988) noted that the TABP–CHD link was strongest in the youngest (under 45 years) of a group of 2,289 patients undergoing coronary arteriography.

Several studies have failed to find a relationship between TABP and CHD in high-risk populations, such as patients undergoing cardiac catheterization or those already diagnosed with CHD. The Multicenter Post-Infarction Research Program (Case, Heller, Case, & Moss, 1985), Aspirin Myocardial Infarction Study (Shekelle, Gale, & Norusis, 1985), and Multiple Risk Factor Intervention Trial (MRFIT; Shekelle, Hulley, et al., 1985) all found no relationship between TABP and CHD or CHD-related mortality. In a follow-up to the Western Collaborative Group Study, Ragland and Brand (1988) showed that individuals diagnosed Type A in 1960 who later developed CHD actually had lower mortality over the next 23 years in comparison with those diagnosed Type B. Rather than a risk factor for CHD, Ragland and Brand suggested, TABP might even be "protective" for subsequent cardiac mortality in those with diagnosed CHD. Similar results were obtained by Barefoot, Peterson, et al. (1989) in a prospective study of 1,467 symptomatic patients undergoing coronary angiography. Among patients with poor left ventricular function, an SI Type A diagnosis was protective for survival. Ahern et al. (1990) reported increased cardiac arrest and death among those diagnosed as Type B, assessed by the Bortner ques-

TABLE 1
Type A Behavior and Prediction of Coronary Heart Disease (CHD): Large-Scale Prospective Clinical Trials

Study	N	Types of subjects	Follow-up (years)	CHD incidence risk ratio, Type A:Type B	Comment
Primary (no prior CHD)					
Western Collaborative Group Study (WCGS; Rosenman et al., 1975)	3,154	Employed California men, age 35–59 years	8.5	2.24	Symptomatic MI
Framingham Heart Study Haynes, Feinleib, & Kannel, 1980	1,674	725 men 949 women age 45–77 years	8	2.9 total CHD, 7.3 MI 2.1 total CHD, 3.6 angina	White-collar men Housewives and employed women
Haynes & Feinleib, 1982	1,330	750 men, 580 women	10	2.4 men, 2.0 women	Total CHD
Eaker, Abbott, & Kannel, 1989	1,289	570 men, 719 women	2	2.2 men, 2.6 women	Angina pectoris only
High-risk subjects					
Williams et al., 1980	2,289	1,610 men, 679 women undergoing coronary angiography	cross-sectional	Strongest SI TAB–CHD relationship among patients < 45	CHD severity similar among Type As and Type Bs 46–54 years old. Increased severity among Type Bs over 55.
Multiple Risk Factor Intervention Trial (Shekelle, Hulley, et al., 1985)	3,110	Subgroup of 12,866 men, age 35–57, in top 10%–15% of CHD risk by blood pressure and serum cholesterol	7.19	NA	No relationship between Type A behavior and CHD endpoints using either Jenkins Activity Survey or SI

Secondary (in those with diagnosed CHD)

Study	N	Description	Years	RR	Findings
Multicenter Postinfarct Group Study (Case, Heller, Case, & Moss, 1985)	516	Subgroup of 866 patients within 2 weeks of acute MI	1–3	NA	No difference in mean Type A scores of survivors versus deaths
Aspirin MI Study (Shekelle, Gale, & Norusis, 1985)	2,314	Subgroup of 2,698 patients given aspirin for prevention of recurrent CHD 30 days–5 years after MI	3	NA	No difference in mean Type A scores of those with and without coronary events
WCGS (Ragland & Brand, 1988)	231	From 231 of 257 WCGS participants who developed angina, silent, or symptomatic MI and survived 24 hours	12	0.58	Type As had better survival rates compared with Type Bs
Duke University Medical Center Study (Barefoot, Peterson, et al., 1989)	1,467	SI assessment of patients hospitalized for cardiac catheterization	4–10	NA	Type As with poor left ventricular function had better survival rates than Type Bs
Cardiac Arrhythmia Pilot Study (Ahern et al., 1990)	353	Post-MI patients with arrhythmia assessed with Bortner Type A Scale	1	0.70	Type As had 0.70 risk of sudden cardiac death in comparison with Type Bs for one standard deviation in scale score

Note. MI = myocardial infarction; SI = structured interview; RR = relative risk ratio; NA = not applicable.

tionnaire, in 353 post-MI patients enrolled in the Cardiac Arrhythmia Pilot Study.

A meta-analysis of 83 studies of the TABP and CHD (Booth-Kewley & Friedman, 1987) provided the following conclusions: (a) TABP does appear to be a risk factor for CHD, approximately doubling risk; (b) depression, anger, and hostility are also related to CHD; (c) SIs are more effective for predicting disease endpoints than are questionnaires; (d) cross-sectional studies have been better predictors than prospective studies; and (e) the Type A effect has been smaller in studies published more recently than in those done in the early days of the hypothesis. It should be noted that there have not been many large-scale epidemiological studies of TABP since the late 1980s.

Summary

Given the variable results of studies attempting to relate TABP to the development of CHD, we offer the following four conclusions.

1. Diagnostic tools vary from study to study and are imperfect. In particular, questionnaires are less powerful than SIs in diagnosing a presumed "virulent core" of the TABP.
2. Diagnostic tools are better used with general populations than with those at high risk for CHD. Pickering (1985) and Miller, Turner, Tindale, Posavac, and Dugoni (1991) have argued that high-risk populations, such as patients undergoing coronary arteriograms, present an unfavorable environment for discovering a potential relationship between TABP (or other behavior patterns) and CHD, for a number of important reasons:

   - Standard cardiologic risk factors, such as serum cholesterol and hypertension, do not correlate well with angiographic assessments of disease severity in many studies because the risk factor is present in a very large proportion of high-risk populations, so why should the TABP?

   - Patients who died before reaching the hospital (about one sixth of patients who have had an MI) are excluded from study and reduce the magnitude of the relationship that can be found between CHD and the risk factor under investigation.

   - Within-CHD groups may be atypical in comparison with the general population, and instruments for diagnosis are insufficiently sensitive to differentiate what may be similar personality styles.

- Beta-blockers, widely used among CHD patients, may blunt TABP and, hence, confound accurate diagnosis.
3. The TABP may vary in importance in subpopulations: Epidemiological evidence appears stronger for TABP as a risk factor for those without clinical CHD (as assessed in the Western Collaborative Group Study, Framingham, and other studies) versus those who already have CHD (Case et al., 1985; Ragland & Brand, 1988; Shekelle, Gale, & Norusis, 1985). After diagnosis of CHD, there seems to be a protective effect associated with TABP, perhaps because individuals diagnosed as Type A may have stronger motivation to change risk factors, which may even include modification of the TABP.
4. Subsets of characteristics of the TABP may not be equally important. As R. B. Williams (1987) and others have hypothesized, it may be that hostility is more important and time-pressured behavior less important, and reliance on overall Type A scores may obscure relationships within one subset.

Meta-analyses and commentaries on the Type A literature have been undertaken by Booth-Kewley and Friedman (1987), Matthews (1988), H. S. Friedman and Booth-Kewley (1988), and Miller et al. (1991) and provide a lively debate on the evolution and importance of this behavior pattern. Thoresen and Powell (1992) provided the most up-to-date review on methodological issues and important suggestions for the design of future research and treatment. (See also chaps. 6 and 10–13 of this book for additional discussions of TABP.)

Anger and Hostility

The word *anger* derives from the Old Norse *angr*, signifying grief, circa 1,000 A.D. Its earliest meanings in English were trouble, affliction, vexation, and sorrow. The *Oxford English Dictionary* (1986) definition—"that which pains or afflicts, or the passive feeling which it produces; trouble, affliction, vexation, sorrow" (p. 325)—was developed in the fourteenth century. Although both *anger* and *angina* derive from the same root word, signifying strangling or choking, the similarity is coincidental. Siegman and Smith (1994) have provided a recent, comprehensive review of the burgeoning literature on anger, hostility, and the heart, which is beyond the scope of this chapter.

One striking demonstration of the effects of anger on the heart was reported by Ironson et al. (1992), who asked study participants with CHD to recall in detail an incident from the past 6 months that still made them "frustrated, angry, irritated or upset." Participants were also given a stressful speech task (defending oneself against an accusation of shoplifting), mental arithmetic, and symptom-limited exercise using a bicycle ergometer. Radionuclide ventriculograms showed that of all conditions, anger recall elicited the greatest impairment in ventricular function, with 7 of the 18 CHD patients showing a drop in ejection fraction $\geq$7%. Notably, only 4 of the 18 patients had a reduction of ejection fraction $\geq$ 7% during symptom-limited exercise. Patients felt their reexperienced anger was only one third to one half as intense as the original feeling.

Using a similar anger recall protocol, Boltwood et al. (1993) studied vasoconstriction in a group of 9 patients during cardiac catheterization. Digital quantitative angiography revealed a significant relationship between experienced anger and vasoconstriction in atherosclerotic, but not in non-atherosclerotic, arterial segments.

Beyond such studies that demonstrate a strong, direct effect of anger on cardiac function for some CHD patients, there is considerable literature on the role of chronic anger and hostility in the development of coronary atherosclerosis. After several studies of the early 1980s failed to uphold a relationship between TABP and CHD, a number of investigators set out in search of a presumed "pathological core" of this behavior pattern. R. B. Williams (1987) coined the term "hostility complex" to describe a cynical, untrusting, and pessimistic orientation to interpersonal interaction and life in general, which he thought might be more strongly related to CHD than the global TABP. The hostility complex is operationally defined by high scores on the Cook–Medley Hostility (Ho) Scale of the Minnesota Multiphasic Personality Inventory (MMPI). Note that the Ho scale was originally devised to differentiate between schoolteachers who maintain positive versus negative rapport with students, not to measure hostility.

Table 2 shows a summary of the major studies on the relationship between Ho scores and CHD. R. B. Williams et al. (1980) first reported a link between the Ho scale and degree of atherosclerosis among patients undergoing cardiac catheterization. Subsequently, the Ho scale predicted CHD- and all-cause mortality in a 25-year study of physicians (Barefoot, Dahlstrom, & Williams, 1984), although an attempted replication by McCranie, Watkins, Brandsma, and Sisson (1986) failed to support this finding. Shekelle, Gale, Ostfeld, and Paul (1983) reported that low-Ho scores were associated with lowest 10-year CHD incidence in a group of initially healthy Western Electric employees. Follow-up after 20 years showed that initial Ho scores were related to subsequent CHD- and all-cause mortality. However, Leon, Finn, Murray, and Bailey (1988); Hearn, Murray, and Leupker (1989); Helmer, Ragland, and Lyme (1991); and Maruta et al. (1993) all failed to find a link between Ho scores and CHD morbidity or mortality. A study by Barefoot, Dodge, Peterson, Dahlstrom, and Williams (1989) continues to uphold the Ho-scale–mortality relation-

TABLE 2

Relationships between the MMPI Cook–Medley Hostility (Ho) Scale and Coronary Heart Disease (CHD)

Study	N	Description	Results
Williams et al., 1980	424	CHD patients awaiting cardiac catheterization	Ho score related to degree of atherosclerosis: >70% stenosis associated with Ho >10
Barefoot, Dahlstrom, & Williams, 1984	255	25 year follow-up of MDs who completed MMPI in medical school	Ho score predictive of both CHD and all-cause mortality
Shekelle, Gale, Ostfeld, & Paul, 1983	1,877	Healthy employed men (Western Electric)	Low Ho score (<10) associated with low CHD event rate. Highest CHD incidence in middle Ho quintile. Ho score related to 20-year overall mortality
McCranie, Watkins, Brandsma, & Sisson, 1986	478	MDs who completed MMPI at medial school admission interview	No relation between Ho score and CHD incidence or mortality. May indicate reluctance to admit hostility at time of evaluation for admission
Leon, Finn, Murray, & Bailey, 1988	280	30-year follow-up of businessmen, mean age 45 years at entry	No relation between Ho score and CHD
Hearn, Murray, & Luepker, 1989	1,399	35-year follow-up of University of Minnesota students who completed MMPI during freshman orientation	No relation between Ho scores and CHD morbidity or mortality
Helmer, Ragland, & Lyme, 1991	158	CHD patients awaiting cardiac catheterization	No relation between Ho score and coronary occlusion

(table continues)

TABLE 2 (Continued)

Study	N	Description	Results
Barefoot, Dodge, Peterson, Dahlstrom, & Williams, 1989	118	Refinement of Ho scale into six subscales; 28-year follow-up of law students	Total Ho scores associated with mortality. Sum of three subscales (cynicism, hostile affect, and aggressive responding) better predicted mortality than did full Ho scale
Maruta et al., 1993	620	620 of 1,145 consecutive general medical patients	No relation between Ho score and CHD after controlling for age and gender
Barefoot, Larsen, Von der Leith, & Schroll, 1995	730	409 male and 321 female residents of Glastrop, Denmark; 50 years old in 1964	High scores on abbreviated Ho scale associated with increased risk of MI and total mortality

Note. MI = myocardial infarction; RR = relative risk ratio; CI = confidence interval; MMPI = Minnesota Multiphasic Personality Inventory.

ship (although sample size was too small [$N = 118$] to find a relationship with CHD mortality). Most recently, Barefoot, Larsen, Von der Lieth, and Schroll (1995) studied 409 male and 321 female residents of Glostrup, Denmark, who were 50 years old in 1964 when they took the MMPI as part of a medical exam. High scores on an abbreviated Ho scale were predictive of future MI ($p = .03$) and total mortality (relative risk ratio = 1.56; 95% confidence interval [CI], 1.05–2.32).

Smith and Barefoot (1993) recently noted methodological problems that may have led to some of these negative findings. The study by McCranie et al. (1986), for instance, assessed Ho scores from MMPIs administered as part of a battery of tests for medical school admission. Not surprisingly, hostility scores in this sample were low relative to other studies, and follow-up failed to find a relationship between scores in this compressed range and subsequent CHD. In the study by Maruta et al. (1993), more than half (57%) of the initial cohort was lost to follow-up, and so results may not accurately reflect the overall study population.

In the latest twist in the Cook–Medley CHD literature, Helmers et al. (1995) administered the Ho scale and the Marlowe–Crowne Social Desirability Scale to CHD patients, according to the hypothesis that defensive denial may be a critical dimension of coronary-prone hostility. Individuals with high Marlowe–Crowne Social Desirability Scale scores are concerned with positive self-representation and tend not to report socially undesirable aspects of themselves, such as hostility. In a series of three experiments, CHD patients with high scores on both the Ho and Marlowe–Crowne Social Desirability scales demonstrated the greatest number of perfusion defects measured by exercise thallium scintigraphy, the most frequent ischemic episodes during ambulatory Holter monitoring, and the most severe mental stress-induced ischemia assessed by echocardiography in comparison with other participants who did not manifest this constellation of high scores on the Ho and Marlowe–Crowne Social Desirability scales.

Questionnaires other than the Ho scale have been used to assess hostility as a risk factor for CHD. In a study of patients undergoing coronary angiography, Siegman, Dembroski, and Ringel (1987) used the Buss–Durkee Hostility Inventory to assess coronary risk. Assault and verbal hostility subscales were positively correlated with CHD severity, whereas "neurotic hostility," defined as suspicion and resentment, was inversely associated. Self-assessments of hostility based on a three-item questionnaire (measuring irritability, ease of anger arousal, and argumentativeness) were used in a study of 3,750 Finnish twin men (Koskenvuo et al., 1988). After 3 years, there was no relationship between CHD and self-appraised hostility in healthy men. However, among men who had CHD and hypertension, hostility increased relative risk of CHD 14.6 times (95% CI, 1.94–110), after smoking, obesity, and alcohol use were controlled for.

Just as negative Type A findings have spawned a search for a "pathological core" of this pattern, so, too, researchers have sought refinement of the Ho scale. Barefoot, Dodge, et al. (1989) found that a composite hostility score, derived from three Ho subscales (cynicism, hostile affect, and aggressive responding), was a better predictor of survival in a group of 118 lawyers than the total Ho score. More recently, Helmers et al. (1993) found that the composite hostility score correlated with perfusion defects and Holter-monitored ST-segment depression among patients under 60 years of age undergoing thallium testing, with relationships strongest for women.

Psychological questionnaires have built-in limitations. Barefoot (1992) has identified self-presentation bias as possibly the major limitation of questionnaires attempting to assess hostility. Many individuals are loathe to admit excessive hostility because it is socially undesirable. In addition, questionnaires generally access an individual's conscious awareness. Many people—perhaps some of the most hostile—are unaware of the extent of their hostility. The environment in which a questionnaire is administered may also have a profound effect on scores. For instance, the medical school applicants in the McCranie et al. (1986) study had low-Ho scores; particularly in that setting, it would seem prudent for those tested to suppress or conceal hostility.

Efforts have been made to overcome the limitations of questionnaires by using SI assessments of hostility, which are summarized in Table 3. Dembroski, MacDougall, Williams, Haney, and Blumenthal (1985) and MacDougall, Dembroski, Dimsdale, and Hackett (1985) scored SIs using potential for hostility (the tendency to become irritated or angered during daily activities) and anger-in (the inability or unwillingness to express anger) as possible criteria of coronary-prone hostility. Both studies showed that Ho scores correlated with degree of atherosclerosis. Two SI analyses of hostility reexamined large-scale studies of coronary-prone behavior. In the MRFIT (Shekelle, Hulley, et al., 1985), which did not find a TABP–CHD association, Dembroski, MacDougall, Costa, and Grandits (1989) reported that 192 participants showing a potential for hostility and an antagonistic interactional style had from 1.5 to 1.7 times the incidence of CHD in comparison with 384 matched control participants. For patients under age 47, elevated SI scores for hostility potential and antagonistic interaction more than doubled CHD risk. In a multivariate reanalysis of SIs from 250 CHD cases and 500 matched control participants from the Western Collaborative Group Study, Hecker, Chesney, Black, and Frautschi (1988) found SI hostility to be the single strongest predictor of CHD incidence.

Barefoot (1992) has separated hostility into cognitive, affective, and behavioral components. He and his colleagues at Duke University Medical Center developed the Interpersonal Hostility Assessment Technique

TABLE 3
Structured Interview (SI) Assessments of Hostility and Coronary Heart Disease (CHD)

Study	N	Description	Results
Dembroski, MacDougall, Williams, Haney, & Blumenthal, 1985	131	Patients with no or severe CHD at cardiac catheterization; scoring of SI into speech stylistics, Type A content, hostility, and anger-in	"Potential for hostility" and "anger-in" related to angiographic severity of CHD (see text for definitions)
MacDougall, Dembroski, Dimsdale, & Hackett, 1985	125	125 catheterization patients; retrospective reanalysis of SI tapes in which no association had been found between Type A behavior and angiographic CHD severity	"Potential for hostility" and "anger-in" related to angiographic disease
Dembroski, MacDougall, Costa, & Grandits, 1989	192 CHD and 384 control patients	Reanalysis of interviews from Multiple Risk Factor Intervention Trial, average 7.1-year follow-up	"Potential for hostility" showed significant relation to CHD. Risk stronger under age 47
Hecker, Chesney, Black, & Farutsch, 1988	250 CHD and 500 control patients	Reanalysis of SIs from Western Collaborative Group Study, 8.5-year follow-up	Hostility significantly related to CHD

(IHAT), which focuses on affective and behavioral components of hostility (in contrast to the Ho scale, which primarily taps into cognitive attitudes and beliefs). The IHAT has been related to coronary artery disease severity during coronary angiography (Barefoot, 1992). In addition, Barefoot, Patterson, Haney, and Cayton (1994) used the IHAT with 49 asymptomatic nonsmoking U.S. Air Force pilots referred for coronary angiography and found higher hostility scores among those with coronary disease, in a study designed to avoid the methodological pitfalls of using high-risk populations (see p. 72 for discussion of this issue).

Several studies have attempted to explain the confusion surrounding the assessment of hostility. Swan, Carmelli, and Rosenman (1989) compared Ho scores with SI hostility and a number of frequently used psychological scales in middle-aged male participants from the National Heart, Lung, and Blood Institute Twin Study. SI ratings of hostility differed considerably from those obtained with the Ho scale. Similarly, Kneip et al. (1993) studied self- and spouse-ratings of anger and hostility in a group of 185 cardiac patients undergoing thallium scans, using the Multidimensional Anger Inventory and the Marlowe–Crowne Social Desirability Scale. After controlling for traditional cardiologic risk factors, Kneip et al. found that only spouse-rated hostility contributed significant predictive power to multiple regression equations for CHD. These variable results clearly demonstrate that hostility assessments derived from interviews and questionnaires share only limited relationship. It appears that self-awareness or willingness to admit hostility may be profoundly limiting factors in the use of questionnaires to assess coronary-prone hostility.

We conclude that some experimental studies, such as Ironson et al.'s (1992), reveal dramatic links between anger and short-term effects on cardiac function. Mittleman et al. (1995) have also demonstrated that episodes of anger can trigger MI in a relatively small percentage of cases (see below). Results of epidemiological studies attempting to link anger or hostility to the long-term development of atherosclerosis are less convincing, although the preponderance of evidence does point to hostility as a risk factor for CHD. As with the Type A literature, initially promising results have been followed by mixed findings. It seems highly likely that the main culprit for this state of confusion is the lack of a standardized assessment methodology.

Psychological Stress

The word *stress* is an alteration of *distress*, derived from the Old French *estresse*, signifying oppression. During the Middle Ages, the term also meant the "pressure exerted on an object" or "the strain of a load." The *Oxford English Dictionary* (1986) definitions of *stress* include "hardship, straits, adversity, [and] affliction" (p. 1110).

The exercise stress test, widely used in clinical cardiology, determines the effects of physical stress on cardiac function with great precision. Psychological stress, however, is an exceedingly complex phenomenon that has been difficult to define, measure, and, hence, study scientifically. One recent definition reveals how easily the term breeds new variables, each of which then requires further exploration: "when demands imposed by events exceed a person's ability to cope, a psychological stress response composed of negative cognitive and emotional states is elicited" (Cohen, Tyrell, & Smith, 1991, p. 606, adapted from Lazarus & Folkman, 1984). In this formulation, *demands, events, coping ability, negative cognitive state,* and *negative emotional state* must all be operationalized to define stress. Nonetheless, interesting findings abound relating various aspects of psychological stress to cardiac function as well as cardiac morbidity and mortality.

In an early attempt to objectively study psychological stress and CHD, Holmes and Rahe (1967) used the Recent Life Change questionnaire. Events such as the death of a spouse, marriage, divorce, or loss of job are considered highly stressful, whereas changes such as working hours, trouble with in-laws, and vacations are thought to be less so. In a 1974 study (Rahe, Romo, Bennet, & Siltanen, 1974), the Recent Life Change questionnaire was administered to 279 survivors of MI and to spouses of 226 cases of sudden cardiac death (SCD) in Helsinki, Finland. Marked elevations in Recent Life Change scores were seen for most cases of MI or SCD for 6 months prior to the event, with results particularly impressive for SCD. Although modifications of the Recent Life Change questionnaire are still used for stress research, this test has not become a standard for assessment.

Using a stress scale "conceived on a purely intuitive basis," Rosengren, Tibblin, and Wilhelmsen (1991, p. 1174) followed a group of 6,935 healthy men, age 47–55 at baseline, in Göteborg, Sweden, for a mean of 11.8 years. The men rated themselves on a variety of psychological problems, such as anxiety, tension, and sleeping difficulties. Among the 5,865 men with the lowest stress ratings, 6% developed a nonfatal MI or died from CHD, whereas 10% of the 1,070 men with the highest stress ratings suffered MI or SCD (odds ratio [OR] = 1.5; 95% CI, 1.2–1.9). In a second, smaller substudy of 1,066 men born in 1933, however, Rosengren et al. failed to replicate the initial finding using the identical stress scale and only a 6-year follow-up.

Few events in human experience create as much stress as war. To study its effects, Sibal, Armenian, and Alam (1989) compared coronary angiograms of 127 CHD patients who had frequent contact with civil war activities in Lebanon with age- and sex-matched control participants who did not. Exposure to acute war events was significantly higher for participants with disease than for control participants. A separate analysis demonstrated even greater risk of atherosclerosis in citizens who had frequently crossed the "green lines" separating warring factions, which was considered a particularly acute stressor because of exposure to snipers' bullets and random shellings without warning. Sibal et al. (1989) concluded that "war related stress may play a role in coronary disease outcome" (p. 630). Similarly, Meisel et al. (1991) noted a sharp increase in the incidence of acute MI and SCD during the first week of the Iraqi SCUD missile attacks on Tel Aviv, Israel, in comparison with five peaceful control periods. Interestingly, coronary event rates returned to normal levels after the first week, despite the continuation of attacks, suggesting that cardiac function is remarkably resilient to ongoing psychological stress for the vast majority of the population. In a related study of a naturally occurring catastrophe, Dobson, Alexander, Malcolm, Steele, and Miles (1991) reported an unusually high incidence of fatal MI and coronary death in the 4-day period following the 1989 Newcastle, Australia, earthquake.

All of these studies lend support to the general hypothesis that psychological stress can play a role in cardiac events, including the precipitation of MI and SCD. Most recent research, however, has focused on particular types of stress and specific biological mechanisms.

Acute Psychological and Behavioral Triggers for MI

One of the hotly debated controversies in twentieth-century cardiology is whether the plaque rupture and ensuing thrombosis responsible for most MIs is a random event or is triggered by identifiable psychological, behavioral, or physiological factors. Although there has been much speculation based on anecdote through the ages, this is an area that has only recently been rigorously investigated. In a preliminary finding that dates only from 1989, Muller, Tofler, and Edelman identified probable psychological and behavioral triggers for MI onset from a number of case histories. Subsequently, Tofler et al. (1990) asked 849 patients to identify possible factors related to their acute MI; triggers were noted by nearly half the patients, with emotional upset and moderate physical activity being the most common. Similarly, Willich et al. (1991) reported that 52% of 224 consecutive acute MI patients noted stress or emotional upset prior to hospital admission. However, all of these studies lacked control groups, and results may have been colored by recall bias.

Expanding on these findings, Muller, Tofler, and Stone (1989) documented circadian variations for a number of physiological processes, including blood pressure, platelet aggregability, heart rate, plasma epinephrine, cortisol, and tissue plasminogen factor (tPA) activity. These physiological processes have been found to correlate with increased rates of MI, SCD, transient myocardial ischemia, and thrombotic stroke (Muller et al., 1985, 1987; Willich, 1990). Changes in these parameters often occur in tandem with changes in activity levels: For instance, all of the above increase with awakening and standing up, as well as with beginning the work week on Monday mornings (intrinsic tPA activity decreases at all of these times; Willich et al., 1992). Thus, Muller, Tofler, and Stone (1989) advanced the theory that physical or mental stress can trigger physiological changes sufficient to rupture a vulnerable plaque, leading to cardiac events, as illustrated in Figure 2.

The ongoing Determinants of Time of Myocardial Infarction Onset Study (hereinafter, *MI Onset study*) has made a number of important discoveries about behavioral and psychological triggers for MI. In a group of 1,228 patients, Mittleman et al. (1993) determined that 4.4% described strenuous physical exertion within 1 hour prior to MI, for an estimated relative risk of 5.9 (95% CI, 4.6–7.7) in comparison with MI patients who reported less strenuous exertion or none during the same period. Among people who habitually exercised less than once, 1–2, 3–4, or 5 or more times per week, the respective risks were 107, 19.4, 8.6, and 2.4, respectively. Thus, the risk of triggering MI in the hour following strenuous physical exertion was greatly reduced if the person had exercised regularly in the months or years before MI. Similar results have been reported in a study from Germany (Willich et al., 1993). Although these findings indicate transient increased risk (immediately postexercise) even for individuals who exercise 5 or more times per week, there is a reduced risk of MI with regular exercise in healthy populations, with an overall reduction of 60% reported in one meta-analysis (Berlin & Colditz, 1990). Thus, although an individual may raise the risk of MI for the hour after each exercise session, the risk is dramatically reduced during the remaining hours of the week.

Another report from the multicenter MI Onset study (Mittleman et al., 1995) revealed that episodes of intense anger in the 2 hours before the onset of MI increased the relative risk to 2.3 (95% CI, 1.7–3.2) in comparison with similar time periods for the same patients when they were not angry. Notably, regular use of aspirin significantly reduced this risk to 1.4 (95% CI, 1.3–2.7). Other findings from the MI Onset study include a 2.1-fold increased risk of MI (95% CI, 1.3–3.3) within 2 hours of sexual activity (Muller et al., 1993) and a 9.5 times increased risk of MI (95% CI, 4.1–22.03, p = .001), with at least one self-rated "extremely meaningful and desirable or undesirable event" within the preceding 26 hours (Jacobs et al., 1992).

These findings provide important data on which to base clinical intervention. Many cardiac patients have an underlying fear that their actions will trigger another MI or even precipitate their own demise. Findings from the MI Onset study can provide reassurance. Generalizing from the results, of the 1 million patients who survive MIs annually in the United States, approximately 3.7% of MIs are precipitated by exertion, 1.3% by anger, and 0.007% by sexual activity (M. Mittleman, personal communication, December 22, 1995). Thus, only a small minority of MIs have

Triggering of Coronary Thrombosis

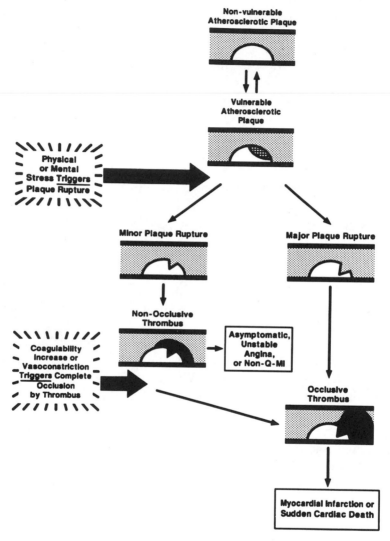

Figure 2. Illustration of a hypothetical method by which daily activities may trigger coronary thrombosis. Three triggering mechanisms: 1) physical or mental stress producing hemodynamic changes leading to plaque rupture, 2) activities causing a coagulability increase, and 3) stimuli leading to vasoconstriction, have been added to the well-known scheme depicting the role of coronary thrombosis in unstable angina, myocardial infarction, and sudden cardiac death. From "Circadian Variations and Triggers of Onset of Acute Cardiovascular Disease," by J. E. Muller, G. H. Tofler, and P. H. Stone, 1989, *Circulation, 79,* p. 739. Copyright 1989 by the American Heart Association. Reprinted with permission.

identifiable behavioral and psychological precipitants. Furthermore, the absolute risk of MI for a 50-year-old man with no coronary risk factors in any given hour is approximately 1 in a million, and an increased relative risk of 2.3 (for instance, within 2 hours of an episode of anger) increases the risk to only 2.3 in a million for 2 hours. Thus, the risk that any single episode of anger will trigger MI is very low. Nonetheless, the individual who becomes angered an average of 4 times a day spends 8 hours each day at greater than twofold increased risk, which translates into a 76% increased risk over the course of a year (M. Mittleman, personal communication, December 22, 1995). It is thus prudent for individuals to develop skills to better manage their anger.

The sensitive clinician must balance the potential harm to a patient from overemphasizing behavioral triggering, such as increasing anxiety, with supportive reassurance about the low likelihood of precipitating an MI with any single activity. Complicating the picture are findings that sexual activity and even "meaningful and desirable" activities appear to increase the risk of MI onset. Nonetheless, cardiac counseling should urge against "weekend warrior" activities (particularly for those who are sedentary) and help individuals to develop good anger-management skills.

Psychological Stress and Myocardial Ischemia

A link between emotional arousal and silent myocardial ischemia using a mental arithmetic stressor was first reported in a laboratory investigation of CHD patients by Deanfield et al. (1984). Subsequently, Barry et al. (1988) noted increased ischemia, much of which was silent, associated with psychological stress in daily life for patients who filled out a behavioral diary. More dramatic findings resulting from a study using sensitive radionuclide ventriculography to link emotional stress directly with myocardial ischemia and cardiac dysfunction were reported by Rozanski et al. in 1988. CHD patients and control participants were subjected to a series of mental and physical tasks: arithmetic; reading; the Stroop Color and Word Test (in which a subject under time pressure reads the name of a color from a card of a different color); and "simulated public speaking," during which each participant gave a 5-minute talk to two white-coated observers about his or her "personal faults and undesirable habits." Quite dramatically, the magnitude of ischemic cardiac dysfunction induced by the stressful simulated public-speaking task was similar to that observed during bicycle exercise. During periods of mental stress, 59% of patients had wall-motion abnormalities, and 36% had a fall in left ventricular ejection fraction of more than 5%. Psychologically induced ischemia was silent in 83% of patients who had wall-motion abnormalities.

Several recent studies have shown that approximately 50% of cardiac patients show evidence of ischemia (usually silent) with mental stress

(Gottdiener et al., 1994; Jain, Burg, Soufer, & Zaret, 1995; Krantz et al., 1994; Legault, Langer, Armstrong, & Freeman, 1995). Gottdiener et al. found increased ischemia during daily life, assessed with a structured diary, for cardiac patients vulnerable to a stressful arithmetic task and simulated public speaking. Legault et al. (1995) discovered more frequent and longer episodes of ambulatory ischemia for patients with CHD vulnerable to Rozanski et al.'s (1988) simulated public-speaking task, which has become somewhat of a standard in laboratory psychological stress testing. In addition, Jain et al. (1995) followed a group of 30 stable patients with CHD for 2 years and discovered that 67% of patients with mental-stress–inducible ischemia had adverse cardiac events (MI or hospitalization for unstable angina) in comparison with only 27% of patients who had no mental-stress–induced dysfunction.

Krantz et al. (1994) suggested recently that the clinical syndrome of exertional chest pain termed *angina pectoris* may be as strongly related to psychological events as to ischemia. They also found much silent ischemia in a group of 63 CHD patients, with 85% of ischemic episodes as measured by ST-segment depression on ambulatory Holter monitoring not associated with anginal pain. Only one third of anginal episodes demonstrated electrocardiogram changes, and anginal pain was more strongly associated with physical exertion and negative emotion than with Holter-diagnosed ischemia. As has been known for some time, the severity or even presence of patient-reported angina is a poor guide to the extent of coronary artery disease, myocardial ischemia, or prognosis.

The most salient psychological implication of silent myocardial ischemia is that an individual is unaware of his or her physiological vulnerability. Because most ischemia is silent for patients who manifest this condition, some warning signal other than anginal pain must limit physical and emotional exertion. Such patients may derive particular benefit from cardiac counseling.

Psychological Stress and SCD

Through the ages, there has been a fascination with dramatic life events that seem to trigger SCD. In his classic paper "Voodoo Death," Cannon (1957) noted that, in 1587, Soares de Souza first reported instances of death apparently induced by fright among South American Indians condemned by a medicine man. Similar observations have been reported by anthropologists living among cultures in Africa, Australia, Haiti, and the islands of the Pacific.

In the popular mind, sudden death is associated with intense fear ("scared to death") as well as anger ("apoplectic with rage"). One extraordinary example of an apparently psychologically precipitated SCD is the case of John Hunter, described above. However, it was not until quite recently that investigators began to study behavioral antecedents that might precipitate SCD. Myers and Dewar (1975) investigated 100 sudden deaths in London and interviewed surviving relatives, using a standardized questionnaire. Twenty-three of the victims were reported to have experienced significant psychological stress within 30 minutes of death, and another 40 within 24 hours. However, as Myers and Dewar (1975) pointed out, "relatives are suggestible and keen to find stress factors to account for disasters as dramatic as sudden death and myocardial infarction" (p. 1140).

There have also been suggestions that a chronic psychological state might influence the propensity to arrhythmia or SCD. Engel (1971) categorized the "life settings" of 170 SCDs reported in newspapers over a 6-year period and found a number of themes: death of a loved one, grief, loss of status or esteem, personal danger or relief from such danger, reunion, triumph, or happy ending. Common to all such life settings was overwhelming excitation, loss of control, and giving up.

Greene, Goldstein, and Moss (1972) interviewed the wives of 26 SCD victims. Interestingly, many wives were angry at their deceased husbands, whom they typically described as foolish for not having consulted a physician earlier. Prodromal symptoms were clearly evident to the wives in nearly every case. Furthermore, most of the wives characterized their husbands as depressed. Greene et al. suggested the hypothesis that SCD may occur in a basically depressed man at high risk for CHD who succumbs to an overwhelming level of arousal.

In a study of 118 patients from Helsinki, Rissanen, Romo, and Siltanen (1978) looked at premonitory signs preceding SCD and found that both acute and chronic stress were most apparent in deaths of those people without a history of CHD. Information was obtained from relatives and gathered according to a uniform protocol. Acute stress was associated with SCD and no detectable MI, whereas chronic stress was more frequently accompanied by definite MI, verified at autopsy.

More recently, using data from the RCPP, Brackett and Powell (1988) reviewed all deaths in this large-scale clinical trial for modifying TABP. After 4.5 years, there were 23 SCDs (death occurring within 1 hour) and 32 nonsudden deaths among the 1,013 post-MI patients. Independent multivariate predictors of SCD were anterior location of infarction, socioeconomic status, and Type A score at entry. Biological factors predominated in nonsudden death, and psychosocial variables were not predictors for these cases. Interpreting the TABP as a chronic endogenous stressor, Brackett and Powell (1988) concluded that their data demonstrated "a direct relation between stress and sudden cardiac death in a large prospective clinical study" (p. 979).

The alternative point of view—that SCD is a chance event with little relationship to psychological stress—has been advanced by Surawicz (1985) and others who note that SCD is rare, even under life's most stressful conditions, such as soldiers marching into battle and panic situations affecting large groups. Hinkle (1985) followed 700 individuals who had 30,000 episodes of ventricular arrhythmia over a 5–10-year period and found death very infrequent, regardless of life circumstances. McIntosh (1985) supported a similar view, asserting that "practically nothing is known about why sudden cardiac death occurs in one but not another person" (p. 105B). Reviewing the data from the Framingham Heart Study, Kannel and Schatzkin (1985) concluded that there are no specific risk factors for SCD independent of those for CHD. A comprehensive review of biobehavioral factors in SCD is provided by Kamarck and Jennings (1991).

Psychological Stress and Cardiac Arrhythmia

Irregular heart rhythms, or arrhythmias, range from benign to deadly. Most SCD results from the arrhythmia of ventricular fibrillation (see chap. 2 of this volume for a discussion of arrhythmias). Even benign arrhythmia can be anxiety provoking for the cardiac patient, requiring considerable explanation and emotional support. There has also been interest in determining whether psychological factors might be involved in the precipitation or exacerbation of arrhythmia.

In one early study, Wellens, Vermeulen, and Durrer (1972) described a young woman in whom the potentially life-threatening arrhythmia of ventricular tachycardia could be regularly precipitated by a ringing alarm clock. A 1981 report from the Lown group (Reich, DeSilva, Lown, & Murowski, 1981) described a "higher nervous activity" task force consisting of psychiatrists, psychologists, and members of a cardiovascular team. Of 117 patients with life-threatening ventricular arrhythmia followed closely by the task force, 25 (21%) had psychological precipitants, 15 within an hour of arrhythmia onset. Triggers included interpersonal conflicts, public humiliation, threat of marital separation, bereavement, business failure, loss of job, and nightmares. According to Lown (1987), three sets of conditions contribute to the occurrence of ventricular arrhythmia: (a) myocardial electrical instability, most often resulting from ischemic heart disease; (b) an acute triggering event, frequently related to mental stress; and (c) a chronic, pervasive, and intense psychological state, often including depression and hopelessness.

Follick et al. (1988) conducted a prospective examination of 125 post-MI patients equipped with transtelephonic electrocardiogram monitors. Patients were followed over a 1-year period after administration of the SCL-90 (Derogatis, Lipman, & Covi, 1973), a questionnaire used to assess psychological distress. A significant relationship was found between ventricular premature contractions and baseline scores on the SCL-90 after cardiac risk, age, and use of beta-blocking drugs were controlled for, suggesting that psychological distress may have prognostic significance for arrhythmia and, presumably, SCD.

Not all investigations of psychological factors have found a positive relationship with arrhythmia. The Cardiac Arrhythmia Pilot Study (Follick et al., 1990) found no relationship between a wide range of questionnaire-assessed psychosocial variables and rates of ventricular premature contractions for 353 patients studied for 1 year. Questionnaires included the State–Trait Anxiety Inventory, Bortner Type-A Scale, Beck Depression Inventory, Anger Expression Scale, and Hassles Scale. A video game designed to provoke cardiovascular reactivity was included, but it also showed no relationship with subsequent arrhythmia.

Animal experiments provide an opportunity to manipulate behavioral variables with far greater freedom and precision than studies involving humans. Such studies support a relationship between psychological stress and vulnerability to cardiac arrhythmia and suggest that if triggering of ventricular arrhythmia occurs, it is related to autonomic imbalance—either increased sympathetic or decreased parasympathetic tone. In a series of experiments with animals, Verrier (1987) had the following results:

1. Psychological stress (aversive conditioning with mild electric shocks while an animal is confined in a sling) substantially reduces the threshold to ventricular fibrillation;
2. Psychological stress increases the incidence of spontaneous ventricular fibrillation after experimental coronary artery occlusion and reperfusion;
3. Beta-adrenergic blockade diminishes or blocks the adverse effects of psychological stress in the above situations, suggesting that sympathetic overactivity is causal; and
4. Vagal blockade substantially increases the adverse effects of psychological stress, suggesting that parasympathetic underactivity may also play a role.

In spite of experimental evidence in animals linking sympathetic overactivity to arrhythmia, known pharmacological actions of catecholamines in humans tending to cause arrhythmia, and several theoretical mechanisms whereby either heightened sympathetic or lowered parasympathetic activity ought to promote arrhythmogenesis, actual demonstration of a major role of autonomic imbalance—either humoral (circulating epinephrine or norepinephrine) or neurological—in the genesis of serious cardiac arrhythmia has been limited.

Psychological Stress and Coronary Artery Function

Vasoconstriction of atherosclerotic coronary artery segments has been demonstrated with psychological stressors (Feigl, 1987), and there has been much interest in the possible role of a endothelial-derived relaxing factor. In their study of 30 CHD patients, Yeung et al. (1991) administered a stressful arithmetic task to patients undergoing cardiac catheterization. A subgroup of patients received intracoronary infusion of acetylcholine, normally a vasodilator if endothelial function is intact. Two coronary artery segments per patient were selected blindly and classified as smooth, irregular, or stenosed. As expected, smooth coronary artery segments dilated in response to both mental stress and acetylcholine. In irregular and atherosclerotic (stenosed) artery segments, however, there was paradoxical constriction with both mental stress and acetylcholine. This suggests that abnormal vasomotor response, probably related to endothelial dysfunction, may be an important determinant of emotionally induced ischemia.

Using an animal model, J. K. Williams, Vita, Manuck, Selwyn, and Kaplan (1991) studied the effects of chronic psychosocial disruption and diet on coronary artery function. Quantitative angiography revealed larger plaques in socially stressed monkeys in comparison with control animals. In addition, socially disrupted monkeys showed paradoxical constriction of coronary arteries in response to acetylcholine in comparison with socially stable controls. Although a low-cholesterol diet reduced the size of arterial plaques, vascular responses of socially stressed animals nevertheless continued to show paradoxical constriction with acetylcholine. Williams et al. concluded that in addition to an atherogenic effect, chronic social stress appears to impair endothelium-dependent vascular responses of coronary arteries.

As the research presented above indicates, impaired coronary artery function has been demonstrated both in humans in response to the acute laboratory stress of mental arithmetic and in cynomolgus monkeys experiencing long-term social disruption.

Psychological Stress and Serum Lipids

Cannon's (1932) "fight or flight response," recast in human terms by M. Friedman and Rosenman (1974) as "free-floating hostility" and "time urgency," suggests that chronic overactivation of the sympathetic nervous system with excess secretion of stress hormones (e.g., catecholamines and cortisol) might be atherogenic. A considerable amount of early work was, therefore, directed at the possible relationship between psychological stress and serum lipids. Indeed, M. Friedman and Rosenman's (1959) seminal research on TABP reported seasonal variations in accountants' cholesterol levels that peaked with the April 15th income tax deadline. Niaura, Stoney, and Herbert (1992) provided a recent review of the stress–lipid literature, with emphasis on research conducted within the past decade, and arrived at several conclusions. First, the results of 62 recent studies of episodic stressors, such as medical school exams or military training exercises, showed positive, though inconclusive, results. Second, some studies of personality traits, such as TABP and hostility, have shown a positive correlation with serum cholesterol levels, although recent studies using the Ho scale did not find such a relationship. Third, most studies of chronic occupational stress have failed to show a relationship between stress and lipids. And, finally, studies of acute laboratory stressors tended to show temporary increases in free fatty acids, although the relationship between such increases and subsequent cholesterol levels is currently unclear.

Animal Studies of Psychosocial Stress and Atherosclerosis

Ongoing, well-controlled research with primates at Bowman-Gray University has provided experimental confirmation for the importance of experimentally manipulated psychological stress in the development of atherosclerosis (see Kaplan, Manuck, Williams, & Strawn, 1993, for the most recent review). In a series of studies, Clarkson, Kaplan, Adams, and Manuck (1987) subjected cynomolgus monkey colonies to stress by repeatedly reshuffling groups, breaking up a stable social structure of dominant and subordinate individuals. In some experiments, high-lipid diets were provided to promote atherosclerosis; in others, the struggle was accentuated by adding a single sexually receptive female to the disorganized group. Dominant monkeys in unstable and stressful social situations developed strikingly increased coronary atherosclerosis in comparison with both subordinates (who presumably did not struggle as hard to achieve dominance) and dominant monkeys in stable (low external stress) groups. Beta-blockers reduced the tendency to develop atherosclerosis.

Summary

The studies cited above represent a sample of the literature on psychological stress and CHD. The stress examined in each of these studies is quite different, including such diverse phenomena as life changes; scores on an intuitively created questionnaire; catastrophic events such as war and earthquake; and a variety of laboratory stressors, such as mental arithmetic, simulated public speaking, mild electric shocks, and experimentally manipulated social disruption of monkey colonies. Our overall assessment of these data is that stressors of many different types do affect a variety of physiological processes that ought to influence clinical manifestations of heart disease. What is not known is what types of stress are most potent or how individual susceptibility, preexisting behavioral profiles, or response to stressors affect the process. It also cannot be determined from the available data how stress does its damage—whether it is modulated through long-term changes in serum cholesterol, blood pressure, or other traditional risk factors or through acute effects on determinants of myocardial ischemia, such as increased heart rate, blood pressure or cardiac contractility, coronary vasoconstriction, the propensity to arrhythmia, increased tendency for thrombosis, or other physiological processes. The physiological mechanisms by which stress affects heart disease need to be studied more closely to provide a better idea of how and where intervention is needed.

Job Strain

Job strain occurs "when individuals have insufficient control over their work situation to be able to satisfactorily deal with the level of demands being placed on them" (Karasek et al., 1988, p. 910). Job strain is the product of high job demands combined with low decision latitude. For example, firemen, cashiers, and freight handlers have high demands but little variability in decisions they are allowed; thus, they have high job strain. Physicians, lawyers, and executives have high demands but also high latitude in decision making, putatively conferring lower job strain. For assessment, Karasek et al. developed both a questionnaire and an "estimation method" that imputes job strain to a number of census-defined occupations (presented in Exhibit 1). A 6-year prospective study of 1,928 Swedish men

EXHIBIT 1
Karasek Job Strain Questionnaire

Statements Used to Define Job Strain

I. Decision latitude
  A. "My job requires that I learn new things."
  B. "My job requires a high level of skill."
  C. "My job requires that I be creative."
  D. "My job requires that I do things over and over."
  E. "I have freedom to decide what I do on the job."
  F. "It is my responsibility to decide how much of the job gets done."

II. Psychological demands
  G. "My job requires working very fast."
  H. "My job requires working very hard."
  I. "I am not asked to do an excessive amount of work."
  J. "I have enough time to get the job done."
  K. "I am free from conflicting demands others make."

Scoring: 1 = strongly disagree, 2 = disagree, 3 = agree, 4 = strongly agree.
From "Job Strain and the Prevalence and Outcome of Coronary Artery Disease," by M. A. Hlatky et al., 1995, *Circulation, 92*, p. 328. Copyright 1995 by the American Heart Association. Reprinted with permission.

(Karasek, Baker, Marxer, Ahlbom, & Theorell, 1981) demonstrated an increased risk of developing CHD with a "hectic and psychologically demanding job" and a relative risk of CHD or cardiovascular death of 4 ($p < .01$; for those with high vs. low job strain). An increased prevalence rate for MI of 2.48 and 3.28, respectively, for two U.S. populations of 2,409 and 2,424 employed men was found using the imputation method (Karasek et al., 1988). In subsequent research using ambulatory blood pressure monitoring, Schnall et al. (1990) determined that job strain is related to workplace diastolic blood pressure and left ventricular mass.

Schnall, Landsbergis, and Baker (1994) have provided a recent, thorough review of the job strain literature. According to their findings, 37 studies were published between 1981 and 1993, and most found a significant positive correlation between either job strain and cardiovascular or all-cause mortality or job strain and risk factors for cardiovascular disease or mortality. Thus far, 11 of 13 published studies have found a positive relationship between job strain and cardiovascular risk factors or cardiovascular disease.

The most recent investigation of job strain, an angiographic study of 1,489 patients by Hlatky et al. (1995), found no relationship between scores on the Karasek questionnaire and severity of cardiac disease or cardiac events over a mean follow-up period of 4 years. In this sample, job strain was more common in patients with normal coronary arteries than in patients with CHD, despite the fact that 84% considered their jobs stressful and 91% believed that job stress could cause a heart attack.

Vital Exhaustion

According to the hypothesis of vital exhaustion, developed in the Netherlands by Appels, Höppener, and Muldur (1987), a debilitated physical and emotional state may be a precursor of MI. The Maastricht Questionnaire was developed to assess vital exhaustion. Items on this questionnaire that are predictive of MI are presented in Exhibit 2.

The vital exhaustion hypothesis was tested in a prospective study of 3,877 city employees in Rotterdam, the Netherlands (Appels & Mulder, 1989). The Maastricht Questionnaire demonstrated an age-adjusted relative risk of 2.28 for MI over 4.2 years. A subsequent analysis (Appels & Schouten, 1991) revealed that frequently "waking up exhausted" conferred a significant independent additional risk beyond "vital exhaustion." Of all the items on the questionnaire, a positive response to "Do you want to be dead at times?" demonstrated the strongest association with age-adjusted relative risk of MI over 4 years.

Most recently, Kop, Appels, Mendes de Leon, de Swart, and Bar (1994) prospectively studied vital exhaustion in a group of 127 patients

EXHIBIT 2
The Maastricht Questionnaire

Medical research is constantly trying to track down the causes of disease. You would help this research by answering the following questions about how you feel lately. Please mark the answers that are true for you. If you don't know or cannot decide circle the ?. There are no "right" or "wrong" answers.

1. Do you often feel tired?	yes	?	no
2. Do you often have trouble falling asleep?	yes	?	no
3. Do you wake up repeatedly during the night?	yes	?	no
4. Do you feel weak all over?	yes	?	no
5. Do you have the feeling that you haven't been accomplishing much lately?	yes	?	no
6. Do you have the feeling that you can't cope with everyday problems as well as you used to?	yes	?	no
7. Do you believe that you have come to a "dead end"?	yes	?	no
8. Do you lately feel more listless than before?	yes	?	no
9. I enjoy sex as much as ever	yes	?	no
10. Have you experienced a feeling of hopelessness recently?	yes	?	no
11. Does it take more time to grasp a difficult problem than it did a year ago?	yes	?	no
12. Do little things irritate you more lately than they used to?	yes	?	no
13. Do you feel you want to give up trying?	yes	?	no
14. I feel fine	yes	?	no
15. Do you sometimes feel that your body is like a battery that is losing its power?	yes	?	no
16. Would you want to be dead at times?	yes	?	no
17. Do you have the feeling these days that you just don't have what it takes any more?	yes	?	no
18. Do you feel dejected?	yes	?	no
19. Do you feel like crying sometimes?	yes	?	no
20. Do you ever wake up with a feeling of exhaustion and fatigue?	yes	?	no
21. Do you have increasing difficulty in concentrating on a single subject for long?	yes	?	no

---

Scoring: Each confirmation of a complaint is coded as 2. All question marks are coded as 1. A negative answer is coded as 0. Note that questions 9 and 14 are reverse-scored (No = 2; ? = 1; Yes = 0). The scale score is obtained by summing the answers.

From "A Questionnaire to Assess Premonitory Symptoms of Myocardial Infarction," by A. Appels, P. Höppener, and P. Muldur, 1987, *International Journal of Cardiology, 17*, p. 24. Copyright 1987 by Elsevier Science Ireland Ltd., Bay 15K, Shannon Industrial Estate, Co. Clare, Ireland. Reprinted with permission.

undergoing successful coronary angioplasty. After controlling for severity of disease and cardiac risk factors, Kop et al. found that 35% of the 43 vitally exhausted patients suffered a new cardiac event in comparison with only 17% of the 84 patients not exhausted during 1.5 years of follow-up (OR = 2.7; 95% CI, 1.1–6.3, p = .02).

Social Support

Social support, or the degree to which one is connected to others in the community, has emerged as an inverse risk factor of considerable magnitude, not only for CHD but for morbidity and mortality from all causes. Of all psychosocial risk factors, the social support literature appears the most consistent in establishing a relationship between heart and mind. Early work in the field focused on the higher death rate of widows and widowers in comparison with the general population (Parkes, 1964; Rees & Lutkins, 1967). Cottington, Matthews, Talbott, and Kuller (1980) reported that loss of a significant other within the past 6 months was more than 6 times as frequent for women who died of SCD than for matched control patients. Chandra, Scklo, Goldberg, and Tonascia (1983) studied the effects of marital status on in-hospital and long-term survival of 1,401 post-MI patients. The in-hospital fatality rate was 19.7% for married men versus 26.7% for unmarried men and 23.2% for married women versus 37.4% for unmarried women. Patterns of improved survival in married patients were consistent over 10 years. The interested reader should consult Broadhead, Kaplan, James, and Wagner's (1983) review of the early literature on social support.

Ruberman, Weinblatt, Goldberg, and Chaudhary (1984) studied social connectedness in a large, post-MI population. Interviews with 2,315 male survivors in the Beta-Blocker Heart Attack Trial showed that those with both high levels of social isolation and a high degree of life stress had a more than fourfold increased risk of total death and SCD over 3 years following MI.

In an analysis of five large-scale prospective studies on the impact of social relationships and health, House, Landis, and Umberson (1988) concluded that lack of social support is a risk factor of major significance. Reviewing data from more than 37,000 people in the United States and Europe, this analysis claimed that lack of social support rivals risks described in the 1964 Surgeon General's report that first established cigarette smoking as a risk factor for morbidity and mortality from a wide range of diseases. Figure 3 shows the relative risk ratios for mortality in the five studies reviewed by House et al. Categories of social ties include marriage, contact with extended family and friends, church membership, and other formal and informal affiliations. Studies had from 8–13 years of follow-up and controlled for a wide range of factors. Increased risks for those with

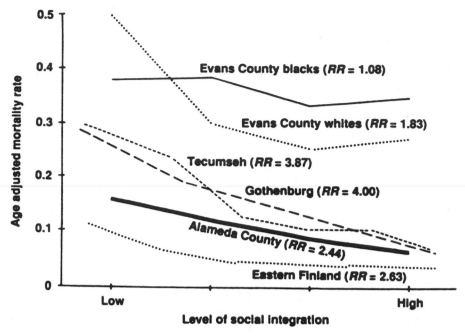

Figure 3. Level of social integration and age-adjusted mortality rate for men in five prospective studies. RR = relative risk ratio for mortality at the lowest versus highest levels of social integration. Evans County is in Georgia, Tecumseh is in Michigan, Alameda County is in California, and Gothenburg is in Sweden.

From "Social Relationships and Health," by J. S. House, K. R. Landis, and D. Umberson, 1988, *Science, 241,* p. 540. Copyright 1988 by the American Association for the Advancement of Science. Reprinted with permission.

lower social support were significant for both men and women, with relative risk ratios higher for men.

Studies on social support have tended to rely on questionnaires or brief interviews about the nature and frequency of interpersonal contacts. Efforts have been made to examine social support more closely to better understand the underlying mechanisms that may promote health or disease. One study (Seeman & Syme, 1987) examined the differences between the structure and function of interpersonal relationships for patients undergoing coronary angiography. The structural aspects of social support were defined as the number of relationships and the frequency of social contacts, whereas the functional aspects related to the quality of those relationships. Results suggested that the functional aspects of relationships and "feeling loved" appear protective for atherosclerosis.

Orth-Gomér, Rosengren, and Wilhelmsen (1993) followed 736 fifty-year-old healthy men born in Göteborg, Sweden, for 6 years. A lack of both emotional support from very close people ("attachment") and support provided by an extended network of people ("social integration") were significant risk factors in multiple logistic regression analysis as predictors of CHD events, after traditional risk factors were controlled for. In fact, lack of social support rivaled cigarette smoking as a risk factor for CHD in this study.

Two large-scale prospective studies have looked at the effects of social isolation on survival after a diagnosis of CHD. In a multicenter investigation, Case, Moss, Case, McDermott, and Eberly (1992) studied living alone and marital disruption in a group of 1,234 patients admitted to coronary care units with documented MI. After 6 months, the recurrent event rate for nonfatal MI or cardiac death was 15.8% for patients living alone versus 8.8% for those living with a partner. Interestingly, marital disruption (divorce, separation, or widowhood) was not a significant independent risk factor for morbid events. Similarly, R. B. Williams, Barefoot, and Califf (1992) studied a consecutive sample of 1,368 patients undergoing cardiac catheterization and discovered that unmarried patients without a confidant had a 3.34 times increased risk of death within 5 years in comparison with patients who either were married or had a close friend in whom they confided.

A well-designed study by Berkman, Leo-Summers, and Horwitz (1992) prospectively followed 100 men and 94 women, 65 years of age or older, who had been hospitalized for acute MI. A large number of physiological variables were controlled for, including severity of disease, comorbidity, and functional status, as well as standard cardiac risk factors. After 6 months, lack of emotional support was associated with significantly increased mortality.

The Case et al. (1992), Williams et al. (1992), and Berkman et al. (1992) studies examined psychosocial support after controlling for a number of important demographic and physiological variables, including left ventricular function. Although the mechanism is poorly understood, social support appears to confer powerful protection against future morbid events after a diagnosis of CHD. In an editorial, Ruberman (1992) urged the adoption of practices that provide social support for isolated cardiac patients, asserting that "for physicians, it is a comforting notion that applying principles to clinical practice that improve the quality of life may yet be shown to extend the length of life as well" (p. 560).

In an attempt to integrate TABP with social support, Blumenthal et al. (1987) studied the interaction of these two factors on 113 patients undergoing coronary angiography. For those diagnosed Type A, the extent of atherosclerosis was inversely related to perceived social support; that is, Type As with high levels of support had the least atherosclerosis, suggesting that social support may moderate the long-term consequences of TABP.

Similarly, Orth-Gomér and Uniden (1990) discovered that lack of social support and social isolation were independent predictors of mortality over 10 years in SI-assessed Type A, but not Type B, men with CHD.

Another study assessed the differences in social support between "maintainers" and "nonmaintainers" of risk factor modification from a subgroup of patients in the MRFIT. O'Reilly and Thomas (1989) reported that maintainers ($n = 63$) and nonmaintainers ($n = 143$) in the Boston area showed highly significant differences for four types of social support that were associated with risk-reduction behavior. Maintainers received more information and advice, appraisal, emotional support, and availability from larger support networks that were family- rather than friendship-centered. This finding suggests the clinical utility of involving family members to support coronary risk-reduction efforts.

We are intrigued by the strength and universality of the relationship between social isolation and CHD in both primary and secondary prevention studies reported to date. As with other psychosocial variables, there is a dearth of hard data on the mechanism or mechanisms by which lack of social support is linked to increased coronary disease. Attractive possibilities include better control of coronary risk factors or earlier responses to premonitory symptomatology because of the influences of family or friends. However, the strength of the protection provided by social support and the often-noted protective effects on noncardiac as well as cardiac mortality suggest that investigations into broader physiological correlates (e.g., possibly autonomic or immunologic) might be highly fruitful for better understanding and therapeutic use of this widely acknowledged major protective factor. Despite the limited knowledge of what physiological mechanisms are involved, the strength and consistency of the data provide a powerful rationale for support groups for CHD patients.

Depression

Depression is a frequent precursor of CHD and often accompanies recovery. In one of the earliest studies, Cassem and Hackett (1973) found objective evidence of depression in 76% of 50 randomly selected patients in a cardiac care unit. Subsequently, one meta-analysis (Booth-Kewley & Friedman, 1987) found that depression, more than any other psychological attribute, had the strongest association with the end results of CHD. (See Fielding, 1991, for a review of this expansive literature.) Writing from a psychiatric perspective, Fernandez (1993) noted that depression is one of the best predictors of poor adherence to lifestyle change and recurrent cardiovascular complications after a cardiac event. He pointed out that depression is typically underdiagnosed and untreated in the 18% to 44% of cardiac patients who suffer from depression severe enough to warrant psychiatric intervention. In a study at two New York City medical centers,

Schleifer et al. (1989) reported that 18% of 283 patients had major depressive disorder and 27% had minor depressive disorder from 8 to 10 days post-MI. Three to 4 months later, 33% met criteria for major or minor depression.

Frasure-Smith, Lesperance, and Talajic (1993) prospectively evaluated the impact of depression on 222 post-MI patients who survived to discharge from a large university hospital in Montreal, Canada. Depression was assessed by using a modified version of the National Institute of Mental Health Diagnostic Interview Schedule while patients were in the hospital. Thirty-five patients (16%) were diagnosed with major depression. After 6 months, 12 patients had died, all from cardiovascular complications, with 6 deaths from among the 35 depressed patients and 6 from among the 187 nondepressed patients. Depression was a significant predictor of mortality, after previous MI and left ventricular dysfunction were controlled for (adjusted hazard ratio = 4.29; 95% CI, 3.14–5.44, p = .013), in the first prospective study to demonstrate an association between major depression and cardiovascular mortality.

In another study of 2,832 initially healthy U.S. adults, questionnaire-assessed depressed affect and hopelessness were associated with increased relative risk of fatal and nonfatal ischemic heart disease over a mean follow-up period of 12.4 years (Anda et al., 1992). Ludwig, Roll, Breithardt, Budde, and Borggrefe (1994) grouped 552 male survivors of acute MI according to depression status and found degree of depression positively related to angina pectoris and maintenance of smoking habits and negatively related to return to work after 6 months. Inversely, "dispositional optimism"—defined as seeing "desired outcomes as attainable"—prior to surgery has been related to both return to work and improved quality of life 6 months after coronary artery bypass graft (CABG) surgery by Scheier et al. (1989).

In the first prospective study to link depression with MI in an initially healthy population, Barefoot and Schroll (in press) found high levels of depressive symptomatology (assessed with the Depression scale of the MMPI) associated with increased risk of MI and mortality in a group of 409 male and 432 female residents of Glostrop, Denmark, all of whom were born in 1914.

There are strong theoretical ties between depressed mood and various coronary-prone behaviors. For instance, the compulsive achievement striving of TABP is thought to be a reaction against an underlying, unconscious depression. As long as the Type A individual is engaged in driven, ambition-related activities, he or she is protected from awareness of the depression. When such activities cease, however, such as after acute MI, depression often becomes unmasked. Clearly, depression is embodied within the cynical and pessimistic orientation to life assessed by the Cook–Medley Ho scale and readily identifiable in many of the items of the Maastricht Questionnaire measuring vital exhaustion. In classic psychoanalytic theory, depression is sometimes considered "anger turned inward," suggesting a strong theoretical link between hostility and depression. It may also be posited that depression contributes to self-destructive behavior and motivates people in the direction of "quick fix" forms of satisfaction, such as cigarettes, alcohol, and fast foods high in saturated fat.

In an attempt to gain greater understanding of the physiological link between depression and CHD outcome, Carney et al. (1995) discovered decreased heart rate variability in 19 depressed CHD patients in comparison with 19 nondepressed control participants, suggesting increased sympathetic nervous system activity or decreased vagal tone as possible physiological mechanisms. Depressed CHD patients with decreased heart rate variability are thus an important target group for psychological treatment.

From these data, which appear quite consistent across many studies, increased attention to psychotherapeutic and psychopharmacological intervention with post-MI and post-CABG depression appears warranted and compelling.

Anxiety

A new hypothesis in cardiac psychology is that anxiety may increase the risk of CHD, particularly SCD. Two prospective studies (Haines, Imeson, & Meade, 1987; Kawachi, Colditz et al., 1994) have demonstrated an association between self-reported symptoms of phobic anxiety (using the Crown–Crisp Index, presented in Exhibit 3) and risk of fatal CHD. The study by Kawachi and associates is noteworthy in that it followed an unusually large sample of 33,999 men over 2 years. They found an increased relative risk of 2.45 from fatal CHD (95% CI, 1.0–5.96) and a 6.08 relative risk of SCD (95% CI, 2.35–15.73) among men with the highest levels of anxiety. A third study (Kawachi, Sparrow, Vokonas, & Weiss, 1994) followed 2,280 men over 32 years and found a similarly increased (although nonsignificant) risk of fatal CHD using a five-item anxiety scale created out of the Cornell Medical Index (OR = 1.94; 95% CI, 0.70–5.41). Here, too, data were more compelling when SCD was the outcome variable (OR = 4.46; 95% CI, 0.92–21.60). Frasure-Smith, Lesperance, and Talajic (1995) reported a relationship between increased anxiety and acute coronary syndromes (unstable angina admissions and recurrent fatal and nonfatal MI) in a sample of 222 post-MI patients.

In a cross-sectional analysis of 381 healthy men enrolled in the Normotensive Aging Study, Kawachi, Sparrow, Vokonas, and Weiss (1995) discovered reduced heart rate variability among men with the highest scores on the Crown–Crisp Index. This finding suggests that phobic anxiety may increase risk of SCD because of diminished heart rate variability, a sign of altered sympathovagal balance in the autonomic regulation of the

EXHIBIT 3
Crown–Crisp Experiential Index

1. Do you have an unreasonable fear of being in enclosed spaces, such as shops, lifts, etc.?
   Answers: Never / Sometimes / Often

2. Do you find yourself worrying about getting some incurable illness?
   Answers: Never / Sometimes / Often

3. Are you scared of heights?
   Answers: Not at all / Moderately / Very

4. Do you feel panicky in crowds?
   Answers: Never / Sometimes / Always

5. Do you worry unduly when relatives are late coming home?
   Answers: No / Yes

6. Do you feel more relaxed indoors?
   Answers: Not particularly / Sometimes / Definitely

7. Do you dislike going out alone?
   Answers: No / Yes

8. Do you feel uneasy travelling on buses or trains even if they are not crowded?
   Answers: Not at all / A little / Definitely

Three individual items were associated with an elevated risk of fatal coronary heart disease: (a) "Always feeling panicky in crowds" (relative risk ratio [RR] 10.8; 95% confidence interval [CI], 2.2–52.5); (b) "Worrying unduly when relatives are late coming home" (RR 2.3; 95% CI, 1.2–4.2); and (c) "Definitely feeling more relaxed indoors" (RR 3.7; 95% CI, 2.1–6.4).

From "Prospective Study of Phobic Anxiety and Risk of Coronary Heart Disease in Men," by I. Kawachi et al., 1994, *Circulation, 89,* p. 1996. Copyright 1994 by the American Heart Association. Adapted with permission.

heart. The relationship between anxiety and CHD, particularly SCD, deserves further scrutiny.

Cardiac Denial

Denial is a psychological coping strategy that allows people to engage in behavior with little conscious awareness of the consequences. Sometimes denial is sufficiently powerful to allow negative behavior in spite of some level of awareness, such as, for example, in patients with CHD who continue to smoke cigarettes. Because denial of a possible cardiac event may lead to delay in seeking medical care, the consequences can be profound: The individual who delays seeking treatment (and, perhaps, not receiving immediate thrombolytic, beta-blocker, or other therapy) risks increased myocardial damage, morbidity, and mortality. The catchphrase "time is muscle" captures the essence of this issue. In addition, life-threatening ventricular arrhythmias often occur in the first few minutes or hours after MI onset. Approximately 60% of out-of-hospital cardiac deaths occur within 2 hours of symptoms (Albarran-Sotelo, Flint, & Kelly, 1988). Overcoming the emotional resistance of cardiac denial may lead to reduced morbidity and mortality for patients with acute coronary syndromes who arrive at the hospital quickly. We speak of emotional resistance because we know of one physician who made love with his wife during the early stages of his MI and refused medical attention for many hours afterward, consequently losing considerable left ventricular function. Although this highly competent physician clearly had the intellectual capacity to diagnose someone else's MI, he was unable to allow the possibility of his own vulnerability to penetrate his emotional defensiveness.

Cardiac denial is a complex phenomenon. Levine et al. (1987) followed 30 men for 1 year post-MI and reported that individuals with high scores on a denial scale spent fewer days in intensive care and had fewer signs of cardiac dysfunction while in the hospital in comparison with those who had low scores. However, after 1 year, high deniers were more noncompliant with treatment recommendations and required more days of rehospitalization. This finding suggests that denial may be adaptive during the acute stages of MI while in the hospital but maladaptive after discharge.

One would think that individuals who have had a cardiac event would be sensitized to the importance of prompt medical care for cardiac symptoms. However, Herlitz et al. (1989) have noted that previous cardiac history was not associated with reduced delay time in seeking medical attention in a number of studies. Furthermore, Wielgosz and Nolan (1991) pointed out that denial has not been definitively linked with delay. One effort to clarify mechanisms of denial was made by Kenyon, Ketterer, Gheorghiade, and Goldstein (1991), who examined factors affecting the time between symptom onset and arrival at the hospital for 103 acute MI patients in Detroit, Michigan. Patients who scored high on a somatic awareness scale and low on an alexithymia scale sought treatment significantly sooner than those with low sensory and emotional awareness scores. The largest source of delay was the time it took patients to decide they were seriously ill. Quite dramatically, only 20% of this patient sample arrived early enough to obtain thrombolytic therapy.

In light of the potential benefit of early thrombolysis, a large-scale media campaign was undertaken in Göteborg, Sweden, in 1987 (Blohm et al., 1992). The HJARTA-SMARTA program pointed out the importance of prompt medical care for chest pain lasting longer than 15 minutes. A 3-week intensive multimedia campaign was followed by newspaper articles and leaflets distributed twice to all households in Göteborg—200,000 leaflets in all. Advertisements were placed on public transportation and radio. All acute MI admissions were reviewed for 21 months before and 13 months after the media campaign began. Median delay time in seeking treatment was reduced from 3 hours before to 2 hours and 20 minutes during the campaign. The percentage of patients receiving thrombolytic therapy increased from 4% before to 13% during the campaign, and infarct size (assessed by cardiac enzymes) was reduced. However, neither in-hospital nor 1-year mortality were significantly affected by this ambitious mass communication effort.

A review by Sirous (1992) traced 21 empirical studies on denial in CHD published in the past 25 years and concluded that denial has a long-term negative effect on health outcome. In 1991, the National Heart, Lung, and Blood Institute began an educational program in the United States, both in the general population and in the medical community, for rapid identification of acute MI patients in an attempt to reduce the time to treatment (National Heart Attack Alert Program Coordinating Committee, 1993). Because of the profound potential benefits of overcoming denial and delay in the era of thrombolytic therapy, this is a subject that deserves much future attention.

PATIENTS WITH NONCARDIAC CHEST PAIN

A related area of likely interest for the mental health practitioner is the large group of patients with chest pain or palpitations who have had CHD ruled out by a standard cardiologic workup. Lantinga et al. (1988) reported that as many as 30% of patients referred for coronary angiography have been found to have normal coronary arteries. At least five studies have discovered that such patients rarely develop clinical CHD, yet a high percentage have a poor quality of life prognosis.

In one series of 94 consecutive referrals to a cardiac clinic in England, 75% of the 51 patients who did not have a cardiac diagnosis reported limitation of activities and continuing concern about their symptoms at both 6-month and 3-year follow-ups (Mayou, Bryant, Forfar, & Clark, 1994). Similarly, in a study of 24 U.S. Veterans Administration patients with angina and normal coronary arteries, Lantinga et al. (1988) found high depression and anxiety, continuing chest pains, and restricted activity 1 year after cardiac catheterization. Knowledge of clean coronary arteries did little to improve the psychosocial status of these patients. Pasternak, Thibault, Savoia, DeSanctis, and Hutter (1980) followed 159 patients with less than 50% coronary stenosis over 43 months and discovered continued episodes of at least once monthly chest pain in 54%, with 17% requiring hospitalization, nearly 50% suffering limitation of activity, and 22% changing jobs or stopping work as a result of chest pain. In this sample, continuing chest pains were more common in women than in men. Similar negative psychosocial findings have also been reported by Channer, Papouchado, James, and Rees (1985); Isner, Salem, Banas, and Levine (1981); and Lavy and Winkle (1979).

Patients with noncardiac chest pain sometimes receive a cardiac diagnosis of microvascular angina, or "Syndrome X," a condition thought to be characterized by vasospasm of the myriad collateral arteries that nourish the heart—arteries that are not visible with cardiac catheterization. Others are thought to be suffering from psychosomatic pains. Still others are labeled with the diagnosis of mitral valve prolapse (or floppy mitral valve), which is quite common in the population and occasionally causes vague cardiac symptoms, but likely is only coincidental in most patients with ongoing chest pain or palpitations who have had a negative workup for other cardiac disease. This diagnostic category represents largely unexplored territory for psychological research and psychotherapy intervention.

CLINICAL TRIALS USING LIFESTYLE INTERVENTION

Clinical trials are traditionally considered the gold standard for scientific validation in both medicine and psychology. One of the strongest arguments for increased attention to cardiac psychology is the reduced morbidity and mortality achieved in several recent clinical trials. Three important trials—the Lifestyle Heart Trial (Gould et al., 1995; Ornish et al., 1990, 1993), the RCPP (M. Friedman et al., 1986, 1987), and Project New Life (Burell, 1993)—are highlighted in separate chapters of this volume (chaps. 9–11, respectively), authored by psychologists central to the research and treatment. Here, we offer brief summaries of these studies and several others.

The Lifestyle Heart Trial has demonstrated angiographic evidence for reversal of coronary atherosclerosis with lifestyle modification. In this prospective study, 48 CHD patients were assigned to either a lifestyle intervention program or routine medical care. The program began with a week-long retreat and became a major focus in participants' lives: Twice-weekly group sessions included exercise, stress management, yoga and meditation, a communal meal, and group support psychotherapy. A spouse or significant other was encouraged to attend these 4-hour evening meetings. Patients ate a vegetarian diet, much of which was provided by the researchers, with only 6.8% of calories derived from fat. The program required daily stretching, relaxation, and meditation for 1 hour and moderate exercise on days when participants did not attend group sessions. Patients underwent coronary arteriograms before entering the study and again at the end of 1 and 4 years, with coronary artery lesions analyzed by quantitative angiography. After 4 years, average stenosis diameter decreased from 43.6% to 39.7% in experimental patients but progressed from 41.6% to 51.4% in the control group (Ornish et al., 1993). After 1 year, 82% of the experimental group showed regression in atherosclerotic lesions, in comparison with only 42% of the control group (Ornish et al., 1990). Patients in the experimental group reported dramatic reductions in frequency, duration, and severity of angina in comparison with increased symptomatology experienced by those in the control group. Regression of lesions was associated with overall adherence to the program in a dose–response relationship, although none of the individual components demonstrated such a relationship. Favorable changes in myocardial perfusion, assessed by positron emission tomography, have been reported recently after 5 years of intervention (Gould et al., 1995).

One important question raised by the Lifestyle Heart Trial is whether so radical a lifestyle change is necessary to delay the progression of atherosclerosis. Schuler et al. (1992) studied a group of 18 patients with stable angina pectoris "with no more than average motivation and discipline" and found regression of CHD with a more modest lifestyle change program that included a low-fat (<20% of calories), low-cholesterol (<200 mg/ day) diet and at least 3 hours of exercise per week. Patients and their spouses participated in four group discussions during the year, and patients were provided with opportunities to talk about personal problems after exercise sessions. At the end of 1 year, 105 stenoses were evaluated by quantitative coronary angiography, which revealed significant regression of atherosclerotic lesions in 7 of 18 patients in the treatment group but in only 1 of the 12 patients receiving the usual care. Progression of atherosclerosis also occurred at a significantly slower rate in treated patients than in control participants.

In Finland, Hamalainen et al. (1989) studied a group of 275 acute MI patients under 65 years of age who were provided with a comprehensive program that included optimal medical care, physical exercise, smoking cessation, dietary advice, and discussion of psychological problems. Intervention was most intensive during the first 3 months after MI, but there was close contact with the health care team for 3 years. Patients were followed for 10 years, at which time there had been 24 (12.8%) SCDs in the intervention group and 43 (23.0%, $p = .01$) in the control group. The number of nonsudden cardiac deaths was similar between groups. It is also notable that benefits were significant 7 years after all intervention had ceased.

The RCPP (M. Friedman et al., 1986) has been the largest behavior modification program to date for secondary prevention of CHD. This study demonstrated a 44% reduction in second MI for 1,013 patients who received 4.5 years of group counseling for the TABP and cardiologic risk factors, in comparison with control participants who received counseling about only traditional cardiac risk factors. Some control group members were subsequently offered Type A counseling and showed a similar reduction in MI recurrence rates over an additional year (M. Friedman et al., 1987). The RCPP also determined that Type A counseling was most protective against cardiac death for patients who had experienced less severe MIs (Powell & Thoresen, 1988), suggesting that psychosocial intervention is most effective when individuals are still relatively healthy but that it may provide less benefit when the disease is severe and physiological processes predominate. Furthermore, in the RCPP, there was a significant reduction in SCD, but not in nonsudden cardiac death for Type A individuals (Brackett & Powell, 1988), providing support for the hypothesis that behavioral factors may be involved in the pathogenesis of lethal arrhythmias.

In an attempt to replicate the RCPP, Burell (1993) randomly assigned 268 nonsmoking post-CABG patients to either a group program for modification of the TABP and cardiac risk factor education or a usual care control group. During the first year, intervention patients met for 17 three-hour group sessions, with 5–6 "booster sessions" in Years 2 and 3. The behavioral treatment was modeled after the RCPP, with patients encouraged to reduce anger, impatience, annoyance, and irritation in daily life. Homework assignments, drills, and relaxation techniques were provided to facilitate self-observation and reduce Type A behavior. At follow-up 4.5 years after surgery, there was a significant difference in total deaths (7 vs. 16, $p = .02$) and a nonsignificant difference in cardiac deaths (5 vs. 8) between treatment and control patients, respectively. There were 14 fatal and nonfatal cardiovascular events (reinfarction, reoperation, or percutaneous transluminal coronary angioplasty) in the intervention group versus 19 in the control group ($p = .04$).

In a creative and practical approach, Frasure-Smith (1991) assessed post-MI patients' stress levels from the General Health Questionnaire administered prior to discharge from the hospital and in monthly telephone interviews. Nurses made home visits and attempted to resolve whatever problems appeared to be causing the patient's distress whenever symptoms exceeded a threshold score. An average of five home visits was made during 1 year of intervention. Patients with high in-hospital stress scores ($n = 61$) had a nearly threefold risk of cardiac mortality over 5 years in comparison with those who had low scores on the initial questionnaire ($n = 168$). However, highly stressed patients who participated in the home-visit intervention did not suffer increased cardiac mortality or recurrent MI in comparison with patients receiving routine medical care. Quite interestingly, intervention provided little benefit for patients who had low in-hospital stress scores, suggesting that only patients who are distressed while in the hospital are likely to benefit from this sort of follow-up. Although this is an encouraging study, randomization problems (e.g., an unexpectedly high proportion of lower socioeconomic individuals in the control group) limit its generalizability (Powell, 1989).

By far the single largest lifestyle modification study has been the MRFIT (Shekelle, Hulley, et al., 1985), a clinical trial for primary prevention of CHD. In this study, 361,662 healthy men were screened to form a cohort of 12,866 high-risk individuals between 35–57 years of age without overt CHD, who were assigned to special intervention programs or to receive usual health care. Special intervention consisted of counseling for smoking cessation, a stepped-care treatment for hypertension, and dietary advice for lowering blood cholesterol levels. In 1982, after an average follow-up of 7 years, risk factor levels declined in both groups, but only slightly more for men in the special intervention group. Mortality was 7.1% lower for this group, but this difference was not statistically significant. One explanation offered by the MRFIT investigators for the disappointing results was the lower than expected mortality of the group receiving usual care. It may be that entry into the study, or living in the risk-factor–conscious society of that time, was sufficient to motivate the control group to change health habits. A higher risk subgroup within the MRFIT cohort, those 12.5% of participants who had abnormal stress tests at entry, showed more favorable results with special intervention. These high-risk participants demonstrated a 57% reduction in CHD mortality with intervention in comparison with those in usual care ($p = .002$; Multiple Risk Factor Intervention Trial Research Group, 1985). An update examining 8,012 participants with hypertension after 10.5 years found an overall reduction of 11% in total deaths and 15% in CHD deaths and, for those with diastolic blood pressure greater than or equal to 100 mmHg, a 36% reduction in total deaths and 50% reduction in CHD deaths (Multiple Risk Factor Intervention Trial Research Group, 1990).

We have argued that CHD is a lifestyle disorder for a substantial segment of the population: those living a coronary-prone lifestyle with little attention to prudent risk factor management (Allan & Scheidt, 1992, 1993). Similar sentiments have been offered by Leaf and Ryan (1990), who pondered,

> Are we developing ingenious, technologically sophisticated and expensive treatment for established disease and ignoring the fact that the malady is potentially preventable and even reversible? . . . Members of the public will need to accept more responsibility for their own health . . . and be disabused of the fantasy that they can indulge in whatever lifestyle they wish and that medicine will make available a pill or operation to erase the adverse health effects of a lifetime of self-abuse. (p. 1418)

Encouragingly, the American Heart Association (1993) has estimated that, between 1964 and 1989, mortality from CHD declined over 50%, an improvement thought to result largely from risk factor modification.

PHYSIOLOGICAL MECHANISMS

If the favorable outcomes of clinical trials incorporating psychological factors represent the current strength of cardiac psychology, then a lack of understanding of physiological mechanisms is surely its chief weakness. Most often, the theoretical networks surrounding the TABP, anger and hostility, vital exhaustion, and job strain hypotheses have invoked chronic increased sympathetic nervous system activity as the primary culprit mechanism. This cardiovascular reactivity hypothesis is thought to be a dispositional tendency, "an individual's propensity to experience cardiovascular reactions of greater or lesser magnitude, compared to those of other persons, when encountering behavioral stimuli experienced as engaging, challenging, or aversive" (as cited in Manuck, 1994, p. 7). In the laboratory, cardiovascular reactivity has been expressed most often as the arithmetic difference from the baseline in responses of heart rate or blood pressure to an eliciting stimulus. Those under psychological stress (as in the life change and job strain models), those who bring about their own frequent psychological stress through Type A behavior or chronic hostility, or those who have reached a stage of vital exhaustion are hypothesized to have had chronically elevated sympathetic nervous system reactions over decades, producing excesses of "stress hormones" such as adrenaline and noradrenaline, testosterone, and cortisol, which are presumably atherogenic. In the latest review of what is now an extensive literature, Manuck (1994) indicated that "on balance, the available evidence is consistent with, but does not confirm, the hypothesis that cardiovascular reactivity is associated with CHD in humans" (p. 25).

Beyond this very general hypothesis of cardiovascular reactivity, however, little is known about the contributions of other physiological mechanisms to various manifestations of cardiac dysfunction. Exhibit 4 shows our summary of some of the possible physiological mechanisms involved in the connection between heart and mind.

CONCLUSION

There seems little doubt that a number of psychosocial variables exert profound influence on cardiac health and disease. It also seems highly likely that psychosocial or lifestyle interventions have enormous potential for

EXHIBIT 4
Possible Physiological Mechanisms Linking Behavioral Factors to Cardiac Dysfunction

1. Increased sympathetic activity (neural, hormonal), causing
   - Increased atherosclerosis through increased activation of macrophages, platelet aggregability, or platelet-derived growth factors
   - Increased ischemia through increased determinants of myocardial oxygen consumption (heart rate, blood pressure, and contractility)
   - Increased ischemia through increased platelet activation, aggregability, and thrombosis
   - Lower ventricular fibrillation threshold
   - Beta-1-epinephrine-mediated hypokalemia
   - Abnormal or increased coronary vasoconstriction or vasospasm
2. Decreased parasympathetic activity, causing
   - Lower VF threshold
3. Increased parasympathetic activity, causing
   - Bradyarrhythmia, including heart block
4. Increased renin-angiotensin-aldosterone activity, causing
   - Hypertension
   - Blood volume expansion (and thus, increased cardiac preload)
   - Excessive vasoconstriction, peripheral and coronary
5. Increased adrenal cortical hormones (especially cortisol), causing
   - Hypertension
   - Blood volume expansion
6. Increased serum cholesterol (from acute or chronic stress)
7. Decreased serum high-density lipoprotein through increased testosterone
8. Increased left ventricular hypertrophy, causing
   - Increased myocardial oxygen needs
   - Increased susceptibility to arrhythmia
9. Possible changes in electrocardiographic QT interval
10. Possible endothelial derived relaxing factor abnormalities
11. Possible bradykinin or atrial natriuretic factor abnormalities
12. Possible spontaneous fibrinolysis abnormalities
13. Changes in standard atherosclerotic risk factors related to behavioral factors (Type A and other)
14. Delays in response to cardiac symptomatology related to denial, depression, lack of social support, and other psychological factors

modifying the course of CHD. Which psychosocial variables are most strongly linked to heart disease, what physiological mechanisms are involved, and where the most powerful and cost-effective interventions should be targeted are subjects for sorely needed study in the next few years.

REFERENCES

Adams, J. (1817). *Memoirs of the life and doctrines of John Hunter*. London: J. Callow.

Ahern, D. K., Gorkin, L., Anderson, J. L., Tierney, C., Hallstrom, A., Ewart, C., Capone, R. J., Schron, E., Kornfeld, D., Herd, J. A., Richardson, D. W., & Follick, M. J. (1990). Biobehavioral variables and mortality in the Cardiac Arrhythmia Pilot Study (CAPS). *American Journal of Cardiology, 66,* 59–62.

Albarran-Sotelo, R., Flint, L. S., & Kelly, K. J. (1988). *Healthcare provider's manual for basic life support.* Dallas, TX: American Heart Association.

Allan, R., & Scheidt, S. (1992). Is coronary heart disease a lifestyle disorder? Part I. *Cardiovascular Reviews & Reports, 13*(12), 13–34.

Allan, R., & Scheidt, S. (1993). Is coronary heart disease a lifestyle disorder? Part II. *Cardiovascular Reviews & Reports, 14*(1), 35–51.

American Heart Association. (1993). *Heart and stroke facts statistics.* Dallas, TX: Author.

Anda, R., Williamson, D., James, D., Macera, C., Eaker, E., Glassman, A., & Marks, J. (1992). Depressed affect, hopelessness, and the risk of ischemic heart disease in a cohort of U. S. adults. *Epidemiology, 4,* 285–294.

Appels, A., Höppener, P., & Muldur, P. (1987). A questionnaire to assess premonitory symptoms of myocardial infarction. *International Journal of Cardiology, 17,* 15–24.

Appels, A., & Mulder, P. (1989). Fatigue and heart disease: The association between "vital exhaustion" and past, present and future coronary heart disease. *Journal of Psychosomatic Research, 33,* 727–738.

Appels, A., & Schouten, E. (1991). Waking up exhausted as a risk indicator of myocardial infarction. *American Journal of Cardiology, 68,* 395–398.

Barefoot, J. C. (1992). Developments in the measurement of hostility. In H. S. Friedman (Ed.), *Hostility, coping, and health* (pp. 13–31). Washington, DC: American Psychological Association.

Barefoot, J. C., Dahlstrom, W. G., & Williams, R. B. (1984). Hostility, CHD incidence, and total mortality: A 25-year follow-up of 255 physicians. *Psychosomatic Medicine, 45,* 59–63.

Barefoot, J. C., Dodge, K. A., Peterson, B. L., Dahlstrom, W. G., & Williams, R. B. (1989). The Cook–Medley Hostility Scale: Item content and ability to predict survival. *Psychosomatic Medicine, 51,* 46–57.

Barefoot, J. C., Larsen, S., Von der Lieth, L., & Schroll, M. (1995). Hostility, incidence of acute myocardial infarction, and mortality in a sample of older Danish men and women. *American Journal of Epidemiology, 142,* 477–484.

Barefoot, J. C., Patterson, J. C., Haney, T. L., & Cayton, T. C. (1994). Hostility in asymptomatic men with angiographically confirmed coronary artery disease. *American Journal of Cardiology, 74,* 439–442.

Barefoot, J. C., Peterson, B. L., Harrell, F. E., Hlatky, M. A., Pryor, D. B., Haney, T. L, Blumenthal, J. A., Siegler, I. C., & Williams, R. B. (1989). Type A behavior and survival: A follow-up study of 1,467 patients with coronary artery disease. *American Journal of Cardiology, 64*, 427–432.

Barefoot, J. C., & Schroll, M. (in press). Symptoms of depression, acute myocardial infarction, and total mortality in a community sample. *Circulation*.

Barry, J., Selwyn, A., Nabel, E., Rocco, M. B., Mead, K., Campbell, S., & Rebecca, G. (1988). Frequency of ST-segment depression produced by mental stress in stable angina pectoris from coronary artery disease. *American Journal of Cardiology, 61*, 989–993.

Berkman, L. F., Leo-Summers, L., & Horwitz, R. I. (1992). Emotional support and survival after myocardial infarction. *Annals of Internal Medicine, 117*, 1003–1009.

Berlin, J. A., & Colditz, G. A. (1990). A meta-analysis of physical activity in the prevention of coronary heart disease. *American Journal of Epidemiology, 132*, 612–628.

Blohm, M., Herlitz, J., Hartford, M., Karlson, B. W., Risenfors, M., Leupker, R. V., Sjolin, M., & Holmberg, S. (1992). Consequences of a media campaign focusing on delay in acute myocardial infarction. *American Journal of Cardiology, 69*, 411–413.

Blumenthal, J. A., Burg, M. M., Barefoot, J., Williams, R. B., Haney, T., & Zimet, G. (1987). Social support, Type-A behavior, and coronary artery disease. *Psychosomatic Medicine, 49*, 331–340.

Boltwood, M. D., Taylor, C. B., Burke, M. B., Grogin, H., & Giacomini, J. (1993). Anger report predicts coronary artery vasomotor response to mental stress in atherosclerotic segments. *American Journal of Cardiology, 72*, 1361–1365.

Booth-Kewley, S., & Friedman, H. S. (1987). Psychological predictors of heart disease: A quantitative review. *Psychological Bulletin, 101*, 343–362.

Bortner, R. W. (1969). A short rating scale as a potential measure of Pattern A behavior. *Journal of Chronic Disease, 22*, 87–91.

Brackett, C. D., & Powell, L. H. (1988). Psychosocial and physiological predictors of sudden cardiac death after healing of acute myocardial infarction. *American Journal of Cardiology, 61*, 979–983.

Broadhead, W. E., Kaplan, B. H., James, S. A., & Wagner, E. H. (1983). The epidemiologic evidence for a relationship between social support and health. *American Journal of Epidemiology, 117*, 521–537.

Burell, G. (1993, September). *Behavior modification in secondary prevention of coronary heart disease: A treatment model that can prolong life after myocardial infarction and coronary artery bypass graft surgery*. Paper presented at the Third National Congress, Italian Society of Cardioneurology, Pavia, Italy.

Cannon, W. B. (1932). *The wisdom of the body*. New York: Norton.

Cannon, W. B. (1957). "Voodoo" death. *Psychosomatic Medicine, 19*, 182–190.

Carney, R. M., Saunders, R. D., Freedland, K. E., Stein, P., Rich, M. W., & Jaffe, A. (1995). Association of depression with reduced heart rate variability in coronary artery disease. *American Journal of Cardiology, 76*, 562–564.

Case, R. B., Heller, S. S., Case, N. B., & Moss, A. J. (1985). Type-A behavior and survival after acute myocardial infarction. *New England Journal of Medicine, 312,* 737–741.

Case, R. B., Moss, A. J., Case, N., McDermott, M., & Eberly, S. (1992). Living alone after myocardial infarction: Impact on prognosis. *Journal of the American Medical Association, 267,* 515–519.

Cassem, N. H., & Hackett, T. P. (1973). Psychological rehabilitation of myocardial infarction patients in the acute phase. *Heart and Lung, 2,* 382–388.

Chandra, V., Scklo, M., Goldberg, R., & Tonascia, J. (1983). The impact of marital status on survival after an acute myocardial infarction: A population based study. *American Journal of Epidemiology, 117,* 320–325.

Channer, K. S, Papouchado, M., James, M. A., & Rees, J. R. (1985). Anxiety and depression in patients with chest pain referred for exercise testing. *Lancet, 12,* 820–826.

Clarkson, T. B., Kaplan, J. R., Adams, M. R., & Manuck, S. B. (1987). Psychosocial influences on the pathogenesis of atherosclerosis among nonhuman primates. *Circulation, 76*(Suppl. 1), 29–40.

Cohen, S., Tyrell, D. A. J., & Smith, A. P. (1991). Psychological stress and susceptibility to the common cold. *New England Journal of Medicine, 325,* 606–612.

Cottington, E. M., Matthews, K. A., Talbott, E., & Kuller, L. H. (1980). Environmental events preceding sudden death in women. *Psychosomatic Medicine, 42,* 567–574.

Deanfield, J. E., Kensett, M., Wilson, R. A., Shea, M., Horlock, P., Wilson, R., DeLandsheere, C. M., & Selwyn, A. (1984). Silent myocardial ischaemia due to mental stress. *Lancet, 2,* 1001–1005.

Dembroski, T. M., MacDougall, J. M., Costa, P. T., & Grandits, G. A. (1989). Components of hostility as predictors of sudden death and myocardial infarction in the Multiple Risk Factor Intervention Trial. *Psychosomatic Medicine, 51,* 514–522.

Dembroski, T. M., MacDougall, J. M., Williams, R. B., Haney, T. L., & Blumenthal, J. A. (1985). Components of Type A, hostility and anger-in: Relationship to angiographic findings. *Psychosomatic Medicine, 47,* 219–233.

Derogatis, L. R., Lipman, R. S., & Covi, L. (1973). SCL–90: An outpatient psychiatric rating scale: Preliminary report. *Psychopharmacology Bulletin, 20,* 13–28.

Dictionary of national biography. (1908). New York: Macmillan.

Dobson, A. J., Alexander, H. M., Malcolm, J. A., Steele, P. L., & Miles, T. A. (1991). Heart attacks and the Newcastle earthquake. *Medical Journal of Australia, 155,* 757–761.

Eaker, E. D., Abbott, R. D., & Kannel, W. B. (1989). Frequency of uncomplicated angina pectoris in Type A compared with Type B persons (the Framingham Study). *American Journal of Cardiology, 63,* 1042–1045.

Engel, G. L. (1971). Sudden and rapid death during psychological stress: Folklore or folkwisdom? *Annals of Internal Medicine, 74,* 771–782.

Feigl, E. O. (1987). The paradox of adrenergic coronary vasoconstriction. *Circulation, 76,* 737–745.

Fernandez, F. (1993). Depression and its treatment in cardiac patients. *Texas Heart Institute Journal, 20,* 188–197.

Fielding, R. (1991). Depression and acute myocardial infarction: A review and reinterpretation. *Social Science and Medicine, 32,* 1017–1027.

Follick, M. J., Ahern, D. K., Gorkin, L., Niaura, R. S., Herd, J. A., Ewart, C., Schron, E. B., Kornfeld, D. S., & Capone, R. J., (1990). Relation of psychosocial and stress reactivity variables to ventricular arrhythmias in the Cardiac Arrhythmia Pilot Study (CAPS). *American Journal of Cardiology, 66,* 63–67.

Follick, M. J., Gorkin, L., Capone, R. J., Smith, T. W., Ahern, D. K., Stablein, D., Niaura, R., & Visco, J. (1988). Psychological distress as a predictor of ventricular arrhythmias in a post-myocardial infarction population. *American Heart Journal, 116,* 32–36.

Foot, J. (1794). *The life of John Hunter.* London: T. Beckett.

Frasure-Smith, N. (1991). In-hospital symptoms of psychological stress as predictors of long-term outcome after acute myocardial infarction in men. *American Journal of Cardiology, 67,* 121–127.

Frasure-Smith, N., Lesperance, F., & Talajic, M. (1993). Depression following myocardial infarction. *Journal of the American Medical Association, 270,* 1819–1825.

Frasure-Smith, N., Lesperance, F., & Talajic, M. (1995). The impact of negative emotions on prognosis following myocardial infarction: Is it more than depression? *Health Psychology, 14,* 388–398.

Friedman, H. S., & Booth-Kewley, S. (1988). Validity of the Type-A construct: A reprise. *Psychological Bulletin, 104,* 381–384.

Friedman, M., & Ghandour, G. (1993). Medical diagnosis of Type A behavior. *American Heart Journal, 126,* 607–618.

Friedman, M., & Powell, L. H. (1984). The diagnosis and quantitative assessment of Type A behavior: Introduction and description of the videotaped structured interview. *Integrative Psychiatry, 2,* 123–129.

Friedman, M., Powell, L. H., Thoresen, C. E., Ulmer, D., Price, V., Gill, J. J., Thompson, L., Rabin, D., Brown, B., Breall, W. S., Levy, R., & Bourg, E. (1987). Effect of discontinuance of Type-A behavioral counseling on Type-A behavior and cardiac recurrence rate of post myocardial infarction patients. *American Heart Journal, 114,* 483–490.

Friedman, M., & Rosenman, R. H. (1959). Association of specific overt behavior pattern with blood and cardiovascular findings: Blood cholesterol level, blood clotting time, incidence of arcus senilis, and clinical coronary artery disease. *Journal of the American Heart Association, 169,* 1286–1296.

Friedman, M., & Rosenman, R. H. (1974). *Type-A behavior and your heart.* New York: Knopf.

Friedman, M., Thoresen, C. E., Gill, J. J., Ulmer, D., Powell, L. H., Price, V. A., Brown, B., Thompson, L., Rabin, D. D., Breall, W. S., Bourg, E., Levy, R., & Dixon, T. (1986). Alteration of Type-A behavior and its effect on cardiac recurrences in post-myocardial infarction patients: Summary results of the Recurrent Coronary Prevention Project. *American Heart Journal, 112,* 653–665.

Friedman, M., & Ulmer, D. (1984). *Treating Type-A behavior and your heart.* New York: Knopf.

Gloyne, S. R. (1950). *John Hunter.* Edinburgh, Scotland: Livingstone.

Gottdiener, J. S., Krantz, D. S., Howell, R. H., Hecht, G. M., Klein, J., Falconer, J. J., & Rozanski, A. (1994). Induction of silent myocardial ischemia with mental stress testing: Relation to the triggers of ischemia during daily life activities and to ischemic functional severity. *Journal of the American College of Cardiology, 24,* 1645–1651.

Gould, K. L., Ornish, D., Scherwitz, L., Brown, S., Edens, R. P., Hess, M. J., Mullani, N., Bolomey, L., Dobbs, F., Armstrong, W. T., Merritt, T., Ports, T., Sparler, S., & Billings, J. (1995). Changes in myocardial perfusion abnormalities by positron emission tomography after long-term, intense risk factor modification. *Journal of the American Medical Association, 274,* 894–901.

Greene, W. A., Goldstein, S., & Moss, A. J. (1972). Psychosocial aspects of sudden death. *Archives of Internal Medicine, 129,* 725–731.

Haines, A. P., Imeson, J. D., & Meade, T. W. (1987). Phobic anxiety and ischaemic heart disease. *British Medical Journal, 295,* 297–299.

Hamalainen, H., Luurila, O. J., Kallio, V., Knuts, L.-R., Arstil, M., & Hakkila, J. (1989). Long-term reduction in sudden deaths after a multifactorial intervention programme in patients with myocardial infarction: 10-year results of a controlled investigation. *European Heart Journal, 10,* 55–62.

Haynes, S. G., & Feinleib, M. (1982). Type A behavior and the incidence of coronary heart disease in the Framingham Heart Study. *Advances in Cardiology, 29,* 85–95.

Haynes, S. G., Feinleib, M., & Kannel, W. B. (1980). The relationship of psychosocial factors to coronary heart disease in the Framingham Study III: Eight-year incidence of coronary heart disease. *American Journal of Epidemiology, 111,* 37–58.

Haynes, S. G., Levine, S., Scotch, N., Feinleib, M., & Kannel, W. B. (1978). The relationship of psychosocial factors to coronary heart disease in the Framingham study. *American Journal of Epidemiology, 107,* 362–383.

Hearn, M. D., Murray, D. M., & Leupker, R. V. (1989). Hostility, coronary heart disease, and total mortality: A 33-year follow-up study of university students. *Journal of Behavioral Medicine, 12,* 105–121.

Hecker, M. H., Chesney, M. A., Black, G. W., & Frautschi, N. (1988). Coronary-prone behaviors in the Western Collaborative Group Study. *Psychosomatic Medicine, 50,* 153–164.

Helmer, D. C., Ragland, D. R., & Lyme, L. S. (1991). Hostility and coronary artery disease. *American Journal of Epidemiology, 133*, 112–122.

Helmers, K. F., Krantz, D. S., Howell, R. H., Klein, J., Bairey, C. N., & Rozanski, A. (1993). Hostility and myocardial ischemia in coronary artery disease patients: Evaluation by gender and ischemic index. *Psychosomatic Medicine, 55*, 29–36.

Helmers, K. F., Krantz, D. S., Merz, C. N. B., Klein, J., Kop, W., Gottdiener, J. S., & Rozanski, A. (1995). Defensive hostility: Relationship to multiple markers of cardiac ischemia in patients with coronary disease. *Health Psychology, 14*, 202–209.

Herlitz, J., Blohm, M., Hartford, M., Halmarsson, A. Holmberg, S., & Karlson, B. W. (1989). Delay time in suspected acute myocardial infarction and the importance of its modification. *Clinical Cardiology, 12*, 370–374.

Hinkle, L. E. (1985). In "Neural control of the heart": Summary of discussion. *Journal of the American College of Cardiology, 5*, 111B.

Hlatky, M. A., Lam, L. C., Lee, K. L., Clapp-Channing, N. E., Williams, R. B., Pryor, D. B., Califf, R. M., & Mark, D. M. (1995). Job strain and the prevalence and outcome of coronary artery disease. *Circulation, 92*, 327–333.

Holmes, T., & Rahe, R. (1967). The social readjustment rating scale. *Journal of Psychosomatic Research, 11*, 213–218.

Home, E. (1794). A short account of the author's life. In J. Hunter, *A treatise on the blood, inflammation, and gun-shot wounds* (pp. xi–lxvii). London: John Richardson.

House, J. S., Landis, K. R., & Umberson, D. (1988, July 29). Social relationships and health. *Science, 241*, 540–545.

Hunter, J. (1792). *Observations in certain parts of the animal oeconomy* (2nd ed.). London: Nicol.

Ironson, G., Taylor, C. B., Boltwood, M., Bartzokis, T., Dennis, C., Chesney, M., Spitzer, S., & Segall, G. M. (1992). Effects of anger on left ventricular ejection fraction in coronary disease. *American Journal of Cardiology, 70*, 281–285.

Isner, J. M., Salem, D. N., Banas, J. S., & Levine, H. J. (1981). Long-term clinical course of patients with normal coronary angiography: Follow-up study of 121 patients with normal or nearly normal coronary arteriograms. *American Heart Journal, 102*, 645–653.

Jacobs, S., Friedman, R., Mittleman, M., Maclure, M., Sherwood, J., Benson, H., & Muller, J. E., for the MI Onset Investigators. (1992). Nine-fold increased risk of myocardial infarction following psychological stress as assessed by a case-control study. *Circulation, 86*(Suppl. 1), 198.

Jain, D., Burg, M., Soufer, R., & Zaret, B. L. (1995). Prognostic implications of mental stress-induced silent left ventricular dysfunction in patients with stable angina pectoris. *American Journal of Cardiology, 76*, 31–35.

Jenkins, C. D., Rosenman, R. H., & Zyzanski, S. J. (1974). Prediction of clinical coronary heart disease by a test for the coronary-prone behavior pattern. *New England Journal of Medicine, 23*, 1271–1275.

Kamarck, T., & Jennings, J. R. (1991). Biobehavioral factors in sudden cardiac death. *Psychological Bulletin, 109,* 42–75.

Kannel, W. B., & Schatzkin, A. (1985). Sudden death: Lessons from subsets in population studies. *Journal of the American College of Cardiology, 5,* 141B–149B.

Kaplan, J. R., Manuck, S. B., Williams, J. K., & Strawn, W. (1993). Psychosocial influences on atherosclerosis: Evidence for effects and mechanisms in non-human primates. In J. Blascovich & E. S. Katkin (Eds.), *Cardiovascular reactivity to psychological stress and disease* (pp. 3–26). Washington, DC: American Psychological Association.

Karasek. R., Baker, D., Marxer, F., Ahlbom, A., & Theorell, T. (1981). Job decision latitude, job demands and cardiovascular disease: A prospective study of Swedish men. *American Journal of Public Health, 71,* 694–705.

Karasek, R. A., Theorell, T., Schwartz, J. E., Schnall, P. L., Pieper, C. F., & Michela, J. L. (1988). Job characteristics in relation to the prevalence of myocardial infarction in the U.S. Health Examination Survey (HES) and the Health and Nutrition Examination Survey (HANES). *American Journal of Public Health, 78,* 910–918.

Kawachi, I., Colditz, G. A., Ascherio, A., Rimm , E. B., Giovannucci, E., Stampfer, M. J., & Willett, W. C. (1994). Prospective study of phobic anxiety and risk of coronary heart disease in men. *Circulation, 89,* 1992–1997.

Kawachi, I., Sparrow, D., Vokonas, P. S., & Weiss, S. T. (1994). Symptoms of anxiety and risk of coronary heart disease. *Circulation, 90,* 2225–2229.

Kawachi, I., Sparrow, D., Vokonas, P. S., & Weiss, S. T. (1995). Decreased heart rate variability in men with phobic anxiety (data from the normative aging study). *American Journal of Cardiology, 75,* 882–885.

Kenyon, L. W., Ketterer, M. W., Gheorghiade, M., & Goldstein, S. (1991). Psychological factors related to prehospital delay during acute myocardial infarction. *Circulation, 84,* 1969–1976.

Kligfield, P. (1980). John Hunter, angina pectoris and medical education. *American Journal of Cardiology, 45,* 367–369.

Kneip, R. C., Delameter, A. M., Ismond, T., Milford, C., Salvia, L., & Schwartz, D. (1993). Self- and spouse ratings of anger and hostility as predictors of coronary heart disease. *Health Psychology, 12,* 301–307.

Kobler, J. (1960). *The reluctant surgeon: A biography of John Hunter.* Garden City, NY: Doubleday.

Kop, W. J., Appels, A., Mendes de Leon, C. F., de Swart, H. B., & Bar, F. W. (1994). Vital exhaustion predicts new cardiac events after successful coronary angioplasty. *Psychosomatic Medicine, 56,* 281–287.

Koskenvuo, M., Kaprio, J., Rose, R. J., Kesaniemi, A., Sarna, S., Heikkila, K., & Langinvainio, H. (1988). Hostility as a risk factor for mortality and ischemic heart disease in men. *Psychosomatic Medicine, 50,* 330–340.

Kostis, J., & Sanders, M. (Eds.). (1991). *The prevention of sudden cardiac death*. New York: Wiley-Liss.

Krantz, D. S., Hedges, S. M., Gabbay, F. H., Klein, J., Falconer, J. J., Bairey Merz, C. N., Gottdiener, J. S., Lutz, H., & Rozanski, A. (1994). Triggers of angina and ST-segment depression in ambulatory patients with coronary artery disease: Evidence for an uncoupling of angina and ischemia. *American Heart Journal, 128*, 703–712.

Lantinga, L. J., Sprafkin, R. P., McCroskery, J. H., Baker, M. T., Warner, R. A., & Hill, N. E. (1988). One-year psychosocial follow-up of patients with chest pain and angiographically normal coronary arteries. *American Journal of Cardiology, 62*, 209–213.

Lavy, E. B., & Winkle, R. A. (1979). Continuing disability of patients with chest pain and normal coronary arteriograms. *Journal of Chronic Diseases, 32*, 191–196.

Lazarus, R. S., & Folkman, S. (1984). *Stress, appraisal, and coping*. New York: Springer.

Leaf, A., & Ryan, T. J. (1990). Prevention of coronary heart disease: A medical imperative. *New England Journal of Medicine, 323*, 1416–1419.

Legault, S. E., Langer, A., Armstrong, P. W., & Freeman, M. R. (1995). Usefulness of ischemic response to mental stress in predicting silent myocardial ischemia during ambulatory monitoring. *American Journal of Cardiology, 75*, 1007–1011.

Leon, G. R., Finn, S. E., Murray, D., & Bailey, J. M. (1988). Inability to predict cardiovascular disease from hostility scores or MMPI items related to Type A behavior. *Journal of Consulting and Clinical Psychology, 56*, 597–600.

Levine, J., Warrenburg, S., Kerns, R., Schwartz, G., Delaney, R., Fontana, A., Gradman, A., Smith, S., Allen, S., & Cascione, R. (1987). The role of denial in recovery from coronary heart disease. *Psychosomatic Medicine, 49*, 109–117.

Lown, B. (1987). Sudden cardiac death: Biobehavioral perspective. *Circulation, 76*(Suppl. 1), 186–196.

Ludwig, K. H., Roll, G., Breithardt, G., Budde, T., & Borggrefe, M. (1994). Postinfarction depression and incomplete recovery 6 months after acute myocardial infarction. *Lancet, 343*, 20–23.

MacDougall, J. M., Dembroski, T. M., Dimsdale, J. E., & Hackett, T. P. (1985). Components of Type A, hostility and anger-in: Further relationships to angiographic findings. *Health Psychology, 4*, 137–152.

Manson, J. E., & Hennekens, C. (Eds.). (1996). *Prevention of myocardial infarction*. New York: Oxford University Press.

Manuck, S. B. (1994). Cardiovascular reactivity in cardiovascular disease: Once more unto the breach. *International Journal of Behavioral Medicine, 1*, 4–31.

Maruta, T., Hamburgen, M. E., Jennings, C. A., Offord, K. P., Colligan, R. C., Frye, R. L., & Malinchoc, M. (1993). Keeping hostility in perspective: Coronary heart disease and the Hostility scale on the Minnesota Multiphasic Personality Inventory. *Mayo Clinic Proceedings, 68,* 109–114.

Matthews, K. A. (1988). Coronary heart disease and Type A behaviors: Update and alternative to the Booth-Kewley and Friedman (1987) quantitative review. *Psychological Bulletin, 104,* 373–380.

Mayou, R., Bryant, B., Forfar, C., & Clark, D. (1994). Non-cardiac chest pain and benign palpitations in the cardiac clinic. *British Heart Journal, 72,* 548–553.

McCranie, E. W., Watkins, L. O., Brandsma, J. M., & Sisson, B. D. (1986). Hostility, coronary heart disease (CHD) incidence and total mortality: Lack of association in a 25-year follow-up study of 478 physicians. *Journal of Behavioral Medicine, 9,* 119–125.

McIntosh, H. D. (1985). The stabilizing and unstabilizing influences of neurogenic and vascular activities of the heart as related to sudden cardiac death. *Journal of the American College of Cardiology, 5,* 105B–110B.

Meisel, S. R., Kutz, I., Dayan, K. I., Pauzner, H., Chetboun, I., Arbel, Y., & David, D. (1991). Effect of the Iraqi missile war on incidence of acute myocardial infarction and sudden death in Israeli civilians. *Lancet, 338,* 660–661.

Miller, T. Q., Turner, C. W., Tindale, R. S., Posavac, E. J., & Dugoni, B. L. (1991). Reasons for the trend toward null findings in research on Type-A behavior. *Psychological Bulletin, 110,* 469–485.

Mittleman, M. A., Maclure, M., Sherwood, J. B., Mulry, R. P., Tofler, G. H., Jacobs, S. C., Friedman, R., Benson, H., & Muller, J. E., for the Determinants of Myocardial Infarction Onset Study Investigators. (1995). Triggering of acute myocardial infarction onset by episodes of anger. *Circulation, 92,* 1720–1725.

Mittleman, M. A., Maclure, M., Tofler, G. H., Sherwood, J. B., Goldberg, R. J., & Muller, J. E. (1993). Triggering of acute myocardial infarction by heavy physical exertion. *New England Journal of Medicine, 329,* 1677–1683.

Muller, J. E., Ludmer, P. L., Willich, S. N., Tofler, G. H., Aylmer, G., & Kanglos, I. (1987). Circadian variation in the frequency of sudden cardiac death. *Circulation, 75,* 131–138.

Muller, J. E., Maclure, M., Mittleman, M., Sherwood, J., & Tofler, G., for the Onset Study Investigators. (1993). Risk of myocardial infarction doubles in the two hours after sexual activity, but absolute risk remains low [Abstract]. *Circulation, 88,* I–509.

Muller, J. E., Stone, P. H., Turi, Z. G., Rutherford, J. D., Czeisler, C. A., Parker, C., Poole, K. W., & Passamani, E., for the MILIS Study Group. (1985). Circadian variations in the frequency of onset of acute myocardial infarction. *New England Journal of Medicine, 313,* 1315–1322.

Muller, J. E., Tofler, G. H., & Edelman, E. (1989). Probable triggers of onset of acute myocardial infarction. *Clinical Cardiology, 12,* 473–475.

Muller, J. E., Tofler, G. H., & Stone, P. H. (1989). Circadian variations and triggers of onset of acute cardiovascular disease. *Circulation, 79,* 733–743.

Multiple Risk Factor Intervention Trial Research Group. (1985). Exercise electro-cardiogram and coronary heart disease mortality in the Multiple Risk Factor Intervention Trial. *American Journal of Cardiology, 55,* 16–24.

Multiple Risk Factor Intervention Trial Research Group. (1990). Mortality after 10 1/2 years for hypertensive participants in the Multiple Risk Factor Intervention Trial. *Circulation, 82,* 1616–1628.

Myers, A., & Dewar, H. A. (1975). Circumstances attending 100 sudden deaths from coronary artery disease with coroner's necropsies. *British Heart Journal, 37,* 1135–1143.

National Heart Attack Alert Program Coordinating Committee, 60 Minutes to Treatment Working Group. (1993). Emergency department: Rapid identification and treatment of patients with acute myocardial infarction. *Annals of Internal Medicine, 23,* 311–329.

Niaura, R., Stoney, C. M., & Herbert, N. (1992). Lipids in psychological research: The last decade. *Biological Psychology, 34,* 1–43.

O'Reilly, P., & Thomas, A. E. (1989). Role of support networks in maintenance of improved cardiovascular health status. *Social Science and Medicine, 28,* 249–260.

Ornish, D., Brown, S. E., Billings, J. H., Armstrong, W. T., Ports, T. A., Merritt, T., Sparler, S., Spaun, L., McLanahan, S., Scherwitz, L. W., Kirkeeide, R., Brand, R. J., & Gould, K. L. (1993). Can lifestyle changes reverse coronary atherosclerosis? Four-year results of the Lifestyle Heart Trial [Abstract]. *Circulation, 88*(Suppl. 1), 385.

Ornish, D., Brown, S. E., Scherwitz, L. W., Billings, J. H., Armstrong, W. T., Ports, T. A., McLanahan, S. M., Kirkeeide, R. L., Brand, R. J., & Gould, K. L. (1990). Can lifestyle changes reverse coronary heart disease? *Lancet, 336,* 129–133.

Orth-Gomér, K., Rosengren, A., & Wilhelmsen, L. (1993). Lack of social support and incidence of coronary heart disease in middle-aged Swedish men. *Psychosomatic Medicine, 55,* 37–43.

Orth-Gomér, K., & Uniden, A. L. (1990). Type-A behavior, social support, and coronary risk: Interaction and significance for mortality in cardiac patients. *Psychosomatic Medicine, 52,* 59–72.

Ottley, D. (1841). Introduction to the life of John Hunter. In J. F. Palmer (Ed.), *The complete works of John Hunter, F. R. S.* (pp. 9–10). Philadelphia: Haswell, Barrington, and Haswell.

Oxford English Dictionary (compact ed.). (1986). Oxford, England: Oxford University Press.

Paget, S. (1797). *John Hunter: Man of science and surgeon.* London: T. Fisher Unwin.

Parkes, C. M. (1964). Effects of bereavement on physical and mental health: A study of the medical records of widows. *British Medical Journal, 2,* 274–279.

Pasternak, R. C., Thibault, G. E., Savoia, M., DeSanctis, R. W., & Hutter, A. M. (1980). Chest pain with angiographically insignificant coronary arterial obstruction. *American Journal of Medicine, 68,* 813–817.

Pickering, T. G. (1985). Should studies of patients undergoing coronary angiography be used to evaluate the role of behavioral risk factors for coronary heart disease? *Journal of Behavioral Medicine, 8,* 203–213.

Powell, L. H. (1989). Unanswered questions in the ischemic heart disease life stress monitoring program. *Psychosomatic Medicine, 51,* 479–484.

Powell, L. H., & Thoresen, C. E. (1988). Effects of Type-A behavioral counseling and severity of prior acute myocardial infarction on survival. *American Journal of Cardiology, 62,* 1159–1163.

Price, V. A., Friedman, M., & Ghandour, G. (1995). Relation between insecurity and Type A behavior. *American Heart Journal, 129,* 488–491.

Ragland, D. R., & Brand, R. J. (1988). Type-A behavior and mortality from coronary heart disease. *New England Journal of Medicine, 318,* 65–69.

Rahe, R. H., Romo, M., Bennet, L., & Siltanen, P. (1974). Recent life changes, myocardial infarction, and abrupt coronary death. *Archives of Internal Medicine, 133,* 221–228.

Rees, W. D., & Lutkins, S. G. (1967). Mortality of bereavement. *British Medical Journal, 4,* 13–16.

Reich, P., DeSilva, R. A., Lown, B., & Murowski, B. J. (1981). Acute psychological disturbances preceding life-threatening ventricular arrhythmias. *Journal of the American Medical Association, 246,* 233–235.

Rissanen, V., Romo, M., & Siltanen, P. (1978). Premonitory symptoms and stress factors preceding sudden death from ischaemic heart disease. *Acta Medica Scandinavica, 204,* 389–396.

Rosengren, A., Tibblin, G., & Wilhelmsen, L. (1991). Self-perceived psychological stress and incidence of coronary artery disease in middle-aged men. *American Journal of Cardiology, 68,* 1171–1175.

Rosenman, R. H., Brand, R. J., Jenkins, C. D., Friedman, M., Straus, R., & Wurm, M. (1975). Coronary heart disease in the Western Collaborative Group Study: Final follow-up experience of 8 1/2 years. *Journal of the American Medical Association, 233,* 872–877.

Rozanski, A., Bairey, C. N., Krantz, D. S., Friedman, J., Resser, K. J., Morell, M., Hilton-Chalfen, S., Hestrin, L., Bietendorf, J., & Berman, D. S. (1988). Mental stress and the induction of silent myocardial ischemia in patients with coronary artery disease. *New England Journal of Medicine, 318,* 1005–1012.

Ruberman, W. (1992). Psychosocial influences on mortality of patients with coronary heart disease. *Journal of the American Medical Association, 267,* 559–560.

Ruberman, W., Weinblatt, E., Goldberg, J., & Chaudhary, B. S. (1984). Psychosocial influences on mortality after myocardial infarction. *New England Journal of Medicine, 311,* 552–559.

Scheier, M. F., Mathews, K. A., Owens, J. F., Magovern, G. J., Lefebvre, R. C., Abbot, R. A., & Carver, C. S. (1989). Dispositional optimism and recovery from coronary artery bypass surgery: The beneficial effects on physical and psychological well-being. *Journal of Personality and Social Psychology, 57,* 1024–1040.

Schleifer, S. J., Macari-Hinson, M. M., Coyle, D. A., Slater, W. R., Kahn, M., Gorlin, R., & Zucker, H. D. (1989). The nature and course of depression following myocardial infarction. *Archives of Internal Medicine, 149,* 1785–1789.

Schnall, P. L., Landsbergis, P. A., & Baker, D. (1994). Job strain and cardiovascular disease. *Annual Review of Public Health, 15,* 381–411.

Schnall, P. L., Pieper, C., Schwartz, J. E., Karasek, R. A., Schlussel, Y., Devereux, R. B., Ganau, A., Alderman, M., Warren, K., & Pickering, T. G. (1990). The relationship between "job strain," workplace diastolic blood pressure and left ventricular mass index. *Journal of the American Medical Association, 263,* 1929–1935.

Schuler, G., Hambrecht, R., Schlierf, G., Grunze, M., Methfessel, S., Hauer, K., & Kubler, W. (1992). Myocardial perfusion and regression of coronary artery disease in patients on a regimen of intensive physical exercise and low fat diet. *Journal of the American College of Cardiology, 19,* 34–42.

Seeman, T. E., & Syme, S. L. (1987). Social networks and coronary artery disease: A comparison of the structure and function of social relations as predictors of disease. *Psychosomatic Medicine, 49,* 541–554.

Shekelle, R. B., Gale, M., & Norusis, M. (1985). Type-A score (Jenkins Activity Survey) and risk of recurrent coronary heart disease in the Aspirin Myocardial Infarction Study. *American Journal of Cardiology, 56,* 221–225.

Shekelle, R. B., Gale, M., Ostfeld, A. M., & Paul, O. (1983). Hostility, risk of coronary heart disease, and mortality. *Psychosomatic Medicine, 45,* 109–114.

Shekelle, R. B., Hulley, S. B., Neaton, J. D., Billings, J. H., Borhani, N. O., Gerace, T. A., Jacobs, D. R., Lasser, N. L., Mittlemark, H. B., & Stamler, J., for the Multiple Risk Factor Intervention Trial Research Group. (1985). The MRFIT Behavior Pattern Study II: Type-A behavior and incidence of coronary heart disease. *American Journal of Epidemiology, 122,* 559–570.

Sibal, A. M., Armenian, H. K., & Alam, S. (1989). Wartime determinants of arteriographically confirmed coronary artery disease in Beirut. *American Journal of Epidemiology, 130,* 623–631.

Siegman, A. W., Dembroski, T. M., & Ringel, N. (1987). Components of hostility and the severity of coronary artery disease. *Psychosomatic Medicine, 49,* 127–135.

Siegman, A. W., & Smith, T. W. (1994). *Anger, hostility and the heart.* Hillsdale, NJ: Erlbaum.

Sirous, F. (1992). Le deni dans la maladie coronarienne [Denial in coronary disease]. *Canadian Medical Association Journal, 147,* 315–321.

Smith, T. W., & Barefoot, J. C., (1993, March). *The assessment of hostility: Implications for research and practice.* Paper presented at the annual meeting of the American Psychosomatic Society, Charleston, SC.

Surawicz, B. (1985). Neural control of the heart: Summary of discussion. *Journal of the American College of Cardiology, 5,* 111B–112B.

Swan, G. E., Carmelli, I., & Rosenman, R. H. (1989). Psychological correlates of two measures of coronary-prone hostility. *Psychosomatics, 30,* 270–278.

Thoresen, C. E., & Powell, L. H. (1992). Type A behavior pattern: New perspectives on theory, assessment and intervention. *Journal of Consulting and Clinical Psychology, 60,* 595–604.

Tofler, G. H., Stone, P. H., Maclure, M., Edelman, E., Davis, V. G., Robertson, T., Antman, E. M., & Muller, J. E. (1990). Analysis of possible triggers of acute myocardial infarction (The MILIS Study). *American Journal of Cardiology, 66,* 22–27.

Verrier, R. L. (1987). Mechanisms of behaviorally induced arrhythmias. *Circulation, 76*(Suppl. 1), 148–156.

Wellens, H. J. J., Vermeulen, A., & Durrer, D. (1972). Ventricular fibrillation occurring in arousal from sleep by auditory stimuli. *Circulation, 46,* 661–665.

Wielgosz, A. T., & Nolan, R. P. (1991). Understanding delay in response to symptoms of acute myocardial infarction. *Circulation, 84,* 2193–2195.

Williams, J. K., Vita, J. A., Manuck, S. B., Selwyn, A. P., & Kaplan, J. R. (1991). Psychosocial factors impair vascular responses of coronary arteries. *Circulation, 84,* 2146–2153.

Williams, R. B. (1987). Refining the Type-A hypothesis: Emergence of the hostility complex. *American Journal of Cardiology, 60,* 27J–32J.

Williams, R. B., Barefoot, J. C., & Califf, R. M. (1992). Prognostic importance of social and economic resources among medically treated patients with angiographically documented coronary artery disease. *Journal of the American Medical Association, 267,* 520–524.

Williams, R. B., Barefoot, J. C., Haney, T. L., Harrell, F. E., Blumenthal, J. A., Pryor, D. B., & Peterson, B. (1988). Type-A behavior and angiographically documented coronary atherosclerosis in a sample of 2,289 patients. *Psychosomatic Medicine, 50,* 139–152.

Williams, R. B., Haney, T. L., Lee, K. L., Kong, Y. H., Blumenthal, J. A., & Whalen, R. E. (1980). Type A behavior, hostility and coronary atherosclerosis. *Psychosomatic Medicine, 42,* 539–549.

Willich, S. N. (1990). Epidemiologic studies demonstrating increased morning incidence of sudden cardiac death. *American Journal of Cardiology, 66,* 18G–21G.

Willich, S. N., Lewis, M., Lowel, H., Arntz, H. R., Schubert, F., & Schroder, R. (1993). Physical exertion as a trigger of acute myocardial infarction. *New England Journal of Medicine, 329,* 1684–1690.

Willich, S. N., Lowel, H., Lewis, M., Arntz, R., Baur, R., Winther, K., Keil, U., & Schroder, R., and the TRIMM Study Group. (1991). Association of wake time and the onset of myocardial infarction. *Circulation, 84*(Suppl. 6), 62–67.

Willich, S. N., Lowel, H., Lewis, M., Arntz, R., Schubert, F., & Schroder, R., and the TRIMM Study Group. (1992). Increased Monday risk of acute myocardial infarction in the working population. *Circulation, 86*(Suppl. 1), 61.

Yeung, A. C., Vekshtein, V. I., Krantz, D. S., Vita, J. A., Ryan, T. J., Ganz, P., & Selwyn, A. P. (1991). The effect of atherosclerosis on the vasomotor response of coronary arteries to mental stress. *New England Journal of Medicine, 325,* 1551–1556.

4

IS THERE A NEED FOR CARDIAC PSYCHOLOGY? THE VIEW OF A PRACTICING CARDIOLOGIST

JEFFREY FISHER

People in American society tend to take the excellence of highly sophisticated and technological medical care for granted. However, many patients rightfully complain of dehumanization in the present medical system (Shorter, 1985). Health psychology has demonstrated the importance of psychological variables in illness and recovery as well as the benefits of psychosocial interventions with patients. The effective physician is one who sees the patient in his or her entirety and devises a medical strategy with the patient's psychosocial needs in mind.

Cardiac psychology may be defined as that branch of health psychology that identifies psychosocial risk factors for the development and perpetuation of cardiovascular disease and the psychological sequelae of cardiac illness. Applied cardiac psychology is a multidisciplinary effort that attempts to prevent or minimize serious medical and psychological complications as a result of these risk factors and, hence, to optimize patients' medical and psychosocial outcomes.

Cardiac psychology has helped broaden perceptions about the technical care that physicians offer patients. Within a decade of the advent of the coronary care unit (CCU), Hackett, Cassem, and Wishnie (1968) had pointed out some of the negative psychological consequences of being treated in such a high-tech environment. Dehumanization and lack of privacy were identified, as well as sleep deprivation and consequently altered

125

sensoria. Although the CCU and its electronic monitors may be reassuring to patients who have experienced acute myocardial infarction (MI), Klein, Kliner, Zipes, Trouper, and Wallace (1968) have shown that there are often profound emotional and physiological responses, such as increased adrenergic tone, when patients transfer out of these units. The increased adrenergic tone can be modified by health care providers who are sensitized to the psychological sequelae of leaving the perceived safety of the CCU and who intervene to provide continuity of care and reassurance to the patient.

Health practitioners who are aware of the importance of cardiac psychology counsel the patient and family to make cardiovascular and psychological function as "normal" as possible. Cardiac psychology can provide educational support for large numbers of men and women with coronary-prone behavior or cardiac disease. Cardiac psychology also encompasses liaison psychiatry in cases where such intervention is required for more serious psychiatric problems, such as major depression and severe anxiety.

Much has been learned in the past 3 decades about coronary-prone behavior and the psychological sequelae of cardiovascular disease. What I attempt to do in this chapter is to offer specific recommendations from my perspective as a clinical cardiologist, citing specific examples from my experience and correlating it with the observations of other clinicians and investigators.

IS CARDIAC PSYCHOLOGY IMPORTANT?

Cardiac psychology is extremely important to the individual as well as to society at large. Cardiovascular illnesses consume a large portion of the nation's health care budget, and in these difficult economic times it is important to provide high-quality and efficient health care. It makes good medical sense to treat the whole patient in order to optimize outcome. Studies have shown that death following MI is increased in patients who have ventricular ectopy (extra heartbeats) and are stressed and socially isolated (Gorkin et al., 1993; Ruberman, Weinblatt, Goldberg, & Chaudhary, 1984). Hence, patients' social support networks need to be mobilized (Cohen, Kaplan, & Manuck, 1994; Dhooper, 1990).

The dynamics of socioeconomic class, education, psychological health, and medical illness have fascinated observers for centuries. The "cardiac patient" may have different psychosocial risk factors for disease than, say, the "cancer patient" or the "ulcer patient." Moreover, the impact of each illness is both general and individual. For instance, loss of limb is disfiguring and both emotionally and mechanically devastating, yet ultimate outcome can differ greatly among individuals. Much of that outcome is affected by an individual's premorbid and postmorbid psychological health. Outcome is improved with good psychological health and strong social support across all illnesses (Backman, 1989). In the absence of an ideal psychosocial milieu, health care providers should maximize existing supports or help create new ones.

PSYCHE AND SOMA

There are obvious and profound connections between people's emotions and their physical reactions. This is particularly obvious in coronary heart disease, where psychophysiological responses have been well documented. Ornish (1990) succinctly described the connections between the brain and heart. Activation of the sympathetic nervous system in the "fight or flight" mode has a profound effect on the blood vessels, including the coronary arteries, lungs, metabolism, and brain. Unfortunately, the stress reaction has become overgeneralized in American society and is a source of illness for some.

There is a normal distribution in how humans express this fight or flight response, and the response is mediated by an extensive interaction among the central and peripheral nervous systems, musculature, gastrointestinal tract, and cardiovascular and neuroendocrine systems (Surwit, Williams, & Shapiro, 1982). Some people are hyperreactors, whereas others are "Cool Hand Lukes." The armed services, when selecting pilots, often use mock combat as an experimental stressor and test for galvanic skin response, a measure of perspiration and pulse rate. Some individuals experience rapid acceleration of their heart rate and sweat profusely when faced with such stress, indicating a hyperresponse. In my practice, I have noted a large number of patients who overreact physiologically during mental or physical stress. There may be a genetic predisposition to hyperreactivity with increased production of or increased sensitivity to stress hormones, perhaps because of some imbalance between the sympathetic and parasympathetic nervous systems. Cardiovascular reactivity has been reviewed extensively by Fredrikson (1985). Some patients have what I term a *hyperkinetic*, or *sensitive*, *heart syndrome*; they respond well to a slow and gradual exercise program, which leads to a reduction in the rapidity of their heart rate to stress and, thus, a reduction in the self-perceived physiological prominence of this reaction. This, in turn, can break the vicious psyche–soma feedback cycle.

ORIGINS OF APPLIED CARDIAC PSYCHOLOGY

The American Heart Association has played a major role in educating the public and health care providers about cardiac disease and, as many have observed, has contributed to the decline in cardiovascular mortality over the past 25 years. The association originated in 1915 in New York City with the creation of "cardiac clinics." These clinics were modeled after tuberculosis clinics, as places where patients could receive specialized care. Cardiac clinics treated patients with rheumatic heart disease and also provided specialized services that included rehabilitation. The Burke Convalescence Home, established in 1915 in White Plains, New York, still serves to rehabilitate cardiac patients, largely after cardiac surgery. Lewis A. Conner, a Cornell Medical School professor, was an early proponent of these clinics and a founder of the American Heart Association. In 1927, Conner reviewed early efforts and cited the importance of social workers for patients' ultimate outcomes. The social workers knew the patients and their families, teachers, and employers. Interdisciplinary strategies were devised that would return patients to school or the workplace without undue cardiopulmonary or emotional strain and, hence, prevent rehospitalization and perpetuation as a "cardiac cripple." The aim of such a such a strategy was more than good medicine, as revealed by Conner's (1927) quote of Dr. Frederic Brush's estimates of savings:

> The care of a heart patient, in the hospitals in the city, in the general medical wards, costs about $30 a week; in a convalescent home, $12 a week; under the care of a physician and visiting nurse from the special Cardiac Clinics or its equivalent, the cost is less than $1 a week. Treating these handicapped patients in the wrong place is practically misappropriating public and private funds. (p. 499)

Although much has changed since 1927, including the mix of cardiac disease and the boom in technological care, the strategy of psychosocial assessment and intervention is no less important. Unfortunately, medicine has become increasingly technical and specialized, resulting in the fragmentation and often the dehumanization of care. Cardiac psychology has the potential of reducing the development of serious cardiovascular disease and improving its outcome with subsequent benefit to the patient's spiritual integrity and his or her family's quality of life. Both the individual and society may benefit economically as well: An increased incidence of returning to work has been demonstrated among patients who have undergone cardiac rehabilitation that emphasized addressing psychological problems (Byrne, 1982; Maeland & Havik, 1987; Riegel, 1993). Thus, the benefits to individuals and society from an organized and integrated cardiac care approach cannot be minimized. Cardiac psychology is fundamental to complete cardiac care.

CONTRIBUTIONS OF CARDIAC PSYCHOLOGY

Numerous studies have investigated the psychological sequelae of acute MI and have been well reviewed by Cromwell and Levenkron

(1984). White (1951) and Hellerstein (1972) believed that most patients admitted to the hospital with MI became depressed. Cassem and Hackett (1977) demonstrated the importance of early physical mobilization in diminishing the anxiety and depression associated with a cardiac event. Hellerstein (1994), one of the pioneers in cardiac rehabilitation, stated that the process of cardiac rehabilitation should begin on the day of admission to the CCU. This is rehabilitation in the broadest sense, and I believe specific suggestions can be made to begin the process of total recovery, even during an acute event. These include (a) offering physical and psychological comfort by pain relief and anxiolytics, including reassurance by a confidence-inspiring staff, and (b) relaying a succinct, understandable diagnosis and treatment plan. In at least one study (Cromwell & Levenkron, 1984), depression and anxiety were determined to be better predictors of recurrent MI than medical data. Similarly, length of stay in the CCU has been related both to care provided by staff and to self-perpetuated care (Cromwell & Levenkron, 1984).

With large numbers of patients undergoing coronary angiography, percutaneous transluminal coronary angioplasty (PTCA), and open-heart surgery, cardiologists need to develop a comprehensive strategy for dealing with the emotional problems that patients bring to the hospital before they are "fixed" and sent home. In cases of coronary heart disease, most cardiological treatment is palliative, and atherosclerosis—the underlying disease process—will progress unless patients change their previous coronary-prone behavior patterns. Applied cardiac psychology must develop a specific agenda to address the complete needs of large numbers of coronary heart disease patients.

INPATIENT AND OUTPATIENT CARE

Much of cardiovascular disease involves acute cardiac problems, including angina, acute MI, cerebrovascular accidents, congestive heart failure, arrhythmias, syncope, and sudden cardiac death. Outpatient care deals with modification of cardiac risk factors, including control of hypertension; important nonpharmacological treatments, such as exercise, weight loss, smoking cessation, and diet change; and minimizing Type A behavior and self-destructive tendencies. Some patients with cardiovascular disease are fortunate enough to never require acute cardiac admission.

The team involved in providing cardiac psychology includes the patient's primary care physician—be it cardiologist, internist, or family practitioner—the nursing staff in the hospital or cardiac rehabilitation service, an exercise physiologist, a nutritionist, a social worker, a psychologist, a psychiatrist, clergy, and ancillary medical personnel (e.g., clerks). The chaplaincy makes an important contribution to emotional comfort in coronary care and postsurgical units.

All personnel dealing with cardiac patients need to be keenly aware of the patient's need for involvement and a sense of control for his or her outcome. Issues that seem small for the medical intern or resident loom large for many patients, and the staff needs to avoid confrontation to effect truly comprehensive and effective care. Patients are often confused because they may get different information from their primary care physician, their cardiologist, a cardiologist assigned to the CCU, or a specialized cardiologist who serves as consultant for cardiac catheterization or electrophysiological testing. In addition, patients sometimes feel that their situation is not as well known to the house staff as they would like. Increased attention must be placed on humanizing hospital care by teaching the importance of reading patients' chart and making sure everyone is knowledgeable about the patients' medical, nursing, and psychological needs.

THE CCU

CCUs, although providing highly sophisticated coronary care, can feel like dangerous places to patients in distress. Imagine being placed inside a small room with electronic monitors and beepers. You are uncomfortable from an intravenous line and may require an arterial catheter, a Swan Ganz catheter through one of the major veins leading into your thorax, and perhaps even a bladder catheter. You quickly develop a surreal sensation as time becomes warped. Your body is at rest, unable to exercise. You may not be allowed out of bed for days. You may have to suffer the humility of using a bedpan. The loss of privacy and control is an enormous assault on the ego (Backman, 1989). Sleep becomes disordered, and you may be confused because of the drugs used for treatment. You may experience sensory deprivation during large periods of the day. Oftentimes, the medical staff may perpetuate this depersonalization by talking about you as the "guy with the anterior MI in Bed 6." Furthermore, you may be angry simply because you have developed an unexpected medical problem.

It is important for staff to humanize CCU treatment as much as possible. Although rules are meant to be kept, it is important that staff listen to patients' requests and try to accommodate their needs as much as possible. I have seen patients become rightfully, and unnecessarily, outraged when a visitor coming from a great distance was not allowed to stay for an extra 5 minutes before a flight home. It is important for the medical and nursing staff to carefully choose their battles and allow a degree of independence, because such self-efficacy aids in the healing process. As one means of promoting more personalized care, I have encouraged patients to have their families put up pictures of themselves in the CCU. Seeing the patient in "street clothes," at home with his or her family, can bring the medical staff back to the reality that they are treating a person, not just a "case."

Transfer Out of the CCU

Often patients are in the CCU for a short period of time, until they are stabilized and are then moved to a step-down unit. The patient's level of anxiety often increases with this move, and at least one study has shown an increased incidence of cardiac events after interunit transfer (Klein et al., 1968). Thus, rather than have an orderly transfer the patient impersonally out of the CCU, whenever possible, it is helpful for the receiving physician or nurse to make the transfer. Patients should be moved from bed to bed as quickly as possible. Having the patient lie on a gurney for a long period of time adds to the sense of helplessness and dehumanization. The patient should be informed that his or her transfer out of the CCU into a step-down unit or general medical bed is a positive sign related to an improvement in condition. The receiving staff should be prepared for symptoms or signs of anxiety, hostility, or depression, and every effort should be made to provide a professional ambience.

Communication

Cromwell and Levenkron (1984) have shown that acute MI patients have shorter hospital stays when they are apprised of their condition and able to anticipate and participate in their treatment. Physicians should provide a rough timetable as to what the patient can expect. For example, a patient admitted with an acute uncomplicated MI should be told that he or she will be observed for several days, will undergo electrocardiograms and blood enzyme tests, and, when stabilized, will undergo a submaximal stress test to see whether there is a residual problem and whether an angiogram is necessary for further assessment. At that juncture, patients may ask questions about the potential for angioplasty or other procedures, including coronary artery bypass graft (CABG) surgery. It is my practice to concentrate on providing information about the procedures that will definitely be used, rather than on those that might be performed. In some instances, a patient's anxieties can be increased if he or she is offered too much technical information.

I am often amazed by the individual peculiarities of patients' needs. Thus, rather than expounding on a patient's problem and possible course, it is often helpful to simply ask the patient "What's on your mind?" "Do you have any questions?" or "Are you confused about anything concerning your care?" It is also reasonable to ask a patient about his or her immediate concerns and anxieties. I vividly recall one middle-aged woman who appeared terrified 1 day following her heart attack. When I asked what her greatest fear was, she expressed a profound concern about who was going to care for her dog. This continued to be her major anxiety during hospitalization, and she was only relieved after a social worker had one of the woman's fellow church members assume care of the animal.

More often than not, critical information can be gained by casual conversation with the patient, rather than through a staccato, detectivelike interrogation. Once the patient is stabilized, it behooves the medical staff to periodically attend the patient, to listen and discuss matters on a one-to-one basis. Such interchanges often yield critically important information and create bonds between the patient and staff that improve mutual understanding and aid in the healing process.

CARDIOVASCULAR CONDITIONS

Following are brief descriptions of various cardiac conditions to provide a background for understanding how psychological interventions can be used with patients undergoing specific procedures. For a more in-depth overview of coronary heart disease, see chapter 2, by Scheidt, as well as various chapters throughout this volume addressing specific conditions and treatments.

Angina Pectoris

A frequent cause of admission to the hospital is angina pectoris—literally, pain in the chest. Chest pain can be caused by cardiac, gastrointestinal, and musculoskeletal disorders, as well as by anxiety and panic. It is critically important to take into account the patient's emotional state when establishing the etiology for such complaints. Furthermore, it is not unusual for a cardiologist to have a patient who has heart disease, esophageal reflux, cholecystitis, cervical radiculopathy, and anxiety or panic disorder. At any given time, one or more of these disorders may lead to symptoms. Knowing the patient's typical pain syndrome for each disorder as well as his or her ambient emotional life can enable one to prescribe the appropriate treatment (Razin, 1985). Taken together, noncardiac chest pain, angina pectoris, and acute MI account for a large proportion of acute hospital admissions in the United States.

Unstable Angina Pectoris

Another frequent cause of hospitalization is unstable angina pectoris. This is a less serious condition than acute MI, as there is no damage to the heart. Nevertheless, the patient is initially treated in much the same way as a heart attack victim. Often patients do not understand why intense treatment is necessary, given that they have not had a heart attack. These patients need to be educated about the potentially serious nature of this disorder without being made to feel like "cardiac cripples." This is done by emphasizing that no permanent damage has occurred because of their "attack" and that, with the appropriate treatment, little or no damage will occur subsequently.

Acute MI

Acute MI is one of the most dramatic of human events. For many patients it is the single most devastating event of their adult life. For some, it is the first time that they have truly had to deal with their own mortality. Once patients arrive in the hospital, they are frequently uncomfortable and extremely anxious. Although numerous studies have investigated the psychological sequelae of acute MI, virtually none have examined intervention, and few guidelines exist regarding psychosocial care during an acute event. Doctors and nurses must learn to deal with the anxiety, anger, irritability, and depression that often occur among patients in this setting. The medical team should provide the patient and family a milieu that exudes competence and caring. The patient should have his or her pain relieved, and the family should be made to feel comfortable. Applied cardiac psychology during acute hospitalization should be empathic and supportive rather than exploratory; such an approach may result in physiological as well as psychological benefits (Razin, 1985). Students of cardiac psychology understand the impact of this life-threatening and life-changing event to the individual and his or her family.

Once a patient is stabilized and made comfortable, staff can obtain more in-depth historical and medical information from the patient and family. It is important to establish the primary medical caretaker and to have that person responsible for transmitting information to the patient and family. All too often, I have witnessed anger and confusion among patients and their families because they have received conflicting information from various physicians, nurses, and staff members.

No two heart attacks are alike. Even though they may involve the same territory of heart muscle in patients of the same age with similar social backgrounds, patients often have widely differing psychological reactions to the event. Those who have had poor premorbid medical and emotional stability and have been socially isolated have poorer prognoses post-MI. Although many patients have objected to being placed in four-bed rooms at the cardiac step-down unit of the New York Hospital–Cornell Medical Center, I have witnessed gratifying relationships develop among such patients recuperating from heart attacks that have continued after discharge. Development of such expanding social networks should be encouraged by the staff, particularly for individuals known to be socially isolated.

Arrhythmia

Abnormal beating of the heart, or arrhythmia, comes in many varieties and involves fast beats (tachyarrhythmias) and slow beats (bradyarrhythmias). When a patient is hospitalized with arrhythmia, investigation into basic heart function is required. The patient needs support and information during hospitalization in order to minimize frustration and anxiety. Arrhythmias are generally investigated with electrophysiology studies (EPSs). However, clues to the cause of an arrhythmia can sometimes be obtained indirectly, as the following vignette from my clinical practice illustrates.

> An elderly woman was admitted to the hospital with a rapid heartbeat. This had occurred several times before over the past year. The cardiologist noticed the patient's address in her chart. He had lived around the corner from the address in a fourth-floor walk-up during his internship. They struck up a casual conversation about the neighborhood, during which the patient volunteered that she had lived in her rent-controlled apartment for 54 years. She also said that both she and her husband were ill and that medication often exceeded twice their monthly rent. With only social security checks for income, they were often left "short" at the end of the month. The patient acknowledged that although she had told previous physicians that she took her medication religiously, she had been ashamed to admit that she often "spread it out" when required by financial circumstances. At those times, her arrhythmias recurred. The cardiologist noted that blood levels of her more expensive medications had been low on this and previous admissions. Furthermore, the previous admissions had all occurred at the end of each month. The patient had even been ashamed to tell her husband about the problem because she felt it would reflect poorly on her abilities as a housewife. Fortunately, the medical staff was able to provide medication on a compassionate basis to prevent a recurrence of this scenario.

In addition to socioeconomic factors such as these in arrhythmogenesis, behavioral, psychological, and environmental factors may contribute to the development, exacerbation, and perpetuation of arrhythmias (Feurstein & Cohen, 1985; Meerson, 1994a, 1994b; Sloan & Bigger, 1991).

Survivors of Cardiac Death

The patient who is resuscitated after a cardiac arrest is in a serious medical as well as emotional condition. Technically, these patients have experienced death and, thus, are called "sudden death survivors." Such patients must undergo extensive cardiovascular tests to establish the cause of their cardiac arrest in order to prevent a recurrence. The psychological sequelae of these experiences are often devastating. Patients and their families may require intensive and often long-term psychosocial support to minimize depression and anxiety. Efforts to humanize the experience, particularly extensive empathic dialogue with the primary care physician, allow the patient to undergo the necessary investigations with a minimum of extra angst. These patients require a well-organized medical and psychological team whose members are fully acquainted with the notion of complete and compassionate care. Such an integrated approach has been outlined by Vlay and Fricchione (1985).

Congestive Heart Failure

Congestive heart failure is a common syndrome that develops as a result of mechanical insufficiency of the heart. Hospital admissions for decompensated congestive heart failure are extremely common, and the economic cost is huge. In 1992, more than 800,000 patients were discharged from hospitals in the United States after a diagnosis of congestive heart failure, and congestive heart failure remains a major cause of cardiovascular mortality (Graves, 1992). There are myriad reasons why people develop congestive heart failure, including poorly controlled hypertension, loss of cardiac muscle power, cardiac muscular stiffness, valvular disorders, and electrical dysfunction of the heart (e.g., arrhythmias). However, congestive heart failure is often precipitated by patients' medication cessation, misunderstanding medication orders, and failure to follow directions for salt and alcohol restrictions. For example, patients often skip taking their diuretics because of the inconvenience of repeated urination. It is important for medical practitioners to inculcate pharmacological therapy into the patient's lifestyle to make it as tolerable as possible. As with other medical conditions, when patients understand the consequences of not taking medication, they are more likely to adhere to a regimen on a long-term basis. It is often helpful, when going over medications, to ask how often the patient is really taking the medication (e.g., "Even though it's prescribed three times a day, how often do you usually take it?") and to assess the patient's understanding of the effects and importance of each medication. Explaining what each pill does in lay language will aid in long-term compliance and likely reduce the incidence of decompensated congestive heart failure.

Cerebrovascular Accidents

Most patients fear the disability of a major cerebrovascular accident more than they fear death itself. The idea of becoming aphasic and immobile with attendant disability and dependence is often terrifying. Patients admitted with transient ischemic attacks, reversible ischemic deficits, and cerebrovascular accidents should be diagnosed and have appropriate treatment begun as quickly as possible. They require early physical and occupational therapy as well as psychosocial intervention to deal with the frustration, anger, and depression that surely follows such devastating illnesses. These patients need to know from the outset that there are facilities for improving their abilities and increasing their independence. For additional information about cardiac illnesses, see chapter 2 of this volume.

PROCEDURES AND INSTRUMENTS

Cardiac Catheterization

Few cardiovascular procedures carry such trepidation as cardiac catheterization and angiography. One of my colleagues put it aptly when he said, "all patients are children when they lie on the cath table." A preparatory strategy of specifically detailing the procedure can reduce patient anxiety (Anderson & Masur, 1989). In addition, it requires technical skill and empathy to perform a cardiac catheterization in which the patient is made to feel comfortable. I have often told patients that there are three unpleasant aspects of cardiac catheterization: (a) the anxiety prior to the procedure—a fear of the unknown; (b) the procedure itself, primarily the "burning" sensation in the chest that typically accompanies insertion of the dye into the coronary arteries and the left ventricle (it is important to advise the patient of this sensation beforehand; if it occurs unexpectedly it will often lead to fear); and (c) the discomfort following the procedure, usually from lying flat with a sandbag on the groin for several hours afterwards. The use of muscle relaxants and analgesics can aid in making cardiac catheterization more tolerable. I have found that patients anticipate the procedure to be much worse than it actually is. Informing patients of such negative anticipation may help to reduce anxiety. Maintaining a conversation with the patient and explaining the procedure as it unfolds often relieve stress. Patients can also use relaxation techniques they have been taught previously or have a cassette player with their favorite music—or even a comedy routine—before and after the procedure to create an "up" mood. During the procedure itself, patients may feel very little discomfort if the cardiologist is oriented to total patient care.

PTCA

In some medical centers PTCA is performed in concert with the diagnostic angiogram, increasing the amount of information that the patient must process, the duration of the procedure, and attendant anxiety as well. When facing this procedure, patients must also be informed of the potential need for emergency CABG surgery. Some patients will not want to have the combined procedure performed at an institution that does not have in-house surgical backup. I have been informed by patients that physicians at some institutions have been angry at them for taking this position, arguing that transportation to a local hospital is available and that such emergencies occur rarely. In my opinion, patients who express such reservations are entitled to them, and arguing with patients does nothing but add to their suspicions about the motives of the cardiology community.

When PTCA is done as a separate procedure, the patient has already experienced cardiac catheterization and is generally less anxious. With PTCA, the patient needs to be informed that he or she may experience angina with the inflation of the balloon and that the sheath through which the catheter is placed may be kept in overnight.

EPSs

Patients with arrhythmias, syncope, and sudden cardiac death may undergo an EPS, an invasive procedure during which the electrical system of the heart is examined. An EPS may take several hours and require drug testing for efficacy in preventing recurrence of potentially lethal arrhythmias. Moreover, the new technique of radio-frequency ablation can be used to eradicate small areas of the electrical system of the heart that lead to abnormal circuits.

Similar to cardiac catheterization, patients undergoing EPS are generally awake but sedated, although in some instances, light general anesthesia is administered. Often the EPS takes many hours, and it may occasionally require electrical cardioversion if other techniques of reverting the arrhythmia fail. These procedures can be extremely frightening to patients, especially survivors of sudden cardiac death, who may have to "relive" the experience. There is no substitute in this case for providing a professional, empathic team. For patients in whom a ventricular arrhythmia is inducible, placement of an automatic implantable cardiodefibrillator (AICD) may be required. This may be done as a single procedure or in conjunction with CABG surgery, valvular repair or replacement, or all of these procedures. Newer AICD units are smaller and less disfiguring than earlier ones. Patients undergoing AICD placement have to deal not only with the need for frequent checks of their devices but also with potential recall or dysfunction of the device. Moreover, many patients who survive sudden death and have such units placed die despite successful electrical intervention, presumably of muscle rather than electrical failure. Given the uncertainties of survival in these patients, their attendant anxiety and depression is understandable. However, many such patients do survive and have good quality of life. Hence, in addition to the medical treatment, they deserve appropriate psychosocial support to maximize the likelihood of their returning to a gainful existence.

Pacemakers

Although not as dramatic as the AICD, a pacemaker is placed in patients who have arrhythmias that usually involve a slow heart rate (brad-yarrhythmia) or complete heart block, and this procedure still carries psychological sequelae. Pacemakers are inserted to substitute for the patient's cardiac "ignition system," which has degenerated. Patients must be monitored and need to be concerned about exposure to microwaves, airport security checks, and other electromagnetic fields. Patients often need a great deal of assurance and at least rudimentary understanding of their pacemakers. I am often struck by the questions asked by pacemaker patients. For example, one 81-year-old woman who had a pacemaker placed for a heart rate of 30 beats per minute associated with fatigue asked if she could travel to Europe, as had been her custom over past summers. She had planned to take this trip before the pacemaker was implanted but was subsequently reluctant to go. That she felt that she was more ill after the procedure than before shows the psychological potency of these surgical procedures. With reorientation, the patient's perception was shifted so that she realized that she was significantly safer with this potentially life-saving device. Such conceptualization often occurs in postoperative patients who, even months after recuperation and rehabilitation following valve or CABG surgery, are less confident in the cardiopulmonary capacity that was second nature to them before surgery. It is important for health practitioners to realize the potency and potential permanence of the "sick role" in patients with cardiovascular disease and to address self-image issues as early as possible.

Cardiac Surgery

CABG surgery is one of the most common surgical procedures in the United States today. Cardiac surgery is also performed in patients with valvular heart disease, congenital heart disease, and occasionally arrhythmias and myopathic disorders. The process of restoring the postoperative patient should begin before surgery. Patients must be made aware that they will feel sicker before they feel better. Even with successful heart surgery, patients are in a weakened condition for many weeks, and aches and pains are common for months, and even years, afterwards. It is important to inform patients that there may be fever, arrhythmias, difficulty in wound healing, pulmonary congestion, weakness, depression, and neuropsychological side effects after surgery (Blacher, 1986; Goldman & Kimball, 1985). Fortunately, in most patients, side effects are few and short-lived. Providing information about potential problems before the surgery may reduce the patient's and family's anxiety afterwards. It is also important to point out that recuperation is not linear and that patients often "take two steps forward and one step back." In addition to teaching how to possibly slow the progression of atherosclerosis, risk factor classes and early cardiac rehabilitation can be extremely valuable because patients are introduced to others with similar problems. Patients often feel relieved when they hear that their problem is common and that others face similar issues. It can also be helpful to inform patients of prominent personalities who have had CABG surgery, pacemakers, and valve replacement and who still lead high-profile, successful lives. Ultimate long-term psychosocial adjustment after CABG (Magni et al., 1987) and valve replacement (Jenkins et al., 1983) is related to a patient's premorbid psychosocial status. Hence, practitioners should identify those in whom postoperative, long-term psychological intervention might improve subsequent quality of life and identify and mobilize appropriate social supports (Cohen et al., 1994; Dhooper, 1990).

Cardiac Transplantation

Cardiac transplantation is an enormous event for patient and family. This procedure is performed in only a few specialized centers, where technical and psychosocial expertise allow maximal outcome. Because the best outcome occurs in those with the most extensive psychological and social supports, patients are selected on the basis of their premorbid adaptation. Nevertheless, a heart transplant does "try the system," and psychiatric distress is typical during the evaluation, waiting period, perioperatively, periods of rejection, and subsequent treatment (Kuhn et al., 1990). Specialized social workers, psychologists, and psychiatrists are required to deal with this difficult process.

INDIVIDUALIZING THERAPY

Tailoring medical therapy to patients' diverse needs is a challenge to the medical practitioner. Maximizing medical therapy, understanding the stresses and strains on the patient's life, anticipating emotional difficulties with consequent medical instability, and being available for patients through difficult times may ultimately result in diminished hospitalization. Patients who are poorly managed, both medically and psychologically, and who are frequently rehospitalized sometimes develop a recalcitrant sick role that becomes progressively more difficult to break. The medical practitioner needs to be aware of such patterns and to seek appropriate consultation from mental health professionals to curtail such ultimately self-defeating behavior.

For many patients with chronic coronary heart disease, cardiac psychology suggests the need for recognition by the patient's primary care physician of the importance of psychosocial factors for the disease. Individual and group cardiac rehabilitation as well as dietary and behavioral counseling may be extremely helpful for a large number of patients who have coronary heart disease.

The Dr. Zhivago Syndrome: Prevention of Unnecessary Cardiac Death

Medical practitioners should aim pharmacological therapy at reducing the amount of myocardial ischemia that patients experience during their usual daily activities and educate patients about the dangers of overdoing it. I often advise patients to avoid the "Dr. Zhivago syndrome," which involves an unusual concurrence of physical and emotional stress. (In the book, Pasternak [1957] described the demise of Dr. Zhivago after he unsuccessfully pursued the woman he believed to be his long-lost love.) Patients should be allowed as much freedom as possible, but they must also be prudent in challenging the limits of their abilities. Unfortunately, a number of my patients have died as a result of MIs apparently triggered by concurrent emotional and physical stress, such as getting anxious about being late and running to catch a train while lugging a heavy suitcase or being provoked into a fight on the street. There is extensive anecdotal and some empirical evidence that sudden cardiac death may be initiated by such factors as psychological challenge (De Silva, 1986; Kamarck & Jennings, 1991). Hence, educating patients about avoiding such stressors is of critical importance.

Cardiac Rehabilitation

Cardiac rehabilitation provides a structured program for recovery from acute cardiac events and serves to transition the patient from the sick role to a normalized life. In addition to progressive exercise and modification of physical risk factors such as obesity, hypertension, hyperlipidemia, and cigarette smoking, individual and group therapy—with specific attention to improvement of stress management skills—appear to improve outcome, although the specific benefits of psychological intervention alone have been difficult to assess (Langosch, 1984). My experience has been that a complete cardiac rehabilitation program can successfully restore patients to their premorbid status and, often, can improve their physical and mental fitness to a higher level than before they became ill. Participation should be particularly urged for socially isolated individuals, who often benefit from social contact as well as other interventions. Cardiac rehabilitation fosters a healthier lifestyle, more realistic expectations, and a return to a rewarding personal and professional life that may reduce the economic burden of cardiovascular illness throughout the country (Squires, Gan, Miller, Allison, & Lavie, 1990).

CONCLUSION

My answer to the question "Is there a need for cardiac psychology?" is an emphatic yes. There is no substitute for each professional understanding the patient as fully as possible (Nichols, 1985). In the hospital, health care workers need to respect the integrity of patients and minimize their dehumanization. From the outset, all those involved need to treat the patient with dignity to prevent a cycle of anger and depression. Patients should be provided with adequate knowledge but not bombarded with overly technical and conflicting information. Pain should be minimized and empathy maximized. Small concessions should sometimes be made to allow patients a degree of control. Finally, health providers need to set realistic limits with difficult patients yet avoid hostility and regressive behavior.

Cardiac psychology means understanding the patient, and this can only occur through communication at a mature and professional level. There is no substitute for time spent at bedside or in the office developing a relationship that may well improve a patient's outcome. The medical and economic costs of unattended psychological distress have recently been documented (Allison et al., 1995).

Although some health care providers may believe that they do not have the time to support the psychological and physiological needs of their patients, they should realize that time spent in developing a trusting therapeutic relationship saves time in the long term. Levinson and Roter (1995) have studied the relationship between physicians' beliefs about psychosocial aspects of patient care and their professional communication. They concluded that patient care is improved when doctors address psychological issues but found no association between concern about psychological factors and length of physician visits. Therefore, inquiring about family and work stresses may only take a moment, yet it provides a window of opportunity to avoid unnecessary, expensive tests when symptoms can be clearly attributed to psychological factors.

Health care providers need to get back in touch with their patients and their family and world. Some patients may require individual psychotherapy with elucidation of psychodynamic issues or the use of relaxation techniques. The majority of patients with cardiac disease will benefit from the understanding, trust, and confidence of a truly therapeutic relationship with their primary health care provider.

In 1968, Duff and Hollingshead identified numerous psychosocial variables that influenced the outcome of medical care. Among their major critiques was the separation of surgeons and internists from the everyday concerns of their patients. They found that physicians generally did not pay attention to personal and family influences on the etiology of the patient's symptoms, diagnosis, or management, and care was profoundly influenced by the social status of the patient. Physicians and nurses did not work closely together, and confusion resulted regarding patient care.

Communication skills in health care providers should not be assumed, nor should their widespread acceptance of psychosocial etiology for illness (Maguire, 1984). To the contrary, studies have demonstrated that our current medical education system is deficient in this regard. What is needed is a reevaluation of the medical mission and a redefinition of total patient care. I believe that all aspects of long-term care of the post-MI patient should remain under the watchful eye of the patient's primary care physician, who can make available a system of community services. Also, specific guidelines need to be developed for in-hospital and outpatient psychosocial and rehabilitative care. Position papers from appropriate organizations (e.g., American Heart Association, American College of Cardiology, and American College of Physicians) delineating this broad approach to care will likely lead to better individual outcome and savings in the U.S. health care system. Cardiac psychology has provided the framework for such a wide-ranging assessment.

REFERENCES

Allison, T. G., Williams, D. E., Miller, T. D., Patten, C. A., Bailey, K. R., Squires, R. W., & Gau, G. T. (1995). Medical and economic costs of psychologic distress in patients with coronary artery disease. *Mayo Clinic Proceedings, 70,* 734–742.

Anderson, K. O., & Masur, F. T. (1989). Psychologic preparation for cardiac catheterization. *Heart and Lung, 18,* 154–163.

Backman, M. E. (1989). *The psychology of the physically ill patient: A clinician's guide.* New York: Plenum Press.

Blacher, R. S. (1986). Psychological aspects of coronary bypass surgery. In R. L. Roessler & N. Decker (Eds.), *Emotional disorders in physically ill patients.* New York: Human Sciences Press.

Byrne, D. G. (1982). Psychological responses to illness and outcome after survived myocardial infarction: A long-term follow-up. *Journal of Psychosomatic Research, 26,* 105–112.

Cassem, N. H., & Hackett T. P. (1977). Psychological aspects of myocardial infarction. *Medical Clinics of North America, 61,* 711–721.

Cohen, S., Kaplan, J. R., & Manuck, S. B. (1994). Social support and coronary heart disease: Underlying psychological and biological mechanisms. In S. A. Shumaker & S. M. Czajkowski (Eds.), *Social support and cardiovascular disease* (pp. 195–221). New York: Plenum Press.

Conner, L. A. (1927). The rehabilitation of cardiac patients through organized effort. *Journal of the American Medical Association, 89,* 496–500.

Cromwell, R. L., & Levenkron, J. C. (1984). Psychological care of acute coronary patients. In A. Steptoe & A. Mathews (Eds.), *Health care and human behaviour* (pp. 209–229). San Diego, CA: Academic Press.

De Silva, R. A. (1986). Psychological stress and sudden cardiac death. In T. H. Schmidt, T. M. Dembroski, & G. Blumchen (Eds.), *Biological and psychological factors in cardiovascular disease* (pp. 155–183). Berlin: Springer-Verlag.

Dhooper, S. S. (1990). Identifying and mobilizing social supports for the cardiac patient's family. *Journal of Cardiovascular Nursing, 5,* 65–73.

Duff, R. S., & Hollingshead, A. B. (1968). *Sickness and society.* New York: Harper & Row.

Feurstein, M., & Cohen, R. (1985). Arrhythmias: Evaluating and managing problems of heart rate and rhythm. In A. M. Razin (Ed.), *Helping cardiac patients: Biobehavioral and psychotherapeutic approaches* (pp. 55–11). San Francisco: Jossey-Bass.

Fredrikson, M. (1985). Behavioral aspects of cardiovascular reactivity in essential hypertension. In T. H. Schmidt, T. M. Dembroski, & G. Blumchen (Eds.), *Biological and psychological factors in cardiovascular disease* (pp. 418–446). Berlin: Springer-Verlag.

Goldman, L. S., & Kimball, C. P. (1985). Cardiac surgery: Enhancing postoperative outcomes. In A. M. Razin (Ed.), *Helping cardiac patients: Biobehavioral and psychotherapeutic approaches* (pp. 113–155). San Francisco: Jossey-Bass.

Gorkin, L., Schron, E. B., Brooks, M. M., Wiklund, I., Kellen, J., Vertner, J., Schoenberger, J. A., Pawitan, Y., Morris, M., & Schumaker, S. (1993). Psychosocial predictors of mortality in the Cardiac Arrhythmia Suppressor Trial-1 (CAST-1). *American Journal of Cardiology, 71,* 263–267.

Graves, E. J. (1992). Summary: National hospital discharge survey. In Klaudia Cox (Ed.), *Vital and health statistics of the center for disease control and prevention* (pp. 1–12). Washington, DC: National Center for Health Statistics, U.S. Department of Health and Human Services.

Hackett, T. P., Cassem, N. H., & Wishnie, H. A. (1968). The coronary care unit: An appraisal of its psychologic hazards. *New England Journal of Medicine, 279,* 1365–1370.

Hellerstein, H. K. (1972). Rehabilitation of the post infarction patient. *Hospital Practice, 7,* 45–53.

Hellerstein, H. K. (1994). *A matter of heart.* Caldwell, ID: Griffith Publishing.

Jenkins, C. D., Babette, A. S., Savageau, J. A., Ockene, I. S., Denlinger, P., & Klein, M. O. (1983). Physical, psychologic, and economic outcomes after cardiac valve surgery. *Archives of Internal Medicine, 143,* 2107–2113.

Kamarck, T., & Jennings, J. R. (1991). Biobehavioral factors in sudden cardiac death. *Psychological Bulletin, 109,* 42–75.

Klein, R. F., Kliner, V. A., Zipes, D. P., Trouper, W. G., & Wallace, A. G. (1968). Transfer from a coronary care unit: Some adverse responses. *Archives of Internal Medicine, 122,* 104–108.

Kuhn, W. F., Brennan, A. F., Lacefield, P. K., Brohm, J., Skelton, V. D., & Gray, L. A. (1990). Psychiatric distress during stages of the heart transplant protocol. *Journal of Heart Transplantation, 9,* 25–29.

Langosch, W. (1984). Behavioral interventions in cardiac rehabilitation. In A. Steptoe & A. Mathews (Eds.), *Health care and human behaviour* (pp. 301–324). San Diego, CA: Academic Press.

Levinson, W., & Roter, D. (1995). Physicians' psychosocial beliefs correlate with their patient communication skills. *Journal of General Internal Medicine, 10,* 375–379.

Maeland, J. G., & Havik, O. E. (1987). Psychological predictors for return to work after a myocardial infarction. *Journal of Psychosomatic Research, 31,* 471–481.

Magni, G., Unger, H. P., Valfre, C., Polesel, E., Cesari, F., Rizzardo, R., Paruzzolo, P., & Galluci, V. (1987). Psychosocial outcome one year after heart surgery: A prospective study. *Archives of Internal Medicine, 147,* 473–477.

Maguire, P. (1984). Communication skills and patient care. In A. Steptoe & A. Mathews (Eds.), *Health care and human behaviour* (pp. 153–173). San Diego, CA: Academic Press.

Meerson, F. Z. (1994a). Stress induced arrhythmia: Disease of the heart. Part I. *Clinical Cardiology, 17,* 362–371.

Meerson, F. Z. (1994b). Stress induced arrhythmia: Disease of the heart. Part II. *Clinical Cardiology, 17,* 422–426.

Nichols, K. A. (1985). Psychological care by nurses, paramedical and medical staff: Essential developments for the general hospital. *British Journal of Medical Psychology, 58,* 231–240.

Ornish, D. (1990). *Dr. Dean Ornish's program for reversing heart disease.* New York: Random House.

Pasternak, B. (1957). *Dr. Zhivago.* New York: Ballantine Books.

Razin, A. M. (Ed.). (1985). *Helping cardiac patients: Biobehavioral and psychotherapeutic approaches.* San Francisco: Jossey-Bass.

Riegel, B. J. (1993). Contributors to cardiac invalidism after acute myocardial infarction. *Coronary Artery Disease, 4,* 215–220.

Ruberman, W., Weinblatt, E., Goldberg, J. D., & Chaudhary, B. S. (1984). Psychological influences on mortality after myocardial infarction. *New England Journal of Medicine, 311,* 552–559.

Shorter, E. (1985). *Bedside manners: The troubled history of doctors and patients.* New York: Simon & Schuster.

Sloan, R. P., & Bigger, J. T. (1991). Biobehavioral factors in the Cardiac Arrhythmia Pilot Study (CAPS). *Circulation, 83*(Suppl. 2), 52–57.

Squires, R. W., Gan, G. T., Miller, T. D., Allison, T. G., & Lavie, C. J. (1990). Cardiovascular rehabilitation: Status. *Mayo Clinic Proceedings, 65,* 731–755.

Surwit, R. S., Williams, R. B., & Shapiro, D. (1982). *Behavioral approaches to cardiovascular disease.* San Diego, CA: Academic Press.

Vlay, S. C., & Fricchione, G. J. (1985). Psychological aspects of surviving sudden cardiac death. *Clinical Cardiology, 8,* 237–243.

White, P. D. (1951). *Heart disease.* New York: Macmillan.

5

CORONARY ATHEROSCLEROSIS: DESCRIPTION, MANIFESTATIONS, AND PREVENTION

WILLIAM CLIFFORD ROBERTS

Atherosclerosis is the biggest killer in the Western world. Approximately 45% of the inhabitants in this portion of the planet will die from its consequences. In the United States alone, an estimated 11,200,000 persons have symptomatic myocardial ischemia resulting from coronary atherosclerosis (American Heart Association, 1995), and countless more suffer from consequences of its attacks on the aorta and the peripheral arteries. The sad thing about atherosclerosis is that in most people it is preventable. It is estimated that only 1 in 500 persons has the genetic disease of heterozygous familial hypercholesterolemia, wherein severe atherosclerosis develops at an early age regardless of lifestyle (M. S. Brown & Goldstein, 1986). The rest, namely 499 of 500 persons, determine themselves whether or not they will develop sufficient quantities of atherosclerotic plaques to narrow their arterial lumens sufficiently to cause organ ischemia or infarction. In this chapter, I review atherosclerosis, with a focus on the coronary arteries, in three main sections. I begin with a description of coronary atherosclerosis that includes the extent of atherosclerosis present in the coronary arteries and the composition of atherosclerotic plaques and the types of lesions that occur in patients with symptomatic myocardial ischemia and the three acute coronary events: unstable angina pectoris (UAP), acute myocardial infarction (AMI), and sudden coronary death (SCD). Next, in describing risk factors for coronary atherosclerosis, I examine the

147

relationship between cholesterol and atherosclerosis and discuss how many direct atherosclerotic risk factors do exist. Finally, in a discussion of the prevention and treatment of coronary atherosclerosis, I note how normal cholesterol levels can be prevented from rising and how elevated levels can be lowered to normal.

DESCRIPTION OF CORONARY ATHEROSCLEROSIS

Extent of Atherosclerosis

The amount of coronary arterial narrowing observed at necropsy in patients with UAP, AMI, and SCD is generally enormous, and certain evidence has suggested that patients with symptomatic myocardial ischemia have as much plaque as those who have died from myocardial ischemia. In a study of 80 patients at autopsy who died from one of these coronary events, an average of 2.9 of the 4 major coronary arteries (right, left main, left anterior descending, and left circumflex) were severely narrowed at some point (>75% decrease in cross-sectional area), and no significant differences were observed among the three coronary subsets of people (Roberts, 1989c).

A more sophisticated approach to determining degrees of luminal narrowing is to examine the entire lengths of the four major epicardial coronary arteries. One technique involves incising each of these arteries transversely at 5-mm intervals and then preparing a histologic section from each 5-mm segment. Normally, the total length of the four major arteries is approximately 27 cm (right = 10 cm, left main = 1 cm, left anterior descending = 10 cm, and left circumflex = 6 cm); thus, approximately fifty-five 5-mm-long segments are available for examination from each heart. Of the 4,016 segments (5 mm in length) studied in the 80 patients from my (Roberts, 1989c, 1994a) studies, 38% of the segments were narrowed 76%–100% in cross-sectional area by plaque alone (compared with a control measure of 3%), 34% were narrowed 51%–75% (control = 22%), 20% were narrowed 26%–50% (control = 44%), and only 7% were narrowed 25% or less (control = 31%). Similar degrees of narrowing by plaque alone in all four categories of narrowing were observed in those who died from AMI and SCD; those with UAP had significantly more severe coronary narrowing than the other two groups (Roberts 1989c; Roberts, Kragel, Gertz, & Roberts, 1994).

The good news is that it takes a huge quantity of plaque before overt myocardial ischemia occurs. The bad news is that, despite the requirement for huge quantities of plaque before problems occur, nearly half of the people in the Western world nevertheless develop these quantities.

Composition of Coronary Atherosclerotic Plaques

Until recently, no detailed information was available concerning the composition of atherosclerotic plaques in the epicardial coronary arteries of patients who had died after coronary events. Using a computerized morphometric system, Kragel and associates (Kragel, Reddy, Wittes, & Roberts, 1989, 1990) determined the various components of atherosclerotic plaques in histologic sections prepared from 1,438 segments (5-mm long) of the four major epicardial coronary arteries in 37 people who had died from coronary artery disease. The dominant component of the coronary atherosclerotic plaques in all three subsets of people was fibrous tissue, comprising about 80% of the plaques in each subset. Extracellular lipid (pultaceous debris) and calcium each made up approximately 5% of the plaques, and several miscellaneous components made up the remainder of the plaques. The cellular component of the fibrous tissue occupied a larger portion of plaque in those with UAP and SCD, and the acellular (dense) component of fibrous tissue occupied a larger portion of the plaque in the group with AMI. In all three subsets, the amount of dense fibrous tissue increased as plaque size increased (or as lumen size decreased).

Acute Coronary Lesions

In recent years, considerable effort has been directed toward understanding the acute coronary events that may be responsible for the development of UAP, AMI, and SCD. From angiographic, angioscopic, and autopsy studies, it has been speculated that plaque rupture and hemorrhage with overlying intraluminal thrombus—which are the acute lesions usually responsible for AMI—are also responsible for UAP and possibly SCD. Kragel, Gertz, and Roberts (1991) examined 3,101 segments (5-mm long) of 268 epicardial coronary arteries from 67 persons who had died after a coronary event. The frequency of intraluminal thrombus was similar in the groups with UAP and SCD (29% in each) and significantly lower than that in the group with AMI (69%). The thrombus was nonocclusive in all who had UAP and in 5 of 6 persons who had SCD, but it was nonocclusive in only 4 of 22 persons who had AMI. The composition of the nonocclusive and occlusive thrombi also was different; that is, the nonocclusive thrombus consisted mainly of platelets and the occlusive thrombus mainly of fibrin. Plaque rupture was found in 33 (49%) of the 67 persons. Its frequency was insignificantly different in the groups with UAP (36%) or SCD (19%). In both groups, the frequency was significantly lower than in the group with AMI (75%). Plaque hemorrhage was observed in 27 (40%) of the 67 studied, and its frequency was significantly lower in the groups who had UAP (21%) and SCD (19%) in comparison with that in the group who had AMIs (63%). Thus, comparison of histologic findings from 67 people who died from coronary artery disease has disclosed that the frequency of three acute coronary lesions (intraluminal thrombus, plaque rupture, and plaque hemorrhage) was similar in patients with UAP and SCD and significantly higher in people who died from a first transmural AMI.

RISK FACTORS FOR CORONARY ATHEROSCLEROSIS

Cholesterol as a Primary Cause

Although the relation between cholesterol and atherosclerosis has been discussed for nearly 90 years, it is only in recent years that sufficient evidence has accumulated to indicate without reasonable doubt that cholesterol plays a major role in the development of atherosclerotic plaques. In this section, I review the various factors linking cholesterol to atherosclerosis.

Feeding high-cholesterol diets to certain nonhuman animals produces atherosclerotic plaques similar to those in humans. The initial connection between cholesterol and atherosclerotic plaques began in 1912, when Anitschkow (1912, 1967) reported finding atherosclerotic plaques similar to those occurring in humans in rabbits fed diets high in cholesterol. Subsequently, atherosclerotic plaques were also produced in other nonhuman animals (e.g., guinea pigs, chickens, and monkeys) by feeding them high-cholesterol diets (Anitschkow, 1967). With this experiment, Anitschkow laid down the dictum that increased cholesterol in the blood was the inciting cause of atherosclerosis. It is not possible to produce atherosclerosis in a carnivore (e.g., dog, cat, lion, or tiger) no matter how much fat or cholesterol is provided unless the thyroid gland is excised before the atherogenic diet is initiated. However, feeding humans a diet high in fat and cholesterol obviously readily produces atherosclerotic plaques. This fact suggests that humans basically are herbivores.

Cholesterol is found both in experimentally induced atherosclerotic plaques in nonhuman animals and in plaques in humans. Three main types of lipid accumulate in atherosclerotic lesions: free sterols (almost exclusively cholesterol), cholesterol esters (mainly cholesteryl linoleate, oleate, and palmitate), and phospholipids (mainly phosphatidylcholine and sphingomyelines; Small, 1988). All three lipids are insoluble in water. These lipids make up about 95% of the total lipids in both normal intima and in atheromatous plaques. Cholesterol esters are nearly absent in newborn intima, but they are a major part of atherosclerotic plaques. Triglycerides are lowest in newborn intima, and they never become a major component of plaques (Small, 1988).

Atherosclerotic plaques large enough to produce clinical problems occur only in people who have serum or plasma total cholesterol levels greater than 150 mg/dl for long periods of time. Most native African, Latin American, and Asian populations have a low frequency of coronary atherosclerosis (Keys, 1970, 1980). Their diets are low in saturated fat, cholesterol, and animal protein. Most adults in these populations have serum total cholesterol levels less than 150 mg/dl (Keys, 1980). Fatal atherosclerotic vascular disease in the United States is rare in anyone who has a serum total cholesterol level less than 150 mg/dl for many years. In the United States, however, only 5% of the population greater than 40 years of age has a serum or plasma total cholesterol level less than 150 mg/dl (Lipid Research Clinics Program, 1979).

The higher the blood total cholesterol level, the greater the chance of having symptomatic and fatal atherosclerotic disease. Although the Framingham study (Castelli, 1984), the Seven Countries study (Keys, 1970, 1980), and the Donolo–Tel Aviv study (Brunner et al., 1987) have demonstrated that people with higher serum total cholesterol levels have higher incidences of atherosclerotic disease than people of similar age and sex with lower levels, I believe that the best study demonstrating the relation between serum total cholesterol level and symptomatic or fatal atherosclerotic disease is the Multiple Risk Factor Intervention Trial (MRFIT; Stamler et al., 1986). The reason is that MRFIT involved over 350,000 persons, whereas the Seven Countries study involved just over 12,000 men from each of seven nations, and the Framingham study involved 5,127 persons. The 356,222 persons without clinical evidence of coronary artery disease sampled in the MRFIT study were divided into deciles on the basis of their serum total cholesterol levels. The 6-year mortality rate from coronary artery disease per 1,000 persons increased as serum total cholesterol levels increased.

What constitutes an elevated total cholesterol level continues to be debated. If an elevated level is that minimal level above which atherosclerotic events occur, then that level would be approximately 150 mg/dl (3.9 mmol/L; Keys, 1970). If it is the level where the risk of atherosclerotic events is substantially increased in comparison with lower levels, then that level would be approximately 200 mg/dl (Stamler et al., 1986). Irrespective of which level is chosen, the higher the level the greater the risk of an atherosclerotic event, and the risk of an atherosclerotic event increases roughly proportional to the level and to the amount of time that this level has been present (Hoeg, Feuerstein, & Tucker, 1994).

In adults in the United States the mean plasma high-density lipoprotein (HDL) level is 45 mg/dl in men and 55 mg/dl in women (Lipid Research Clinics Program, Epidemiology Committee, 1979). Data, especially from Framingham, Massachusetts, have shown that high levels of HDL are associated with decreased risk and that low levels are associated with increased risk of atherosclerotic events (Castelli et al., 1986; Gordon, Castelli, Hjortland, Kannel, & Dawber, 1977). The evidence is convincing that high HDL is good and low HDL is bad. But what is the risk of a serum HDL level of 20 mg/dl if the low-density lipoprotein (LDL) cholesterol is less than 100 mg/dl and the serum total cholesterol is less than 150 mg/dl? The answer is no risk (Roberts, 1989a). Is an HDL of 100 mg/dl protective when the total cholesterol is 300 (ratio = 3) and LDL cholesterol is near 200 mg/dl? The answer is probably no. Whether the HDL cholesterol is an independent risk factor (i.e., independent of the LDL cholesterol level) is not yet clear. It is reasonable to view a low HDL cholesterol as an additive atherosclerotic risk factor if the LDL cholesterol is elevated, but not as an additive atherosclerotic risk factor if the LDL cholesterol is low.

Although it is perhaps a controversial assertion, in my view the only absolute, unequivocal, independent atherosclerotic risk factor is an elevated serum total cholesterol level or LDL cholesterol level either alone or in combination with a low HDL cholesterol level.

The higher the serum total and LDL cholesterol levels, the greater the extent of the atherosclerotic plaques. The International Atherosclerosis Project quantified the extent of coronary and aortic atherosclerotic plaques at necropsy in 23,207 persons in 14 countries (McGill, 1968). The extent of the atherosclerotic plaques differed markedly among populations, and the mean serum total cholesterol level correlated positively with the severity of the atherosclerotic plaques.

Lowering the blood total cholesterol and LDL cholesterol levels decreases the chances of fatal or nonfatal atherosclerotic disease. The Lipid Research Clinics–Coronary Primary Prevention Trial (LRC–CPPT; using cholestyramine; Lipid Research Clinics Program, 1979, 1984a, 1984b; Roberts, 1984), the Helsinki Primary Prevention Trial (using gemfibrozil; Frick et al., 1987; Huttunen et al., 1987), and the West of Scotland Coronary Prevention Trial (using pravastatin; Shepherd et al., 1995) have provided evidence that lowering the blood total and LDL cholesterol levels reduces the frequency of fatal and nonfatal coronary artery disease. All three studies were randomized, double-blind, placebo-controlled, multicenter, primary prevention trials analyzed through the intention-to-treat method.

The LRC–CPPT included 3,806 men aged 35 to 59 years (M = 48 years) at entry with plasma total cholesterol levels greater than or equal to 265 mg/dl (after dieting): Half of the participants received cholestyramine (24 g a day), and the other half received placebo. The cholestyramine group (n = 1,899) had average total and LDL cholesterol reductions by the end of the 7th year of 12% (from 292 to 257 mg/dl) and 19% (216 to 175 mg/dl), respectively. In contrast, the placebo group (n = 1,907), also on a cholesterol-lowering diet, had average total and LDL cholesterol reductions of 5% (from 292 to 277 mg/dl) and 9% (216 to 198 mg/dl), respectively. The primary end results—fatal coronary artery disease or non-fatal AMI—were reduced 19% at 7 years (Frick et al., 1987; Huttunen et al., 1987; Lipid Research Clinics Program, 1979, 1984a, 1984b; Roberts, 1984).

The Helsinki trial included 4,081 men aged 40 to 55 years ($M = 47$ years) at entry with serum non-HDL cholesterol levels above 200 mg/dl. The mean serum total cholesterol level for the 4,081 men was 290 mg/dl, and the mean HDL cholesterol level was 48 mg/dl. Half of the men received gemfibrozil (1.2 g a day), and the other half received a placebo (1.2 g a day). The gemfibrozil group had average total and LDL cholesterol reductions of 9% during the first 2 years and during the last 3 years of the study (reductions from 270 to 245 mg/dl for total level and 189 to 173 mg/dl for LDL level, respectively). The HDL cholesterol rose during both the first 2 years and the last 3 years of study by 9% (from 47 to 52 mg/dl). In contrast, the placebo group, also on a cholesterol-lowering diet, had no change in either serum total (from 270 to 273 mg/dl) or LDL cholesterol (48 to 47 mg/dl) during the entire 5 years of the trial. The primary end results—fatal coronary artery disease or nonfatal AMI—were reduced 34%.

The West of Scotland trial included 6,595 men aged 45 to 64 years with mean total serum cholesterol levels at entry of 272 mg/dl (after dieting). Half of the men received pravastatin (40 mg a day), and the other half received a placebo. Pravastatin lowered total serum cholesterol by 20% and LDL by 26%, whereas there was no change with the placebo. Nonfatal MI or CHD death—the primary endpoints—were reduced 31%, and total deaths were reduced 22% ($p = .051$).

All three trials demonstrated that lowering the blood total and LDL cholesterol levels reduces the incidence of fatal and nonfatal coronary artery disease. The LRC–CPPT and Helsinki primary prevention trials, when analyzed by the intention-to-treat method, showed that every 1% reduction in serum total cholesterol resulted in a 2% reduction in the frequency of MI over a 5- to 7-year period. If the trials had been analyzed by comparing those who actually took the drugs in the prescribed amounts to those who did not take the drug, then the studies would have shown at least a 3% reduction in MI frequency for every 1% reduction in serum total cholesterol (see Figure 1).

Atherosclerotic plaques may regress or fail to progress when high total and LDL cholesterol levels are lowered. Several experimental studies in nonhuman animals have shown that atherosclerotic plaques regress when blood lipid levels fall after atherogenic diets are eliminated (Armstrong & Megan, 1972). Several studies of humans, most published in this decade, have demonstrated that lipid lowering both retards the rate of progression of angiographically demonstrated coronary arterial narrowing and causes reduction in the size of atherosclerotic plaques (as evidenced by increased

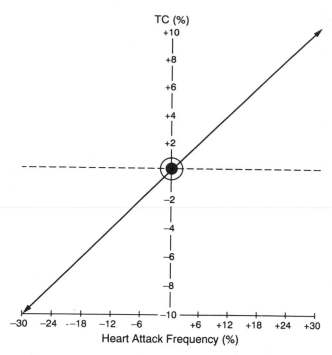

Figure 1. Effect of increasing or decreasing serum total cholesterol level on the frequency of fatal coronary artery disease or nonfatal acute myocardial infarction (AMI). These data were derived primarily from the Helsinki Heart Study (Frick et al., 1987). For every 10% decrease in the serum total cholesterol level there is a 30% decrease in AMI frequency. The reverse also is true: For every 10% increase in the serum total cholesterol level, there is a 30% increase in the frequency of AMI.

luminal diameters), as well as usually decreases the frequencies of recurrences of atherosclerotic events (Blankenhorn et al., 1987, 1993; Brensike et al., 1984; B. G. Brown et al., 1990; B. G. Brown, Xue-Qiao, Sacco, & Albers, 1993; Buchwald et al., 1990; Cashin-Hemphill et al., 1990; Duffield et al., 1983; Haskell et al., 1994; Kane et al., 1990; R. I. Levy et al., 1984; MAAS Investigators, 1994; Ornish et al., 1990; Schuler et al., 1992; Waters et al., 1994; Watts et al., 1992). For plaque progression to cease, it appears that the serum total cholesterol needs to be lowered to 150 mg/dl. In other words, the serum total cholesterol must be lowered to the level maintained by the average pure vegetarian. Because relatively few people are willing to abide by the vegetarian lifestyle, lipid-lowering drugs are required for most people to reach the 150 mg/dl level.

There no longer is any controversy about the role of cholesterol in atherosclerosis. In my view, physicians should provide a clear and united voice to the public regarding the dangers of elevating the blood LDL cholesterol level. Every person needs to know his or her serum or plasma total cholesterol level and, if it is elevated, every attempt should be made to lower it. I believe that the most effective means of improving the health of the largest percentage of Americans is for each person to lower his or her LDL cholesterol level.

Other Risk Factors

Several factors have been considered to predispose people to developing atherosclerosis, including elevated LDL cholesterol or low levels of HDL cholesterol (or both), systemic hypertension, cigarette smoking, family history of atherosclerotic disease, obesity, diabetes mellitus, and being a male (National Cholesterol Education Program Expert Panel, 1988). The key question is how many of these factors are direct. If *direct* means that this risk factor must be present for atherosclerosis to occur, then all but one of these factors can be eliminated. Atherosclerosis of severe degree may occur in individuals with normal blood pressures, in nonsmokers, in nonobese people, in those with normal glucose metabolism, and in women. Thus, all of these factors are indirect and so may worsen the atherosclerotic process, but in the absence of the direct factor they do not cause atherosclerosis. Next, I examine each of these other atherosclerotic risk factors to see if it is a direct or an independent factor.

Systemic Hypertension

In nonhuman experimental animals fed atherogenic diets (high in fat and cholesterol), those previously made hypertensive developed more atherosclerotic plaques than did the normotensive animals (Wenger & Schlant, 1990). Hypertensive people with total and LDL cholesterol levels similar to those in normotensive people also have a higher frequency of atherosclerotic events in comparison with normotensive people (D. Levy, Wilson, Anderson, & Castelli, 1990). These two facts have been used to support the contention that systemic hypertension is an atherosclerotic risk factor. However, most studies describing the benefits of antihypertensive therapy have not demonstrated a reduction in coronary or peripheral atherosclerotic events by such therapy. There is no evidence that systemic hypertension accelerates atherosclerosis if the serum total cholesterol level is below 150 mg/dl. It appears, then, that systemic hypertension is a cholesterol-dependent risk factor, because a person's serum total cholesterol level must be above 150 mg/dl before hypertension has the ability to accelerate atherosclerosis and, therefore, that hypertension is not an independent atherosclerotic risk factor.

Cigarette Smoking

Although it is incompatible with good health, cigarette smoking does not, in and of itself, produce atherosclerotic plaques. In populations where serum total cholesterol levels are below 150 mg/dl, atherosclerotic events are rare even when cigarette smoking is widespread. In Japan for instance, cigarette smoking is common, but atherosclerotic events are relatively uncommon. The average serum total cholesterol level in adults in Japan is about 170 mg/dl, which is not a level associated with a high frequency of atherosclerotic events (Hatano, 1989). Many Japanese adults have serum total cholesterol levels below 150 mg/dl. In populations where the average serum total cholesterol level in adults is greater than 200 mg/dl (such as the United States) smoking cigarettes appears to accelerate atherosclerosis, but this acceleration seems to be a cholesterol-dependent phenomenon.

Family History

When atherosclerotic events occur in people under 55 years of age, it generally means two things: (a) The affected individuals have serum total cholesterol levels considerably higher than people of similar age and sex who have not had atherosclerotic events, and (b) the affected individuals have total cholesterol levels much higher than those found in older individuals who experienced atherosclerotic events. In people with untreated familial hypercholesterolemia of the heterozygous type, serum total cholesterol levels are usually from 300 to 400 mg/dl, and these individuals usually have atherosclerotic events between 31 and 50 years of age (M. S. Brown & Goldstein, 1986; Goldstein & Brown, 1987). In untreated individuals with familial hypercholesterolemia of the homozygous variety, the serum total cholesterol levels are usually above 800 mg/dl, and these individuals usually have atherosclerotic events before they are 20 years of age (M. S. Brown & Goldstein, 1986; Goldstein & Brown, 1987). Thus, individuals who have atherosclerotic events before age 50 generally have higher total LDL cholesterol levels than do individuals who have atherosclerotic events later in life, and the genetic forms of hyperlipidemia are primarily in these younger groups. A young age at the time of an atherosclerotic event simply denotes very high serum total cholesterol levels. It is the cholesterol level—not the patient's age or the presence of atherosclerotic events in other family members—that is the villain.

Severe Obesity

In general, people who are obese have higher total and LDL cholesterol levels than do nonobese people of similar age and sex (Garrison &

Castelli, 1985). This fact is not surprising of course, because obese people eat more fat than do nonobese people. Although few individuals exist to study, I am not aware that adults who are obese and have serum total cholesterol levels below 150 mg/dl have any increased risk for development of atherosclerotic events. Thus, obesity is a cholesterol-dependent risk factor, not an independent risk factor.

Diabetes Mellitus

Patients with juvenile diabetes clearly have more atherosclerotic plaques and a higher frequency of atherosclerotic events than do individuals of similar age and sex who do not have diabetes (Crall & Roberts, 1978; Mautner, Lin, & Roberts, 1992). But those with juvenile diabetes usually have higher serum total and LDL cholesterol and lower HDL levels than do their nondiabetic counterparts. Likewise, people with adult-onset diabetes have more atherosclerosis and a higher frequency of atherosclerotic events than do people without diabetes who are of similar age and sex (Waller, Palumbo, Lie, & Roberts, 1980). Moreover, those with adult-onset diabetes have higher serum total and LDL cholesterol, triglyceride, and lower HDL cholesterol levels than do their nondiabetic counterparts (Cowie, Howard, & Harris, 1994). There is no evidence that people with diabetes who have serum total cholesterol levels under 150 mg/dl have an increased frequency of atherosclerotic events in comparison with nondiabetic counterparts who have similar cholesterol levels. Indeed, there is no evidence that people with diabetes who have low serum total cholesterol levels have atherosclerosis of any significance. Thus, diabetes mellitus also appears to be a cholesterol-dependent risk factor.

Male Sex

As many women die from atherosclerotic events as do men (Roberts, 1990a, 1990b). The average age of death from atherosclerotic coronary artery disease in men (who have not had angioplasty or bypass) is 60 years; in women the average is 68 years (Roberts, 1990a, 1990b). Men have higher total and LDL serum cholesterol levels earlier in life than do women, but later in life, women have higher levels than do men (Lipid Research Clinics Program, 1979). However, neither men nor women have atherosclerotic events unless their total cholesterol levels rise above 150 mg/dl. The higher the level, the greater the chance of an event and the earlier the event occurs, irrespective of sex. Thus, it is a person's blood cholesterol level, not their sex, that determines whether an atherosclerotic event will occur. Male sex thus cannot be viewed as an independent atherosclerotic risk factor.

Psychosocial Factors

I have not been convinced that psychosocial factors alone actually cause plaques, but they do play a major—perhaps the major—role in determining when atherosclerotic events occur. In addition, psychosocial factors are of the utmost importance in the 499 of 500 persons who determine themselves whether or not significant atherosclerosis will develop, by choosing a healthy or unhealthy diet, exercise or a sedentary lifestyle, obesity or thin habitus, and the like.

PREVENTION AND TREATMENT OF ATHEROSCLEROSIS

Control of Serum Cholesterol

To prevent symptomatic or fatal atherosclerosis in those people with serum total cholesterol levels of about 150 mg/dl, the level must be prevented from rising. To prevent symptomatic or fatal atherosclerosis in people with elevated serum total cholesterol levels, the level must be reduced to the 150 mg/dl area. The best news about atherosclerosis is that it can be prevented in 499 of 500 persons by keeping the total cholesterol in the 150 mg/dl area and that it can be arrested by lowering an elevated level to the 150 mg/dl level.

The mean serum total cholesterol of the umbilical blood of newborns is about 75 mg/dl (1.9 mmol/L). Within 2 weeks of life, that value rises to a mean of 150 mg/dl (3.9 mmol/L), and it remains at that level until about 20 years of age, when it gradually starts to rise (Expert Panel on Blood Cholesterol Levels in Children and Adolescents, 1991). The average serum total cholesterol level in the United States among people 20 to 74 years of age is 215 mg/dl, and the average for people in coronary care units after an AMI is 225 mg/dl (Sempos et al., 1993). Men have higher levels earlier in life, and women have higher levels in later life. More than 50% of American adults have serum total cholesterol levels above 200 mg/dl (>5.2 mmol/L), and 20% of the U.S. population has serum total cholesterol levels above 240 mg/dl (American Heart Association, 1995). To keep a normal cholesterol level normal or return an elevated level to normal, one must restrict dietary intake of cholesterol, fat, and total calories or take one or more lipid-lowering drugs, or do both.

Cholesterol Intake

The average adult in the United States consumes about 500 mg of cholesterol daily. To picture 500 mg—hardly a calorie—it may be useful to picture a toothpick. The average toothpick weighs about 100 mg, so people consume the equivalent of five toothpicks of cholesterol daily. Dietary cholesterol is derived exclusively from animals and their products, so limiting the intake of these products automatically reduces the intake of cholesterol. Nearly 50% of the direct cholesterol consumed by adults in the United States comes from the visible and nonvisible eggs eaten, so giving up eggs eliminates nearly one half of one's direct cholesterol intake. Beef accounts for nearly 30% of direct cholesterol intake, so giving up both egg and beef products essentially eliminates the direct cholesterol intake problem. Men and women in the United States consume similar amounts of cholesterol, but through slightly different sources: Men consume more meat, and women consume more cheese. The cholesterol content of most meat eaten by humans is similar. A 100-g portion of muscle from a cow, pig, deer, chicken, turkey, or fish contains approximately 85 mg of cholesterol; thus switching from one meat to another has little impact on cholesterol intake. Fish is advantageous in that it contains relatively little fat, whereas the meat of cows and pigs—at least those raised in the United States—is laden with fat. In addition, fish contains the so-called omega-3 fatty acids, which may be beneficial to the cardiovascular system through other mechanisms.

Fat Intake

Most adults in the United States consume over 100 g of fat daily, many over 150 g daily. Yet, no one should consume over 75 g of fat daily—the equivalent of a deck of cards—and, ideally, men should consume no more than 60 g and women no more than 50 g of fat daily. There are two problems with fat: (a) All fats possess a saturated component, and (b) all fats are high in calories. All fatty acids contain a polyunsaturated component, a monounsaturated component, and a saturated component. A *polyunsaturated fat* is one in which the polyunsaturated component is dominant, and the remainder is divided between the monounsaturated and saturated components; a *monounsaturated fat* is one in which the monounsaturated component is dominant. The saturated fatty acids (coconut oil, palm kernel oil, and beef fat) raise the serum total cholesterol level, and the polyunsaturated (safflower, cottonseed, corn, sesame, soybean, and fish oils) and monounsaturated (olive, peanut, and avocado) fatty acids either lower the level or have a neutral effect on the total cholesterol level. The reason that the saturated fat component is so dangerous is that it is essentially converted into cholesterol as it is broken down in the body. Thus, for an individual who consumes 120 g of fat daily, usually about 40 g is saturated, and when that 40 g enters the body it is essentially converted into cholesterol. The saturated fat can be identified by its being solid at room temperature; the polyunsaturated and monounsaturated fats are soft or liquid at room temperature. All three fatty acids are very high in calories (9 cal/g).

Although there are many sources of fat, in contrast to the relatively few sources of direct cholesterol, a major source of fat (about 30%) in the United States is meat, primarily because of the way that cattle are raised. Cows for slaughter are placed in feedlots in their last 4 to 6 months of life and fed 20–25 lb (9.08–11.35 kg) of various grains and soybeans each day. The purpose of this heavy feeding is to make the animals fat, so that they taste better when cooked. Once they are fat enough, we kill the cows—and then they kill us. This cycle is the merry-go-round of unhealthiness.

Fast-Food Restaurants

One of the easiest means of rapidly acquiring a heavy dose of fat and cholesterol is the fast-food restaurant (Roberts, 1987, 1992). In America, $5 of every $10 spent on restaurant food is spent at a fast-food restaurant. Over 160,000 fast-food restaurants are available in the United States, and over $70 billion is spent at them each year. In fact, fast-food restaurants outnumber traditional restaurants in the United States. One of 5 persons in America visits a fast-food restaurant every day, and 4 of 5, every month (Roberts, 1992). More than 50% of the U.S. population lives within 3 minutes of a McDonald's. McDonald's alone has employed more than 8 million workers (7% of the U.S. workforce) and has replaced the U.S. Army as America's largest job-training organization. McDonald's is the world's largest owner of commercial real estate.

The *Fast-Food Guide*, by Jacobson and Fritschner (1986, 1991), details the amount of calories, fat, sodium, sugar, and other "nutrients" in the foods and liquids sold by the 15 largest fast-food chains in the United States. The champion hamburger (as of 1991) is Carl's Double Western bacon cheeseburger, which contains 1,030 calories, 14 teaspoons of fat, and 1,800 mg of sodium. This is truly the coronary artery bypass special. The Burger King chicken sandwich (the bird champ) contains nearly 700 calories, 9 teaspoons of fat, and 1,415 mg of sodium. Carl's Jr. fish sandwich contains 560 calories, 7 teaspoons of fat, and 1,220 mg of sodium. The Dairy Queen Health Blizzard, regular size (champ among shakes and malts), contains 820 calories, 8 teaspoons of fat, 410 mg of sodium, and 14 teaspoons of sugar. A Taco Bell taco salad with shell (the salad champion) contains 905 calories, 14 teaspoons of fat, and 910 g of sodium. These fast foods lead to quick plaques. Other Mexican dishes are no better (Hurley & Schmidt, 1994; Roberts, 1994b). A chile relleno dinner (cheese-stuffed, deep-fried pepper, topped with cheese and red sauce) contains as much saturated fat as 27 slices of bacon and is much fattier than a cup of Häagen-Dazs Exträs Cookie Dynamo ice cream. Two crispy chicken tacos (crisp corn tortillas stuffed with chicken, cheese, lettuce, and tomato) with refried beans and rice amount to 1,042 calories (36% of which come from fat), 42 g of fat (including 13 g of saturated fat), and 2,260 mg of sodium. Unlike Chinese or Italian restaurant food, it is tough to make Mexican dishes less fatty and less salty.

Excessive Body Weight

The tremendous quantity of fat consumed in the United States displays itself by the largeness of people in this society. In 1990, 60% of Americans aged 18 years and over were considered overweight, and 30% were frankly obese (>20% above their ideal body weight). No society has ever been as overweight as the present United States, and the percentage of those overweight continues to increase (Kuczmarski, Flegal, Campbell, & Johnson, 1994). Four national surveys between 1960 and 1991 of 6,000–13,000 U.S. adults showed that 33% were overweight (>120% of desirable weight) during the last survey (1988–1991). Overweightness frequency increased 8% between the 1976–1980 and the 1988–1991 surveys. The mean body weight during this approximate 10-year period increased 8 lb (3.6 kg). For the first time in 15 years, neither losing weight nor stopping smoking was the Number 1 New Year's resolution in 1994. Instead, people were most concerned with managing their personal finances better.

There is no better monitor for fat consumption than body weight. The first road to health is the maintenance of ideal or near ideal body weight. The more we weigh, the sooner we die (Manson, Stampfer, Henneken, & Willett, 1987). Anyone can identify the exception, such as Sir Winston Churchill. Physicians need to set the example here. But losing weight is so difficult. A pound of body fat contains about 3,500 calories. To lose 1 lb (0.454 kg) of fat, 3,500 more calories must be burned than are consumed. One pound can be lost each week by burning 500 more calories each day than are consumed. Since walking or running a mile each consumes about 400 calories, combining exercise with reduced calorie consumption may speed weight reduction.

Calculating Daily Calories and Fat to Maintain Ideal Body Weight

To help maintain or achieve an ideal or near ideal body weight, it is useful to know how many calories are permissible each day (Roberts, 1994c). Most adults in the Western world need from 11 to 18 calories per pound per day to sustain an ideal weight: 11 for the near-sedentary individual (+), 13 for the moderately active (++), 15 for the moderate exerciser or physical laborer (+++), and 18 for the extremely active exerciser or physical worker (++++). Because I am 6-feet tall and like to weigh no more than 170 lb (77.18 kg) and am moderately active (++), I need about 2,300 calories daily: For me, a diet where 30% of the calories are from fat would be 690 calories from fat (2,300 × 0.30); at 20% fat, 460 calories (2,300 × 0.20); and at 10% fat, 230 calories (2,300 × 0.10). Given the new food-labeling regulations, which provide grams of fat on food labels, it is better to calculate the grams of fat rather than the percentage of calories from fat in each of the various percentage-of-calories-from-fat diets. Thus, the maximum grams of fat that I should consume can readily be determined by dividing the number of calories derived from fat by 9 (the number of calories in 1 g of fat), were I to consume a diet consisting of (a) 30% calories from fat (690 ÷ 9 = 75 g), 20% calories from fat (460 ÷ 9 = 50 g), or 10% calories from fat (230 ÷ 9 = 25 g). Total calories is the important factor from the standpoint of body weight, but fat calories or fat grams is the important item from the standpoint of atherosclerotic disease. If everyone consumed no more than 25 g of fat daily, then no one would have atherosclerosis of clinical significance. Unfortunately, few people are pure vegetarians, which is a near requirement for maintaining a 25-g fat intake. At 50 g of fat daily (a little <2 ounces), one's risk of significant atherosclerotic disease is also small. At 75 g it is greater. If the quantity of fat consumed could be closer to 50 g daily, people's arteries would be cleaner and then atherosclerosis and excessive body weight would not be so prevalent. Unfortunately, most American adults consume more than 100 g of fat daily—many over 140 g—and so their body weights increase, and their risk for developing significant atherosclerosis is enormous.

Meat Consumption

If clinically significant atherosclerosis is to be prevented or arrested, then the amount of fat consumed must be diminished. An easy way to decrease fat consumption is to decrease meat consumption. The ideal is a pure vegetarian–fruit diet that provides no more than about 10% of calories from fat. Not many people in the Western world want to become vegetarians, however (either pure ["vegans"] or the ovolacto type), but that should be the goal. For atherosclerotic health to improve, however, people must at least decrease the quantity of meat they consume. With 21 meals a week, people must make more of them meatless. The type of meat consumed also must be altered. Bovine and porcine muscle are the most heavily laden with fat, and therefore their quantity must be decreased the most. In general, the higher the grade of meat, the more fat it contains. Regardless of the grade or cut, the fat of all red meats is predominantly saturated (about 45% of the fat), and only 2% of the fat is polyunsaturated. Ground beef contributes more saturated fat to the average American diet than any other single food. The fat-ladened skin of chickens and turkeys must be avoided. Fish is the preferred meat because it contains relatively little fat and also contains some potentially favorable fatty acids in contrast to those in the meat of cows, pigs, chickens, turkeys, and sheep. Additionally, people need to avoid snacks between meals, because many of them are laden with fat and calories, and desserts, except on special occasions. Snacks just before bedtime are rarely fat- or calorie-friendly.

Characteristics of Carnivores and Herbivores

Humans basically are not carnivores. If several characteristics of carnivores and herbivores are compared, then human beings clearly have more characteristics of herbivores than carnivores. The appendages of carnivores contain claws, whereas herbivores have hands or hoofs. The teeth of carnivores are sharp, but those of herbivores are mainly flat (for grinding). The intestinal tract of carnivores is short, but that of herbivores is long. (The small intestine in humans is 26-ft [7.62 m] long.) Carnivores lap fluids, and herbivores sip them. Carnivores cool their bodies by panting; herbivores, by sweating. Carnivores make their own vitamin C, whereas herbivores obtain their vitamin C from their diet. Most humans believe themselves to be carnivores (because they eat meat), but fundamentally, our characteristics more closely resemble the herbivores. There are probably only three foods intended for Homo sapiens: starches (rice, corn, potatoes, beans, and pasta), vegetables, and fruits.

Human beings who eat exclusively a vegetarian and fruit diet for many decades (assuming that consumption of the fatty acids high in saturated fat, such as coconut oil and palm kernel oil, are avoided) infrequently develop the diseases so commonly observed in human meat eaters (Trowell & Burkitt, 1981). Diseases very uncommon in vegetarians include atherosclerosis; systemic hypertension (at least 60 of the 160 million persons in the United States over 20 years of age have systemic arterial pressures >140/90 mm Hg); cancer of the breast and colon, and possibly cancer of the prostate gland; diabetes mellitus (with onset after age 50 years); obesity; peptic ulcer, appendicitis, diverticulitis, and irritable bowel syndrome; osteoporosis and osteoarthritis; gallstones and kidney stones; and salmonellosis and trichinosis.

Diets and Diseases of Human Stone-Age Ancestors

Most diseases that vegetarians do not get were apparently rare or very uncommon among human Stone Age or Paleolithic ancestors and remain uncommon among the few remaining groups of hunter–gatherers still living on earth. Eaton, Konner, and Shostak (1988a, 1988b) have made some observations about our Stone Age ancestors, some of which I summarize below (see also Roberts, 1988).

Lack of genetic change and enormous environmental change. The gene pool has changed little since anatomically modern humans, or Homo sapiens, became widespread about 35,000 years ago. From a genetic standpoint, current humans are still late Paleolithic preagricultural hunter–gatherers. Our genetic makeup was selected, over geological eras, to ultimately fit the lifestyle of Paleolothic humans. Thus, we have Stone Age bodies in an Atomic Age.

The increasing industrialized affluence of the past 200 years has affected human health both beneficially and adversely. Improved housing, sanitation, and medical care have ameliorated the impact of infection and trauma, which were the chief causes of death from the Paleolithic era until 1900. The result is that average life expectancy is now approximately double what it was for preagricultural humans. Concomitantly, the past century has accelerated the biological estrangement that has increasingly differentiated humans from other mammals for over 2 million years. In today's Western nations, people have little need for exercise, but they consume foods quite different from those available to other mammals and expose themselves to harmful agents such as alcohol and tobacco. Westernized people have crossed an epidemiological boundary and entered a watershed in which disorders such as atherosclerosis, systemic hypertension, obesity, diabetes mellitus, and certain cancers have become common in contrast to their rarity or near nonexistence among remaining preagricultural humans.

The late Paleolithic lifestyle. The period from 35,000 to 20,000 years ago is the last time period during which the collective human gene interacted with bioenvironmental circumstances typical of those for which it had been originally selected. Thus, the diet, exercise patterns, and social adaptions of that time have continuing relevance today.

Nutrition. The dietary requirements of all Stone Age people were met exclusively by uncultivated vegetables and wild game. The amount of protein was great, probably 33% of calories, in comparison with that in the current American diet, which derives 12% of its calories from protein. Because game animals are lean, Paleolithic humans ate much less fat than Americans and Europeans do today. Stone Age people ate more polyunsaturated than saturated fat, although their cholesterol intake equaled or exceeded that now common in industrialized nations. Stone Age people ate much more dietary fiber than do most Americans. They also obtained far more potassium than sodium from their food (as do all other mammals). Finally, because they had no domesticated animals, they had no dairy foods; despite this, their calcium intake far exceeded that consumed today.

Physical exercise. The hunter–gatherer way of life generated high levels of physical and aerobic fitness. Strength and stamina were characteristic of both sexes at all ages. The hunter–gatherers were stronger and more muscular than succeeding agriculturalists.

Alcohol. Alcoholic beverages were infrequently consumed by Stone Age people, and those available—all products of natural fermentation—

were far less potent than present-day distilled liquors. Solitary, addictive drinking apparently did not occur.

Tobacco. Tobacco was practically unavailable until agriculture appeared in the Americas about 5,000 years ago. Pipes and cigars were the only methods used for smoking until about 1850, when cigarettes first appeared. The major impact of tobacco abuse is a postcigarette phenomenon.

Obesity. Stone Age people were lean, and leanness today in the Western world is nearly the exception. Most food today is calorically concentrated in comparison to the wild game and uncultivated fruits and vegetables that constituted the Paleolithic diets. In eating a given volume, enough to create a feeling of fullness, Paleolithic humans consumed fewer calories than those consumed in a similar volume in the Western world today. Most beverages consumed today provide a significant caloric load. Paleolithic humans, in contrast, drank water. Energy expenditure (i.e., calories burned) by modern humans is much less than that of humans in the Stone Age.

Systemic Hypertension

There are still some cultures on earth whose members do not have essential hypertension and the concomitant rise in blood pressure with age. When people living in these remaining preliterate cultures adopt a Western lifestyle, however, either by migration or acculturation, they first develop a tendency for their blood pressure to rise with age and then an increasing tendency to develop systemic hypertension (Eaton et al., 1988a, 1988b). The diets of these normotensive preliterate people are low in sodium, high in potassium, high in calcium, and low (if not completely lacking) in alcohol.

Diabetes Mellitus

Obesity and maturity-onset diabetes are among the first disorders to appear when unacculturated people undergo economic development. The overall prevalence of noninsulin-dependent diabetes among adults in industrialized countries ranges from 3% to 10%, but among unacculturated native populations it is 0%–2%. The most powerful risk factor for diabetes is obesity, and excessive weight gain is virtually absent in unindustrialized societies. Obese people have reduced numbers of cellular insulin receptors, a relative tissue resistance to insulin, and higher blood insulin levels than do lean people. Conversely, high-level physical fitness, characteristic of aboriginal people, is associated with an increased number of insulin receptors and better insulin binding, both of which enhance the body's sensitivity to insulin. Diets containing ample amounts of nonnutrient fiber and complex carbohydrates lower both fasting and postprandial blood glucose levels, and these types of diets are the rule among unindustrialized societies, but are the exception in Western nations.

Thus, the message from Eaton and associates is this: We need to eat and exercise like the Stone Age people. If we do, our health will improve substantially, and our medical bills will decrease substantially.

Effectiveness of Diet in Lowering Total and LDL Cholesterol Levels

The effectiveness of diet in lowering total and LDL cholesterol levels is nearly directly dependent on the percentage of calories from fat in the diet. The average American adult consumes a diet containing nearly 40% of calories from fat, one third of which is of the saturated variety. The most commonly prescribed diet by physicians in the United States is the National Cholesterol Education Program Step 2 Diet, which is a 30%-of-calories-from-fat diet with saturated fat less than 7% and cholesterol less than 200 mg/day (National Cholesterol Education Program Expert Panel, 1993). This diet, however, is relatively ineffective in reducing the total and LDL cholesterol levels. With this diet, which provides a 25% reduction in percentage of calories from fat, the average serum total cholesterol level is reduced by only 5% (e.g., from 240 to 228 mg/dl [6.2 to 5.9 mmol/L], and the average serum LDL cholesterol level also is reduced an average of 5% (e.g., from 160 to 152 mg/dl [4.1 to 3.9 mmol/L]; Hunninghake et al., 1993; Roberts, 1994d). A reduction in the percentage of calories from fat from 40% to 20% (e.g., with the American Heart Association Phase III Diet) decreases the serum total cholesterol by about 20% (e.g., from 240 to 192 mg/dl [6.2 to 5.0 mmol/L] and the LDL cholesterol by about 20% (e.g., 160 to 128 mg/dl [4.1 to 3.3 mmol/L]; Grundy, Nix, Whelan, & Franklin, 1986). Most Americans, however, are not willing to reduce the percentage of calories from fat in their diet to the 20% level. A reduction of the percentage of calories from fat from 40% to 10% can reduce the serum total cholesterol level in people without familial hypercholesterolemia to the 150 mg/dl (3.9 mmol/L) area, a level achieved for practical purposes only by those following a vegetarian–fruit diet, but a level where atherosclerotic plaques do not form and where those that are present shrink in size. Incidentally, the diet of the Japanese historically has included only 10% of calories from fat, and significant atherosclerosis has seldom been observed among the Japanese people (Keys, 1980). Today, the Japanese are consuming a diet averaging about 23% of calories from fat, and the consequence has been a significant increase in the frequency of symptomatic atherosclerosis (Hatano, 1989). Thus, for diets to be very effective in lowering the serum total and LDL cholesterol levels, the percentage of calories from fat must be reduced to 20% and, ideally, to 10%.

If all adults in the United States were to reduce their percentage of calories from fat by 25% (from 40% to 30% of calories from fat), then the frequency of symptomatic and fatal atherosclerosis and the extent of atherosclerosis would decrease in the population as a whole. For an individual, however, the percentage of calories from fat must be reduced to about 20% before the risk of a first or subsequent atherosclerotic event will be substantially reduced. And in individuals who have already had an atherosclerotic event, where the challenge is to decrease the chances of a subsequent atherosclerotic event, a reduction of 50% of the percentage of calories from fat (and also of dietary cholesterol) is necessary to significantly reduce the risk of a further event. For Americans who have consumed approximately 40% of their calories from fat for 40 years to suddenly reduce that percentage by half is a burden that most are not willing to tackle. Thus, lipid-lowering drugs have assumed a major role in lowering cholesterol levels in the United States.

Lipid-Lowering Drugs

For people with familial hypercholesterolemia, diet alone will not be adequate to lower the total and LDL cholesterol levels sufficiently to substantially reduce the risk of having an atherosclerotic event. Furthermore, for people who have had an atherosclerotic event, lipid-lowering drug therapy is recommended unless they are willing to reduce the percentage of calories from fat in their diets to about 10% (Roberts, 1989b). Finally, for people who have very high serum total and LDL cholesterol levels—not produced by an identifiable cause, such as a drug (e.g., diuretic), hepatic disease, renal disease, or hypothyroidism—a lipid-lowering drug may be required if diet therapy is ineffective.

Primary Prevention

Except for the person with familial hypercholesterolemia, the first and ideally the only step required to lower total and LDL cholesterol levels adequately is diet, followed by diet, and then more diet. Each succeeding step of diet means lowering of the quantity of fat and cholesterol consumed further. If the diet alone does not lower the total and LDL cholesterol levels adequately, then the lipid-lowering (altering) drugs are useful.

Secondary Prevention

In my view, people who have had an atherosclerotic event should be on one or more cholesterol-lowering drugs irrespective of their serum or plasma lipid levels, because whatever their levels, people who have had such events have levels that are too high (Roberts, 1989b). This recommendation is not made lightly, because there are about 7 million persons in the United States alone with symptomatic myocardial ischemia, plus many others with limb or cerebral ischemia from atherosclerosis. Nevertheless, there is increasing evidence that lipid-lowering medicines taken after MIs may be even more beneficial than aspirin, beta-blockers, angiotensin converting enzyme inhibitors, and calcium antagonists in preventing subsequent atherosclerotic events (Rossouw, Lewis, & Rifkind, 1990; Scandinavian Simvastatin Survival Study Group, 1994). Furthermore, if lipid-lowering drugs can bring a person's serum total cholesterol level down to the 150–160 mg/dl area and the LDL cholesterol level down below 100 mg/dl, then they can prevent or at least retard atherosclerotic progression and produce some regression. The use of lipid-lowering drugs, of course, does not negate the necessity of adherence to a low-cholesterol, low-fat diet, because each of these interventions appears to work synergistically. Even in patients who refuse to follow the low-cholesterol, low-fat diet, however, the lipid-lowering drugs produce substantial reductions in serum total cholesterol levels (Hunninghake et al., 1993) and decrease the chances of first and subsequent events (see Figure 2).

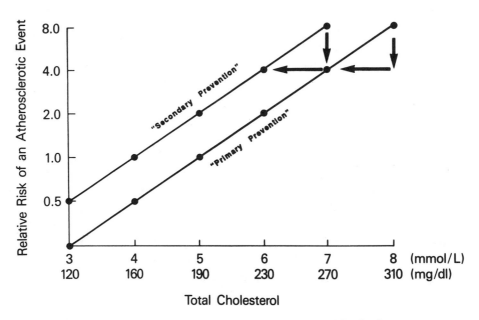

Figure 2. Effects of serum total cholesterol reduction on the risk of a first or subsequent atherosclerotic event. Primary prevention refers to average risk, in that the person has not had an atherosclerotic event. Secondary prevention refers to high risk, for someone who has had an atherosclerotic event. The occurrence of an event shifts the line to the left. Nevertheless, wherever the serum total cholesterol level is, a reduction of that level by approximately 40 mg/dl (or 1 mmol/L) reduces the relative risk of an atherosclerotic event (either a first or subsequent event) by half. Thus, large benefits result from reducing one's serum total cholesterol level.

Types of Lipid-Lowering Drugs

The first-line lipid-lowering drugs, in my view, should be the 3-hydroxy–3-methylglutaryl coenzyme A (HMG-CoA) reductase inhibitors (the statins), for several reasons: They are the best LDL cholesterol lowering drugs, they are the sole lipid-lowering drugs that can be taken only once a day, they are well tolerated, and they have few side effects. Four statin drugs are presently available in the United States; more than 70% of the patients on these drugs are taking only 1 tablet daily, and few patients are taking the maximal recommended doses of these drugs. Equivalent doses of these drugs are as follows: 10 mg of simvastatin = 20 mg lovastatin = 20 mg pravastatin = 40 mg fluvastatin. These drugs not only lower the serum LDL cholesterol and total cholesterol levels but also raise the serum HDL cholesterol level (about 6%) and lower the triglyceride level (about 20%). Side effects of the statins at low doses are extremely uncommon.

The vitamin niacin, when taken in high doses (generally 1.5–3.0 g daily), may be thought of as a poor person's HMG-CoA reductase inhibitor because it too has favorable effects on all four lipoproteins. Niacin is the best HDL cholesterol raiser of the lipid-lowering agents. However, its side effects—flushing, itching, and pounding headaches—limit its use in most patients.

Gemfibrozil, the only fibrate available in the United States, lowers the triglyceride level more effectively than any of the other lipid-lowering drugs, but it has only a modest effect on the LDL cholesterol level and, not infrequently, actually raises rather than lowers the LDL cholesterol level.

Cholestyramine and colestipol, the bile-acid resins, are the safest of the lipid-altering drugs, but these medicines must be taken in large amounts (about 30 gm/day) to have the same effects on LDL cholesterol as do smaller doses of the statin drugs. Furthermore, these drugs raise the triglyceride level, and they have small (4% or lower) effects on HDL cholesterol level. Recently, both cholestyramine and colestipol became available in 1-g-sized tablets. The addition of 4 g of these drugs to the lower-dose statin drugs increases the favorable impact on the serum lipoproteins.

Probucol, an antioxidant, has not been demonstrated to prevent or retard atherosclerosis, and it is rarely used now in the United States. This drug lowers (23% or less) HDL cholesterol level and has no effect on the triglyceride level, and its LDL cholesterol level lowering effect is only modest. Other antioxidants, such as vitamins E, C, and A, have yet to show evidence of either preventing or retarding atherosclerosis.

A major problem with the lipid-lowering drugs is compliance. About 50% of people started on these drugs quit taking them within a year, and this is true whether the drug is one easily tolerated, like the statins, or one with disturbing side effects, such as niacin or the bile-acid resins. Another problem with lipid-lowering drugs is that most of the people needing them are not taking them because they have not been prescribed. Probably no more than 1 million of the 7 million persons with symptomatic myocardial ischemia in the United States, and no more than 1 million of the 40 million persons in the United States with serum total cholesterol levels above 240 mg/dl, are taking one or more lipid-lowering drugs (Pearson, 1989).

Getting Cardiologists Interested in Lipid-Lowering Drugs

Most cardiologists appear to be hesitant in prescribing lipid-lowering drugs to their patients, even for patients who have had one or more atherosclerotic events. Several surveys have shown that cardiologists rank only slightly above general internists, general practitioners, and the general public in considering cholesterol of major importance for the development of atherosclerosis. The reasons why physicians heretofore have been less than enthusiastic about drug reduction of cholesterol are many, and likely include (a) confusion from the older published literature about risks and benefits of drug therapy; (b) the fact that drug therapy is long term and "unexciting," without dramatic witnessed results; and (c) the expense and possible side effects of long-term drug therapy (Roberts, 1993). Nonetheless, recent studies—particularly the stunning results of the Scandinavian Simvastatin Survival Study (1994)—make it clear that the benefits of drug therapy for elevated cholesterol in those who already have clinical coronary heart disease far outweigh the risks.

SUMMARY

The good news about coronary atherosclerosis is that it takes a great deal of plaque before symptoms of myocardial ischemia occur. The bad news is that, despite the need for large quantities of plaque before symptoms occur, nearly half of of the people in the United States develop the necessary quantity. Atherosclerosis is infrequently solely a hereditary condition. Most people get atherosclerosis because they consume too much fat, cholesterol, and calories. The consequence is an elevated (>150 mg/dl) serum total cholesterol level, and the higher the number above 150 mg/dl, the greater the quantity of plaque deposited in the arteries. If the serum total cholesterol level can be prevented from rising above 150 mg/dl, then plaques are not laid down. If elevated levels are lowered to 150 mg/dl, then further plaque does not form, and parts of those present may vanish. A fruit–vegetarian–starch diet is necessary as a rule to achieve the 150 mg/dl level in most adults. Lipid-lowering drugs are required for patients who have familial hypercholesterolemia and for most patients who have experienced atherosclerotic events. The best news about atherosclerosis is that it can be prevented in people who do not have it in hereditary form, and it can be arrested by lowering elevated serum total cholesterol to the 150 mg/dl level.

REFERENCES

American Heart Association. (1995). *Heart and stroke facts: 1995 statistical supplement*. Dallas, TX: Author.

Anitschkow, N. N. (1912). Lesions of organs under lipid infiltration. *Proceedings of the Medical Society of Petersburg, 80,* 1.

Anitschkow, N. N. (1967). A history of experimentation on arterial atherosclerosis in animals. In H. T. Blumenthal (Ed.), *Cowdry's arteriosclerosis: A survey of the problem* (2nd ed., pp. 21–44). Springfield, IL: Charles C Thomas.

Armstrong, M. L., & Megan, M. B. (1972). Lipid depletion in atheromatous coronary arteries in rhesus monkeys after regression diets. *Circulation Research, 30,* 675–680.

Blankenhorn, D. H., Azen, S. P., Kramsch, D. M., Mack, W. J., Cashin-Hemphill, L., Hodis, H. N., DeBoer, L. W. V., Mahrer, P. R., Masteller, M. J., Vailas, L. I., Alaupovic, P., Hirsch, L. J., & the MARS Research Group. (1993). Coronary angiographic changes with lovastatin therapy: The Monitored Atherosclerosis Regression Study (MARS). *Annals of Internal Medicine, 119,* 969–976.

Blankenhorn, D. H., Nessim, S. A., Johnson, R. L., Sanmarco, M. E., Azen, S. P., & Cashin-Hemphill, L. (1987). Beneficial effects of combined colestipol–niacin therapy on coronary atherosclerosis and coronary venous bypass grafts. *Journal of the American Medical Association, 257,* 3233–3240.

Brensike, J. F., Levy, R. I., Kelsey, S. F., Passamani, E. R., Richardson, J. M., Loh, I. K., Stone, N. J., Aldrich, R. F., Battaglini, J. W., Moriarty D. J., Fisher, M. R., Friedman, L., Friedwald, W., Detre, K. M., & Epstein, S. E. (1984). Effects of therapy with cholestyramine on progression of coronary arteriosclerosis: Results of the NHLBI Type II Coronary Intervention Study. *Circulation, 69,* 313–324.

Brown, B. G., Albers, J. J., Fisher, L. D., Schaefer, S. M., Lin, J.-T., Kaplan, C., Zhao, X.-Q., Bisson B. D., Fitzpatrick, V. F., & Dodge, H. T. (1990). Regression of coronary artery disease as a result of intensive lipid-lowering therapy in men with high levels of apolipoprotein B. *New England Journal of Medicine, 323,* 1289–1298.

Brown, B. G., Xue-Qiao, X., Sacco, D. E., & Albers, J. J. (1993). Lipid lowering and plaque regression: New insights into prevention of plaque disruption and clinical events in coronary disease. *Circulation, 87,* 1781–1791.

Brown, M. S., & Goldstein, J. L. (1986). A receptor-mediated pathway for cholesterol homeostasis. *Science, 232*, 34–47.

Brunner, D., Weisbort, J., Meshulam, N., Schwartz, S., Gross, J., Saltz-Rennert, H., Altman, S., & Loebl, K. (1987). Relation of serum total cholesterol and high-density lipoprotein cholesterol percentage to the incidence of definite coronary events: Twenty-year follow-up of the Donolo-Tel Aviv prospective coronary artery disease study. *American Journal of Cardiology, 59*, 1271–1276.

Buchwald, H., Varco, R. L., Matts, J. F., et al. & the POSCH Group. (1990). Effect of partial ileal bypass surgery on mortality and morbidity from coronary heart disease in patients with hypercholesterolemia: Report of the Program on the Surgical Control of the Hyperlipidemias (POSCH). *New England Journal of Medicine, 323*, 946–955.

Cashin-Hemphill, L., Mack, W. J., Pogoda, M. J., Sanmarco, M. E., Azen, S. P., & Blankenhorn, D. H. (1990). Beneficial effects of colestipol–niacin on coronary atherosclerosis. *Journal of the American Medical Association, 264*, 3013–3017.

Castelli, W. P. (1984). The epidemiology of coronary heart disease: The Framingham study. *American Journal of Medicine, 76*, 4–12.

Castelli, W. P., Garrison, R. J., Wilson, P. W. F., Abbott, R. D., Kalousdian, S., & Kannel, W. B. (1986). Incidence of coronary heart disease and lipoprotein cholesterol levels: The Framingham study. *Journal of the American Medical Association, 256*, 2835–2838.

Cowie, C. C., Howard, B. V., & Harris, M. I. (1994). Serum lipoproteins in African Americans and Whites with non-insulin-dependent diabetes in the U.S. population. *Circulation, 90*, 1185–1193.

Crall, F. V., Jr., & Roberts, W. C. (1978). The extramural and intramural coronary arteries in juvenile diabetes mellitus: Analysis of nine necropsy patients aged 19 to 38 years with onset of diabetes before age 15 years. *American Journal of Medicine, 64*, 221–230.

Duffield, R. G. M., Lewis, B., Miller, N. E., Jamieson, C. W., Brunt, J. N. H., & Colchester, A. C. F. (1983). Treatment of hyperlipidaemia retards progression of symptomatic femoral atherosclerosis: A randomized controlled trial. *Lancet, 2*, 639–641.

Eaton, S. B., Konner, M., & Shostak, M. (1988a). *The Paleolithic prescription.* New York: Harper & Row.

Eaton, S. B., Konner, M., & Shostak, M. (1988b). Stone Agers in the fast lane: Chronic degenerative diseases in evolutionary perspective. *American Journal of Medicine, 84*, 739–749.

Expert Panel on Blood Cholesterol Levels in Children and Adolescents. (1991). *Report of the Expert Panel on Blood Cholesterol Levels in Children and Adolescents, National cholesterol education program* (Publication No. 91–2732). Rockville, MD: National Institutes of Health.

Frick, M. H., Elo, O., Haapa, K., Heinonen, O. P., Heinsalmi, P., Helo, P., Huttunen, J. K., Kaitaniemi, P., Koskinen, P., Manninen, V., Maenpaa, H., Malkonen, M., Manttari, M., Norola, S., Pasternack, A., Pikkarainen, J., Romo, M., Sjoblom, T., & Nikkila, E. A. (1987). Helsinki Heart Study: Primary-prevention trial with gemfibrozil in middle-aged men with dyslipidemia: Safety of treatment, changes in risk factors, and incidence of coronary heart disease. *New England Journal of Medicine, 317,* 1237–1245.

Garrison, R. J., & Castelli, W. P. (1985). Weight and 30-year mortality of men in the Framingham study. *Annals of Internal Medicine, 106,* 1006–1009.

Goldstein, J. L., & Brown, M. S. (1987). Regulation of low-density lipoprotein receptors: Implications for pathogenesis and therapy of hypercholesterolemia and atherosclerosis. *Circulation, 76,* 504–507.

Gordon, T., Castelli, W. P., Hjortland, M. C., Kannel, W. B., & Dawber, T. R. (1977). High density lipoprotein as a protective factor against coronary heart disease. *American Journal of Medicine, 62,* 707–714.

Grundy, S. M., Nix, D., Whelan, M. F., & Franklin, L. (1986). Comparison of three cholesterol-lowering diets in normolipidemic men. *Journal of the American Medical Association, 256,* 2351–2355.

Haskell, W. L., Alderman, E. L., Fair, J. M., Maron, D. J., Mackey, S. F., Superko, H. R., Williams, P. T., Johnstone, I. M., Champagne, M. A., Krauss, R. M., & Farquhar, J. W. (1994). Effects of intensive multiple risk factor reduction on coronary atherosclerosis and clinical cardiac events in men and women with coronary artery disease: The Stanford Coronary Risk Intervention Project (SCRIP). *Circulation, 89,* 975–989.

Hatano, S. (1989). Changing CHD mortality and its causes in Japan during 1955–1985. *International Journal of Epidemiology, 18*(Suppl. 1), S149–S158.

Hoeg, J. M., Feuerstein, I. M., & Tucker, E. E. (1994). Detection and quantitation of calcific atherosclerosis by ultrafast computed tomography in children and young adults with homozygous familial hypercholesterolemia. *Arteriosclerosis and Thrombosis, 14,* 1066–1074.

Hunninghake, D. B., Stein, E. A., Dujovne, C. A., Harris, W. S., Feldman, E. B., Miller, V. T., Tolbert, J. A., Laskarzewski, P. M., Quiter, E., Held, J., Taylor, A. M., Hopper, S., Leonard, S. B., & Brewer, B. K. (1993). The efficacy of intensive dietary therapy alone or combined with lovastatin in outpatients with hypercholesterolemia. *New England Journal of Medicine, 328,* 1213–1219.

Hurley, J., & Schmidt, S. (1994, July–August). Mexican food: Oilé. *Nutrition Action Healthletter, 21*(1), 4–7.

Huttunen, J. K., Kaitaniemi, P., Koskinen, P., Manninen, V., Maenpaa, H., Malkonen, M., Norola, S., Pasternack, A., Pikkarainen, J., Roma, M., Sjoblom, T., & Nikkila, E. A. (1987). The Helsinki Heart Study: Basic design and randomization procedure. *European Heart Journal, 8*(Suppl. I), 1–29.

Jacobson, M. F., & Fritschner, S. (1986). *Fast-food guide.* New York: Workman.

Jacobson, M. F., & Fritschner, S. (1991). *The completely revised and updated fast-food guide* (2nd ed.). New York: Workman.

Kane, J. P., Malloy, M. J., Ports, T. A., Phillips, N. R., Diehl, J. C., & Havel, R. J. (1990). Regression of coronary atherosclerosis during treatment of familial hypercholesterolemia with combined drug regimens. *Journal of the American Medical Association, 264,* 3007–3012.

Keys, A. (Ed.). (1970). Coronary heart disease in seven countries. *Circulation, 41*(Suppl. I), 1–211.

Keys, A. (1980). *Seven countries: A multivariate analysis of death and coronary heart disease.* Cambridge, MA: Harvard University Press.

Kragel, A. H., Gertz, S. D., & Roberts, W. C. (1991). Morphologic comparison of frequency and types of acute lesions in the major epicardial coronary arteries in unstable angina pectoris, sudden coronary death and acute myocardial infarction. *Journal of the American College of Cardiology, 18,* 801–808.

Kragel, A. H., Reddy, S. G., Wittes, J. T., & Roberts, W. C. (1989). Morphometric analysis of the composition of atherosclerotic plaques in the four major epicardial coronary arteries in acute myocardial infarction and in sudden coronary death. *Circulation, 80,* 1747–1756.

Kragel, A. H., Reddy, S. G., Wittes, J. T., & Roberts, W. C. (1990). Morphometric analysis of the composition of coronary arterial plaques in isolated unstable angina pectoris with pain at rest. *American Journal of Cardiology, 66,* 562–567.

Kuczmarski, R. J., Flegal, K. M., Campbell, S. M., & Johnson, C. L. (1994). Increasing prevalence of overweight among U.S. adults: The National Health and Nutrition Examination Surveys, 1960–1991. *Journal of the American Medical Association, 272,* 205–211.

Levy, D., Wilson, P. W. F., Anderson, K. M., & Castelli, W. P. (1990). Stratifying the patient at risk from coronary disease: New insights from the Framingham Heart Study. *American Heart Journal, 119,* 712–717.

Levy, R. I., Brensike, J. F., Epstein, S. E., Kelsey, S. F., Passamani, E. R., Richardson, J. M., Loh, I. K., Stone, N. J., Aldrich, R. F., Battaglini, J. W., Moriarty, D. J., Fisher, M. L., Friedman, L., Friedewald, W., & Detre, K. M. (1984). The influence of changes in lipid values induced by cholestyramine and diet on progression of coronary artery disease: Results of the NHLBI Type II Coronary Intervention Study. *Circulation, 69,* 325–336.

Lipid Research Clinics Program. (1979). Design and implementation: Coronary Primary Prevention Trial. *Journal of Chronic Disease, 32,* 609–631.

Lipid Research Clinics Program. (1984a). Lipid Research Clinics Coronary Primary Prevention Trial results: I. Reduction in incidence of coronary heart disease. *Journal of the American Medical Association, 251,* 351–364.

Lipid Research Clinics Program. (1984b). Lipid Research Clinics Coronary Primary Prevention Trial results: II. The relationship of reduction in incidence of coronary heart disease to cholesterol lowering. *Journal of the American Medical Association, 251,* 365–374.

Lipid Research Clinics Program, Epidemiology Committee. (1979). Plasma lipid distributions in selected North American populations: The Lipid Research Clinics Program Prevalence Study. *Circulation, 60,* 427–439.

MAAS Investigators. (1994). Effect of simvastatin on coronary atheroma: The Multicentre Anti-Atheroma Study (MAAS). *Lancet, 344,* 633–638.

Manson, J. E., Stampfer, M. J., Hennekens, C. H., & Willett, W. C. (1987). Body weight and longevity: A reassessment. *Journal of the American Medical Association, 257,* 353–358.

Mautner, S. L., Lin, F., & Roberts, W. C. (1992). Composition of atherosclerotic plaques in the epicardial coronary arteries in juvenile (Type I) diabetes mellitus. *American Journal of Cardiology, 70,* 1264–1268.

McGill, H. C., Jr. (Ed.). (1968). *The geographic pathology of atherosclerosis.* Baltimore: Williams & Wilkins.

National Cholesterol Education Program Expert Panel. (1988). Report of the National Cholesterol Education Program Expert Panel on detection, evaluation, and treatment of high blood cholesterol in adults. *Archives of Internal Medicine, 148,* 36–69.

National Cholesterol Education Program Expert Panel. (1993). Expert Panel on detection, evaluation, and treatment of high blood cholesterol in adults (Adult Treatment Panel II): Summary of the second report of the National Cholesterol Education Program (NCEP). *Journal of the American Medical Association, 269,* 3015–3023.

Ornish, D., Brown, S. E., Scherwitz, L. W., Billings, J. H., Armstrong, W. T., Ports, T. A., McLanahan, S. M., Kirkeeide, R. L., Brand, R. J., & Gould, K. L. (1990). Can lifestyle changes reverse coronary artery disease? The Lifestyle Heart Trial. *Lancet, 336,* 129–133.

Pearson, T. A. (1989). Influences on CHD incidence and case fatality: Medical management of risk factors. *International Journal of Epidemiology, 18*(Suppl 1), S217–S222.

Roberts, W. C. (1984). Reducing the blood cholesterol level reduces the risk of heart attack. *American Journal of Cardiology, 53,* 649.

Roberts, W. C. (1987). Fast foods and quick plaques. *American Journal of Cardiology, 59,* 721–723.

Roberts, W. C. (1988). Stone Agers in the atomic age: Lessons from the Paleolithic life-style for modern man. *American Journal of Cardiology, 61,* 1365–1366.

Roberts, W. C. (1989a). Atherosclerotic risk factors: Are there ten or is there only one? *American Journal of Cardiology, 64,* 552–554.

Roberts, W. C. (1989b). Lipid-lowering therapy after an atherosclerotic event. *American Journal of Cardiology, 64,* 693–695.

Roberts, W. C. (1989c). Qualitative and quantitative comparison of amounts of narrowing by atherosclerotic plaques in the major epicardial coronary arteries at necropsy in sudden coronary death, transmural acute myocardial infarction, transmural healed myocardial infarction, and unstable angina pectoris. *American Journal of Cardiology, 64,* 324–328.

Roberts, W. C. (1990a). The best antiarrhythmic agent will be a lipid-lowering agent. *American Journal of Cardiology, 66,* 1402.

Roberts, W. C. (1990b). We think we are one, we act as if we are one, but we are not one. *American Journal of Cardiology, 66,* 896.

Roberts, W. C. (1992). More on fast foods and quick plaques. *American Journal of Cardiology, 70,* 268–270.

Roberts, W. C. (1993). Getting cardiologists interested in lipids. *American Journal of Cardiology, 72,* 744–745.

Roberts, W. C. (1994a). Calculating the percentage of calories from fat and the grams of fat consumed daily to maintain an ideal body weight. *American Journal of Cardiology, 73,* 719–720.

Roberts, W. C. (1994b). The ineffectiveness of a commonly recommended lipid-lowering diet in significantly lowering the serum total and low-density lipoprotein cholesterol levels. *American Journal of Cardiology, 73,* 623–624.

Roberts, W. C. (1994c). Mexican food: Oilé. *American Journal of Cardiolology, 74,* 974–975.

Roberts, W. C. (1994d). Retail costs of the statin lipid-lowering drugs. *American Journal of Cardiology, 74,* 1181.

Roberts, W. C., Kragel, A. H., Gertz, S. D., & Roberts, C. S. (1994). Coronary arteries in unstable angina pectoris, acute myocardial infarction, and sudden coronary death. *American Heart Journal, 127,* 1588–1593.

Rossouw, J. E., Lewis, B., & Rifkind, B. M. (1990) The value of lowering cholesterol after myocardial infarction. *New England Journal of Medicine, 323,* 1112–1119.

Scandinavian Simvastatin Survival Study Group. (1994). Randomised trial of cholesterol lowering in 4,444 patients with coronary heart disease: The Scandinavian Simvastatin Survival Study (4S). *Lancet, 344,* 1383–1389.

Schuler, G., Hambrecht, R., Schlierf, G., Niebauer, J., Hauer, K., Neumann, J., Hoberg, E., Drinkmann, A., Bacher, F., Grunze, M., & Kubler, W. (1992). Regular physical exercise and low-fat diet: Effects on progression of coronary artery disease. *Circulation, 86,* 1–11.

Sempos, C. T., Cleeman, J. I., Carroll, M. D., Johnson, C. L., Bachorik, P. S., Gordon, D. J., Burt, V. L., Briefel, R. R., Brown, C. D., Lippel, K., & Rifkind, B. M. (1993). Prevalence of high blood cholesterol among U.S. adults: An update based on guidelines from the second report of the National Cholesterol Education Program Adult Treatment Panels. *Journal of the American Medical Association, 269,* 3009–3013.

Shepherd, J., Cobbe, S. M., Ford, I., Isles, C. G., Lorimer, A. R., Macfarlane, P. W., McKillop, J. H., & Packard, C. J., for the West of Scotland Coronary Prevention Study Group (1995). Prevention of coronary heart disease with pravastatin in men with hypercholesterolemia. *New England Journal of Medicine, 333,* 1301–1307.

Small, D. M. (1988). Progression and regression of atheriosclerotic lesions: Insights from lipid physical biochemistry. *Arteriosclerosis, 8,* 103–129.

Stamler, J., Wentworth, D., & Neaton, J. D., for the MRFIT Research Group. (1986). Is relationship between serum cholesterol and risk of premature death from coronary heart disease continuous and graded? Findings in 356,222 primary screenees of the Multiple Risk Factor Intervention Trial (MRFIT). *Journal of the American Medical Association, 256,* 2823–2828.

Trowell, H. C., & Burkitt, D. P. (Eds.). (1981). *Western diseases: Their emergence and prevention.* Cambridge, MA: Harvard University Press.

Waller, B. F., Palumbo, P. J., Lie, J. T., & Roberts, W. C. (1980). Status of the coronary arteries at necropsy in diabetes mellitus with onset after age 30 years: Analysis of 229 diabetic patients with and without clinical evidence of coronary heart disease and comparison to 183 control subjects. *American Journal of Medicine, 69,* 498–506.

Waters, D., Higginson, L., Gladstone, P., Kimball, B., LeMay, M., Boccuzzi, S. J., & Lespérance, J., for the CCAIT Study Group. (1994). Effects of monotherapy with an HMG-CoA reductase inhibitor on the progression of coronary atherosclerosis as assessed by serial quantitative arteriography: The Canadian Coronary Atherosclerosis Intervention Trial. *Circulation, 89,* 959–968.

Watts, G. F., Lewis, B., Brunt, J. N. H., Lewis, E. S., Coltart, D. J., Smith, L. D. R., Mann, J. I., Swan, A. V. (1992). Effects on coronary artery disease of lipid-lowering diet, or diet plus cholestyramine, in the St. Thomas' Atherosclerosis Regression Study (STARS). *Lancet, 339,* 563–569.

Wenger, N. K., & Schlant, R. C. (1990). Prevention of coronary atherosclerosis. In J. W. Hurst, R. C. Schlant, C. E., Rackley, E. H., Sonnenblick, & N. K. Wenger (Eds.), *The heart* (7th ed., pp. 893–923). New York: McGraw-Hill.

6

DIAGNOSIS OF TYPE A BEHAVIOR PATTERN

MEYER FRIEDMAN, NANCY FLEISCHMANN,
and VIRGINIA A. PRICE

In this chapter, we describe in detail the videotaped clinical examination (VCE) that is currently used to diagnose Type A behavior pattern (TABP) in men and women. Included is a new scale for the assessment of insecurity, which is at the heart of this behavior pattern. Prior to describing TABP and the scale, we review the confusion concerning the relationship of Type A behavior (TAB) to coronary heart disease (CHD), which we believe has chiefly resulted from the reliance on questionnaires or stereotyped questions for diagnosis of TABP.

In 1959, Friedman and Rosenman first observed a significantly greater prevalence of clinical CHD in people who exhibited time urgency and free-floating hostility—a disorder they labeled *TABP*. Subsequent studies (Rosenman et al., 1964, 1975) revealed that otherwise healthy people with this disorder later had clinical CHD significantly more frequently than those (Type B) who did not exhibit symptoms and signs of TABP. More recently, an attempt was made to modify the intensity of TAB in two thirds of 1,013 postinfarction patients in the Recurrent Coronary Prevention Project (RCPP), a randomized clinical trial (Friedman et al., 1982, 1986, 1987). The recurrence rate of another myocardial infarction was 44% lower in the treated group than in control participants and was associated with a reduction in TAB. This close relationship between TAB and CHD has been confirmed not only by individual studies conducted by a number of investigators (Caffrey, 1969; Carruthers, 1969; Haynes, Feinleib, & Kannel, 1980; Review Panel on Coronary-Prone Behavior and Coronary Heart Disease, 1981) but also by two meta-analyses (Booth-Kewley & Friedman, 1987; Matthews, 1988) of the Type A literature.

There have, however, also been epidemiological studies in which no correlation was found between TAB and CHD (e.g., Case, Heller, Case, & Moss, 1985; Ragland & Brand, 1988a, 1988b; Ruberman, Weinblatt, Goldberg, & Chaudhary, 1984; Shekelle et al., 1985). In some of the negative epidemiological studies (Case et al., 1985; Ruberman et al., 1984; Shekelle et al., 1985), the investigators apparently were unaware of reports (by Chesney & Black, 1988; Friedman, 1969, 1988; Friedman & Rosenman, 1959; Lacy, Robbins, & Kostis, 1988; Powell, Dennis, & Thoresen, 1988; and Rosenman et al., 1964, 1975) that pointed out that a correct diagnosis of TAB cannot be made unless, as in any other medical disorder, an examination is performed in which both the psychomotor signs are observed and the specific traits or symptoms of the behavior are elicited (e.g., time urgency and free-floating hostility). Unfortunately, these negative studies (Case et al., 1985; Ruberman et al., 1984; Shekelle et al., 1985) depended exclusively on the subjective responses of the participants. Repeatedly, we have observed that because of either lack of awareness or reluctance to admit to impatience or easily aroused hostility, those with TABP often deny having either of these two components and would have been designated Type B *were it not for their exhibiting the psychomotor signs of TABP.*

The lack of awareness of many of the psychomotor signs and more arcane traits and symptoms of TAB may be chiefly responsible for the otherwise unnecessary controversy concerning the relationship between TAB and the pathogenesis of CHD. We enumerate in this chapter the symptoms, traits, and psychomotor signs that we presently look for when diagnosing TAB.

FINDINGS ON THE TIME-URGENCY COMPONENT

Contrary to recent trends in the literature emphasizing the contribution of hostility to coronary-prone behavior, in a recent study, Friedman and Ghandour (1993) found that the symptoms, traits, and psychomotor signs of the time-urgency component of the total VCE proved more efficient than seeking only the free-floating hostility manifestations. It is of interest that the use of an optimal diagnostic cutoff score of the time-urgency component of the VCE was almost as efficient as the total VCE cutoff score in diagnosing both male and female coronary patients with TAB and men who were known to be Type B. However, use of the optimal diagnostic cutoff score of just the free-floating hostility component was found to be a relatively poor diagnostic tool, in that it resulted in the diagnosis that 18 of the 99 coronary patients had Type B behavior (Friedman & Ghandour, 1993). When the psychomotor signs of the free-floating hostility component were disregarded, the diagnostic cutoff score of this component performed even more poorly, yielding a false diagnosis in 44 of 99 patients with CHD (the correct diagnosis was achieved when the total VCE score was used; Friedman & Ghandour, 1993). These findings agree with those of other researchers (Hearn, Murray, & Leupker, 1989; Leon, Finn, Murray, & Bailey, 1988; McCranie, Watkins, Brandsma, & Sisson, 1986) who, using the Cook–Medley questionnaire (also used by Barefoot, Dahlstrom, & Williams, 1983; Shekelle, Gale, Ostfeld, & Oglesby, 1983; and Williams et al., 1980), found no causal relevance of hostility to either the prevalence or the incidence of CHD.

These discordant conclusions by no means rule out the probability that hostility, as Friedman and colleagues have long insisted (Friedman, 1988; Friedman & Rosenman, 1959, 1974), plays a significant role in the enhancement of the course of CHD. What these inconsistencies do demonstrate, however, as suggested by Hearn et al. (1989), is the basic fallibility of attempting to detect the presence of TAB or any other medical disorder without ascertaining the psychomotor signs as well as the symptoms and traits.

What should be emphasized is that when 99 successive postmyocardial infarction patients were subjected to the VCE, all but 2 exhibited TAB (Friedman & Ghandour, 1993). In other words, a person under 60 years of age who suffers an infarction almost always exhibits TAB.

VCE: THE NEW, IMPROVED DIAGNOSTIC TOOL

Friedman and colleagues have attempted to improve the sensitivity, specificity, and efficiency of an examination for the detection of TAB ever since the "structured interview" was first introduced in 1959 (Friedman & Rosenman, 1959). In 1979, these researchers developed the videotaped structured interview (VSI) for diagnostic use in the RCPP (Friedman et al., 1982, 1986). Videotaping was added not to increase the efficiency of the examination but to permit the feasibility of further diagnostic scrutiny and also to obtain a permanent record, thus allowing a means of documenting possible future changes in the intensity of TAB by comparison of initial and later videotaped examinations.

The progressive, increased efficiency in the diagnosis of TAB was accomplished by observing additional psychomotor signs in people who already had been diagnosed as Type A by elicitation of the already known symptoms and traits of TABP.

The examination we describe in this chapter, the VCE, has been renamed because earlier diagnostic procedures (Friedman & Powell, 1984) were neither "structured" nor an "interview," because examiners never confined themselves to a rigidly prescribed set of questions but often varied the questions they asked. More important, with the new VCE, we seek to detect psychomotor signs of TAB as carefully as we initially sought symptoms and traits.

The VCE differs from the previously used VSI in its scoring system and its search for six additional symptoms of TAB (feeling that one is not liked by others, sleeplessness, difficulty with children, intramarital difficulties or competition, and easily provoked irritability) as well as in the deletion of five diagnostic items (substitution of numerals for metaphors, horizontal eyeball movements, rapid eyeball movements, competition with children, and humming). In addition, four new psychomotor signs have been added (eye bulge, inappropriate laughter, teeth grinding, and shoulder tic). These new TAB signs and symptoms have been observed over the past several decades. The complete VCE is outlined in Exhibit 1.

It is also important for accuracy in the diagnosis of TAB that the examiner have sufficient training and intrinsic capabilities (a) to elicit the correct responses to his or her examination of a person and (b) to detect the often subtle psychomotor signs exhibited by the person with TAB (see Figures 1–4). In short, we believe in the veracity of the following statement with which Rosenman et al. concluded their 1964 report:

> Certainly, it cannot be stressed too greatly that the correct classification of a subject depended far more upon the motor and emotional qualities accompanying his responses to specific questions than the actual content of his answers. To minimize or to misunderstand this last differential is to fail in the correct behavior assessment of a subject. (p. 15)

We believe that, if these words had been heeded, much of the present confusion concerning the relationship between TAB and CHD would not have occurred. We also believe that this confusion will disappear when qualified examiners search as diligently for the psychomotor signs of TAB as they have for the symptoms and traits of this behavior pattern. Finally, we feel that a sense of time urgency (or impatience) will be recognized to be equally or even more involved than hostility in the pathogenesis of clinical CHD. After all, historians and philosophers, such as Toynbee (1961) and deToqueville (1904), were as impressed with the increasing sense of time urgency and impatience in human lives as with their increasing hostility.

A few final caveats are in order. VCE scores of 400 to 150 are considered "very severe," those of 149 to 100 are "severe," and those from 99

EXHIBIT 1
The Videotaped Clinical Examination for Type A Behavior

I. Manifestations of the presence of time urgency
  A. Symptoms and traits
    1. Self-awareness of time urgency [20]
    Eliciting query: Do you believe that you are in a hurry to get things done more often than not?
    2. Warning by others to slow down [15]
    Eliciting query: Does your spouse or any close friend ever tell you to slow down, take it easier, or become less tense?
    3. Haste in walking [5], eating [5], and leaving the table [5; possible total of 5–15]
    Eliciting queries:
      ■ Do you walk fast? [5]
      ■ Do you eat fast? [5]
    4. Indulgence in polyphasic activities (doing more than one thing at a time) [possible total of 5–15]
    Eliciting queries:
      ■ Do you like to look at television, read a magazine or newspaper, and eat at the same time? [5]
      ■ Do you like to look at your mail or do other things while listening to someone on the phone? [5]
      ■ Do you regularly think of other matters while listening to your spouse or others? [5]
    5. Intense dislike of waiting in lines [10]
    Eliciting query: Do you very much mind waiting in grocery checkout, bank, or theater lines or waiting to be seated in a restaurant? [An emphatically expressed dislike is considered a scored response.]
    6. Fetishistic punctuality [10]
    Eliciting query: If you make an appointment with someone, say at 4 p.m., will you be there? [A scored response to this query is one of the following statements emphatically expressed: "I'm always on time," "I'll be there on the button or even before 4 p.m.," or "I'll be there and I resent it if the other person keeps me waiting"; the Type B person would calmly respond "usually" or "I'll try to be there."]
    7. Infrequent recall of memories, observation of natural phenomena, or daydreaming [10]
    Eliciting query: Do you find that you have time just to sit and daydream, to meditate or recall old memories, or to carefully scrutinize flowers, trees, birds, or animals? [A scored response is failure of the examinee to do any of these things.]
  B. Psychomotor signs
    Unlike elicitation of symptoms and traits of either time urgency or free-floating hostility, detection of psychomotor signs of Type A behavior may take many hours of training and instruction. Just as it takes many hours of listening to heart murmurs for a medical student to acquire the acoustic skills to differentiate

(continues)

EXHIBIT 1 *(Continued)*

one valvular murmur from another, so it may take a long time for a person to diagnose some of the more subtle psychomotor signs indicating the presence of impatience or hostility.

1. Chronic facial tension [20]

   This sign springs from tautness of the maxillomasseter muscle complex and is often accompanied by moderate contraction of the frontalis muscle; the eyelids are often narrowed.

2. Ticlike elevation of eyebrows [5]

   If present at all, appears 3–10 times during the 15- to 20-minute examination period.

3. Ticlike elevation or retraction of one or both shoulders [5].

   This usually appears with similar frequency as eyebrow elevation.

4. Tense posture—abrupt, rapid, jerky movements [5]

   Three questions are asked by the examiner, after he or she first relates in a tedious, pleonastic manner (e.g., redundant; using more words than necessary) a mundane circumstance, which should enhance the impatience of the person being questioned. Having done this, the examiner then tediously poses the question, but before finishing it he or she begins to stutter. The examiner notes whether the examinee, aware of the context of the question, becomes proleptic. For example: the examiner begins by saying, "most working people usually arise before 8 a.m. during the week." The examiner then purposely becomes pleonastic by adding, "that is, Monday through Friday. Of course, on Saturday and Sunday, they may sleep later." Having said this, the examiner then begins to stumble, saying "uh-uh-uh." The test is positive if the examinee interrupts by answering the question before it has been completely presented. This questioning procedure is performed at three different times during the examination and a different question is used for each presentation. If the examinee interrupts the examiner's questioning two out of three times, then the test is considered a scored response. Examinee sits tensely and/or movements are hurried and abrupt.

5. Rapid speech [10]

   Examinee speaks at 140 or more words per minute, sometimes making comprehension difficult.

6. Hastening speech of others [20]

   Examinee frequently—and unconsciously—utters rapidly "uh huh, uh huh" or "mmh, mmh," to hasten the rate of speech of others.

7. Prolepsis (anticipation and answering of an argument before one's opponent has put it forward) [20]

8. Tongue–teeth clicking [5–20]

   This clicking sound is created by abrupt separation of the front part of the tongue from its prior adhesion to the back

EXHIBIT 1 *(Continued)*

of the upper incisors when the mouth is opened to speak. The tongue pressure against these upper teeth reflexly occurs when the maxillomasseter muscle complex becomes tense. If this latter tension becomes habitual and prolonged, tongue-to-teeth pressure occurs, not infrequently, but permanently causing indentations or extrusions of the tongue. [If just clicking is heard the score is 5, but if there is also tongue disfiguration, then the score is 15.]

9. Audible, forced inspiration of air [10]
   The examinee is observed at times, particularly when speaking rapidly, to suck in a breath of air as he or she continues to speak.

10. Expiratory sighs [5–20]
    Although Type B subjects sometimes emit an expiratory sigh, if an examinee sighs more than once during the examination period, then a score of 5 is given; if more than 5 times, then a score of 20 is given.

11. Excessive facial perspiration [40]
    Chronic extrusion of beads of perspiration from the skin of the forehead and upper lip at normal room temperature, in an otherwise apparently healthy person is not observed frequently; when observed it should be considered an ominous sign of a hyperactive sympathetic nervous system. (Note: Whether this manifestation results from time urgency, free-floating hostility, or both remains to be determined; however, it is not to be confused with the cold facial perspiration that sometimes accompanies angina pectoris.)

12. Frequent eyelid blinking [5]
    A positive response is 25 or more eyeblinks per minute.

II. Manifestations of free-floating hostility
    A. Symptoms or traits
       1. Frequent loss of temper while driving [10]
          Eliciting query: Do you get upset when driving, particularly while commuting? Does your spouse ever tell you to cool or calm down when driving with you? Do you swear at other drivers? [An affirmative response to any of these questions is a scored response.]

       2. Disbelief in altruism [5]
          Eliciting query: Do you believe that most people are basically dishonest and not eager to help others? [An affirmative answer is a scored response.]

       3. Sleeplessness because of anger or frustration [10]
          Eliciting query: Do you often find it difficult to fall asleep or to continue to sleep because you are upset about something a person has done? [A scored response is one in which the examinee relates that this is a common event.]

       4. Chronic difficulty in filial relationships [10]
          Eliciting query: Do you find (or have you found) it difficult to deal with your children? [Almost every parent may en-

(continues)

EXHIBIT 1 *(Continued)*

counter some difficulties in dealing with their children, particularly when the latter are adolescents. Therefore the examiner should not be content with asking a single question but should ask a sufficient number to get a clear idea of the filial relationships. Also, careful note should be made of the possible emergence of psychomotor signs as the examinee responds to this question. For example, if the person's voice becomes strident or his or her face clouds up as he or she discusses this question, then a scored response is indicated regardless of the content of the discussion.]

5. Intramarital tension or competition [15]
   Eliciting query: Do you have any feelings that your spouse is competing against you or is too critical of your faults? [A scored response is made only if the examinee states that he or she has these feelings often or if his or her voice becomes bitter and face perturbed as he or she answers the query.]

6. Teeth grinding (25)
   Eliciting query: Do you grind your teeth? Has your dentist ever told you that you do so?

7. Easily provoked irritability or discomfort on encountering trivial errors of commission or omission by others [15]
   Eliciting query: Can you tell me what things annoy or upset you? [A quick answer by the examinee in which he or she lists, frequently in an unpleasant voice, several or more trivial events (e.g., the driving errors of others, the indifference of store clerks, or the tardiness of the mail) is a scored response.]

B. Psychomotor signs
   Psychomotor signs suggestive of the presence of free-floating hostility, such as those suggestive of time urgency or impatience, must be searched for from the beginning until the very end of the videotaped clinical examination and regardless of what query has been presented to the examinee.

   1. Facial hostility [25]
      The physiognomy indicative of hostility is created by a combination of subtle but definite contractions of the orbital muscles, the muscles surrounding the mouth, and the masseter muscles.

   2. Periorbital pigmentation [25]
      A diffuse and permanent deposit of melanin usually involving the skin of the lower eyelid, although not infrequently, a deposit also occurs in the upper eyelid.

   3. Ticlike retraction of upper (and sometimes lower) eyelid [25]
      A quick, abrupt, partial retraction of the upper eyelid (sometimes accompanied by a similar retraction of the lower eyelid) that briefly exposes the sclera above the iris.

EXHIBIT 1 *(Continued)*

4. Hostile vocal qualities [25]
   A speaking voice that is grating, harsh, irritating, or generally unpleasant or excessively loud warrants a positive
   score.
5. Ticlike bilateral retraction of buccinator and orbicularis oris
   muscles [25]
   Quick, short drawing back of the sides of the mouth,
   sometimes sufficient to expose the teeth.
6. Clenched hand in casual conversation [5]
   This physical sign, although frequently observed in coronary patients, is also occasionally observed in healthy Type
   B subjects.
7. Hostile laugh [10]
   A very loud, explosive, unpleasant, quasi-humorous, jarring outburst of sound.

The total examination score is computed by adding the numbers in brackets that
follow each eliciting query that was positively scored. From "The Medical
Diagnosis of Type A Behavior," by M. Friedman and G. Ghandour, 1993, *American
Heart Journal, 126,* pp. 608–609. Copyright 1993 by Mosby–Year Book. Reprinted
with permission.

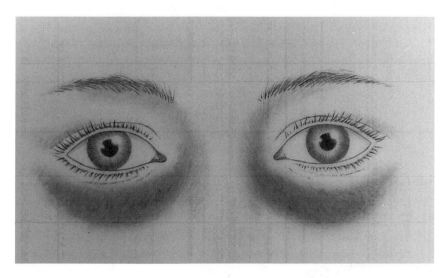

Figure 1. Shading of the lower eyelid depicts bilateral deposition of melaninlike
pigmentation observed in varying degrees of intensity in approximately 27% of people
with Type A behavior. Pigmentation often involves the upper eyelid and may also
involve the upper area of the cheeks. From "The Medical Diagnosis of Type A
Behavior," by M. Friedman and G. Ghandour, 1993, *American Heart Journal, 126,* p.
609. Copyright 1993 by Mosby–Year Book. Reprinted with permission.

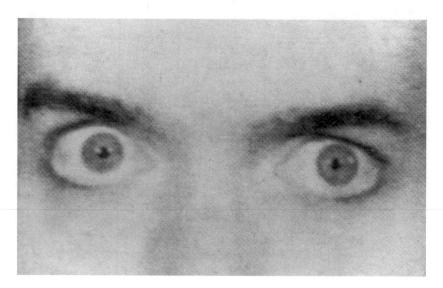

Figure 2. Ticlike exposure of sclera around the iris is caused by retraction of upper and lower eyelids. Most often, only the upper eyelid retracts, exposing the sclera above the upper portion of the iris. From "The Medical Diagnosis of Type A Behavior," by M. Friedman and G. Ghandour, 1993, *American Heart Journal, 126,* p. 609. Copyright 1993 by Mosby–Year Book. Reprinted with permission.

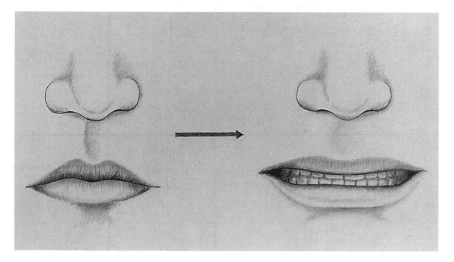

Figure 3. Ticlike retraction of bilateral portions of the lips toward the ears is shown leading to partial opening of the mouth, sometimes sufficient to expose the distal ends of teeth. Sometimes retraction is extensive and may last several seconds. From "The Medical Diagnosis of Type A Behavior," by M. Friedman and G. Ghandour, 1993, *American Heart Journal, 126,* p. 609. Copyright 1993 by Mosby–Year Book. Reprinted with permission.

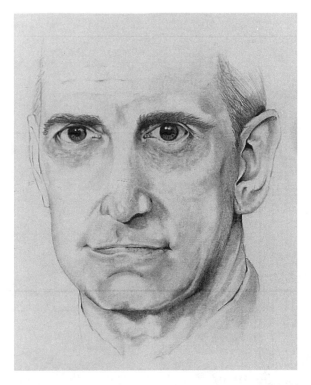

Figure 4. Hostility portrayed in this drawing is created by a combination of subtle but definite contractions of the orbital muscles, the muscles surrounding the mouth, and the masseter muscles. Glaring of eyes is created by retraction of the upper eyelids through the action of the levator palpebrae muscles; this results in exposure of a larger portion of the iris. In addition, the lacrimal segment of the orbicularis oculi muscles appears to raise the medial third of the lower lid slightly, thereby increasing the intensity of stare. The corrugator portion of orbicularis oculi muscles lowers the eyebrows to achieve further accentuation of perceived glare. Combined with bilateral pulling of the risorius muscles, thinning of the vermillion surface of the lips occurs, and a "pseudosmile" appears. Glare of eyes, pseudosmile, and slight bulge of tensed masseter muscles of the jaw create a look of anger under the thin veneer of civility.

From "The Medical Diagnosis of Type A Behavior," by M. Friedman and G. Ghandour, 1993, *American Heart Journal, 126,* p. 613. Copyright 1993 by Mosby–Year Book. Reprinted with permission.

to 0 are "moderate to nil." A VCE score of 45 or above indicates the presence of TAB but not necessarily CHD. However, a low score (i.e., below 45) not only indicates the absence of TAB but also predicts a relative protection against the future premature incidence of CHD. We state this last point because of the rarity, in our clinical experience, of ever finding a low VCE score in a patient who has CHD. It might also be noted that, in our current research—the 10-year prospective Coronary and Cancer Prevention Project (CCPP), a Type A intervention for primary prevention (i.e., in healthy individuals)—we use the VCE as a treatment tool, pointing out Type A symptoms and signs and providing participants with examples of healthy, less stressful behaviors that they may then incorporate into their own lifestyles.

We believe that insecurity is the "nucleus" of the TABP and have recently developed an insecurity scale to assess this crucial parameter (see Exhibit 2; Price, Friedman, Ghandour, & Fleischmann, 1995). This scale has been validated on a group of 204 men and women who are participating in the CCPP in San Francisco, California.

EXHIBIT 2
The Insecurity Scale

1. Do most of the people you know like you quite a bit?
   Yes = 0; *No* = 5
2. Most Type A people say that they did not receive sufficient or unconditional affection from both their parents. Did you?
   Yes = 0; *No* = 15
3. On entering a room filled with your acquaintances or business associates, do you ever feel that too few of them wish to talk with you or sit next to you at a lunch or dinner table?
   Never = 0; *Sometimes* = 5; *Very often* = 15
4. In conversations with three or more other persons, do you feel that they speak to each other more than to you?
   No = 0; *Occasionally* = 5; *Frequently* = 10
5. At your funeral or memorial service, do you believe a large number of persons will attend?
   Yes = 0; *No, I knew so few people* = 3; *No, vague reason* = 5
6. Do you, like most people, have insecurities about your finances, your marriage, or your career?
   Never = 0; *Sometimes* = 5; *Often* = 10; *Constantly, or "too often"* = 20
7. Would you say your inner sense of security is more like a triangle sitting on its apex or more like a triangle sitting on its base?
   Base = 0; *Apex* = 15
8. What qualities of your own do you wish your children will not possess?
   Insecurity or poor self-esteem = 5
9. Do you find it difficult to just sit and daydream or recall memories?
   No = 0; *Yes* = 10
10. William James wrote that if one finds the happiest man, the one most envied by the world, nine times out of ten, in his innermost consciousness is a sense of failure. Is this true in your case?
    No = 0; *Somewhat* = 5; *Frequently* = 15; *Always* = 20

HOW TO ADMINISTER THE VCE

We believe that the best way for psychologists to learn how to administer the VCE is through individualized training. Clinicians should learn to proceed with the examination using a "light hand" and allowing for digressions. It is important for examiners to be nonjudgmental, open to argument, friendly, accepting, and, occasionally, even witty when administering the VCE. Such a posture may seem "unscientific" to some, but this is far from the case. One is much more likely to gain truthful or uncensored responses in a relaxed atmosphere, especially when talking about behavior that is, at some level of consciousness, known to be frowned on or thought of as downright bad for one's health.

This seemingly casual examination produces a valid assessment that is stable over time and has shown very high interrater reliability (Friedman & Powell, 1984). Through many thousands of examinations, Friedman and colleagues have refined the precise definition of Type A indicators, and through many more thousands of hours of treatment of patients with CHD, they have documented the insecurity and lack of self-esteem that they have long believed are initiating causes of the behavior.

It is behavior that is the primary focus of this examination and behavior that is scored. Furthermore, the examinee's self-assessment, as on questionnaires, is not always congruent with his or her behavior. What does it mean, for instance, when a person says, "No, damn it, I never get angry!"? You cannot know unless you see and hear the person. When you can see and hear the person, you can note the anger, or lack of anger, in his or her voice and many other signs giving meaning to this statement. These signs are precisely defined and not subjective at all. Speech characteristics, facial expressions, signs of physical tension, and so on are all vital clues to the patient's status.

Clinicians are highly trained and close observers, but even so, they sometimes take the literal answer and leave it at that. Consider the case of a person queried about a possible anger-producing situation. He or she could have any of the following reactions:

1. Smiles and agrees that such situations are unfortunate.
2. Frowns, but denies any personal irritation. [If the frown is a grimace, it is scored as a psychomotor sign of hostility.]
3. Quickly shifts in seat, and clenches fist [psychomotor signs of time urgency and hostility]; Makes pejorative comments about "such people," but still denies anger.
4. Admits anger and begins to tell of a similar incident in his or her past.

Option 2 would alert an experienced observer to pursue the matter, possibly to a positive response, possibly not. Option 3 would receive a positive score by an experienced rater but might be missed by the novice because of the denial. Option 4 would be positively scored by any observer, but it might have been denied on a self-questionnaire (e.g., "I only get angry sometimes", or "My anger is justified and therefore is not real anger").

The above illustration deals with hostility because it is much easier to describe. Ironically, time urgency is so pervasive in U.S. society that almost no one can recognize it. And because so many people behave in a time-urgent fashion, it is often considered normal even when recognized. In our opinion, one source of hostility is the accumulation of years, sometimes decades, of frustrated time urgency. Thus, hostility is the endpoint in the worsening of TAB, not the cause. Furthermore, according to the data (Friedman & Ghandour, 1993), hostility by itself will not predict coronary morbidity or mortality nearly as well as time urgency does.

When rationalizations for time urgency are offered, they may often be deemed reasonable by both the subject and an untrained observer. What does it mean when you think of other things when your spouse is talking to you? Easy rationalizations are "She repeats herself," or "He never gets to the point." What about when your children are talking to you? Harder (but still possible) rationalizations may arise ("I must get my briefcase from the office"). What does it mean when you leave your first choice of restaurant because of a long wait and go to a second, or third choice? One common rationalization is "they only want you to spend money at the bar." Is the frustration of waiting more important than your aesthetic choices? What does it mean when you swear at traffic delays? You may think "My taxes paid for this —— road!" What does it mean when you cease to explore the world around you? Perhaps you rationalize thus: "We don't travel much. I need to be handy for emergencies at the office." What does it mean when you never reflect on even today's events, much less the course of your life? You are perennially focused on getting somewhere, almost certainly with no clear idea where that place is. You are time urgent without a target that is clearly defined, except that of doing more and more and having less and less time to do it in.

Rapid speech, anticipating questions, hastening the speech of the interviewer, and abrupt movements are specific identifying characteristics of people who want to get out of the present moment and into the next.

We do not believe that it is possible for an examiner to use the VCE method of assessing TAB without personal instruction; few medical diagnoses of even the most basic sort can adequately be taught by written word alone. Thus, we strongly urge anyone who hopes to use the VCE in diagnosing TAB to visit a psychologist who is presently using this procedure. The physical signs of TAB must be seen to be properly evaluated (see Figures 1–4). We present the VCE here so that clinicians and researchers can gain some familiarity with the correct diagnosis of TAB.

SUMMARY

We have described the ideology behind the revision of a method of examining people for TABP. It is our hope that the extensive use of the VCE will do away with the unnecessary confusion concerning the relationship of TAB to CHD. Once a clinician learns how to diagnose the presence of TAB, he or she will find almost without exception that a patient (under 60 years of age) who suffers from CHD also exhibits TAB. Conversely, any person who exhibits Type B behavior is relatively immune to clinical CHD before the age of 60.

REFERENCES

Barefoot, J. C., Dahlstrom, W. G., & Williams, R. B. (1983). Hostility, CHD incidence and total mortality: A 25-year follow-up study of 255 physicians. *Psychosomatic Medicine, 45,* 59–63.

Booth-Kewley, S., & Friedman, H. S. (1987). Psychological predictors of heart disease: A quantitative review. *Psychological Bulletin, 101,* 340–362.

Caffrey, C. B. (1969). Behavior patterns and personality characteristics related to prevalence rates of coronary heart disease in American monks. *Journal of Chronic Disease, 22,* 93–99.

Carruthers, M. E. (1969). Aggression and atheroma. *Lancet, 2,* 1170–1171.

Case, R. B., Heller, S. S., Case, N. B., & Moss, A. J. (1985). Type A behavior and survival after acute myocardial infarction. *New England Journal of Medicine, 313,* 737–741.

Chesney, M. A., & Black, G. W. (1988). Type A behavior and mortality from coronary heart disease [Letter]. *New England Journal of Medicine, 319,* 116–117.

deToqueville, A. (1904). *Democracy in America.* New York: Appleton-Century-Crofts.

Friedman, M. (1969). *The pathogenesis of coronary artery disease.* New York: McGraw-Hill.

Friedman, M. (1988). Type A behavior: A frequently misdiagnosed and rarely treated disorder. *American Heart Journal, 115,* 930–936.

Friedman, M., & Ghandour, G. (1993). Medical diagnosis of Type A behavior. *American Heart Journal, 126,* 607–618.

Friedman, M., & Powell, L. (1984, July). The diagnosis and quantitative assessment of Type A behavior: Introduction and description of the videotaped structured interview. *Integrative Psychiatry,* 123–129.

Friedman, M., Powell, L., Thoresen, C. E., Ulmer, D., Price, V. A., Gill, J. J., Thompson, L., Rabin, D. D., Brown, B., Breall, W. S., Levy, R. A., & Bourg,

E. (1987). Effect of discontinuance of Type A behavioral counseling on Type A behavior and cardiac recurrence rate of post-myocardial infarction patients. *American Heart Journal, 114*, 483–490.

Friedman, M., & Rosenman, R. H. (1959). Association of specific behavior pattern with blood and cardiovascular findings. *Journal of the American Medical Association, 169*, 1286–1296.

Friedman, M., & Rosenman, R. H. (1974). *Type A behavior and your heart.* New York: Knopf.

Friedman, M., Thoresen, C. E., Gill, J. J., Ulmer, D., Powell, L. H., Price, V. A., Brown, B., Thompson, L., Rabin, D. D., Breall, W. S., Bourg, E., Levy, R., & Dixon, T. (1986). Alteration of Type A behavior and its effect on cardiac recurrences in post-myocardial infarction patients: Summary results of the Recurrent Coronary Prevention Project. *American Heart Journal, 112*, 653–665.

Friedman, M., Thoresen, C. E., Gill, J. J., Ulmer, D., Thompson, L., Powell, L., Price, V., Elek, S. R., Rabin, D. D., Breall, W. S., Piaget, G., Dixon, T., Bourg, E., Levy, R. A., & Tasto, D. L. (1982). Feasibility of altering Type A behavior pattern after myocardial infarction. Recurrent Coronary Prevention Project study: Methods, baseline results and preliminary findings. *Circulation, 66*, 83–92.

Haynes, S. G., Feinleib, M., & Kannel, W. B. (1980). The relationship of psychosocial factors to coronary heart disease in the Framingham study, III. Eight-year incidence of coronary heart disease. *American Journal of Epidemioliogy, 111*, 37–58.

Hearn, M. D., Murray, D. M., & Leupker, R. V. (1989). Hostility, coronary heart disease, and total mortality: A 33-year follow-up study of university students. *Journal of Behavioral Medicine, 12*, 105–121.

Lacy, C. R., Robbins, M. L., & Kostis, J. B. (1988). Type A behavior and mortality from coronary heart disease [Letter]. *New England Journal of Medicine, 319*, 114–115.

Leon, G. R., Finn, S. E., Murray, I., & Bailey, J. M. (1988). The inability to predict cardiovascular disease from hostility scores of MMPI items related to Type A behavior. *Journal of Consulting and Clinical Psychology, 56*, 567–600.

Matthews, K. A. (1988). Coronary heart disease and Type A behavior: Update on and alternatives to the Booth-Kewley and Friedman quantitative review. *Psychological Bulletin, 104*, 373–380.

McCranie, E. W., Watkins, L., Brandsma, J., & Sisson, B. (1986). Hostility, coronary heart disease (CHD) incidence and total mortality: Lack of association in a 25-year follow-up study of 478 physicians. *Journal of Behavioral Medicine, 9*, 119–125.

Powell, L. H., Dennis, C. A., & Thoresen, C. E. (1988). Type A behavior and mortality from coronary heart disease [Letter]. *New England Journal of Medicine, 319*, 114–115.

Price, V. A., Friedman, M., Ghandour, G., & Fleischmann, N. (1995). Relation between insecurity and Type A behavior. *American Heart Journal, 129*, 488–491.

Ragland, D. R., & Brand, R. J. (1988a). Coronary heart disease mortality in the Western Collaborative Group Study. *American Journal of Epidemiology, 127*, 462–475.

Ragland, D. R., & Brand, R. J. (1988b). Type A behavior and mortality from coronary heart disease. *New England Journal of Medicine, 318*, 65–69.

Review Panel on Coronary-Prone Behavior and Coronary Heart Disease. (1981). Review Panel on Coronary-Prone Behavior and Coronary Heart Disease: A critical review. *Circulation, 63*, 1199–1215.

Rosenman, R. H., Brand, R. J., Jenkins, C. D., Friedman, M., Straus, R., & Wurm, M. (1975). Coronary heart disease in the Western Collaborative Group Study: Final follow-up experience of 8 1/2 years. *Journal of the American Medical Association, 23*, 872–877.

Rosenman, R. H., Friedman, M., Strauss, R., Wurm, M., Kositcheck, R., Hahn, W., & Werthessen, N. T. (1964). A predictive study of coronary heart disease. *Journal of the American Medical Association, 189*, 15–22.

Ruberman, W., Weinblatt, E., Goldberg, J. D., & Chaudhary, B. S. (1984). Psychosocial influences on mortality after myocardial infarction. *New England Journal of Medicine, 311*, 552–559.

Shekelle, R. B., Gale, M., Ostfeld, A. M., & Oglesby, P. (1983). Hostility, risk of coronary disease, and mortality. *Psychosomatic Medicine, 45*, 219–228.

Shekelle, R. B., Hulley, S. B., Neaton, J. D., Billings, J. H., Borhani, N. O., Gerace, T. A., Jacobs, D. R., Lasser, N. L., Millemark, M. B., & Stamler, J. (1985). The MRFIT behavior pattern study, II. Type A behavior and incidence of coronary heart disease. *American Journal of Epidemiology, 122*, 559–570.

Toynbee, A. (1961). *A study of history* (Vol. 12). London: Oxford University Press.

Williams, R. B., Haney, T. L., Lee, K. L., Kong, Y., Blumenthal, J. A., & Whalen, R. E. (1980). Type A behavior, hostility and coronary atherosclerosis. *Psychosomatic Medicine, 42*, 539–549.

7

THE CARDIAC PSYCHOLOGY OF WOMEN AND CORONARY HEART DISEASE

SUE C. JACOBS and JANE B. SHERWOOD

In this chapter, we address the psychology of women and coronary heart disease (CHD). We start with three assumptions common to cardiac psychology: (a) Women's minds, emotions, and the entirety of their psychosocial experience affect the health of their hearts; (b) the health of women's hearts and cardiovascular systems affects their minds, emotions, and mental health; and (c) these mind–body or mind–heart interactions will be in operation throughout the course of CHD. These assumptions also hold for men. Because there are known gender differences throughout the course of CHD, we make two additional assumptions: There are gender differences in the CHD mind–body link, and an awareness of these differences is important to both the women with CHD and their health service providers.

There is not a great deal of literature on the relationship between women and mind–body factors in CHD, because most research has been done with men. What literature there is, however, suggests that the interrelationships between gender differences in CHD and a variety of psychological factors are complex. There are many ways to conceptualize the relationships between gender, CHD, and psychological factors. One could consider either psychological factors or CHD the endpoints. If one considers CHD the endpoint, as we do here, then one could look at the effect of gender on the relationship between CHD and psychological variables.

We have decided to focus, however, on how psychological factors may potentially mediate gender differences in CHD. We do this both because the relationship between gender and CHD is better established than that between any psychological variable and CHD and because we are more interested in the impact of the mind on the body than vice versa. Moreover, we think that this perspective will be most useful to the health provider working with women who have or are at high risk for CHD.

There are three basic aims in this chapter. The first is to sketch out some of what is known about CHD in women and known differences with men. The second is to look at known or potential gender differences in risk factors, triggers, treatment, and prognosis over the course of CHD. The third aim is to raise questions about current assumptions and research directions in cardiac psychology, which have come primarily from studies with men, and to encourage caution when applying these assumptions to women.

CHD IS NOT JUST A MAN'S DISEASE

Cardiovascular disease, of which CHD is one type, is the leading cause of death for women in the United States, accounting for half of all deaths of women age 50 and over (American Heart Association, 1995). CHD kills more women than cancer, AIDs, osteoporosis, and domestic violence combined (American Medical Women's Association, 1995). From 1988 to 1990, women had more visits to physicians, nearly as many hospitalizations, and more deaths than men because of cardiovascular disease (Higgins & Thom, 1993). Twenty-four percent of all women's deaths from cardiovascular disease are attributable to CHD (Higgins & Thom, 1993).

For years, there was a misconception that heart disease, especially CHD, was a middle-aged man's disease. This belief had been around at least since William Heberden characterized CHD as a problem afflicting men in his 1768 *Communication on the History and Care of Diseases* (cited in Wenger, 1993). Such misperception is partially attributable to the fact that myocardial infarction (MI) and CHD occur, present more severely, and result in death at an earlier age for men than women. Women's onset of CHD is about 10 years later than men's (American Heart Association, 1995).

Fortunately, public and practitioner awareness of women and cardiovascular disease has slowly increased. This is due in large part to an American Heart Association (1989) educational campaign on women and heart disease. However, there is still much less known about CHD in women than in men. Women have been excluded from many clinical trials and other research on CHD in the past. This deficit is now being addressed by the National Heart, Lung, and Blood Institute (NHLBI), as evidenced by the 1992 research conference "Cardiovascular Health and Disease in Women" (Wenger, Speroff, & Packard, 1993).

Even less is known about the psychology of women and CHD. This was highlighted in a conference convened by the NHLBI in 1991, titled "Women, Behavior, and Cardiovascular Disease" (Czajkowski, Hill, & Clarkson, 1994). Again, many—perhaps most—studies in cardiac psychology have excluded women. In studies that have included women, sample sizes have often been too small to detect gender differences (Frasure-Smith, Lespérance, & Talajic, 1995; Mittleman et al., 1995). The limited research that has focused on the psychology of women and CHD or on gender differences in psychological factors and CHD is also questionable because it has been based on assumptions derived from research with men (Chesney, 1993; Eaker, 1989; Rodin & Ickovics, 1990) or has been based on small samples (Powell et al., 1993).

GENDER DIFFERENCES IN CHD

The prevalence of CHD in the United States is high for both men and women, although it has been decreasing in recent times. However, independent of gender differences in risk factors, men die younger and at a faster rate than women. In 1992, about one in four Americans (58,920,000) had one or more forms of cardiovascular disease (including CHD, stroke, high blood pressure, and rheumatic heart disease); 11,200,00 had CHD (American Heart Association, 1995). Final mortality rates for 1991 indicated that there were 479,358 women's deaths from cardiovascular disease and 446,702 men's deaths (American Heart Association, 1995). There were 2.5 million hospitalizations and 32 million physicians' office visits related to cardiovascular disease for women and 2.7 million hospitalizations and 25 million office visits for men (Higgins & Thom, 1993). Although heart disease, particularly CHD, is the leading cause of death for women in the United States, at age 55 and under men have MIs or die from CHD from 2 to 3 times more often than do women. This gender difference decreases with increasing age, with more deaths from cardiovascular disease among elderly women than elderly men. The following known gender differences in CHD were summarized at the 1992 NHLBI-sponsored conference "Cardiovascular Health and Disease in Women" (Wenger et al., 1993):

1. The prognosis for women with MI is worse than for men (women die at earlier ages).
2. With both conventional medical and surgical therapies, the prognosis for CHD is worse for women than men.

3. Women have an excess of silent myocardial ischemia and unrecognized MI; however, data on the frequency and consequences of these are lacking.
4. Women undergo fewer invasive procedures than men, although it is uncertain whether this means that women are undertreated or men are overtreated.
5. There are few data on efficacy for women or gender differences for medications or revascularization for CHD; however, women gain the same survival benefits as men following MI from thrombolytic therapy, although they bleed more and receive as much protection as men against reinfarction after MI with aspirin and beta-blocking drugs.
6. Gender differences, if any, in long-term management programs for secondary prevention of CHD are unknown because women have largely been underrepresented in past clinical trials.
7. Fewer women than men participate in cardiac rehabilitation programs, and women drop out more often than men (because of comorbidities, family responsibilities, and possibly other psychosocial factors), although benefits appear to be equal for men and women.

In a book chapter on anger, hostility, gender, and CHD, Stoney and Engebretson (1994) listed four major hypotheses used by others to explain gender differences in CHD mortality rates: Men may be less biologically fit than women; men may engage in more health-damaging roles and behaviors than women; estrogen and other reproductive hormones have a protective effect in women; and men may exhibit greater physiological and cardiovascular reactivity to stress than women, resulting in more CHD if such reactivity is, in fact, related to the disease process. None of these explanations has been adequately tested and none alone is adequate to account for observed gender differences, yet all are worth considering.

Etiology and Risk Factors for CHD

Factors that increase the risk of CHD for women are similar to those for men. Between the ages of 20 and 74, 29% of women (26% of men) have high serum cholesterol, 36% (45% of men) have hypertension, 23% (28% of men) smoke cigarettes, and 33.5% (32% of men) are overweight (National Center for Health Statistics, 1990, as cited in Higgins & Thom, 1993). Risk ratios calculated for 55-year-old men and women in the Framingham Heart Study, where the average risk was equal to 100, were as follows: 83 for women with no major risk factors (68 for men), 113 for women who smoke cigarettes (98 for men), 175 for women who both have elevated blood cholesterol and smoke cigarettes (136 for men), and 288 for women who have high blood pressure, have elevated blood cholesterol, and smoke cigarettes (200 for men; American Heart Association, 1995).

Of the risk factors for CHD, hypertension (Frohlich, 1993; Krieger, 1994), cigarette smoking (Gritz, 1994; Ockene, 1993; Rosenberg, 1993), and high cholesterol predict CHD for women as well as men, whereas diabetes (7% of women vs. 6% of men), triglyceride levels, and high-density lipoprotein levels are more predictive of risk for women (Higgins & Thom, 1993). High-density lipoprotein cholesterol—a major protective rather than risk factor—is considerably higher in women, at least before menopause, than in men. And postmenopausal women more often have higher serum cholesterol levels than men (Krauss, 1993). Also, in post-menopausal women, the use of estrogen has been associated with both lower morbidity and mortality from CHD (LaRosa, 1993; Ravnikar, 1993; Speroff, 1993; Stampfer et al., 1991; Sullivan, 1993).

Minority, less well-educated, and less affluent women and men are disproportionately affected by CHD risk factors (Krieger, 1994). Hypertension is especially a problem for Black women, and obesity is a problem for Black, Hispanic, and Native American women (Jeffery, 1994; Stefanick, 1993; Wing, 1993). Major weight gain has been found to be twice as high for women as men, with Black women more likely to become overweight than White women (Stefanick, 1993). Increasing this risk even more is physical inactivity (King, 1994; Stefanick, 1993), especially among those who are less well educated and who have lower family incomes.

It is important to note that there is less direct evidence that reducing risk factors will result in reduced CHD risk for women. Women have not been included in some of the large clinical trials designed to assess the effects of reducing risk factors by medical or behavioral interventions. Nonetheless, there is some evidence supporting the efficacy of behavioral interventions with women in reducing such risk factors as cigarette smoking (Gritz, 1994; Ockene, 1993; Rosenberg, 1993), obesity (Jeffery, 1994; Stefanick, 1993; Wing, 1993), or lack of exercise (King, 1994).

Risk of CHD Among Women in the Framingham Heart Study

A 20-year follow-up of 749 women in the Framingham Heart Study (Eaker, Pinsky, & Castelli, 1992) found the following to be predictors of MI or CHD death after age, cigarette smoking, systolic blood pressure, diabetes, cholesterol, and body mass index were controlled for ($ps < .05$ for all variables): overall predictors were low educational level, tension, and lack of vacations; among employed women an additional predictor was perceived low financial status; and among homemakers predictors were loneliness during the day, difficulty falling asleep, housework affecting health, and the belief that one is prone to heart disease. In a classic review of prospective studies of CHD from Framingham that included women, Eaker (1989) noted that lower socioeconomic status was related to CHD in women across ages and in different populations.

Relationship of Social Support and Social Isolation to CHD Risk

Other sociocultural factors found to affect the long-term mortality risk of CHD in men and women include the availability of social support and social networks (Berkman, 1994; Berkman, Vaccarino, & Seeman, 1993). Berkman et al. (1993) found that social networks or ties are related to CHD mortality; however, social networks and social support do not appear to account for gender differences in CHD risk, at least not on the basis of data presently available. They suggested that social isolation and lack of emotional support are important to both men and women. Another study even suggested that the loss of emotional support can precede death from CHD. Cottington, Matthews, Talbott, and Kuller (1980) found that, in comparison with matched control participants, 81 women ages 25 to 64 who died suddenly from atherosclerotic heart disease were 6 times as likely to have experienced the death of a significant other within the previous month.

Job Strain and Multiple Roles of Women

Job strain has been considered a risk factor for CHD; however, women have been excluded from most studies where this factor has been investigated (Eaker, 1989). In evaluating the risk not only for CHD but for overall cardiovascular disease in 13,779 Swedish male and female workers, Hall (1994) found the highest prevalence of cardiovascular disease among blue-collar men who had high job demands, low social support, and low work control (prevalence ratio = 7.22; 95% confidence interval [CI]); the highest prevalence of cardiovascular disease for women was among white-collar women with high job demands and low social support (prevalence ratio = 2.06; 95% CI).

The multiple roles of caring for a family and working outside the home have been considered as explanations for gender differences in CHD risk. Theorell (1991), for example, hypothesized that an increased risk among women was due to their double roles (at home and paid work). Dixon, Dixon, and Spinner (1991) found in a study of 202 professional women that what differentiated between women with and without cardiovascular disease ($p < .01$) was the tension between career world (career sacrifices) and interpersonal commitments to spouses, children, and friends (interpersonal sacrifices).

Hostility, Anger, and Type A Behavior in CHD Etiology

The relationship between hostility and the incidence of CHD has been reviewed (Friedman, 1992; Helmers, Posluszny, and Krantz, 1994;

Smith, 1992) and is discussed at length in chapter 3 of this book. A link between chronic hostility and CHD has been shown for men (Dembroski, MacDougall, Costa, & Grandits, 1989; Hecker, Chesney, Black, & Frautschi, 1988) and suggested for women in a study by Barefoot, Haney, Hershkowitz, & Williams (1991). Type A behavior was found to be an independent predictor of angina pectoris, but not of MI or fatal coronary events, in both men and women in the 20-year Framingham Heart Study follow-up report (Eaker, Abbott, & Kannel, 1989). In the Population Study of Women, 795 middle-age urban women living in Göteborg, Sweden, were followed for 12 years; Type-A-related measures derived from the Eysenck Personality Inventory and Cesarec–Marke Personality Schedule predicted neither angina pectoris nor MI. However, low ratings of aggression predicted electrocardiographic changes consistent with ischemic heart disease (Hällström, Lapidus, Bengtsson, & Edström, 1986).

A number of studies have also found that self-reported hostility at a younger age predicted both CHD and all-cause mortality in men (Barefoot, Dahlstrom, & Williams, 1983; Barefoot, Dodge, Peterson, Dahlstrom, & Williams, 1989; Koskenvuo et al., 1988; Shekelle, Gale, Ostfeld, & Paul, 1983). We know of no longitudinal studies begun long enough ago to see whether hostility at younger ages predicts CHD in women. However, Adams (1994) has been studying students who attended the Mills College for Women. She has reported that hostility at ages 24, 27, 43, and 52 was negatively correlated with general health at age 52 for 105 women. When possible mediator variables at age 43 were controlled for (i.e., cigarette smoking, excessive alcohol intake, body mass index, negative life events, and social role satisfactions), hostility at each age remained a significant predictor of health at age 52. We would not yet expect to find a significant incidence of CHD in this young cohort since CHD does not present until about age 65 for most women, 10 years later than for men (American Heart Association, 1995).

The cardiac psychology literature has suggested that hostility and anger may contribute to the development of CHD because of exaggerated cardiovascular and hemostatic reactivity in response to behavioral stressors by people who are chronically hostile (Blascovich & Katkin, 1993). Most reactivity studies have been with men, but studies with women have also supported the hypothesis that hostile people exhibit excessive cardiovascular reactivity to stress that evokes anger-related emotional states (Suarez, Harlan, Peoples, & Williams, 1993). A number of studies have documented complex differences in physiological and cardiovascular reactivity to different kinds of stressors in men and women. For example, men have shown greater elevations than women in blood pressure, plasma norepinephrine, and low-density lipoprotein cholesterol in response to laboratory stress (Stoney, Matthews, McDonald, & Johnson, 1988). Allen, Stoney, Owens, and Matthews (1993) found men to be "vascular" reactors—to respond with greater total peripheral resistance and systolic and diastolic blood pressure—in comparison with women on a number of stressful laboratory tasks. By contrast, they found women to be "cardiac" reactors, responding with larger increases in heart rate than men to stressful tasks. Although attitudinal hostility, measured by the Cook–Medley Hostility Scale and other personality measures, showed gender differences, these measures did not contribute to the gender differences in cardiovascular response to stress.

Several recent reviews (e.g., Stoney & Engebretson, 1994; Thoresen & Low, 1990; Weidner, 1994) have summarized findings related to hostility, anger, or Type A behavior and women's risk of CHD. In general, the role of behavior reflecting hostility or anger constructs for women's development of CHD remains unclear; however, it apparently operates in a different way for men than for women and differently for women in different situations. Stoney and Engebretson (1994) have provided a summary of tentative gender differences in anger and hostility. Their review suggested that: (a) there are no gender differences in the emotional experience of anger and hostility, as measured by either self-report or other-rater behavioral observation; (b) males have higher levels of attitudinal hostility in comparison with females, based on such measures as the Cook–Medley Hostility Scale; and (c) there are gender differences in anger expression—with males inhibiting and females expressing feelings of anger—and in aggression, with males more physically aggressive than females.

Relationship of Depression to CHD Risk

Although much research in cardiac psychology has focused on the role of hostility and Type A behavior in the etiology of CHD, there is evidence that depression may play a role as well (Booth-Kewley & Friedman, 1987; Carney, Freedland, Smith, Rich, & Jaffe, 1994). This may be especially true for women, who are twice as likely to be depressed as men and who manifest a comorbidity between depression and cardiovascular disease (Dimsdale, 1993). Evidence from a community-based study of women in Göteborg, Sweden, supports this hypothesis. Depressed women were found to be 5 times more likely to develop angina over a 12-year interval than nondepressed women (Hällström et al., 1986).

Vital Exhaustion and CHD

Another link between psychosocial factors and CHD risk for women has been suggested by Dutch research on "vital exhaustion." *Vital exhaustion,* according to Appels and Mulder (1989), is a debilitated emotional and physical state characterized by fatigue, increased irritability, and feelings of demoralization. It is measured by the Maastricht Questionnaire (MQ), a 21-item self-administered checklist (Appels, Höppener, & Mulder,

1987; see also p. 94, this volume). In a prospective study of 3,877 male city employees in Rotterdam, the MQ demonstrated an age-adjusted relative risk (RR) of 2.28 for MI over 4.2 years (Appels & Mulder, 1989). In another study (Appels, Falger, & Schouten, 1993), a retrospective form of the MQ was administered to 79 women hospitalized with first MI and, for comparison purposes, 90 women hospitalized in the departments of general and orthopedic surgery at a hospital in The Netherlands. After age, smoking, coffee consumption, diabetes, hypertension, nonanginal pain, and menopausal status were controlled for, the relative risk for MI associated with vital exhaustion was 2.75 (95% CI, 1.28–5.81, $p < .01$). Long-lasting conflicts, unemployment, and family financial problems during childhood and adolescence were positively related to vital exhaustion. A number of factors in adulthood were also positively associated, including unwanted childlessness, educational problems with children, financial difficulties, and prolonged marital problems. Women who both held jobs and took care of households with children under age 16 had significantly higher MQ scores in comparison with working women without those household responsibilities ($t = 4.25$, $p < .001$). This finding corresponds with a strong association between vital exhaustion and prolonged overtime for men (Falger & Schouten, 1992).

Stressful Life Events

Stressful life events have been associated with MI onset in a number of studies (e.g., Magni et al., 1983), but these studies did not look at gender differences. Other research, however, has shown that men and women differ little in the number of stressful life events they experience at the same ages, although single men experience more stressful life events than do single women or married men and women (Mulvey & Dohrenwend, 1983). In secondary analyses of five epidemiological surveys of the general population, Kessler and McLeod (1984) found that women's vulnerability (increased psychological distress) to life events was largely confined to "network" events: events that occur not to the women themselves but to those around them. They suggested that the "emotional cost of caring" is responsible for a substantial part of the overall relationship between gender and distress.

Gender Differences in Triggers of Acute Onset of Coronary Events

Events or activities that trigger the acute onset of cardiac events have only recently come under scientific investigation (Muller, Tofler, & Stone, 1989). According to the American Heart Association (1995), there was no previous evidence of CHD in 63% of women or 48% of men who died suddenly of CHD. Although researchers do not yet know what accounts for this apparent gender difference in sudden cardiac death, research into triggering events may provide some clues. In the Multicenter Investigation of Limitation of Infarct Size Study, Tofler et al. (1990) found that, of 849 male and female patients, men were more likely to report a precipitating factor for their MIs than were women ($p < .02$). The most common precipitating factor reported by both women (20.7%) and men (17.5%) was emotional upset. In addition, men were more likely to report heavy physical activity as a possible trigger for MI than were women (11.4 vs. 1.7%, respectively, $p < .001$). Men were also found more likely to have an acute MI triggered during moderate or marked physical activity ($p < .01$) in the Thrombolysis in Myocardial Infarction II Study (Tofler et al., 1992). Similarly, more men than women had apparent external triggers for MI in an Israeli study (Behar et al., 1993). The apparently greater susceptibility of men to triggers may be because women have a later onset of CHD and may be less likely to engage in strenuous exertion.

In the Determinants of Time of Myocardial Infarction Onset Study (hereinafter, *MI Onset Study*; Maclure et al., 1991) no gender differences were found in the timing of onset of MI; the risk of MI onset in the 2 hours after awakening was 2.3 times higher than during other times of the day (95% CI, 1.9–2.7). Interviews with 1,228 patients in this same study, using data based on a case-crossover design, showed the relative risk of MI 1 hour after heavy exertion, in comparison with less strenuous or no activity, to be 5.9 (95% CI, 4.6–7.7). The number of women who had an episode of heavy exertion in the 1 hour hazard period was too small to determine whether or not gender modified the results (Mittleman et al., 1993).

Psychologically Meaningful Life Events

Psychologically stressful events have been found to occur frequently as triggers of MI in the ongoing MI Onset Study. Jacobs, Maclure et al. (1992) found a high frequency of both positive (highly desirable) and negative (highly undesirable) psychologically stressful events preceding MI onset, with no gender differences. A case-control study of 129 patients from the MI Onset Study and community controls (matched for age, gender, neighborhood, and onset time) found a significantly increased risk of psychologically stressful events in both the 2 hours and the day before the onset of the symptoms of MI (Jacobs, Friedman et al., 1992), with no gender effects.

Expressed Anger

Episodes of anger have been found to increase the risk of MI onset (Mittleman et al., 1995). Using two types of self-matched control data based on a case-crossover design for the 1,623 patients (501 women) interviewed, Mittleman et al. found the RR of MI in the 2 hours after an episode of anger to be 2.3 (95% CI, 1.7–3.2). Further analysis indicated a trend ($p < .09$, ns) for men's risk to be lower (RR = 1.9; 95% CI) than women's (RR = 3.3; 95% CI).

Gender Differences in Treatment of CHD

There are a number of gender differences in the treatment of CHD, such as referral patterns (Shaw et al., 1994; Sherwood, Maclure, Goldberg, Tofler, & Muller, 1992), length of hospital stay, diagnostic and invasive procedures performed, and outcome from treatments (Welty, 1994). Only 10%–25% of patients participating in most clinical trials are women, even though CHD is as common for women as men (Detre & Stone, 1993). This limits conclusions about women's responses to therapy for acute coronary events or recovery from them.

Only about 20% of patients referred for cardiac catheterization have been women (Detre & Stone, 1993). In addition, gender differences have been found in a cohort of 3,975 middle-aged patients referred for outpatient testing (Shaw et al, 1994). Among the 840 evaluated noninvasively for suspected CHD, 47% were women. Of those referred for an initial stress test evaluation, 63% of the men were given additional diagnostic tests compared with only 38% of the women. Coronary revascularization procedures were performed less frequently in women (2.0% vs. 4.9% in men, $p < .03$), who also had MI or sudden cardiac death more often during 2 years of follow-up (6.9% vs. 2.4% in men, $p = .002$). In the Swedish Follow-Up of Chest Pain Study (Wiklund et al., 1993), women were referred less often to coronary care units for post-MI chest pain (82.2% vs. 91.7% of men; $p < .05$) even though they more often had a previous history of heart failure ($p < .05$) and angina ($p < .05$) than men. In the U. S., once in the hospital, women have been found to be referred later (4.5 days) than men (2.9 days) from community hospitals to university or other tertiary-care hospitals for cardiac dysfunction ($p < .01$; Sherwood et al., 1992).

At older ages, women are twice as likely as men to die within a few weeks of MI (American Heart Association, 1995). Even though women have a higher post-MI mortality rate than men, they are referred less often for either percutaneous transluminal coronary angioplasty (PTCA) or coronary artery bypass graft (CABG) surgery. The reasons for this are unclear, although some suggest that it may be because of an assumption that the procedures may not be safe for women (Welty, Mittleman, Healy, Muller, & Shubrooks, 1994). Others suggest that men are referred too often for these invasive procedures. Studies investigating gender differences in invasive procedure morbidity and mortality and in long-term mortality following PTCA or CABG have shown mixed results. A number of studies, including those based on the NHLBI Coronary Angioplasty Registry (Cowley et al., 1985; Holmes et al., 1988; Kelsey et al., 1993), have shown significantly higher risks for women; a few others, however, found no differences in PTCA success rates for men and women (Cowley, Kelsey, Cosgigan, & Detre, 1987; McEniery et al., 1987). Welty et al. (1994) found no significant gender differences in a group of 505 patients (164 women) followed for 34 months in PTCA success rate, referral for CABG, repeat PTCA, reinfarction, or death. Women did have more recurrent angina than men (54% vs. 42.5%, $p < .01$).

Cardiac psychology has begun to address psychological stress during acute treatment for life-threatening cardiac events. For example, patients with high levels of in-hospital psychological stress have shown a threefold increased risk of cardiac mortality over the next 5 years ($p < .0003$) and a 1.5-fold increased risk of reinfarction ($p = .09$) among men (Frasure-Smith, 1991). Similarly, a pattern of social isolation and high life stress have been shown to result in a fourfold increase in risk of mortality after acute MI (Jenkinson, Madeley, Mitchell, & Turner, 1993). Although these investigations did not include women or did not report gender differences, another study comparing levels of stress experienced at post-MI hospital discharge (Toth, 1993) found no differences between men and women in stress scores or identified stressful concerns.

More recently, Frasure-Smith, Lespérance, and Talajic (1995) assessed a number of negative emotions in 222 post-MI patients (49 women) over 12 months. Multivariate analysis showed that depressive symptoms, anxiety, and history of depression all significantly predicted subsequent cardiac events, independent of cardiac disease severity. The only nonpsychological variable in this study to predict recurrent acute coronary syndromes was gender; however, the role of gender was somewhat reduced after a history of depression and anxiety was accounted for. The authors concluded that "women's greater tendency to express depression and anxiety" and other unknown gender-related factors may "place them at increased risk for the thrombogenic events represented by recurrent acute coronary syndromes following MI" (Frasure-Smith et al., 1995, p. 395).

Gender Differences in CHD Rehabilitation and Prognosis

Forty-four percent of women in comparison with 27% of men will die within 1 year following MI (American Heart Association, 1995). Older women who have MIs are twice as likely as men to die within a few weeks (American Heart Association, 1995). Still, women are greatly underrepresented in studies of secondary prevention. There is evidence that women are more likely than men to be anxious, depressed, stressed, and unhappy with social support following acute MI (Frank & Taylor, 1993). They are also less likely to enter cardiac rehabilitation programs and more likely to drop out (Downing & Littman, 1994; Haskell, 1993).

The Cardiac Arrhythmia Suppression Trial (Schron, Pawitan, Shumaker, & Hale, 1991) found that post-MI women were more limited in social functioning, were less satisfied with their current life situations, and reported more emotional and physical stress symptoms than men, regardless of age and severity of disease. Wiklund et al. (1993) investigated gender differences in the Follow-Up of Chest Pain study in Göteborg, Sweden. One year after MI, women had significantly more psychological and psychosomatic complaints. These included feeling pressed for time, waking up too early, and waking up during the night ($p < .05$), as well as anxiety, difficulty falling asleep, difficulty in relaxing, increased use of sleeping tablets, and headaches ($p < .01$).

In an exploratory study of the 83 female participants in the Recurrent Coronary Prevention Project, Powell et al. (1993) looked at psychosocial predictors of mortality in the 6 women who died over an average of 8.5 years of follow-up. In a multivariate stepwise logistic regression analysis, independent psychosocial predictors of mortality included being divorced, being employed without a college degree, and the inverse of time urgency and "emotional arousability." Because of their small sample, Powell et al. saw their results as primarily offering hypotheses for further investigation. However, they indicated that their findings did suggest that the women tended to have "unmet expectations" for the roles they opted for in the 1940s and 1950s; were forced to work because of economic circumstances; and were resentful, lonely, and dissatisfied.

Women not only participate less in cardiac rehabilitation programs, but also report more cardiac symptoms, have decreased ability to perform activities of daily living, return to work less often, and are more depressed than their male counterparts after a cardiac event (Downing & Littman, 1994; Haskell, 1993; Thoresen & Low, 1994). This may be, in part, because rehabilitation programs are designed to fit men's schedules and not the "double duty" of home and work in women's lives (Thoresen & Low, 1994).

IMPLICATIONS FOR CARDIAC PSYCHOLOGY AND HEALTH CARE PROVIDERS

From our overview it is clear not only that women are at high risk for CHD but that CHD is the major killer of women, who have poorer prognoses following MI than men (American Heart Association, 1995; Eaker, Pinsky, & Castelli, 1992; Higgins & Thom, 1993). This situation is slowly changing, with more public attention being drawn to women and CHD and to research and treatment issues (e.g., ongoing large-scale studies, such as the Post-Menopausal Estrogen Progestin Investigation, the Women's Health Initiative, and the Hormone Replacement Study [cited in Czaj-kowski et al., 1994; Shumaker & Smith, 1995; Wenger et al., 1993]; see also Orth-Gomér, Chesney, & Wenger, in press). However, women have either not been included as often as men or have been a small part of the sample population in studies of the etiology, primary prevention, treatment, or secondary prevention of CHD. This is as true for studies in cardiac psychology as for clinical trials or epidemiological studies in cardiology.

Much of what is known about women and CHD has been framed in models developed primarily from research on men. A number of researchers—including Eaker (1989), Rodin and Ickovics (1990), and Chesney (1993)—have challenged the practice of applying to women those models developed solely from research investigating the relationship of psychological factors and CHD in men. Recent studies suggest that gender-limited paradigms may be impeding progress in how health care providers view and treat CHD in both men and women. One example of progress made when such paradigms are transcended is the use of hormone replacement therapy as a "cardiac" medication for women with CHD (Rav-nikar, 1993; Speroff, 1993; Stampfer et al., 1991). Obviously, this practice would not have even been considered if research based only on men was consulted.

Recent studies or models such as those set forth by Powell et al. (1993), Frasure-Smith et al. (1995), and Stoney and Engebretson (1994) provide examples of how breaking out of gender-limited, male-based paradigms may help increase knowledge about mind–body aspects of CHD in both men and women. The current importance of these studies lies more in the questions they raise than in their actual research findings. Such studies suggest that cardiac psychology needs to give increased attention to women's roles, role stress, social isolation, anxiety, depression, vital exhaustion, "unmet expectations," and expression of anger and other emotions.

We end this chapter with three very basic recommendations to health-care providers working with women with or at high risk for CHD. These suggestions are particularly important given the long-standing myth that CHD is a man's disease. Our suggestions assume the premises of the mind–body link for both men and women. They also assume, even with the current dearth of information about the cardiac psychology of women, that there are gender differences in the mind–body link and, thus, encourage clinicians and researchers to pay attention to such possible differences. Specifically, we recommend that health care providers

- Educate women about cardiovascular disease, especially CHD. Inform them of their risk factors and that CHD is as deadly for them as it is for their husbands and brothers. Teach women how to identify signs and symptoms of CHD and to not minimize their symptoms, so that they seek prompt medical attention.

- Examine their own cultural or social assumptions for biases that could affect either the information they obtain from women or the delivery of care. Remember that CHD is the Number 1 killer of women in the United States, so it is important for health care providers to take women's reports of cardiac symptoms seriously and not simply view them as psychosomatic complaints.

- Use the continuing-education materials and the counseling and health education materials on women and CHD available from such organizations as NHLBI, the American Heart Association, and the American Women's Medical Association. The understanding of women and CHD and the role of psychological variables may change quickly as data from new studies become available.

We hope that these suggestions will not only enhance the quality of interventions with patients but also encourage more research that focuses on gender-related similarities and differences in risks, interventions, and prognoses. Such continued research is needed in both cardiac psychology and cardiology to expand the frontiers of both disciplines and provide more hope for patients—both men and women.

REFERENCES

Adams, S. H. (1994). Role of hostility in women's health during midlife: A longitudinal study. *Health Psychology, 13*, 488–495.

Allen, M. T., Stoney, C. M., Owens, J. F., & Matthews, K. A. (1993). Hemodynamic adjustments to laboratory stress: The influence of gender and personality. *Psychosomatic Medicine, 55*, 505–517.

American Heart Association. (1989). *Silent epidemic: The truth about women and heart disease.* Dallas, TX: Author.

American Heart Association. (1995). *Heart and stroke facts: 1995 statistical supplement.* Dallas, TX: Author.

American Medical Women's Association. (1995, September 16). *The difference in a woman's heart* [Live videoconference]. Irving, TX: VHA Satellite Network.

Appels, A., Falger, P. R. J., & Schouten, G. W. (1993). Vital exhaustion as a risk indicator for myocardial infarction in women. *Journal of Psychosomatic Research, 37*, 881–890.

Appels, A., Höppener, P., & Mulder, P. (1987). A questionnaire to assess premonitory symptoms of myocardial infarction. *International Journal of Cardiology, 17,* 15–24.

Appels, A., & Mulder, P. (1989). Fatigue and heart disease: The association between vital exhaustion and past, present and future coronary heart disease. *Journal of Psychosomatic Research, 33,* 727–738.

Barefoot, J. C., Dahlstrom, W. G., & Williams, R. B. (1983). Hostility, coronary heart disease incidence, and total mortality: A 25-year follow-up study of 255 physicians. *Psychosomatic Medicine, 45,* 59–63.

Barefoot, J. C., Dodge, K. A., Peterson, B. L., Dahlstrom, W. G., & Williams, R. B. (1989). The Cook–Medley hostility scale: Item content and ability to predict survival. *Psychosomatic Medicine, 51,* 46–57.

Barefoot, J. C., Haney, T. L., Hershkowitz, B. D., & Williams, R. B. (1991, March). *Hostility and coronary artery disease in women and men.* Paper presented at the Twelfth Annual Meeting of the Society of Behavioral Medicine, Washington, DC.

Behar, S., Halabi, M., Reicher-Reiss, H., Zion, M., Kaplinsky, E., Mandelzweig, L., & Goldbourt, U. (1993). Circadian variation and possible external triggers of onset of myocardial infarction: SPRINT Study Group. *American Journal of Medicine, 94,* 395–400.

Berkman, L. F. (1994). Social support and cardiovascular disease morbidity and mortality in women. In S. M. Czajkowski, D. R. Hill, & T. B. Clarkson (Eds.), *Women, behavior, and cardiovascular disease* (NIH Publication No. 94-3309, pp. 159–166). Rockville, MD: National Institutes of Health.

Berkman, L. F., Vaccarino, V., & Seeman, T. (1993). Gender differences in cardiovascular morbidity and mortality: The contribution of social networks and support. In N. K. Wenger, L. Speroff, & B. Packard (Eds.), *Cardiovascular health and disease in women* (pp. 217–223). Greenwich, CT: Le Jacq Communications.

Blascovich, J., & Katkin, E. S. (Eds.). (1993). *Cardiovascular reactivity to psychological stress and disease.* Washington, DC: American Psychological Association.

Booth-Kewley, S., & Friedman, H. (1987). Psychological predictors of heart disease: A quantitative review. *Psychological Bulletin, 101,* 110–112.

Carney, R. M., Freedland, K. E., Smith, L. J., Rich, M. W., & Jaffe, A. S. (1994). Depression and anxiety as risk factors for coronary heart disease in women. In S. M. Czajkowski, D. R. Hill, & T. B. Clarkson (Eds.), *Women, behavior, and cardiovascular disease* (NIH Publication No. 94-3309, pp. 117–126). Rockville, MD: National Institutes of Health.

Chesney, M. A. (1993). Social isolation, depression, and heart disease: Research on women broadens the agenda [Editorial comment]. *Psychosomatic Medicine, 55,* 434–435.

Cottington, E. M., Matthews, K. A., Talbott, E., & Kuller, L. H. (1980). Environmental events preceding sudden death in women. *Psychosomatic Medicine, 42,* 567–574.

Cowley, M. J., Kelsey, S. F., Cosgigan, T. M., & Dtere, K. M. (1987). Percutaneous transluminal coronary angioplasty in women: Gender differences in outcome. In E. Eaker, B. Packard, N. K. Wenger, T. B. Clarkson, & H. A. Tyroler (Eds.), *Coronary heart disease in women: Proceedings of an NIH workshop*. New York: Haymarket Doyma.

Cowley, M. J., Mullin, S. M., Kelsey, S. F., Kent, K. M., Gruentzig, A. R., Detre, K. M., & Passamani, E. R. (1985). Sex differences in early and long-term results of coronary angioplasty in the National Heart, Lung, and Blood Institute's PTCA Registry. *Circulation, 71*, 90–97.

Czajkowski, S. M., Hill, D. R., & Clarkson, T. B. (Eds.). (1994). *Women, behavior, and cardiovascular disease* (NIH Publication No. 94-3309). Rockville, MD: National Institutes of Health.

Dembroski, T. M., MacDougall, J. M., Costa, P. T., & Grandits, G. A. (1989). Components of hostility as predictors of sudden death and myocardial infarction in the Multiple Risk Factor Intervention Trial. *Psychosomatic Medicine, 51*, 514–522.

Detre, K. M., & Stone, P. H. (1993). Working group report: Management of coronary heart disease in women. In N. K. Wenger, L. Speroff, & B. Packard (Eds.), *Cardiovascular health and disease in women* (pp. 99–101). Greenwich, CT: Le Jacq Communications.

Dimsdale, J. E. (1993). Influences of personality and stress-induced biological processes on etiology and treatment of cardiovascular diseases in women. In N. K. Wenger, L. Speroff, & B. Packard (Eds.), *Cardiovascular health and disease in women* (pp. 225–230). Greenwich, CT: Le Jacq Communications.

Dixon, J. P., Dixon, J. K., & Spinner, J. C. (1991). Tensions between career and interpersonal commitments as a risk factor for cardiovascular disease among women. *Women and Health, 17*, 33–57.

Downing, J., & Littman, A. (1994). Gender differences in response to cardiac rehabilitation. In S. M. Czajkowski, D. R. Hill, & T. B. Clarkson (Eds.), *Women, behavior, and cardiovascular disease* (NIH Publication No. 94-3309, pp. 353–354). Rockville, MD: National Institutes of Health.

Eaker, E. D. (1989). Psychosocial factors in the epidemiology of coronary heart disease in women. *Psychiatric Clinics of North America, 12*, 167–173.

Eaker, E. D., Abbott, R. D., & Kannel, W. B. (1989). Frequency of uncomplicated angina pectoris in Type A compared to Type B persons (the Framingham study). *American Journal of Cardiology, 63*, 1042–1045.

Eaker, E. D., Pinsky, J., & Castelli, W. P. (1992). Myocardial infarction and coronary death among women: Psychosocial predictors from a 20-year follow-up of women in the Framingham study. *American Journal of Epidemiology, 135*, 854–864.

Falger, P. R. J., & Schouten, E. G. W. (1992). Exhaustion, psychological stressors in the work environment, and acute myocardial infarction in adult men. *Journal of Psychosomatic Research, 36*, 777–786.

Frank, E., & Taylor, C. B. (1993). Psychosocial influences on diagnosis and treatment plans of women with coronary heart disease. In N. K. Wenger, L. Speroff, & B. Packard (Eds.), *Cardiovascular health and disease in women* (pp. 231–237). Greenwich, CT: Le Jacq Communications.

Frasure-Smith, N. (1991). In-hospital predictors of psychological stress as predictors of long-term outcome after acute myocardial infarction in men. *American Journal of Cardiology, 67,* 121–127.

Frasure-Smith, N., Lespérance, F., & Talajic, M. (1995). The impact of negative emotions on prognosis following myocardial infarction: Is it more than depression? *Health Psychology, 14,* 388–398.

Friedman, H. S. (Ed.). (1992). *Hostility, coping, and health.* Washington, DC: American Psychological Association.

Frohlich, E. D. (1993). Coronary prevention therapy: Hypertension. In N. K. Wenger, L. Speroff, & B. Packard (Eds.), *Cardiovascular health and disease in women* (pp. 145–148). Greenwich, CT: Le Jacq Communications.

Gritz, E. R. (1994). Biobehavioral factors in smoking and smoking cessation in women. In S. M. Czajkowski, D. R. Hill, & T. B. Clarkson (Eds.), *Women, behavior, and cardiovascular disease* (NIH Publication No. 94-3309, pp. 53–67). Rockville, MD: National Institutes of Health.

Hällström, T., Lapidus, L., Bengtsson, C., & Edström, K. (1986). Psychosocial factors and risk of ischemic heart disease and death in women: A 12-year follow-up of participants in the population study of women in Gothenburg, Sweden. *Journal of Psychosomatic Research, 30,* 451–459.

Hall, E. M. (1994). Multiple roles and caregiving stress in women. (1994). In S. M. Czajkowski, D. R. Hill, & T. B. Clarkson (Eds.), *Women, behavior, and cardiovascular disease* (NIH Publication No. 94-3309, pp. 167–178). Rockville, MD: National Institutes of Health.

Haskell, W. L. (1993). Cardiac rehabilitation and secondary prevention: Issues of participation and benefit for women. In N. K. Wenger, L. Speroff, & B. Packard (Eds.), *Cardiovascular health and disease in women* (pp. 123–128). Greenwich, CT: Le Jacq Communications.

Hecker, M., Chesney, M., Black, G., & Frautschi, N. (1988). Coronary-prone behaviors in the Western Collaborative Group Study. *Psychosomatic Medicine, 50,* 153–164.

Helmers, K. F., Posluszny, D. M., & Krantz, D. S. (1994). Associations of hostility and coronary artery disease: A review of studies. In A. W. Siegman & T. W. Smith (Eds.), *Anger, hostility and the heart* (pp. 215–237). Hillsdale, NJ: Erlbaum.

Higgins, M., & Thom, T. (1993). Cardiovascular disease in women as a public health problem. In N. K. Wenger, L. Speroff, & B. Packard (Eds.), *Cardiovascular health and disease in women* (pp. 15–19). Greenwich, CT: Le Jacq Communications.

Holmes, D. R., Holubkov, R., Vilestra, R., Kelsey, S. F., Reeder, G. S., Dorros, G., Williams, D. O., Cowley, M. J., Faxon, D. P., & Kent, K. M. (1988). Comparison of complications during percutaneous transluminal coronary angioplasty from 1977 to 1981 and from 1985 to 1986. *Journal of the American College of Cardiology, 12,* 1149–1155.

Jacobs, S. C., Friedman, R., Mittleman, M., Maclure, M., Sherwood, J., Benson, H., & Muller, J. E., for the Myocardial Infarction Study Onset Investigators. (1992). Nine-fold increased risk of myocardial infarction following psychological stress as assessed by a case-control study. *Circulation, 86,* 789.

Jacobs, S. C., Maclure, M., Sherwood, J., Tofler, G. H., Friedman, R., Goldberg, R. J., Benson, H., & Muller, J. E., for the Myocardial Infarction Onset Study Investigators. (1992, March). *High frequency of positive or negative psychologically stressful events possibly trigger onset of myocardial infarction.* Paper presented at the annual meeting of the Society of Behavioral Medicine, Washington, DC.

Jeffery, R. W. (1994). Biobehavioral influences on diet, obesity, and weight control strategies in women. In S. M. Czajkowski, D. R. Hill, & T. B. Clarkson (Eds.), *Women, behavior, and cardiovascular disease* (NIH Publication No. 94-3309, pp. 89–96). Rockville, MD: National Institutes of Health.

Jenkinson, C. M., Madeley, R. J., Mitchell, J. R., & Turner, I. D. (1993). The influence of psychosocial factors on survival after myocardial infarction. *Public Health, 107,* 305–317.

Kelsey, S. F., James, M., Holubkov, A. L., Holubkov, R., Cowley, M. J., & Detre, K. M. (1993). Results of percutaneous transluminal coronary angioplasty in women: 1985–1986 National Heart, Lung, and Blood Institute's Coronary Angioplasty Registry. *Circulation, 87,* 720–729.

Kessler, R. C., & McLeod, J. D. (1984). Sex differences in vulnerability to undesirable life events. *American Sociological Review, 49,* 620–631.

King, A. C. (1994). Biobehavioral variables, exercise, and cardiovascular disease in women. In S. M. Czajkowski, D. R. Hill, & T. B. Clarkson (Eds.), *Women, behavior, and cardiovascular disease* (NIH Publication No. 94-3309, pp. 69–88). Rockville, MD: National Institutes of Health.

Koskenvuo, M., Kaprio, J., Rose, R. J., Kesaniemi, A., Sarna, S., Heikkila, K., & Langinvainio, H. (1988). Hostility as a risk factor for mortality and ischemic heart disease in men. *Psychosomatic Medicine, 50,* 330–340.

Krauss, R. M. (1993). Effects of hormones on lipids and lipoproteins. In N. K. Wenger, L. Speroff, & B. Packard (Eds.), *Cardiovascular health and disease in women* (pp. 161–167). Greenwich, CT: Le Jacq Communications.

Krieger, N. (1994). Influence of social class, race, and gender on the etiology of hypertension among women in the United States. In S. M. Czajkowski, D. R. Hill, & T. B. Clarkson (Eds.), *Women, behavior, and cardiovascular disease* (NIH Publication No. 94-3309, pp. 191–206). Rockville, MD: National Institutes of Health.

LaRosa, J. C. (1993). Some aspects of coronary risk and prevention factors in women. In N. K. Wenger, L. Speroff, & B. Packard (Eds.), *Cardiovascular health and disease in women* (pp. 31–35). Greenwich, CT: Le Jacq Communications.

Maclure, M., Sherwood, J., Mittleman, M., Goldberg, R., Tofler, G. H., & Muller, J. E. (1991). Increased risk of myocardial infarction onset within the two hours after wakening [Abstract]. *Circulation, 82*(Suppl.), I118.

Magni, G., Corfini, A., Berto, F., Rizzardo, R., Bombardelli, S., & Miraglia, G. (1983). Life events and myocardial infarction. *Australian and New Zealand Journal of Medicine, 13,* 257–260.

McEniery, P. T., Hollman, J., Knezinek, V., Dorosti, K., Franeo, I., Simpfendorfer, C., & Whitlow, P. (1987). Comparative safety and efficacy of percutaneous transluminal coronary angioplasty in men and in women. *Catheterization and Cardiovascular Diagnosis, 13,* 364–367.

Mittleman, M. A., Maclure, M., Sherwood, J. B., Mulry, R. P., Tofler, G. H., Jacobs, S. C., Friedman, R., Benson, H., & Muller, J. E., for the Determinants of Time of Myocardial Infarction Onset Study Investigators. (1995). Triggering of acute myocardial infarction onset by episodes of anger. *Circulation, 92,* 1720–1725.

Mittleman, M. A., Maclure, M., Tofler, G. H., Sherwood, J. B., Goldberg, R. J., & Muller, J. E., for the Determinants of Time of Myocardial Infarction Onset Study Investigators. (1993). Triggering of acute myocardial infarction by heavy physical exertion: Protection against triggering by regular exercise. *New England Journal of Medicine, 329,* 1677–1683.

Muller, J. E., Tofler, G. H., & Stone, P. H. (1989). Circadian variation and triggers of onset of acute cardiovascular disease. *Circulation, 79,* 733–744.

Mulvey, A., & Dohrenwend, B. S. (1983). The relation of stressful life events to gender. *Issues in Mental Health Nursing, 5,* 219–237.

Ockene, J. K. (1993). Preventing smoking and promoting smoking cessation among women across the life span. In N. K. Wenger, L. Speroff, & B. Packard (Eds.), *Cardiovascular health and disease in women* (pp. 247–257). Greenwich, CT: Le Jacq Communications.

Orth-Gomér, K., Chesney, M. A., & Wenger, N. K. (in press). *Women, stress, and heart disease.* Hillsdale, NJ: Erlbaum.

Powell, L. H., Shaker, L. A., Jones, B. A., Vaccarino, L. V., Thoresen, C. E., & Pattillo, J. R. (1993). Psychosocial predictors of mortality in 83 women with premature acute myocardial infarctions. *Psychosomatic Medicine, 55,* 426–433.

Ravnikar, V. A. (1993). Hormone replacement therapy in the primary prevention of cardiovascular disease: Benefits, risks and compliance issues. In N. K. Wenger, L. Speroff, & B. Packard (Eds.), *Cardiovascular health and disease in women* (pp. 181–187). Greenwich, CT: Le Jacq Communications.

Rodin, J., & Ickovics, J. R. (1990). Women's health: Review and research agenda as we approach the 21st century. *American Psychologist, 45,* 1018–1034.

Rosenberg, L. (1993). Cigarette smoking and cardiovascular disease in women. In N. K. Wenger, L. Speroff, & B. Packard (Eds.), *Cardiovascular health and disease in women* (pp. 139–143). Greenwich, CT: Le Jacq Communications.

Schron, E. B., Pawitan, Y., Shumaker, S. A., & Hale, C. (1991). Health quality of life differences between men and women in a postinfarction study. *Circulation, 84,* (Suppl. II), 245.

Shaw, L. J., Miller, D. D., Romeis, J. C., Kargi, D., Younis, L. T., & Chaitman, B. R. (1994). Gender differences in the noninvasive evaluation and management of patients with suspected coronary artery disease. *Annals of Internal Medicine, 120,* 559–566.

Shekelle, R. B., Gale, M., Ostfeld, A. M., & Paul, O. (1983). Hostility, risk of coronary heart disease and mortality. *Psychosomatic Medicine, 45,* 109–114.

Sherwood, J., Maclure, M., Goldberg, R. J., Tofler, G., & Muller, J. E. (1992). Women are referred later than men for tertiary care following myocardial infarction [Abstract]. *Circulation, 86,* 39.

Shumaker, S. A., & Smith, T. R. (1995). Women and coronary heart disease: A psychological perspective. In A. L. Stanton & S. J. Gallant (Eds.), *The psychology of women's health: Progress and challenges in research and application* (pp. 25–49). Washington, DC: American Psychological Association.

Smith, T. W. (1992). Hostility and health: Current status of a psychosomatic hypothesis. *Health Psychology, 11,* 139–150.

Speroff, N. F. (1993). The impact of oral contraception and hormone replacement therapy on cardiovascular disease. In N. K. Wenger, L. Speroff, & B. Packard (Eds.), *Cardiovascular health and disease in women* (pp. 37–45). Greenwich, CT: Le Jacq Communications.

Stampfer, M. J., Colditz, G. A., Willett, W. C., Manson, J. E., Rosner, B., Speizer, F. E., & Hennekens, C. H. (1991). Postmenopausal estrogen therapy and cardiovascular disease. Ten-year follow-up from the nurses health study. *New England Journal of Medicine, 325,* 756–762.

Stefanick, M. L. (1993). The roles of obesity, regional adiposity, and physical activity in coronary heart disease in women. In N. K. Wenger, L. Speroff, & B. Packard (Eds.), *Cardiovascular health and disease in women* (pp. 149–156). Greenwich, CT: Le Jacq Communications.

Stoney, C. M., & Engebretson, T. O. (1994). Anger and hostility: Potential mediators of the gender difference in coronary heart disease. In A. W. Siegman & T. W. Smith (Eds.), *Anger, hostility and the heart* (pp. 215–237). Hillsdale, NJ: Erlbaum.

Stoney, C. M., Matthews, K. A., McDonald, R., & Johnson, C. A. (1988). Sex differences in lipoprotein, cardiovascular, and neuroendocrine responses to acute stress. *Psychophysiology, 25,* 645–656.

Suarez, E. C., Harlan, E., Peoples, M. C., & Williams, R. B. (1993). Cardiovascular and emotional response in women: The role of hostility and harassment. *Health Psychology, 12,* 459–468.

Sullivan, J. M. (1993). Hormone replacement in the secondary prevention of cardiovascular disease. In N. K. Wenger, L. Speroff, & B. Packard (Eds.), *Car-*

diovascular health and disease in women (pp. 189–194). Greenwich, CT: Le Jacq Communications.

Theorell, T. (1991). Psychosocial cardiovascular risks: On the double loads in women. *Psychotherapy and Psychosomatics, 55,* 81–89.

Thoresen, C. E., & Low, K. G. (1990). Women and the Type A behavior pattern: Review and commentary. *Journal of Social Behavior and Personality, 5,* 117–133.

Thoresen, C. E., & Low, K. G. (1994). Psychosocial interventions in female cardiovascular disease patients. In S. M. Czajkowski, D. R. Hill, & T. B. Clarkson (Eds.), *Women, behavior, and cardiovascular disease* (NIH Publication No. 94-3309, pp. 329–342). Rockville, MD: National Institutes of Health.

Tofler, G. H., Muller, J. E., Stone, P. H., Forman, S., Solomon, R. E., Knatterud, G. L., & Braunwald, E. (1992). Modifiers of timing and possible triggers of onset of acute myocardial infarction in the TIMI II population. *Journal of the American College of Cardiology, 20,* 1045–1055.

Tofler, G. H., Stone, P. H., Maclure, M., Edelman, E., Davis, V. G., Robertson, T., Antman, E. M., Muller, J. E., & the MILIS Study Group. (1990). Analysis of possible triggers of acute myocardial infarction (the MILIS study). *American Journal of Cardiology, 66,* 22–27.

Toth, J. C. (1993). Is stress at hospital discharge after acute myocardial infarction greater in women than in men? *American Journal of Critical Care, 2,* 35–40.

Weidner, G. (1994). The role of hostility and coronary-prone behaviors in the etiology of cardiovascular disease in women. In S. M. Czajkowski, D. R. Hill, & T. B. Clarkson (Eds.), *Women, behavior, and cardiovascular disease* (NIH Publication No. 94-3309, pp. 103–106). Rockville, MD: National Institutes of Health.

Welty, F. K. (1994). Gender differences in outcome after diagnosis and treatment of coronary artery disease. In S. M. Czajkowski, D. R. Hill, & T. B. Clarkson (Eds.), *Women, behavior, and cardiovascular disease* (NIH Publication No. 94-3309, pp. 285–310). Rockville, MD: National Institutes of Health.

Welty, F. K., Mittleman, M. A., Healy, R. W., Muller, J. E., & Shubrooks, S. J. (1994). Similar results of percutaneous transluminal coronary angioplasty for women and men with postmyocardial infarction ischemia. *Journal of American College of Cardiology, 23,* 35–39.

Wenger, N. K. (1993). Coronary heart disease in women: An overview (myths, misperceptions, and missed opportunities). In N. K. Wenger, L. Speroff, & B. Packard (Eds.), *Cardiovascular health and disease in women* (pp. 21–29). Greenwich, CT: Le Jacq Communications.

Wenger, N. K., Speroff, L., & Packard, B. (Eds.). (1993). *Cardiovascular health and disease in women.* Greenwich, CT: Le Jacq Communications.

Wiklund, I., Herlitz, J. H., Johansson, S., Bengtson, A., Karlson, B. W., & Persson, N. G. (1993). Subjective symptoms and well-being differ in women and men after myocardial infarction. *European Heart Journal, 14,* 1315–1319.

Wing, R. R. (1993). Obesity and related eating and exercise behaviors. In N. K. Wenger, L. Speroff, & B. Packard (Eds.), *Cardiovascular health and disease in women* (pp. 239–246). Greenwich, CT: Le Jacq Communications.

8

PSYCHOLOGICAL ISSUES AND CORONARY ARTERY BYPASS SURGERY

JEFFREY P. GOLD

Coronary artery bypass graft (CABG) surgery, or coronary revascularization, has become one of the most common surgical procedures, with an estimated 468,000 procedures performed on 309,000 patients in the United States in 1992 and 800,000 to 850,000 operations performed yearly worldwide (American Heart Association, 1995). The present operative mortality rate, approximately 1%–2% in low-risk patients, is better than that of open gall bladder surgery and is approaching that of a routine tonsillectomy. The morbidity of CABG surgery has also dramatically decreased in the nearly 30 years since the procedure's initial clinical application. Pulmonary, cardiac, renal, and visceral complications have been studied and the outcomes improved, but much less attention has been focused on quality of life, cognitive, psychological (e.g., depression), and neurological changes. These four major areas of central nervous system functioning are the focus of this chapter.

A significant percentage of the information presented in this chapter has been derived from the preliminary analysis of a cohort of 248 patients undergoing elective myocardial revascularization as part of the Cornell Coronary Artery Bypass Outcome Trials Group. This is a multidisciplinary, multi-institutional 3-year federally funded study for which I am the primary investigator. This extremely homogeneous population (in terms of age, gender, percentage of retired persons, and medical history) has been studied from many perspectives and to a large extent forms the basis for the analysis of the psychological issues associated with CABG surgery that are described here.

QUALITY OF LIFE

Quality of life has been more difficult to study and define than many physiological variables associated with recovery from surgery, and only recently have researchers begun to focus on questions of lifestyle and quality of life after coronary revascularization. Older studies have often used late postoperative morbidity (death more than 6–12 months after the operation) and return to work as measures for evaluating quality of life, but return to work and late morbidity are complex matters that are not directly related to quality of life.

A 1983 study that was part of the Seattle Heart Watch Project demonstrated that many more patients retired following CABG surgery than did similar patients treated with medication alone, in spite of the finding that, in objectively measured stress tests, the bypass patients had better exercise tolerance than those treated with medications alone. Both of the well-known randomized trials of medical versus surgical treatment of angina—the European Coronary Surgery Study (European Coronary Surgery Study Group, 1982) and the Coronary Artery Surgery Study (Coronary Artery Surgical Study Principal Investigators, 1984)—also found very high rates of retirement within a few years after bypass surgery, in spite of good exercise tolerance, when measured objectively by stress testing. (In these two trials, both medically and surgically treated patients retired at the same high rate: Approximately 50% retired within 5 years of surgery.) This high incidence of retirement has been attributed to societal and family pressures, as well as poorly defined psychological issues, rather than to postoperative cardiac or other physical limitations. One apparent psychological issue is that some patients tend to blame "stress on the job" for their heart attacks or need for bypass surgery, and they may have been encouraged to think this way by their families or physicians. Others may see the surgery as an occasion to examine their lives and break away from boring, unstimulating, or stressful work routines. Finally, some companies place barriers in the way of patients who wish to return to work and encourage retirement, particularly if the job involves substantial physical activity. Thus, return to work after CABG surgery is associated with a large number of factors, adding impetus to recent research that uses psychological tools to measure various aspects of quality of life.

Some of the carefully validated comprehensive health survey instruments that have been used to study quality of life in coronary bypass patients include the Short Form Health Index Questionnaire (SF-36); the

Sickness Impact Profile; Functional Status Questionnaire; Duke–University of North Carolina Health Profile; Rand Health Insurance Measures; Index of Well-Being; National Health and Nutrition Examination Survey; and the Spitzer, Dobson, and Hall Quality of Life Index. The SF-36 is one of the most useful, because it is relatively easy to administer and assess quality of life in seven separate domains of function (social function, role function, energy, bodily pain, general health, mental health, and physical function).

Several large studies enrolling as many as 13,000 respondents have served to validate the SF-36 in many different types of populations (e.g., Jenkinson, Coulter, & Wright, 1993). In particular, this measure has been used with patients who have diabetes mellitus, peptic ulcers, varicose veins, chronic back pain, osteoarthritis of the hip, congestive heart failure, and myocardial infarction, as well as many other health problems. The SF-36 asks questions such as these: "How limited are you in performing vigorous activities such as running, lifting heavy objects, and participating in sports?" (responses ranging from *severely limited* to *not limited at all*) and "How frequently do you participate in community activities?" (responses ranging from *more than once a week* to *never*). In addition, it has been cross-validated by gender, age, socioeconomic status, ethnicity, education, demographics, source, and symptom severity, as well as for primary languages. All of these factors make the SF-36 an extremely useful instrument.

In one large Cornell Coronary Artery Bypass Outcome Trial (CCABOT; Gold et al., 1995), at 6 months following coronary revascularization, 61% of patients were working part- or full-time, in comparison with 59% preoperatively—not a significant difference. However, with pre- and postoperative SF-36 evaluation, the same patients were demonstrated to have significant improvement in all seven domains of functioning postoperatively. Thus, return to work is not necessarily correlated with improved quality of life. Several studies have shown that women report greater impairment of health status than men both preoperatively and postoperatively. In a population of 140 CABG patients, women scored significantly lower than men preoperatively in the physical and mental health domains of the SF-36, and 6 months postoperatively, women reported significantly more impairment than men in the physical, mental health, and role domains (Peterson et al., 1993a, 1993b). In the CCABOT study mentioned above (Gold et al., 1995), men and women demonstrated comparable improvement on the SF-36 after coronary bypass. The 6-month postoperative outcomes for women appeared less favorable only because they began at a lower preoperative level than their male counterparts.

Advanced age has also been implicated as a factor for adverse outcome following CABG surgery. In a prospective randomized study of 178 patients ages 39–88 years who were undergoing elective CABG surgery (Gold et al., 1993), the impact of age on outcome was carefully examined with the standard SF-36 health survey instrument. Patients were tested preoperatively, at 7 days postoperatively, and at 6 months following their surgery. In this particular CCABOT group of patients, the perioperative mortality rate was 2%, and the rate of combined cardiac and neurological complication was 7%. Logistic regression analyses confirmed that increased age was related to cardiac and neurological morbidity. Overall, the elderly patients improved significantly in every domain of the SF-36, and there was no difference between the younger and older patients for this quality of life improvement. Although age does remain a significant predictor of cardiac and neurological complications in patients with coronary artery disease, significant improvement in functional status was observed in all age groups. In the light of these findings, one can expect CABG to improve functional status, as measured by the SF-36, in older as well as younger patients.

A similar, large-prospective CCABOT study using the SF-36 (Gold et al., 1995) examined quality of life outcome in patients with severe hypertension and in patients with treated diabetes. In both of these subsets, the impact of CABG surgery on postoperative quality of life was not altered. Indeed, patients with diabetes and hypertension fared as well and demonstrated as much improvement in quality of life as patients who were neither diabetic nor hypertensive.

COGNITIVE STATUS CHANGES

Within the neurological and behavioral medicine literature, there is ongoing controversy about the best test battery for assessment of cognitive function, particularly in patients undergoing surgical procedures. Selection of a cognitive test battery is difficult because the ground rules for distribution of domains, duration of testing, and reproducibility must all be integrated with difficulties associated with multiple languages and fatigue. Different groups have assembled different test batteries, all making various claims about the applicability of cognitive function testing in patients who have had CABG surgery as well as those who are in other surgical and medical disease states.

Although many measures may be used in a given cognitive test battery, they tend to fall into separate domains. The assessment of psychomotor, linguistic, and memory function is usually done before and after intervention. All of these cognitive tests have been standardized, and norms are well established. In addition, a clinically important difference needs to be defined, and this varies from study to study and from center to center. There is presently no consensus on what constitutes a clinically important difference in patients undergoing CABG surgery. Furthermore, these tests need to be validated in many behavioral science settings as well as in the perioperative setting. Confounding variables such as patients' age, gender, level of education, and fluency in English need to be removed as determinants of test accuracy.

A limited short- and long-term deterioration in cognitive function as assessed by serial neuropsychological test batteries has been reported. It is not known whether this deterioration is peculiar to the specific aspects of cardiac surgery and cardiac anesthesia or is due more to the stresses of surgery, independent of the organ system or the type of anesthesia used. Numerous studies of noncardiac surgery have demonstrated some significant deterioration in many of the domains of cognitive function tested. Even procedures done under local or regional anesthesia for noncardiac diagnoses are associated with significant functional deterioration. Fortunately, these changes are reversible and improve significantly within the first several months following surgery.

POSTOPERATIVE DEPRESSION

Depression following CABG surgery and other major surgical procedures is common, but it is often not looked for and, thus, insufficiently recognized. It may last a few days or a few months and affects not only the patient's quality of life, but his or her health and perception of recovery. Depression can be particularly severe in patients who have also suffered a recent loss of a family member and in those who have a history of preoperative psychological disorders. It does frequently occur in patients who have been emotionally stable preoperatively.

The relationship between depression and functional status was studied in a group of CCABOT patients undergoing elective CABG surgery. Preoperatively and at 6 months postoperatively, patients completed extensive questionnaires that included outcome parameters as described by the SF-36 health survey (in the seven domains). Patients also underwent repeated testing with the Center for Epidemiological Studies—Depression Scale (CES–D), which has been cross-validated in many subsets of the population and across many different disease states. In this particular CCABOT study, the mean age was approximately 66 years, and 22% of the participants were women. Most of the patients had relatively good health status, and most had little or no comorbidity. The depression scores increased significantly postoperatively, representing an increase in depressive symptoms; this was in spite of SF-36 scores that increased significantly in all seven domains, indicating an improvement in functional status and quality of life. An increase in the CES–D score, indicating an increase in depressive symptoms, was associated with a significantly lesser degree of improvement in the SF-36 functional status at 6 months of follow-up. A multivariate analysis of possible predictors (age, comorbid illness, and perioperative complications, among others) of an increase in the CES–D score confirmed that only lesser improvement in the SF-36 scores was associated with increases in the CES–D score. A lesser degree of improvement in functional status (quality of life) was therefore the only factor that was found to be associated with an increase in depressive symptoms following CABG surgery.

Social isolation and depression have been associated with adverse long-term prognosis after myocardial infarctions and other illnesses. The relationship between depression and outcome as related to social support was studied in 178 CCABOT patients undergoing CABG surgery. Depression was assessed with the CES–D; outcome was assessed with the SF-36 health survey. Age, gender, and comorbidity scores as well as the Canadian Cardiovascular Scale were similar at baseline across this study population. Preoperatively, approximately 40% of the patients had a CES–D score suggesting depression, and a multivariate analysis showed that patients with preoperative depression were more commonly women, had been recently bereaved, and had low perceived social support. The absence of friends with whom a patient could share joys or sorrows (not having a special person who cared about his or her feelings) was associated with this higher incidence of measured depression preoperatively (Peterson, 1994). At 6 months, however, approximately 68% of all patients scored in the depressive range of the CES–D. New-onset depression accounted for nearly one half of these patients. Multivariate analysis showed that only social isolation was associated with new-onset depression. Depressed patients scored lower on the SF-36 health survey both preoperatively and postoperatively, but the degree of improvement on the SF-36 was similar to that of nondepressed patients. Depression, therefore, was not related to functional outcome following CABG surgery.

Overall mortality rates were similar, at 3% in the nondepressed and 4% in the depressed group, which is not a significant difference. Immediate postoperative cardiac and neurological complications were similar, whereas complication rates in the period between hospital discharge and 6-month assessment were extremely low and did not differ between depressed and nondepressed patients. Approximately 40% of patients who were depressed before surgery remained depressed after surgery. Only 4% improved postoperatively such that they no longer scored in the depressive range on the CES–D. One third of the patients who were not depressed preoperatively became depressed postoperatively. Many of the patients who became depressed after the surgery did so definitively.

It is not surprising that CABG surgery does not alleviate depression, especially when it is known that preoperative depression is related to personality issues, life events, and circumstances that would be unlikely to change after surgery. Surprisingly, though, nearly half of patients with postoperative depression are newly depressed. In a population of newly depressed patients in one CCABOT study, there were no significant differences in the SF-36 health survey quality of life indicators to predict new onset of postoperative depression. When preoperative factors—such as age, gender, cardiac ejection fraction, symptom duration, treatment duration, previous myocardial infarction, presence of congestive heart failure, stroke, comorbid illness and recent isolation, bereavement, or lack of perceived social support—were carefully studied, only isolation was found to be a significant predictor of an increase in depressive symptomatology and CES–D scores after surgery.

It has not been possible in the CCABOT studies to predict the development of postoperative depression from such factors as number of grafts placed, hours in intensive care unit, length of hospital stay, or cardiac and neurological morbidity. When return to work was studied as a potential predictive parameter for postoperative depression, it was found to be nonsignificant. Again, only isolation—defined as not being involved in religious or organizational activities and having limited social interaction with friends or relatives—has had a clear-cut ability to predict the postoperative increase in depression (Peterson et al., 1993a; Pirraglia, 1993).

Postoperative depression is therefore a real entity following CABG surgery, and it is not yet possible to predict which subset of the previously nondepressed patient population will develop this problem after surgery. It is important for both cardiologists and psychologists to be aware of this high incidence of depression because such patients may, in fact, be responsive to treatment. The presence or absence of postoperative depression does not relate to transient cognitive or neuropsychological difficulties, nor does it prevent these patients from obtaining the same substantial improvement in overall functional status as their nondepressed peers. This finding suggests the usefulness of screening patients preoperatively for social isolation. Perhaps providing isolated patients with social support within the community before they go through CABG surgery would be a valuable addition to their care. Mended Hearts, cosponsored by the American Heart Association and local medical centers, is a national nonprofit organization that provides peer support and educational services to people who have heart conditions.

NEUROLOGICAL CHANGES

Stroke is perhaps the most devastating complication of CABG surgery. Over the nearly 30 years of coronary revascularization surgery, stroke incidence rates varying between 1% and 10% for major fixed focal neurological deficits and higher frequencies for minor fixed or transient neurological deficits have been reported. Interestingly, in spite of significant refinement of cardiac surgical and anesthetic techniques, these numbers have not changed over the past 3 decades. With the recent advent of high-quality imaging that makes use of transesophageal echocardiography and middle cerebral artery transcranial Doppler assessments, it has been possible to study both embolic and hemodynamic events associated with coronary revascularization.

Embolic events resulting from aortic debris are thought to be an important cause of fixed neurological events in patients undergoing cardiac surgery. Several studies have demonstrated a correlation between severity of aortic atherosclerotic disease as assessed by transesophageal echocardiography and stroke (Hartman et al., 1994; Katz et al., 1992; Marshall et al., 1992). The strong correlation between stroke incidence and aortic disease as assessed by transesophageal echocardiography suggests that this diagnostic technique is important and should be used more often, although it is not clear what preventive techniques should be used if severe aortic atheromatous disease is present and the patient requires CABG surgery. The use of transcranial middle cerebral artery Doppler assessments has further enhanced the understanding of some of the mechanical events associated with CABG surgery. Standard intraoperative maneuvers, such as cannulation of the aorta and clamping of the ascending aorta as well as the creation of the proximal aortic anastamoses, are commonly associated with cerebral embolic events that can be detected by transcranial Doppler signals. The aggregate number of these embolic events appears to correlate quite closely with the frequency and severity of fixed neurological and cognitive defects following coronary surgery. In one CCABOT study of 46 patients undergoing CABG surgery instrumented with transcranial Doppler assessments as well as transesophageal echocardiographic probes, an association was found between the number of embolic signals detected with transcranial Doppler at the aortic clamp removal and the transesophageal echocardiographically determined grade of aortic arch atheroma (Barbut et al., 1994). This finding strengthens the hypothesis that these embolic signals represent debris dislodged from the aortic wall by the placement and removal of the clamps. The implication is that a modification of the surgical technique could potentially minimize the number of embolic events and, therefore, the incidence of postoperative strokes. The correlation between the number of cerebral microemboli, degree of aortic atheromata, and postoperative cognitive dysfunction suggests that removal of clamps may liberate dislodged fragments of atheromatous plaque from the aortic wall and that cerebral emboli may not represent air bubbles or platelet clumps trapped within the blood vessels or within the extracorporeal circuitry of the heart, as has been previously hypothesized.

Blauth et al. (1988) have shown that cardiopulmonary bypass may be associated with platelet–fibrin emboli that are 25 to 35 microns in diameter, in spite of a 40-micron filter that is commonly added to the cannula returning from the machine to the patient. A prospective study of 38 patients undergoing elective coronary revascularization demonstrated very small numbers of platelet–fibrin emboli before surgical incision but increasing numbers of these emboli during the start and completion of the cardiopulmonary bypass run (Pugsley et al., 1994). Platelet–fibrin emboli represent another potential source of postoperative cerebral dysfunction. It is not clear whether the platelet–fibrin emboli are related to the heart–lung machine or to other factors. The exact role of emboli versus cerebral-perfusion-related injury remains unclear, and so requires further intensive scrutiny.

The importance of closer control of pressure and flow during CABG surgery has also been previously underestimated as it relates to the development of postoperative fixed neurological injury. In a recently reported CCABOT study (Gold et al., 1995), 248 patients undergoing elective coronary revascularization were randomly assigned to undergo one of two intraoperative blood pressure treatment strategies. In the control group, the perfusion pressures were maintained at a mean arterial pressure range of 40–50 mm Hg, whereas in the experimental group, the pressures ranged between 80 and 100 mm Hg (much closer to their preoperative mean blood pressure). With the exception of the mean arterial pressure on cardiopulmonary bypass, participants in the two study groups underwent identical perioperative management. Although there were many differences when the patients were assessed 7 days after surgery, fixed neurological deficits were the most striking differences that remained at the 6-month evaluation. In patients assigned randomly to a higher mean operative blood pressure while undergoing CABG surgery, the incidence of fixed postoperative neurological deficit was dramatically reduced (1.6% vs. 6.4%, for lower vs. higher mean operative blood pressure, respectively). When this same subset of patients was carefully scrutinized with echocardiography and divided according to the severity of their ascending and descending aortic atherosclerosis, a more striking correlation emerged. A severalfold increase in the fixed stroke rate was found in patients who had advanced atherosclerosis of the aorta when managed at a lower blood pressure range in comparison with those who had the equivalent degree of aortic atherosclerosis when managed in a pressure range closer to their preoperative mean blood pressure. Thirty-three percent of the patients with advanced aortic atherosclerotic cardiovascular disease had strokes with lower intraoperative perfusion pressure, as opposed to only 10% of those in the higher perfusion pressure groups.

POSTOPERATIVE REHABILITATION

If the CABG patient and his or her family understand the process and stresses associated with coronary revascularization, and both have realistic expectations for postoperative functional status associated with a rational chronology for recovery, then their ability to deal with the emotional roller coaster of postoperative life is greatly enhanced. Most patients and families report that the use of educational materials, augmented by support groups and education classes, serve to improve satisfaction with the process and improve their ability to cope with this situation.

Postoperative cardiac physical rehabilitation (whether individual or group structured) further serves to reinforce the successful aspects of the patient's surgical procedure, improves self-esteem, and improves the patient's ability to participate in day-to-day activities. The early recognition and aggressive treatment of true postoperative depression are also essential for optimizing the psychological outcome of coronary revascularization. Waiting for the patient or family to report the classic symptoms and signs of depression significantly delays the effectiveness of intervention. In my clinical experience with the CCABOT studies, patients who have developed depression after cardiac surgery have tended to be quite receptive to counseling as well as to pharmacological intervention. Awareness on the part of the cardiologist and cardiac surgeon and knowledge of the early signs and symptoms of clinical depression thus become more important as increasing numbers of physicians and other health care providers interact with each patient and family. Perhaps the routine use of standardized psychometric testing in the postoperative setting would be a potential surrogate for the more time-consuming and expensive formal psychiatric evaluation as a means of detecting and treating depression early on. A strong long-term relationship between the primary care physician and the patient and his or her family allows them to come forward with nonphysical complaints and concerns and sets the stage for frank and honest discussions about such issues as depression, quality of life, and perceived cognitive and neurological alterations. Reassurance and early intervention for medical and psychiatric problems serve to markedly limit potential deaths incurred from these problems. In addition, mere acknowledging to patients and families that these phenomena are common, amenable to treatment, and extremely short lived for the most part tends to relieve much anxiety associated with these issues.

Clinicians and researchers in many fields are just beginning to explore the diagnosis, prevention, and treatment of the neurological, psychological, cognitive, and functional changes associated with CABG surgery. As new and different modalities are developed to treat ischemic cardiac disease, similar studies will be needed to confirm the safety and efficacy of these modalities, not only from a cardiac perspective but also with regard to their psychological and neurological risk. It will only be through refined and careful study that the optimal outcome associated with all types of treatment modalities for ischemic cardiac disease can be defined and long-term morbidity from such disease truly minimized.

REFERENCES

American Heart Association (1995). *Heart and stroke facts: 1995 statistical supplement*. Dallas, TX: Author.

Barbut, D., Hinton, R. B., Hartman, G. S., Bruefach, M., Hahn, R., Szatrowski, T. P., Charlson, M. E., & Gold, J. P. (1994, September). *Number of emboli detected by TCD during CABG is related to aortic atheroma as assessed by TEE*. Presented at the Third International Conference of the Brain and Cardiac Surgery, Key West, FL.

Blauth, C., Arnold, J., Schulenberg, W., et al. (1988). Cerebral microembolism during cardiopulmonary bypass. *Journal of Thoracic Cardiovascular Surgery, 95*, 668–676.

Coronary Artery Surgery Study principal investigators and their associates. (1984). Myocardial infarction and mortality in the Coronary Artery Surgery Study (CASS) randomized trial. *New England Journal of Medicine, 310*, 750–758.

European Coronary Surgery Study Group. (1982). Long term results of prospective randomised study of coronary artery bypass surgery in stable angina pectoris. *Lancet, 2*, 1173–1180.

Gold, J. P., Charlson, M. E., Williams-Russo, P., et al. (1995). Improvement of outcomes after coronary artery bypass: A randomized trial comparing intraoperative high versus low mean arterial pressure. *Journal of Thoracic Cardiovascular Surgery, 110*, 1302–1314.

Gold, J. P., Hayes, J. G., Charlson, M. E., Williams-Russo, P., Peterson, J. C., Pirraglia, P., Mattis, S., Krieger, K., & Isom, O. W. (1993). Preservation of neurocognitive function after CABG: The impact of age. *Circulation, 88*, I-638.

Hartman, G. S., Bruefach, M., III, Yao, F. S., Barbut, D., Szatrowski, T. P., & the CCABOT Group (1994). Relationship between TEE assessed atheromatous disease of the descending aorta and stroke in CABG patients [Abstract]. *American Society of Anesthesiology.*

Jenkinson, C., Coulter, A., & Wright, L. (1993). Short form 36 (SF-36) health survey questionnaire: Normative data for adults of working age. *British Medical Journal, 306*, 1437–1440.

Katz, E. S., Tunick, P. A., Rusinek, H., Ribakove, G., Spencer, F. C., & Kronzon, I. (1992). Protruding aortic atheromas predict stroke in elderly patients undergoing cardiopulmonary bypass: Experience with intraoperative transesophageal echocardiography. *Journal of the American College of Cardiology, 20,* 70–77.

Marshall, K., Kanchuger, M., Kessler, K., et al. (1992). Superiority of transesophageal echocardiography in detecting aortic arch atheromatous disease: Identification of patients at increased risk of stroke during cardiac surgery. *Journal of Cardiothoracic Anesthesia, 8,* 5–13.

Peterson, J. C. (1994). Functional outcomes after coronary bypass surgery: The impact of gender. *Clinical Research, 42,* 247A.

Peterson, J. C., Gorkin, L., Rothballer, K. B., Pirraglia, P. A., Gold, J. P., & Charlson, M. E. (1993a). Pre-operative depression predicts outcome among cardiac patients. *Clinical Research, 41,* 121A.

Peterson, J. C., Rothballer, K. B., Pirraglia, P., Williams-Russo, P., Gold, J. P., Hayes, J. G., & Charleson, M. E. (1993b). The relationship between gender and functional status in bypass patients. *Circulation, 88,* I-577.

Pirraglia, P. A. (1993, October). *Onset of depression after cardiac surgery hinders improvement of functional status.* Paper presented at the Eastern Conference of the American Federation for Clinical Research.

Pugsley, W., Linger, L., Paschalis, C., Treasure, T., Harrison, M., & Newman, S. (1994). The impact of microemboli during cardiopulmonary bypass on neuropsychological functioning. *Stroke, 25,* 1393–1399.

II

CLINICAL TRIALS

9

THE LIFESTYLE HEART TRIAL: COMPREHENSIVE TREATMENT AND GROUP SUPPORT THERAPY

JAMES H. BILLINGS, LARRY W. SCHERWITZ, RICK SULLIVAN, STEPHEN SPARLER, and DEAN M. ORNISH

In the first part of this chapter, we present our research on the effects of an intensive lifestyle change program on patients with coronary heart disease (CHD). Lifestyle changes in this program include a low-fat vegetarian diet, moderate aerobic exercise, stress management practice, and group support. To date, two pilot studies and two randomized trials have implemented this program with patients who have CHD (Gould et al., 1995; Ornish et al., 1990; Ornish, Gotto, Miller, Rochelle, & McAllister, 1979; Ornish et al., 1983; Scherwitz & Kesten, 1994). A major focus of this chapter is the Lifestyle Heart Trial because this trial involved long-term treatment and follow-up of patients who undertook the lifestyle change program and end results were measured using both quantitative coronary angiography (QCA) and positron emission tomography (PET). It was in the Lifestyle Heart Trial that we refined the group support tech-

This study was supported by grants from the National Heart, Lung, and Blood Institute of the National Institutes of Health (R01 HL42554), the Department of Health Services of the State of California (No. 1256SC-01), Gerald D. Hines Interests, the Houston Endowment, Inc., the Henry J. Kaiser Family Foundation, the John E. Fetzer Institute, Continental Airlines, the Enron Foundation, the Nathan Cummings Foundation, the Pritzker Foundation, the First Boston Corporation, Quaker Oats Company, Texas Commerce Bank, Corrine and David Gould, Pacific Presbyterian Medical Center Foundation, General Growth Companies, Arthur Andersen and Company, and others.

We gratefully acknowledge the many helpful comments from volume editors Robert Allan and Stephen Scheidt. From our institute we thank volunteers Deborah Kesten, Glenn Perelson, and Tim Regoli for editing this manuscript.

niques of the program. To provide a full account of this group process, in the second part of this chapter we discuss the rationale for group support and the techniques we have used to foster group cohesiveness among patients with CHD.

In the past, we have focused much attention on reporting the diet, exercise, and stress management techniques of the program. However, some participants have regarded the group support process as the most important aspect of the program. Group support began as a forum to monitor and promote adherence to the other program components. Over the course of 4 years, the group process deepened and evolved into a therapy to address the psychosocial aspects of CHD, including self-involvement, hostility and anger, alienation, isolation, and loneliness. The Lifestyle Heart Trial was not designed to assess the impact of group support, so we have no empirical data to verify its importance. However, the group support component was an integral part of the therapy and helped participants learn better interpersonal skills, enabling them to develop strong emotional bonds, which are often missing among patients who have CHD.

PAST STUDIES

In 1977 and 1980, Ornish and collaborators conducted two studies to assess the short-term effects of lifestyle change on patients with CHD (Ornish et al., 1979, 1983). These studies provided reasonable evidence that comprehensive lifestyle change without drugs or surgery may improve myocardial perfusion (blood flow to the heart) and left ventricular function.

Pilot Study

The 1977 study involved a 1-month residential intervention with 10 patients (no control group) who were housed in a hotel. During this time, patients ate a very low-fat, low-cholesterol diet, practiced stress management techniques (including stretching and breathing exercises, meditation, visualization, and progressive relaxation) for 2 hours each day, stopped smoking, and began a walking program. After 1 month, patients reported a 90% reduction in frequency of anginal episodes. Objective results included a 62.5% increase in treadmill time and decreases in systolic and diastolic blood pressures, ventricular premature beats, plasma cholesterol, and plasma triglycerides. All of these improvements were statistically significant when each patient was used as his or her own control (in paired t tests). Exercise thallium-201 scintigraphy was performed in only 4 patients (due to a lack of resources), of whom 2 showed improved myocardial perfusion and 2 were unchanged.

First Randomized Clinical Trial

Ornish et al. (1983) next conducted a randomized clinical trial to more thoroughly evaluate the short-term effects of comprehensive lifestyle change in patients with CHD. They compared the cardiovascular status of 24 patients who changed their lifestyle in a 24-day retreat setting with 24 patients who received the usual cardiac care. After 24 days, patients who changed their lifestyle had a 44% mean increase in duration of exercise and a 55% mean increase in total work performed. Exercise radionuclide ventriculography revealed somewhat improved left ventricular regional wall motion during peak exercise in 19 of 24 patients in the experimental group and a net improvement in the left ventricular ejection fraction from rest to maximum exercise of +6.4%. Also, they found a 20.5% mean decrease in total and low-density lipoprotein cholesterol; a reduction in Type A behavior (measured by interview), anxiety, and depression; and a 91.0% mean decrease in frequency of anginal episodes. All of these differences were statistically significant when compared with the usual-care control group. In summary, the findings indicated that even short-term comprehensive lifestyle change not only dramatically reduced risk factors but also greatly improved functioning of the heart and psychological status.

LIFESTYLE HEART TRIAL

The findings from the first two residential studies on the beneficial effects of lifestyle change on CHD raised two important questions: Could patients maintain a vigorous lifestyle change program on a long-term, free-living basis? and Would lifestyle changes halt or even reverse the progression of coronary artery stenosis as measured by QCA?

Study Design

The Lifestyle Heart Trial was designed as a single-blinded, randomized, controlled clinical trial. Sample size calculations based on prior work indicated that a treatment effect of 8% absolute percentage of diameter stenosis between the two groups could be detected, with an estimated power of 90%, by using data from 40 patients at 1-year follow-up.

Patient Recruitment

A cardiac care nurse screened consecutive patients in two San Francisco cardiac catheterization laboratories using criteria specified elsewhere (Ornish et al., 1990). Over a period of 3 years, 93 patients met eligibility requirements for entry into the study. We began by using the classic controlled clinical trial procedure of randomly assigning patients to experimental or control groups after baseline testing. However, we encountered difficulties when patients expressed a strong desire to be assigned to the experimental group. This occurred, in part, because some of these patients either did not have the option of coronary artery bypass graft (CABG) surgery or angioplasty or assiduously wanted to avoid these invasive procedures. It became clear that the internal validity of the study would be seriously compromised by dropouts and crossovers from disappointed patients who were assigned to the control group. Because we expected that more patients would refuse to make intensive lifestyle changes than would refuse to be in the control group, the project biostatistician used a target invitation ratio of five experimental to four control patients to assign patients to groups. Of the 93 eligible patients, 53 were randomly assigned to the experimental group and 40 to the control group, whose members would simply be under the usual care of their own physicians. Patients were then contacted and invited to participate in the study; 28 (53%) and 20 (50%) agreed to participate in the experimental and control groups, respectively.

Measures and Bias Control

The methods for measuring risk factors, program adherence, changes in CHD by QCA, and changes in myocardial blood flow in the trial have been described elsewhere (Gould et al., 1995; Ornish et al., 1990). To reduce the possibility that knowledge of group assignment might bias outcome measurements, technicians responsible for all medical tests were unaware of patients' group assignments.

Description of the Lifestyle Change Intervention

Overview

To acquaint patients and their spouses or partners with the lifestyle change program, intervention began with a week-long residential retreat at a local resort hotel. During the retreat, participants received daily lectures that provided the scientific rationale for the diet, exercise, stress management, and group support components of the program. The retreat also provided two 1-hour stress management sessions per day, aerobic exercise, and evening group support meetings. Most patients began to experience substantial improvements in symptoms (decreased angina, increased energy, and improved well-being) during this week, thereby increasing credibility and motivation. After the retreat, patients attended meetings every Tuesday and Thursday. Each meeting consisted of four 1-hour activities: aerobic exercise, stress management, sharing a low-fat vegetarian dinner, and a support group meeting. The sequence of the evening schedule prepared participants for the often emotionally challenging group process at the end of the evening. The hour each of exercise and stress management promoted relaxation and focused attention, whereas sharing a tasty, healthful meal gave participants an opportunity to socialize.

Aerobic Exercise

Our exercise prescription followed the guidelines of the American College of Sports Medicine (1987). Each patient was prescribed an exercise level according to a baseline treadmill exercise stress test; these levels were updated during each of the following 4 years when subsequent treadmill tests were performed. Patients were asked to exercise a minimum of 3 hours per week and to spend a minimum of 30 minutes per session exercising within their prescribed target heart rates or perceived exertion levels. The target heart rates were calculated at 50%–80% of maximal heart rate achieved during the treadmill test, using the Karvonen formula. If ischemia occurred during the baseline stress test, then the heart rate at which 1 mm of ST-segment depression first occurred was designated the maximum heart rate. In addition, patients were trained to identify exertion levels by means of the Borg Perceived Exertion Scale and asked to maintain exertion levels of 11–14 (*fairly light* to *somewhat hard*) on the 6- to 20-point scale. Most patients' exercise consisted of walking, although some swam or bicycled.

Stress Management Techniques

The stress management practices integrated stretching, relaxation, yogic breathing techniques, meditation, and guided imagery (Ornish, 1982, 1990; Ornish et al., 1983). Each technique was selected for the purpose of enhancing a patient's sense of relaxation, concentration, and awareness of internal states.

Specifically, patients were taught a series of 12 yoga poses designed to stretch and tone the body while developing internal awareness (Ornish, 1990). During the poses, participants were asked to stretch gently and slowly while focusing on their breath, movement, and corresponding sensations. Following the stretching phase, participants lay on their backs for 15 minutes of deep relaxation, using three techniques: (a) squeezing and relaxing individual muscle groups, beginning with the feet and moving toward the head; (b) without moving, mentally focusing on each body part while directing it to relax; and (c) concentrating on breathing followed by meditating on a sense of peace.

Following the relaxation, patients sat in a comfortable upright position and practiced breathing techniques designed to energize the body and relax and balance mental awareness. Then patients sat for 5 minutes to focus on one object or process such as the breath, a word, a prayer, or a sense of peace. As the last technique, patients were asked to visualize their arteries dilating with increased blood flow to the heart. Patients were asked to practice the five stress management techniques for at least 1 hour per day, using an audiocassette for home practice.

Diet

Patients and their spouses prepared food at home and brought it to the twice-weekly group meetings for the evening meal. Their creativity in preparing raw fruits and vegetables as well as cooked vegetables, beans, grains, and legumes was inspiring for both staff and visitors. The diet excluded caffeine and limited animal products to egg whites and one cup of nonfat milk or yogurt daily; this averaged 10 mg of cholesterol intake per day. Alcohol, which was not served or encouraged, was restricted to one drink (one cocktail or a glass of wine or beer) per day for those without prior alcohol abuse. Sodium intake was restricted only for hypertensive patients or those with congestive heart failure or renal disease. Meals contained approximately 10% of daily calories from fat, 15% from protein, and 75% from complex carbohydrates.

Group Support Meetings

After dinner, participants gathered in groups of 8–14 people, then formed a circle sitting in chairs. In this format, the participants and staff members spent an hour talking and listening to one another. Following a description of the Lifestyle Heart Trial findings, we discuss the group process and specific techniques in detail.

Results

Lifestyle Changes After 1 Year

Results indicated that patients could make and maintain comprehensive lifestyle changes. Fat intake was reduced from 30.8% of total calories at baseline to 7.0% at 1 year, exercise increased from 19.7 to 40.2 minutes per day, and stress management practice increased from 6.2 to 77.1 minutes per day. In the control group, patients maintained prior fat intake (29.3% to 29.4% of total calories) and made little change in prior exercise levels (from 18.4 to 20.6 minutes per day) or stress management practices (from 1.7 to 4.3 minutes per day).

Weight and Chest Pain

Consistent with the low-fat dietary and exercise changes, lifestyle change patients lost an average of 20.5 lb in the first year; they also reduced their angina frequency from 6.38 to 0.56 attacks per week. In contrast, control group patients gained 3 lb the first year, and their angina frequency increased from 1.43 to 4.00 attacks per week.

Coronary Artery Lesion Changes After 1 Year

In the 28 patients enrolled in the experimental group, 154 lesions with narrowings greater than 20% were identified, 54 of which were more than 50% stenosed, and 21 of which were totally occluded, indicating that these patients had severe CHD. Each patient had at least one lesion greater than 50% stenosed, and most had more severe lesions. Of the 20 patients in the control group, 132 lesions greater than 20% were identified, 33 of which were more than 50% blocked, of which 7 were totally occluded. Stenosis, measured by the percentage of the narrowing of coronary luminal diameter, decreased from 40.0% to 37.8% in the lifestyle change group yet progressed from 42.7% to 46.1% in the control group ($p = .001$, two-tailed). When stenotic lesions greater than 50% were analyzed, average stenosis regressed from 61.1% to 55.8% in the experimental group but progressed from 61.7% to 64.4% in the control group ($p = .03$, two-tailed). Although 82% of patients in the experimental group had average changes in the direction of regression of coronary atherosclerosis, approximately 53% of patients in the usual-care group had changes in the direction of progression of stenosis. Furthermore, in an analysis combining the experimental and control groups, the degree of lifestyle change was positively correlated with changes in coronary atherosclerosis ($r = .45$, $p = .01$).

Lifestyle Changes After 4 Years

After 4 years, results revealed adequate adherence by program participants, especially to the diet, but some reduction in exercise and a somewhat greater drop in the practice of stress management. Analysis of 3-day diet diaries indicated that lifestyle group patients consumed an average of 8.3% of calories from fat and 38.9 mg cholesterol in comparison with control patients, who consumed 28.0% of calories from fat and 154.1 mg of cholesterol. Patients in both groups exercised 4 times per week for a similar duration. Patients in the lifestyle change group practiced an average of 3.2 stress management techniques per day for a mean of 43.7 minutes, in comparison with control group patients, who practiced an average of 0.63 techniques for a mean of 9.8 minutes per day.

Psychosocial Changes at 1 and 4 Years

The lifestyle change intervention appears to have had a strong and consistent positive effect on reducing the psychosocial risk factors of anger and hostility. Lifestyle change group patients had a significant reduction in Spielberger trait anger compared with no change in the control group at 1 year ($p = .05$); this effect was maintained at the 4-year follow-up. Likewise, Type A behavior, assessed by interview, was reduced in the lifestyle change group more than in the control group at both 1- and 4-year follow-ups, although the difference was not statistically significant. However, within the total Type A score, an interview-derived rating of hostility at 1 year decreased significantly more in the lifestyle change group than in the control group, and this effect was maintained after 4 years ($p = .05$). We did not actively try to alter Type A behavior as part of the intervention or group process.

Lesion Changes and Cardiac Perfusion Results at 4 Years

After 4 years of lifestyle change therapy, percentage of diameter stenosis continued to improve, but at a slower rate than during the first year, although minimum diameter (a measure of the most stenosed artery segment) remained unchanged. Conversely, in the control group, coronary stenosis worsened by both lesion measures. Lesions regressed from 38.9% diameter stenosis to 35.9% in the lifestyle change group but progressed from 42.5% to 54.3% in the control group ($p = .001$). Minimum diameter remained unchanged from a baseline of 1.64 mm in the lifestyle change group but narrowed from 1.74 to 1.44 mm in the control group ($p = .05$). Regression of coronary atherosclerosis was most remarkable in those patients who adhered best to the diet, exercised more than 3 times per week, and practiced more than 1 hour of stress management each day. There was a dose–response relationship between adherence to the intervention and change in percentage of diameter stenosis in both experimental and control groups at 1 year and after 4 years.

Findings for coronary artery stenosis were corroborated with PET scans measuring perfusion of blood to the heart (Gould et al., 1995). PET scans revealed that the size and severity of perfusion abnormalities (quantitatively measured by computer) during hand-grip exercise and dipyridamole infusion improved in the lifestyle change group but worsened in the control group. Specifically, the percentage of the left ventricle with perfusion abnormalities more than 2.5 standard deviations below normal decreased by 5.1% in the lifestyle group but increased by 10.3% in the control group ($p = .02$). Similarly, the percentage of left ventricle activity below 60% of maximum increased 13.5% in the control group and decreased 4.2% in the experimental group ($p = .004$).

Cardiac Events

All 48 patients were followed after 4 years to determine the incidence of myocardial infarctions (MIs), coronary angioplasties and CABG surgeries, cardiac-related hospitalizations, and deaths. Results showed a substantially higher percentage of patients having coronary events as well as a higher total number of events in the control group than in the experimental group. Control patients were more likely to have had coronary angioplasty and CABG surgery or to have been hospitalized for cardiac-related problems than were experimental patients. The number of patients with MIs was similar (2 in each group), although the number of MIs was twice as high in the control group because 2 patients each had two subsequent reinfarctions.

Discussion

The results indicate that selected heart patients can maintain intensive lifestyle changes for 4 years. In the Lifestyle Heart Trial and three other studies of shorter duration (Ornish et al., 1979, 1983; Scherwitz & Kesten, 1994), patients adhered well to the program. A primary reason for such adherence may be the immediacy with which patients experienced benefits from following the regimen. Experiencing these benefits is a strong reinforcement for adhering to the program, and witnessing such benefits in others is also encouraging.

A second aspect that may promote adherence is harder to define. We think it may have been the feeling of community that came from participating in the program. This sense of community was fostered most in the group support meetings. Indeed, encouraging results from other clinical trials have shown that group-based therapies alone may positively influence the outcome of chronic diseases. The group therapy most researched is the cognitive-behavioral approach to reducing Type A behavior (Levenkron & Moore, 1988; Nunes, Frank, & Kornfeld, 1987; Price, 1988). Most notably, in the Recurrent Coronary Prevention Project (Friedman et al., 1986), a 44% reduction in recurrent MI was reported among patients with CHD who received counseling for Type A behavior and CHD risk factors in comparison with those who received counseling only about standard risk factors (see also chaps. 10 and 11, this volume). Also, in a study consisting of 86 metastatic breast cancer patients, those who participated in a weekly "supportive–expressive" group averaged a 36.6-month survival time compared with 18.9 months for patients in a routine-care control group (Spiegel, Bloom, Kraemer, & Gottheil, 1989).

As far as we know, no other research project has requested as much lifestyle change as we have through this program. Why were the required changes so great? In designing the Lifestyle Heart Trial it was not known how much lifestyle change would be required to stop the progression of coronary disease; therefore, our minimum guidelines consisted of substantial changes. Had this program not shown dramatic results, we would have been more confident that lifestyle change alone is not sufficient to halt disease progression. Correlational analyses assessing the relationship of program adherence to lesion changes indicated that our minimum guidelines were just enough to stop the progression of disease. Those who did more than 3 hours of exercise per week, practiced more than 1 hour of stress management techniques daily, and most closely followed the diet improved the most. These results support an intensive approach and raise the possibility that even more regression is possible with more lifestyle change than our minimum guidelines.

We want to be clear that all patients are not motivated to make intensive lifestyle changes. Difficulty in following our program depends on participants' life experience, insight, and willingness to change. From talking with patients who have been most successful in terms of disease reversal, it is clear that they have not viewed the program as difficult to follow. At the beginning, through study and self-examination, the program offered patients the opportunity to identify ways in which lifestyle had contributed to their disease. They responded by placing their health and well-being as a top priority, simplifying their lives, leaving out what was harmful, and taking the time to adhere to the program fully. For these individuals, following the program became a way of life. Some patients, on the other hand, may struggle at first to follow the guidelines and then subsequently experience markedly reduced angina, increased peacefulness, greater joy, and closer ties with friends, which will reinforce the program's approach and make following it a priority.

The QCA and PET results provided convincing evidence in this study population that a program of intensive lifestyle change reversed the progression of CHD and increased blood flow to the heart. In the control group, the percentage of diameter stenosis progressed from 42.5% at baseline to 54.3% at 4 years—a diameter increase of 11.8%—even though diet and exercise among control participants were close to conventionally recommended American Heart Association and National Cholesterol Education Program guidelines. Evidently, moderate risk-factor changes were inadequate to halt CHD progression in this population. Thus, an absolute increase of 11.8% of diameter stenosis is our best estimate of what would have happened to the experimental group patients had they not adopted intensive lifestyle changes. However, they showed a decreased absolute change of 3.1% of diameter stenosis (significant by pre- and post-t test for the experimental group, $p = .02$). Although this is a modest change in the direction of reversal, when added to the 11.8% progression that was presumably halted, it equals an absolute difference of 14.9% of diameter stenosis, which is good evidence of a strong and clinically significant treatment effect.

PET results showed an even stronger treatment effect at 4- to 5-year follow-up. It appears that myocardial perfusion, a crucial factor, increased even more than one would expect from the angiographic changes. Other mechanisms, including endothelial-mediated vasodilatation of epicardial arteries and changes in coronary microcirculation, may contribute to these differences (Harrison, Armstrong, Freiman, & Heistad, 1987; Kuo, Davis, Cannon, & Chilian, 1992; Zeiher, Drexler, Wollschlager, & Just, 1991).

We are frequently asked which component of the lifestyle change program was most clinically effective. The Lifestyle Heart Trial was not designed to assess the relative impact of each component, and all components may have worked together synergistically to produce the benefits found. For example, many people overeat fatty foods during times of stress, so stress management may enhance dietary adherence. Nevertheless, both dietary fat and cholesterol as well as amount of stress management practice were significantly correlated with changes in percentage of diameter stenosis measured at both 1 and 4 years, providing some support that both of these components were important for obtaining regression. However, these components were confounded with exercise, stress management, and group support, so we cannot be certain about their relative importance for the treatment effect. There is good evidence that dietary adherence could not have accounted for all the clinical benefits: Within the experimental group, all but one patient closely followed the diet, yet those who did more stress management practice had more regression than those who did less. Stress management practice was also significantly correlated with decreases in low-density lipoprotein cholesterol and hostility, providing two possible pathways that could have affected lesion change. Behavioral studies that attempt to vary only one independent variable are difficult to implement, because cardiac patients tend to change lifestyle in multiple ways, thus confounding the intervention. Also, for any given individual, the relative importance of each component may vary.

Because half of the patients who were invited refused to participate, the study may not be representative of all patients who have CHD. The strategy of the Lifestyle Heart Trial was to maximize internal validity—to motivate patients to make intensive changes in lifestyle—and then to assess the effects of those changes with the best available measures. Now that we know there is a clinical benefit, at least with the population studied, further studies are needed to determine whether other intervention teams can be trained to implement the program in diverse populations and whether these populations, including women, minorities, and the less educated, would be willing to undergo such intensive lifestyle change.

Currently, we are conducting a multicenter lifestyle heart trial with 600 patients in eight hospitals in a variety of areas in the United States. This study will assess whether other teams can implement the program on a cost-effective basis and whether they can motivate patients to adhere to the program. Assessment will include the extent to which such patients can reduce risk factors, avoid coronary events, and reduce the need for CABG surgery, coronary angioplasty, and cardiovascular medications.

THE SUPPORT GROUP AS THERAPY

The Importance of Group Therapy With Cardiac Patients

Patients who have CHD seem especially prone to the cultural emphasis on individualism and accomplishment, characteristics that promote isolation rather than interpersonal connection. They often are so absorbed with "comparing" and "doing" that there is little inclination or ability to connect and relate to others. Results from our studies and others have shown that patients with CHD are self-involved (Scherwitz, Graham, Grandits, Buehler, & Billings, 1986; Scherwitz et al., 1983), socially isolated (Ruberman, Weinblatt, Goldberg, & Chaudhary, 1984), inattentive to others (Friedman & Rosenman, 1974), and often harbor impatience, competitiveness, hostility, and depression (Friedman & Powell, 1984). Thus, the rationale of our group support therapy is that if lack of social support, self-involvement, and hostility are contributing factors in CHD, then social connectedness and greater emotional intimacy may help patients to heal (Berkman & Syme, 1979; Ornish, 1990; Orth-Gomér, Rosengren, & Wilhelmsen, 1993).

From a sociological perspective, the support group process may help to counter the self-involvement, loneliness, and alienation that is so common in American culture because of the breakdown in social networks (e.g., extended families, neighborhoods, and religious institutions). American culture, and perhaps much of Western culture, tends to prize individualism and downplay relatedness, especially for men (Bellah, Madsen, Sullivan, Swidler, & Typton, 1985; Guisinger & Blatt, 1994).

Given the wealth of experimental evidence for the high prevalence of psychosocial problems in patients with CHD (Allan & Scheidt, 1992, 1993) and their history of poor adherence to risk-factor reduction, it has been our experience that a group support component is very helpful to (a) greatly increase adherence to other parts of the treatment protocol; (b) reduce hostility, depression, and social isolation, which are risk factors for recurrent cardiac events; and (c) produce other effects that are not fully understood but that may relate to both improved quality of life and clinical outcome.

Description of Group Support Therapy

Meetings with patients in the experimental group of the Lifestyle Heart Trial typically began with a brief meditation that included closing the eyes and focusing on breathing. This provided a transition from social interaction at dinner to the task of focused talking and listening. Next, the group leader often suggested recalling an event or experience in the last week that was upsetting, uplifting, or otherwise stimulated a feeling or set of emotions. The group leader then suggested that participants choose one word that best characterized their feelings. After members opened their eyes, the leader asked each participant to share the word that he or she had chosen. Group members could then ask one another to explain or expand on the feelings characterized by their words.

This sharing of feelings and focused listening continued for most of the hour. Usually several participants had a chance to speak at length, and all were allowed to share their experience if they chose. Given the typical psychosocial characteristics of patients with CHD, it was not surprising that it was often challenging to motivate our research participants to speak genuinely about their feelings and to listen with empathy and compassion. This type of communication may be difficult for an action-oriented CHD patient because it triggers introspection, which is often unpleasant and difficult to put into words.

Additionally, these patients may be less familiar with the experiences of stillness and openness that may facilitate the ability to listen to others with empathy and compassion. Stillness involves calming the mind. Openness requires holding the other's experience in consciousness, even when unpleasant, long enough to find one's own personal response to what has been expressed. Practicing this type of communication is often contrary to many CHD patients' tendencies to isolate themselves by emphasizing differences and ignoring similarities between themselves and others.

At first, many of our research participants were acutely aware of differences in socioeconomic and marital status, race, education, religion, verbal fluency, psychological development, and sexual preference. We encouraged patients to look for similarities rather than the differences among group members. As patients began to experience their similarity in feelings, they often developed greater empathy, compassion, connection, and community with each other. Listening to other group members express feelings sometimes makes it easier for listeners to recognize their own feelings; it can also be less threatening than expressing one's own feelings. However, active listening can be also be tedious and tension filled, particularly for those who are not used to this process. We think the stress management techniques were useful in helping patients develop the stillness and openness required to listen and respond. It also may have helped them to become more aware of their own feelings and thoughts that were at the threshold of their awareness.

The interactive process of talking and listening served to shift the focus from the leader to the participants, helping participants to develop the skill to express empathy toward one another. Sessions ended with patients joining hands, closing their eyes, and sitting for a moment of silence. The group leader often closed with a few sentences designed to summarize the issues raised by members and to emphasize the similarities among the expressed feelings and experiences.

Communication Skills

Focus on Feelings

Our major activity in the group meetings was the practice of speaking and listening to one another sincerely express feelings. We used feelings as the medium of communication for several reasons. In interpersonal communication, feelings are less likely to be disputed than thoughts, more likely to be accepted at face value, and less likely to be heard as criticism. The participants' search for compassionate responses from their own experience provided much needed practice for finding similarities rather than differences among themselves. Focusing on feelings in the group also gave the participants an understandable reason to develop the ability to identify how they felt. It helped give them the sense that they were having feeling responses to things much of the time, even when they were unaware of them.

Another goal was to emphasize the process of being with people rather than doing anything with or for them. Being silent and listening to another person's feelings without giving advice or trying to solve his or her problem is a key to experiencing intimacy and connectedness.

To enhance participants' learning about interpersonal communication, we divided the process of speaking and listening into four stages or skills (in accordance with Ornish, 1990):

Self-communication:
1. Identification of feelings.
2. Expression of feelings.
Other communication:
3. Listening with empathy and compassion.
4. Expression of empathy and compassion.

Identification of Feelings

In our framework, it is axiomatic that the ability to identify and experience emotions is essential to communicate successfully in the group. Although this appears to be simple in theory, it was often difficult for the patients in practice. When dealing with personal problems and issues, patients who have CHD tend to think, solve, and then move on. Feelings are generally disregarded as irrelevant, uninteresting, or destructive. When restricted from forming opinions and problem solving, it was not unusual for patients to become somewhat anxious or irritated, asking, "What am I supposed to do here?" When this occurred, the group leader suggested that they pay attention to how they were feeling and reminded them that the problem to be solved in the group was how to heal isolation and enhance intimacy.

To identify a feeling, one must detect it in awareness and sometimes locate it as a physical sensation. An effective technique for accessing feelings that are subtle or not immediately apparent is to become quiet and relaxed, focusing one's attention on breathing and then on one's general feeling state. Time and focus are needed to translate a sensation of the inner state into the language of emotion. It is also necessary to learn a vocabulary of emotional expression as well as both the ability and inclination to reflect on one's own emotional history. To accomplish this, we worked to distinguish feelings from thoughts in the group. This was often a challenge, because thoughts can masquerade as feelings (e.g., "I feel that I'm right.").

Additionally, participants practiced identifying judgments, which can be particularly isolating thoughts, such as, "I feel you should . . . ," "You never . . . ," or "You always . . . ." To further develop the skill of identifying feelings, staff urged participants to monitor feelings and tensions throughout the day, making these feelings the focus of attention while breathing deeply and relaxing.

Expression of Feelings

It is not difficult for patients with CHD to express such "big muscle" emotions as anger, frustration, or impatience; to express sensitive or tender feelings is much more challenging, however. This is due in part either to a lack of awareness of subtle feelings or to the belief that revealing tender feelings brings with it a sense of vulnerability and inadequacy. Hence, we focused on the self-affirming properties of self-expression.

We began with simple practices. For instance, group meetings often started by having participants spend a few moments meditating on their feeling state. Then the leader might ask each group member to complete just one sentence beginning with "I feel. . . ." All the while, the group leader listened for clues that distinguished thoughts from feelings. For example, it was likely to be a thought masquerading as a feeling if a participant's answer began with "I feel as if," or "I feel that," or if his or her answer contained a judgment, such as "I feel ignored." An alternative technique, which was simpler but required more discipline, was for participants to choose just one word to express how they were feeling. This expression was succinct enough so that all could speak, and it often raised curiosity so that participants encouraged each other to elaborate. Asking another to expand on a feeling is often perceived as a gesture of support as well as an invitation to talk. A third approach was for someone to tell a significant feeling experience. This provided a deeper listening practice for everyone as there was more detail and more time to explore one's own feeling reactions.

Listening With Empathy and Compassion

One guideline in group support situations is that everything that takes place in the group is important. A joke, silence, or sarcasm all mean something. Although many people may be educated to be good speakers, it is not likely that they have been taught to listen actively. Becoming a good listener begins with concentration on what the speaker is saying, both verbally and nonverbally. To concentrate requires the listener to penetrate a screen of psychological distractions and stay focused on the speaker.

One major distraction was often the CHD patients' impulse to fix the speaker's problem. A frequent tendency was to give opinions or unsolicited advice. We do not consider this type of response as empathic, and it is often unpleasant for the person whose problem is being discussed. Giving opinions and advice can easily isolate the person with the problem from the person offering the advice. First, it highlights an inadequacy, namely, that one hasn't solved his or her own problem. Second, the advice-giver may assume a position of superiority, which exacerbates this sense of inadequacy. The result is often a loss of self-esteem and withdrawal from the advice-giver.

Instead, we encouraged patients to listen carefully and scan their past experience for a similar situation or feeling and relive it briefly in their imagination before responding. The task was to balance the moments of "leaving oneself" and stepping into someone else's life with finding an empathic and compassionate response from one's personal experience.

Expression of Empathy and Compassion

The next phase, the expression of an empathic and compassionate response, enhanced the connection we were seeking in the group process. This connection happens when the person talking knows that another person understands his or her feelings. To remove some of the more common obstacles to experiencing and expressing empathy and compassion, we asked participants to follow some simple rules: (a) Do not give advice unless it is asked for, (b) do not give reassurance unless it is requested, and (c) do not give testimonials about your successful or unsuccessful experience with a problem that someone else is bringing up unless the point you are making is your understanding of the person's feelings.

Empathic responses usually take the form of sharing a feeling. This feeling can be a physical sensation, such as "I felt queasy while I was listening to you describe that." Or the feeling could be an emotion, such as "I feel sad that I can't express all of the feelings I have about what you're saying" or "I feel frustrated that I can't make it better for you." Sometimes the response might be a memory of a similar experience that can be shared simply and directly.

Group Session Excerpt

The following excerpt from a group meeting illustrates the brevity of exchanges, the expression and content of everyday feelings, and the leader's role in encouraging listening with empathy and compassion. At the beginning of the session, each person in the group was asked to describe, using one word, how he or she was feeling.

Participant P (67-year-old spouse of a CHD patient): "I would like to hear more about the feeling 'competitive' expressed by Participant M."

Participant M (72-year-old female CHD patient who had used the word *competitive* to express her feeling): "I feel almost embarrassed to say this, it's so silly. I know I shouldn't feel this way but . . . I love to garden and I have a garden. It's a lovely garden, but I can't quite get myself to finish it. I know when I finish it I will invite several other real gardeners to see it. I know how they will see it, and when I see my garden through their eyes, what I'll see is what is wrong or missing. It will make me feel competitive and inadequate."

Participant F (70-year-old male CHD patient whose significant other does not participate in the program): "Are [these people] really that good?"

Participant M: "Oh yes, I'm pretty good but they are world-class gardeners; they are world-class everything. They are lively, energetic, and are doing so many wonderful things with their lives. They are busy, active, and productive. Great gardening is just one of the things they do."

Participant L (67-year-old single male CHD and stroke patient): "So, it's more than just gardening, it's their life compared to yours."

Participant M: "Yes, it's more than just gardening. I admire them but I also know that what they do is just not me. Sometimes I wish it were but I know it's not."

Participant H (the 70-year-old husband of P, who opened the discussion): "What would you like to hear from them when they see your garden?"

Participant M: "I don't want them to say anything. I know what they will think, and I don't want them to say something that I know they don't believe just to be nice. That would be awful."

Participant P (spouse of H): "I'm sure your garden is really wonderful and being concerned about what they will think spoils your experience of your garden."

Group Leader (GL [the clinical psychologist]): "You want M to feel differently than she does about this. You want her to feel better?"

[Participant P smiles and nods.]

GL: "Let's take a quiet moment to reflect on what M is telling us and how she feels. Can you think of a situation where you know that what you're feeling is not what you should feel? In this case it feels bad that no matter how well you do something, you know someone else can do it better. You know how easy it is to get stuck in that feeling and how hard it is to get out, even when you know it's crazy."

[Many participants nod their heads in a gesture of understanding.]

Participant H: "I understand how that feels, and I also was aware that I would feel upset if I came to see your garden and I felt I couldn't say I liked it . . . that you wouldn't believe me."

Participant M: "I hadn't thought of that. I understand, but it would be hard for me to hear that."

GL: "Can everybody understand that feeling? How hard it is to get a compliment and just accept it?"

[Most participants smile and nod; 30 seconds of silence follow.]

GL to Participant M: "Is there more that you would like to say about any of this?"

Participant M: "No. It's a big issue for me. I need to keep working on it."

[30 seconds of silence.]

Stress management teacher (SMT) to Participant H: "I want to hear more about your word, *happy*."

Participant H (who retired 2 years before because of job-related stress): "I just got back from a trip to China. I did some work and felt good. I used my brain and it still worked. That felt really good. It just felt good to be alive and feel alive—to feel productive. It's been a long time since I felt that way. It feels really good to feel happy again."

[Group members smile and clap spontaneously because all have been with H through difficult times; 50 seconds of silence follow.]

Participant G to SMT: "I would like to hear about your word, *helix*. What is a helix feeling?"

SMT: "I don't know if *helix* is the right word. It was the symbol that came to mind when I was trying to find my feeling word. I feel all twisted in circles. I feel both happy and sad. My youngest daughter, whom I adore, is graduating from high school and will be leaving home soon. She is ready to go and I am prepared to say goodbye to this period of our lives together. I feel sad because she is my last physical link to Fred, her father and my deceased husband. He has somehow been alive in the stories that I tell her about her father. I think I'm going to miss that a lot."

GL: "It's like losing Fred again."

SMT: [Nods tearfully.]

[The group is silent, its attention focused intensely on SMT's feelings. Many participants are teary-eyed; the silence is unusually long. This exchange, occurring near the end of the hour, initiates the group closing.]

Role of the Leader

The group leader should act as a clinician, educator, coach, and role model. As a clinician, the group leader should screen potential participants and identify those who are not likely to succeed in following the program and those who would be disruptive to the group process. We have found that patients with highly unsupportive spouses or those currently manifesting self-destructive addictions such as cigarette smoking, alcoholism, or drug abuse are less likely to succeed in our program.

As a therapist and educator, the group leader should be experienced and well informed about all components of the lifestyle program in order to teach and reinforce program adherence. Also, the leader should be conversant with group-related psychological concepts so that he or she can answer such questions as "What is empathy?" "Why is giving advice discouraged?" or "What does any of this have to do with heart disease?" As a clinician, he or she needs to be familiar with the pathophysiology of CHD, its clinical manifestations, and the epidemiological and clinical research on psychosocial and standard risk factors. As a coach, the group leader's primary role is that of facilitating the emotional connection or bonding among participants. This involves reminding participants when they are straying from the practice of the four communication skills.

The group leader also needs to be experienced at handling interpersonal conflict. Patients who have CHD tend to be intense and hostile, especially in the early stages of the program. Anger is often directed at the group leader and at other participants. The group leader should remind participants that tension is related to the emergence of differences in the group, and that the task is to reconcile oneself to the inevitability of differences in any group, to accept the differences, and to seek to understand the other person's perspective and feelings.

As a role model and a participant in the lifestyle heart program, the group leader is also expected to follow all aspects of the program and to disclose personal and intimate information when appropriate in the group setting. We think that this level of involvement and openness, along with the leader's accessibility during dinner and informal talks, enhances the group experience.

CONCLUSION

These observations, impressions, and speculations on the group support process, bolstered by the success apparent from results of the Lifestyle Heart Trial, are just a beginning. Clearly, there is something special about the intimate connections of group meetings for patients who have CHD that is not fully understand. We encourage clinicians to use group support techniques as an enriching experience that will help participants make and maintain behavioral and risk-factor changes. Furthermore, we hope that our experience stimulates investigators to research group processes by developing measures of progress and by correlating such measures with behavioral and clinical outcomes.

REFERENCES

Allan, R., & Scheidt, S. (1992). Is coronary heart disease a lifestyle disorder? A review of psychologic and behavioral factors: I. *Cardiovascular Reviews and Reports, 13,* 13–53.

Allan, R., & Scheidt, S. (1993). Is coronary heart disease a lifestyle disorder? A review of psychologic and behavioral factors: II. *Cardiovascular Reviews and Reports, 14,* 35–51.

American College of Sports Medicine. (1987). *Guidelines for exercise testing and prescription.* Philadelphia: Lea & Febiger.

Bellah, R. N., Madsen, R., Sullivan, W. M., Swidler, A., & Typton, S. M. (1985). *Habits of the heart.* New York: Harper & Row.

Berkman, L. F., & Syme, S. L. (1979). Social networks, host resistance and mortality: A nine-year follow-up study of Alameda County residents. *American Journal of Epidemiology, 109,* 186–204.

Friedman, M., & Powell, L. H. (1984). The diagnosis and quantitative assessment of Type A behavior: Introduction and description of the videotaped structured interview. *Integrative Psychiatry, 2,* 123–129.

Friedman, M., & Rosenman, R. (1974). *Type A behavior and your heart.* New York: Knopf.

Friedman, M., Thoresen, C. E., Gill, J. J., Ulmer, D., Powell, L., Price, V., Brown, B., Thompson, L., Rabin, D., Breall, W. S., Bourg, E., Levy, R. L., & Dixon, T. (1986). Alteration of Type A behavior and its effect on cardiac recurrences in post-myocardial infarction patients: Summary results of the Recurrent Coronary Prevention Project. *American Heart Journal, 112,* 653–665.

Gould, K. L., Ornish, D., Scherwitz, L., Brown, S., Edens, R. P., Hess, M. J., Mullani, N., Bolomey, L., Dobbs, F., Armstrong, W. T., Merritt, T., Ports, T., Sparler, S., & Billings, J. (1995). Changes in myocardial perfusion abnormalities by positron emission tomography after long-term, intense risk factor modification. *Journal of the American Medical Association, 274,* 894–901.

Guisinger, S., & Blatt, S. J. (1994). Individuality and relatedness: Evaluation of a fundamental dialectic. *American Psychologist, 49,* 104–110.

Harrison, D. G., Armstrong, M. L., Freiman, P. C., & Heistad, D. D. (1987). Restoration of endothelium-dependent relaxation by dietary treatment of atherosclerosis. *Journal of Clinical Investigation, 80,* 1801–1811.

Kuo, L., Davis, M. J., Cannon, S., & Chilian, W. M. (1992). Pathophysiological consequences of atherosclerosis extend into the coronary microcirculation. *Circulation Research, 70,* 465–476.

Levenkron, J. C., & Moore, G. L. (1988). Type A behavior pattern: Issues for intervention research. *Annals of Behavioral Medicine, 10,* 78–83.

Nunes, E., Frank, K. A., & Kornfeld, D. S. (1987). Psychologic treatment for Type A behavior pattern and coronary heart disease: A meta-analysis of the literature. *Psychosomatic Medicine, 48,* 159–173.

Ornish, D. M. (1982). *Stress, diet, and your heart*. New York: Holt, Rinehart & Winston.

Ornish, D. M. (1990). *Dr. Dean Ornish's program for reversing heart disease*. New York: Random House.

Ornish, D. M., Brown, S. E., Scherwitz, L. W., Billings, J. H., Armstrong, W. T., Ports, T. A., McLanahan, S. M., Kirkeeide, R. L., Brand, R. J., & Gould, K. L. (1990). Can lifestyle changes reverse coronary heart disease? The Lifestyle Heart Trial. *Lancet, 336*, 129–133.

Ornish, D. M., Gotto, A. M., Miller, R. R., Rochelle, D., & McAllister, G. K. (1979). Effects of a vegetarian diet and selected yoga techniques in the treatment of coronary heart disease. *Clinical Research, 27*, 720A.

Ornish, D. M., Scherwitz, L. W., Doody, R. S., Kesten, D., McLanahan, S. M., Brown, S. E., DePuey, E. G., Sonnemaker, R., Haynes, C., Lester, J., McAllister, G. K., Hall, R. J., Burdine, J. A., & Gotto, A. M. (1983). Effects of stress management training and dietary changes in treating ischemic heart disease. *Journal of the American Medical Association, 249*, 54–59.

Orth-Gomér, K., Rosengren, A., & Wilhelmsen, L. (1993). Lack of social support and incidence of coronary heart disease in middle-aged Swedish men. *Psychosomatic Medicine, 55*, 37–43.

Price, V. A. (1988). Research and clinical issues in treating Type A behavior. In B. K. Houston & C. R. Snyder (Eds.), *Type A behavior pattern: Research, theory and intervention* (pp. 275–311). New York: Wiley.

Ruberman, W., Weinblatt, E., Goldberg, J., & Chaudhary, B. S. (1984). Psychosocial influences on mortality after myocardial infarction. *New England Journal of Medicine, 311*, 552–559.

Scherwitz, L., Graham, L. E., Grandits, G., Buehler, J., & Billings, J. (1986). Self-involvement and coronary heart disease incidence in the Multiple Risk Factor Intervention Trial. *Psychosomatic Medicine, 48*, 187–199.

Scherwitz, L., & Kesten, D. (1994). The German Lifestyle Change Pilot Project: Effects of diet and other lifestyle changes on coronary heart disease. *Homeostasis, 35*, 198–204.

Scherwitz, L., McKelvain, R., Laman, C., Patterson, J., Dutton, L., Yusim, S., Lester, J., Draft, I., Rochelle, D., & Leachman, R. (1983). Type A behavior, self-involvement, and coronary atherosclerosis. *Psychosomatic Medicine, 45*, 47–57.

Spiegel, D., Bloom, J. R., Kraemer, H. C., & Gottheil, E. (1989). Effect of psychosocial treatment on survival of patients with metastatic breast cancer. *Lancet, 2*, 888–891.

Zeiher, A. M., Drexler, H., Wollschlager, H., & Just, H. (1991). Endothelial dysfunction of the coronary microvasculature is associated with impaired coronary blood flow regulation in patients with early atherosclerosis. *Circulation, 84*, 1984–1992.

10

REDUCING TYPE A BEHAVIOR PATTERNS: A STRUCTURED-GROUP APPROACH

PAUL E. BRACKE and CARL E. THORESEN

In the worry and strain of modern life, arterial degeneration is not only very common but develops often at a relatively early age. For this I believe that the high pressure at which men live and the habit of working the machine to its maximum capacity are responsible rather than excesses in eating and drinking. (Sir William Osler, 1897, p. 153)

Despite substantial advances in controlled research as well as clinical practice over the past 3 decades, diseases of the cardiovascular system remain the leading cause of death in the United States and other Western industrial cultures (American Heart Association, 1991). According to a recent World Health Organization study comparing coronary deaths and nonfatal heart attacks at 38 research centers in 21 industrialized nations, the United States ranked in the top third, with the 10th highest rate for men and 8th highest for women (Tunstall-Redoe et al., 1994). Although age-specific mortality rates in the United States from cardiovascular disease, especially coronary heart disease (CHD) for those under 70, have declined about 35% since the late 1960s, the total proportion of death due to CHD has not changed significantly (Sutherland, Pershy, & Brody, 1990). CHD remains the leading overall cause of mortality in men and women, accounting for six times more deaths than cancer. Furthermore, women who suffer a heart attack have twice the death rate as do men (Mattsen & Herd, 1988).

We are greatly indebted to Meyer Friedman, MD, the principal investigator of the Recurrent Coronary Prevention Project, for his support and encouragement, as well as to the many colleagues at the Meyer Friedman Institute, Mt. Zion Medical Center, University of California, San Francisco. We remain solely responsible, however, for what appears in this chapter.

Support for part of the research reported here was provided by Grant 2R01H34396 to Carl E. Thoresen from the National Heart, Lung, and Blood Institute.

In this chapter, we discuss a treatment for reducing the Type A behavior pattern (TABP) and, consequently, reducing coronary recurrences in postcoronary patients, as well as improving psychosocial health. After a brief introduction to TABP and its role in CHD, we describe the results of the Recurrent Coronary Prevention Project (RCPP), a controlled 4.5-year intervention study (1977–1982) treating over 1,000 post-myocardial infarction (MI) patients, as well as a 4-year follow-up study. Since the RCPP, the treatment has been modified and is used by others to help postinfarct patients, as well as reasonably healthy people, reduce TABP and improve their health and quality of life. In this chapter, the treatment rationale and the nature of significant changes in treating TABP are also presented. After a comprehensive discussion of the treatment, we propose some additional ways of conceptualizing TABP that may aid further improvement of existing treatments.

Although increasingly understood, the etiology of CHD still remains unclear. In prospective studies, established risk factors for CHD—including age, hypertension, diabetes, cigarette smoking, and elevated serum cholesterol—have predicted CHD. However, these factors do not explain the majority of the new cases of CHD (Jenkins, 1971; National Center for Health Statistics, 1989). Given the continuing failure of traditional risk factors to explain most CHD cases, the possible role of personality, along with behavior and social–cognitive factors in CHD, reemerged in the 1960s and remains a lively if not contentious topic (M. Friedman & Ulmer, 1984; Henry & Stephens, 1977; Ornish et al., 1990; Thoresen & Powell, 1992).

THE EARLY TYPE A STORY

In 1959, Meyer Friedman and Ray Rosenman identified what they called a specific action–emotion complex, or a clinical syndrome, on the basis of extensive clinical observations in young and middle-aged male coronary patients. A chronic struggle to accomplish often vague goals or acquire more and more material symbols of success seemed to dominate these patients. They did not appear to be the neurotic, anxious individuals who commonly presented themselves for psychotherapy but, instead, were observed to be less psychologically minded extroverts whose style was often to take immediate action and not give much reflection to their problems. Following the medical model—patients typically viewed as positive or negative for a disease—these people were labeled *Type A* and were contrasted with those generally lacking TABP or *Type B*. More recently, Rosenman, Swan, and Carmelli (1988) summarized persons with TABP as follows:

- Intense, sustained drive to achieve self-selected but often poorly defined goals
- Profound eagerness to compete and need to "win"
- Persistent desire for recognition and advancement
- Continuous involvement in multiple and diverse activities under time constraints
- Habitual tendency to increase the rate of doing most physical and mental activities
- Extreme mental and physical alertness
- Pervasive aggressive and hostile feelings

Rosenman et al. (1988) viewed this pattern in terms of a combination of behavioral dispositions (e.g., aggressiveness), specific behaviors (e.g., rapid and emphatic speech), and emotional responses (e.g., quickness to anger). Other researchers (e.g., Price, 1982; Strube, 1990) have emphasized more specific cognitive processes, including self-evaluative factors and underlying beliefs (e.g., "I must constantly prove my worth to others") as fundamental Type A characteristics.

A series of studies examining TABP was conducted in the late 1950s and throughout the 1960s (e.g., M. Friedman & Rosenman, 1959; M. Friedman, St. George, Byers, & Rosenman, 1960; Rosenman & Friedman, 1961). These early studies suggested that men and women classified as Type A evidenced the following: (a) higher levels of total serum cholesterol in the absence of any changes in diet, (b) faster blood clotting, (c) greater "sludging" of red blood cells after ingesting high-fat meals, (d) higher levels of norepinephrine and adrenocorticotrophin-releasing hormone, and (e) greater signs and symptoms of clinical heart disease when compared with non-Type A persons.

The most significant early study, the Western Collaborative Group Study (WCGS), involved 3,154 healthy men between the ages of 39 and 59, who were followed for 8.5 years (Rosenman, Brand, Sholtz, & Friedman, 1976). This prospective study clearly showed that men classified as Type A by a structured audiotaped interview were two times more likely to develop clinical CHD than men assessed as Type B over the 8.5 years. (Rosenman et al., 1976). These differences were not explained by differences in serum cholesterol level, blood pressure, smoking, diabetes, or other CHD risk factors. In other words, TABP was shown in multivariate analysis to be a significant independent risk factor for CHD.

Collectively, these earlier correlational and descriptive studies created a portrait of CHD risk associated with TABP for White men and, in a few studies, for White women (Booth-Kewley & Friedman, 1987). The TABP also seemed to be associated with CHD as well as with other factors that increase the risk of CHD (e.g., smoking). However, evidence showing that

TABP was causally related to CHD was lacking. Furthermore, subsequent studies of the TABP–CHD connection did not always find a positive or significant relationship (Booth-Kewley & Friedman, 1987). If, however, it could be shown that reductions in TABP were directly linked to reductions in CHD within a controlled, experimentally designed study, then support for TABP as a possible causal factor in CHD would be strengthened.

Since the early 1980s, several correlational studies have reported null findings: Type A behavior pattern does not always predict greater CHD over time. Ragland and Brand (1988a), for example, reported a 22-year follow-up of the original WCGS participants. They found that TABP failed to predict cardiac mortality over 2 decades, whereas hypertension and elevated cholesterol did predict mortality. However, Ragland and Brand (1988a) did not examine cardiac morbidity (e.g., suffering a nonfatal MI)—a much more likely cardiac event in individuals who were initially healthy. More important, they did not reassess levels of TABP in participants, which may have changed over a 22-year period. Consequently, some participants initially rated as Type B in the WCGS may have become more Type A because of life changes and experiences. Furthermore, refinement of TABP assessment has emerged since the early 1960s, especially in assessing the hostility component, something not emphasized earlier (Friedman & Powell, 1984). Thus, some WCGS participants may have been misclassified initially—as Type B—in the 1960s, when the WCGS was conducted. Schweritz (1988), for example, demonstrated empirically this problem of misclassification of participants as Type B in the Multiple Risk Factor Intervention Trial (MRFIT), another major study reporting no relationship between TABP and coronary morbidity and mortality. Interestingly, Dembroski, MacDougall, Costa, and Grandits (1989) did show a strong predictive relationship of TABP for CHD in the MRFIT study when the hostility component of TABP was separately assessed by reanalyzing audiotaped structured interviews, but only for men under 50 years old and not those who were initially over 50.

Several reasons may explain why TABP has inconsistently predicted CHD, including conceptual, assessment, and research design problems (Thoresen & Powell, 1992). For example, TABP has often been assessed only by self-report measures using a dichotomous rating: A person was labeled globally as either Type A or Type B. Doing so has undoubtedly led to many misclassifications, given the considerable range of characteristics among people labeled as Type A. Furthermore, the failure of self-reports to assess TABP validly and reliably over time has added to the problem.

Booth-Kewley and Friedman (1987), as well as Matthews (1988), provided excellent quantitative reviews of predictive studies using meta-analysis. These reviews included several studies failing to find a predictive relationship between TABP and CHD outcomes (e.g., Ragland & Brand, 1988a, 1988b). Both reviews concluded that the overall weight of evidence, despite some failures to predict, still clearly demonstrates a significant relationship between TABP and CHD for White men, but only when the Type A structured interview (and not self-report measures) has been used to assess TABP, and then only in general-population–type studies, and not those homogeneous studies assessing men with advanced CHD. However, evidence that TABP predicts CHD for women or for non-White men remains lacking (Graff-Low, Thoresen, King, Pattillo, & Jenkins, 1995; Thoresen & Graff-Low, 1994).

Other methodological problems may also account for failures to find a predictive relationship between TABP and CHD outcomes. All studies that reported null findings used only cardiac death as the outcome, and not cardiac morbidity, such as a nonfatal MI. Furthermore, most studies that showed no TABP–CHD relationship examined men who were already suffering serious levels of coronary disease. The power of any psychosocial or behavioral factor to predict death, including TABP, measured as a dichotomy in samples of high-risk or seriously diseased men is severely limited. Miller, Turner, Tindale, Posavac, and Dugoni (1991) argued persuasively that the failure of TABP to predict cardiac mortality in several studies was, in large part, due to the "indirect range restriction" problem. That is, if studies of high-risk persons, such as postcoronary patients, use factors that are highly correlated to what is being predicted to select participants (e.g., using degree of CHD or smoking to predict cardiac death), then the statistical power to find significant relationships between other factors, such as TABP, is reduced. Miller et al.'s argument also finds support from meta-analyses of Booth-Kewley and Friedman (1987) and Matthews (1988).

Despite failures of some studies to find predictive relationships between TABP and subsequent cardiac death, the proverbial "proof of the pudding" may lie in results of well-controlled experiments. Correlational studies, even when assessing large samples, commonly create uncertainty when it comes to trying to clarify what may have caused the observed relationships (Feinstein, 1988).

For example, what if, by means of an experimental research design, TABP was reduced in persons with advanced CHD, and what if that reduction in TABP resulted in significantly fewer fatal and nonfatal coronary recurrences? If so, then strong evidence is provided for a relationship between TABP and CHD (cf. Nunes, Frank, & Kornfeld, 1987, for a meta-analysis of TABP intervention studies).

THE RECURRENT CORONARY PREVENTION PROJECT

In 1974, planning started on an experimentally designed intervention study to determine if TABP could be reduced and, in doing so, if CHD recurrences of MI could be reduced. To answer this, 928 adult male and 84 adult female post-MI volunteers were recruited for a 5-year intervention study.

Before treatment, all participants received a complete physical examination, including a resting 12 lead electrocardiogram, as well as the videotaped structured interview to assess TABP. In addition, participants completed several self-report scales, including an extensive questionnaire on TABP; measures of anger, social support, work satisfaction, and self-efficacy; and ratings about ability to relax and eat, talk, and walk slowly. Participants' average age was 53.2 years. Participants were randomly assigned to either of two treatment conditions, Type A counseling ($n = 592$) or cardiac counseling ($n = 270$), or to a nonrandomized comparison group that received no treatment ($n = 150$). Differences on 20 variables, such as sociodemographic factors and CHD risk factors, were examined between the two randomized conditions. None differed significantly between the two treatment groups at the beginning of the RCPP.

Within the Type A counseling assignment, a total of 60 groups (with approximately 10 participants per group) met over 4.5 years, compared with 22 groups (of approximately 12) in the cardiac counseling group. Originally, 5 years were planned, but results were so clear after 4 years that treatment was discontinued at 4.5 years at the request of the funding agency. In the Type A counseling group, 28 sessions of 90 minutes each were held during the first year, with approximately monthly sessions thereafter for 3.5 years for a total of 62 sessions. The focus in these sessions was on becoming more aware of the signs and symptoms of TABP in everyday situations in oneself and in others. Another focus was on learning how to alter selected behaviors, attitudes, and beliefs using self-management techniques. The cardiac counseling condition groups met approximately bimonthly over the 4.5 years (33 sessions in all), with a focus on medical issues as well as diet and nutrition. However, no attention was given to TABP or chronic stress.

Major Results of the RCPP

By the end of the third year, the total coronary recurrence rate (fatal plus nonfatal events) was 7.2% for the Type A counseling group, compared with 13% for the cardiac counseling group ($p < .005$). This 40% difference was due primarily to fewer nonfatal cardiac events occurring in the Type A counseling group. Differences between the two treatments in cardiac death, however, were not statistically significant.

Greater reductions in TABP were also found for the Type A counseling intervention. For example, of those staying active in both treatment groups, 31.7% in the Type A counseling group had markedly reduced their

TABP (defined as more than 1 standard deviation reduction on two independent measures of TABP), compared with only 7.2% in the cardiac counseling treatment. Furthermore, those who markedly reduced their TABP had a total coronary recurrence rate of 1.7%, compared with 8.6% for those who showed less or no reductions in TABP—a fivefold difference ($p < .05$). Figure 1 displays the cumulative annualized total-recurrence rate for both treatments over the 4.5-year course of treatment.

These reductions in coronary events paralleled reductions in TABP as assessed by the VSI (see Figure 2). In addition, Type A rating scales were also completed by participants, as well as by spouses and work colleagues about the participants. All of these methods of measurement yielded similar results (M. Friedman et al., 1986).

Roughly, 1 out of 4 participants who entered the RCPP already had undergone coronary artery bypass graft surgery (CABG; $n = 247$). Those who received the Type A counseling showed dramatic change. Only 14.0%

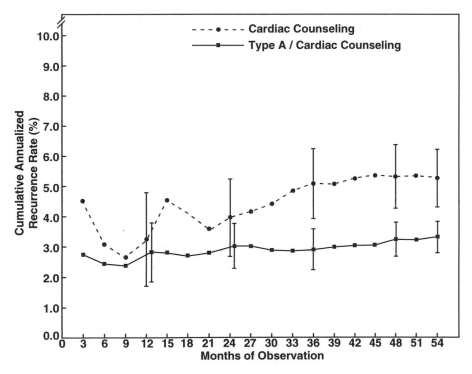

Figure 1. Cumulative annualized recurrence rate in cardiac-counseled and Type A/cardiac-counseled participants calculated quarterly for 4.5 years. Note that 95% confidence limits of quarterly calculated cardiac recurrence rates no longer intersect at the end of 36 months.

From "Alteration of Type A Behavior and Its Effect on Cardiac Recurrences in Post-Myocardial Infarction Patients: Summary Results of the Recurrent Coronary Prevention Project," by M. Friedman et al., 1986, *American Heart Journal, 112,* p. 659. Copyright 1986 by Mosby–Yearbook. Reprinted with permission.

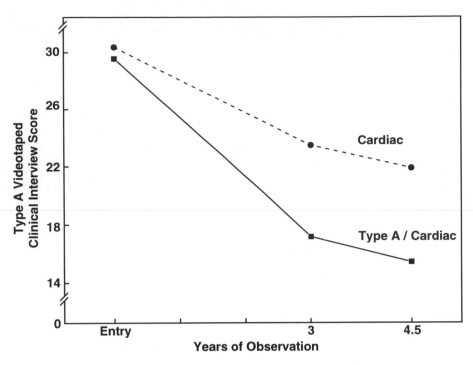

Figure 2. Reductions in observed Type A behavior at 3 years and at end of treatment (4.5 years). Within-group and between-group changes were significant at 3 years ($p < .001$). From "Alteration of Type A Behavior and Its Effect on Cardiac Recurrences in Post-Myocardial Infarction Patients: Summary Results of the Recurrent Coronary Prevention Project," by M. Friedman et al., 1986, *American Heart Journal, 112,* p. 658. Copyright 1986 by Mosby–Yearbook. Reprinted with permission.

of the bypass participants in Type A counseling suffered recurrent MI, compared with 30.3% of those in cardiac counseling ($p < .05$), a difference of over 50%.

Overall, the Type A counseling treatment failed to significantly lower cardiac death, compared with the cardiac counseling treatment. However when the degree of coronary disease at the beginning of the study was considered (i.e., the severity of the damage to the myocardium caused by the prior infarction), those with less myocardial pathology who received the Type A counseling treatment suffered significantly fewer cardiac deaths ($p < .05$; Powell & Thoresen, 1988). Note that roughly two thirds of the RCPP sample at entry had mild to moderate cardiac disease pathology. These results seem to parallel those of Spiegel, Bloom, Kraemer, and Gottheil (1989), showing that women with less advanced breast cancer pathology survived longer after 12 monthly psychosocial group treatment sessions.

In addition, the risk of sudden cardiac death (i.e., death within 60 minutes of the onset of symptoms) was found to be predicted by "emotional arousability," a simplified measure of TABP assessed by the videotaped structured interview (Powell, Simon, Bartzokis, Pattillo, & Thoresen, 1994). Perhaps most surprising was the impact of reduced depressive affect on lowering coronary recurrences over the 4-year follow-up. For example, those who significantly reduced their self-reported depression had 59% fewer cardiac deaths (Powell et al., 1995) compared with those who showed little or no reduction.

These findings about CABG participants and sudden cardiac death represent post hoc discoveries. They were not predicted in advance and therefore need to be interpreted with caution. Still, they merit careful consideration. Indeed, these surprising findings exemplify the crucial need to focus more sharply on specific factors within persons and within situations rather than relying entirely on global predictors (e.g., TABP vs. TABP) and global outcomes (e.g., only total mortality). As will be noted, the conceptual oversimplification of the TABP as a global measure has created a great deal of confusion in the literature about this clinical syndrome (Thoresen & Powell, 1992).

Follow-Up Results of the RCPP

Roughly 4 years after the RCPP treatment program ended, a comprehensive evaluation of participants was conducted (Thoresen, 1990, 1996). Significant differences were found between the two treatments in coronary recurrences at follow-up as well as differences in reduced TABP levels.

In multivariate analyses adjusted for standard CHD risk factors and several psychosocial factors, the following three coronary-prone factors were found to significantly predict the recurrence of total cardiac events 4 years after treatment ended: (a) overall reduction in TABP (assessed by videotaped interview), (b) reduction in self-reported depression, and (c) increases in self-efficacy (confidence to act successfully; e.g., physically relax, eat more slowly, and listen more to others).

Any controlled study, regardless of sample size, duration, and results, requires replication before firm conclusions are valid. Furthermore, no study offers completely unambiguous data, typically due to methodological limitations. Some features of the RCPP merit comment on this point.

Participants were volunteers for a 5-year study. As such, they obviously may not be representative of all post-MI participants. Furthermore, they were, on average, in their early 50s when they entered the study, somewhat younger than many first-time surviving MI patients. In addition, there were differences in treatment length over the 4.5 years. Those in the Type A counseling condition were offered 62 scheduled sessions (and attended an average of 38), compared with 33 sessions (average attendance of 25) for the cardiac counseling condition. Attendance in both groups averaged about 60% of all sessions. Thus, it is conceivable that Type A counseling treatment proved more effective in reducing coronary events simply because more sessions were attended and therefore more social support was experienced (Orth-Gomér & Unden, 1990).

However, when participants were divided in terms of coronary recurrences into the lowest, middle, and highest thirds (tertiles), no relationship of attending sessions was found in the cardiac counseling treatment among level of attendance, change in any psychosocial measure, such as social contact and social support, and reduced cardiac events (Mendes de Leon, Powell, & Kaplan, 1991). Furthermore, when those in each treatment who attended the same number of sessions were compared, only those in the Type A counseling condition showed significant and positive changes in psychosocial measures. Finally, after treatment was finished, a crossover treatment procedure was used for those who were in the cardiac counseling condition. Of those available, 91% of former cardiac counseling participants volunteered to participate in a 1-year condensed version of the Type A counseling program.

To assess the effect of this treatment, the patterns of total coronary events were compared for the 4.5 years before with the 12-month treatment period. A dramatic shift was observed: No fatal or nonfatal recurrences were observed for former cardiac counseling participants during the 1 year, a significant reduction from the accelerating trend of events during the previous 4.5 years (Gill et al., 1985). Thus, the conjecture that a larger number of sessions in the Type A counseling condition or changes in social support might explain the changes observed in the RCPP seems questionable. A more likely explanation lies in the value of learning about TABP and developing skills in how to reduce TABP in daily living.

Overall, the effect of Type A intervention programs are encouraging. Despite the very small number of intervention studies, compared with literally hundreds of correlational studies (cross-sectional and prospective), intervention studies have demonstrated promising changes in TABP (Nunes et al., 1987; Thoresen & Powell, 1992). These findings deserve replication with comparably aged participants, as well as those in their 60s and older. Burell (1995) recently replicated these findings with 268 middle-aged CABG patients in Sweden, using a shorter Type A counseling treatment (see chap. 11, this volume). In addition, Wolff, Thoresen, Venter, and Viljoen (1994) reported some early findings of a small-scale RCPP replication in South Africa, involving 150 post-MI participants. Conceivably, variations of Type A group counseling may prove to be especially cost-effective interventions.

Ketterer's (1993) analysis of the effects of several cognitive–behavioral interventions for coronary patients also sheds encouraging light. He found—by analyzing a variety of interventions focused on TABP, depression, anger, anxiety, and other psychosocial factors—that on average, those treated had 39% fewer nonfatal recurrences and 33% fewer cardiac deaths than did patients in control conditions.

We are still quite far from understanding just how the processes of change work in small, structured counseling groups. Yet some, perhaps many, with coronary disease can be successfully helped to reduce disease risk and substantially improve their quality of life. Such programs probably work best if they offer a fairly broad focus, including reduction in standard risk factors as well as in psychosocial risk factors.

ALTERING TYPE A: TREATMENT OVERVIEW

A group-treatment program for altering TABP first emerged in the 1970s with the RCPP. Designed originally as a multiyear behavioral intervention, this treatment approach has evolved over the years in at least two major ways:

- The limitations of a more narrowly focused behavioral approach have been recognized, giving way to an expanded cognitive–behavioral perspective, coupled with more emphasis on existential, spiritual, and philosophical issues.
- The length and format of treatment has changed to accommodate programs that last from 9 months to 2 years rather than 4.5 years. Dramatic reductions in the videotaped clinical examination (VCE; see chap. 6, this volume) as well as clinical observations strongly indicate that some participants can make meaningful changes after 9 to 12 months of group treatment, whereas others require ongoing participation spanning several years.

The RCPP treatment program was originally created to help post-MI participants gain a better understanding of how and why TABP may impact them physically, socially, and emotionally at work, at home, and in the community and, subsequently, to reduce their TAB. Currently, a modification of the RCPP treatment is being applied in a large, multiyear intervention study, the Coronary and Cancer Prevention Project, involving over 3,000 asymptomatic participants. In addition, the RCPP program has been extensively and effectively used with many people who are healthy but who are trying to reduce TABP and the resulting chronic distress and struggle that characterize their life.

As we describe the structured-group treatment, our conjectures and recommendations are based on our repeated clinical observations and conclusions and those of many other psychologists and psychiatrists who have successfully altered TABP in the RCPP, the Coronary and Cancer Prevention Project, and other controlled studies, as well as in private clinical programs for more than 15 years. All of these programs focus on the following major themes:

- Pathophysiology of TABP and CHD
- Diagnostic signs and symptoms of TABP
- Type A-related emotions, attitudes, and beliefs
- Case examples of people exhibiting TABP
- Role of self-esteem and feelings of self-worth
- Increasing patience, empathy, compassion, forgiveness, and love (i.e., more Type B qualities)
- Reduction of impatience, competitiveness, and hostility.

To deal with these themes, a dynamic format for group sessions is used. In the first few weeks, for example, the format is highly structured, focusing on conveying information and increasing understanding of TABP and CHD. Initially, the group leader serves primarily as a teacher. As the group develops, the focus shifts gradually to the experiences of participants surrounding their efforts to apply what they have discussed, observed, and read. For example, the "driving game" is one of the first group exercises through which participants become more aware of how they typically feel and react while driving a car. These reactions include physiological changes, overt behavior, specific thoughts and feelings, and the impact of other drivers' actions on participants' levels of stress and TABP.

Later, group members, who have developed a greater sense of trust and respect for others in the group, increasingly bring current problems and issues (e.g., conflict with family members, problems at work, or relationship problems) to the group. Although such problems become a major focus, attention is still given to being less Type A, through practicing daily relaxation, using focused self-awareness, and using specific cognitive–behavioral exercises to reduce TABP.

Along with participating in the group, members are asked to take action between group sessions. The point is made repeatedly to participants that the success of the program depends on what each person does between group sessions. It is not enough to attend sessions, because the real work and benefit come primarily from making changes in daily living. To facilitate the changes, a variety of audiovisual and print material is used. Each participant, for example, receives a "Drill Book" of daily cognitive–behavioral exercises, as well as reading material related to modifying TAB. Initially, chapters are assigned in M. Friedman and Ulmer's (1984) *Treating Type A Behavior and Your Heart*. This reading serves as a focus for discussion. Later, a variety of books are suggested, including biographies of famous people whose lives illustrate TABP, such as *Lyndon Johnson and the American Dream* (Kearns, 1976). Participants also contribute newspaper articles and cartoons illustrating Type A characteristics.

In addition, every group session commences with a brief relaxation exercise (about 10 minutes) that illustrates the value of taking time to slow down, to become more calm, to focus attention, and to be more alert and attentive in the group. Participants are repeatedly encouraged to practice relaxation every day for 20 to 30 minutes.

Attendance is taken at every session, and group leaders typically will call a participant who was absent to ask about how things are going and to mention that the person was missed at the last meeting. The message conveyed and almost always appreciated by the participant is clear: We care about you, we missed you, and we hope you will attend the next session. This process only begins to illustrate the group leader's crucial role in the successful treatment of TABP.

Essential Qualities of Effective Group Leaders

The talent and humanity of the group leader are critical to the success of treatment. Although effective group leaders may come from a variety of theoretical orientations, we believe that effective leaders must be able to do the following:

- Convey expertise and authority to participants who are often hypercritical, defensive, and resistant to change. A group leader needs a substantial understanding of the pathophysiology of CHD, especially as related to the TABP and chronic stress.
- Direct, motivate, and support participants' efforts to reduce their TAB. The leader needs expertise in the principles of cognitive and behavior change.
- Personally understand TABP by being actively involved in observing and modifying his or her own TAB.
- Cultivate group cohesion and a positive atmosphere and use participants' interactions in a therapeutic manner. The leader needs expertise in group therapy.

We believe that understanding their own TABP enables leaders to empathize with participants' difficulties in trying to change. It also facilitates recognition of the perceptions, attitudes, and beliefs underlying participants' TABP. Treatment effectiveness may be severely undermined if leaders lack sufficient insight into their own behavior, are not willing to disclose these insights to their group, and are not actively committed and involved in modifying their own TAB.

The personal qualities of a group leader, such as sensitivity and flexibility, become even more important as the role of the leader changes over time. In the course of group treatment over several months, the leader assumes the various roles of teacher, consultant, guide, and companion. All roles remain essential, but some predominate at different phases of treatment. Initially, for example, the leader functions primarily as a caring teacher. After a few months, the role gradually shifts to that of a consultant, guide, and, finally, a companion. Each role requires different expertise and personal qualities. Given these requirements, group leaders selected for the RCPP were experienced clinicians who were able to present themselves as mature, respected, and successful professionals. They avoided technical jargon, communicated in a simple and sincere manner, and exhibited the same gentle sense of humor about their own foibles and incongruities as they did toward those of participants. Indeed, an easy and comfortable sense of humor proved invaluable if not essential to promoting change.

Alteration of TAB requires improvement of participants' self-esteem. A group leader needs to experience and actively express a genuine caring toward group members. Doing so can be a formidable challenge when confronted with the often hypercritical hostility of some participants, especially in the first few months. Thus, group leaders' caring must often have the qualities of a disciplined compassion: the ability to set limits and engage in firm confrontations while still retaining empathy and understanding. Helping others to change their TAB consistently challenges the leader to intervene with as much presence, caring, and respect as is humanly possible.

Goals of Group Treatment

The goals and therapeutic approaches of the treatment program grew directly out of the conceptualization of TABP. Chronic TAB generates excessive physical, emotional, and behavioral arousal. Thus, a primary aim of treatment is to reduce the arousal that accompanies the pervasive impatience and free-floating hostility that characterize TABP. However, because TAB is generated by a particular view of one's self and the world, effective treatment must also help participants examine and change their underlying attitudes and beliefs. Furthermore, whereas what might be called a "Type A world view" includes such qualities as suspiciousness, cynicism, and alienation, it appears to be generated and maintained by anxiety, insecurity, and precarious self-esteem. Reducing insecurity and enhancing self-esteem are thus essential for the effective treatment of TAB.

Because we are essentially seeking to help participants begin the process of changing a world view and style of coping that is often lifelong, the treatment program is designed to do the following:

- Increase participants' awareness of TABP and its pervasive consequences
- Develop greater self-awareness of one's personal manifestation of TABP (i.e., use of the self-monitor)

- Teach participants strategies for physical and psychological relaxation
- Help participants develop healthy alternatives to time urgency and hostility
- Provide behavioral exercises by which participants can develop healthier Type B behaviors
- Help participants recognize and modify Type A attitudes and beliefs
- Reduce participants' insecurity and foster healthier ways of maintaining self-esteem
- Help participants improve relationships with spouses, family, friends, and coworkers
- Develop a healthier philosophy of living for dealing with life's fundamental and unavoidable dilemmas and spiritual issues.

Although it is important to clearly identify healthier alternatives to TAB, excessively rigid, unrealistic, or prescriptive goals can stifle participants' creativity in developing personally relevant goals. Worse, unrealistic goals may create a sense of failure when they are not reached, thus promoting self-criticism, resentment, and discouragement—and consequently, promoting a Type A perspective.

Furthermore, although goals are necessary to achieve significant and lasting change, we have continually observed that the rate and process of change remain exquisitely idiosyncratic. For instance, some participants are able to initiate significant changes surprisingly soon after developing the ability to monitor their TAB. Others, however, need repeated and intensive work to examine and modify underlying attitudes and beliefs. Unfortunately, some participants seem hopelessly trapped and enslaved by their Type A beliefs, regardless of everyone's best efforts to facilitate change. A profound fear of relinquishing control and tolerating the anxiety inherent in change seems to entrench some in their Type A patterns. Still, the vast majority who make a genuine commitment, and show patient effort, succeed in making life-enhancing and, in many instances, life-saving changes.

Treatment Format and Approach

We believe that TAB is best treated in a small-group format using an approach that combines elements of cognitive–behavioral and existential–humanistic orientations (e.g., Bandura, 1986; Bracke & Bugental, 1995; Powell & Thoresen, 1987). The small group (approximately 10–12 participants), meeting in sessions of 1.5 to 2 hours, offers the following advantages over individual treatment:

1. The small group provides an excellent opportunity to experience the benefits of ongoing social support.

2. Participants' learning is enhanced vicariously by listening to the problems and successes of others.
3. Almost all of the participants can improve their weak active-listening skills and their pervasive distractibility.
4. Feedback from several peers is often perceived as more valid than that from only one person, especially a "professional."

The optimal atmosphere in the group is one of mutual trust, respect, and support. This atmosphere, however, must be persistently cultivated by the group leader, given the well-established hostile and cynical outlooks of many participants. Such an atmosphere enables participants to begin expanding their self-awareness, a prerequisite for reducing TAB.

Developing Greater Awareness: "Bomb and Fuses" and the Self-Monitor

To increase self-awareness and self-understanding in people with TAB, the *Type A self-monitor* was developed. More than most people, those with TABP seem to have lost much of their innate ability to be subjectively aware of themselves (i.e., to know what's going on within and around themselves). The most serious consequence of this loss is that participants too often direct their lives in mindless attempts to please, impress, or protect themselves from others. Many participants have chronically ignored their feelings (e.g., exhaustion, insecurity, and loneliness) in order to strive aggressively for more professional status and economic gain. They often appear numb to their feelings. To change, participants need to develop the ability to access and remain aware of their unique internal experience. We try to accomplish this through an ongoing combination of meditation and relaxation, self-monitoring exercises, and the supportive feedback of group members and the group leader.

Initially, participants often deny that TABP is a distinct syndrome and seriously doubt its contribution to CHD risk. Or they may believe that TAB only affects others (Powell & Thoresen, 1987). As a means of confronting participants' denial and increasing adherence to the treatment regimen, the *bomb and fuses* metaphor was developed (M. Friedman & Ulmer, 1984). The bomb was identified as a participants' original MI, their occluded coronary arteries, and their cardiac denial. The bomb was portrayed as subject to detonation by any of the following fuses: (a) TAB, especially anger and impatience; (b) excessive and prolonged physical exertion at a high altitude (i.e., above 5,000 ft); (c) excessive and prolonged physical activity to a state of exhaustion; (d) one extremely heavy-fat meal; (e) chronic mental and emotional exhaustion; (f) excessive use of caffeine; and (g) chronic abuse of alcohol. Group leaders consistently inquired about each participant's avoidance of these fuses. If a member "lit a fuse," he or she was asked to describe the situation to the group and how that situation might be avoided in the future. These commonly experienced fuses were depicted as risky situations that over time might put the participant in jeopardy of exacerbating his or her cardiac disease risk.

Just as TAB obscures awareness of one's subjective state, it also blinds many participants to their behavior at home, at work, and in the community. Without an accurate and reliable awareness of their own TAB, participants are seriously hampered in making informed and healthier choices about how they respond to the situations they encounter. The cultural glamour sometimes associated with TAB can be eliminated by reducing TABP to its essential features and effects. To do this, the acronym "AIAI" (anger, irritation, aggravation, impatience) was created to facilitate a greater awareness of the actual nature and consequences of TABP.

Derived from behavioral research on self-monitoring (Thoresen & Mahoney, 1974), the Type A self-monitor procedure was developed to help participants detach from the personal distress in a situation by refocusing their attention more objectively on the occurrence of distress itself. For example, when a person impatiently waits in a slow bank line, the person may start criticizing the incompetence of the teller or the bank's deplorable understaffing. The self-monitor ideally would intervene at this point with the awareness of the hypercritical and impatient feelings and suggest that patience, rather than criticism, is a more desirable response. The self-monitor might, for example, note that "waiting in line gives me the opportunity to reflect on some interesting thing I could do this weekend or could remind me to observe specific Type A signs of others waiting in line or relax." Essentially, the participant develops a *meta-cognition*—an observing and more objective "third-person" perspective, one that optimally provides an intimate awareness of the participant's emotional responses, fears, and rationalizations, as well as behaviors (Powell & Thoresen, 1987).

Development of a self-monitor begins with group discussions that comprehensively describe the specific behavioral signs and symptoms of TABP. Videotapes and audiotapes illustrating speech and psychomotor behaviors are used to provide concrete examples. In addition, participants complete a variety of self-monitoring exercises. Perhaps the most effective means of developing the self-monitor comes from the immediate feedback about specific TAB that participants receive from others as they discuss provocative topics (e.g., reactions to a rude driver or a critical colleague at work). A primary responsibility of the group leader in this process is to cultivate an atmosphere of trust, respect, and mutual support, so that participants can explore possible underlying beliefs as well as give and accept feedback on their behavior.

The group leader must also establish that both impatience and anger are natural emotional responses that impact health and well-being most when they are intense, prolonged, and chronic. Unless this view of anger and impatience can be accepted, many participants will suppress and deny their TAB to impress the group leader and compete with other participants (e.g., look like they are changing their TAB more or faster). The consequence of such denial and premature suppression of TAB is a crucial loss of opportunities to examine and modify the basic beliefs and emotional reactions that stimulate TAB. We encourage participants to develop a self-monitor that is respectful, curious, and interested in understanding the self, rather than the harsh, rigid, and perfectionistic internal critic that usually lies at the core of the TABP. A helpful self-monitor observes behaviors, attitudes, and emotions and generally chooses to respond in a patient, calm, and reassuring manner. Development of such self-awareness is essential to helping participants begin to reduce their chronic physical arousal.

Reducing Arousal: Relaxation and Meditation Training

Developing the ability to reduce the physical and emotional arousal created by TABP is highly beneficial both directly and indirectly. The health value of using relaxation and meditation consistently over time to reduce physiological hyperarousal has been suggested for some stress-related diseases (Henry & Stephens, 1977; Price, 1988). Many participants who exhibit TAB have, for example, great difficulty in modulating their "engines at full speed ahead" and easing off their hard-driving behavior. The chronic sympathetic nervous system hyperarousal associated with TAB can be significantly reduced by practicing relaxation or meditation in a systematic fashion. Progressive muscle relaxation, for example, has been shown to reduce sympathetic arousal, including accelerated heart rate and elevated blood pressure (Cottier, Shapiro, & Julius, 1984). Several other procedures (e.g., *autogenic training*, or self-hypnosis; breath meditation; and guided imagery) can also be effective in helping participants reduce their general arousal and focus on group activities.

However, it is unrealistic to expect that all participants have the motivation and discipline necessary to practice formal relaxation or meditation procedures in daily life. Typically, at first, only a few in any group will make the effort. Thus, relaxation training can be used as a "primer" with less ambitious goals (e.g., reduce arousal and increase focus in the group). Group sessions always begin with some form of relaxation or meditation that helps focus attention, create physical comfort, and provide an experience of mental calm and peacefulness that usually contrasts dramatically with the physical and emotional tension that participants very often experience. Because many have become deeply habituated to the tense feelings of chronic arousal, relaxation often sensitizes participants to the experiential differences between the two states.

Typically, the group leader initially demonstrates a particular relaxation procedure to instruct and model its most effective use. Because relaxation or meditation of any type is usually an unfamiliar feeling, participants often experience some discomfort during initial exercises (e.g., "I feel more tense than I did before"). The group leader can use such experiences to discuss the intensity of participants' chronic arousal and possible resistance to slowing down, as well as a competitive struggle to relax "better than others." After a relaxation strategy has been demonstrated and practiced at a group session, members are instructed to practice the procedure daily between group sessions and discuss their experiences at the next meeting.

A variety of relaxation strategies, including abdominal breathing, progressive muscle relaxation, autogenics, and guided imagery, are presented to allow participants to select a procedure or combination of procedures that works best for them. The goal is to help each participant to develop a proficient personal style of relaxing and to be able to use a relaxation response in daily situations that provoke impatience and anger. Responding in a more relaxed manner also helps participants begin to change specific TABs.

Practicing Type B Behaviors: Daily Drills

Replacing the time-urgent and hostile behaviors associated with TABP requires that participants experience and practice healthier alternative behaviors. A set of daily drills was developed to provide participants with structured exercises that involve acting and thinking in healthier ways.

Figure 3 illustrates a page from the participants' drill book. Daily drills include exercises aimed at modifying actions and attitudes in the areas of impatience (e.g., eat more slowly); hostility (e.g., purposely say "maybe I'm wrong"); self-esteem (e.g., contemplate your positive achievements for 10 minutes); and improving relationships (e.g., ask a family member about his or her day's activities). In addition to the daily exercises, each week's drills are accompanied by philosophical and spiritual concepts that participants are asked to reflect on and discuss at group sessions.

The group leader plays an essential role in helping participants develop and maintain the motivation and discipline needed to consistently complete the drills. Initially, participants' motivation can be increased by presenting the general rationale for the drills and the specific value of completing individual exercises. In addition, the group leader points out that although completing all drills is most beneficial, the difficulties and resistances that participants may encounter are important to observe and understand, even if a specific drill has not been completed. Through this guidance, members become increasingly aware of their own personal version of TABP as well as how they resist changing. Time is reserved in group sessions for discussion of experiences during drills to emphasize the positive effects that members report, provide support, and share suggestions on how difficult drills might be successfully accomplished. Throughout these discussions, the group leader can reiterate the importance and rationale for

---

MONDAY: Alter one of your usual habits or ways of doing things.

TUESDAY: Ask a member of family about their day's activities.

WEDNESDAY: Leave watch off.

THURSDAY: Walk more slowly.

FRIDAY: Verbalize affection to spouse/children

SATURDAY: Eat more slowly.

SUNDAY: Practice smiling as you remember
two to three happy events of the past.

---

1.   "For every minute you are angry, you lose 60 seconds of happiness." - Ralph W. Emerson

2.   "Contempt for others is a weed that can flourish in only one very special kind of soil, that composed of self contempt."-Anonymous

3.   "One can stroke persons with words." - F. Scott Fitzgerald.

4.   "When a fixed idea makes its appearance, a great ass also makes its appearance." - Nietzsche.

Figure 3. Example from the Recurrent Coronary Prevention Project drill book used in structuring daily behavioral exercises.

completing drills and provide ongoing encouragement and reinforcement. In time, participants create their own drills, tailored to their particular situations, problems, and concerns. Although the daily drills do enable participants to begin changing many behaviors, they are not sufficient to effectively reduce the core components of their TAB.

Reducing Time Urgency

In addition to the daily drills, group discussions and specific exercises are needed to reduce participants' chronic impatience. Initially, the nature of time urgency, its causes, and its destructive effects are discussed, to promote self-awareness and increase motivation to change. Time urgency, the frenetic drive to accomplish an unrealistic number of tasks in progressively less time, is believed to be the result of covert insecurity and an unstable or inadequate level of self-esteem (M. Friedman & Ulmer, 1984). Such insecurity arises in part from the fear that one will be unable to cope with a task and will consequently lose status with peers, superiors, or family.

The general manifestations of this insecurity include the following:

- A chronic inability to say no to requests from others for help with nonessential tasks
- An extreme reluctance or refusal to delegate tasks and to reduce overall workload
- An apparent greed to acquire an unrealistic number of responsibilities, material possessions, or symbols of achievement in trying to prove self-worth
- A preoccupation with personal shortcomings and "weaknesses," coupled with a devaluing of strengths and positive feedback from others.

By contrast, it is crucial that the time pressure of excessive tasks and deadlines that are actually imposed by superiors be validated by the group leader as "real." The cultural influences that virtually worship speed and hurriedness must also be acknowledged when discussing factors that promote time urgency and impatience.

To help reduce time urgency, participants must first develop an awareness of their own specific manifestations of impatience and become sensitized to the oppressive subjective experience that characterizes "hurry sickness." This is best accomplished through self-observation exercises, group discussion of specific impatient behaviors, and the examination of participants' experience of greater calmness created through relaxation. That is, participants are asked to report on the subjective experience of relaxation as compared with the tension of chronic time urgency. Identifying the specific time-urgent behaviors of participants that occur during group sessions is an extremely potent means of developing self-awareness.

Discussions are also used to expose the consequences of the chronic impatience that participants are unaware of or deny. For instance, many participants deny the likelihood that impatience may actually promote errors rather than greater productivity. This is especially true when polyphasing (i.e., doing more than one task at a time) occurs. It is essential to confront participants with the reality that their impatience often encourages them to view others as "obstacles" in their way, thus promoting hostile behavior. This hostility can, in turn, erode or destroy relationships with others, depriving the individual of social support, a critical source of self-esteem. This vicious cycle lies at the root of TABP and helps perpetuate it. Although such discussions are useful, the crucial factor lies in increasing participants' awareness of their own particular time-urgent behaviors and their specific attitudinal causes. Without this personal awareness, significant change will not occur.

Specific exercises are used to help participants become aware of the personal beliefs that generate time urgency and, more important, to develop more realistic attitudes and healthier strategies for coping with demands. Cognitive restructuring is based on the principle that an emotional reaction is produced by one's *perception* of the requests and demands made by others (Bandura, 1986). Because participants' perceptions play a major role in their emotional arousal and coping behavior, exposing, examining, and modifying these Type A perceptions are essential for successful treatment. For example, participants are asked to list the causes of a major professional or personal success. Through such analyses, members begin to realize that they have succeeded despite their impatience and that time urgency often impedes rather than enhances a career.

Through other exercises, participants realize that their extreme reluctance to delegate is often due to an excessive need to retain control in a misguided effort to raise self-esteem. Participants examine Type A beliefs such as these:

- My worth depends on the quantity, not the quality, of my achievements.
- I must constantly prove my worth again and again, because my past accomplishments don't count.
- I must do more than others to be worthy.

Through such awareness and reflection, participants begin to develop and apply healthier and more personally congruent beliefs, which help them to reduce chronic overscheduling.

Similarly, the necessity to engage in genuine prioritizing of one's activities is established by exercises that illustrate the fallacy of "Type A prioritizing": All tasks are crucial and must be accomplished today! Participants must learn to distinguish tasks that are truly urgent from those that are only important. Furthermore, most participants appear to use an approach to managing their time that views others as objects to be controlled and is not based on their vision or values (Covey, Merrill, & Merrill, 1994). Role-play exercises are used to develop participants' abilities to assertively reject the unrealistic demands of others and to modify the demands they place on themselves. Examining and reducing time urgency naturally lead to a greater awareness of anger and hostility. (See chap. 13, this volume, for additional discussion of treatment of time pathologies.)

Reducing Anger and Hostility

Research that has examined the components of TABP suggests that hostility may be its most toxic element (e.g., Matthews & Haynes, 1986; Williams, Barefoot, & Shekelle, 1984). Although it is clear from a clinical perspective that time urgency is a pervasive antecedent of hostility and must be modified, the treatment program does consider the reduction of hostility a predominant goal. Because we are seeking to help participants modify a hostile Type A world view and style of coping, treatment focuses on the following:

- Increasing the individual's understanding of Type A hostility
- Developing a pervasive awareness of one's personal manifestations of hostility
- Identifying specific situations that immediately evoke hostility
- Identifying situations that create anxiety, insecurity, and stress, which in turn promote displaced hostility
- Understanding and modifying the personal beliefs that generate hostility
- Developing, practicing, and applying healthier methods of dealing with provocative situations.

Initially, the nature and specific behavioral manifestations of Type A hostility must be comprehensively described and discussed. The group leader needs to establish that anger is a naturally occurring and often healthy emotional response to threat, anxiety, or frustration. It is important that participants avoid the tendency to suppress and deny their hostile reactions so that they appear to be "reasonable and in control." Thus, it is necessary for participants to learn that the problem with Type A anger is not simply that anger occurs, but that it occurs more frequently, often more intensely, and lasts for longer periods of time. The potential "abuse" of anger is described, that is, some participants have essentially become "addicted" to the immediate physiological arousal that accompanies anger. This dependency on the energizing effects of anger's physiological arousal presents a major challenge.

Groups begin by discussing the essential features of Type A anger and hostility—a hypercritical world view, cynicism, distrust, suspiciousness, and attribution of malevolence by others. To avoid participants' defensiveness about their hostile attitudes, initial discussions focus primarily on general behavioral signs and symptoms and gradually move to the identification of participants' own hostile behaviors. To monitor their Type A hostility, participants become aware of more subtle manifestations, such as sarcasm, facial grimacing, hypercritical generalizations about groups (e.g., other ethnic or racial groups, women, or professions), persistent teasing, and explosive or jarring laughter.

A particularly fertile microcosm that may be used to identify participants' angry and hostile beliefs is automobile driving. Group members describe provocative driving experiences with the goals of identifying specific signs and symptoms of anger, exposing underlying hostile attitudes, and developing alternative ways of perceiving and responding to the automotive idiosyncrasies of others. Participants are asked to practice more reflective, cooperative, and calm approaches to driving (e.g., driving in the slow lane and yielding to oncoming traffic) and to become more accepting of, and even compassionate about, other drivers. The continued development and pervasive use of the self-monitor cannot be overemphasized as an essential skill in reducing anger and hostility.

The Bait and Hook Metaphor

An extremely useful therapeutic metaphor for helping to reduce anger and hostility is that of *bait and hooks* (Powell & Thoresen, 1987). Participants learn that as they move through the unpredictable waters of daily life, they, like fish, encounter obstacles and provocative situations that, like bait, invite aggressive responses. The crucial concept for participants to understand is that their own perception of an event is the hook that evokes their hostility. To increase awareness of provocative situations, participants examine a series of situations that often elicit Type A hostility with the goal of assessing which baits are most personally provocative. With increased awareness and reflection many participants start to avoid situations when possible or respond without Type A anger. An example of a bait–hook exercise is presented in Exhibit 1. It is essential that participants, through such exercises as well as self-monitoring and group discus-

EXHIBIT 1
Examples of the "Bait and Hook" Metaphor

- Bait situation: Others making trivial mistakes.
  Examples: Spouse forgets to pick up shirts from laundry, or colleague makes an insignificant error in the office.
  Type A "Hook" attitude: How dare you make a mistake that inconveniences me! Your mistake clearly indicates your general incompetence and my general superiority.
- Bait situations: Ideology (political, religious, etc.).
  Examples: Friends express different political views, or patient reads an article describing the religious or cultural beliefs of a different group.
  Type A "Hook" attitude: How can these people be so incredibly stupid to believe that stuff? How dare these people question my beliefs by believing differently than me?
- Bait situations: Being pressed for time or under a deadline.
  Example: Project deadline at work, or struggling to arrive for an appointment on time.
  Type A "Hook" attitude: I have the right to push everything and everyone out of my way. It is grossly unfair that I do not have all the time I need.

sion, become aware of the personal beliefs that promote their hostility. (See chap. 12, this volume, for an expanded discussion of the hook.)

Narcissism and TABP

Type A hostility often appears to arise from an excessive sense of entitlement, a hypersensitivity to perceived disapproval, or an exaggerated need for control (Bracke & Bugental, 1995; Bugental & Bracke, 1992; Thoresen & Pattillo, 1988). Lasch (1978) describes the neonarcissism that characterizes much of the Type A perspective: fiercely competitive for approval, superficially cooperative while restraining anger, and demanding immediate gratification yet perpetually unsatisfied. Within this context, Type A hostility seems understandable. If a person is exhausting himself or herself to complete more and more productive tasks and trying to do so in less and less time, but still feeling unloved and unappreciated, if not ignored, then hostility and cynicism seem very justified (Bugental & Bracke, 1992). Furthermore, it has been our consistent clinical observation that the narcissism of many participants exceeds that of the less intense and more situational "cultural narcissism" and strongly indicates a more pervasive, extreme, and enduring narcissistic personality disorder.

Although each person will have an idiosyncratic set of beliefs, the following are examples of typical implicit narcissistic assumptions:

- People ought to have the same beliefs, values, and perceptions that I have.
- Unlike others, I don't deserve to suffer life's obstacles and inconveniences.
- My anger is justified and caused by the ignorance and incompetence of others.
- Giving and receiving love and affection are signs of weakness.
- Because of my intellectual, economic, or moral superiority, I should never be questioned, challenged, or criticized.
- It's a dog-eat-dog world, and people are not to be trusted.

As with time urgency, therapeutic intervention supports participants as they reconsider their hostile beliefs and subsequently develop healthier attitudes, which are based on humility, understanding, compassion, and forgiveness.

In addition to examining and modifying personal beliefs, participants learn how to respond assertively rather than aggressively. Participants are confronted with the perspective that although hostile responses may achieve short-term compliance from others, the long-term consequences of hostility are often severe. Hostility promotes counterattacks, rejection, and feelings of guilt. Assertiveness requires that participants learn to reduce the emotional intensity of their responses, take time to consider a situation, and respect both their needs and those of others. Furthermore, participants learn to monitor the psychomotor phenomena that accompany their assertive responses, use appropriate volume and emphasis in their speech, and structure their requests in a manner intended to resolve a conflict (Bower & Bower, 1976). Assertive responses can be developed and practiced in group sessions using actual conflict situations that participants have encountered.

The goal of treatment is not to impose cognitive restructuring on all situations that provoke anger. Instead, participants are encouraged to respond assertively to situations marked by clear moral and ethical transgressions, as compared with trivial aggravations. Our goal is to help participants assess situations more accurately and choose carefully from an expanded range of response options, with compassion and understanding in mind. In effectively achieving such changes, participants do in fact reduce the dynamics that underlie TABP.

Enhancing Self-Esteem and Reducing Insecurity

Because TABP appears to be motivated by covert insecurity (Price & Friedman, 1995) or fragile self-esteem, reducing insecurity and enhancing self-esteem are essential for effective treatment. Self-esteem may be conceptualized as comprising three major components: (a) the perception of some degree of control (Glass, 1977); (b) a relatively strong general sense of self-efficacy or personal competence in one's life (Bandura, 1982); and (c) a positive perception of one's worth as a person (Branden, 1969). Treatment enhances participants' perceptions of control and self-efficacy by increasing their ability to (a) identify and avoid unwanted TAB; (b) reduce physical tension and create calmness by applying relaxation strategies; (c) improve relationships and resolve conflicts using assertiveness training; and (d) identify, examine, and mindfully alter Type A beliefs.

Participants' feelings of self-worth are enhanced through a variety of exercises and processes. Because the self-worth of many participants is excessively dependent on career achievement, participants are encouraged to identify and develop other sources of self-esteem (e.g., strengthening family relationships and broadening aesthetic and spiritual interests through involvement in hobbies, music, literature, and art). Greater self-acceptance is promoted through an active and realistic evaluation of achievements and performance expectations. Although many participants have accomplished a great deal, their self-esteem has received surprisingly little validation because of perfectionistic expectations and excessively harsh self-criticism.

The relationship among self-esteem, achievements, and expectations was well described by William James (1890):

$$\text{Self-esteem} = \frac{\text{Achievements}}{\text{Expectations}}$$

Thus, a person can increase self-esteem by either increasing achievements or reducing expectations. This way of thinking about self-esteem becomes the focus of group discussions and daily exercises.

Developing a Healthier Philosophy of Living

The insecurity that promotes Type A overscheduling and aggressive, hostile reactions to others can be reduced by helping participants identify, understand, and deal more effectively with life situations that create their underlying anxiety. Recently, it has been proposed that it is indeed therapeutic to help participants distinguish between those situational anxieties that they can exert effective control over (e.g., anxiety over a business presentation) and those that are inherent in living (e.g., anxiety regarding our ultimate aloneness, fate, or death; Bracke & Bugental, 1995).

Self-esteem and security are greatly increased by helping participants develop and improve their relationships with family and friends. Reducing aversive TAB and learning the skills necessary for more genuine and intimate relationships serve to lessen the isolation that participants usually experience and to increase the affection and validation that so powerfully nourish self-worth. In addition to using these healthier means of increasing security and self-esteem, participants are taught that insecurity and inadequate self-esteem cannot be ameliorated solely by the acquisition of material objects. Gradually these insights begin to undermine underlying beliefs that have supported fear and insecurity.

The supportive and caring environment of the group, accompanied by the acceptance of the group leader, helps provide a powerful boost for participants' self-esteem and for much needed personal reflection. Within this context, participants begin to reflect on the broader issues and values in their lives and to develop a healthier and more authentic personal philosophy. Although behavioral drills and cognitive-restructuring exercises are extremely effective in reducing the destructive effects of the TABP, such approaches by themselves are limited in helping participants create more meaningful and satisfying lives (Bracke & Bugental, 1995; Bugental & Bracke, 1992).

As treatment progresses, participants begin to explore basic spiritual questions, such as, What is truly important to me, and why? To what have I committed my life? Do I believe in a higher power or force in the world? Can I love myself as I am? What are my responsibilities to others, to the earth? What am I doing to live a more spiritually healthy life? Can I at times put the needs of others first? Although it is extremely important for participants who have chronically struggled with life to reach the point where they ask, Is this worth dying for? it is truly crucial that they also ask, What is worth living for? The final goal of treatment is to help participants develop a healthy personal philosophy for living that will maintain and extend the progress made during the program.

The spiritual dimension of treatment is explicitly acknowledged at the end of each group session. Participants stand in a circle, holding hands, while the following closing statement is read slowly by one of the group members:

> We are here because we realize that we all need more help than we can give ourselves. We need each other. So may all our efforts be of benefit to each one. And may friendship and love bring enrichment to all our lives, and to all those whose lives are in our care. We acknowledge this gratefully. Amen.

Improving Treatment: The Need to Expand Theory

Conceptual development is urgently needed if we are to extend our understanding and improve our treatment of TABP (Bracke & Bugental, 1995; H. Friedman, Hawley, & Tucker, 1994; Thoresen & Powell, 1992). Although a comprehensive discussion of basic conceptual problems is beyond the scope of our presentation, we suggest the following perspectives as highly consistent with clinical observations and empirical studies and, thus, as essential additions to the traditional cognitive–behavioral model of TABP. As a syndrome defined by behavior, TABP encompasses a wide array of individual patterns, which are promoted, precipitated, and maintained by many cultural, developmental, and existential factors. It is not a uniform, "one size fits all" disorder that is readily assessed with a self-report measure and easily treated in a few individual sessions.

Expanding Type A as a Concept

Although TABP was once thought to be a very distinct psychological–behavioral disorder, we have consistently observed that Type A characteristics, such as time urgency, impatience, and hostility, vary greatly among people diagnosed as Type A. These primary Type A characteristics vary in degree and intensity as well in the situations that elicit them (Thoresen & Powell, 1992). For instance, whereas some participants pervasively exhibit blatant hostility, others primarily display anxious and depressive symptoms, usually related to extreme time pressure. Many, on careful observation, display a quality of intenseness, often tied to a sense of impatience or time urgency. Such individual differences must be considered and addressed if an intervention program is to be effective.

Some contend that only the hostility component of TABP promotes CHD (e.g., Williams & Barefoot, 1988). Others believe that TABP relates to CHD only in concert with other factors, such as social isolation, expression of negative emotions, or conflicted dependence on others (e.g., H. Friedman et al., 1994; Howard, Rechnitzer, Cunningham, Wong, & Brown, 1990; Orth-Gomér & Undén, 1990). Still others conceptualize TABP at the macro level of cultural values (e.g., Margolis, McLeroy, Runyon, & Kaplan, 1983; Van Egeren, 1991). Each of these perspectives holds some truth. None alone appears valid.

Furthermore, TABP cannot usefully be viewed as a fixed personality trait or solely as a matter of an intrapsychically troubled or hostile self. Nor is TABP a categorical medical disorder in the sense that one is either "infected" or not. TABP emanates from transactions between an individual's beliefs, perceptions, and behavior and those of others in particular situations (Thoresen & Öhman, 1987). Add to this the documented impact of age, gender, socioeconomic status, ethnicity, and educational level on CHD risk, and a much more complex conception of TABP emerges (Pincus & Callahan, 1995).

Cultural Constrictions

In many ways, TABP represents a culturally created and socially sanctioned lifestyle, an often destructive way of coping with demands and challenges of living that too often is respected, even admired (Bracke & Bugental, 1995; Thoresen & Bracke, in press). Van Egeren (1991) proposed that TABP is a culturally sanctioned "success trap" created by a classic approach–avoidance dilemma. That is, although the highly individualistic, hostile, and impatient thoughts and actions of TABP can produce positive short-term results, the ongoing and long-term consequences may be pervasively negative. Thus, the person who generally uses the Type A style becomes trapped in an inconsistent system of rewards and disappointments. Tragically, the person becomes enmeshed in a series of futile challenges and perceived threats, prompting hopeless and helpless feelings and promoting a deep resentment and pervasive hostility (Van Egeren, 1991). For some, the tragic effects of TABP may be tempered by personal or social relationships, such as intimate friendships and socially supportive groups (Orth-Gomér & Undén, 1990), but we believe that the overall impact on health over the life span diminishes quality of life and endangers survival.

The recent emergence in our culture of a pervasive sense of emptiness that often develops into what has been described as neonarcissism (Lasch, 1978) broadly promotes TABP (Bugental & Bracke, 1992). Economic, social, and political forces have reduced the importance of being one's self and having an internal locus of control. Concurrently, excessive individuality ("I, me, my, mine") has been increasingly exalted as a cultural ideal (Bellah, Madsen, Sullivan, Swidler, & Tipton, 1985). The result of such factors has been self-absorption, a deep alienation, emptiness, and a loss of self-direction in many persons. Advertising has capitalized on such alienation and emptiness to promote acquisition of material goods as the answer to loneliness and the path to fulfillment (Lasch, 1978). Within this cultural context, TABP may reasonably be viewed as a futile and frustrating attempt to eliminate the distress of emptiness by overfilling one's life with work and home projects and material symbols of "success" (Bracke & Bugental, 1995). To ignore such cultural, economic, and political realities weakens treatment efforts and may encourage a blaming of the Type A victim, without implicating those cultural or corporate factors that encourage TABP.

Avoiding Existential Dilemmas

The role of anxiety deriving from life's basic conditions (i.e., existential factors) in promoting TAB, has not been well incorporated into Type A theory (Bracke, 1992). Through awareness, we implicitly experience the basic conditions of living, each of which confronts us with a particular challenge or dilemma that creates existential anxiety. If this anxiety is tolerated and integrated into one's life, it becomes a healthy motivation to live fully and in accord with one's needs and values (Bugental, 1965). If, however, one finds life's basic issues too overwhelming, then an existential phobia may develop as a means of attempting to avoid this anxiety. An existential phobia reduces anxiety by limiting awareness and choices and severely constricting one's life—often by a compulsive immersion in work, social, or domestic activities (i.e., *compulsive doing*).

In essence, a person who is unable to confront an existential dilemma may become hooked on Type A workaholism as a means of trying to avoid existential anxiety (Bracke & Bugental, 1995). Wittingly or not, many corporations capitalize on the pervasive anxiety born of alienation and emptiness, and promote greater dependence on addiction to work as an answer to dealing with life's difficult issues, by seeming to promise a path to fulfillment and meaning.

At the core of this existential phobia is a dread-inspired obsessiveness that promotes a near-total immersion in work and an addiction to sheer compulsive doing. Thus, TAB may be, for many, an existential phobia used to manage the acute or chronic distress about life's fundamental anxieties (Bracke & Bugental, 1995).

SOME CONCLUDING THOUGHTS

Structured small-group treatment programs for reducing TAB and related psychosocial factors (e.g., depressive affect) offer promise for avoiding coronary recurrences and, we hope, for reducing overall CHD incidence. The results of the RCCP, as well as other research findings, provide encouraging evidence that changing TABP is feasible and can be a powerful intervention for reducing cardiac disease. Efforts to replicate the RCPP, as well as variations of that treatment, deserve prompt attention. For too long, cardiac rehabilitation programs have been meager in number and have compromised in focus by limiting their efforts to smoking, diet, and exercise. The chronic struggle and arousal along with the emotional distress that influence smoking, poor diet, and physical inactivity deserve a place in cardiac rehabilitation programs. Surprisingly, such programs may prove to be cost-effective when compared with repeated CABG, angioplasty, and long-term medication (Powell, Weir, & Thoresen, 1994).

In many ways, TABP represents a cultural canon for presumably successful living in our increasingly time-urgent, competitive, and materialistic culture. Within such a cultural context, the intimate friendships and strong attachments that promote health and happiness are too often sacrificed because they require time, patience, nurturing, listening, and reduced self-absorption. For many, the TABP may also be an attempt to avoid pervasive distressing feelings of emptiness, alienation, and meaninglessness. Thus, programs that bring people together in a consistent, genuine, and caring fashion to help each other can offer very powerful medicine.

Needed are treatment programs that recognize the multidimensional nature of the TABP and other coronary-prone factors and, thus, are sensitive to important individual differences in the life circumstances, motivation, and personality of the people who seek help. The challenge and opportunity of cardiac psychology as an emerging human science are to apply the power of behavioral medicine more effectively and efficiently to the varieties of experience that injure as well as strengthen the human heart.

REFERENCES

American Heart Association. (1991). *Heart facts*. Dallas, TX: Author.

Bandura, A. (1982). Self-efficacy mechanism in human agency. *American Psychologist, 37*, 122–147.

Bandura, A. (1986). *Social foundations of thought and action: A social cognitive theory*. Englewood Cliffs, NJ: Prentice-Hall.

Bellah, R., Madsen, R., Sullivan, W., Swidler, A., & Tipton, S. (1985). *Habits of the heart: Individualism and commitment in American life*. Berkeley: University of California Press.

Booth-Kewley, S., & Friedman, H. S. (1987). Psychosocial predictors of heart disease: A quantitative review. *Psychological Bulletin, 101*, 343–362.

Bower, G., & Bower, S. (1976) *Asserting yourself: A practical guide for positive change*. Reading, MA: Addison-Wesley.

Bracke, P. E. (1992, March). *An existential–humanistic view of the Type A behavior pattern*. Paper presented at the Society of Behavioral Medicine Meeting, New York.

Bracke, P. E., & Bugental, J. F. T. (1995). Existential addiction: A new conceptual model for Type A behavior and workaholism. In T. Pauchant (Ed.), *In search of meaning* (pp. 65–93). San Francisco: Jossey-Bass.

Branden, N. (1969). *The psychology of self-esteem*. New York: Bantam Books.

Bugental, J. F. T. (1965). *The search for authenticity: An existential–analytic approach to psychotherapy*. New York: Holt, Rinehart & Winston.

Bugental, J. F. T., & Bracke, P. E. (1992). The future of existential–humanistic psychotherapy. *Psychotherapy, 29*, 28–33.

Burell, G. (1995). *Behavior modification after CABG surgery: Effects on cardiac morbidity, mortality, Type A behavior, and depression*. Unpublished manuscript, Centre for Caring Sciences, Uppsala University, Sweden.

Cottier, C., Shapiro, K., & Julius, S. (1984). Treatment of mild hypertension with progressive muscle relaxation: Predictive value of indexes of sympathetic tone. *Archives of Internal Medicine, 144*, 1954–1958.

Covey, S. R., Merrill, A. R., & Merrill, R. R. (1994). *First things first*. New York: Simon & Schuster.

Dembroski, T. M., MacDougall, J. M., Costa, P. T., & Grandits, G. A. (1989). Components of hostility as predictors of sudden death and myocardial infarction in the Multiple Risk Factor Intervention Trial. *Psychosomatic Medicine, 51*, 514–522.

Feinstein, A. R. (1988). Scientific standards in epidemiologic studies of the menace of daily life. *Science, 242*, 1257–1263.

Friedman, H., Hawley, P. H., & Tucker, J. H. (1994). Personality, health, and longevity. *Current Directions in Psychological Science, 3*, 37–41.

Friedman, M., & Powell, L. H. (1984). The diagnosis and quantitative assessment of Type A behavior: Introduction and description of the Videotaped Structural Interview. *Integrative Psychiatry 1*, 123–129.

Friedman, M., & Rosenman, R. H. (1959). Association of specific overt behavior pattern with blood and cardiovascular findings. *Journal of the American Medical Association, 169*, 1286–1296.

Friedman, M., St. George, S., Byers, S. O., & Rosenman, R. H. (1960). Excretion of 41 catecholamines, 17-ketosteroids, 17-hydroxycorticoeds, and 5-hydroxyindole in men exhibiting a particular behavior pattern (A) associated with high incidence of clinical coronary artery disease. *Journal of Clinical Investigation, 39*, 758–764.

Friedman, M., Thoresen, C. E., Gill, J., Ulmer, D., Powell, L. H., Price, V. A., Brown, B., Thompson, L., Rabin, D., Breall, W. S., Bourg, W., Levy, R., & Dixon, T. (1986). Alteration of Type A behavior and its effect on cardiac recurrences in postmyocardial infarction patients: Summary results of the Recurrent Coronary Prevention Project. *American Heart Journal, 112*, 653–665.

Friedman, M., & Ulmer, D. K. (1984). *Treating Type A behavior and your heart.* New York: Knopf.

Gill, J. J., Price, V. A., Friedman, M., Thoresen, C. E., Powell, L. H., Ulmer, D., Brown, B., & Drews, F. R. (1985). Reduction in Type A behavior in healthy American army officers. *American Heart Journal, 110,* 503–514.

Glass, D. C. (1977). *Behavior patterns, stress, and coronary disease.* Hillsdale, NJ: Erlbaum.

Graff-Low, K., Thoresen, C. E., King, A., Pattillo, J. R., & Jenkins, C. (1995). Anxiety, depression and heart disease in women. *International Journal of Behavioral Medicine, 1,* 305–319.

Henry, J., & Stephens, P. (1977). *Stress, health and the social environment.* New York: Springer-Verlag.

Howard, J. H., Rechnitzer, P. A., Cunningham, D. A., Wong, D., & Brown, H. (1990). Type A behavior, personality, and sympathetic regime. *Behavioral Medicine, 16,* 149–160.

James, W. (1890). *The principles of psychology* (Vols. 1 & 2). New York: Dover.

Jenkins, C. D. (1971). Psychologic and social precursors of coronary disease. *New England Journal of Medicine, 294,* 974–994.

Kearns, D. (1976). *Lyndon Johnson and the American dream.* New York: Harper & Row.

Ketterer, M. (1993). Secondary prevention of ischemic heart disease: The case for aggressive behavioral monitoring and intervention. *Psychosomatics, 34,* 478–484.

Lasch, C. (1978). *The culture of narcissism: American life in an age of diminishing expectations.* New York: Norton.

Margolis, L. H., McLeroy, K. K., Runyon, C. W., & Kaplan, B. H. (1983). Type A behavior: An ecological approach. *Journal of Behavioral Medicine, 6,* 245–258.

Matthews, K. A. (1988). CHD and Type A behaviors: Update on and alternatives to the Booth-Kewley and Friedman quantitative review. *Psychological Bulletin, 104,* 373–380.

Matthews, K. A., & Haynes, S. G. (1986). Type A behavior pattern and coronary disease risk: Update and critical evaluation. *American Journal of Epidemiology, 123,* 923–960.

Mattsen, M. E., & Herd, J. A. (1988). Cardiovascular disease. In E. Bleichman & K. Browned (Eds.), *Handbook of behavioral medicine for women* (pp. 160–174). Elmsford, NY: Pergamon Press.

Mendes de Leon, C. F., Powell, L. H., & Kaplan, B. H. (1991). Change in coronary-prone behaviors in the Recurrent Coronary Prevention Project. *Psychosomatic Medicine, 53,* 407–419.

Miller, T. Q., Turner, C. W., Tindale, R. S., Posavac, E. J., & Dugoni, B. L. (1991). Reasons for the trend toward null findings in research on Type A behavior. *Psychological Bulletin, 100,* 469–485.

National Center for Health Statistics. (1989). (DHHS Publication No. CHS 45042). Washington, DC: U.S. Government Printing Office.

Nunes, E. V., Frank, K. A., & Kornfeld, D. S. (1987). Psychologic treatment for Type A behavior pattern and for coronary heart disease: A meta-analysis of the literature. *Psychosomatic Medicine, 48,* 159–173.

Ornish, D., Brown, S. E., Scherwitz, L. S., Billings, J. H., Armstrong, W. T., Ports, T. A., McLanahan, S. M., Kirkeeide, R. L., Brand, R. J., & Gould, K. L. (1990). Can lifestyle changes reverse coronary artery disease? *Lancet, 336,* 129–133.

Orth-Gomér, K., & Unden, A. L. (1990). Type A behavior, social support, and coronary risk: Interaction and significance for mortality in cardiac patients. *Psychosomatic Medicine, 52,* 59–72.

Osler, W. (1897). *Lectures on angina pectoris and allied states.* New York: Appelton-Century-Crofts.

Pincus, T., & Callahan, L. F. (1995). What explains the association between socioeconomic status and health: Primarily medical access or mind–body variables? *Advances, 11,* 5–36.

Powell, L. H., Mendes de Leon, C., Thoresen, C. E., Pattillo, J. R., Simon, S., & Kaplan, B. (1995). *Change in depressed affect predicts cardiac events in male survivors of acute myocardial infarction.* Unpublished manuscript.

Powell, L. H., Simon, S. S., Bartzokis, T. C., Pattillo, J. R., & Thoresen, C. E. (1994). *Emotional arousability predicts sudden cardiac death in post-myocardial infarction men.* Unpublished manuscript.

Powell, L. H., & Thoresen, C. E. (1987). Small group treatment of Type A behavior. In J. A. Blumenthal & D. C. McKee (Eds.), *Applications in behavioral medicine and health psychology: A clinician's source book* (pp. 174–208). Sarasota, FL: Professional Resource Exchange.

Powell, L. H., & Thoresen, C. E. (1988). Effects of Type A behavioral counseling on severity of prior acute myocardial infarction on survival. *American Journal of Cardiology, 62,* 1159–1163.

Powell, L. H., Weir, D. R., & Thoresen, C. E. (1994, April). *Comparison of cost effectiveness of behavioral, pharmacological and surgical treatment for post–myocardial infarction patients.* Paper presented at the Annual Meeting of the Society of Behavioral Medicine, Boston.

Price, V. A. (1982). *Type A behavior pattern: A model for research and practice.* San Diego, CA: Academic Press.

Price, V. A. (1988). Research and clinical issues in treating Type A behavior. In B. H. Houston & R. Snyder (Eds.), *Type A behavior pattern: Current research and future trends* (pp. 275–311). San Diego, CA: Academic Press.

Price, V. A., & Friedman, M. (1995). The relationship between insecurity and Type A behavior. *American Heart Journal, 129,* 488–491.

Ragland, D. R., & Brand, R. (1988a). Coronary heart disease mortality in the Western Collaborative Group Study. *American Journal of Epidemiology, 127,* 462–475.

Ragland, D. R., & Brand, R. (1988b). Type A behavior and mortality from coronary heart disease. *New England Journal of Medicine, 318,* 65–69.

Rosenman, R. H., Brand, R. J., Sholtz, R. L., & Friedman, M. (1976). Multivariate prediction of coronary heart disease during 8.5-year follow-up in the Western Collaborative Group Study. *American Journal of Cardiology, 37,* 903–910.

Rosenman, R. H., & Friedman, M. (1961). Association of specific behavior pattern in women with blood and cardiovascular findings. *Circulation, 24,* 1173–1184.

Rosenman, R. H., Swan, G. E., & Carmelli, D. (1988). Definition, assessment, and evolution of the Type A behavior pattern. In B. K. Houston & C. R. Snyder (Eds.), *Type A behavior pattern: Research theory and intervention* (pp. 8–31). New York: Wiley.

Scherwitz, L. (1988). Interviewer behaviors in the Western Collaborative Group Study and the Multiple Risk Factor Intervention Trial Structured Interviews. In B. Houston & C. R. Snyder (Eds.), *Type A behavior pattern: Research, theory, and intervention* (pp. 146–167). New York: Wiley.

Spiegel, D., Bloom, J. R., Kraemer, H. C., & Gottheil, E. (1989). Effect of psychosocial treatment on survival of patients with metastic breast cancer. *Lancet, 2,* 888–891.

Strube, M. J. (Ed.). (1990). *Type A behavior.* Corte Madera, CA: Select Press.

Sutherland, J. E., Pershy, V. W., & Brody, J. A. (1990). Proportionate mortality trends: 1950 through 1986. *Journal of the American Medical Association, 264,* 3178–3184.

Thoresen, C. E. (1990, June). *Long-term effects of Type A group treatment in the Recurrent Coronary Prevention Project.* Paper presented at the First International Society of Behavioral Medicine Meeting, Uppsala, Sweden.

Thoresen, C. E. (1996). *Effects of reducing coronary-prone behavior in postmyocardial infarction patients: A four-year follow-up.* Unpublished manuscript, Stanford University, School of Education.

Thoresen, C. E., & Bracke, P. E. (in press). Reducing coronary recurrence and coronary prone behavior: A structured group approach. In J. Spira (Ed.), *Group therapy for the medically ill.* New York: Guilford Press.

Thoresen, C. E., & Graff-Low, K. (1994). Psychosocial interventions in female cardiovascular disease patients. In S. M. Czajkowski, D. R. Hill, & T. B. Clarkson (Eds.), *Women, behavior, and cardiovascular disease* (NIH Publication No. 94-3309, pp. 329–342). Rockville, MD: National Institutes of Health.

Thoresen, C. E., & Mahoney, J. M. (1974). *Behavioral self-control.* New York: Holt, Rinehart & Winston.

Thoresen, C. E., & Ohman, A. (1987). Type A behavior pattern: A person–environment interaction perspective. In D. Magnussen & A. Ohman (Eds.), *Psychopathology: An interaction perspective* (pp. 325–346). San Diego, CA: Academic Press.

Thoresen, C. E., & Pattillo, J. R. (1988). Exploring the Type A behavior pattern in children and adolescents. In B. K. Houston & Snyder, C. R (Eds.), *Type*

A behavior pattern: Research, theory and intervention (pp. 98–145). New York: Wiley.

Thoresen, C. E., & Powell, L. H. (1992). Type A behavior pattern: New perspectives on theory, assessment and intervention. *Journal of Consulting and Clinical Psychology, 60,* 595–604.

Tunstall-Redoe, H., Kueslasman, K., Amonyel, P., Arveiler, D., Rajakangas, A., & Pajak, A., (1994). Myocardial infarction and coronary deaths in the World Health Organization MONICA Project. *Circulation, 90,* 581–612.

Van Egeren, L. F. (1991). A "success trap" theory of Type A behavior: Historical background. In M. Strube (Ed.), *Type A behavior* (pp. 45–58). Corde Madera, CA: Select Press.

Williams, R. B., & Barefoot, J. C. (1988). Coronary-prone behavior: The emerging role of the hostility complex. In B. K. Houston & C. R. Synder (Eds.), *Type A behavior pattern: Research, theory, and intervention* (pp. 189–211). New York: Wiley.

Williams, R. B., Barefoot, J. C., & Shekelle, R. B. (1984). The health consequences of hostility. In M. A. Chesney & R. H. Rosenman (Eds.), *Anger, hostility and behavioral medicine* (pp. 173—186). New York: McGraw-Hill.

Wolff, E., Thoresen, C. E., Venter, E., & Viljoen, H. (1994, April). *The Recurrent Coronary Prevention Project: Some initial findings in the South African replication.* Paper presented at the Annual Meeting of the Society of Behavioral Medicine, Boston.

11

GROUP PSYCHOTHERAPY IN PROJECT NEW LIFE: TREATMENT OF CORONARY-PRONE BEHAVIORS FOR PATIENTS WHO HAVE HAD CORONARY ARTERY BYPASS GRAFT SURGERY

GUNILLA BURELL

Coronary heart disease (CHD) is highly influenced by the way people live. Well-known risk factors such as smoking, diet, a sedentary lifestyle, and socioeconomic position belong to this realm (Campeau et al., 1984; Fitzgibbon, Leach, & Kafka, 1987; Kaplan, Sallis, & Patterson, 1993; Lie, Lawrie, & Morris, 1977; Solymoss, Nadeau, Millette, & Campeau, 1988). Lifestyle factors also include behavioral and emotional characteristics, such as social isolation, depression, anxiety, and the Type A behavior pattern (TABP; Booth-Kewley & Friedman, 1987; Friedman & Rosenman, 1974). Medical and surgical procedures have been developed that are quite effective for ameliorating acute symptoms and manifestations of CHD (CASS Principal Investigators and Associates, 1983; European Coronary Surgery Study Group, 1979; Takaro, Hultgren, Lipton, & Detre, 1976). However, to influence the course of the disease in the long run, behavioral interventions may well be necessary.

Secondary prevention can be conceptualized as the development and implementation of long-term strategies for patients who already have CHD, with the objective of decreasing cardiac events, improving quality of life, and prolonging life. Lifestyle change after a cardiac event is sometimes difficult, and patient compliance is often low (Kaplan et al., 1993). Thus, there is an opportunity for health professionals to create an educational and therapeutic setting to help patients initiate and maintain behavior changes that will promote their health. Simply telling a patient what he or she should do, or distributing a leaflet, will not be sufficient for achieving this goal. Physicians and other health professionals need to provide opportunities for behavioral and cognitive skills training. By shaping behavior, psychotherapists can help patients develop a new behavioral repertoire that they can use in their daily lives.

THE NEW LIFE TRIAL

Project New Life is a behavioral secondary prevention program aimed at modifying coronary-prone behavior in postcoronary artery bypass graft (CABG) patients. The New Life trial was a randomized study to evaluate the effects of behavioral intervention for CABG surgery patients in several hospitals in middle and north Sweden; I served as the principal investigator of the study as well as the leader for most of the groups. In this chapter, I describe the design and results of the study as well as the therapeutic goals, content, and methods of the program. I also discuss some conclusions from the application and implementation of the program in the regular clinical setting.

To a large extent, coronary-prone behavior is defined as the TABP. The reasons for this are partly historical, partly because many of the key features of what is now considered coronary-prone behavior (e.g., potential for hostility, impatience, and time urgency) were first characterized in studies of TABP (Review Panel on Coronary-Prone Behavior and Coronary Heart Disease, 1981), and partly because the interventions used in Project New Life were patterned after the Recurrent Coronary Prevention Project (RCPP), developed by Friedman (Friedman et al., 1986, 1987), who in large part conceptualized the TABP. I have evaluated the treatment design and techniques used in Project New Life in a previous, small study (see Burell et al., 1994). Contemporary conceptions of coronary-prone behavior also embrace such issues as social isolation, depression, anxiety, low self-esteem, and job strain. In addition to focusing on the modification of the TABP, the Project New Life therapeutic intervention dealt explicitly with the issues of social support, techniques for ensuring successful coping, combating depression, and maximizing self-actualization.

Evaluation of long-term outcome of CABG surgery has shown a return of cardiac symptoms in a substantial number of patients and a need for reoperation in as many as 25% (CASS, 1983; Mayou, 1986). Furthermore, the surgery has been shown to have negative effects on patients' quality of life (CASS, 1983; Jenkins, Stanton, Savageau, Denlinger, & Klein, 1983; Kinchla, 1985; Kolata, 1981; Mayou & Bryant, 1987; Oberman & Kouchoukos, 1979; Robinson, Froelicher, & Utley, 1984). For some patients, depression and cognitive deficits create problems for returning to a normal life. A number of cardiac rehabilitation programs for post-myocardial infarction (MI) patients have been scientifically evaluated (Oldenburg, Perkins, & Andrews, 1985); however, specific programs for post-surgery patients have been rare. Many post-CABG patients feel that people in their environment, including their physicians, regard them as "fixed, and ready to function 100%." This demand may be difficult to manage when one is confronted with physical weakness, a variety of pains and aches, worries, and a low energy level. The starting point for the New Life trial was to investigate whether behavioral intervention aimed at modification of Type A behavior and improvement of coping skills following CABG could decrease morbidity and mortality in comparison with routine care.

Method

Participation in the study was offered to male and female patients who had undergone CABG 3–12 months prior to recruitment. Patients were referred from the University Hospital of Uppsala and 13 other Swedish hospitals. Patients who suffered from diabetes mellitus, other severe somatic or psychiatric disease, or alcoholism and those who were non-Swedish speaking were excluded. Patients were required to be nonsmokers at the time of entry into the study. Patients who were judged eligible were invited by mail to participate. Each was sent a letter that described conditions of participation and randomization and extended an invitation to an information meeting, where details of the study would be described. Such information meetings were held for about 20 patients at a time. After these procedures, 261 patients (37 women and 224 men) agreed by written informed consent to participate. The mean age of all participants was 58 years.

From the total sample, 128 of the patients were randomly assigned to 1 year of behavioral group treatment, to be followed by five to six "booster sessions" during each of Years 2–3. One hundred thirty-three patients were randomly assigned to a routine-care control condition. Patients were recruited consecutively, and randomization took place at each treatment center whenever there was a sufficient number of participants to form a new group. No attempt was made to interfere with routine care, which varied among hospitals. Thus, both experimental and control patients had access to rehabilitation programs that were regularly offered by their hospitals.

Treatment groups consisted of 5–9 patients, some of mixed gender. Three-hour group sessions were held every third week over 1 year, for a total of 17 sessions. The first phase of the treatment (6 sessions) was focused on education about CHD, surgical issues, risk factors and risk behaviors, psychological factors that influence well-being, and Type A behavior. From the very first session, participants were given homework assignments related to observation of health behaviors (e.g., eating, alcohol consumption, and smoking [in case of relapse]) and coronary-prone behaviors (e.g., Type A behavior, depressive reactions, and anxiety). The remainder of the sessions were targeted at modifying TABP in participants: developing and applying new reactions and behaviors that entailed less impatience, irritation, hostility, depression, and distress. Homework assignments provided much of the material for group discussion. The agenda for each session included a brief relaxation procedure, review of homework assignments, introduction and discussion of new ideas, and preparation for new homework. A cardiologist and a nutritionist were each responsible for conducting one session. The remaining sessions were led by a clinical psychologist.

Results

The results at 5–6.5 years after surgery showed a significant difference in total mortality among patients who had been in behavioral group treatment and those who had received only routine care (7 vs. 16 deaths; $p = .02$ on Gehan's Wilcoxon Test; see Table 1). There were also differences in cardiovascular mortality, MI, reoperation, and angioplasty (a total of 14 vs. 19 events; $p = .045$, Gehan's Wilcoxon Test). Fewer patients in behavioral group treatment suffered cardiac events, and they remained event-free considerably longer (see Figure 1). None of the patients in behavioral group treatment died during the treatment year (see Figure 2).

There were no differences in cardiac history, risk factors, or surgery parameters that could explain these treatment differences. Experimental and control patients were compared with regard to gender, age, and family history of CHD as well as hypertension and smoking. The control patients

TABLE 1
Cardiovascular Events Among Participants in the New Life Trial at 5–6.5 Years After CABG Surgery

	Group	
Event	Experimental	Control
Total mortality	7	16
Cardiovascular mortality	5	8
Nonfatal reinfarction	2	8
Reoperation	6	2
Angioplasty	1	1
Total cardiovascular events	14	19
Number of days in coronary care unit	243	416

Note. CABG = coronary artery bypass graft.

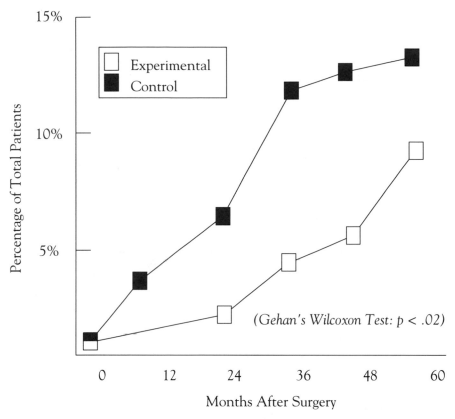

Figure 1. Proportion of cardiac events among patients participating in the New Life trial after coronary artery bypass graft surgery.

were somewhat older (59 vs. 56 years), and the experimental patients tended to have a larger genetic risk as defined by family history of CHD. However, none of these factors turned out to be related to recurrent events during the study. Disease status at study entry was established by number of prior MIs, left ventricular function, left ventricular failure, number of diseased vessels, left main coronary artery stenosis, and New York Heart Association classification. No significant differences were found in these variables. Likewise, operative parameters such as number of grafts placed or total number of distal anastomoses did not differ. The only background factors that were related to new cardiac events during the trial were number of MIs prior to surgery and number of diseased vessels, and there were no significant differences between experimental and control patients with regard to these factors.

Significant reductions in self-rated Type A behavior were evident after treatment, according to analysis of covariance (ANCOVA; $p < .0003$).

CUMULATIVE MORTALITY

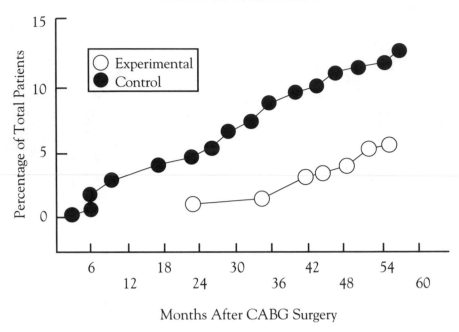

Figure 2. Cumulative mortality among patients who participated in the New Life trial after coronary artery bypass graft (CABG) surgery.

The experimental patients changed significantly ($t = 8.5$), whereas the control patients remained the same. There was also a significant reduction in Beck Depression Inventory scores for experimental patients, which differed significantly from controls (ANCOVA $p < .008$).

These results point to the promising conclusion that participating in behavioral group treatment that is aimed at reducing Type A behavior and other psychosocial risk factors can reduce morbidity and mortality in post-CABG patients.

SIMILARITIES AND DIFFERENCES BETWEEN THE RCPP AND THE NEW LIFE TRIAL

The RCPP enrolled patients after MI, whereas the New Life trial recruited patients after CABG surgery. However, the RCPP included many surgery patients, and many of the New Life patients had suffered MIs. Project New Life excluded patients who had experienced surgery complications, had diabetes mellitus, or were still smoking.

It is sometimes claimed that CABG and MI patients are different in terms of their disease progression and mechanisms. However, in terms of behavioral problems and treatment targets, the two populations are quite similar. The RCPP patients were recruited primarily at workplaces in urban areas, which probably entailed an upward socioeconomic selection. The New Life patients were representative of the average post-CABG patient population in Sweden, residing in urban and rural areas in mid- and north Sweden and, on the average, 5 years older than those in the RCPP. Their socioeconomic background most likely varied more than that of the RCPP patients. These differences would tend to increase generalizabilty of the results.

Both the RCPP and Project New Life were randomized trials. The RCPP offered group intervention for control patients by providing cardiac counseling about standard risk factors but not about Type A behavior reduction. However, this was not feasible with the New Life patients, because 14 hospitals were involved, dispersed over two thirds of the area of Sweden.

Outcome Measures

Both the RCPP and New Life studies used total and cardiac mortality, cardiac morbidity, and change of Type A behavior measured by the video-taped clinical examination, self-ratings, and spouse ratings. In addition, the RCPP used ratings by coworkers, which New Life did not use because a substantial proportion of the participants were no longer part of the work-force.

The New Life trial also assessed a number of other psychological variables: depression, anxiety, anger, social support, marital satisfaction, and health quality of life. A medical examination included New York Heart Association classification, cardiac symptoms, risk factor status, and cardiac function determined by a bicycle workload test.

Intervention

The groups in the New Life Trial had fewer participants, generally 7–8, compared with 10–12 in the RCPP. Both programs had gender-mixed groups. The dropout rate was lower in the New Life trial, possibly because of the smaller size of the groups and the close collaboration with hospitals and cardiologists. The RCPP used alternative group counseling (about the "standard" risk factors for CHD) as a control condition. In the New Life trial, the control patients received "routine care," which varied among the participating hospitals, some providing physical rehabilitation or dietary advice (or both) and others providing virtually nothing. Thus, the RCPP controlled for the effect of group participation per se. The basic treatment of the New Life trial was 1 year, with four to five follow-up sessions for each of the next 2 years. The RCPP program lasted considerably longer, for 4.5 years, although the frequency of sessions was once a month for most of the treatment period. On the basis of clinical observations from Project New Life, I believe that the frequency of sessions should ideally be every week for the first 2 or 3 months and biweekly for the rest of the year, with a less frequent maintenance program for subsequent years.

There are important similarities in the content and treatment format of the two trials. Both used the same format for behavioral treatment sessions: a brief relaxation procedure, review and discussion of homework assignments, introduction of new ideas and material built on previous therapeutic work, and new assignments. Also, a very important tool in both programs was the requirement of daily behavioral drills.

Results

Both studies were successful in significantly reducing recurrent cardiac events. The RCPP demonstrated that results could be maintained over a longer follow-up period. Project New Life supported the idea that reduction of Type A behavior can reduce cardiac morbidity and may prolong life.

PROJECT NEW LIFE

The components of the New Life program can be summarized as follows:

1. Developing knowledge about behavior and CHD.
2. Increasing awareness of one's own reactions and behaviors, which can be described as creating an "inner voice" to guide and monitor behavior.
3. Practicing new behavioral skills.
4. Identifying and changing belief systems.
5. Reflecting on spiritual issues.
6. Utilizing group social support.

The program is very practical and relies much on homework assignments and monitoring behavior. Following is a description of the clinical content of the New Life program.

Developing Knowledge

The awareness that "stress is bad" may not provide sufficient motivation for individuals to change their behavior. Information alone often has little impact. However, for patients who are involved in a change process, knowledge that is personalized can become very important in guiding the therapeutic process. Detailed knowledge about what has happened to one's heart can decrease anxiety and increase a sense of self-efficacy.

The first sessions of the program were devoted to fairly structured teaching. Photographs, slides, films, and written material were used to describe MI, CABG surgery, and the relevant anatomy and physiology. Even if the patient had been instructed about these issues earlier, such information had probably been given during the emergency phase of the illness, when emotional interference with learning was at a peak. In group sessions, each individual had the opportunity to discuss his or her own history and experience. This included the opportunity to share the emotional consequences of having undergone CABG surgery and, possibly, having had an MI. Many patients had experienced periods of anxiety, worry, and depression, emotions that in some cases were strange to them. Because many patients had been very active and independent people, the sometimes prolonged feelings of weakness and vulnerability after CABG were especially frightening for them. By becoming aware that such reactions are common and would not always be so prominent, many patients experienced a sense of relief and began to feel more secure and optimistic. By sharing with others, group members developed a sense of acceptance, support, and cohesiveness.

Patients were also educated about standard risk factors, health behaviors, and other factors that may influence the course of CHD. Relevant research was discussed, and even though the New Life program did not include specific suggestions for dietary change or physical exercise, there was encouragement to change these behaviors as well.

The core of the educational phase was to learn how Type A behaviors manifest and how they may be related to CHD. By means of audiovisual and written material, through observation of the behavior of others, and by self-observation assignments and discussion of case illustrations, patients developed recognition and insight into the symptoms and signs of Type A behavior. The relationship between behavior and its effect on the heart was continually emphasized. A therapeutic "bottom line" was that whatever rational reasons one may have for being angry, it might precipitate a cardiac event and even death (Mittleman et al., 1995).

The general goals of the education phase can be summarized as developing knowledge about each of the following: basic anatomy and physiology of the cardiovascular system, the signs and symptoms of Type A behavior, and the relationship between Type A behavior and CHD.

Creating an Inner Voice

Monitoring one's own behavior and recognizing stimuli that elicit TABP were cornerstones of change in Project New Life. Metaphors were used to illustrate this process. For instance, counselors emphasized the need for patients to develop a new "behavioral track," and in order to know when it is appropriate to "change tracks," they must attend to a warning sign indicating that they are on the "wrong track." The warning sign might be a rush of anger; a hostile thought; or physical manifestations such as increased heart rate, a clenched fist, or muscular tension. Structured self-observation in the form of diaries, homework assignments, and discussion and feedback in the group were effective tools for fostering self-awareness of these warning signs. Early in the therapeutic process, patients typically became aware of their reactions some time after an upsetting event had taken place. After training in self-observation (e.g., by recording warning signs, reactions, and consequences in a diary), patients were able to shorten the time lag between an upsetting event and the awareness of how they reacted. Eventually, awareness occurred more often during the event itself. In the case of recurring stimuli for stressful or angry reactions, patients frequently learned to recognize early warning signs and avoided troubling situations or coped differently.

The group leader plays a vital role as the original inner voice for members. Often patients remarked, "I realized I was beginning to get angry, but then I thought of you, the group leader, and relaxed." Another patient described an unforeseen, upsetting situation in which this thought came to mind: "What is it that K. [the group leader] wants me to do?" Gradually, the inner voice may become the patient's own voice. Also, behavior observed during group sessions was used to foster awareness of TABP. In summary, the general goals for the development of awareness involved (a) becoming more alert to bodily signals, such as muscular tension, heart rate, and motorizations, and (b) observing, reflecting, and drawing conclusions about contingencies of behavior.

Skills Training

Project New Life used the following metaphor to help patients develop new behavioral skills:

> Suppose you want to travel by train from Point A to Point B, and there is no track. What would you have to do to get to Point B by train? Motivation alone will not be sufficient. If you get on a train at A and just wish to go to B, you will end up somewhere else—until a new track has been built. Change of behavior comes about similarly; it is a question of building a new behavioral track, which takes time, labor, and endurance.

The alternative to the Type A track is not passivity. Many coronary patients alternate between a pattern of despair and depression and a pattern of aggressive activity, in which hostility or anger appears to serve as a source of physical and mental energy. Concomitant release of catecholamines may mask bodily signals of exhaustion that result from relentless hard-driving behavior. Catecholamines can act as a self-released stimulant drug, and initial attempts to slow down may create withdrawal symptoms. Therapists in the New Life program reinforced the idea that behavior can be energized by such positive emotions as enthusiasm, curiosity, and love. The goals of Type A behavior modification include not only the reduction of self-destructive behavior but also the development of problem-solving and communication skills, improvement of self-esteem, and trust in other people. The general goal of skills training in the New Life program can be summarized as improving patients' ability to cope with daily life.

Similar to the RCPP, the New Life trial made use of daily behavioral drills aimed at reducing mental and physical tension, reducing time-urgent and aggressive behaviors, and changing Type A attitudes and beliefs. The rationale for daily behavioral practice was that manifestations of the TABP are very habitual. To break such unhealthy habits, patients needed to create new ones that would eventually become natural, automatic, and rewarding. Behaviors are shaped in small concrete steps, by repetition and positive reinforcement. One example is to improve patients' attention to their behavior. However, simply saying "be more attentive" is too vague and general; the patient may respond "I can't do that; it's impossible for me." However, to practice one specific attention exercise on one specific day is usually more feasible and provides a way to overcome obstacles that a patient might have to even trying a new behavior. For example, Monday might entail observing a flower, Tuesday observing facial expressions, and Wednesday listening without interrupting. The next week, the same behavioral exercises are repeated on the same days, until the next month, when a new set of exercises is practiced. One immediate reward for undertaking the exercises is an improvement of quality of life. Another is the feedback and emotional support from the group. Fairly soon, most of the exercises become reinforced by improved social interaction and a sense of self-efficacy. Once the "daily drill book" has been introduced, it is used ever after, providing topics for discussion and feedback during group sessions. Because behavior is very much under the influence of immediate consequences, frequent social and emotional feedback from the group and the group leader is a crucial motivating factor for patients to try behaviors that may at first seem alien. The shaping process suggests that the group leader will not criticize or punish but, instead, will support and reward progress, however small it may seem. It is also important to maintain an atmosphere of positive and unconditional regard for every individual in the group. Thus, it is the group leader's task to detect and focus on good will and positive efforts. The group leader is one of the most important models for alternatives to Type A behavior. The ability to deal with very difficult personal issues is also crucial for the leader.

In summary, the goals of skills training are to cultivate the following behaviors:

- Reduction of physical and emotional tension
- Avoidance of exhaustion
- Reduction of irritation, anger, frustration, impatience, time urgency, and distress
- Coping with negative emotions such as worry, anxiety, and depression
- Expression of thoughts and emotions directly, honestly, and in a caring manner
- Improvement of communication skills
- Responding and acting, rather than reacting, to everyday problems of living.

Cognitive Patterns and Belief Systems

Type A thinking is characterized by an excessive awareness of time and deadlines, competitiveness, perfectionism, extreme demands that can never quite be met, a need for control over events and other people, and free-floating hostility. Typical of the Type A "inner dialogue" are absolute judgments (involving the terms *always, never,* or *everybody*), overgeneralizations, hostile generalizations, devaluation of self and others, negative predictions, and exaggeration of the importance of trivial events (Friedman & Ulmer, 1984). Just as they do with overt behaviors, patients must learn to recognize cognitive patterns and what triggers them. With homework assignments that include self-monitoring and group discussion, patients learn to understand that certain ways of thinking increase distress and irritation. A diary may be useful and should include registration of particular events that elicited irritation, noting what the person was thinking, what he or she did, and what happened afterward. Irritating events can generally be conceptualized in three categories. The first category includes minor, trivial, temporary occurrences with few long-term consequences. Examples include irritation at a red light, with the clothes of an unknown teenager, or with a waiter whose service is less than perfect. Systematic self-observation often leads to a decrease in reactions to such stimuli. A second category encompasses events that are beyond an individual's control, for instance, irritation at other other motorists or actors on television. Patients must practice letting go of the struggle for control in such situations. This is accomplished by reporting, reviewing, and reinterpreting events in group discussions, where others' insightful comments are often of great value. The third category includes the real, sometimes major problems that occur in family or workplace relationships. What is needed in these situations is the development of active and constructive problem-solving and communication skills, to allow the person to take action instead of just reacting. Group sessions create opportunities for patients to review and reinterpret events as well as find alternative ways of coping. What is most essential is the application of new principles in everyday life.

People exhibiting Type A behavior typically place extreme demands on themselves, often demands that can never be met. They can always do things "better, faster, or differently." Life is a constant struggle to prove their worth as human beings. There is rarely a feeling of real satisfaction, because there is an ongoing uncertainty as to whether anything is ever "good enough." Such rigid judgments of self and others must be replaced with greater acceptance and flexibility. Group discussion thus must attend to the issues of self-esteem and self-acceptance. The unconditional acceptance provided in the group and modeled by the group leader is crucial for helping patients change their negative self-image. An atmosphere where members can share all thoughts and feelings, including the "darker side" of themselves, yet still be accepted can provide a fundamental therapeutic experience and contribute to a profound change of outlook.

The general goals of cognitive restructuring can be summarized as developing all of these behaviors:

- The ability to cope with the unexpected
- Self-respect and self-esteem
- Tolerance, acceptance, and respect for people different from oneself
- Taking one's own basic needs seriously
- Trust in others
- Positive emotions, such as joy, enthusiasm, curiosity, love, and optimism.

Spiritual Issues

Patients who have undergone CABG have an awareness of having been close to death. For most people, the heart has a profound emotional and symbolic value. Some patients will say "I was dead for an hour," referring to the time of extracorporeal circulation. Many patients have had ruminations about the possibility of not waking up again. Some have even prepared for their own funerals. After surgery there is often a heightened sense of the preciousness of life. However, many people avoid thinking about or discussing the issues of death and the meaning of life. Group sessions with cardiac patients provide a setting in which such discussions are natural. When patients begin to change behavior, experience more positive feedback, and review their belief systems, there is often a change of self-image and refocusing one's life on what is truly important.

Later sessions in the New Life program were devoted to discussion of knowing oneself and reflecting on the question of what one wants to do with the rest of one's life. Some of the drills relate to these issues, for instance, when angry or upset, asking "Is this worth dying for?" Other, related drills include spending time alone, observing the beauty of nature, and reflecting on dreams. In one exercise, participants were asked to list 10 characteristics of themselves and to evaluate whether the list was positive or negative. Too many negatives evoke a discussion of self-image. Another exercise asked patients to describe "some things [they] would really like to do." This allowed wishes to surface that might have never been revealed before. Discussion and acceptance by other group members created and enhanced optimism for a worthwhile future. Patients were also asked to reflect on "the three things that you consider most important to make your life meaningful." Most patients gave answers centered around the themes of physical well-being, a meaningful job or activity, relationships, and love. Still, many Type A patients have lived in ways that have prevented fulfillment of such life goals. They have damaged their health, emptied their activities of joy by being relentlessly hard driving, and have never been able to express and accept love. The program stressed that "now is the time to turn life around" and find out what is needed to approach these profound goals and values.

Goals for the discussion of spiritual and life values in Project New Life included finding a balance between work, family, health, pleasurable activities, and spiritual interests; developing new interests; developing joy, enthusiasm, and hope; and accepting and giving love.

WORKING WITH WOMEN WHO HAVE CHD

Groups in Project New Life either consisted exclusively of male participants or were gender mixed, because the women were the minority. In a group of, for instance, seven men and two women, it was often difficult for the women to create space for themselves to speak up. It is becoming increasingly obvious that the backgrounds and panorama of risk factors differ for men and women with CHD. Women have higher mortality rates from MI and surgery (Eaker et al., 1988), perhaps because it takes longer before they receive adequate care (Ayanian & Epstein, 1991; Steingart et al., 1991). Women under 65 who have CHD are a statistical minority partly because of protection from estrogen; thus, women who do develop CHD at a younger age often have more risk factors and greater severity of disease. Pain relief after CABG surgery is often less pronounced in women. Also, the psychological and social consequences of suffering an MI or going through CABG are different for men and women. Groups remained gender mixed throughout the New Life trial. One result of this experience has been to offer separate groups for men and women in current clinical interventions. There are specific pressures and life problems that women share that may not be relevant to men. Of course, the opposite situation is also true: Men share some profound life experiences that are gender unique.

Consider this excerpt from Freudenberger and North's (1986) book about women's burnout:

> Are there situations in your life in which you are tired, hurting, but push harder to compensate for those weaknesses? Do you alternate between feeling pressured and drained, panicked and driven? Are you often irritable, harassed, and anxious, and some mornings just don't want to get out of bed? Are you often agitated from constantly anticipating the spoken and unspoken demands from those considered important? Tired from acting the resident nurturer at home, at work, and with friends? Frustrated from jumping from role to role and finding yourself even further behind? Do you feel that no matter how good you are, you're still not good enough? (p. 6)

Without using the concepts of coronary-prone or Type A behavior, this quote captures the experience of many participants in women's groups for those with CHD. Type A behavior is "a continuous struggle, an unremitting attempt to accomplish or achieve more and more things or participate in more and more events in less and less time, frequently in the face of opposition—real or imagined—from other persons" (Friedman & Ulmer, 1984, p. 33). This struggle has different manifestations for men and women. For instance, whereas a man may struggle to achieve status, physical strength, and omniscience, a woman's pressures may be more in the domain of relationships. She may struggle to be perfect in caring for everyone else's needs, to the point where she neglects her own. According to Price (1988), common female roles are the giver, the mediator, and the perfectionist. One female executive with severe angina pectoris shared that what stressed her most in her job was to keep everybody around her happy and prevent all conflicts, not only between herself and others, but among everyone. Several women in my clinical groups who had husbands with CHD neglected themselves in their attempts to keep their husbands alive. One woman even kept her anginal attacks hidden because it would cause her husband too much anxiety to hear about them. Thus, the demand for perfectionism, and an incessant struggle for control over the uncontrollable, with high emotional involvment, may finally lead to exhaustion, physical breakdown, and disease (Appels, Falger, & Schouten, 1993).

Hostility may manifest itself differently in men and women. Few women are blatantly aggressive in their overt behavior. Instead, a woman's anger and frustration may more likely take the form of resentment, bitterness, nervous agitation, or depression (Dearborn & Hastings, 1987; Eaker et al., 1992; Hällström, Lapidus, Bengtsson, & Edström, 1986). Some of the women in the female groups that have developed out of Project New Life have expressed disgust for themselves, for instance, at the sight of themselves in the mirror. One professional and highly successful woman felt that she was "cheating" other people whenever she was perceived as competent. The women in our groups, more openly than the men, exhibited devaluation, low self-esteem, and feelings of despair.

A number of studies have shown Type A behavior to be more common in employed women than in housewives and more common in women with higher education (Dearborn & Hastings, 1987; Thoresen & Graff-Low, 1990). However, most of these studies have used questionnaires to assess Type A behavior, which might have led to an emphasis on job involvement scores—which probably does not indicate coronary-prone behavior—and a general underestimation of anger and frustration, as expressed by nonverbal behaviors. Nevertheless, it is clear that employed women have dual stresses and strains. Frankenhaeuser (1991) showed that secretion of catecholamines increases in women at the end of the day, that is, by the time of their second or third jobs, as mothers, wives, and homemakers. Such a life situation may be expected to facilitate and reinforce whatever tendencies to time urgency and impatience a woman might have. However, an interactional view necessitates the study of how different women cope with this modern reality. A coronary-prone woman, with harsh self-demands, may drive herself to exhaustion by never being quite satisfied with her performance and by not allowing herself adequate rest.

CHD is less common in women with higher education and professional jobs than in women in lower positions (Eaker et al., 1992; Hazuda et al., 1986; Matthews, Kelsey, Meilahn, Kuller, & Wing, 1989). This could be taken to imply that it is not "dangerous" for a woman to be employed outside her home. The pathogenic situation involves some combination of a woman's double or triple burdens: her own and her family's demands and role expections, her lack of control and lack of social support, and her inability to set limits and balance her life (Appels et al., 1993; Frankenhaeuser, 1991; Theorell, 1991). These conditions can apply to women regardless of their employment status.

What are the factors that may trigger MIs in coronary-prone women? The following observations and reflections are based on my experiences from group treatment of women with CHD after MI or CABG surgery. Many women were very unhappy when they first came to group sessions. They often blamed themselves for their disease. Conversely, many of our male patients seemed to cope fairly well; they were active and in a good mood after the surgery, eager to start something new (which is perhaps a positive aspect of their Type A behavior). Such optimism and eagerness were extremely rare in women with CHD. Women were often worse off medically and might have justified reasons for worry. Very often they were depressed, anxious, and very bitter regarding the inadequate medical treatment that too many women still encounter. They were lonely and had no one to talk to about their situation; often, they did not want to talk, to avoid burdening family and friends. Many women did not expect their families to accommodate their needs. Change of diet was often not supported, and time off for physical excercise was hard to obtain. In a number of cases, women's desires for more personal attention were negatively received, especially by husbands.

What might be the psychological setup that triggers a manifestation of CHD? Perhaps exhaustion (Appels et al., 1993): Many women carry an extreme burden in caring for others daily, not only for the family but also for elderly or handicapped relatives or neighbors. An incessant struggle is perhaps met with too few gratifications, so the overall balance is negative. Also, coronary-prone women in my groups seemed to have encountered severe personal losses more often than expected, such as the death of children or other very close family members, sometimes under traumatic circumstances. One woman had lost an infant, a young adult son, and her husband. This woman had given up the expectation that life, or people, would ever provide her with something good and worthwhile. She suffered from chronic grief.

The group leader needs to be particularly observant to certain potential problems in groups of female CHD patients. Some women may have difficulties in dealing with socially dominant people and may be hesitant to express their ideas and feelings in the presence of such people. Thus, if a woman in a group is very talkative and socially dominant, others may feel frustrated or inferior in verbal skills. A woman can dominate by talking about herself a great deal without listening to others, by presenting herself as superior in handling her life, by denying problems, by challenging homework assignments, or by controlling other group members by organizing activities for them or being "helpful" in an insensitive way. I have experienced how such patterns led to members forming subgroups of two or three, who would talk privately to each other and not in the group. It is certainly constructive to form personal bonds of friendship, but not to the exclusion of work in the group. It is the group leader's obligation to detect such dynamics quickly and create a more secure and well-balanced group interaction. The inability to accept others as they are and to be honest and direct in communication, a fear of confrontation, a lack of self-esteem, and the tendency to talk secretly with one's allies to the exclusion of others in many cases are profound problems in women's daily lives. Thus, these patterns should be dealt with as vital therapeutic targets in women's groups.

CONCLUSION

Project New Life demonstrated that a behavior modification program after CABG can reduce cardiac mortality and morbidity. This program focused on modification of coronary-prone Type A behavior—that is, hard-driving, competitive, and time-pressured behavior and easily aroused anger and irritation. The intervention format was a group-based 1-year treatment program, with booster sessions in Years 2 and 3. Treatment components included learning to recognize and monitor one's own behavior; techniques for developing new behavioral skills for becoming less overreactive, angry, hostile, and distressed; and changing Type-A-related values and belief systems. It is increasingly recognized that the progression of CHD is highly influenced by behavior and lifestyle. Secondary prevention risk-factor-modification programs for CHD patients should thus offer comprehensive behavioral treatment for patients whose behaviors place them at risk for recurrent cardiac events.

REFERENCES

Appels, A., Falger, P. R. J., & Schouten, E. G. W. (1993). Vital exhaustion as risk indicator for myocardial infarction in women. *Journal of Psychosomatic Research, 37*, 881–890.

Ayanian, J. Z., & Epstein, A. M. (1991). Differences in the use of procedures between women and men hospitalized for coronary heart disease. *New England Journal of Medicine, 325*, 221–225.

Booth-Kewley, S., & Friedman, H. S. (1987). Psychological predictors of heart disease: A quantitative review. *Psychological Bulletin, 101*, 343–362.

Burell, G., Öhman, A., Sundin, Ö., Ström, G., Ramund, B., Culhed, I., & Thoresen, C. E. (1994). Modification of Type A behavior patterns in post myocardial infarction patients: A route to cardiac rehabilitation. *International Journal of Behavorial Medicine, 1*(1), 32–54.

Campeau, L., Enjalbert, M., Lespérance, J., Bourassa, M. G., Kwiterovich, P., Jr., Wacholder, S., & Sniderman, A. (1984). The relation of risk factors to the development of atherosclerosis in saphenous-vein bypass grafts and the progression of disease in the native circulation: A study 10 years after aorto-coronary bypass surgery. *New England Journal of Medicine, 311*, 1329–1332.

CASS Principal Investigators and Associates. (1983). A randomized trial of coronary artery bypass surgery: Quality of life in patients randomly assigned to treatment groups. *Circulation, 68*, 951–960.

Dearborn, M. J., & Hastings, J. E. (1987, Summer). Type A personality as a mediator of stress and strain in employed women. *Journal of Human Stress*, 53–60.

Eaker, E. D., Packard, B., Wenger, N. K., Clarkson, T. B., & Tyroler, H. A. (1988). Coronary artery disease in women. *American Journal of Cardiology, 61*, 641–644.

Eaker, E. D., Pinsky, J., & Castelli, W. P. (1992). Myocardial infarction and coronary death among women: Psychosocial predictors from a 20-year follow-up of women in the Framingham study. *American Journal of Epidemiology, 135,* 854–864.

European Coronary Surgery Study Group. (1979). Coronary artery surgery in stable angina pectoris: Survival at two years. *Lancet, 1*(8122), 889–893.

Fitzgibbon, G. M., Leach, A. J., & Kafka, H. P. (1987). Atherosclerosis of coronary artery bypass graft and smoking. *Circulation, 136,* 45–47.

Frankenhaeuser, M. (1991). The psychophysiology of workload, stress and health: Comparison between the sexes. *Annals of Behavorial Medicine, 13,* 197–204.

Freudenberger, H. J., & North, G. G. (1986). *Women's burnout.* New York: Penguin.

Friedman, M., Powell, L. H., Thoresen, C. E., Ulmer, D., Price, V. A., Gill, J. J., Thompson, L., Rabin, D. D., Brown, B., Breall, W. S., Levy, R., & Bourg, E. (1987). Effect of discontinuance of Type A behavorial counseling on Type A behavior and cardiac recurrence rate of post myocardial infarction patients. *American Heart Journal, 114,* 483–490.

Friedman, M., & Rosenman, R. H. (1974). *Type A behavior and your heart.* New York: Fawcett Crest.

Friedman, M., Thoresen, C. E., Gill, J. J., Ulmer, D., Powell, L. H., Price, V. A., Brown, B., Thompson, L., Rabin, D., Breall, W. S., Bourg, E., Levy, R., & Dixon, T. (1986). Alteration of Type A behavior and its effect on cardiac recurrences in post-myocardial infarction patients: Summary results of the Recurrent Coronary Prevention Project. *American Heart Journal, 112,* 653–665.

Friedman, M., & Ulmer, D. (1984). *Treating Type A behavior and your heart.* Englewood Cliffs, NJ: Knopf.

Hällström, T., Lapidus, L., Bengtsson, C., & Edström, K. (1986). Psychosocial factors and risk of ischemic heart disease and death in women: A twelve-year follow-up of participants in the population study of women in Gothenburg, Sweden. *Journal of Psychosomatic Research, 30,* 451–459.

Hazuda, H. P., Haffner, S. M., Stern, M. P., Knapp, J. A., Eifler, C. W., & Rosenthal, M. (1986). Employment status and women's protection against coronary heart disease. *American Journal of Epidemiology, 123,* 623–639.

Jenkins, C. D., Stanton, B.-A., Savageau, J. A., Denlinger, P., & Klein, M. D. (1983). Coronary artery bypass surgery: Physical, psychological, social and economic outcomes six months later. *Journal of the American Medical Association, 250,* 782–788.

Kaplan, R. M., Sallis, J. F., & Patterson, T. L. (1993). *Health and human behavior.* New York: McGraw-Hill.

Kinchla, J. (1985). Psychologic and social outcomes following coronary artery bypass surgery. *Journal of Cardiopulmonary Rehabilitation, 5,* 274–283.

Kolata, G. B. (1981). Consensus on bypass surgery. *Science, 211,* 42–43.

Lie, J. T., Lawrie, G. N., & Morris, G. C. (1977). Aortocoronary bypass saphenous vein graft atherosclerosis: Anatomic study of 99 vein grafts from normal and hyperlipoproteinemic patients up to 75 months postoperatively. *American Journal of Cardiology, 40*, 906–914.

Matthews, K. A., Kelsey, S. F., Meilahn, E. N., Kuller, L. H., & Wing, R. R. (1989). Educational attainment and behavorial and biologic risk factors for coronary heart disease in middle-aged women. *American Journal of Epidemiology, 129*, 1132–1144.

Mayou, R. (1986). Invited review: The psychiatric and social consequences of coronary artery surgery. *Journal of Psychosomatic Research, 30*, 255–271.

Mayou, R., & Bryant, B. (1987). Quality of life after coronary artery surgery. *Quarterly Journal of Medicine, 62*, 239–248.

Mittleman, M. A., Maclure, M., Sherwood, J. B., Mulry, R. P., Tofler, G. H., Jacobs, S. C., Friedman, R., Benson, H., & Muller, J. E. (1995). Triggering of acute myocardial infarction onset by episodes of anger. *Circulation, 92*, 1720–1725.

Oberman, A., & Kouchoukos, N. T. (1979). Working status of patients following coronary bypass surgery. *American Heart Journal, 98*, 132–133.

Oldenburg, B., Perkins, R. J., & Andrews, G. (1985). Controlled trial of psychological intervention in myocardial infarction. *Journal of Consulting and Clinical Psychology, 53*, 852–859.

Price, V. A. (1988). Research and clinical issues in treating Type A behavior. In B. K. Houston & C. R. Snyder (Eds.), *Type A behavior pattern* (pp. 275–333). New York: Wiley.

Review Panel on Coronary-Prone Behavior and Coronary Heart Disease. (1981). A critical review. *Circulation, 63*, 1199.

Robinson, G., Froelicher, V. F., & Utley, J. R. (1984). Rehabilitation of the coronary artery bypass graft surgery patient. *Journal of Cardiac Rehabilitation, 4*, 74–86.

Solymoss, B. C., Nadeau, P., Millette, D., & Campeau, L. (1988). Late thrombosis of saphenous vein coronary bypass grafts related to risk factors. *Circulation, 78*, 1140–1143.

Steingart, R. M., Packer, M., Coglianese, M. E., Gersh, B., Geltman, E. M., Sollano, J., Katz, S., Moye, L., & Basta, L. L. (1991). Sex differences in the management of coronary artery disease. *New England Journal of Medicine, 325*, 226–230.

Takaro, T., Hultgren, H. N., Lipton, M. J., & Detre, K. M. (1976). The VA cooperative randomized study of surgery for arterial occlusive disease, II: Subgroups with significant left main lesions. *Circulation, 54*(Suppl. 3), 107.

Theorell, T. (1991). Psychosocial cardiovascular risks: On the double loads in women. *Psychotherapy and Psychosomatics, 55*, 81–89.

Thoresen, C. E., & Graff-Low, K. (1990). Women and the Type A behavior pattern: Review and commentary. *Journal of Social Behavior and Personality, 5*, 117–133.

III

CLINICAL TECHNIQUE
AND INTERVENTION

12

THE HOOK: A METAPHOR FOR GAINING CONTROL OF EMOTIONAL REACTIVITY

LYNDA H. POWELL

The Recurrent Coronary Prevention Project (RCPP) was a 4.5-year clinical trial of an intervention aimed at altering Type A behavior and the risk of recurrent cardiac events in post-myocardial infarction (MI) patients. The Type A behavioral intervention was based upon the principles of cognitive–social learning theory (Bandura, 1986) and emphasized the role of change in basic beliefs and attitudes as a way to promote an enduring change in lifestyle (Powell & Thoresen, 1987).

During the course of this trial, the RCPP research team developed a number of intervention strategies aimed at promoting a shift in basic beliefs and attitudes. One of these strategies came to be known as the *Hook*. The Hook is a cognitive exercise that helps participants replace thoughts associated with emotional reactivity with an alternative that is associated with stress resistance. Because of its popularity and efficacy at promoting an immediate shift in cognition, it was presented to all of the approximately 500 patients who received the Type A behavioral counseling. At the conclusion of the 4.5-year treatment, as part of a final evaluation of the program, these participants were asked to respond to the open-ended question "What helps most in reducing irritabilities and anger?" The strategy that received the largest number of endorsements was the Hook.

The process used to change behavior in the RCPP was to begin by helping participants to recognize traditional Type A behaviors in others

313

and then in themselves. Next, exercises were developed to help participants to behave in ways consistent with Type B behavior. Finally, exercises
were developed to promote cognitive change in beliefs and attitudes that
formed the basis of the outward manifestations of Type A behavior. The
Hook served as a first exposure to cognitive change, that is, the concept
that it is possible to purposefully change the way one thinks about things.
The basic elements of the theory and technique behind the Hook are
presented below.

EMOTIONAL REACTIVITY AND THE HEART

The target of the Hook intervention is chronic emotional reactivity
to minor, unexpected stressors. This reactivity most commonly takes the
form of anger, irritation, aggravation, or impatience (referred to as *AIAI*
during the RCPP). Theoretically, any strong emotion, of a negative or even
a positive nature, could have an adverse impact on the heart. There was
more concern with anger and its concomitants because they occur with
more daily regularity than do the strong positive emotions, such as joy,
excitement, and ecstasy. This is an unfortunate by-product of modern life.

References to a connection between strong emotions and heart attacks, or MIs, have been recorded throughout history and described by
Engel (1971) as follows. In the Bible, Ananias fell down dead when
charged by Peter, "You have not lied to man, but to God." The emperor
Nerva died of a "violent excess of anger" against a senator who offended
him. Pope Innocent IV succumbed suddenly to the effects of grief soon
after the overthrow of his army. Chilon of Lacedaemon died from joy while
embracing his son who had borne away the prize at the Olympic Games.

Perhaps the story of the cardiotoxic effects of strong emotion that is
told most often is that of John Hunter, the eighteenth-century surgeon and
anatomist, who, at the time of his death, was studying the connection
between angina pectoris and coronary artery disease. As told by his student,
Edward Jenner:

> Wrath, to which John was so prone, exposed him to the direst attacks.
> A tardy coachman, an inattentive secretary, would throw him into
> volcanic rages. He realized his danger, yet was powerless to control his
> temper. "My life," he said, "is at the mercy of any rogue who chooses
> to provoke me." (Kligfield, 1980, p. 368)

These reports raise the possibility that acute cardiac events may be
triggered by transitory, acute psychological stressors. A number of animal,
case, and epidemiologic studies have supported this. Lown and colleagues
(Lown, Verrier, & Corbalan, 1973; Verrier, Hagestad, & Lown, 1987)
showed that the threshold for ventricular fibrillation in dogs was lowered

when dogs were stressed or angered, both in cases where coronary arteries were and were not experimentally occluded. Case studies with coronary patients who had been undergoing ambulatory monitoring at the time of fatal arrhythmia reveal that intense emotional states associated with watching a championship sporting event or losing one's wallet were accompanied by increased heart rate, premature ventricular contractions (PVCs), and, in one case, ST depression, followed by sinus tachycardia, ventricular tachycardia, and ventricular fibrillation (Gradman, Bell, & DeBusk, 1977; Lown, DeSilva, Reich, & Murawski, 1980). The emotional state and its concomitant catecholamines, either alone or in conjunction with ischemia, appeared to create a setting in which generally nonlethal PVCs initiated a degeneration to ventricular fibrillation.

Retrospective studies also suggest the importance of psychological triggers of fatal or near-fatal cardiac events. Cardiac arrhythmias have been shown to be more strongly and consistently related to intense emotional experiences, such as job interviews and public speaking, than they are to chronic signs of stress, such as hostility and anxiety (Kamarck & Jennings, 1991). Anger appears to be the most common, but not the only, emotional state associated with arrhythmias (Reich, DeSilva, Lown, & Murawski, 1981). A preliminary analysis of interviews with patients who were in the hospital recovering from MI revealed that 14% experienced moderate or greater anger in the 24 hours before the MI, most frequently caused by fights with family (25%) or conflicts at work (22%; Mittleman et al., 1994). These studies must be interpreted with caution, however, because of possible recall bias in subjects who have had an event and may need to find some justification for it.

In our own work with the RCPP cohort, we found that a rescore of the Videotaped Structured Interview for Type A behavior (Friedman & Powell, 1984), which focused only on whether or not a participant became emotionally aroused during the course of the interview, was associated with 2.3 times the incidence of sudden cardiac death in 929 post-MI men (Powell, Simon, Bartzokis, Pattillo, & Thoresen, 1991). Taken together, these reports suggest that some acute coronary events can be triggered by acute emotional states.

STRESSORS THAT TRIGGER EMOTIONAL REACTIVITY

In their early descriptions of Type A behavior, Friedman and Rosenman (1974) emphasized the importance of minor, everyday stressors as precipitants of the Type A struggles against time and other people. The importance of minor stressors as precipitants of emotional reactivity was more recently supported by a review of sudden cardiac death which revealed that stressors that precipitate lethal arrhythmias are most commonly small, unexpected "hassles" occurring within 1 hour before the episode (Kamarck & Jennings, 1991). Approximately 30 of these hassles occur each day for the average urbanite (Stroebel, 1982). The nature of the emotion they precipitate appears to be less important than its abrupt onset and intensity (Reich et al., 1981). Although these hassles are small and generally not remembered by the day's end, the abrupt onset of emotion is related to the fact that they are unexpected. Unexpected stressors are associated with more distress (Suls, Gastorf, & Witenberg, 1975) and poor coping (Lazarus, 1966; Staub, Tursky, & Schwartz, 1971). Among the unexpected stressors that have been linked to fatal or near-fatal cardiac arrhythmias are watching a sporting event on TV, losing one's wallet, rough-housing with children, and winning the lottery (Gradman et al., 1977; Lown et al., 1980).

BELIEFS AND ATTITUDES UNDERLYING EMOTIONAL REACTIVITY TO MINOR STRESSORS

Two key beliefs underlie chronic emotional hyperreactivity to minor stressors (Powell, 1992). The first belief, in technical terms, is a belief in *pure environmental determinism*. Pure determinism postulates that human behavior is a function of environmental stimuli. The environment shapes, orchestrates, and controls behavior and is the instigator against which individuals counteract (Bandura, 1986). In B. F. Skinner's (1971) words, "A person does not act upon the world, the world acts upon him" (p. 211). The implication of this personal belief is that regulation of one's own behavior can be accomplished only by a regulation of its situational determinants. The attitude that follows a belief in pure determinism is *other blame*, that is, that other people and things are responsible for one's distress (Tennen & Affleck, 1990). This attitude can be detected in a person's immediate perception of unexpected stressors, which often takes the form of "Unfair!" or "Why me?"

A second key belief associated with chronic, emotional reactivity is the belief that the environment is always malleable: That is, environmental forces are subject to one's personal control and can be changed through personal efforts as long as one persists. This belief is a logical extension of the first belief. Because behavior (e.g., distress) is under environmental control, a desired change in behavior (e.g., reduction in distress) must come from countercontrol over the environment (e.g., the source of the problem). To believe that the environment cannot be controlled would undermine one's sense of personal control and efficacy. Attitudes that are symptomatic of a belief in the malleability of the environment include "I'll show you," "Try harder," and "We have only just begun to fight."

When an unexpected, minor stressor occurs, the first belief mobilizes the search for someone or something to blame, and the second belief mobilizes an attempt to correct the situation by changing the blamed person or object. For example, when a person is unexpectedly caught behind a tediously slow person in a long line at a grocery store, the belief in pure determinism is manifested as the perception of the situation as unfair. It is this perception that is closest to the patient's awareness and, thus, most accessible for intervention. This perception triggers emotional reactivity (in this case, impatience/irritation), which then mobilizes the second belief, that the situation can be changed. This could take the form of a verbal protest to the slow person for not being prepared or to the cashier for not having enough checkout lines open, or a nonverbal protest in which, through body language and/or sighs of exasperation, it is clear to those around that the situation is unacceptable.

BELIEFS AND ATTITUDES INCOMPATIBLE WITH EMOTIONAL REACTIVITY TO MINOR STRESSORS

A more expanded view of causality is a belief in *reciprocal determinism* (Bandura, 1986). According to this view, any particular human action (in this case, emotional reactivity) can be explained by personal (i.e., behavioral, cognitive, emotional, and physiological) and environmental influences, all of which operate interactively, as determinants of each other. A complete explanation of a particular event considers the contribution of all of these factors (i.e., the other person's role, the situation itself, one's own behavior in the situation, one's perception of the situation, and one's physiological and emotional response to the situation). When this belief of causality is followed, the concept of blame (either blaming others or blaming oneself) is meaningless:

> Viewed from the perspective of reciprocal determinism, the practice of searching for the ultimate environmental cause of behavior is an idle exercise. This is because, in an interacting process, the one and the same event can either be an environmental stimulus, response, or reinforcer, depending upon where and on which side of the ongoing exchange one happens to look first in the flow of events. (Bandura, 1986, p. 26)

The more expanded the view one has of causality, the more potential targets there are for intervention.

A second, related belief is that the environment *may not be* malleable. In this belief, it is accepted that there are many environmental factors that are intransigent and beyond one's personal control. Therefore, efforts to exert direct change over such factors are futile. Control over intransigent stressors requires a cognitive strategy in which the control is shifted from direct control over the event to control over the way one perceives the event (i.e., cognitive control).

THE HOOK INTERVENTION

The Hook is a cognitive restructuring strategy that aims to replace an attitude associated with reactivity to a stressor with an alternative attitude that is associated with stress resistance. Specifically, the attitude of other-blame, which manifests itself as the immediate perception of "Unfair!" and mobilizes anger or irritation, is replaced with an alternative perception (i.e., "Hook!"), which is associated with less reactivity to stressors. The process of making this perceptual shift makes it possible to explore attitudes that underlie the old perception, to make superficial the belief in pure environmental determinism, and to replace it with a belief in reciprocal determinism and its related attitudes.

These theoretical concepts are complex and generally not of interest to participants. Thus, the therapist must use creativity and skill to get the basic points across in ways that are accessible. To do this, powerful metaphors have been developed that carry great personal meaning for participants. The Hook is one of these metaphors. The Hook intervention is presented as a progression of three general questions. These questions are written on the blackboard, and the therapist works interactively with the participants to arrive at answers, to use examples to provide meaning to the answers, and to reinforce the answers continually throughout the session. The first question introduces participants to the general idea of cognitive change; that is, one has the ability to remain in control of a situation by changing the way one thinks. The second question sensitizes participants to the types of stressors that are likely to promote anger or impatience/irritation, using an exercise in which they experience a small, unexpected stressor (i.e., a hook). The third question provides participants with a cognitive strategy that can be used to replace their characteristic response to the stressor with an alternative that is associated with less reactivity. In the RCPP, this strategy was used in a group-counseling format, but the principles are easily adaptable for presentation to individuals.

Question 1: What is Behavior Modification?

The therapist begins the session by asking all participants to review the events of the day and to describe an incident in which they became angered, irritated, or impatient. The therapist notes the situation and the response for each participant.

Figure 1 presents the first question, which is intended to introduce patients to the theory behind cognitive change. The question that is put on the board and posed to participants is, "What is behavior modification?" To develop an answer to this question, the therapist draws two circles, one of which represents a person and the other of which represents his or her environment. The person is composed of his or her actions and thoughts; the environment is composed of other people and other things. The Skinnerian view of causality, called *determinism*, is demonstrated by connecting the person and the environment circles with an arrow that points from the environment to the person; that is, the environment determines the person's behavior, or "the environment made me do it." Then the therapist floods the participants with examples of this view of causality by going back to the irritating situations that were described earlier by the participants and reinterpreting them using this view of causality. For example, if a participant described a situation in which he or she became irritated because he or she could not find a parking space, then the deterministic view of causality would seek to lay blame—on the administrators for failing to provide adequate parking spaces, on one's boss for failing to let him or her leave work early enough to find a space, and so on. The important point to bring out when the arrow points from the environment to behavior is the attitude that "someone or something made me angry."

An alternative view of causality, called *reciprocal determinism*, is then depicted by adding an arrow pointing from the person to the environment. Now the arrow is bidirectional. According to this model, the anger or irritation described earlier by the participants can be explained either in

WHAT IS BEHAVIOR MODIFICATION?

To be in control, you have a <u>choice.</u>

You can:

Change others

<u>or</u>

Change the way you <u>think</u> about others.

Figure 1. The first discussion question in the Hook intervention.

terms of the environmental stressor or in terms of one's response to the stressor. Here, the therapist works with the participants to reinterpret their irritation from the perspective of multiple causality. Going back to the parking space situation, the participant may be particularly "on edge" today because he or she failed to finish an important report at work and thus was more easily irritated than usual.

The main point—and the answer to the first question—is the concept of choice. One can reduce anger or irritation by choosing either to change the environmental stressor or to change one's response to the stressor (Figure 1). This enhances one's feelings of control because even when faced with a stressor that is inherently uncontrollable (which the majority of daily stressors are), one can use the second strategy of changing one's thoughts about the stressor and sustain the feeling of control.

At this point, the therapist tries to bring this theoretical explanation to life by using a real example in which a person became angered because he or she had a deterministic view of causality and could not change the stressor. I used a particularly potent example that I personally observed of a woman attending her son's graduation, where, despite arriving at an early hour and procuring a seat with an excellent view, she was not able to see because a large number of latecomers, who had no choice but to stand in front of her seat, blocked her view. The woman was stuck in an unfair situation, where her choice was to try and exert direct control over this stressor or to exert indirect control over it by altering her reactivity to it. This example tends to bring out a number of coping styles, which can then be relabeled by the therapist in terms of the preceding discussion.

The first question ends with participants having been exposed in theory to the concept that one has the ability to change one's thoughts about an event. The next question is one in which the participant actually experiences, in the here and now, how it feels to be hooked by an unexpectedly stressful situation.

Question 2: What Is Impatience/Irritation?

The second question is written on the board, and the answer is written with blanks for three words: A _____ response to a _____ and _____ stressor (see Figure 2).

The answer to the first blank is that one thing that characterizes impatience, irritation, or anger is that this response is quick. When a stressor strikes, one's reaction is immediate, and it is often erroneously thought that the reaction is automatic and not mediated through thoughts. In fact, the reaction does follow an immediate perception of the situation. The implication of this is that to intervene on impatience, irritation, or anger, one must use a simple strategy that can be called upon quickly.

WHAT IS IMPATIENCE / IRRITATION?

A <u>quick</u> response to a
<u>small</u> and <u>unexpected</u> stressor

Figure 2. The second discussion question in the Hook intervention.

The answer to the second blank is that one aspect of situations that generally provoke impatience, irritation, or anger is that they are small and relatively insignificant hassles. Most often, these hassles will not be remembered at the end of the day or the end of the week. The implication of this is that they are the ubiquitous by-products of everyday life. Indeed, one way of thinking about everyday life is that it is characterized by recurring hassles: as many as 30 hassles in any particular day.

The answer to the third blank is that another characteristic of situations that provoke irritation, impatience, and anger is that they are unexpected. What makes them difficult to manage is that they cannot be predicted but seem to emerge when least expected.

At this point, the therapist creates the metaphor of the hook to describe irritation, impatience, and anger reactions. The therapist might say something like this:

> You wake up each morning, and you are like a fish, swimming down a stream in clear water. Then, all of a sudden, a hook drops (the hook being a small, unexpected hassle). You then make a decision to bite into the hook, and become irritated or annoyed, or to pass the hook by. But whatever decision you make when faced with this hook is relatively unimportant because there will be another hook, and another, as we go throughout our day. In fact, as many as 30 hooks are likely to drop in front of you on any typical day.

To solidify the learning and demonstrate the concept in the here and now, the therapist throws out a hook to 1 or 2 participants. The therapist normally does this by accusing them of not paying attention during the session:

> Now I would like to stop here for a minute and point out that John and Bill don't seem to be paying much attention to what I am talking about now. I simply want to ask them to try and pay more attention, because these concepts are very important to the goals we are trying to accomplish.

John and Bill may protest and defend themselves or may simply flush. The therapist waits for a few seconds, until the entire group has a reaction to the hook, and then poses the question, "What did I just do?" John and Bill (who actually were paying close attention during the entire session) are generally the first to observe that the therapist threw out a hook. It was indeed a *small* hook, and one that will generally not be remembered the following week. It was certainly *unexpected*, in that they had no idea that it was coming and therefore could not prepare for it. Finally, their reaction to it was *immediate*: They argued, protested, or had a flush of anger or embarrassment. If the therapist expands the experience to the entire group, it is likely that more members than just John and Bill will have bitten into the hook.

The critical question to raise is how the patients perceived the hook. In most cases, they will have had a cognition that is consistent with other-blame, such as "Unfair!" or "Why me?" It is critical to bring to the surface the cognition that preceded the emotion, because this is the target of the hook intervention.

Question 3: What Can We Do About It?

The therapist puts the third question on the board and draws the correct answer, as presented in Figure 3. The first part of the answer is the lightbulb. He or she explains:

> This signifies that *at the time the hook drops*, not even 2 seconds later, we do something. The lightbulb reminds us that our habitual response will be immediate, and, therefore, our intervention should be immediate. The second part of the answer is the fish hook. Once the hook drops, the lightbulb goes on, and we say to ourselves "Hook!" What we are doing is identifying a hook as a hook.

No other intervention is needed, but participants should watch and reflect on what happens after the hook is identified.

What is of interest to most participants is that the process of labeling a stressor as a hook, rather than as an unfair situation, neutralizes its arousal effect. It appears to be more like a predictable by-product of everyday life than a reason for emotional arousal. What is also of interest is that the process of identifying hooks is actually a process of enjoying enhanced control. In this case, the control is not over other people (which actually seldom occurs) but over *one's response* to other people. The enhanced perception of control is associated with enhanced self-esteem. The recognition of hooks, therefore, is synonymous with building self-esteem.

Common Concerns Raised During the Hook Intervention

The spirit behind the Hook intervention is to learn to change one's perception of the stressor, not to change the stressor itself. Patients often

WHAT CAN WE DO ABOUT IT?

Figure 3. The third discussion question in the Hook intervention.

misunderstand this and happily embrace the concept of the hook, seeing it as a new weapon to be used in their battles to change other people. This may be evident, for example, when certain participants indicate that they are going to tell their spouse not to hook them. This use of the metaphor is associated with persistence in a deterministic view of life and a commitment to the strategy of attempting to change others as a way to keep reactivity down. The true spirit of the hook is that no attempt to change others is made; the change is simply in one's perception of an event. No one else will ever know the intervention is taking place.

Some patients may respond negatively to the hook strategy because they believe that this intervention will make them nonreactive to *all* events. They may argue that in certain situations they want to counter the action of the aggressor. It is important to reinforce that, indeed, one must have the skills to take action against an aggressor and, in fact, that is the most common coping response. The hook should not replace this strategy, it simply should augment it. By learning about how cognitive change works, and the situations in which it can be most effective, one is augmenting one's coping repertoire. By so doing, one expands control. In many cases, taking counteraction against a stressor will be useful, and the stressor will be amenable to change. In a great many other cases, however, no matter how persistent and strong one's efforts are, the stressor is not amenable to change. In these cases, the availability of a cognitive-change strategy in which one reduces one's reactivity to the stressor may be the most effective.

After The Hook

The Hook intervention promotes a major shift in thinking for most patients. It is important to reinforce this learning in the hours after the session occurs. The therapist should suggest to participants that it is likely that a hook will drop within the next few hours after the session is over and that this is an important time in which they can identify their first hook. If they can identify a hook on their own, soon after the session, when the concepts are fresh in their minds, it is likely that they will be positively and immediately reinforced by feelings of enhanced control and self-esteem. This will provide motivation to continue to identify other hooks and further solidify learning.

To further reinforce this learning I sent each participant a postcard, drawn by hand, such as that presented in Figure 4. This serves as a reminder for patients between therapy sessions that their task is to watch out for hooks and to identify them.

At subsequent therapy sessions, learning can be further solidified by using the hook metaphor as a way to reinterpret events in patients' lives. I use a card on which the picture in Figure 5 is drawn, and, once the therapist or a group member suspects that another member has bitten a hook, she or he takes the card from the middle of the table and places it in front of the group member.

Have you recognized a hook today??

Figure 4. Example of a postcard sent to participants to reinforce the concept of the Hook.

Figure 5. The card used to reinforce the concept of the Hook during subsequent counseling sesssions.

In the context of the larger process of therapy, the Hook session provides a framework for discussions of the role of cognitions in determining behavior. Subsequent discussions can include the role of other basic beliefs about the world and others and how they mobilize characteristic styles of coping (see Powell, 1992, for a review of a number of basic beliefs that underlie coronary-prone behaviors). Once patients learn and apply the notion of cognitive change to daily experiences, they may express interest in learning how to be more effective at influencing others in their lives. In this case, assertiveness skills can be helpful, in which patients are taught to exert direct influence over others but without using aggression and its accompanying emotional arousal (Bower & Bower, 1976). Note, however, that the patient will have a preference for changing others rather than changing himself or herself. Switching prematurely to assertiveness training runs the risk of losing the opportunity to promote a true appreciation of the benefits to be gained from embracing the cognitive-change strategies.

The Hook counseling session is one in which the aim is to expand the coping repertoire of the patient. The essence of effective coping is found in the Serenity Prayer (Niebuhr, 1943), which asks for "courage to change what can be changed, serenity to accept what can't be changed, and wisdom to know the difference." When this wisdom is practiced, chronic negative emotions can be managed, and risk of acute cardiac events may be reduced. The Hook is a route to attaining this wisdom.

REFERENCES

Bandura, A. (1986). *Social foundations of thought and action: A social cognitive theory.* Englewood Cliffs, NJ: Prentice Hall.

Bower, S. A., & Bower, G. H. (1976). *Asserting yourself: A practical guide for positive change.* Reading, MA: Addison-Wesley.

Engel, G. L. (1971). Sudden and rapid death during psychological stress: Folklore or folk wisdom? *Annals of Internal Medicine, 74,* 771–782.

Friedman, M., & Powell, L. H. (1984). The diagnosis and quantitative assessment of Type A behavior: Introduction and description of the videotaped structured interview. *Integrative Psychiatry, 2,* 123–136.

Friedman, M., & Rosenman, R. H. (1974). *Type A behavior and your heart.* New York: Knopf.

Gradman, A. H., Bell, P. A., & DeBusk, R. F. (1977). Sudden death during ambulatory monitoring. Clinical and electrocardiographic correlations. Report of a case. *Circulation, 55,* 210–211.

Kamarck, T., & Jennings, J. R. (1991). Biobehavioral factors in sudden cardiac death. *Psychological Bulletin, 109,* 42–75.

Kligfield, P. (1980). John Hunter, angina pectoris and medical education. *American Journal of Cardiology, 45,* 367–369.

Lazarus, R. S. (1966). *Psychological stress and the coping process.* New York: McGraw-Hill.

Lown, B., DeSilva, R. A., Reich, P., & Murawski, B. J. (1980). Psychologic factors in sudden cardiac death. *American Journal of Psychiatry, 137,* 1325–1335.

Lown, B., Verrier, R., & Corbalan, R. (1973). Psychologic stress and threshold for repetitive ventricular response. *Science, 182,* 834–836.

Mittleman, M. A., Maclure, M., Sherwood, J. B., Mulry, R. P., Tofler, G. H., Jacobs, S. C., Friedman, R., Benson, H., & Muller, J. E., for the Determinants of Myocardial Infarction Onset Study Investigators. (1994). Triggering of myocardial infarction onset by episodes of anger. *Circulation, 92,* 1720–1725.

Niebuhr, R. (1943). The Serenity Prayer. *Bulletin of the Federal Council of Churches.*

Powell, L. H. (1992). The cognitive underpinnings of coronary-prone behaviors. *Cognitive Therapy and Research, 16,* 123–142.

Powell, L. H., Simon, S. R., Bartzokis, T. C., Pattillo, J. R., & Thoresen, C. E. (1991). Emotional arousability predicts sudden cardiac death in post-MI men [Abstract]. *Circulation, 83,* 722.

Powell, L. H., & Thoresen, C. E. (1987). Changing the Type A behavior pattern: A small group treatment approach. In J. A. Blumenthal & D. M. McKee (Eds.), *Applications in behavioral medicine: A clinician's sourcebook* (Vol. 1, pp. 171–206). Sarasota, FL: Professional Resource Exchange.

Reich, P., DeSilva, R. A., Lown, B., & Murawski, B. J. (1981). Acute psychological disturbance preceding life-threatening arrhythmias. *Journal of the American Medical Association, 246,* 233–235.

Skinner, B. F. (1971). Beyond freedom and dignity. New York: Knopf.

Staub, E., Tursky, B., & Schwartz, G. E. (1971). Self-control and predictability: Their effects on reactions to aversive stimulation. *Journal of Personality and Social Psychology, 18,* 157–162.

Stroebel, C. F. (1982). *QR: The quieting reflex. A six-second technique for coping with stress anytime, anywhere.* New York: Putnam.

Suls, J., Gastorf, J. W., & Witenberg, S. H. (1975). Life events, psychological distress and the Type A coronary-prone behavior pattern. *Journal of Psychosomatic Research, 25,* 315–319.

Tennen, H., & Affleck, G. (1990). Blaming others for threatening events. *Psychological Bulletin, 108,* 209–232.

Verrier, R. L., Hagestad, E. L., & Lown, B. (1987). Delayed myocardial ischemia induced by anger. *Circulation, 75,* 249–254.

13

TREATMENT OF TIME PATHOLOGIES

DIANE K. ULMER and LEONARD SCHWARTZBURD

At the earliest moment at which we catch our first glimpse of Man on earth we find him not only on the move but already moving at an accelerating pace. This crescendo of acceleration is continuing today. In our generation it is perhaps the most difficult and dangerous of all the current problems of the race. (Arnold Toynbee, 1961, p. 603)

Historian Toynbee's observation was made over 30 years ago, but it may be more percipient than ever. There seems to be a widespread belief, at least in this country, that the pace of life has increased considerably within the last few decades. Surveys have indicated that Americans say they have less leisure time today than they did 10 years ago (Gibbs, 1989; Robinson, 1990). People complain that they do not have enough time to do all that needs to be done and that lack of time is a source of stress for them. Yet, driven in great part by the keenly competitive nature of business and other cultural factors, there seems to be a continued inexorable push to accelerate, to be more efficient, to do more in less time.

This acceleration of pace is abetted by the ever more rapid evolution of technology, which allows and encourages people to do things faster. And it is compounded by the explosion of information and choices to which people are exposed.

These forces can, and do, seduce people into overscheduling their days and overstimulating their minds (Keyes, 1991; Toffler, 1970). The inevitable sense of time pressure that follows encourages frenetic activity and racing thoughts. Given that humans, for millennia, have lived in accord with their own biorhythms and nature's cycles, is the impact of this recent exponential increase in life's pace harmful? Should clinicians be concerned about a rapid-paced lifestyle and the stress of time pressure in their patients?

CLINICAL OBSERVATIONS

The answer to both of the questions above, we believe, is a qualified yes, based primarily on nearly 2 decades of clinical experience. However, these conclusions are supported by biomedical and psychosocial research. The yes is qualified because we have observed that whereas some people appear to have a pathological response to time-pressure stressors, some people do not. Therefore, at this time, we cannot say that a rapid-paced lifestyle with its attendant time pressures is always harmful. But we can say that such a lifestyle has the potential to erode health and well-being, and for many people, it has done so.

We have observed this detrimental impact in three areas. The first is interpersonal. A busy lifestyle conducted at a rapid pace may contribute to the fragmentation of relationships and support systems. Emotionally satisfying relationships require time to develop and time to sustain. It is a complex process that does not easily accommodate rushing or shortcuts. The result of a time-pressured lifestyle is often a lack of emotional closeness and increased isolation. The research literature is clear about the correlation between isolation, poor social support systems, and increased morbidity and mortality from all causes, including coronary disease (Berkman, 1984; Berkman & Syme, 1979; Cobb, 1976; Kaplan, Cassel, & Gore, 1977; Medalie & Goldbourt, 1976; Raab, 1966; see also chap. 3, this volume).

The second area of observation is intrapersonal. This lifestyle can lead to a decreased sense of self-worth, largely, we believe, because in the long run, quantitative accomplishments are not as self-esteem enhancing as nourishing relationships. Our clinical experience also supports the observation that on a deeply personal level, a rapid-paced lifestyle significantly erodes one's spiritual sense of self. Inner peace and time urgency are quite incompatible. Therefore, we hypothesize that if people find tranquillity and inner contentment to be elusive, they may often become attached to the stimulation of "busyness" as a substitute.

The third area concerns physical health. We have observed that some people are overly physiologically reactive to time pressures; that is, they respond with heightened arousal. This arousal, as mediated by the sympathoadrenomedullary and pituitary-adrenocortical systems, can cause significant physiological changes in the body, as a whole, and in the cardiovascular system, in particular. Because many people report chronic feelings of time urgency, they may also be suffering from chronic overarousal (Chrousos & Gold, 1981). We believe that it is this chronicity of arousal, often accompanied by exhaustion, combined with a degradation or lack of emotionally satisfying relationships that leads to ill health and disease.

TIME PATHOLOGIES DEFINED

It is first important to define our terms with greater precision. There are distinctions to be made among *time pressure*, *time urgency*, and *hurry sickness*, the last a term used by Friedman and Rosenman (1974). Although time urgency and hurry sickness have been used somewhat interchangeably in earlier writings (Friedman & Ulmer, 1984), on the basis of ongoing clinical observation, we propose that it is useful to regard hurry sickness as a more severe form of time urgency with a discrete symptomatology.

Time Pressure

Time pressure is the perception that there is insufficient time to accomplish a specific task (or specific tasks), which often leads to subsequent feelings of anxiety and tension.

Time Urgency

Time urgency is the frequent experience of time pressure with a corresponding conviction that one needs to hurry or speed up the rate at which one is doing things. This is encouraged by the rationale that if there is insufficient time to accomplish everything, the solution is to do everything faster. With time urgency, a person's behaviors often become more rapid (e.g., faster speaking, walking, eating, and thinking) and include attempts to do more than one thing at a time (polyphasic activity). Impatience and inability to wait or tolerate delay are also often seen.

The feeling of time urgency can become chronic, if experienced routinely, and hurried behaviors can become habitual. Thus the feeling can exist and the behaviors can be manifested in the absence of actual time pressures.

Hurry Sickness

Severe and chronic feelings of time urgency that have brought about changes affecting personality and lifestyle are known as *hurry sickness*. The following are three major symptoms:

1. Deterioration of the personality, marked primarily by loss of interest in aspects of life except for those connected with

achievement of goals and by a preoccupation with numbers, with a growing tendency to evaluate life in terms of quantity rather than quality.

2. Racing-mind syndrome, characterized by rapid, shifting thoughts that gradually erode the ability to focus and concentrate and create disruption of sleep.

3. Loss of ability to accumulate pleasant memories, mainly due to either a preoccupation with future events or rumination about past events, with little attention to the present. Focusing on the present is often limited to crises or problems; therefore memories accumulated tend to be of unpleasant situations.

Time Pathologies

For the sake of conceptual unity and brevity, we propose the term *time pathologies* to refer to the toxic continuum of disordered behaviors, perceptions, and states running the gamut from mild time urgency to severe hurry sickness.

RESEARCH REVIEW

In examining the possible relationship of time pathologies to coronary artery disease (CAD), four areas deserve close study. The first three are addressed in the research literature: (a) physiological reactivity in response to time pressure, (b) fatigue and exhaustion associated with chronic arousal, generated in an attempt to sustain peak performance, and (c) loss of social support systems. The fourth can be described as a personal, perhaps even spiritual, barrenness or emptiness spawned by the chronic struggle to accomplish tasks, which can lead to a rather joyless existence and give rise to covert self-destructive behaviors. This area has received very little attention in the empirical literature. Accordingly, it is addressed in the section titled "Rationale for Treatment."

Physiological Reactivity

A number of studies examined the effects of time-pressure stressors on research subjects within the laboratory setting. Many of these studies compared the reactivity of people demonstrating the Type A behavior pattern (TABP), of which time urgency is a major component, to those manifesting Type B behavior (generally defined as the absence of Type A behavior). A few studies simply looked at the physiological effects of time pressure on general groups of people.

One of the first of these studies of groups (Friedman, Rosenman, & Carroll, 1958) showed that accountants' cholesterol levels rose, and blood-clotting time (presumed risk factors for myocardial infarction [MI]) decreased, during the pressures of tax time, despite dietary control. In a more recent study (Malkoff, Muldoon, Zeigler, & Manuck, 1993), 40 healthy young men were asked to participate in a 20-minute mental task with a deadline and built-in impediments. The experimental groups had significant ($p < .05$) elevations in heart rate (HR), blood pressure (BP), and blood-platelet adenosine-5-triphosphate (ATP) secretion, compared with a control group, which sat quietly during the testing period. The control group had no rise in HR, BP, or ATP. ATP release is thought to spur a cascade of reactions that can encourage artery wall damage and blood-vessel narrowing, in addition to coronary thromboses (Mustard, Packham, & Kinlough-Rathbone, 1990; Ross, 1986; Vanhoutte & Houston, 1985). Krantz and associates (1991) observed that under laboratory-controlled time-pressure tasks, patients with severe CAD experienced greater ischemic wall-motion abnormalities of their hearts than did those with less severe disease. These patients also had higher systolic blood pressure (SBP) and catecholamine levels during testing than did patients with less severe disease.

A problem with the studies mentioned in the previous paragraph, which document increased physiological arousal under laboratory-induced time pressure, is the difficulty in generalizing isolated results from the laboratory to everyday time pressures. Do such findings indicate that time pressures that trigger arousal play a role in the development of CAD?

Light, Dolan, Davis, and Sherwood (1992) attempted to address this problem, known in behavioral medicine as the controversial "reactivity hypothesis," which holds that "high cardiovascular reactivity to behavioral stressors may play a role in the long-term pathogenesis of sustained arterial hypertension and/or coronary heart disease" (p. 217). The researchers recruited 51 men who were tested 10 to 15 years before for cardiovascular reactivity (SBP, diastolic blood pressure [DBP], and HR) during a reaction-time test involving the threat of electric shock. By means of stethoscopic and ambulatory monitoring during work, social activities, and leisure activities, they found that higher reactivity during the early testing was a good predictor of higher blood pressures a decade later. For example, those who reacted originally with high SBP now had higher SBP ($p < .002$), high reactive DBP predicted elevated DBP ($p < .0006$), and high HR predicted higher HR ($p < .04$), SBP ($p < .035$), and DBP ($p < .005$). Elevated blood pressure is one of the well-accepted, standard risk factors for CAD.

A recent study (Schnall, Schwartz, Landsbergis, Warren, & Pickering, 1992) looking at male subjects in highly demanding, stressful jobs (defined as needing to work fast and hard with little authority) found that they not only manifested greater blood pressure (an average of 137/85 vs. 129/83) at work, compared with other workers, but their blood pressures tended to remain high, even while sleeping. The researchers speculated that the cumulative effect of exposure to stressors over time may permanently raise blood pressure.

Manuck, Olsson, Hjemdahl, and Rehnquist (1992) followed 13 post-MI patients who previously participated in a placebo group of a secondary intervention trial. On completion of the trial, BP, HR, and catecholamines were evaluated at rest and in response to a reaction-time test on two occasions. Upon follow-up at 39 to 64 months, 5 patients had suffered new cardiovascular events (MI or stroke). These 5 patients had shown significantly higher SBP ($p < .0001$) and DBP ($p < .04$) in response to the test, although catecholamines in this group were higher on only 1 of the 2 testing days. The two groups of patients did not differ in baseline measurements, cardiovascular response to exercise testing, lipids, glucose, age, or follow-up time.

Sherwood, Hinderliter, and Light (1995) evaluated the hemodynamic basis of blood pressure reactivity in normotensives and in borderline hypertensives. Blood pressure increases were greater ($p < .05$) in the borderline hypertensive subjects during an active coping reaction-time test, but not during a passive cold pressor test. The researchers believed that their observations "further support the view that the early stages of hypertension are characterized by sympathetic nervous system hyperreactivity, but only with tasks that elicit active behavioral coping responses. The extent to which these responses are elicited by typical daily events may be an important determinant of whether borderline hypertension matures to its established form" (Sherwood et al., 1995, p. 384).

The Recurrent Coronary Prevention Project (see chap. 10, this volume), a large ($N = 1,012$), 4.5-year intervention trial to reduce TABP in coronary patients, found that treated subjects, compared with controls, had significant ($p < .001$) reductions in time urgency and impatience and sustained 44% fewer new coronary events (Mendes de Leon, Powell, & Kaplan, 1991).

These five studies add supporting data to the small knowledge base about the long-term impact of chronic time pressure on health and support the hypothesis that there is a relationship between cardiovascular reactivity and hypertension, a major risk factor for CAD. There is also some indication that increased reactivity to time pressure can lead to an increase in cardiac events (Manuck et al., 1992) and that decreases in time-pressured behavior may lead to reductions in recurrent MI (Friedman et al., 1986; Mendes de Leon et al., 1991). More research in this area is needed to further clarify the importance of the relationship between time pathologies and the development of CAD.

Exhaustion

The second area that deserves close attention is the relationship between time pathologies and the state of exhaustion. We have observed a number of pre- and post-CAD patients reaching a state of exhaustion, thought to be a result of reduced cardiac vigor due to advancing atherosclerosis, as a result of their incessant struggles to do more things in less time. A state of excessive exhaustion has been observed as an important and common premonitory symptom of MI and sudden cardiac death (Crisp, Queenan, & D'Souza, 1984; Feinleib, Simon, Gillum, & Marjolis, 1975; Klaboe, Otterstad, Winsness, & Espeland, 1987; Kuller, Cooper, & Perper, 1972). However, our clinical experience has suggested that for some of our time-urgent patients, exhaustion seems to be a risk for a coronary event rather than a result of worsening disease processes.

Freeman and Nixon (1985) made a similar clinical observation and believe that when patients fatigue themselves by over-doing and foregoing appropriate rest, a state of physiological hyperarousal is necessary to enable them to maintain their pace. They hypothesized that, under conditions of chronic arousal, cardiac events such as angina or MI could be triggered by stressful breathing patterns. Forced hyperventilation has even been used to provoke coronary artery spasm in the cardiac catheterization laboratory (Girotti et al., 1982). Nixon (1986) described the type of arrhythmic hyperventilation that might trigger a cardiac event as subtle and often missed clinically. It is characterized by shallow upper-chest breathing at a slightly rapid rate that compromises homeostasis through its chronicity. Sucking air when speaking, expiratory sighing, and tense, slightly elevated shoulders are diagnostic signs. People who suffer from the more severe forms of time pathologies often exhibit such signs and report symptoms of sleep disturbances, fatigue, struggle against environmental resistances, abnormal breathing patterns, irritability, and a depressive state, among others (see Exhibits 1 and 2).

The way people progress from experiencing time pressure to more severe states of chronic time urgency and hurry sickness leading to exhaustion seems to be a complex interaction among physiological, psychological, and sociological processes. We believe that it begins with the adoption of a belief system that is almost a cultural imperative in this country: the belief that one's worth as a person is dependent on one's accomplishments. How this belief has the potential to lead to CAD is well described by Robert Eliot (1984), a cardiologist, in his book *Is It Worth Dying For?* Recounting his life before his heart attack, he wrote,

> My body cried out for rest, but my brain wasn't listening. I was behind
> schedule. My timetable read that by the age of 40 I should be the chief

EXHIBIT 1
Physical Signs of Time Pathologies

1. Rapid behaviors (e.g., walking, talking, and eating fast). Speech is often dysrhythmic.
2. Shallow upper-chest breathing. Often accompanied by sucking in air while speaking, expiratory sighing, and slightly elevated shoulders.
3. Tics: eyebrow, shoulders; rapid eye blinking is sometimes seen.
4. Nervous repetitive movements (e.g., knee jiggling, finger tapping, nail biting, teeth grinding).
5. Smacking or clicking sound as mouth opens to speak, due to tense jaw muscles.
6. Hurrying the speech of others, interrupting.
7. Head nodding while speaking; excessive head nodding while listening.
8. Facial tautness, expressing tension and anxiety.
9. Tuneless humming.
10. Periorbital pigmentation, due to excessive ACTH production from chronic struggle.

of cardiology at a major university. I was 43 when I left the University of Florida and accepted the position of Chief of Cardiology at the University of Nebraska. All I had to do was run a little faster and I'd be back on track. I came to feel that the walls were closing in on me and that I would never break free to make my dream a reality. Desperately I did what I had been doing all my life. I picked up the pace. . . . I had no time for family and friends, relaxation, and diversion. When [my wife] bought me an exercise bike for Christmas, I was offended. How could I possibly find time to sit down and pedal a bicycle? I was often overtired, but I put that out of my mind. I wasn't concerned about my health. . . . I was an expert in diseases of the heart and I knew I didn't have any of the risk factors. . . . But I was running a big risk for other reasons. I had been pushing too hard for too long. Now all my efforts seemed futile. . . . A feeling of disillusionment descended on me, a sense of invisible entrapment. I didn't know it then, but my body was continuously reacting to this inner turmoil. . . . [The heart attack] came two weeks after my 44th birthday. (pp. 1–2)

Dr. Eliot's story is not unique. In nearly 2 decades of clinical experience, we have heard this story with variations many times.

Loss of Social Support

A third area in which time pathologies do harm to people's health is in the degradation of relationships and, thus, social support networks. Lack

EXHIBIT 2
Psychological Symptoms of Time Pathologies

1. Impatience with the rate at which things happen; irritable when kept waiting.
2. Difficulty relaxing—feels guilty or restless.
3. Experiences a "racing mind"; may report sleep disturbances because of it.
4. Reports frequent attempts to do more than one thing at a time; difficulty listening without thinking of other things.
5. Makes a fetish out of being on time or, conversely, is chronically late.
6. Reports chronic feelings of time pressure.
7. Reports feeling overburdened or overwhelmed with all that needs to be done; may report often being overtired.
8. May admit to poor relationships; lack of close friends.

of time often prevents people from sustaining and nourishing relationships, sometimes leading to strain and misunderstanding. Friendships may be eroded from lack of attention, and family members are frequently resentful that the time-urgent person seems to continually place a higher priority on doing things than spending time with them. Further compounding this phenomenon is the fatigue that many sufferers of time pathologies often develop, promoting irritability and a lack of tolerance. All too often these emotional tendencies come to dominate relationships. Hurt and anger can easily flare, leading the time-urgent person to feel misunderstood, unsupported, and, ultimately, isolated.

We have also observed that when time-urgent individuals' relationships start to erode, they will often attempt to achieve even more, in an effort to compensate for the loss of self-esteem suffered from the troubled relationships. The increased effort requires higher levels of energy expenditure, which can, in turn, promote the state of exhaustion. Thus, it is possible for people suffering from time pathologies to get themselves into a driven state, in which their feelings of self-worth are totally dependent on their accomplishments, they are exhausted, and their support networks are tattered. Added to the known risk of fragmented social support systems and isolation is the physiological arousal that comes with combating growing fatigue and the hurt and anger generated by the stress and strain of troubled relationships.

The physiological mechanism by which emotional isolation and poor social support systems contribute to coronary disease and other illnesses is not precisely known. Nevertheless, the preponderance of available data shows a strong correlation between them (e.g., Berkman, 1984; Berkman & Syme, 1979; Cobb, 1976; Kaplan et. al. 1977; Medalie & Goldbourt,

1976; Raab, 1966). Much of this data comes from epidemiological studies. There are, however, several studies that have looked at social support from the perspective of cardiovascular reactivity. The following study is representative of the few in the literature. Gerin, Pieper, Levy, and Pickering (1992) studied normotensive college students ($N = 40$) for cardiovascular reactivity during a discussion task in which there was either support or no support during challenge conditions. Baseline SBP, DBP, and HR were obtained for both the supported group and the nonsupported group. The volunteers were continuously monitored during a group discussion in which the experimental group received support from another member of the group when challenged on their opinions. The nonsupported group had no allies during the group discussion when challenged and registered higher SBP, DBP, and HR. The difference in cardiovascular reactivity between the supported and nonsupported group was significant ($p < .0005$). Data from studies such as this one raise the question of whether the morbidity and mortality associated with poor social support could be mediated by heightened physical reactivity provoked by various forms of distress.

RATIONALE FOR TREATMENT

Treatment of time pathologies can help reduce (a) the intensity of a person's reactivity to time pressures, (b) the frequency with which a person is exposed to time pressure stressors through lifestyle changes, and (c) the tendency for susceptible patients to become overly fatigued and exhausted. Treatment can also provide emotional support as well as teach patients how to strengthen their relationships.

Last, we have seen treatment of time pathologies positively affect a fourth area of concern: a personal barrenness, which leads to a rather joyless existence, encouraging covert, self-destructive behaviors, such as noncompliance to medical regimens; food, alcohol, and substance abuse; exhausting schedules; being accident-prone; and sabotage of careers or support systems through poor judgment and alienating behaviors. This state often revolves around the belief that one's worth as a person is dependent on one's accomplishments. The belief encourages development of time pathologies, because more accomplishments translate into more self-worth.

Such reinforcement leads a person to take on more and more things to do. However, many patients report that the good feelings after an accomplishment tend to be fleeting rather than cumulative or lasting, adding to the need for continual, and often improved, accomplishment. Patients talk about their need to "up the ante" in terms of goals they set for themselves. Time realities run head-on into this insatiable need to accomplish more—and the realities prevail. To cope, people start speeding up their pace. They begin to experience frustration with perceived delays and typically feel impatient and irritable.

When time urgency becomes chronic, habitual, and severe, the symptoms of hurry sickness begin to emerge. People become so consumed and preoccupied with their goals, projects, and tasks that they lose the ability to be interested in others or other things in their environment. Their personality may start to deteriorate. They are often too busy for hobbies, cultural events, books, or even vacations. Their relationships suffer, and they become more isolated. They often feel alone and misunderstood in their strivings.

Frequently, hurry-sickness sufferers fall into the habit of evaluating their lives in terms of "how much" or "how many," instead of qualitative values. The growing dependence on numbers in their thought processes often supplants the richness of imagery, fantasy, and metaphor. Creative thinking, which takes time, can fall victim to hurry sickness.

With the increase in the pace of their life, people often develop racing-mind syndrome, which seems to exacerbate the tension associated with this condition. A racing mind can interfere with sleep, either by preventing it or by interrupting it in the middle of the night, and can keep a person awake for several hours. This phenomenon seriously contributes to a growing state of exhaustion. The racing mind also erodes the ability to concentrate on one thing at a time. When this occurs, people's efficiency subtly deteriorates, making it more difficult to accomplish things quickly. To compensate for their inability to stay focused, people will often wait until the last moment to get things done because the pressure of an approaching deadline turns on the "fight-or-flight" arousal response. In this hyperalert state, their mind can focus better on the "threat": the deadline. People begin to believe and say that they work better under pressure.

Finally, because their minds are so often preoccupied with future events, goals, and tasks, the present slides by with little attention paid to it unless there is some sort of crisis or acute problem. From our clinical experience, this results in people accumulating many memories of upsetting, negative, and stressful events. The rest of their life slips by relatively unnoticed and unenjoyed.

Unwittingly, they rob themselves of the very things that make life rich and enjoyable—the time to savor lovely aspects of their milieu, the companionship of good friends, pleasant memories, or free-floating curiosity about a variety of nonproductive interests that can provide delight and enrichment. In the words of one patient, "We render the events of our lives meaningless by the pace at which we go at them."

With lives devoid of richness and joy, with the tyranny of pressured schedules, with minds ceaselessly racing, and with the constant driven need to perform and succeed, it is not surprising that hurry sickness can lead to emotional and physical exhaustion, anger, and frustration. At this point, we observe an increasing tendency for people to engage in self-destructive behaviors.

Clinicians who have worked with coronary patients have no doubt heard some say that they knew their heart attack was coming and they were relieved that it had happened. Nurses in coronary care units are accustomed to hearing such comments from their patients. An MI can provide an honest and face-saving reason for bowing out of the "rat race." Patients may be able to feel as though they did not necessarily fail, but that their bodies let them down, which is an "honorable" way out.

Treatment of time pathologies can open new avenues and a vision of how to live a more healthful, enjoyable, and productive life. Patients can gain an understanding of the driven nature of their behavior and their approach to life. As they slow down their pace, they may feel more in control. They can discover other yardsticks by which to measure themselves besides quantitative productivity, which allows them to experience ambition and drive without feeling driven. As they take the time to nourish their relationships or to develop new ones, their worth as a person is mirrored back to them by newfound regard they see in the eyes of loved ones and friends.

In our clinical experience, most people who participate in treatment programs report enhanced feelings of self-esteem and improved physical relaxation with a corresponding decrease in feelings of anger and frustration and in their perceived stress levels. Their families usually report that they are easier to live with, more pleasant, and show far fewer self-destructive tendencies.

On a deeper personal level, hurry-sickness sufferers often wrestle with a profound dilemma in which they want to feel good about themselves and experience inner peace and contentment. However, the main way in which they experience positive feelings of worth is by doing many things. By being constantly busy, they can suppress unpleasant and painful feelings of poor self-worth that tend to become conscious when they are idle, but frenetic activity is incompatible with a sense of tranquillity or peace.

Treatment of time pathologies can encourage people to risk slowing down and developing a deeper, more accurate awareness of the true basis for their self-worth. We have seen many patients develop a sense of inner peace and enhanced self-esteem as a result of behavioral changes. We speculate that a paradigm shift in the way patients view themselves may provide significant protection against the ravages of CAD (Kaplan, 1991; Ornish, 1990).

Although the treatment of time pathologies has many psychological benefits, it also has important physiological benefits. Controlled intervention studies that attempt to reduce time urgency in coronary patients, although few, have consistently achieved positive results. These results include reduced CAD symptomatology and reduced coronary events (nonfatal MIs; Friedman et al., 1986; Ibrahim et al., 1974; Rahe, Ward, & Hayes, 1979) as well as evidence of atherosclerotic regression (Ornish et al., 1990). The treatments provided in these studies address issues in addition to time pathologies, but slowing down and learning to be more relaxed were significant elements of the treatment protocols.

The treatment program for time pathologies described below is based in great part on the protocol used in the Recurrent Coronary Prevention Project (Friedman et al., 1986), in which time urgency was significantly reduced ($p < .001$) and recurrent MI was 44% less in the treatment group compared with the control group. The treatment group ($n = 592$) consisted of male and female post-MI patients from all socioeconomic groups. In an extension of this study, a subset of the control group ($n = 104$) received 1 year of the same treatment (Friedman et al., 1987). This group's recurring coronary event rate dropped from 6.8% in the previous year to 1.9% during the treatment ($p < .05$).

The following treatment protocol for time pathologies has also been influenced by the work of others (Benson, Rosner, Marzetta, & Klemchuk, 1974; Nixon, 1986, Ornish, 1990).

OVERVIEW OF TREATMENT

The goals of treatment for time pathologies include the following: (a) reduced physiological arousal to perceived time-pressure demands and stressors through cognitive reframing, behavior and lifestyle changes, and relaxation response skills; (b) avoidance of exhaustion by maintaining balance in lifestyle, changing perspective, and enhancing self-worth; (c) strengthening relationships and social support through self-monitoring of feelings and communication and allowing more time for relationship building; (d) developing the ability to be introspective; and (e) fostering the capacity to feel inner contentment. The overall goal of treatment is enhancement of health and enjoyment of life, with specific attention to prevention of CAD or, in the case of CAD patients, prevention of further CAD events.

Factors Affecting Outcome

We have identified three important factors that significantly affect the success of treatment. The first is the therapeutic approach. We believe group therapy for time pathologies is usually more effective than individual treatment. We strongly recommend that a multidimensional approach be used, borrowing from several disciplines, and that the therapist work with patients in small groups of 6 to 12.

The group program has a number of advantages besides cost-effectiveness. Many participants comment on the "mirror" effect of seeing themselves by observing the behavior of others in the group. Over time, the group can become a powerful social support tool and influence members' behavior through positive peer pressure, facilitating change while reducing isolation. In addition, the group can be a safe place in which to share experiences and feelings and can also be a forum for discussing broader philosophical issues that few actively consider.

The multidisciplinary approach includes cognitive therapy, behavior modification, psychodynamic theory, and relaxation response training, in addition to education about cardiac risk factors, the wisdom of great thinkers, and common sense.

We strongly encourage a somewhat structured approach, especially in the beginning phases of the program, for structure seems to comfort many patients. Because of time urgency, many do not wish to "waste time." Two examples of wasting time that have been repeatedly brought to our attention are attending a session in which the therapist did not have an agenda or some specific material to share and having to listen to other people talk too much. Initially, patients respond favorably to leaving each session with some bit of new information or a nugget of wisdom presented by the therapist or synthesized from the discussions. Also, it is important for the therapist to realize that those who suffer from racing-mind syndrome will have great difficulty listening to others and remembering what is discussed. Therefore, material often needs to be repeated, and there is a better chance of retention if it is also presented with visual aids.

A second factor for success is length of time in treatment. Encouraging long-lasting change in habitual reactions to environmental stressors and changing old beliefs requires time, as does integration of these changes into a person's life. Change will occur in many people over a 3- to 6-month period, but from our observations, the durability of those changes is often suspect. Our clinical experience suggests that for most people the time in treatment should be 1 year at a minimum, with 2 years being more desirable (e.g., Friedman et. al., 1986; Ornish et al., 1990). Some may require a longer treatment time. Weekly sessions for 2 to 3 months, moving to twice a month for a total time of 2 years is a treatment program that seems to work well. Some clinicians advocate starting with an intensive period, such as a weekend (or longer) retreat. This intensive beginning often "jump starts" the change process and promotes faster bonding between participants, which is certainly desirable but not absolutely necessary for a successful treatment program.

A third variable for success is the therapist, that is, his or her skills and qualities. Friedman (1979) listed the qualities he believes necessary for therapists to work successfully with time-urgent Type As, to which we subscribe: (a) The therapist must not be severely afflicted with time urgency unless actively working to modify it. (b) The therapist must be able to diagnose and understand time pathologies and also be able to differentiate them from the psychopathology seen by most mental health providers. (c) The therapist needs a working understanding of CAD to be able to speak with some authority. (d) The therapist should have "an armamentarium of metaphors, aphorisms, and quotations that will allow [the penetration of] the obdurate and emotional barriers presented by severely afflicted" (Friedman, 1979, p. 245) coronary patients with this behavior. (e) The therapist needs patience to facilitate the repetition needed for change. (f) Courage aids the therapist in gently but frankly confronting patients with their behaviors and the nature of their destructiveness. (g) The therapist must have the capacity to care for the patient, to be aware of the person behind the behavior pattern, and to demonstrate that caring.

We would add two other recommendations to this list. The therapist needs to be a teacher at times, presenting educational material, sometimes with diagrams and demonstrations, and checking routinely on behavioral assignments. It is crucial that the therapist not get "hooked" into engaging challenging or hostile patients in arguments, but to therapeutically point out their behaviors as part of the affliction needing to be modified.

Treatment Components

Education

We recommend that patients be educated in at least three areas and that this take place early in the treatment program. The first area is the psychomotor signs and the symptoms of time pathologies (Friedman & Ghandour, 1993; Friedman & Powell, 1984; see also Exhibits 1 and 2). Second, patients should have a general knowledge of the pathophysiology of CAD, including what is known about the effects of tension and emotional factors on the cardiovascular system. Third, patients will benefit from increasing their knowledge of human behavior.

Cognitive Therapy

This discipline, along with behavior modification, seems to work well with this patient population. We assume this is because of its rational approach, practical application, and often rapid effects, all of which appeal to the time-pressured person. Self-talk (e.g., "Will this make any difference in my life in a week? in a year?"), cognitive filters (e.g., the "hook," see chap. 12, this volume), and cognitive reframing (e.g., "Perhaps the driver who just cut me off didn't see me") are among the techniques introduced as soon as feasible, usually within the first 6 weeks. This often enables patients to experience some change early in the treatment program, which is motivating and encouraging. The length of the program also gives them time to become somewhat skillful in the application of these techniques.

Behavior Modification

The practical nature of this discipline also tends to appeal to these patients due, in great part, we suspect, to the action or "doing" involved. We recommend that patients be given behavioral exercises or drills throughout the treatment, for we have found them to be of particular value in helping patients to physically slow down, which seems to have a positive impact on people's emotional state and reduces the tension associated with rapid behaviors.

Relaxation Response Training

The benefits of relaxation response training have been described in other writings (Benson et al., 1974). Although very beneficial for them, patients with hurry sickness often struggle with these techniques in the beginning and get discouraged. The racing-mind syndrome hinders focusing and experiencing the desired calming effects. A well-structured relaxation exercise, such as progressive muscle relaxation, has the best chance of initial success because it is an active process and the focus changes from muscle group to muscle group. It is also important to teach relaxed breathing techniques, such as diaphragmatic breathing, to provide a relaxation skill that can be used in nearly all situations. We have noted that many coronary patients who exhibit time pathologies seem to develop a kind of alexithymic (Taylor, Bagby, & Parker, 1991) condition, in which their tension level becomes so habitual that they no longer feel it and it seems like a normal state. One simple and inexpensive feedback device we have found helpful is skin-temperature-sensitive "biodots." Participants wear them during group sessions and monitor their stress level according to the color changes. It is a crude biofeedback device, but patients are often impressed to see the dot darken after they have talked about an upsetting event and lighten when they feel more relaxed. For some, the visual cue can help increase awareness of internal tension.

Psychodynamic Theory

Although the core of treatment is behavior change, knowledge of psychodynamics is valuable. As used here, the term *psychodynamic* refers to the understanding of the personality as a complex interaction among various levels or components. These include drives, psychological defenses, unconscious processes, values and beliefs, and inferred ego states such as self-esteem.

From our clinical experience, severe time pathologies can be viewed, in part, as a defense against underlying psychological and emotional problems such as depression and anxiety. In some, these problems are far from awareness, but in others, they are easily acknowledged. Some individuals, for whom hurry sickness was successful in keeping depression and anxiety suppressed, have been observed to become overtly depressed or to experience increased anxiety as they give up time-pressured behaviors. For such patients, additional individual therapy may be necessary. However, we have seen some people experience a lifting of depression and anxiety as they begin to use more effective, changed behaviors. They tend to receive positive reinforcement from others in the form of greater acceptance and otherwise improved interpersonal relations. This in turn can result in enhanced self-esteem, better control over what happens to them, and a consequent increased probability of meeting their own expectations.

Common Sense and Wisdom

The importance of a liberal application of common sense and wisdom to the treatment of this disorder cannot be overestimated. Some time-urgent patients can be helped to be more sensible in the way they schedule their days when faced with the objective evidence that they rarely allow enough time for tasks and consequently set themselves up for time pressure. The treatment is also enhanced by stripping the behavior of some of its glamour or desirability by asking penetrating questions that bring into relief the flaws of many commonly held assumptions about the utility of rapid-paced, time-urgent behaviors. One way to do this is to critically examine the attributes for success. The therapist can be greatly aided by sharing the wisdom of great thinkers, writers, poets, and philosophers, such as the quote from Lord Chesterfield, "He who is in a hurry shows that the thing he is about is too big for him," or that from Thomas Edison, "The best thinking is done in solitude. The worst is done in turmoil." See Appendix A for a list of other quotes that can be useful in treating time pathologies.

Motivational Issues

One of the first challenges to the clinician working with people who suffer from time pathologies is motivating them to spend time in a program of some duration. A coronary event often provides substantial motivation for many patients. However, not all patients seize the opportunity provided by illness to make sweeping changes in their lifestyles. Some make certain changes, such as modifying their diets or exercising regularly. Others escape myocardial damage by the timely application of modern technology, such as angioplasty or bypass surgery, and perhaps believe that their problem is "fixed." The younger male patient sometimes refuses to admit that stress is a problem, because he's "handling it." Finally, we think that a certain percentage of our patients exhibit a kind of addiction to the stimulating effects of the catecholamines (e.g. adrenaline and noradrenaline), which are often elevated with feelings of time pressure.

One effective way to break through patients' denial about the need to reduce their time-pressure stress is for the therapist to become clinically skilled in the diagnosis of time pathologies. The overt psychomotor signs, such as knee jiggling, finger tapping, or teeth grinding, can be pointed out to the patient, with the explanation of their meaning, as objective evidence of tension. As a general rule, patients are receptive to this approach and will truly listen, often with a degree of curiosity.

To overcome patients' reluctance to commit to long-term treatment, it is helpful to describe the program in terms of skills that can be learned to accomplish goals, without such a toll on the cardiovascular system. To be skilled in anything takes time and so does overcoming lifelong habits. Also, with the results of the Ornish (e.g., Ornish et al., 1990) study, patients can have the hope of reversing their CAD, and this is a goal many will embrace, sometimes with the same single-mindedness that they brought to their vocational pursuits. Here again, the quick fix is not an option. Just as coronary disease took time to become manifest, so does reversal.

Our clinical experience strongly indicates that, once patients are involved in the treatment program, the vast majority find it intriguing and helpful enough that length of treatment is no longer an issue. Indeed, a certain number complain when the frequency of sessions decreases, and many participants stay in the program for more than 2 years.

For those few who declare that they like the pace at which they live, that it's exciting, the therapist can point out that they may be addicted to their own stress hormones (the catecholamines). Addiction suggests that the person is being manipulated by something not under his control, a concept some will find abhorrent. Anecdotally, one participant, a brilliant health professional, resisted all rationales for changing his behavior. It was only when the concept of being addicted to his own stress hormones was presented that he embraced the need to change. He now reports that he avoids giving himself a "fix" about 90% of the time. His family has also reported benefits from his change.

Beginning Treatment

It is recommended that the therapist set the tone of the group at the start. At the first session, it is important to briefly review the aims of the program and to remind participants that the focus is changing unhealthy behaviors and habits, and not changing their personalities. Also, briefly reviewing pertinent research findings relating to lifestyle and behavior change and their impact on coronary disease aids in reinforcing program credibility. Participants need to be apprised of their responsibilities, such as regular attendance, confidentiality, and participation. The therapist's responsibilities should also be reviewed. These include facilitation, role modeling, making the group a "safe" place, and providing the structure and guidance for learning and change. It is helpful to provide these responsibilities in written form. We also provide a workbook, which will be described further.

Also in the first session are introductions by the participants. We recommend the following instructions: "When you introduce yourself, please tell us something about yourself without telling us what you do for a living. Then tell us what you hope to gain from the program. Then, finally, if you wish, you can tell us what you do." It is often confounding for people who base their identity on their vocation to describe themselves without reference to their work. Their struggle provides an opportunity for enlightenment. We usually use this opportunity to remark that after all, "We are human beings, not human doings." This is one of the activities of the first session that helps to set the fundamental tone of what the treatment is about—namely, helping participants find self-worth in ways other than quantitative accomplishment, which may in turn reduce their pathology about time.

Other techniques used in the first session are an introductory relaxation exercise and a self-observational assignment. We often assign observation of psychomotor signs and symptoms of time urgency. For example, we have participants report on how stressed they become while driving. Many individuals in coronary groups will admit to experiencing driving stresses. This is one area in which changes can be made rapidly, lending encouragement for further behavior change.

Within the first 6 sessions, other topics include (a) pathophysiology of CAD and the impact of emotional stress on the heart; (b) contingency planning in case of another coronary event—how to distinguish between various pains; (c) education about the importance of prompt medical attention and the immense value of early thrombolytic therapy if a person may be having an MI; (d) what kinds of activities increase risk of MI (having a cardiologist assist is helpful); (e) if evaluated for time pathologies with the videotaped clinical examination (see chap. 6, this volume), discussion of scores can serve as good feedback and possible motivation; (f) developing a "self-monitor" for behaviors and body tension levels; (g) application of "self-talk" and other cognitive techniques to reduce driving and other stressors; and (h) an introduction to behavioral drills.

Other subjects have been found to be valuable early in the treatment regimen. The concept that the locus of control for emotional reactivity is within the individual, rather than the external environment, is useful, particularly for psychologically unsophisticated individuals. There is frequent discussion of success, with a focus on the actual, rather than time-urgent, qualities that typically foster achievement. These topics are interwoven with subjects that arise as the therapist follows up on the patients' efforts to monitor time-pressured behaviors, their ability to reduce driving stress, and their experiences with the behavioral drills.

Moving on through the year, the therapist can initiate discussions of time management and time awareness, which we define as a sense of inner peace; reducing frustration and anger generated by time pressures; self-esteem issues; developing or restoring the ability to use images, fantasy, and metaphors; impoverishment and restoration of the facets of one's personality; ways to find joy in living; enhancing relationships; fostering relaxation and inner peace; and objective analysis of personal belief systems.

Many patients in coronary groups will want to talk about their disease and what it is like to cope with it. It is difficult for many patients to talk about their feelings. As a result, they will often begin by asking practical questions about symptoms, medications, procedures, and other medical topics. It is important for the therapist to provide opportunities and encouragement for expressing feelings about living with heart disease. If one person does so, often others feel safe in following. In discussions such as these, the therapist may notice a peculiar tendency for patients, when asked about how they *feel* about certain situations, to answer in terms of what they would *do*.

Because of this tendency to strongly identify with what they do and because it becomes apparent that certain of their behaviors are negative and harmful, some patients will become depressed as they see themselves more clearly, or as the glamour they had previously attached to their time-pressured behavior is lost. We feel that this is related to the way that the frenetic behaviors serve to mask underlying depression. The best approach we have found is to make distinctions between the person and behavior, which is changeable, and to remind patients that time pathology is a treatable affliction. Sometimes we have even used the following analogy: "If your business was not doing well and you brought in a consultant who pointed out that certain activities were harmful, would you assume that the business was no good, or would you work to make the necessary changes?"

Last, it may be necessary to call on people in the group to assure everyone's participation. In checking on the behavioral drills, it is desirable for each person to report on his or her experience, as well as how well they have practiced the drills.

Treatment Tools

The Therapist as a Role Model

One of the most powerful tools is the behavior of the therapist, which can serve as a model. The therapist's willingness to forthrightly examine his or her own behavior and to practice what is preached has an importance that cannot be overestimated.

Philosophic Precepts, Quotes, Aphorisms, and Other Writings

By using the wisdom passed down through the ages, as well as the writings of recent authors and poets, the therapist can strengthen the impact of therapeutic messages. It may be easy for a patient to challenge something the therapist says, but it is not so easy to challenge the time-honored words of Lincoln, Franklin, Shakespeare, or Socrates. Their wisdom has survived because it has been valued over generations; the odds are great that the patients will find their quotations valuable as well.

A list of some helpful quotes can be found in Appendix A. In addition, we find William James's writings (1890/1950) on changing "undesirable emotional tendencies" (p. 463) to be persuasive in discussing the value of behavior modification, as well as the autobiographies of Benjamin Franklin (1793/1868; on changing his own behavior) and Charles Darwin (1887/1958; on deterioration of his personality). We encourage the therapist to search the literature for additional pertinent writings. Emerson's essays (Emerson & Forbes, 1909/1968) have been found to be effective, especially his thought-provoking comments on the meaning of success. A hidden benefit is that the therapist, too, gains expanded knowledge and enriched thought as a result of such a literature search.

Behavioral Drills

The behavioral drills are a cornerstone of our program. We have listed them in Appendix B. To emphasize their importance, we have the drills listed in a workbook and assign them weekly. The importance of drills is reinforced by reading philosophic precepts and quotes, reporting research and biochemical findings related to behavior change, and describing what seems to be a feedback loop in our bodies connecting the mind with the quality of motor activity (Ekman, Levenson & Friesen, 1983). By deliberately reducing the speed at which something is done, such as walking or talking more slowly, one can reduce the feeling of urgency, as though the feedback from slowed motor activity has a dampening effect. Conversely, speeding up the rate at which one does something seems to exacerbate feelings of time urgency. This may appear somewhat paradoxical to participants, but if they practice slowing down, it will often decrease anxiety and tension. In the words of one participant, "Slowing down has the side effect of reducing anxiety. And although I can't prove it and it seems counter-intuitive, I think I'm getting as much done."

The therapist must be disciplined enough to follow up on assignments. Failure to do so conveys the message that they are not important, and participants will not practice them. The successes and problems patients report in their drilling efforts provide rich material for discussion and often an opportunity for insights.

Our approach is to encourage a sense of mastery of the behavioral drills. This requires that the therapist explain why such mastery is desirable. This can be done from the perspective of enhanced physical and coronary health (e.g., reduction of biochemical arousal and reduced bodily tension and anxiety) and also from the perspectives of a better sense of control and inner peace. For example, the drill "Practice standing in a long line" often perturbs patients when first presented. They frequently demand to know why they should deliberately expose themselves to such a stressor! First, the therapist can point out that even though participants may be able to avoid waiting in line most of the time, there will come a time when it is necessary or inevitable. At that point, will the patient have mastery over the situation, or will impatience and irritation and the attendant physiological arousal occur? The therapist can have patients discuss their usual cognitive process during this activity and guide them into choosing new ways to look at it. We have announced that some people have even come to experience a sort of enjoyment when waiting in line. This statement is always met with disbelief. But it is true. Some people, through mastery, have found that the time they spend waiting can be an unexpected gift of free time, which can be used to think creatively about all sorts of things, and that this can be a relaxing and even enriching experience. We also often tell patients that while waiting, they have only their thoughts for company. Perhaps they need to ask themselves why they find themselves so boring. For many, this is a novel concept, which gives the therapist a fertile opportunity to point out how hurry sickness can adversely affect their personalities and rob them of the ability to have absorbing, interesting, and rich thoughts.

Blackboard or Flipchart

Essentially, the therapist's main tools are words and the mirrorlike effect of the group experience. But our clinical experience indicates that patients who suffer from time pathologies usually learn better from what they see than from what they hear. Some have real difficulty listening, so distracted are they by their polyphasic thoughts. Therefore, to the extent it is feasible for the therapist to use diagrams or visual aids, we recommend it.

Workbook

Although not crucial to the success of a treatment program, we believe a workbook certainly enhances it. The behavioral drills, philosophic precepts, and other writings are kept in the workbook. And our patients are often given handouts, which they can keep in it for future reference. The workbook becomes, over time, a helpful manual for participants, reflective of the treatment program.

Videotaped Clinical Examination (VCE)

This is a tool found to be helpful, but it is not crucial to the success of the treatment program. If the therapist has the resources and time, we recommend that before beginning treatment, each patient be examined for the diagnostic signs and symptoms of time urgency and hurry sickness. Chapter 6 provides a description of the VCE for TABP, which contains both hostility and time-pressure subscores. The VCE also allows for measurement of change in intensity of the TABP, including the time-pressure component. With this examination, the clinician has a baseline record on which a patient's progress can be measured with some objectivity. Diagnostic testing can be repeated at the end of a year. Sometimes the "before" and "after" videotapes document remarkable change. The therapist will find that "numbers-oriented" patients will be intrigued with their scores and often motivated to "improve" them. We find it valuable for the patient to see the VCE midway through the program. For group work, we show portions (with prior permission) of each person's videotape during a session. Often this exercise can have a dramatic and enlightening impact.

Other Group Activities

A group exercise that aids in bonding and helps clarify the meaning of success is one in which participants are instructed to think of one success they have had and share it with the group at the next session. They are also asked to think about the qualities they brought to bear in that situation that were responsible for their success. During the exercise, the therapist makes a list on the board of all the qualities for success mentioned by participants. At the end of the exercise, the therapist will have an impressive list of positive qualities responsible for success, often including hard work, good judgment, the ability to communicate, and the capacity for creative thinking. Although some patients may initially believe that their speed of doing things was responsible for their success, this is the time to point out that impatience, irritation, frenzied activity, and similar behaviors are not on the list. We recommend that this be done about 2 months into the treatment program.

Group discussions focused on uncovering patients' belief systems can also be very fruitful. Often patients are initially stymied in getting at their underlying beliefs. One technique that helps is for the therapist to provide guidance with analytical questions. As an example, a patient may say that he gets tense when he is going to be late. The therapist can ask, "What do you worry will happen if you are late?" The patient may respond that he worries people will think he's disrespectful. The therapist can then ask what would happen if that occurred. This kind of guided questioning continues until the patient cannot go any further.

Some examples of the beliefs underlying time pathologies that have been articulated by our patients are listed below:

1. If I'm late, I'm a failure.
2. Other people's opinions of me are of crucial importance.
3. I am what I do. If I am not doing anything, I am nothing.
4. I'm a good person if I get everything done. If I don't, I'm a bad person.
5. If I do something wrong or don't get something done, I'm a bad person.
6. I'm not permitted to relax until I'm finished or exhausted.
7. Wasting time is a sin.
8. If I make a mistake, something bad will always happen.

When a patient is successful in uncovering such beliefs, they can often be seen as illogical. The therapist can guide and encourage replacing these harmful beliefs with more healthful ones. Devising such healthful beliefs can also be a group activity.

RELATIONSHIP BETWEEN TIME PATHOLOGIES AND ANGER

There have been recent challenges to the role of time urgency as a risk factor for CAD, as anger, cynicism, and hostility have been designated as reifying the core of coronary-prone behavior (Williams et. al., 1980, 1982). From a theoretical perspective, anger may be more "toxic" to the cardiovascular system than time pathologies. From a practical perspective, however, time pressure cannot be ignored because it can trigger frustration that leads to anger and hostility. Frustration often begets aggression; much research was done more than 50 years ago to validate the "frustration aggression hypothesis" (Dollard, Miller, Mowrer, & Sears, 1939; Miller et. al., 1941; Rosenzweig, 1944). As described by a patient, "I find myself setting these arbitrary, almost meaningless deadlines, and then the pressure, anxiety, and resentment build up. If anything gets in the way, like even a signal light turning red, I'm angry, for no reason." Another patient declared, "Nothing makes me angrier than to be kept waiting." Our clinical experience suggests that time-related anger occurs more intensely when the behaviors of others or events frustrate the achievement of goals and when self-worth is overly connected to the achievement of those goals.

Time-urgent patients, then, can be seen as persons with a driving ambition to engage in behaviors that will enhance their self-esteem. Anyone or anything that slows them down often creates frustration and anger, which further elevate the chronic state of flight or fight. Thus, although anger may be the primary emotional toxic factor in coronary-prone behavior, time pathology is, at the very least, its handmaiden. The relationship between anger and time pathologies should receive more theoretical and research attention in the future.

SUMMARY

Time-pressured lifestyles are prevalent in American society. Research suggests that time pressure can heighten cardiovascular reactivity and alter neurohormonal states (Gibbs, 1989; Keyes, 1991; Rifkin, 1987; Robinson, 1990). Severe chronic reactivity combined with excessive struggle to accomplish goals can lead to fatigue and exhaustion, which have been implicated as prodromal symptoms of a cardiac event. Time pathologies encourage degradation of relationships and social support networks and can erode self-worth and inner contentment. Interventional trial research suggests that treatment can be both valuable and desirable from physical and emotional perspectives and can alter the course of CAD. The group-treatment program described is one that has resulted in a high degree of change in unhealthful behaviors for many patients, can reduce recurring coronary events, and can improve quality of life.

Just as current mind–body research is slowly eroding the separateness of the emotional and physical self, it is helping practitioners view the person as interconnected and whole. Treatment of time pathologies can have a ripple effect, touching many aspects of a person's life. The result is a person who is healthier and more whole.

REFERENCES

Benson, H., Rosner, B. A., Marzetta, B. R., & Klemchuk, H. M. (1974). Decreased blood pressure in pharmacologically treated hypertensive patients who regularly elicited the relaxation response. *Lancet, 1*, 289–291.

Berkman, L. F. (1984). Assessing the physical health effects of social networks and social support. *Annual Review of Public Health, 5*, 413–432.

Berkman, L. F., & Syme, S. (1979). Social networks, host resistance and mortality. A nine-year follow-up study of Alameda County residents. *American Journal of Epidemiology, 109*, 186–204.

Chrousos, G., & Gold, P. (1981). The concepts of stress and stress system disorders: Overview of physical and behavioral homeostasis. *Journal of the American Medical Association, 267,* 1244–1252.

Cobb, S. (1976). Social support as a moderator of life stress. *Psychosomatic Medicine, 38,* 300–314.

Crisp, A., Queenan, M., & D'Souza, M. (1984). Myocardial infarction and emotional climate. *Lancet, 1,* 616–619.

Darwin, C. (1958). *Autobiography* (N. Barlow, Ed.). New York: Harcourt, Brace, Jovanovich. (Original work published 1887)

Dollard, J., Miller, N. E., Mowrer, O. H., & Sears, R. R. (1939). *Frustration and aggression.* New Haven, CT: Yale University Press.

Ekman, P., Levenson, R., & Friesen, W. (1983). Autonomic nervous system activity distinguishes among emotions. *Science, 221,* 1208–1210.

Eliot, R. (1984). *Is it worth dying for?* New York: Bantam Books.

Emerson, R. W., & Forbes, W. (Eds.). (1968). *The journals of Ralph Waldo Emerson.* New York: Doubleday. (Original work published 1909)

Feinleib, M., Simon, A., Gillum, R., & Marjolis, J. (1975). Prodromal symptoms and signs of sudden death. *Circulation, 51*(Suppl. 1), 155–159.

Franklin, B. (1868). *The autobiography of Benjamin Franklin.* New York: Heritage Press. (Original work published 1793)

Freeman, L., & Nixon, P. (1985). Dynamic causes of angina pectoris. *American Heart Journal, 110,* 1087–1092.

Friedman, M. (1979). Qualities of patient and therapist required for successful modification of coronary-prone (Type A) behavior. *Psychiatric Clinics of North America, 2,* 243–248.

Friedman, M., & Ghandour, G. (1993). Medical diagnosis of Type A behavior. *American Heart Journal, 126,* 607–618.

Friedman, M., & Powell, L. (1984, July–August) The diagnosis and quantitative assessment of Type A behavior: Introduction and description of the videotaped structured interview. *Integrative Psychiatry,* 123–129.

Friedman, M., Powell, L., Thoresen, C., Ulmer, D., Price, V., Gill, J., Thompson, L., Rabin, D., Brown, B., Breall, W., Levy, R., & Bourg, E. (1987). Effect of discontinuance of Type A behavioral counseling on Type A behavior and cardiac recurrence rate of post myocardial infarction patients. *American Heart Journal, 114,* 483–490.

Friedman, M., & Rosenman, R. (1974). *Type A behavior and your heart.* New York: Knopf.

Friedman, M., Rosenman, R., & Carroll, V. (1958). Changes in the serum cholesterol and blood clotting time in men subjected to cyclic variation of occupational stress. *Circulation, 17,* 852–861.

Friedman, M., Thoresen, C., Gill, J., Ulmer, D., Powell, L., Price, V., Brown, B., Thompson, L., Rabin, D., Breall, W., Bourg, E., Levey, R., & Dixon, T.

(1986). Alteration of Type A behavior and its effect on cardiac recurrences in post infarction patients: Summary results of the Recurrent Coronary Prevention Project. *American Heart Journal, 112,* 653–665.

Friedman, M., & Ulmer, D. (1984). *Treating Type A behavior and your heart.* New York: Knopf.

Gerin, W., Pieper, C., Levy, R., & Pickering, T. (1992). Social support in social interaction: A moderator of cardiovascular reactivity. *Psychosomatic Medicine, 54,* 324–336.

Gibbs, N. (1989, April 24). How America has run out of time. *Time Magazine,* pp. 58–67.

Girotti, L., Crosatto, J., Messutti, H., Kaski, J., Dyszel, E., Rivas, C., Araujo, L., Vetulli, H., & Rosenbaum, M. (1982). The hyperventilation test as a method for developing successful therapy in Prinzmetal's angina. *American Journal of Cardiology, 49,* 834–839.

Ibrahim, M. A., Feldman, J. G., Sultz, H. A., Staiman, M. G., Young, L. J., & Dean, D. (1974). Management after myocardial infarction: A controlled trial of the effect of group psychotherapy. *International Journal of Psychiatry Medicine, 5,* 253–268.

James, W. (1950). *The principles of psychology.* New York: Dover. (Original work published 1890)

Kaplan, B. H. (1991). Social health and the forgiving heart: The Type B story. *Journal of Behavioral Medicine, 15,* 3–14.

Kaplan, B. H., Cassel, J. C., & Gore, S. (1977). Social support and health. *Medical Care, 15,* 47–58.

Keyes, R. (1991). *Timelock.* New York: HarperCollins.

Klaboe, G., Otterstad, J., Winsness, T., & Espeland, N. (1987). Predictive value of prodromal symptoms in myocardial infarction. *Acta Medica Scandinaica, 222,* 27–30.

Krantz, D. S., Helmers, K. F., Bairey, C. N., Nebel, L. E., Hedges, S. M., & Rozanski, A. (1991). Cardiovascular reactivity and mental stress-induced myocardial ischemia in patients with coronary artery disease. *Psychosomatic Medicine, 53,* 1–12.

Kuller, L., Cooper, M., & Perper, J. (1972). Epidemiology of sudden death. *Archives of Internal Medicine, 129,* 714–719.

Levenson, R., Ekman, P., & Friesen, W. (1990). Voluntary facial action generates emotion-specific autonomic nervous system activity. *Psychophysiology, 27,* 363–384.

Light, K., Dolan, C., Davis, M., & Sherwood, A. (1992). Cardiovascular responses to an active coping challenge as predictors of blood pressure patterns 10 to 15 years later. *Psychosomatic Medicine, 54,* 217–230.

Malkoff, S. B., Muldoon, M. F., Zeigler, Z. R., & Manuck, S. B. (1993). Blood platelet responsivity to acute mental stress. *Psychosomatic Medicine, 55,* 477–482.

Manuck, S. B., Olsson, G., Hjemdahl, P., & Rehnquist, N. (1992). Does cardio-vascular reactivity to mental stress have prognostic value in post-myocardial infarction patients? A pilot study. *Psychosomatic Medicine, 54,* 102–108.

Medalie, J., & Goldbourt, U. (1976). Angina pectoris among 10,000 men: II. Psychosocial and other risk factors as evidenced by a multivariate analysis of a five year incidence study. *American Journal of Medicine, 60,* 910–921.

Mendes de Leon, C., Powell, L., & Kaplan, B. (1991). Change in coronary-prone behaviors in the Recurrent Coronary Prevention Project. *Psychosomatic Medicine, 53,* 407–419.

Miller, N. E., Maslow, A. H., Sears, R. R., Berteson, G., Levy, D. M., Hartmann, G. W., Mowrer, O. H. Doob, L. W., & Dollard, J. (1941). Symposium on the effects of frustration. *Psychological Review, 48,* 337–366.

Mustard, J., Packham, M., & Kinlough-Rathbone, R. (1990). Platelets, blood flow, and vessel wall. *Circulation, 81*(Suppl. 1), 24–27.

Nixon, P. G. F. (1986). Exhaustion: Cardiac rehabilitation's starting point. *Physiotherapy, 72,* 224–228.

Ornish, D. (1990). *Reversing heart disease.* New York: Ballantine/Random House.

Ornish, D., Brown, S. E., Scherwitz, L. W., Billings, J. H., Armstrong, W. T., Ports, T. A., McLanahan, S. M., Kirkeeide, R. L., Brand, R. J., & Gould, K. L. (1990). Can lifestyle changes reverse coronary heart disease? *Lancet, 336,* 129–133.

Ornish, D., Scherwitz, L. W., Doody, R. S., Kesten, D., McLanahan, S., Brown, S., DePuey, G., Sonnemaker, R., Haynes, C., Lester, J., McAllister, G., Hall, R., Burdine, J., & Gotto, A. (1983). Effects of stress management training and dietary changes in treating ischemic heart disease. *Journal of American Medical Association, 249,* 54–59.

Raab, W. (1966). Emotional and sensory stress factors in myocardial pathology. *American Heart Journal, 72,* 538–564.

Rahe, R. H., Ward, H. W., & Hayes, V. (1979). Brief group therapy in myocardial infarction rehabilitation. *Psychosomatic Medicine, 41,* 229–242.

Rifkin, J. (1987). *Time wars.* New York: Henry Holt.

Robinson, J. P. (1990, February). The time squeeze. *American Demographics,* 30–33.

Rosenzweig, S. (1944). An outline of frustration theory. In E. Hunt (Ed.), *Personality and the behavior disorders* (Vol. 1, pp. 379–388). New York: Ronald Press.

Ross, R. (1986). The pathogenesis of atherosclerosis—An update. *New England Journal of Medicine, 314,* 488–500.

Schnall, P. L., Schwartz, J. E., Landsbergis, P. A., Warren, K., & Pickering, T. G. (1992). Relation between job strain, alcohol, and ambulatory blood pressure. *Hypertension, 19,* 488–494.

Sherwood, A., Hinderliter, A., & Light, K. (1995). Physiological determinants of hyperreactivity to stress in borderline hypertension *Hypertension, 55,* 384–390.

Taylor, G. J., Bagby, R. M., & Parker, J. (1991). The alexithymia construct: A potential paradigm for psychosomatic medicine. *Psychosomatics, 32,* 153–164.

Toffler, A. (1970). *Future shock.* New York: Random House.

Toynbee, A. (1961). *A study of history* (Vol. 12). London: Oxford University Press.

Vanhoutte, P., & Houston, D. (1985). Platelets, endothelium, and vasospasm. *Circulation, 72,* 728–734.

Williams, R. B., Haney, T. L., Lee, K. L., Kong, Y. H., Blumenthal, J. A., & Whalen, R. E. (1980). Type A behavior, hostility and coronary atherosclerosis. *Psychosomatic Medicine, 42,* 539–549.

Williams, R. B., Jr., Lane, J. D., Kuhn, C. M., Meosh, W., White, A. D., & Schanberg, S. M. (1982). Type A behavior pattern and elevated physiological and neuroendocrine responses to cognitive tasks. *Science, 218,* 483–485.

Appendix follows on the next page.

APPENDIX A
QUOTES, APHORISMS, AND PHILOSOPHICAL PRECEPTS TO AID IN THE TREATMENT OF TIME PATHOLOGIES

1. "He who is hurried cannot walk gracefully."
   —*Old Chinese proverb*

2. "There are two creatures in nature that exhibit impatience—people and puppies. Even a spring bud knows restraint in a prolonged cold spell."

3. "He who is in a hurry shows that the thing he is about is too big for him."
   —*Lord Chesterfield, 1740*

4. "And when all the clocks and calendars have stopped their counting for you, what then has your life added up to?"

5. "Nothing is so vulgar as to be in a hurry."
   —*Oliver Wendell Holmes*

6. "One's voice sounds lovely only when one possesses an inner repose."

7. "Beware the mind-destroying drug of constant activity."
   —*Loren Eisley*

8. "Success is a result; it must not be a goal."
   —*Gustave Flaubert*

9. "Do not say things. What you are thunders so, that I cannot hear what you say to the contrary."
   —*Ralph Waldo Emerson*

10. "Beware of the tyranny of the 'Dark Goddess of Continual Accomplishment'."

11. "The greatest waste of time is to spend it being irritated."

12. "When a man cannot distinguish a great from a small event, he is of no use."
    —*Winston Churchill*

13. "Habit is the hardiest of all the plants in human growth."
    —*Marcel Proust*

14. "Wisdom cometh to the learned man through the opportunity of leisure."
    —*Ecclesiastes*

15. "Life is an 'unfinishedness'."
    —*Meyer Friedman*

16. "The creative act is the defeat of habit by originality."
    —*Arthur Koestler*

17. "Success is getting what you want. Happiness is wanting what you get."
    —*Bertrand Russell*

18. "The stature of a man can be measured by the size of the event that preoccupies him."

19. "We render the events in our lives meaningless by the pace at which we go at them."
    —*L. Moglen (treatment participant)*

20. "The best thinking is done in solitude. The worst is done in turmoil."
    —*Thomas Edison*

21. "The urgent things are seldom important and the important things are seldom urgent."

22. "God's greatest gift to me is the ability to be astonished anew by the almost incredible beauty of a dandelion plant in full bloom."
    —*Charles Ephraim Burchfield*

23. "Good conversation should be a dialogue, not a dual of monologues."

24. "Every good habit that is worth possessing must be paid for in strokes of daily effort."
    —*William James*

25. "Our life is frittered away by detail . . . simplicity, simplicity, simplicity."
    —*Henry David Thoreau*

26. "When there are no events, there is no time."
    —*Albert Speer*

27. "A mind continually preoccupied with the future garners nothing in its memory."

28. "God gave us memory so we could have roses in the winter."
    —*Percy Bysshe Shelley*

29. "A person who can remember what he has seen can never be lonely or be without food for thought."
    —*Vincent van Gogh*

30. "We are shaped and fashioned by what we love."
    —*Johann Wolfgang von Goethe*

31. "If you make the organization your life, you are defenseless against the inevitable disappointments."
    —*Peter Drucker*

32. "Those who rush arrive first at the grave."
   —*Spanish proverb*

33. "Why not learn by getting down to the actual practice?"
   —*Mahatma Gandhi*

34. "A mind that is fast is sick. A mind that is slow is sound. A mind that is still is divine."
   —*Meher Baba*

35. "What we nurture in ourselves will grow. This is Nature's eternal law."
   —*Johann Wolfgang von Goethe*

36. "The beginning of wisdom is the realization that what is of concern today won't seem important tomorrow."
   —*Old Chinese proverb*

37. "If you treat every situation as a life-and-death matter, you'll die a lot of times."
   —*Dean Smith*

38. "Why use ten dollars' worth of energy on ten cent problems?"
   —*Participant in U.S. Army War College research program*

39. "To make anything a habit, do it; to not make it a habit, do not do it; to unmake a habit, do something else in place of it."
   —*Epictetus*

40. "The Indian Summer of life should be a little sunny and a little sad, like a season, and infinite in wealth and depth of tone—but never hurried."
   —*Henry B. Adams*

APPENDIX B
DRILLS TO REDUCE TIME PATHOLOGIES

1. **Walk, talk, and eat more slowly:** Gives calmer, less tension-filled feedback from the body to the brain, which helps to reduce feelings of time pressure.

2. **Practice doing one thing at a time:** Reduces time pressure as described above, enhances feeelings of control, and also helps to restore the ability to focus on one thing, which counteracts the racing-mind syndrome.

3. **Practice listening without interrupting:** Teaches patience and listening skills. Helps develop interest in others' thoughts and ideas, which counteracts egocentrism.

4. **Linger at the table after eating:** Enhances interpersonal relationships and patience.

5. **Drive in one of the slow lanes:** Establishes a slower pace and generally less tension with driving, encourages less attention on speed, and reduces some excessive competitiveness in driving situations.

6. **Stand in a long line and use your mind creatively to take advantage of the wait:** Develops patience and a sense of mastery in waiting situations; encourages creativity for pleasurable thoughts, rather than impatient ones.

7. **Refrain from projecting your time urgency on others:** Helps develop internal monitor, plus encourages awareness of the impact one's behavior has on others.

8. **Create gaps in your daily schedule to allow for unexpected events or to give you free time:** Counteracts tendency to overschedule; helps facilitate a more relaxed pace during daily activities.

9. **Leave off watch:** Curbs habitual attention to time, which reduces the feeling of being controlled by time; helps one be more relaxed during the day. (*Note:* Direct participants who insist they need a watch to place it in a pocket or handbag, so it is available with some extra effort.)

10. **Practice *thinking* about one thing at a time:** Slows racing-mind syndrome; also encourages skills in concentration and focusing.

11. **Routinely practice a meditation or relaxation exercise:** Helps to develop a relaxation response, which can be called on in times of stress.

12. **Listen to soothing music for 30 minutes and do nothing else:** Encourages relaxation, slowing of the mind, and focusing skills.

13. **Practice focusing on the process, rather than just the completion of a task:** Encourages focus on the present rather than the future (i.e., the finish). Also allows for experiencing the process, which may include some pleasurable or joyful moments. Facilitates the retention of memories of the process.

14. **Try to schedule your morning before work so it is not rushed; ideally, give yourself a little idle time:** Allows the day to start with a more relaxed pace, which can often influence the pace of the day; gives feelings of control, because rushing makes one feel out of control.

15. **Tape record conversations at dinner with the family and listen to yourself:** Aids in development of self-monitor, helps "seeing" oneself as others do; this enhances understanding of others' responses.

16. **Take small breaks during long periods of work:** Allows more effective management of pace and tension of work; encourages mental rest and refreshes one's energy level.

14

THE RELAXATION RESPONSE: USE WITH CARDIAC PATIENTS

RICHARD FRIEDMAN, PATRICIA MYERS, SHARON KRASS, and HERBERT BENSON

From time immemorial, it has been suspected that there is an important relationship between psychological stress and cardiovascular disease. Even the ancient philosophers appreciated that strong emotions, especially anger and anxiety, bring with them physiological reactions that can adversely affect both psychological and physical well-being. Consider the following observations: "But the present world is a different one. Grief, calamity, and evil cause inner bitterness . . . there is disobedience and rebellion. . . . Evil influences strike from early morning until late at night . . . they injure the mind and reduce its intelligence and they also injure the muscles and the flesh." Despite the contemporary tone of these comments, they were made 4,600 years ago in China (Huang, 2,697 B.C./ 1966). Although the immutable relationship between psychological events and physical health was consistently appreciated throughout history, it took the seventeenth-century English physician, William Harvey, to describe the special relationship between emotions and the cardiovascular system. In 1628, Harvey offered the following, now famous, case history:

> A strong man who, having received an injury and affront from one more powerful than himself, and upon whom he could not have his revenge, was so overcome with hatred and spite and passion, which he yet communicated to no one, that at last he fell into a strange distemper, suffering from extreme oppression and pain of the heart and

363

breast [from which the patient shortly died]. (Harvey, 1628, pp. 172–173)

There is an important symmetry to this stress–cardiovascular relationship. That is, calmness or relaxation may have beneficial effects on the cardiovascular system. Despite the historic hypothesized association among stress, relaxation, and cardiovascular events, only recently have attempts been made to systematically and empirically determine the veracity of these putative relationships. This volume is intended to broadly examine the significance of these relationships against the background of current scientific research. The goals of this chapter are much more circumscribed. The relaxation response is defined, the rationale for its use with cardiac patients is described, and finally, evidence supporting its incorporation into comprehensive cardiac care is presented.

THE RELAXATION RESPONSE

The relaxation response is believed to be an integrated hypothalamus response that results in a generalized decrease in sympathetic nervous system arousal. Hess first described the reaction as the *trophotropic response* and found through his experiments on cats that it could be elicited by electrically stimulating the anterior hypothalamus (Hess, 1957). Stimulation of what Hess termed the *trophotropic zone* resulted in signs of reduced sympathetic nervous system arousal, such as decreased muscle tension, blood pressure, and respiration. This trophotropic response, or relaxation response, was the opposite of what he termed *ergotropic reactions*, which increased sympathetic nervous system arousal and prepared the body for emergencies. The ergotropic reaction corresponds to the heightened state of sympathetic nervous system arousal first described by Walter B. Cannon and popularly known as the *fight-or-flight response* (Cannon, 1914).

Cannon observed that when most animals in the wild are faced with life-threatening situations, their bodies respond with a predictable physiologic arousal pattern, which prepares them to either fight a threat or run away from it. The response prepares the body for vigorous muscular activity by stimulating physiological changes to facilitate a high level of functioning of the skeletal muscles. Within the cardiovascular system, sympathetic nervous system arousal increases heart rate, increases contractile force, and constricts arteries. A rapid heart beat increases the rate of blood flow to the muscles to meet their demand for increased oxygen, nutrients, and waste removal. Vasoconstriction of the surface arteries helps to minimize blood loss in the event of an injury. The combined effect of elevated cardiac output and peripheral vasoconstriction causes arterial blood pressure to rise. Blood platelet activity also increases, to prepare the body for a potential injury that might result in blood loss (Grignani et al., 1991). Sympathetic nervous system stimulation causes the platelets to change shape and secrete a variety of chemicals designed to constrict and repair damaged vessels, both of which tend to reduce bleeding. The increased sympathetic nervous system activity responsible for the physiological sequelae associated with the fight-or-flight response is mediated by the release of norepinephrine at myoneural junctions and by the release of epinephrine by the adrenal medullae (Guyton, 1991). Acutely, blood pressure rises and heart rate increases during such periods of stress. It has been hypothesized that if such stress-induced increases in blood pressure and heart rate are repeatedly or persistently elicited but not used for running or fighting, then chronic cardiovascular damage may ensue.

The fight-or-flight response was necessary for primitive man's survival when confronted by wild beasts. Today, the same response is stimulated to varying degrees when a person is faced with everyday stresses. It has been suggested that repeated or prolonged elicitation of the fight-or-flight response can contribute to cardiac disease (see Eliot, 1992, for a review of this perspective).

The relaxation response is the behavioral and physiological opposite of the fight-or-flight response. An examination of the early experimental work of Cannon (1914) and Hess (1957)—combined with the more recent observations of Wallace, Benson, and Wilson (1971) and Wallace and Benson (1972)—suggests an important symmetrical relationship between the stress-induced flight-or-flight response and the relaxation response. Whereas the fight-or-flight response involves central and peripheral nervous system changes that prepare the organism for action, the relaxation response involves central and peripheral nervous system changes that prepare the organism for calmness and behavioral inactivity. Whereas repeated or prolonged elicitation of the fight-or-flight response has been implicated in pathogenesis of medical illness related to stress and arousal, repeated or prolonged elicitation of the relaxation response has been implicated in prevention or amelioration of stress-related disease. Finally, there are numerous psychological events that could automatically elicit the fight-or-flight response. Perception of physical danger is one such event. However, in today's world, ego threats associated with being kept waiting in line or on the phone, the perception of disrespect, or time pressures can also automatically elicit the fight-or-flight response. Similarly, there are numerous ways to elicit the relaxation response. Progressive muscle relaxation, focused attention, yoga, meditation, prayer (Benson, Beary, & Carol, 1974), or even repetitive exercise (Benson, Dryer, & Hartley, 1978) all can result in the same physiological response pattern labeled the *relaxation response* (Benson & Stuart, 1992).

The earliest attempts to formally examine the physiology of the relaxation response were conducted on meditators. In New Delhi, Anand,

Chhina, and Singh (1961) examined a yoga practitioner as he was confined in a sealed metal box. Through meditation, the yogi was able to markedly reduce his oxygen consumption and carbon dioxide elimination. In 1966, two Japanese scientists, Kasamatsu and Hirai, at the University of Tokyo, found that during meditation Zen monks could increase their cortical-alpha-wave activity (i.e., slow their brain waves). These findings supported the general hypothesis that certain behavioral, that is, meditative, practices could result in important central and peripheral nervous system changes. Furthermore, these physiological changes were in the opposite direction of those observed during periods of stress. Such findings suggested to Western researchers that individuals could possibly learn to change what had been considered the involuntary activity of the autonomic nervous system. This had important clinical implications. Activation of the sympathetic branch of the autonomic nervous system had been considered an automatic reaction to the perception of stress. Because hyperreactivity of the sympathetic branch is considered an important risk factor for cardiovascular disease, the ability to bring these reactions under voluntary control could have important implications for the development and treatment of these problems.

Benson and his colleagues were among the first to study the physiology of meditation using Western experimental standards and among the first to describe the potential utility of meditative practices in medicine. For example, Wallace et al. (1971) studied 36 volunteers at Harvard University and the University of California at Irvine. Participants served as their own controls and spent time during the experiment in both meditative and nonmeditative states. Measurements of blood pressure, heart rate, rectal temperature, skin resistance, and electroencephalographic events were taken at 10-minute intervals. Relative to sitting quietly, decreases in oxygen consumption, carbon dioxide elimination, respiratory rates, minute ventilation (the amount of air inhaled and exhaled by the lungs in a 1-minute period), and arterial blood lactate levels (an indication of anaerobic metabolism) were recorded during meditation (see Figure 1). These acute changes are all compatible with reduced sympathetic nervous system activity (Wallace & Benson, 1972).

More recent and direct evidence of the effect of the relaxation response on central nervous system indexes of arousal has been presented by Jacobs, Benson, and Friedman (1993). This study examined the efficacy of a multifactor behavioral intervention for chronic sleep-onset insomnia. The intervention included education about sleep (e.g., stages and sleep architecture) and sleep hygiene (e.g., refraining from use of alcohol, caffeine, and nicotine in the evening), sleep scheduling, and modified stimulus control (using the bed for sleep only). Patients were taught relaxation-response techniques and were instructed to practice relaxation at bedtime. Results showed that compared with normal sleepers, the insomnia patients showed a greater reduction in sleep-onset latency. The most important

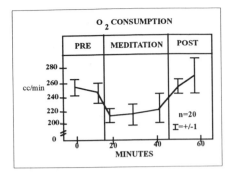

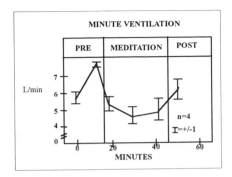

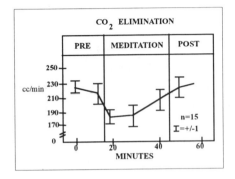

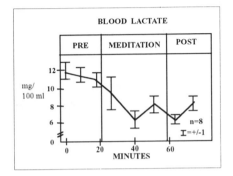

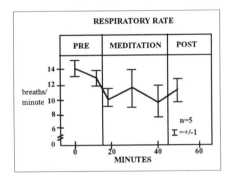

Figure 1. Some of the acute effects of the relaxation response.

result, however, was that the insomnia group showed a greater reduction in cortical arousal, as assessed by electroencephalograph power spectra analyses. More specifically, a reduction in cortical arousal was observed from pre- to posttreatment. It is probable that the relaxation-response training mediated the reductions in cortical arousal. Furthermore, these reductions in cortical arousal were likely responsible for the dramatic reductions in sleep-onset latency obtained in the study. These results, although obtained on people with insomnia, support the contention that regular elicitation of the relaxation response results in physiological changes that are opposite in direction (i.e., reduced cortical arousal) to those observed during the fight-or-flight response (i.e., increased cortical arousal).

The study by Jacobs and his coworkers affords the opportunity to address a common misconception about the physiological and therapeutic aspects of the relaxation response, specifically, its relationship to sleep. It has been suggested by Benson (1975) and others that regular elicitation of the relaxation response would result in significant and beneficial physiological changes. However, if the physiological changes associated with elicitation of the relaxation response were the same as those associated with sleep, then what extra benefits could be expected above and beyond those derived from sleeping? Actually, the physiological changes associated with the relaxation response and those associated with sleep have little resemblance. As indicated in Figure 2, whereas oxygen consumption drops rapidly within the first few minutes of elicitation of the relaxation response (in this case through meditation), during sleep, the consumption of oxygen decreases appreciably only after several hours. During sleep, the concentration of carbon dioxide in the blood increases significantly, indicating a

O_2 CONSUMPTION DURING SLEEP AND THE RELAXATION RESPONSE

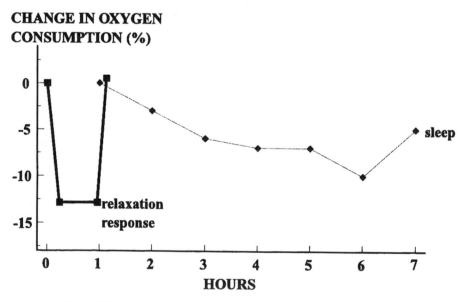

Figure 2. Time differences in oxygen consumption during elicitation of the relaxation response and sleep.

reduction in respiration. There is a slight increase in the acidity of the blood, which is due to the decrease in ventilation and not to a change in metabolism as occurs during meditation. The electrical conductivity of the skin tends to increase during sleep, suggesting a reduction in sympathetic activity. However, the rate and magnitude of sleep-related increases in skin conductivity are much smaller that those observed during meditation (Das & Gastaut, 1957; Hawkins, Puryeur, Wallace, Deal, & Thomas, 1962; Tart, 1967; see Wallace & Benson, 1972, for a review). Hence, it seems that regular elicitation of the relaxation response results in a pattern of sympathetically mediated physiological changes that are not the same as those observed during sleep. Similarly, Jacobs and Lubar (1989) have demonstrated that the central nervous system effects of elicitation of the relaxation response are different than those observed during sleep.

On the basis of the early physiological observations, Benson and others began to examine the potential medical benefits of regular elicitation of the relaxation response. The research literature indicates that elicitation of the relaxation response is effective in the treatment of other noncardiac-related conditions—including chronic pain (e.g., Caudill, Schnable, Zuttermeister, Benson, & Friedman, 1991), insomnia (e.g., Jacobs et al., 1993), the side effects of cancer chemotherapy (e.g., Vasterling, Jenkins, Tope, & Burish, 1993), the side effects of AIDS therapy (e.g., Carson, 1993), hostility (e.g., Muskatel, Woolfolk, Carrington, Lehrer, & McCann, 1984), premenstrual syndrome (e.g., Goodale, Domar, & Benson, 1990), infertility (e.g., Domar, Seibel, & Benson, 1990), surgical preparation (e.g., Mandle et al., 1990), anxiety (e.g., Fasko, Osborne, Hall, Boerstler, & Kornfeld, 1992) and depression (e.g., Blanchard et al., 1986).[1] One controlled study indicated that cognitive–behavioral stress-management training, which includes relaxation training, may result in positive changes in immunological functioning in recently notified HIV-positive gay men. Furthermore, statistical analyses suggested that the positive psychological and immunological effects may be attributable to, among other things, relaxation skills learned (Antoni et al., 1991). There is even some evidence that the survival rate among breast cancer patients may be positively influenced

---

[1]The effects of elicitation of the relaxation response on anxiety and depression require additional comment. These two disorders are usually considered psychological problems as opposed to somatic or biomedical problems. Without addressing the appropriateness of making this type of distinction between mental and physical illness, it is worth pointing out that an American Psychiatric Association task force on treatment strategies for psychiatric disturbances clearly endorses the use of relaxation training for both anxiety and depression (American Psychiatric Association, 1989). This endorsement was based on a review of the literature that was supportive of the efficacy of relaxation training for symptom reduction. The adjunctive use of relaxation training with medically ill patients for whom anxiety and depression are precipitants or consequences of the illness is a logical extension of this endorsement.

by behavioral treatment programs that include regular elicitation of the relaxation response (Fawzy & Fawzy, 1994).

ELICITATION OF THE RELAXATION RESPONSE

There are numerous ways to elicit the relaxation response, including meditation, progressive muscle relaxation, autogenic training, yoga, exercise, and hypnosis. Although we have frequently commented on the commonality of physiological response to a variety of instructional sets (Benson & Stuart, 1992), the issue is still confusing to some. In clinical practice, we have found it very useful to ask patients to elicit the relaxation response in a way that is compatible with their belief system and customary practices. Hence, a religious patient might be comfortable using a familiar repetitive prayer, whereas a patient interested in physical exercise might be comfortable eliciting the relaxation response during repetitive exercise. This way, adherence to relaxation regimens will be maximized. In our experience, the manner in which the response is elicited is immaterial because the psychological and physiological results are the same. The clinician's responsibility is to help the patient develop a personally relevant and effective technique. Two components appear to be absolutely necessary: mental focusing and the adoption of a passive attitude toward distracting thoughts. As long as the technique used includes these two basic steps, the relaxation response will occur.

Benson et al. (1975) incorporated elements common to various historical strategies and developed the following instructional set for eliciting the response:

1. Sit quietly in a comfortable position and close your eyes.
2. Deeply relax all your muscles, beginning at your feet and progressing up to your face. Keep them deeply relaxed.
3. Breathe through your nose. Become aware of your breathing. As you breathe out, say the word "one" silently to yourself. For example, breathe in . . . out, one; in . . . out, one; etc. Continue for 20 minutes. You may open your eyes to check the time, but do not use an alarm. When you finish, sit quietly for several minutes at first with closed eyes and later with opened eyes.
4. Do not worry about whether you are successful in achieving a deep level of relaxation. Maintain a passive attitude and permit relaxation to occur at its own pace. Expect other thoughts. When distracting thoughts occur, ignore them by thinking "Oh well" and continue repeating "one." With practice, the response should come with little effort. Practice

the technique once or twice daily, but not within two hours after any meal, since the digestive processes seem to interfere with the subjective changes.

For many Americans, formal relaxation is simply outside their definition of medical treatment, and therefore, they will not be enthusiastic about practicing. When this resistance is coupled with financial responsibility for learning techniques that elicit the relaxation response, adherence can be depressingly low. However, it is the clinician's responsibility to engage the patient by communicating that formal relaxation training can initially be perceived as difficult. Clinical experience suggests that after some practice, it is frequently perceived as a brief and welcome respite from the stresses and strains of everyday life. Furthermore, if patients can be motivated to get through the initial period of doubt, cynicism, and difficulty, regular elicitation of the relaxation response can become a self-reinforcing daily activity.

This issue of stress as a perceived event requires some discussion at this juncture. We have not offered a formal definition of stress in this chapter because the issue of stress itself is a hotly debated topic and could not have been adequately discussed in this forum. However, we consider stress to result from any dangerous or threatening situation that may require behavioral adjustment. When such an adjustment occurs, the fight-or-flight response tends to occur even if running away or fighting are not appropriate responses. Much of the stress in a person's life is due to the perception of a necessity for change even though no adjustment is necessary. *Cognitive restructuring*, *reframing*, and other terms are used in stress management to describe a process whereby patients are helped to reduce the number of events that are perceived as stressful. Elicitation of the relaxation-response results in peripheral nervous system changes that are opposite to those observed during stress (Wallace et al., 1971). In addition, as we have suggested, elicitation of the relaxation response results in central nervous system changes as well. It has been suggested by Benson—and backed up by some experimental evidence (e.g., Kutz, Borysenko, & Benson, 1985; Orme-Johnson & Haynes, 1981)—that these central effects may facilitate the cognitive-restructuring process (see Benson, 1987). However, the evidence that elicitation of the relaxation response facilitates cognitive change is still tentative. At any rate, the use of the relaxation response in stress management for cardiovascular disease or for any other illness should be considered part of a total stress-management program. It has not been suggested that the relaxation response alone will necessarily result in maximal alteration in perceptions or will result in behavioral changes. Rather it has been suggested that using the relaxation response along with cognitive restructuring and behavior modification will maximize the efficacy of the latter interventions (see Benson & Stuart, 1992).

THE RATIONALE FOR THE USE OF THE RELAXATION RESPONSE WITH CARDIAC PATIENTS

The Physiological Rationale

The physiological rationale for the use of the relaxation response with cardiac patients is straightforward and is based on the symmetrical relationship between the stress response and the relaxation response. To the extent that stress-induced increases in sympathetic nervous system activity contribute to cardiovascular disease, relaxation-response–induced decreases in sympathetic nervous system activity might prevent and treat cardiac disease (see chap. 3 of this volume for a review).

The Relaxation Response and Cardiovascular Disease

The data regarding the effects of stress management, in general, and the efficacy of the relaxation response, in particular, in decreasing cardiac disease are limited. A Medline database search of articles published within the last 4 years listed 76 related to myocardial infarction and psychological stress. However, only 6 related relaxation-response training with myocardial infarction.

Although the literature on relaxation and cardiovascular disease is small, the relationship between relaxation and one risk factor for cardiovascular disease, namely hypertension, has been extensively investigated. Indeed, the use of the relaxation response as a treatment for hypertension is perhaps the most extensively evaluated topic in psychosomatic medicine. The efficacy of the relaxation response on the treatment of hypertension remains under debate. A meta-analysis by Kaufmann et. al. (1988) noted that studies that try to evaluate the effectiveness of behavioral interventions among hypertensive patients are generally confounded by the fact that patients with higher blood pressures are medicated. Studies need to analyze treatment results from medicated and nonmedicated patients separately. Furthermore, a demonstration of an effect of behavioral interventions would require an analysis that would account for the effects of medications throughout treatment and follow-up. Kaufmann et al. also suggested that a true measure of treatment effectiveness may be limited by several factors, including the fact that people evaluated in outcome studies are frequently only mildly hypertensive and the fact that results showing reductions in blood pressure are often based on entry-level readings. (The low entry-level blood pressures would preclude observation of substantial reductions in blood pressure following treatment.) Furthermore, Kaufmann et al. indicated that studies in their meta-analysis did not account for individual differences among hypertensive people and suggested that if such differences were considered, results of treatment effectiveness may have been amplified.

Another meta-analysis reported by Eisenberg et al. (1993) concluded that cognitive interventions (e.g., biofeedback, relaxation, or meditation) for essential hypertension are better than no treatment at all but not more effective than credible sham interventions or self-monitoring alone. However, a more recent meta-analysis came to a much different conclusion (Linden & Chambers, 1994). Linden and Chambers found that nondrug approaches to the treatment of hypertension, including cognitive–behavioral psychological therapy such as relaxation techniques, were "particularly effective and did not differ from drug treatment in observed raw effect sizes for systolic blood pressure" (p. 35). Drug therapies were initiated at higher initial blood pressure levels than nondrug treatments, and after adjustment for these initial pressure differences, the effect of individualized psychological treatment matched the effect of drug treatment for both systolic and diastolic blood pressure. Linden and Chambers concluded that nondrug therapies such as relaxation approaches may be more effective than commonly believed.

Clearly, the scientific community has not reached a general consensus regarding the effects of relaxation as a treatment for hypertension. As Benson, Stuart, and Friedman (1994) pointed out, meta-analyses such as these are important but do not address the issue from a clinical perspective. Such analyses, of necessity, examine the independent efficacy of relaxation techniques and other therapies alone. However, in clinical practice, relaxation approaches are integrated with other stress-management techniques, behavior-modification approaches, and pharmacotherapy. Furthermore, none of these meta-analyses concentrated on the great variability of response exhibited by hypertensive patients to any treatment intervention.

Hypertensive patients vary widely in the underlying pathophysiology of their condition. Hence, it is unlikely that relaxation-response training or any other intervention would be universally effective. For example, weight loss is a particularly useful intervention for some obese hypertensive patients. However, it would certainly not be very effective for nonobese hypertensive patients. Yet, in many studies, the efficacy of relaxation procedures has been evaluated without regard to individual differences (Friedman, Siegal, Jacobs, & Benson, 1992). Jacob et al. (1992) emphasized this point in a study evaluating the effects of relaxation training for hypertensive patients. The only patients who exhibited significant reductions in blood pressure after relaxation training were those whose blood pressure tended to peak in the physician's office. Thus, these "white-coat" hypertensive patients may be particularly good candidates for relaxation training.

The number of patients with white-coat hypertension may be substantial. Pickering et al. (1988) estimated that as many as 20% of all hypertensives may exhibit this effect. The point here is that responses vary. Relaxation-response training may be an effective treatment for some hypertensive patients. Relaxation-response training may be a more effective treatment for subcategories of patients suffering from other kinds of cardiovascular diseases as well. Biopsychosocial characteristics need to be identified that would be predictors of those subpopulations most likely to respond to relaxation-response interventions.

The Relaxation Response and Cardiac Reactivity

As indicated above, hypertension has been studied in relation to relaxation techniques more than has any other cardiovascular disease. However, some important studies have examined the effects of the relaxation response on cardiac events directly. Benson, Alexander, and Feldman (1975) examined the effects of elicitation of the relaxation response on premature ventricular contractions in patients with proven, stable ischemic heart disease. They observed that after 4 weeks, 8 of the 11 patients exhibited a reduction in the frequency of premature ventricular contractions.

Lown et al. (1976) published an important case study regarding a 39-year-old man who twice experienced ventricular fibrillation and numerous ventricular premature beats. Given the normality of his coronary arteries and the lack of impaired cardiac function found on catheterization, Lown et al. concluded that the ventricular premature beats were related to "higher" nervous system activity. Significantly, these ventricular premature beats were provoked by psychological stress and reduced by meditation.

More recently, Leserman and her coworkers reported that relative to a control intervention, regular elicitation of the relaxation response before and after cardiac surgery reduced the incidence of postoperative supraventricular tachycardia ($p = .04$; Leserman, Stuart, Mamish, & Benson, 1989a). Patients who practiced the relaxation training also reported greater reductions in psychological tension ($p = .04$) and anger ($p = .04$) compared with controls. However, because the experimental group began with higher tension levels relative to the control group, these results may have been due to a regression to the mean. Still the results support the notion that relaxation-response training may be helpful in lowering the anxiety levels of surgical patients.

Physiological effects of the relaxation response were examined in a recent study that evaluated cardiac parasympathetic tone by measuring the frequency components of heart-rate variability (Sakakibara, Takeuchi, & Hayano, 1994). Elicitation of the relaxation response was associated with enhanced cardiac parasympathetic tone. Enhanced vagal tone (i.e., an index of increased parasympathetic activity) represents a potentially beneficial clinical event because such enhancements might result in cardiovascular events opposed to those that occur coincidently with sympathetic stimulation. Heart function and respiration were monitored in 16 college students, who were assigned to either a relaxation-response group or a resting control group. Autogenic training was used to elicit the relaxation response. Specifically, participants in the relaxation-response condition were given audiotaped instructions to calm their feelings and to increase the feelings of heaviness and warmth in muscles. Results showed that whereas there was no difference in respiration between the relaxation-response and control groups, the relaxation-response group showed an increase in the high-frequency component of heart-rate variability, which is an indication of increased cardiac parasympathetic tone.

These results are important when considered in conjunction with the prior literature. There is considerable clinical evidence that reduced cardiac parasympathetic tone is an important risk factor in cardiac disease. Myers et al. (1986) and Martin et al. (1987) demonstrated that a decrease of heart-rate variability (i.e., an indication of decreased parasympathetic tone) was associated with an increased risk of sudden cardiac death. Furthermore, a reduction in heart-rate variability is a significant predictor of mortality during the first 4 years after an acute myocardial infarction (Kleiger, Miller, Bigger, Moss, & the Multicenter Post-Infarction Research Group, 1987). These observations, relating decreased heart-rate variability and decreased parasympathetic tone, support the hypothesis that an increase in cardiac vagal tone may help prevent cardiovascular disease. Therefore, results that indicate that elicitation of the relaxation response increases heart-rate variability and enhances parasympathetic tone are relevant.

In addition to laboratory studies on the effects of relaxation training on cardiac function, studies have examined this relationship in real-life settings. For example, Toivanen, Lansimies, Jokela, & Hanninen (1993) examined the effect of relaxation approaches on cardiac reactivity related to work strain. Ninety-eight female employees of either a hospital cleaning unit or a bank were randomly assigned to either a relaxation intervention or a control group. For 6 months, relaxation training sessions were conducted in 15-minute sessions during work breaks once each day. A microcomputer-based system was used to record heart-rate variability during periods of relaxation and stress at the work site. Participants were trained in deep breathing exercises, tension and relaxation of the abdominal muscles, and deep relaxation with focus on calm breathing. Participants were asked to practice relaxation at other times during the day and before falling asleep. In addition, half the experimental participants participated in group relaxation sessions three times per week for the entire 6-month training period, whereas the other half participated in only four group sessions. Increases in heart-rate variability were recorded from pretreatment to posttreatment and compliance to continue practicing was enhanced in the group that participated in support sessions throughout the 6-month period.

It is important to emphasize that regular elicitation of the relaxation response results in chronic physiological changes. That is, the physiological benefits associated with elicitation of the relaxation response are not restricted to periods when patients are actually eliciting the response. The chronic nature of relaxation-mediated physiological changes (i.e., reduced responsivity to plasma norepinephrine) was experimentally demonstrated by Hoffman and his coworkers (Hoffman et al., 1982) and by Morrell and Hollandsworth (1986).

In summary, numerous studies implicate psychological stress as an important stimulus that can contribute to pathogenesis of sympathetically mediated cardiovascular events. Furthermore, there is a consistent literature indicating that elicitation of the relaxation response results in reduced sympathetic activity and a small number of controlled studies that indicate that elicitation of the relaxation response results in cardiovascular alterations such as increased parasympathetic activity that may be beneficial (Sakakibara et al., 1994). However, more studies are required to document the actual clinical benefits associated with relaxation-mediated changes in autonomic activity.

The Psychological Rationale

The psychological rationale for the use of the relaxation response with cardiac patients is that regular elicitation of the relaxation response reduces negative psychological symptoms. For example, Leserman et al. (1989b) demonstrated that in hypertension patients, a behavioral intervention program was successful at reducing blood pressure levels and psychological symptoms from pre- to posttreatment. The program included training in elicitation of the relaxation response as well as nutritional counseling, exercise, and stress management. In addition to significant decreases in systolic and diastolic blood pressure levels, there were reductions in measures of anxiety and depression. Total psychological symptoms as measured on the Symptom Distress Checklist (Derogatis, 1977) were also significantly lowered ($p < .01$). Improvements were maintained at 5-year follow-up. As previously indicated, there is an extensive literature substantiating the beneficial effects of relaxation training in reducing negative psychological symptoms (see American Psychiatric Association, 1989).

Psychological effects of relaxation-response training in cardiac patients were reported in a recent controlled study by Trzcieniecka-Green and Steptoe (1994), in which a 12-week relaxation-based stress-management program was evaluated. Participants were 78 patients who had myocardial infarction, coronary artery bypass surgery, or coronary angioplasty. Reductions in chest pain and symptoms of anxiety and depression were found pre- to posttreatment. By means of standardized assessments, improvements were also observed in psychological well-being, activities in daily living, social activity, quality of interactions, and satisfaction with sexual relationships. Improvements were maintained to a large degree at 6-month follow-up.

The Behavior-Modification Rationale

In addition to the beneficial effects of relaxation training on physical symptoms, psychological symptoms, and quality of life, there is another compelling reason for its use with cardiovascular patients. Relaxation-response training may facilitate the realization and maintenance of the behavior-modification goals that are core components of primary and secondary cardiac disease prevention programs. One important way in which relaxation-response training may help maintain behavioral goals is by reducing the *stress disinhibition effect*, which describes the observation that increases in stress and anxiety in turn increase the likelihood of patients engaging in acute anxiety-reducing behaviors, such as smoking and eating high-fat foods (Marlatt, 1985). Relaxation training has been demonstrated to be a very effective acute coping strategy for anxiety reduction (see American Psychiatric Association, 1989). Consequently, to the extent that patients can reduce their stress, they may reduce the likelihood of engaging in unhealthy anxiety-reducing behaviors. This point requires some amplification. Evidence suggests that many patterns of self-regulation break down when people are under stress. Presumably, this stress-induced breakdown in self-regulatory capacity is the result of a depletion in the cognitive and emotional resources required to maintain self-regulation (Baumeister, Heatherton, & Tice, 1993). Coping with stress and anxiety has a "psychic cost" that takes the form of lowered self-regulatory capacity (e.g., Glass, Singer, & Friedman, 1969). As people become more stressed and anxious, they are more likely to increase smoking, break diets, abuse alcohol or drugs, or otherwise engage in immediately gratifying, but ultimately damaging, behaviors (Heatherton & Renn, 1995).

To the extent that relaxation-response training reduces stress and anxiety, the likelihood of these stress-related relapses occurring is reduced. An example was recently reported by Wynd (1992), who examined relapse behavior in 76 smokers who had completed smoking-cessation programs. Failure rates for smoking-cessation programs are often 60%–80%, and stress has been identified as a major factor contributing to relapse. Smokers were assigned to either a relaxation-training ($n = 39$) or control group ($n = 37$). The groups met for 3 months after completion of smoking-cessation programs. The relaxation-based intervention included guided-imagery training, with audiotapes provided for practice at home. Participants in the relaxation group were asked to practice for 20 minutes a day, for a minimum of 4 times per week. Relaxation-trained participants showed reduced stress as measured by the Perceived Stress Scale (Cohen, Kamarck, & Mermelstein, 1983), enhanced imagery effectiveness, and perhaps most important, greater smoking abstinence, as compared with control participants not exposed to the relaxation training. At 3 months posttreatment, only 28% of the relaxation-trained participants relapsed. However, 49% of the control participants had relapsed.

THE RELAXATION RESPONSE IN COMPREHENSIVE CARE

Few studies have provided evidence that elicitation of the relaxation response itself reduces the frequency of major cardiac events such as myocardial infarction. However, the physiological rationale is compelling. Researchers (e.g., Eliot, 1992) generally conclude that psychological stress can cause sympathetically mediated events that are relevant to cardiovascular pathophysiology. Furthermore, there is evidence that regular elicitation of the relaxation response results in reduced sympathetic activity, which has relevance to cardiovascular disease. The absence of large-scale epidemiology-type studies examining the effects of elicitation of the relaxation response on the incidence of myocardial infarctions is likely the result of funding decisions. To conduct such studies would be very expensive and, from a methodological perspective, very hard to control.

In addition to the physiological rationale, there is another good reason to use relaxation-response training in comprehensive cardiac care: It makes logical sense to patients. In a recent study by Tofler et al. (1990), when patients were asked what stimulus most likely triggered their myocardial infarctions, the most frequently mentioned event was mental stress. Patients expect that mental stress will be addressed as part of their cardiac care, and relaxation-response training is a logical component of such treatment.

In virtually all studies on comprehensive care, it is very difficult to separate the degree to which relaxation training alone is responsible for beneficial cardiovascular outcomes independent of changes in diet and exercise. The most successful cardiovascular programs focus on all three components because they seem to work synergistically. For example, the Lifestyle Heart Trial (Ornish et al., 1990), described in chapter 9, is a popular, scientifically based intervention that combines all three components without any attempt to assess independent contributions.

The integrative perspective was emphasized in a study in which relaxation-response training appeared to enhance the effects of other therapy components. Van Dixhoorn, Duivenvoorden, Pool, and Verhage (1990) examined the psychological impact of exercise combined with relaxation-response training and exercise alone in a group of 156 myocardial infarction patients. Patients were randomized into a group that was given physical exercise training alone or a group given both physical exercise and relaxation training. Patients completed the State–Trait Anxiety Inventory (a 40-item standardized anxiety inventory; Van Der Ploeg, Defares, & Spielberger, 1980), a Sleeping Habits Questionnaire (a 10-item questionnaire about hours of sleep and sleep quality; Visser, Hofman, & Kumar, 1979), and a Functional Complaints Questionnaire (a 25-item inventory that questions participants about complaints frequently mentioned by cardiac patients). Also administered was the Heart Patients Psychological Questionnaire (Erdman, 1981) which includes four scales: (a) Well-Being (includes statements such as "I feel at ease nowadays" and "I feel healthy"), (b) Subjective Invalidity (e.g., feelings of inadequacy and an inability to fulfill role function; includes items such as "I could do a lot more work formerly" "I don't have enough stamina"), (c) Displeasure (includes items such as "I'm often out of sorts without knowing why"), and (d) Social Inhibition (includes items such as "I don't like having a lot of people around me"). Patients in the exercise-only group exhibited no change in psychological measures, whereas the group given relaxation training exhibited reductions in anxiety and feelings of invalidity. Physical outcomes, as measured by exercise testing, also distinguished the two groups. More positive physical outcomes were recorded in the relaxation-training and exercise group compared with the exercise-only group.

Note that in much the same way as stress management should not be separated from exercise and low-fat diet regimens in the treatment of cardiac disease, relaxation-response training should not be taught independently from the other core aspects of stress management.

CONCLUSION

The relaxation response is a physiological state associated with a reduction in sympathetic nervous system activity. Regular elicitation of the relaxation response has resulted in the remediation of a wide variety of medical symptoms. The data on independent effects of the relaxation response alone on cardiac disease are not complete, and its use along with other risk-factor-reduction interventions is most appropriate. There is some suggestion that relaxation training alone may help some patients with hypertension (e.g., Jacob et al., 1992). However, given (a) the inherent logic of its inclusion in comprehensive cardiac care, (b) the degree to which patients perceive stress as a causative factor in cardiac disease, (c) the known effects of the relaxation response on the sympathetic and parasympathetic nervous systems, (d) its beneficial effects on negative psychological symptoms, and (e) its positive effects on behavior modification goals, relaxation training should be an essential component of cardiac disease prevention and cardiac care.

REFERENCES

American Psychiatric Association. (1989). Treatment of psychiatric disorders. *Task report of the American Psychiatric Association* (pp. 1856, 2429–2430). Washington, DC: Author.

Anand, B. K., Chhina, G. S., & Singh, B. (1961). Some aspects of electroencephalographic studies in Yogis. *Electroencephalography and Clinical Neurophysiology, 13*, 452–456.

Antoni, M. H., Baggett, L., Ironson, G., LaPerriere, A., August, S., Klimas, N. Schneiderman, N., & Fletcher, M. A. (1991). Cognitive–behavioral stress management intervention buffers distress responses and immunologic changes following notification of HIV–1 seropositivity. *Journal of Consulting and Clinical Psychology, 59*, 906–915.

Baumeister, R. F., Heatherton, T. F., & Tice, D. M. (1993). When ego threats lead to self-regulation failure: Negative consequences of high self-esteem. *Journal of Personality and Social Psychology, 64*, 141–156.

Benson, H. (1975). *The relaxation response.* New York: Morrow.

Benson, H. (1987). *Your maximum mind.* New York: Random House.

Benson, H., Alexander, S., & Feldman, C. L. (1975). Decreased premature ventricular contractions through use of the relaxation response in patients with stable ischaemic heart-disease. *Lancet, 2*, 380–382.

Benson, H., Beary, J. F., & Carol, M. P. (1974). The relaxation response. *Psychiatry, 37*, 37–45.

Benson, H., Dryer, T., & Hartley, L. H. (1978). Decreased oxygen consumption during exercise with elicitation of the relaxation response. *Journal of Human Stress, 4*, 38–42.

Benson, H., & Stuart, E. M. (1992). *The wellness book.* New York: Simon & Schuster.

Benson, H., Stuart, E. M., & Friedman, R. (1994). Non-pharmacologic treatment of hypertension [Letter to the editor]. *Annals of Internal Medicine, 230*, 91.

Blanchard, E. B., Andrasik, F., Appelbaum, K. A., Evans, D. D., Myers, P., & Barron, K. D. (1986). Three studies of the psychologic changes in chronic headache patients associated with biofeedback and relaxation therapies. *Psychosomatic Medicine, 48*, 73–83.

Cannon, W. B. (1914). The emergency function of the adrenal medulla in pain and the major emotions. *American Journal of Physiology, 33*, 356–372.

Carson, V. B. (1993). Prayer, meditation, exercise, and special diets: Behaviors of the hardy person with HIV/AIDS. *Journal of the Association of Nurses in AIDS Care, 4*, 18–28.

Caudill, M., Schnable, R., Zuttermeister, P., Benson, H., & Friedman, R. (1991). Decreased clinic utilization by chronic pain patients after behavioral medicine intervention. *Clinical Journal of Pain, 7*, 305–310.

Cohen, S., Kamarck, T., & Mermelstein, R. (1983) A global measure of perceived stress. *Journal of Health and Social Behavior, 24*, 385–396.

Das, N. N., & Gastaut, H. (1957). Variations de L'activite electrique du cerveau, du coeur et des muscles squelletiques au cours de la meditation et de l'extase Yogique. [Variations of the electrical activity of the brain, the heart, and the skeletal muscles during the course of meditation and yogic trance]. *Electroencephalography and Clinical Neurophysiology* (Suppl. 6), 211–219.

Derogatis, L. R. (1977). *SCL-90 revised version manual.* Baltimore: Author.

Domar, A. D., Seibel, M. M., & Benson, H. (1990). The Mind/Body Program for Infertility: A new behavioral treatment approach for women with infertility. *Fertility and Sterility, 53,* 246–249.

Eisenberg, D. M., Delbanco, T. L., Berkey, C. S., Kaptchuk., T. J., Kupelnick, B., Kuhl, J., & Chalmers, T. C. (1993). Cognitive behavioral techniques for hypertension: Are they effective? *Annals of Internal Medicine, 118,* 964–972.

Eliot, R. S. (1992). Stress and the heart: Mechanisms, measurement, and management. *Postgraduate Medicine, 92,* 237–248.

Erdman, R. (1981). *Welberinden bij hartpatienten.* Lisse, The Netherlands: Swets & Zeitlinger.

Fasko, D., Osborne, M. R., Hall, G., Boerstler, R. W., & Kornfeld, H. (1992). Comeditation: An exploratory study of pulse and respiration rates and anxiety. *Perceptual and Motor Skills, 74,* 895–904.

Fawzy, F. I., & Fawzy, N. W. (1994). A structured psychoeducational intervention for cancer patients. *General Hospital Psychiatry, 16,* 149–192.

Friedman, R., Siegal, W. C., Jacobs, S. C., & Benson, H. (1992). Distress over the non-effect of stress [Letter to the editor]. *Journal of the American Medical Association, 268,* 198.

Glass, D. C., Singer, J. E., & Friedman, L. N. (1969). Psychic cost of adaptation to an environmental stressor. *Journal of Personality and Social Psychology, 12,* 200–210.

Goodale, I. L., Domar, A. D., & Benson, H. (1990). Alleviation of premenstrual syndrome symptoms with the relaxation response. *Obstetrics and Gynecology, 75,* 649–655.

Grignani, G., Soffiantino, F., Zucchella M., Pacchiarini, L., Tacconi, F., Bonomi, E., Pastoris, A., Shaffi, A., Fratino, P., & Tavazzi, L. (1991). Platelet activation by emotional stress in patients with coronary artery disease. *Circulation, 83*(Suppl. 2), 128–136.

Guyton, A. (1991). *Textbook of medical physiology* (8th ed.). Philadelphia: W. B. Saunders.

Harvey, W. (1928). *Anatomical studies on the motion of the heart and blood* (C. D. Leake, Trans.). Springfield, IL: Charles C Thomas. (Original work published 1628)

Hawkins, D. R., Puryeur, H. B., Wallace, C. D., Deal, W. B., & Thomas E. S. (1962). Basal skin resistance during sleep and "dreaming." *Science, 136,* 321–322.

Heatherton, T. F., & Renn, R. J. (1995). Stress and the disinhibition of behavior. *Mind/Body Medicine, 1,* 72–81.

Hess, W. R. (1957). *Functional organization of the diencephalon*. New York: Grune & Stratton.

Hoffman, J. W., Benson, H., Arns, P. A., Stainbrook, G. L., Landsbery, L., Young, J. B., & Gill, A. (1982). Reduced sympathetic nervous system responsivity associated with the relaxation response. *Science, 215*, 190–192.

Huang, T. N. C. S. W. (1966). *The yellow emperor's classic of internal medicine* (I. Veith, Trans.). Berkeley: University of California Press. (Original work ca. 2,697 B.C.)

Jacob, R. G., Shapiro, A. P., O'Hara, P., Portser, S. Kruger, A. Gatsonis, C., & Ding, Y. (1992). Relaxation therapy for hypertension: Setting-specific effects. *Psychosomatic Medicine, 54*, 87–101.

Jacobs, G. D., Benson, H., & Friedman, R. (1993). Home-based central nervous system assessment of a multifactor behavioral intervention for chronic sleep-onset insomnia. *Behavior Therapy, 24*, 159–174.

Jacobs, G. D., & Lubar, J. R. (1989). Spectral analysis of the central nervous system effects of the relaxation response elicited by autogenic training. *Behavioral Medicine, 15*, 125–132.

Kasamatsu, A., & Hirai, T. (1966) An electroencephalographic study on the Zen meditation (Zazen). *Folia Psychiatrica Neurologica Japonica, 20*, 315–336.

Kaufmann, P. G., Jacob, R. G., Ewart, C., Chesney, M. A., Mnenz, L. R., Doub, N., Mercer, W., & HIPP investigators. (1988). Hypertension intervention pooling project. *Health Psychology, 7*(Suppl.), 209–224.

Kleiger, R. E., Miller, J. P., Bigger, J. T., Jr., Moss, A. J., & the Multicenter Post-Infarction Research Group. (1987). Decreased heart rate variability and its association with increased mortality after acute myocardial infarction. *American Journal of Cardiology, 59*, 256–262.

Kutz, I., Borysenko, J. Z., & Benson, H. (1985). Meditation and psychotherapy: A rationale for the integration of dynamic psychotherapy, the relaxation response and mindfulness meditation. *American Journal of Psychiatry, 142*, 1–8.

Leserman, J., Stuart, E. M., Mamish, M. E., & Benson, H. (1989a). The efficacy of the relaxation response in preparing for cardiac surgery. *Behavioral Medicine, 15*, 111–117.

Leserman, J., Stuart, E. M., Mamish, M. E., Deckro, J. P., Beckman, R. J., Friedman, R., & Benson, H. (1989b). Nonpharmacologic intervention for hypertension: Long-term follow-up. *Journal of Cardiopulmonary Rehabilitation, 9*, 316–324.

Linden, W., & Chambers, L. (1994). Clinical effectiveness of non-drug treatment of hypertension: A meta-analysis. *Annals of Behavioral Medicine, 16*, 35–45.

Lown, B., Temte, J. V., Reich, P., Gaughan, C. Regestein, Q., & Hal, H. (1976). Basis for recurring ventricular fibrillation in the absence of coronary heart disease and its management. *New England Journal of Medicine, 294*, 623–629.

Mandle, C. L., Domar, A. D., Harrington, D. P., Leserman, J., Bozadjian, E. M., Friedman, R., & Benson, H. (1990). Relaxation response in femoral angiography. *Radiology, 174*, 737–739.

Marlatt, G. A. (1985). Relapse prevention: Theoretical rationale and overview of the model. In G. A. Marlatt & J. R. Gordon (Eds.), *Relapse prevention* (pp. 3–70). New York: Guilford Press.

Martin, G. J., Magid, N. M., Myers, G., Barnett, P. S., Schaad, J. W., Weiss, J. S., Lesch, M., & Singer, D. H. (1987). Heart rate variability and sudden death secondary to coronary artery disease during ambulatory electrocardiographic monitoring. *American Journal of Cardiology, 60,* 86–89.

Morrell, E. M., & Hollandsworth, J. G., Jr. (1986). Norepinephrine alterations under stress conditions following the regular practice of meditation. *Psychosomatic Medicine, 48,* 270–277.

Muskatel, N., Woolfolk, R. L., Carrington, P., Lehrer, P. M., & McCann, B. S. (1984). Effect of meditation training on aspects of coronary-prone behavior. *Perceptual and Motor Skills, 58,* 515–518.

Myers, G. A., Martin, G. J., Magid, N. M., Barnett, P. S., Schaad, J. W., Weiss, J. S., Lesch, M., & Singer, D. N. (1986). Power spectral analysis of heart rate variability in sudden cardiac death: Comparison to other methods. *IEEE Transactions on Biomedical Engineering, 33,* 1149–1156.

Orme-Johnson, D. W., & Haynes, C. T. (1981). EEG phase coherence, pure consciousness, creativity, and TM-Sidhi experiences. *Neuroscience, 13,* 211–217.

Ornish, D., Brown, S. E., Scherwitz, L. W., Billings, J. H., Armstrong, W. T., Ports, T. A., McLanahan, S. M., Kirkeeide, R. L., Brand, R. J., & Gould, K. L. (1990). Can lifestyle changes reverse coronary heart disease? The Lifestyle Heart Trial. *Lancet, 336,* 129–133.

Pickering, T. G., James, G. D., Boddie, D., Harshfield., G. A., Blank, A., & Laragh, J. H. (1988). How common is white coat hypertension? *Journal of the American Medical Association, 259,* 225–228.

Sakakibara, M., Takeuchi, S., & Hayano, J. (1994). Effect of relaxation training on cardiac parasympathetic tone. *Psychophysiology, 31,* 223–228.

Tart, C. T. (1967). Patterns of basal skin resistance during sleep. *Psychophysiology, 4,* 35–39.

Tofler, G. H., Stone, P. H., Maclure, M., Edelman, E., Davis, V. G., Robertson, T., Antman, E. M., & Muller, J. E. (1990). Analysis of possible triggers of acute myocardial infarction (the MILIS study). *American Journal of Cardiology, 66,* 22–27.

Toivanen, H., Lansimies, E., Jokela, V., & Hanninen, O. (1993). Impact of regular relaxation training on the cardiac autonomic nervous system of hospital cleaners and bank employees. *Scandinavian Journal of Work, Environment and Health, 19,* 319–325.

Trzcieniecka-Green, A., & Steptoe, A. (1994). Stress management in cardiac patients: A preliminary study of the predictors of improvement in quality of life. *Journal of Psychosomatic Research, 38,* 267–280.

Van Der Ploeg, H., Defares, P., & Spielberger, C. (1980). *Manual for the State–Trait Anxiety Inventory.* Lisse, The Netherlands: Swets & Zeitlinger.

Van Dixhoorn, J., Duivenvoorden, H. J., Pool, J., & Verhage, F. (1990). Psychic effects of physical training and relaxation therapy after myocardial infarction. *Journal of Psychosomatic Research, 34,* 327–337.

Vasterling J., Jenkins, R. A., Tope, D. M., & Burish, T. G. (1993). Cognitive distraction and relaxation training for the control of side effects due to cancer chemotherapy. *Journal of Behavioral Medicine, 16,* 65–80.

Visser, P., Hofman, W. F., & Kumar, A. (1979). Sleep and mood: Measuring sleep quality. In R. G. Priest, A. Pletscher, & J. Ward (Ed.), *Sleep research.* Lancaster, PA: MTP Press.

Wallace, R. K., & Benson, H. (1972). The physiology of meditation. *Scientific American, 226,* 84–90.

Wallace, R. K., Benson, H., & Wilson, A. F. (1971). A wakeful hypometabolic physiologic state. *American Journal of Physiology, 221,* 795–799.

Wynd, C. A. (1992). Relaxation imagery used for stress reduction in the prevention of smoking relapse. *Journal of Advanced Nursing, 17,* 294–302.

15

EXERCISE AND THE PATIENT WITH CORONARY HEART DISEASE

RICHARD A. STEIN

Exercise is often thought of as a "two-edged sword" with respect to the patient who has coronary heart disease (CHD). On one side, the stress to the heart during vigorous exercise represents a small but definite risk to the patient during and immediately after exercise (Siscovick, Weiss, & Fletcher, 1984). On the other side, regular, repeated bouts of exercise (exercise training) offer a clear protective effect in people who do not have clinical CHD (Morris, Heady, & Raffle, 1953) and may do so as well in patients with CHD (Rechnitzer et al., 1983). In addition, regular exercise is associated with an impressive improvement in functional status and in clinical well-being for the patient who has CHD.

In this chapter, I review the physiology and practical considerations of developing an exercise program for the patient who has CHD. I then discuss the epidemiology of exercise and exercise training with respect to CHD (e.g., Does exercise training prevent CHD?). Finally I address the relationship of regular exercise to selected personality and psychosocial characteristics.

THE PHYSIOLOGY OF EXERCISE AND EXERCISE TRAINING

I begin my lecture on exercise to my second-year medical students with the following scenario:

John has just arrived in the lobby on the morning of an important final exam—a course in which he has not, so far, done well. John is 9 minutes late, and the exam has started, but between him and the elevator are 30 well-dressed medical school applicants on a tour of the campus. Having no choice, John takes the steps and climbs quickly and at an ever-increasing pace up to the 8th floor.

The work of climbing the steps is done for the most part by the leg muscles (primarily the gastrocnemius and the quadriceps muscles). Initially the muscles can contract and relax using stored energy in the form of high-energy phosphates (e.g., adenosine triphosphate). This supply will be exhausted within a few seconds however, and the muscle cells must therefore generate increasing amounts of new high-energy phosphates to permit the muscular work to continue and to increase.

Muscle cells generate high-energy phosphates by metabolizing free fatty acids and carbohydrates (Olson, 1986). During step climbing and other "aerobic exercises," the muscle fully metabolizes the fuel sources, using oxygen in a process termed *oxidative phosphorylation*. The muscle cells can do this so quickly as to permit continued contractile work, but they require a continued supply of (and with increasing work, an increase in) oxygen- and substrate-rich blood. The mechanisms and the consequences of the mechanisms that the body uses to provide an increasing supply of oxygen and blood to the working muscles during exercise make up much of the body of knowledge known as "exercise physiology."

The first of the three major components of this exercise response is the shunting of blood away from nonworking muscles and organs to the working muscles. This shunting can supply from 600 to 900 ml a minute of additional blood to the working muscles (Ehsani, 1987). This occurs as a consequence of the body's increase in sympathetic nervous system activity and an increase in circulating adrenaline and noradrenaline. The result is a generalized constriction in the blood vessels leading to muscles and some organs. The working muscles, however, override this effect by producing by-products of oxidative metabolism that cause local vasodilation. This results in an enhanced supply of blood reaching the working muscles.

The second component of the exercise response is a threefold increase in the extraction of oxygen by the working muscles going from rest to peak exercise levels. At rest, your calf muscle (the gastrocnemius) extracts 5 cc of oxygen from every 100 ml of blood that perfuse the muscle (Clausen, 1976). This increases during exercise to 15 cc of oxygen from every 100 ml of blood that perfuse the muscle.

The third component of the exercise response is by far the most important. This is an increase in the amount of blood pumped by the heart each minute (the cardiac output). Whereas the impact of the first two adaptive responses is modest and occurs early in an increasing amount of exercise, the increase in cardiac output is critical and, in the setting of an increasing workload (e.g., climbing steps in a progressively faster fashion), will increase continually until near exhaustion. Once you exceed moderate-intensity exercise, the major adaptive response to further increases in work intensity is an increase in cardiac output.

Cardiac output is the product of the amount of blood ejected from the heart with each beat (the stroke volume) and the heart rate (Cardiac Output = Stroke Volume × Heart Rate). Stroke volume increases by about 25% from rest, but, again, this occurs early in the progressive exercise load (American College of Sports Medicine, 1991). The major factor in the increase in cardiac output is heart rate. In normal individuals, the heart rate can increase 300% (e.g., from 60 beats/minute at rest to 180 beats/minute at peak exercise; Clausen, 1976).

The important consequence of this increase in heart rate is that the heart muscle itself, in order to beat faster and work harder to eject more blood, needs more oxygen-rich blood. The change in the product of heart rate and systolic blood pressure is an estimate of the increase in myocardial oxygen requirements during exercise (Katz, 1992). At rest, with a heart rate of 70 and a systolic blood pressure of 120, the "double product" (Heart Rate × Systolic Blood Pressure) is 8,400. If the patient exercises to a heart rate of 150 and a systolic blood pressure of 160 mmHg, then the peak double product becomes 24,000. The peak exercise load has thus increased the myocardial oxygen requirement to almost 3 times the requirement at the resting level. Unlike the muscle of the legs, which can increase oxygen extraction with exercise, the heart is always extracting at near-maximal level, and so any increase in oxygen requirement must be met by increases in coronary blood flow. This can only occur with a dilation (and thus, a fall in resistance) of the heart's own arteries, the coronary arteries. When dilation occurs normally, the blood flow to the heart will increase fourfold from rest to maximal exercise. Where this is limited by atherosclerotic plaque that narrows the coronary artery lumen, the requirement for oxygen-rich blood will exceed supply capability, and a state of imbalance—ischemia—will exist. Ischemia induces the chest pressure and pain (known as *angina pectoris*) that is a common presentation of CHD.

Let us go back for a moment to our student.

John has reached the 8th floor, but he is so out of breath and his pulse is so fast that he has to rest for a few minutes before he can sit down to take the exam. After the exam he is more upset about his physical condition than his anticipated score and comes into the building every day before classes to exercise. This includes running up the steps.

Six months into this program, John is again late for an exam and must climb the same steps, at the same rate, with the same body weight (if he lost a few pounds, he could carry some extra books to keep the total weight the same). This time, however, he reaches the classroom without being breathless, at a lower heart rate (135 beats/minute in comparison with the 160 beats/minute of the first time), and is able to sit right down to his exam.

The changes that have occurred as a consequence of John's regular exercise are termed the *training response*. This response is a significant part of the rationale for prescribing regular exercise for patients who have CHD.

Two changes have occurred that have allowed John and, indeed, allow older men or women with CHD to have a lower heart rate and thus, as noted above, a lower cardiac oxygen requirement with exercise as a result of exercise training. One change, seen for the most part only in younger healthy people, is a training-related increase in the stroke volume at rest and throughout an increasing exercise load. The stroke volume increases as a consequence of both an increase in resting diastolic volume and an enhanced ejection fraction. These changes are called "central" and are usually seen in young, healthy individuals who exercise train. The second adaptive response is seen in all people (and patients) who effectively exercise train: an increase in the oxygen-extraction ability of the working muscles. The result of both of these changes is to reduce heart rate at any given workload as a result of exercise training. The central changes permit any given cardiac output to be delivered at a higher stroke volume and thus a lower heart rate (again, Cardiac Output = Stroke Volume × Heart Rate) and the peripheral change—the enhanced oxygen-extraction ability of the working muscles—permits any given muscle workload and associated oxygen requirement to be met with a lower cardiac output and, thus, by a lower heart rate (Clausen, 1976).

Because heart rate is a major determinant of the myocardial oxygen requirement, the reduced exercise heart rate at any given work level that results from exercise training is associated with a concomitant fall in the heart's oxygen requirement. For the patient with coronary artery occlusive disease, this will result in the ability to perform increased external work (e.g., to climb more steps at a faster pace) without exceeding his or her angina threshold (the oxygen requirement that exceeds the supply capability of the diseased artery). Multiple clinical studies of patients with angina pectoris and those with a history of myocardial infarction (MI) have shown that effective exercise training will increase maximal exercise capacity prior to chest pain in patients who have angina (Chaitman, 1992) and will increase maximal exercise capacity in patients who have had MIs (Ehsani, Heath, Hagberg, Sobel, & Holloszy, 1981). Indeed, studies from Israel that measured post-MI work capacity after patients had participated in a cardiac rehabilitation program for 3.5 years showed that these values exceeded those of an age-matched control group of healthy individuals (Kellerman, 1982).

PRACTICAL CONSIDERATIONS AND COMPONENTS OF AN EXERCISE-TRAINING PROGRAM

Development of an exercise-training program for patients with CHD will involve the following decisions:

1. Type of exercises.
2. Frequency of exercise sessions.
3. Duration of exercise sessions.
4. Format of exercise sessions.
5. Intensity of exercises.

Type of Exercises

Exercise for patients who have CHD may be low resistance, involving significant limb motion against relatively low resistance. Such activity is often called *aerobic* because the involved muscles use Type II fibers that are rich in mitochondria and generate the required high-energy phosphates by using oxygen through the Krebs cycle and oxidative phosphorylation pathways. Such low-resistance, or aerobic, exercise is associated with a significant increase in cardiac output and moderate increases in systolic blood pressure.

Exercise that involves slow and limited motion against high resistance, such as weight lifting or use of muscle-building resistance machines, is deemed *high-resistance exercise*. High-resistance exercise uses more Type I fibers that have relatively scarce mitochondria and generate required high-energy phosphates through anaerobic (glycolytic) pathways. High-resistance or anaerobic exercise is associated with only small increases in cardiac output but large increases in systolic blood pressure.

Cardiac rehabilitation and prevention exercise programs usually take advantage of low-resistance (aerobic) exercises because it is this type of exercise training (in contrast to resistance training, which increases strength and muscle size) that is associated with an increase in maximal oxygen consumption, peak work capacity, and a reduction in heart rate at given exercise levels. Good exercise choices thus include walking, jogging, cycling, aerobic exercise classes or routines, swimming, or rowing.

Exercise should ideally involve all major muscle groups in all four extremities. This is because, as noted above, the increase in oxygen extraction that is the major physiological basis for the training response is specific to the muscle that is exercise trained. Thus, an individual who trained only by brisk walking would not demonstrate any significant training benefit when given an arm exercise task to perform. In contrast, someone who had trained using all four extremities on a rowing or cross-country-ski exercise device or someone who had supplemented his or her walking program with regular arm calisthenics (with or without light hand weights) would show a training response during arm exercise.

Frequency of Exercise Sessions

Data from the Astrand study of the relative effectiveness of different frequencies of training sessions in Scandinavian cross-country skiers are the basis for the recommended three sessions per week used in cardiac exercise programs (Astrand & Rodahl, 1977). Training will take longer at a frequency of only two sessions per week, and may be somewhat speeded up with four sessions of training per week, but this frequency is often associated with muscle soreness and soft-tissue injuries or complaints. One exercise session a week does not result in a significant training effect.

Duration of Exercise Sessions

Exercise sessions should last from 20 to 50 minutes. Again, longer sessions may enhance the training effect but will also increase the likelihood of muscle and joint soreness.

Format of Exercise Sessions

On the basis of my experience, each session should begin with a warm-up that consists of several minutes of stretching and a 2- to 5-minute period of gradually increasing the selected exercise or exercises to the training intensity. This physiological component of the warm-up is associated with an enhanced sense of comfort during the training load, and in athletes the warm-up has been associated with increased performance (Balady, 1994).

Following the warm-up, the individual continues into a 15- to 30-minute period of exercise at the selected training intensity. This training workload can be sustained (e.g., 25 minutes of cycling) or it can be interspersed with 3- to 5-minute exercise training loads separated by 1–2 minutes of slow-pedaling "rest" loads. Both techniques are of equal value in achieving a training response. The interval method allows for alternating exercise activities (such as in an aerobics class; Astrand & Rodahl, 1977).

At the end of each session, the individual should slowly (over 3–5 minutes) decrease the intensity of the exercise ("cool down") and should repeat the same stretches used in the warm-up. Studies have reported various data with regard to the benefits of warm-up and cool-down stretching, but most programs still incorporate these components.

Intensity of the Training Exercises

A training effect has been associated with regular exercise performed at 60% to 90% of an individual's maximal intensity (American College of Sports Medicine, 1994). Most cardiac rehabilitation and prevention programs aim for 70% to 85% of maximum intensity, because this is associated with a rapid training response and is in a range that most patients find acceptable, if not comfortable. For the patient with CHD, the intensity must be selected after an exercise electrocardiographic (ECG) exam and is usually set below the exercise intensity level (and its associated double product) at which significant ECG ischemia, symptoms, or hemodynamic abnormalities are noted. Exercise intensity can be controlled by the individual in one of two ways. The patient can be given either a target heart rate (Zohman & Tobias, 1970), which represents 70% to 85% of the heart rate achieved on a maximal exercise ECG exam, or the rate below which he or she manifested ECG or clinical findings. If this heart rate is divided by 6, then a 10-second pulse-rate target is arrived at, and the individual can take his or her 10-second pulse (at the radial or carotid artery) during exercise or at the start of a rest interval. An acceptable range is the 10-second target plus or minus 10% (e.g., for a target heart rate of 130 beats/minute, the 10-second target range would be 19–23 beats/10 seconds). The second—and in my experience, the preferred—method to control exercise intensity is through use of the Rated Perceived Exertion (RPE) Scale, developed by Borg (1982). This is a scale of 6 to 20 (or a modified scale of 1–10), with descriptions of the perceived intensities (e.g., *hard*, *very hard*, or *exhaustive*) assigned to each number. The patient exercises at 12 to 13 out of 20 (or 6–8 out of 10) on the RPE Scale. Studies have shown a remarkably direct relationship between score on the RPE Scale and objective indexes of work or cardiac response (Borg, 1982).

It is extremely important to focus on avoiding injury in CHD exercise programs, including overuse injury, which results in muscle or joint soreness. The reason for this concern about minor soft-tissue injury is that it can be a major cause of patients dropping out of exercise programs. Cardiac rehabilitation and prevention programs have a poor track record as far as compliance is concerned. Oldridge, Wicks, Hanley, Sutton, and Jones (1978) and others have reported that 50% of patients are no longer actively exercising after 1 year, and only 20% to 30% continue to exercise by the 2-year mark.

Individual and program factors that predict compliance are the focus of ongoing behavioral science investigations. To a relatively small degree, all of the following have been shown to predict exercise program compliance: patients' understanding of the impact of their disease and the value of exercise as reflected in their score on a health belief model (Mirotznick,

Feldman, & Stein, 1995), the source of the decision to exercise and its relationship to patients' locus of control, and patients' "readiness to change" position on the transtheoretical model. Although there are few effective strategies, one clear factor that affects compliance failure (dropout) is injury. In my experience, patients stop exercising (sometimes on their physician's advice) until they "feel better" after an injury, and then they never start again. Thus, my admonition to avoid injury and, if possible, overuse symptoms.

EXERCISE AND THE PREVENTION OF CHD

Studies of the value of regular exercise in the prevention of CHD have focused on two settings: primary prevention (the value of exercise in preventing the onset of CHD in presumably healthy people) and secondary prevention (the value of exercise in preventing further clinical episodes in patients who have CHD).

Primary prevention studies have repeatedly shown that moderate and vigorous physical activity is associated with a reduced incidence of CHD. For instance, Morris, Everitt, Pollard, and Chave (1980) reported a reduced incidence of CHD in active versus sedentary British civil servants. Methodological and design concerns about this type of study, however, have limited its impact. Wider acceptance of the protective effect of regular exercise followed two well-designed and controlled studies by Paffenbarger. In the first study (Paffenbarger, Laughlin, Gima, & Black, 1970), San Francisco Bay dockworkers who performed heavy labor (before the days of container shipping) were compared to those who only performed light activities or were sedentary at their jobs. When major CHD risk factors (cholesterol was only included in the later part of the study) were considered in the analysis, a clear protective effect of occupational exercise was seen. The second study looked at Harvard University alumni (Paffenbarger, Hyde, Wing, & Hsieh, 1986). The authors collected data and accounted for CHD risk factors. Daily activity was calculated from patients' reports, and calories burned in exercise were calculated for each patient. Again, a clear protective effect of exercise was seen. This protective effect was demonstrated even in the presence of other significant risk factors (e.g., smoking more than 20 cigarettes a day). Of equal importance was the finding that the greater the caloric expenditure in exercise the lower the incidence of CHD. Paffenbarger et al. noted a clear dose-response–type curve of up to 3,000 Kcal per day. The danger of a sedentary lifestyle and the protective effects of exercise with regard to CHD were formally recognized in 1993, when the American Heart Association specifically included sedentary lifestyle as a major risk factor for CHD.

The issue of exercise effects on secondary prevention of CHD is less clear. It is often difficult to separate the effects of exercise from dietary changes or pharmacological management (especially aspirin and beta-blockers) in post-MI patients. In addition, because exercise is now included in the general good management of post-MI patients, it is difficult to get a pure sedentary control group for such studies. A number of studies of exercise training and survival or incidence of clinical events have been randomly assigned and controlled (e.g., Wilhelmsen et al., 1975). These studies looked at exercise in combination with dietary and risk-factor modification as opposed to only dietary and risk-factor modification. Several studies showed a trend toward increased survival in the exercise group, but the outcomes did not achieve statistical significance. However, a meta-analysis of several of the largest and best controlled studies did achieve significance with regard to increased survival in the exercising group (O'Conner et al., 1989). With the current use of lipid-lowering agents, stress reduction, and lifestyle modification in post-MI patients, it is difficult to perform a "clean study" on the independent effects of exercise in the secondary prevention of CHD. Current studies of the effects of dietary modification and lipid-lowering agents have documented small changes in the direction of regression of anatomic coronary atherosclerosis (through quantitative coronary angiography). The same studies, however, have shown significant improvements in stress myocardial perfusion (according to positron emission tomography scanning; Ornish et al., 1990). The independent effect of exercise in such study populations could not be assessed.

PSYCHOLOGICAL EFFECTS OF REGULAR EXERCISE

Exercise training and an active lifestyle have been postulated to have a variety of psychological benefits, including a reduction in depression and anxiety, an improved sense of well-being, and the modification of Type A behavior.

Clinical studies, although not consistent or conclusive, have pointed to an antidepressant effect of regular exercise. Griest et al. (1979) and others have performed randomly assigned and controlled studies of exercise training versus psychotherapy (in a variety of formats) and have shown regular exercise to be as efficacious as psychotherapy for clinical depression and the improvement of depression scores on interview and self-completion instruments. Postulated mechanisms for exercise-related improvement in depression include such psychodynamic mechanisms as enhancement in self-efficacy, distraction during exercise, and the social support provided from participating in group exercise classes. Biochemical postulates include exercise-related increases in brain levels of catecholamines and beta-endorphins.

Anxiety has been evaluated with self-completion and interview instruments in clinical studies of joggers versus sedentary people (Francis & Carter, 1982). A study of active versus sedentary students (Hayden & Allen, 1984) has noted a reduction in anxiety scores with regular exercise. Likewise, a controlled, randomly assigned study of a 3-month exercise program in Danish men showed significant improvement in anxiety scores in the exercising group (Fasting & Gronningsaeter, 1986). Psychodynamic mechanisms that have been postulated are the same as those noted for depression above (self-efficacy, distraction, and social support).

An intriguing area of investigation is the effect of regular exercise on a person's sense of well-being and Type A behavior. This could have a significant impact on large sections of the population. One randomly assigned and controlled study of moderate-intensity exercise (Moses, 1989) has noted an improved sense of well-being in the exercising group. Several studies have measured the components of Type A behavior in patients with and without regular exercise. A positive, but not consistent, correlation has been found with regular exercise and reduced Type A scores, especially in hostility scores, as noted in a study by Shaeffer, Krantz, and Weiss (1988).

CONCLUSION

In summary, data on exercise and psychological patterns and presentations are promising but, to date, are not conclusive. The proposed psychodynamic and biological basis of such changes are intriguing, yet remain to be validated. The outcome of exercise training for patients with CHD is, however, a clear "win." The patient who exercises regularly at a moderate or greater intensity will, in general, note an enhanced exercise tolerance and a reduced sense of fatigue at any given submaximal workload. The patient will also most probably experience less depression and anxiety. In short, if exercise were a pill, all physicians would prescribe it (and probably take it).

REFERENCES

American College of Sports Medicine. (1991). *Clinical exercise physiology in ACSM guidelines for exercise testing and prescription* (4th ed.). Philadelphia: Lea & Febiger.

American College of Sports Medicine. (1994). *Exercise for the patient with coronary heart disease: American College of Sports Medicine position stand.* Indianapolis, IN: Author.

Astrand, P. O., & Rodahl, K. (1977). *Textbook of work physiology.* New York: McGraw-Hill.

Balady, G. J. (1994). Practical guidelines for exercise in patients with normal ventricular function. In G. H. Fletcher (Ed.), *Cardiovascular response to exercise* (pp. 431–432). New York: American Heart Association.

Borg, G. A. (1982). Psychosocial basis of perceived exertion. *Medical Science and Sports Exercise, 14,* 377–387.

Chaitman, B. (1992). Exercise stress testing. In E. Braunwald (Ed.), *Heart disease* (4th ed., p. 171). Philadelphia: W. B. Saunders.

Clausen, J. P. (1976). Circulatory adjustments to dynamic exercise and effect of exercise training in normal subjects and patients with ischemic heart disease. *Progress in Cardiovascular Disease, 18,* 459–495.

Ehsani, A. A. (1987). Cardiovascular adaptation to endurance training in ischemic heart disease. *Exercise and Sport Science Reviews, 15,* 53–66.

Ehsani, A. A., Heath, G., Hagberg, J., Sobel, B. E., & Holloszy, J. O. (1981). Effects of 12 months of intensive exercise training on ischemic ST depression in patients with coronary artery disease. *Circulation, 64,* 1116–1124.

Fasting, K., & Gronningsaeter, H. (1986). Unemployment, trait anxiety and physical exercise. *Scandinavian Journal of Sports Science, 8,* 99–103.

Francis, K., & Carter, R. (1982). Psychological characteristics of joggers. *Journal of Sports Medicine, 24,* 69–74.

Griest, J., Klein, M. H., Eischens, R. R., Faris, J., Gurman, A. S., & Morgan, W. P. (1979). Running as treatment for depression. *Comprehensive Psychiatry, 20,* 41–54.

Hayden, R., & Allen, G. (1984). Relationship between aerobic exercise, anxiety and depression: Convergent validation by knowledgeable informants. *Journal of Sports Medicine, 24,* 69–74.

Katz, A. (1992). *Physiology of the heart* (2nd ed.). New York: Raven Press.

Kellerman, J. J. (1982). *Comprehensive cardiac rehabilitation.* Basel, Switzerland: Karger.

Mirotznick, J., Feldman, L., & Stein, R. (1995). The Health Belief Model and adherence with a community center based supervised coronary heart disease exercise program. *Journal of Community Health, 20,* 233–247.

Morris, J. N., Everitt, M. G., Pollard, P., & Chave, S. P. W. (1980). Vigorous exercise in leisure time: Protection against coronary heart disease. *Lancet, 11,* 1207–1210.

Morris, J. N., Heady, J. A., & Raffle, P. A. B. (1953). Coronary heart disease and physical activity of work. *Lancet, 20,* 1053–1057.

Moses, J. (1989). The effects of exercise training on mental well-being in the normal population: A controlled trial. *Journal of Psychosomatic Research, 33,* 47–61.

O'Conner, G. T., Buring, J. E., Yusuf, S., Goldhaber, S. Z., Olmstead, B. A., Paffenbarger, R. S., & Hennekens, C. H. (1989). An overview of randomized trials of rehabilitation with exercise after a myocardial infarction. *Circulation, 80,* 234–243.

Oldridge, N. B., Wicks, J. R., Hanley, C., Sutton, J. R., & Jones, N. L. (1978). Non-compliance in an exercise rehabilitation program for men who have suffered a myocardial infarction. *Canadian Medical Association Journal, 118,* 361–364.

Olson, M. S. (1986). Bioenergetics and oxidative metabolism. In T. M. Delvin (Ed.), *Textbook of biochemistry* (pp. 212–220). New York: Wiley.

Ornish, D., Brown, S. E., Scherwitz, L., Billings, J. H., Armstrong, W. T., Ports, T. A., McLanahan, S. M., Kirkeeide, R. L., Brand, R. J., & Gould, K. L. (1990). Can lifestyle changes reverse coronary heart disease? The Lifestyle Heart Trial. *Lancet, 336,* 129–133.

Paffenbarger, R. S., Hyde, R. T., Wing, A. L., & Hsieh, C. C. (1986). Physical activity, all cause mortality and longevity of college alumni. *New England Journal of Medicine, 314,* 605–613.

Paffenbarger, R. S., Laughlin, M. E., Gima, A. S., & Black, R. A. (1970). Work activity of longshoremen as related to death from coronary heart disease and stroke. *New England Journal of Medicine, 282,* 1101–1114.

Rechnitzer, P. A., Cunningham, D. A., Andrew, G. M., Buck, C. W., Jones, N. L., Kavanagh, I. T., Oldridge, N. B., Parker, J. O., Shephard, R. J., Sutton, J. R., & Donner, A. P. (1983). Relationship of exercise to the recurrence rate of myocardial infarction in men. *American Journal of Cardiology, 51,* 65–69.

Shaeffer, M. A., Krantz, D. S., & Weiss, S. M. (1988). Effects of occupational–based behavioral counseling and exercise interventions on Type A components and cardiovascular reactivity. *Journal of Cardiologic Rehabilitation, 10,* 371–377.

Siscovick, D. S., Weiss, N. S., & Fletcher, R. H. (1984). Incidence of primary cardiac arrest during vigorous exercise. *New England Journal of Medicine, 311,* 874–877.

Wilhelmsen, L., Sanne, H., Elmfeldt, D., Grimby, G., Tibblin, G., & Wedel, H. (1975). A controlled trial of physical training after myocardial infarction. *Preventive Medicine, 4,* 491–508.

Zohman, L., & Tobias, J. (1970). *Cardiac rehabilitation.* New York: Grune & Stratton.

16

PSYCHOPHARMACOLOGY AND CARDIAC DISEASE

KATAYOUN TABRIZI, ANDREW LITTMAN,
REDFORD B. WILLIAMS, JR., and STEPHEN SCHEIDT

This chapter encompasses two major areas of concern: (a) drugs used for psychiatric conditions common in patients who have cardiac disease and (b) the possible psychiatric side effects of drugs commonly used for patients who have heart disease. As noted elsewhere in this volume, substantial numbers of patients with cardiac disease suffer from psychiatric symptoms (primarily depression or anxiety) for which treatment may include medications. Therefore, it is important for professionals working with patients who have cardiac disease to consider the medical and, particularly, cardiovascular effects of these medications. The other side of the coin is the increasing awareness of psychiatric side effects from many drugs that are commonly used to treat cardiovascular disease. Mental health professionals and cardiologists alike need to recognize the risks and benefits of drug therapy in this patient population.

In this chapter, we emphasize the importance and adverse prognosis of depression in cardiac patients and consider possible mechanisms underlying depression, particularly relating to serotonin in the central nervous system. We discuss the diagnosis and differential diagnosis of depression and summarize the medications useful in therapy, including selective serotonin reuptake inhibitors (SSRIs), tricyclic antidepressants (TCAs), monoamine oxidase inhibitors (MAOIs), and a miscellaneous group of antidepressants. We follow this summary with a brief discussion of the treatment of anxiety and panic disorder. Next, we consider the possible psychiatric side effects of drugs used to treat patients who have cardiac disease: specifically, beta-blockers, calcium blockers, nitrates, angiotensin converting enzyme (ACE) inhibitors, and antilipid agents.

DEPRESSION AND CORONARY ARTERY DISEASE

Depression and cardiac disease are both so common in the U.S. population that many patients will have both simply by coincidence. It is also likely that significant cardiac disease is in many patients causally associated with depression, whether the cardiac condition and its attendant disabilities lead to depression or whether possible shared pathologic mechanisms make depressed patients more likely to develop coronary artery disease (CAD). It has been estimated that 20% to 40% of patients with CAD exhibit depressive symptoms (Cay, Vetter, Philip, & Dugard, 1972; Kavanagh, Shephard, & Tuck, 1975; Kurosawa, Shimizu, Nishimatsu, Hirose, & Takamo, 1983; Lloyd & Cawley, 1978; Stern, Pascale, & Ackerman, 1977; Wishnie, Hackett, & Cassem, 1971).

Recent research has clearly documented that increased levels of depressive symptomatology adversely affect a person's survival. One study (Frasure-Smith, Lespérance, & Talajic, 1993) persuasively demonstrated that patients who met criteria for major depressive disorder following myocardial infarction were 5 to 6 times more likely to die during the ensuing 6 months (a 16% mortality rate for depressed patients in comparison with 3% for nondepressed patients). In a more recent presentation (Frasure-Smith, Lespérance, & Talajic, 1995), the same authors reported that even lesser degrees of depression (Beck's Depression Inventory scores >10) that did not meet criteria in the revised third edition of the *Diagnostic and Statistical Manual for Mental Disorders* (American Psychiatric Association, 1987) for major depression were still associated with an increased mortality rate at 18 months. Despite the high prevalence of depression and associated increased risk of death in CAD patients, depression is infrequently diagnosed or treated in this population.

The mechanisms by which depression might increase mortality or morbidity in patients with CAD are only speculative. Veith et al. (1994) have documented increased sympathetic nervous system activity in patients who have major depression. Other studies have shown depressed patients to have reduced levels of parasympathetic activity as well (Carney et al., 1988). Increased sympathetic and decreased parasympathetic activity, both of which might plausibly promote dangerous arrhythmias, have been implicated in increased mortality among CAD patients who have depression (Frasure-Smith et al., 1993) Another biological pathway that could increase mortality, likely associated with the known sympathetic nervous system and cortisol excess in depression, is suppression of the immune system (Evans et al., 1992). Depression has also been found to be associated with an increase in health-damaging behaviors, such as smoking and alcohol consumption (Anda et al., 1990; Glassman et al., 1990; Hartka et al., 1991).

There is a striking overlap between these patterns and those found in hostile individuals. It has been documented that highly hostile people exhibit enhanced sympathetically mediated cardiovascular responses when angered by various experimental challenges in the laboratory setting (Smith & Allred, 1989; Suarez & Williams, 1989). In addition to their excessive sympathetic reactivity to stress, hostile individuals also show reduced parasympathetic nervous system antagonism of sympathetic effects on the heart (Fukudo et al., 1992). Ambulatory studies have confirmed a reduced level of parasympathethic activity among hostile individuals (Sloan et al., 1994).

The biobehavioral patterns found in depressed as well as hostile individuals have been linked to serotonin system dysfunction. A hypothesis, based on a considerable body of research from both human and animal studies, suggests that reduced central nervous system serotonin activity is capable of mediating all of the biobehavioral characteristics found in highly hostile individuals. Serotonin in the central nervous system has long been suspected to play a role in depression (Meltzer & Lowy, 1987). Therefore a serotonin-dysfunction hypothesis could explain the clustering of these biobehavioral characteristics in individuals with psychosocial risk factors as well as those patients with depressive disorders or even subclinical depressive symptoms. Such an hypothesis, if confirmed with further research, will have important implications for pharmacological approaches to treatment and, perhaps, for prevention of psychosomatic factors that adversely affect the course of CAD. One major intervention suggested by this hypothesis is the use of SSRIs for treating depression in patients who have CAD. Ultimately, such agents deserve further consideration in primary prevention programs among populations at high risk for development of CAD, perhaps particularly for those who are diagnosed as excessively hostile or depressed.

Other chapters in this book focus on psychotherapeutic interventions in patients with CAD. In this chapter, we review some of the clinical issues relevant to the pharmacotherapy of depression in patients who have CAD, especially using the SSRIs. As noted above, there is a rational basis to believe that the SSRIs might be particularly beneficial not only in treating the depression associated with CAD but also, perhaps, in reducing the health-damaging effects of high hostility seen in some patients with CAD.

Making an accurate diagnosis is the essential first step to effective treatment. Unfortunately, some clinical misconceptions interfere with the diagnosis and treatment of major depression in patients with CAD. First, depression is considered by too many clinicians to be a "normal" reaction to a major medical illness such as a coronary event. Even though there has been no systematic study of the effect of treatment on mortality and morbidity in depressed patients with CAD, one could argue that, considering the indirect evidence, depression in patients who have CAD should be treated as seriously as, say, hypovolemic shock in a patient suffering from acute bleeding. That is, although shock may be a common reaction to the blood loss, no one would consider it normal. There is also some fear regarding the side effects of psychotropic medications in these patients. Yet, given the understanding of the pharmacotherapy of depression, these medications can be safely and effectively administered to the vast majority of patients who have CAD.

The diagnostic criteria for major depression from the fourth edition of the *Diagnostic and Statistical Manual for Mental Disorders* (American Psychiatric Association, 1994) are listed in Figure 1. To make an accurate diagnosis, one must rule out a variety of other diagnoses (see Figure 2). A helpful mnemonic for remembering those conditions that can mimic or contribute to depressive symptoms is DEMENTIA:

- Drugs (including prescription medications, illicit substances, and, most important, alcohol) are one of the most common organic causes of depression. Many medications can be associated with depression, especially certain antihypertensives and corticosteroids (see below).
- Endocrine conditions, especially hypothyroidism and hyperthyroidism, adrenal insufficiency, and hyperparathyroidism.
- Metabolic conditions, such as hyponatremia and hypokalemia.
- Neurological disorders, such as multiple sclerosis and Alzheimer's disease.
- Trauma, especially if a subdural hematoma or intracerebral bleeding is present (an ever-present danger in cardiac patients treated with thrombolytic agents, heparin, aspirin, and a variety of powerful antithrombin, anticoagulant, and antiplatelet medications).
- Infections, in particular, the subacute central nervous system infections.
- Avitaminosis, such as B12 deficiency.

After the diagnosis of major depression has been established, a variety of therapeutic interventions are available, including drug therapy, one of the most effective and well-studied treatment options. Antidepressant medications can be classified in four groups: the SSRIs, the tricyclics and heterocyclics, the MAOIs, and the atypical or the miscellaneous antidepressants. Almost any of the available antidepressants in therapeutic doses can significantly reduce depressive symptoms (especially neurovegetative symp-

■ **Criteria for Major Depressive Episode**

A. Five (or more) of the following symptoms have been present during the same 2-week period and represent a change from previous functioning; at least one of the symptoms is either (1) depressed mood or (2) loss of interest or pleasure.

Note: Do not include symptoms that are clearly due to a general medical condition, or mood-incongruent delusions or hallucinations.

(1) depressed mood most of the day, nearly every day, as indicated by either subjective report (e.g., feels sad or empty) or observation made by others (e.g. appears tearful). **Note:** In children and adolescents, can be irritable mood.

(2) markedly diminished interest or pleasure in all, or almost all, activities most of the day, nearly every day (as indicated by either subjective account or observation made by others)

(3) significant weight loss when not dieting or weight gain (e.g., a change of more than 5% of body weight in a month), or decrease or increase in appetite nearly every day. **Note:** In children consider failure to make expected weight gains.

(4) insomnia or hypersomnia nearly every day

(5) psychomotor agitation or retardation nearly every day (observable by others, not merely subjective feelings of restlessness or being slowed down)

(6) fatigue or loss of energy nearly every day

(7) feelings of worthlessness or excessive or inappropriate guilt (which may be delusional) nearly every day (not merely self-reproach or guilt about being sick)

(8) diminished ability to think or concentrate, or indecisiveness, nearly every day (either by subjective account or as observed by others)

(9) recurrent thoughts of death (not just fear of dying), recurrent suicidal ideation without a specific plan, or a suicide attempt or a specific plan for committing suicide

B. The symptoms do not meet criteria for a Mixed Episode (see p. 355).

C. The symptoms cause clinically significant distress or impairment in social, occupational or other important areas of functioning.

D. The symptoms are not due to the direct physiological effects of a substance (e.g., a drug of abuse, a medication) or a general medical condition (e.g., hypothyroidism).

E. The symptoms are not better accounted for by Bereavement, i.e., after the loss of a loved one, the symptoms persist for longer than 2 months or are characterized by marked functional impairment, morbid preoccupation with worthlessness, suicidal ideation, psychotic symptoms, or psychomotor retardation.

Figure 1. Criteria for major depressive episode. From *Diagnostic and Statistical Manual of Mental Disorders* (4th ed., p. 327), by the American Psychiatric Association, 1994, Washington, DC: American Psychiatric Association. Copyright 1994 by the American Psychiatric Association. Reprinted with permission.

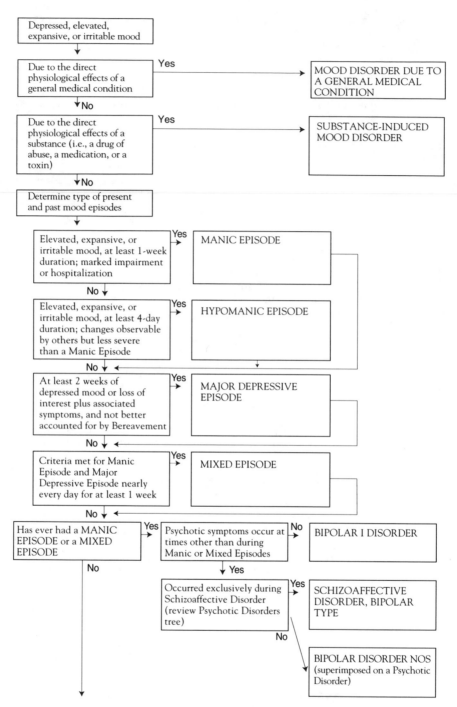

Figure 2. Differential diagnosis of mood disorders. From *Diagnostic and Statistical Manual of Mental Disorders* (4th ed., p. 696), by the American Psychiatric Association, 1994, Washington, DC: American Psychiatric Association. Copyright 1994 by the American Psychiatric Association. Reprinted with permission.

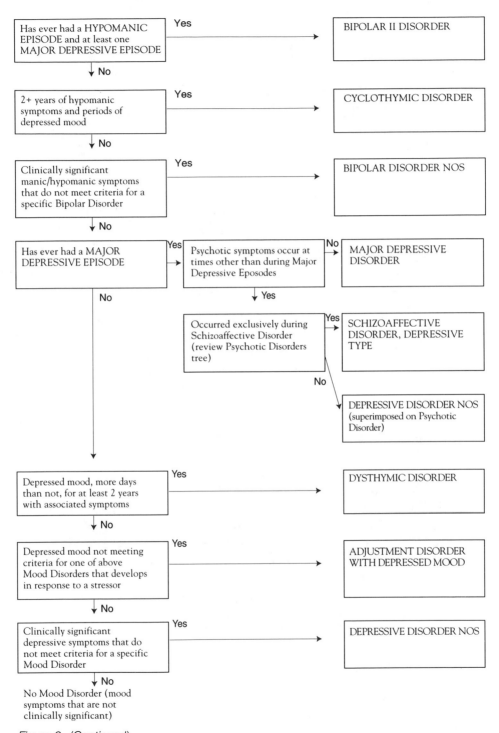

Figure 2. (Continued)

toms) in 65% to 75% of patients who have major depression (Nemeroff, 1994). With the exception of antimicrobial agents and a few other classes of drugs, antidepressants have better efficacy than most other medication groups, a fact that is unfortunately not always fully appreciated. Because almost all antidepressants have the same rate of efficacy, the major considerations in choosing one over another are their side effect profiles and costs. This is especially important for patients who have other medical illnesses and are on other medications that could possibly interact with the antidepressants.

It should be emphasized that psychotherapy is also an effective treatment for depression. Indeed, the treatment of mild depressive states can proceed without pharmacotherapy; but for moderate to severe depression, data suggest that a combined approach of medications and psychotherapy is the most effective choice (Depression Guideline Panel, 1993).

Antidepressants

SSRIs

The serotonin system is one of the oldest neurotransmitter systems, found in all vertebrates and most invertebrates that have been studied (Jacobs, 1991). Serotonergic neurons originate in the midline of the brain stem and project diffusely throughout the brain with considerable interaction between the serotonin and other neurotransmitter systems. Therefore, there is no medication that is truly "selective" for the serotonin system. The SSRIs, or more accurately, SRIs, are selective in their inhibition of synaptic reuptake of serotonin, but this does not mean they have no effect on other neurotransmitters. There is a great deal of evidence supporting the role of serotonin in the pathophysiology of depression (Owens & Nemeroff, 1994); indeed, all of the effective treatments against depression (SSRIs, TCAs, and MAOIs; the atypical antidepressants; electroshock therapy; and lithium) influence serotonergic neurotransmission.

The most common side effects with SSRIs are nausea, diarrhea, anxiety ("jitteriness"), and insomnia (see Table 1). Another bothersome side effect of SSRIs is their tendency to cause sexual dysfunction, mainly delayed ejaculation or inability to ejaculate in men and anorgasmia in women. These medications are very safe in overdose, and because they have very little effect on adrenergic, histaminergic, or cholinergic receptors, the common side effects seen with the blockade of these receptors (orthostatic hypotension, sedation, dry mouth, urinary retention, and blurred vision) are rare with SSRIs. Therefore, discontinuation of treatment because of adverse effects is much lower with SSRIs than with TCAs.

All SSRIs are potent inhibitors of different isoenzymes of the cytochrome P450 system, the hepatic mechanism that is responsible for the

TABLE 1
Incidence of Primary Side Effects of Selective Serotonin Reuptake Inhibitors

Side effect	Fluoxetine	Sertraline	Paroxetine
Nausea	+++	+++	+++
Diarrhea or loose stools	+++	+++	++
Anxiety	++	+	+
Nervousness	++	+	+
Sexual dysfunction	++	++	++
Insomnia	++	++	++
Tremor	+	++	+
Headaches	+++	+++	+++
Constipation	+	+	++
Dry mouth	+	++	++
Somnolence	+	+	++
Weakness or fatigue	++	++	++
Anorexia	++	+	+

Note. + denotes incidence of 1%–9%; ++ denotes incidence of 10%–19%; +++ denotes incidence of 20% and above. From "Evolutionary Trends in the Pharmacotherapeutic Management of Depression," by C. B. Nemeroff, 1994, *Journal of Clinical Psychiatry, 55*(Suppl.), p. 10. Copyright 1994 by Physicians Postgraduate Press. Reprinted with permission.

metabolism of many medications. Therefore, a variety of medications can potentially interact with SSRIs. Table 2 shows some of the clinically significant interactions between SSRIs and other drugs (DeVane, 1994).

The efficacy of SSRIs is comparable to that of TCAs, but given their more favorable side-effect profile, these medications should be used as the first line of treatment in major depression, especially for patients who have cardiac disease. Currently, there are three SSRIs commonly used for treatment of depression: fluoxetine, sertraline, and paroxetine. A fourth SSRI, fluvoxamine, recently became available for treatment of obsessive–compulsive disorder.

Fluoxetine (Prozac) is the first SSRI that became available in the United States. The usual starting dose is 20 mg per day, but the effective dose range is 20–80 mg per day, usually given in one morning dose. Fluoxetine's half-life is about 3 days, but its active metabolite, norfluoxetine, has a half-life of 4–16 days. Therefore, after the drug is discontinued, its active metabolite will be present in the body for up to 5 weeks. This can be an important clinical feature, especially in cases of intolerable side effects or drug interactions. One good example is the contraindication for coadministration of MAOIs and SSRIs. This combination can cause a potentially fatal serotonergic syndrome characterized by muscle rigidity, myoclonus, diaphoresis, hyperthermia, and autonomic instability. It is therefore recommended that, when switching from an SSRI to an MAOI, a washout period be observed, for at least 5 weeks in the case of fluoxetine. Fluoxetine and norfluoxetine are both potent inhibitors of the hepatic isoenzyme P450

TABLE 2
Potentially Significant SSRI–P450 Isoenzyme Drug Interactions

SSRI	P450 isoenzyme inhibited	Potential interactive drug
Fluoxetine	2C	Phenytoin
	2D6	Tricyclics, antipsychotics, Type 1C antiarrhythmics
	3A4	Carbamazepine
Sertraline	2D6	Tricyclics, antipsychotics, Type 1C antiarrhythmics
	2C	Tolbutamide
	3A4	Carbamazepine
Paroxetine	2D6	Tricyclics, antipsychotics, Type 1C antiarrhythmics
Fluvoxamine	1A2	Theophylline, caffeine, tricyclics
	3A4	Carbamazepine, alprazolam, triazolam, terfenadine, astemizole

Note. This is a noninclusive list based on case reports, literature documentation, Federal Drug Administration–approved product labeling, or isoenzyme-specific pathway interactions. Additional interactions can occur. Significance depends on dosage, length of therapy, and various factors related to the patient's clinical state. SSRI = selective serotonin reuptake inhibitor.

From "Pharmacogenetics and Drug Metabolism of Newer Antidepressant Agents," by C. L. DeVane, 1994, *Journal of Clinical Psychiatry, 55*, p. 42. Copyright 1994 by Physicians Postgraduate Press. Reprinted with permission.

2D6; thus, inhibition of the hepatic enzyme by SSRIs will interfere with degradation and increase the plasma level of certain other drugs that may be administered at the same time, such as TCAs, antipsychotics, and carbamazepine (Tegetrol).

Sertraline (Zoloft) is usually started at a 50 mg daily dose; the average therapeutic range is 50–200 mg per day. Its main side effects include nausea, diarrhea, insomnia, and sexual dysfunction. There are no cardiotoxic effects or electrocardiogram abnormalities reported with sertraline, and, like other SSRIs, it is quite safe in overdose. Sertraline is also a potent inhibitor of P450 2D6 and so might increase levels of concomitantly administered medications; potential drug interactions should be considered when it is used (see Table 2). In comparison with fluoxetine, sertraline has a much shorter half-life (26 hours) and no active metabolite, making it safer for medically ill patients or in cases where untoward side effects or drug interactions might require rapid withdrawal of the antidepressant.

Paroxetine (Paxil) also does not have any effect on heart rate, blood pressure, or electrocardiogram time intervals. It has a much shorter half-life in comparison with fluoxetine and no active metabolite. Its main side effects are nausea, headache, sedation or insomnia, and, occasionally, dry mouth. Usually the side effects subside with continued use. Paroxetine is also a potent inhibitor of P450 2D6 and may increase the plasma levels of certain drugs. The usual starting dose for paroxetine is 10–20 mg per day. The dose can be increased by 10 mg per 1–2 weeks after at least 3–4 weeks of treatment. The dose range for paroxetine is 20–50 mg per day administered in a single morning dose.

TCAs and Heterocyclic Antidepressants

These agents are not the first option in the treatment of depression, especially in elderly patients and in those with cardiac disease. In addition to their unfavorable side-effect profile (sedation, orthostatic hypotension, blurred vision, dry mouth, constipation, urinary retention, and sexual dysfunction), they have a number of potentially cardiotoxic effects. Even though they possess some quinidinelike antiarrhythmic properties, their other cardiac effects (such as conduction delay and sinus tachycardia) make them potentially problematic for use with cardiac patients. The other major problem with TCAs is their narrow therapeutic index. All of these medications can be lethal in overdose. In fact, they have been reported to be the third most common cause of drug-related death and the number one cause of suicide by overdose in the United States (Callaham & Kassel, 1985; Kapur, Mieczkowski, & Mann, 1992). This fact and other side effects mentioned above have lead to the rather common practice of prescribing these medications in subtherapeutic doses, especially by nonpsychiatric physicians and nurse practitioners. Some patients may be labeled as "refractory" or "treatment resistant," whereas, in fact, they have never had an adequate trial of an antidepressant medication. Generally, the tertiary amines (amitriptyline, imipramine, doxepine, and trimipramine) cause more side effects than the secondary amines (nortriptyline and desipramine). Table 3 shows the common side effects of TCAs.

MAOIs

The observation that the antituberculosis drug iproniazide caused mood elevation in some patients led to the discovery of MAOIs, the first antidepressants, nearly 40 years ago. Although the other three groups of antidepressants (TCAs, SSRIs, and the atypical group) act by inhibiting presynaptic reuptake or by blocking postsynaptic receptors of certain neurotransmitters, such as norepinephrine, serotonin, and dopamine, MAOIs inhibit the degradation of these neurotransmitters.

Currently, three MAOIs are available in the United States: phenelzine (Nardil), tranylcypromine (Parnate), and isocarbaxizid (Marplan). These medications require the patient to be on a low-tyramine diet by avoiding certain foods (such as aged cheeses, red wine, chocolate, beer, dry sausage, liver, smoked fish, and fava beans) and to avoid certain medications, such as sympathomimetics and meperidine (Demerol). In addition to these limitations, MAOIs have a lower therapeutic response rate (50%

TABLE 3
Common Side Effects of Tricyclic Antidepressants (TCAs)

TCA	Anticholinergic effects	Orthostatic hypotension	Sedation	Insomnia	Agitation and restlessness	Nausea	Headaches and migraine	Sexual dysfunction	Weight gain
Amitriptyline	+++	+++	+++	0	0	0	+	++	++
Desipramine	+	++	+	0	+	0	+	+	+
Doxepin	++	+++	+++	0	0	0	+	++	++
Imipramine	++	+	++	0	+	0	+	++	++
Nortriptyline	+	+++	++	0	+	0	+	+	+
Protriptyline	+++	+++	+	0	+	0	+	++	++
Trimipramine	+++	++	+++	0	+	0	+	++	++

Note. +++ = frequently; ++ = occasionally; + = rarely; 0 = not reported. From "Evolutionary Trends in the Pharmacotherapeutic Management of Depression," by C. B. Nemeroff, 1994, Journal of Clinical Psychiatry, 55(Suppl.), p. 6. Copyright 1994 by Physicians Postgraduate Press. Reprinted with permission.

to 60%) than the other classes of antidepressants and, therefore, have limited utility in the treatment of depression, especially in patients with cardiac problems.

Other Antidepressants

Additional antidepressants include trazodone, bupropion, nefazodone, and venlafaxine, each of which has unique pharmacology and so cannot be included with other classes of antidepressants.

Trazodone (Desyrel) is a triazolopyridine derivative with a yet-unknown mechanism of action. Its major metabolite, m-chlorophenyl-piperazine (m-CPP), is an antagonist for a number of serotonin receptor subtypes. In comparison with SSRIs, it is a weak inhibitor of serotonin reuptake. Even though its efficacy in clinical trials has been comparable to that of TCAs and fluoxetine, its sedating quality limits its clinical use as an effective antidepressant. It can cause significant orthostatic hypotension through alpha-1-adrenergic blockade and, therefore, is of limited use for the treatment of depression in the patient with cardiac disease. Trazodone can occasionally be helpful in symptomatic treatment of severe insomnia associated with major depression. An uncommon but important side effect in men is priapism, which should be treated as a medical–surgical emergency. Trazodone has also been associated with arrhythmias in cardiac patients. It has a rather wide therapeutic range (150–600 mg per day) and should be given in divided doses, considering its short half-life of 3–9 hours.

Nefazodone (Serzone) is chemically related to trazodone but is a more potent 5-hydroxytryptamine antagonist at the postsynaptic level. It has a more favorable side-effect profile in comparison with trazodone, with weaker alpha-1-adrenergic blockade and, thus, fewer problems with orthostatic hypotension. It has almost no cardiotoxic, anticholinergic, or histaminergic activity. Its main side effects include sedation, dizziness, weakness, dry mouth, nausea, constipation, and amblyopia (Fontaine, 1992). The short half-lives of the parent compound (2–5 hours) and its active metabolites—OH-nefazodone (2–5 hours) and m-CPP (4.5 hours)—require twice daily dosing (Nemeroff, 1994). Its usual therapeutic dose is 400–600 mg per day.

Venlafaxine (Effexor) was recently approved for clinical use. It is unrelated to other antidepressants. Its main mechanism of action is believed to be related to both norepinephrine and serotonin reuptake blockade by the parent compound and its main metabolite, O-desmethylvenlafaxine. Both are weak inhibitors of alpha-1-adrenergic, cholinergic, and histaminergic receptors. Its side effects include nausea, sexual dysfunction, and sustained hypertension. The blood pressure increase appears to be dose dependent, with an incidence of 3% for low doses (>100 mg per day), 5%–

7% at mid-dose range (100–300 mg per day), and 13% at higher doses (>300 mg per day). Blood pressure should be monitored at least once a day, and the dose should be lowered or the drug discontinued if hypertension occurs. Because of these side effects, venlafaxine should be used as a second-line drug for treatment of depression in patients with cardiac problems. It should be noted that some clinical trials have shown venlafaxine to be particularly effective in certain treatment-resistant patients (Montgomery, 1993).

Bupropion (Wellbutrin) has no significant effect on reuptake of serotonin or norepinephrine, but it is a weak blocker of dopamine reuptake. However, this property does not seem to explain its antidepressant effect, which is comparable to TCAs for treatment of major depression. It has also been favorably compared to fluoxetine in treatment of moderate-to-severe depression in a study of outpatients (Feighner et al., 1991). Bupropion has a favorable side-effect profile in comparison with TCAs. It does not cause orthostatic hypotension or any anticholinergic side effects, and it has very few cardiovascular or sexual problems. Its only significant adverse effect in the clinical setting is its propensity to induce seizures at high therapeutic dosages, especially in those with a predisposition to seizure disorder (alcoholism or history of head injury). Because this effect is dose related, the drug should be administered in divided doses (2 or even 3 times per day, especially when the total daily dose is higher than 200–300 mg). The incidence of seizure in one study has been estimated at 0.24% among more than 3,300 patients on 225–450 mg per day of bupropion (Johnston et al., 1991). Bupropion should be reserved as a viable second choice in cardiac patients with depression, especially for those who experience untolerable sexual dysfunction on SSRIs.

Other Psychopharmacological Medications

Antianxiety agents are commonly prescribed for patients who have CAD. Benzodiazepine antianxiety agents are very useful for the treatment of panic disorder, which is commonly seen in patients who are treated by cardiologists for atypical chest pain but who have normal coronary arteries. Antidepressants of both tricyclic and SSRI types, as well as cognitive–behavioral psychotherapy, are also useful treatments for panic disorder.

Antianxiety agents of the benzodiazepine type are also commonly used to treat sleep disorders, but they should be used only for a brief period. The treatment of sleep disorders with benzodiazepines for a prolonged period is, in many cases, the partial treatment of a posttraumatic, depressive, or anxiety disorder, and such patients should be evaluated more intensively for these disorders. It should be noted that benzodiazepines can be "disinhibiting," or paradoxically, may enhance aggressiveness in some patients (Wilkinson, 1985).

The nonbenzodiazepine antianxiety agent buspirone (Buspar), a selective serotonin-1A partial agonist, is a nonaddictive agent useful in the treatment of generalized anxiety disorder. The role of low levels of central serotonin has been linked to the increased impulsivity and hostility manifested in individuals who have mood and personality disorders as well as those who have these symptoms but do not have a formal psychiatric diagnosis. Buspirone has been found to be an effective agent in treating hostility, irritability, and impatience in CAD patients without a psychiatric diagnosis (Littman, 1993). In addition, anger outbursts, or "anger attacks," commonly seen in those individuals with depressive disorders (in 44% of patients) have been shown to be effectively treated with SSRIs (Tollefson, 1995).

Discussion of the use of psychostimulants, lithium, and the antipsychotic agents in patients with CAD is beyond the scope of this chapter, but these have been recently reviewed by Littman (1993).[1]

CARDIAC DRUGS WITH PSYCHIATRIC SIDE EFFECTS

Beta-Blockers

Beta-blockers have multiple uses in treating cardiovascular disease. They are commonly prescribed for angina pectoris (wherein they balance coronary artery blood supply diminished because of atherosclerotic disease, with decreased myocardial oxygen demands produced by beta-blockers' effects of lowering blood pressure, heart rate, and cardiac contractility). They are also effective antihypertensive agents. They are good antiarrhythmic agents for both atrial and ventricular arrhythmias and reduce the rate of sudden cardiac death in some patients predisposed to this problem (Beta-Blocker Heart Attack Trial Research Group, 1982; Norwegian Multicenter Study Group, 1981). Beta-blockers may be "cardioprotective," in that they possibly reduce the size of a myocardial infarct if administered immediately after the onset of symptoms (MIAMI Trial Research Group, 1985). They also reduce the reinfarction rate, when used continuously for several years after a first myocardial infarction (Beta-Blocker Heart Attack Trial Research Group, 1982; Norwegian Multicenter Study Group, 1981).

The side effects of beta-blockers include excessive bradycardia (slowing of the heart rate, which occasionally causes dizziness or even fainting), rare heart block (an electrical disorder of conduction between the atria and the ventricles, which can also cause excessively slow heart rates, dizziness, and fainting), and rare precipitation or exacerbation of congestive heart failure in patients who have preexisting diminished cardiac function.

---

[1]For further discussion, consult Shader's (1994) *Manual of Psychiatric Therapeutics*.

Beta-blockers often have slightly unfavorable effects on serum lipids (they tend to lower high-density lipoprotein—the "good" cholesterol—and raise serum triglyerides slightly). They tend to cause vasoconstriction of smaller peripheral blood vessels, which often leads patients to complain of cold hands, feet, ears, or nose. The major side effects limiting the use of beta-blockers, however, are psychological. Possibly through their interference with the sympathetic nervous system, beta-blockers cause nightmares, insomnia and other sleep disorders, sexual dysfunction (mainly, loss of libido but occasionally erectile dysfunction), fatigue, and difficulties with concentration and mental alertness—all of which are often irreverently summed up as the "beta-blocker blahs." The published literature has cited rather low levels for such side effects. For example, the large randomized Beta-Blocker Heart Attack Trial (Beta-Blocker Heart Attack Trial Research Group, 1982) studied 3,837 patients for more than 2 years after acute myocardial infarction and had to withdraw study medication because of "tiredness" in 1.5% of patients on high doses of propranolol and 1.0% of those on placebo (ns); "depression" in 0.4% on propranolol and 0.4% on placebo (ns); "nightmares" in 0.1% and 0.2%, respectively (ns); "insomnia" in 0.2% and 0.0% (ns); and reduced sexual activity in 0.2% and 0.0% ($p < .05$). Alternatively, the number of patients reporting such complaints at any time during the trial was much higher: tiredness in 66.8% on propranolol and 62.1% on placebo ($p < .005$); reduced sexual activity in 43.2% and 42.0%, respectively (ns); and depression in 40.7% and 39.8% (ns). Regardless of published data from clinical trials involving close follow-up and dedicated personnel who went to great lengths to keep patients in the trial, many practicing physicians in clinical settings get so many complaints about the psychiatric side effects of beta-blockers that they tend to avoid these medications. An alternative explanation is that physicians focus on beta-blockers as culprits but do not identify and treat the depression that is so commonly seen in patients with CAD.

It has been suggested that psychiatric side effects might be avoided with more water-soluble beta-blockers that have more difficulty in penetrating the lipid-rich blood–brain barrier to enter the central nervous system. Given this hypothesis, physicians will often use (or switch to) nadolol (Corgard) or atenolol (Tenormin), which are two of the most water-soluble (and least lipid-soluble) beta-blockers. It has also been suggested that central nervous system side effects might be lessened with beta-blockers that have intrinsic sympathomimetic activity. These drugs do not interfere with the sympathetic nervous system at low levels of sympathetic activity and block only at high levels of sympathetic activation (e.g., during exercise or mental stress). Drugs with intrinsic sympathomimetic activity include pindolol (Visken) and acebutolol (Sectral).

Calcium Blockers

Calcium blockers have few psychiatric side effects. Nifedipine (Procardia and Adalat) and other dihydropyridines (e.g., nicardipine [Cardene]), which are powerful peripheral vasodilators, can cause reflex tachycardia, which can be distressing to the patient (often reported as "palpitations" or as being "aware of my heart"). Depending on the general anxiety level of the patient, however, being aware of the heart can sometimes raise anxiety considerably, and patients may be much relieved by stopping these agents. Rarely, excessive hypotension and, thus, dizziness or fainting may occur. All calcium blockers, but especially verapamil, can cause or exacerbate heart failure in patients with baseline poor cardiac function, which can lead to shortness of breath, orthopnea, nocturnal dyspnea, or leg edema. The newer dihydropyridines—amlodipine (Norvasc), felodipine (Plendil), and isradipine (Dynacirc)—have very little direct effect on the heart and are less likely to cause any cardiac or secondary psychological side effects (*Physicians' Desk Reference*, 1995).

Recently, a scientific controversy has erupted over the possibility that calcium blockers, particularly nifedipine, might actually increase mortality or myocardial infarction rates in patients with CAD. (Furberg, Psaty, & Meyer, 1995; Psaty et al., 1995). Needless to say, this has caused enormous anxiety among both cardiac patients and their physicians. The scientific issue is not settled as this chapter is written, and so readers need to pay close attention to the emerging scientific literature. Many cardiologists are switching away from nifedipine, particularly the (older and rarely used) short-acting form of the drug, in patients with CAD. There is much less evidence that other calcium blockers pose any problem, and few cardiologists are making changes without further evidence in patients successfully treated with diltiazem or verapamil, those on long-acting nifedipine (Procardia XL), or those without CAD in whom calcium blockers are prescribed for hypertension. In all patients treated with these drugs, reassessment of currently understood risks and benefits and patient reassurance are generally indicated.

Nitrates

Nitrates have no psychiatric side effects, but they frequently cause headaches and may cause considerable hypotension in some patients, with attendant reflex tachycardia, palpitations, dizziness, or syncope (fainting). It is our clinical observation that there is an important psychological issue related to nitroglycerin use: the reluctance of many patients to use the drug properly. Sublingual nitroglycerin is not a painkiller and does not "mask" myocardial ischemia. Rather, nitroglycerin and other oral nitrates actually reduce or eliminate myocardial ischemia.

For reasons that are not always clear, many patients resist using nitroglycerin when they experience anginal pain. In some cases, there may be a fear that others, spouse or coworkers, will become aware of angina and be unduly alarmed, and force the patient to reduce activities, go to the doctor or a hospital, or cause similar inconveniences. Other patients seem to have a "macho" attitude that they are able to bear the pain, which is usually transient, and so need not bother to take medication. At times, patients seem to feel that overcoming pain without medication is somehow therapeutic, in the sense that, just as regular physical exercise might increase tolerance, perhaps bearing anginal pain might in some way condition the heart and improve its ability to deal with angina in the future. These and other rationalizations are surprisingly frequent, enough so that all cardiologists should discuss the proper use of nitroglycerin periodically with patients. It seems likely that suboptimal use of nitroglycerin is often a manifestation of denial in patients with CHD. Contrary to popular thought, repeated ischemia does not appear to grow new collaterals, improve exercise tolerance, or do anything else beneficial. Continuous electrocardiographic monitoring suggests that even though anginal pain may last only a minute or two after the patient stops walking or whatever activity precipitated angina, electrocardiographic changes (and thus, presumably abnormal physiology within heart muscle) sometimes last for 20 minutes or more. Thus, patients need to be encouraged to take sublingual nitroglyercin promptly at the first appearance of angina and to repeat the dose 2 minutes after the first pill (and a third time, 2 minutes after that) if angina persists.

ACE Inhibitors

ACE inhibitors—prescribed for hypertension, congestive heart failure, and postmyocardial infarction in those with considerable myocardial damage—have no particular psychiatric side effects; their major side effect is a dry cough. Examples of ACE inhibitors include benazepril (Lotensin), captopril (Capoten), enalapril (Vasotec), fosinopril (Monopril), lisinopril (Prinivil, Zestril), quinapril (Accupril), ramipril (Altace), and almost anything else that ends with "pril."

Adrenergic Blockers

Alpha-blockers are a type of adrenergic (sympathetic) blocker used for hypertension and also to improve urinary flow so that a patient's sleep will not be disrupted by frequent nighttime urination. These medications have no particular psychiatric side effects but do cause orthostatic hypotension and dry mouth. This group includes prazosin (Minipress), doxazosin (Cardura), and terazosin (Hytrin). An older group of antihypertensives can cause depression and, perhaps rarely, suicide. The best known example, which is rarely used these days, is reserpine; another, more often used and less likely to cause depression, is alpha-methyl-dopa (Aldomet). A newer drug is clonidine (Catapres), which can cause serious and even life-threatening rebound hypertension if abruptly discontinued. This is emphatically not the drug to prescribe for poorly compliant patients.

Anticoagulants

Anticoagulants (e.g., warfarin [Coumadin]) are used for patients with atrial fibrillation, artificial cardiac valves, and after large myocardial infarctions. Antiplatelet agents such as aspirin and ticlopidine (Ticlid)—used in primary prevention of CAD in high-risk individuals as well as for secondary prevention after acute myocardial infarction, coronary bypass surgery, and coronary angioplasty—have no psychiatric side effects, but the possibility of central nervous system hemorrhage should be kept in mind. Neurological or psychiatric changes (especially if acute in onset) in patients taking these medications should be thoroughly evaluated on an emergency basis. One recent study (Mittleman et al., 1995) reported that aspirin seems to block (or mediate) the increased risk of acute MI produced by anger.

Antilipid Agents

Antilipid agents have an interesting history of psychosocial concerns. At least two older trials of anticholesterol drugs—the Helsinki Primary Prevention Trial, using gemfibrozil (Frick et al., 1987), and the Lipid Research Clinics Coronary Primary Prevention Trial (Lipid Research Clinics Progam, 1984)—have found a reduction in cardiovascular morbidity and mortality balanced by an increase in violent deaths (homicides, suicides, and accidents). Although the numbers were small, the findings did cause disquiet in the cardiological and epidemiological communities for some years. This concern has almost entirely evaporated with the stunningly favorable findings of the Scandinavian Simvastatin Survival Study (1994), as well as the West of Scotland Study (Shepherd et al., 1995). In the first trial, simvastatin (Zocor) was given to 4,444 hyperlipidemic patients with prior CAD. In the second, pravastatin (Pravachol) was given to 6,595 individuals with high serum cholesterol but no prior heart disease. In both studies, low-density lipoprotein was reduced 26%–35%, total cholesterol was reduced 20%–25%, and the statin drugs—over a 5-year period—demonstrated 25%–30% declines in total deaths, myocardial infarcts, need for bypass surgery or coronary angioplasty, and several other favorable outcomes (with no adverse effects regarding cancer, violent deaths, or noncardiovascular deaths). There have been poorly documented claims that some statin drugs may cause occasional sleep disturbances, but this seems an insignificant problem compared with the major reductions in serum cholesterol and adverse clinical events that these powerful agents (lovastatin [Mevacor], simvastatin [Zocor], pravastatin [Pravachol], and fluvastatin [Lescol]) have been able to achieve. In some cases, switching from one statin drug to another may ameliorate the sleep problem.

CONCLUSION

Depression is a common but frequently underdiagnosed and undertreated psychiatric illness in patients who have CHD. Data suggest that comorbid depressive illness will increase mortality in these patients. Antidepressants, especially SSRIs, offer an effective mode of treatment. In fact, they may also be helpful in modifying the health-damaging biobehavioral patterns seen in hostile individuals, given the possible role of serotonin in both depression and hostility. Outcome studies are needed to prove the beneficial effect of antidepressant treatment on morbidity and mortality of CHD. Until these are done, it is our recommendation that every patient with CHD be evaluated for depression and that appropriate treatment (psychotherapy, medication, or a combination of both) be offered to those suffering from this serious and potentially fatal illness.

REFERENCES

American Psychiatric Association. (1987). *Diagnostic and statistical manual of mental disorders* (3rd ed., rev.). Washington, DC: Author.

American Psychiatric Association. (1994). *Diagnostic and statistical manual of mental disorders* (4th ed.). Washington, DC: Author.

Anda, R. F., Williamson, D. F., Escobedo, L. G., Mast, E. E., Giovino, G. A., & Remington, P. L. (1990). Depression and the dynamics of smoking: A national perspective. *Journal of the American Medical Association, 264,* 1541–1545.

Beta-Blocker Heart Attack Trial Research Group. (1982). A randomized trial of propranolol in patients with acute myocardial infarction: I. Mortality results. *Journal of the American Medical Association, 247,* 1707–1714.

Callaham, M., & Kassel, D. (1985). Epidemiology of fatal tricyclic antidepressant ingestion: Implications for management. *Annals of Emergency Medicine, 14,* 1–9.

Carney, R. M., Rich, M., TeVelde, A., Saini, J., Clark, K., & Freedland, K. E. (1988). The relationship between heart rate, heart rate variability and depression in patients with coronary artery disease. *Journal of Psychosomatic Research, 32,* 159–164.

Cay, E. L., Vetter, N., Philip, A. E., & Dugard, P. (1972). Psychological status during recovery from an acute heart attack. *Journal of Pyschosomatic Research, 16,* 425–435.

Depression Guideline Panel. (1993). *Clinical practice guideline number 5: Depression in primary care, 2. Treatment of major depression* (AHCPR Publication No. 93-0551). Rockville, MD: U.S. Department of Health and Human Services, Agency for Health Care Policy and Research.

DeVane, C. L. (1994). Pharmacogenetics and drug metabolism of newer antidepressant agents. *Journal of Clinical Psychiatry, 55,* 38–45.

Evans, D. L., Folds, J. D., Pettito, J. M., Golden, R. N., Pedersen, C. A., Corrigan, M., Gilmore, J. H., Silva, S. G., Quade, D., & Ozer, H. (1992). Circulating natural killer cell phenotypes in men and women with major depression: Relation to cytotoxic activity and severity of depression. *Archives of General Psychiatry, 49,* 388–395.

Feighner, J. P., Gardner, E. A., Johnston, J. A., Batey, S. R., Khayrallah, M. A., Ascher, J. A., & Lineberry, C. G. (1991). Double-blind comparison of bupropion and fluoxetine in depressed outpatients. *Journal of Clinical Psychiatry, 52,* 329–335.

Fontaine, R. (1992). Novel serotonergic mechanisms and clinical experience with nefazodone. *Clinical Neuropharmacology, 159*(Suppl. 1, Pt. A), 99A.

Frasure-Smith, N., Lespérance, F., & Talajic, M. (1993). Depression following myocardial infarction: Impact on 6-month survival. *Journal of the American Medical Association, 270,* 1819–1825.

Frasure-Smith, N., Lespérance, F., & Talajic, M. (1995). Depression and 18-month prognosis after myocardial infarction. *Circulation, 91,* 999-1005.

Frick, M. H., Elo, O., Haapa, K., Heinonen, O. P., Heinsalmi, P., Helo, P., Huttunen, J. K., Kaitaniemi, P., Koskinen, P., Manninen, V., Maenpaa, H., Malkonen, M., Manttari, M., Norola, S., Pasternack, A., Pikkarainen, J., Romo, M., Sjoblom, T., & Nikkila, E. A. (1987). Helsinki Heart Study: Primary prevention trial with gemfibrozil in middle-aged men with dyslipidemia: Safety of treatment, changes in risk factors, and incidence of coronary heart disease. *New England Journal of Medicine, 317,* 1237–1245.

Fukudo, S., Lane, J. D., Anderson, N. B., Kuhn, C. M., Schanberg, S. M., McCown, N., Muranaka, M., Suzuki, J., & Williams, R. B. (1992). Accentuated vagal antagonism of beta-adrenergic effects on ventricular repolarization: Evidence of weaker antagonism in hostile Type A men. *Circulation, 85,* 2045–2053.

Furberg, C. D., Psaty, B. M., & Meyer, J. V. (1995). Nifedipine: Dose-related increase in mortality in patients with coronary heart disease. *Circulation, 92,* 1326–1331.

Glassman, A. H., Helzer, J. E., Covey, L. S., Cottler, L. B., Stetner, F., Tipp, J. E., & Johnson, J. (1990). Smoking, smoking cessation, and major depression. *Journal of the American Medical Association, 264,* 1546–1549.

Hartka, E., Johnstone, B., Leino, E. V., Motoyoshi, M., Temple, M. T., & Fillmore, K. M. (1991). A meta-analysis of depressive symptomatology and alcohol consumption over time. *British Journal of Addiction, 86,* 1283–1298.

Jacobs, B. H. (1991). Serotonin and behavior: Emphasis on motor control. *Journal of Clinical Psychiatry, 52*(Suppl.), 17–23.

Johnston, J. A., Lineberry, C. G., Ascher, J. A., Davidson, J., Khayrallah, M. A., Feighner, J. P., & Stark, P. (1991). A 102-center prospective study of seizure in association with bupropion. *Journal of Clinical Psychiatry, 52,* 450–456.

Kapur, S., Mieczkowski, T., & Mann, J. J. (1992). Antidepressant medications and the relative risk of suicide attempt and suicide. *Journal of the American Medical Association, 268,* 3441–3445.

Kavanagh, I. T., Shephard, R. J., & Tuck, J. A. (1975). Depression after myocardial infarction. *Canadian Medical Association Journal, 113,* 23–27.

Kurosawa, H., Shimizu, Y., Nishimatsu, Y., Hirose, S., & Takamo, T. (1983). The relationship between mental disorders and physical severities in patients with acute myocardial infarction. *Japanese Circulation Journal, 47,* 723–728.

Lipid Research Clinics Program. (1984). The Lipid Research Clinics Coronary Primary Prevention Trial results: I. Reduction in incidence of coronary heart disease. *Journal of the American Medical Association, 251,* 351–364.

Littman, A. B. (1993). Review of psychosomatic aspects of cardiovascular disease. *Psychotherapy and Psychosomatics, 60,* 148–167.

Lloyd, G. G., & Cawley, R. H. (1978). Psychiatric morbidity in men one week after first acute myocardial infarction. *British Medical Journal, 2,* 1453–1454.

Meltzer, H. Y., & Lowy, M. T. (1987). The serotonin hypothesis of depression. In H. Y. Meltzer (Ed.), *Psychopharmacology: The third generation of progress* (pp. 513–526). New York: Raven Press.

MIAMI Trial Research Group. (1985). Metoprolol in Acute Myocardial Infarction (MIAMI): A randomised placebo-controlled international trial. *European Heart Journal, 6,* 199–226.

Mittleman, M. A., Maclure, M., Sherwood, J. B., Mulry, R. P., Tofler, G. H., Jacobs, J. C., Melman, A., Benson, H., & Muller J. E. (1995). The Determinants of Myocardial Infarction Onset Study Investigators: Triggering of acute myocardial infarction onset by episodes of anger. *Circulation, 92,* 1720–1725.

Montgomery, S. A. (1993). Venlafaxine: A new dimension in antidepressant pharmacotherapy. *Journal of Clinical Psychiatry, 54,* 119–126.

Nemeroff, C. B. (1994). Evolutionary trends in the pharmacotherapeutic management of depression. *Journal of Clinical Psychiatry, 55*(Suppl.), 3–15.

Norwegian Multicenter Study Group. (1981). Timolol-induced reduction in mortality and reinfarction in patients surviving acute myocardial infarction. *New England Journal of Medicine, 304,* 801–807.

Owens, M. J., & Nemeroff, C. B. (1994). Role of serotonin in the pathophysiology of depression: Focus on the serotonin transporter. *Clinical Chemistry, 40*(2), 288–295.

Physicians' desk reference (49th ed.). (1995). Montvale, NJ: Medical Economics Data Company.

Psaty, B. M., Heckbert, S. R., Koepsell, T. D., Siscovick, D. S., Raghunathan, T. E., Weiss, N. S., Rosendaal, F. R., Lemaitre, R. N., Smith, N. L., Wahl, P. W., Wagner, E. H., & Furberg, C. D. (1995). The risk of myocardial infarction associated with antihypertensive drug therapies. *Journal of the American Medical Association, 274*, 620–625.

Scandinavian Simvastatin Survival Study Group. (1994). Randomised trial of cholesterol lowering in 4444 patients with coronary heart disease: The Scandinavian Simvastatin Survival Study (4S). *Lancet, 344*, 1383–1389.

Shader, R. I. (Ed.). (1994). *Manual of psychiatric therapeutics* (2nd ed.). New York: Little, Brown.

Shepherd, J., Cobbe, S. M., Ford, I., Isles, C. G., Lorimer, A. R., Macfarlane, P. W., McKillop, J. H., & Packard, C. J. (1995). The West of Scotland Coronary Prevention Study Group: Prevention of coronary heart disease with pravastatin in men with hypercholesterolemia. *New England Journal of Medicine, 333*, 1301–1307.

Sloan, R. P., Shapiro, P. A., Bigger, J. T., Jr., Bagiella, E., Steinman, R. C., & Gorman, J. M. (1994). Cardiovascular autonomic control and hostility in healthy subjects. *American Journal of Cardiology, 74*, 298–300.

Smith, T. W., & Allred, K. D. (1989). Blood pressure responses during social interaction in high and low cynically hostile men. *Journal of Behavioral Medicine, 12*, 135–143.

Stern, M. J., Pascale, L., & Ackerman, A. (1977). Life adjustment postmyocardial infarction: Determining predictive variables. *Archives of Internal Medicine, 137*, 1680–1685.

Suarez, E. C., & Williams, R. B., Jr. (1989). Situational determinants of cardiovascular and emotional reactivity in high and low hostile men. *Psychosomatic Medicine, 51*, 404–418.

Tollefson, G. D. (1995). Anger, aggression, and depression. *Journal of Clinical Psychiatry, 56*, 489–491.

Veith, R. C., Lewis, N., Linares, Q. A., Barnes, R. R., Raskind, M. A., Villacres, E. C., Murburg, M. M., Ashleigh, E. A., Castillo, S., Peskind, E. R., Pascualy, M., & Halter, J. B. (1994). Sympathetic nervous system activity in major depression: Basal and desipramine-induced alterations in plasma norepinephrine kinetcis. *Archives of General Psychiatry, 51*, 411–422.

Wilkinson, C. J. (1985). Effects of diazepam (Valium) and trait anxiety on human physical aggression and emotional state. *Journal of Behavioral Medicine, 8*, 101–114.

Wishnie, H. A., Hackett, T. P., & Cassem, N. H. (1971). Psychological hazards of convalescence following myocardial infarction. *Journal of the American Medical Association, 215*, 1292–1296.

17

THE PATIENT IN THE CCU WAITING ROOM: IN-HOSPITAL TREATMENT OF THE CARDIAC SPOUSE

MARIANNE DELON

The early morning visitor, alone in the waiting room of a coronary care unit (CCU), is a familiar sight to most health care professionals. The visitor, frequently a spouse, appears to have kept vigil, for hours, on the other side of a door that separates him or her from the patient. In most cases, this door will remain closed to the spouse until visiting time, hours after he or she has arrived. While the patient is ministered to by a seemingly endless stream of medical professionals, the spouse waits. Occasionally, a doctor or nurse will emerge to ask a question or update the patient's condition, but essentially the spouse is alone and in crisis.

Providing psychological treatment for the spouse of a cardiac patient in a CCU is not a novel concept; social workers have been offering such intervention for decades. What I suggest in this chapter is a paradigm developed after years of interaction with spouses of cardiac patients. My discussion of the role of the social worker in the CCU is followed by a description of the crisis as it is typically experienced by the "cardiac spouse." I identify areas of assessment and present recommendations for individual and group intervention. I conclude by offering thoughts for providing this program in the current era of health care reform.

Numerous arguments have been made for promoting the inclusion of the spouse in a patient's hospital treatment plan (Klein, Dean, & Bogdon-off, 1967). Systems theory proposes that the illness of one member cannot be viewed in isolation of the family as a whole (Chavez & Faber, 1987). The significance of the systems concept is further reinforced by the spouse's ability to affect a critically ill patient's hospital course (Chatham, 1978). Through effective coping choices, the spouse can be instrumental in shaping the patient's adjustment so that acceptance of the illness, adherence to the treatment plan, and decision-making abilities are all enhanced. In addition to affecting the patient's experience, a medical crisis can impose considerable strain on a spouse's psychological, social, and economic functioning. The psychological toll can even be heavier than that on the patient (Bohachick & Anton, 1990), and for some spouses, the patient's recovery precedes his or her own (Crawshaw, 1974). Finally, the CCU environment is affected by a spouse's response to the crisis. Inadequate coping can negatively influence interactions with the CCU staff and, in extreme cases, threaten the integrity of the unit. Ultimately, how easily a spouse moves from one end of the crisis to the other will depend on the success of his or her coping choices. Through early assessment, intervention, and team involvement, a spouse can be helped to eliminate barriers to effective coping and to move through the crisis in as healthy a way as possible.

ROLE OF THE SOCIAL WORKER

A treatment plan devised to address the needs of a cardiac spouse in crisis is essential and one that CCU social workers—with their proficiency in psychosocial assessment, therapeutic intervention, and the delivery of concrete services and referrals—are well suited to implement. As members of the CCU team, social workers often function as liaisons between staff and family. Social workers can satisfy the spouse's need to interact with someone whose professional role is to take "a personal interest in their well-being" and with whom time spent is not perceived as "an imposition" (Hampe, 1975). Assessment and treatment planning for the patient are more easily accomplished within the context of this supportive interaction with the spouse.

The social worker frequently relies on the involvement of the multidisciplinary CCU team in assessing and treating the cardiac spouse. A prerequisite to the team's involvement is a unitwide understanding of the spouse's needs and a commitment to providing therapeutic intervention. It is imperative that staff recognize that people use a wide variety of coping mechanisms, with varying degrees of success. When a spouse's coping mechanisms are alienating and counterproductive, such as with displaced anger or severe acting out, staff may respond with avoidance, which in turn can render any treatment plan difficult to implement. Attempts must be made to align with the spouse who copes poorly. This can be accomplished only through an empathic understanding of individual limitations and the belief that, through interaction, change to effective coping is possible. The social worker can promote such understanding through interdisciplinary communication and teaching.

Doctors, nurses, and support staff are, for the social worker, invaluable referral sources. In-service training and informal discussion can accomplish the task of educating staff about the indications for appropriate referral of spouses. Follow-up communication is key to involvement in treatment plans that require staff collaboration. Weekly social work rounds, with the nurse manager and CCU attending physician or fellow, provide an opportunity for follow-up regarding earlier referrals and, when indicated, development of staff interventions.

THE CARDIAC SPOUSE IN CRISIS

As used in this chapter, the term *spouse* may connote a variety of relationships in which there is an expected degree of exclusivity, support, and caring, such as wife, husband, or same-sex or opposite-sex partner. However the relationship is defined, the onset of cardiac illness in one partner is a crisis that threatens a couple in unique ways.

The crisis state, though finite, is one in which the individual finds that his or her usual coping skills are insufficient. The life-threatening nature of cardiac illness raises the specter of loss of the partner and family roles and jeopardizes economic stability, to name but a few consequences (Bedsworth & Molen, 1982; Nyamathi, 1987). Compounding these stresses may be the daily demands of work, child care, and such preexisting problems as debt, unemployment, or the illness of another family member (Craven & Sharp, 1972). The spouse must also learn to navigate the CCU environment. Fast-paced and highly technical, the CCU is a subculture with its own language, hierarchy, rules, and values. It is an environment that may increase the spouse's sense of powerlessness and anxiety and leave him or her feeling like an "outsider" (Speedling, 1980). Timely and thorough understanding of the patient's diagnosis, treatment options, and prognosis are crucial to the medical decisions that a spouse is often asked to make, sometimes without benefit of the patient's input and frequently with only limited understanding of the particular illness.

Lazarus and Folkman (1984) have described *cognitive appraisal* as the process by which an individual evaluates a stressor in order to select from an array of coping strategies. According to this model, one aims to regulate the emotional response to the crisis (emotion-focused coping) or to minimize stress through cognitive and behavioral methods (problem-focused coping). The spouse's cognitive appraisal of the patient's admission to the CCU and subsequent coping strategies are determined by both the real and the perceived severity of illness and individual coping abilities. These in turn may affect or be affected by the spouse's psychological, marital, and economic status, as well as his or her cultural references and religious beliefs. Capacity for realistic appraisal and appropriate choice of coping strategies varies greatly and, for some spouses, can be severely limited.

ASSESSMENT OF THE CARDIAC SPOUSE

Assessment and treatment are not discrete processes. Within the context of an assessment interview, the mere availability of an empathic, nonjudgmental professional can relieve stress and, therefore, be viewed as an intervention.

A comprehensive assessment of the cardiac spouse's needs should explore the areas of physiological and psychological functioning, marital dynamics, social support, economic status, religious beliefs, and cultural norms. Assessment, generally, is an ongoing process. However, the time that an ongoing assessment requires is not always available and may fail to address the immediate needs of the spouse in crisis. In many instances, the initial interview provides the only opportunity in which the social worker can evaluate needs and formulate a treatment plan. Ultimately, an adequate assessment is one that focuses on the most critical areas of need or dysfunction.

Physiological Functioning

Careful observation can often provide information about a spouse's state of health. Being accompanied by an attendant or the use of a cane are obvious, if incomplete, indicators of physical limitations. It is important to examine the necessity for assistance and whether needs are being adequately met. Less apparent are the illnesses that may develop as a result of the crisis. Exacerbation of preexisting illness or the emergence of new symptoms in a spouse is not uncommon during a partner's illness. Disturbances of sleep, appetite, and concentration have been frequently reported (Nyamathi, 1987; Skelton & Dominian, 1973), as have somatic complaints, such as chest pain, palpitations, headaches, and gastrointestinal disorders (Skelton & Dominian, 1973). Symptoms that do not abate after a few days should be evaluated by an appropriate medical professional. Some, such as potential cardiac symptoms, should be evaluated immediately.

Psychological Functioning

As with physical illness, preexisting psychiatric illness can become exacerbated by crisis. Individuals with psychotic or borderline diagnoses, in particular, may be especially vulnerable in a crisis. Immediate assessment must be made in the presence of such psychotic symptoms as extreme paranoia, delusional thinking, and hallucinations, with attention paid to disturbed mood, affect, reality testing, thought processes, and the use of blatant denial. Suicidal ideation, or references to prior attempts, must be fully explored. Fact gathering should be conducted through focused, yet sensitive, questioning.

Cognitive appraisal of the crisis and selection of coping strategies are influenced by one's mental status and the defenses that one uses. Paranoia, for instance—whether indicative of psychosis or characterological style—may impede a spouse's ability to trust the validity of medical information received, the motives of staff, or the medical community in general. Denial, a frequently used defense, may distort understanding of the patient's medical status. Assessment of the spouse's cognitive appraisal ability can be accomplished by eliciting his or her version of the patient's diagnosis, prognosis, and treatment recommendations early in the initial interview.

Marital Dynamics

The equilibrium of a marriage, or any similar intimate relationship, can be jeopardized by the onset of a partner's cardiac illness. The state of marriage distinguishes the spouse's experience of the event from others in the patient's orbit, such as friends or associates, who may be less emotionally involved. Assessment of marital dynamics should involve discussion of the roles assigned to each partner. Role theory provides some concepts that are useful in assessing this area of functioning.

A role is a "patterned sequence of learned actions . . . performed by a person in an interaction situation" (Davis, 1986, p. 544). Some of the stress experienced by a spouse is often predicated on the belief that alteration, reassignment, or loss of a role that may result from a partner's illness cannot be tolerated. The patient's recovery and full capacity may be necessary to the maintenance of social and financial status (social position), whereas the spouse, perhaps temporarily, may be forced to assume roles incompatible with those that he or she routinely performs (role conflict). For example, a conflict may arise when a spouse who usually enacts a passive, dependent role is asked to make medical decisions for a partner too ill to do so. The spouse may need to undertake additional roles, including some formerly fulfilled by the patient, such as financial management and child care, and this can be burdensome (resulting in role overload). The prospect of the patient's death, and with it the need to withdraw one's reliance on another (role discontinuity), may present the greatest threat. An exploration of a couple's preexisting marital problems, when they are present, is an important aspect of assessment. In my years of clinical experience with couples in and outside of hospital settings, I have observed that guilt, anger, and resentment—often a feature of unresolved marital conflicts—may heighten during a cardiac crisis.

Social Support

Assessment of a spouse's need for and ability to accept support begins with inquiry about the scope and quality of his or her familial and social networks. The existence of family and friends, however, does not always imply the availability of effective support. Friends or family may be unable or unwilling to accept a supportive role, whereas previously strained family relationships can worsen during a medical crisis. Although some spouses are capable of coping adequately despite a dearth of support, others are unable to solicit the help available to them. Assessment should bring about distinctions between those who can and cannot mobilize needed support. Feelings about dependency, autonomy, and control will often determine the degree to which a spouse can accept or reject support from others.

Economic Status

Economic difficulties and concerns related to medical insurance frequently generate the first meeting between a social worker and spouse. Insurance status is critical to a smooth and safe discharge plan and may be especially relevant for the patient whose CCU stay is prolonged. Financial hardship, either preexisting or caused by the patient's admission, may require immediate intervention by the social worker.

Cultural Norms and Religious Beliefs

Cultural norms and religious beliefs are areas that are often overlooked during assessment, yet they may offer insight into a range of feelings, behaviors, and coping choices. Cultural differences may increase anxiety and feelings of alienation, particularly when there is a language barrier. Religious beliefs and the practice of attendant rituals (especially by and for the patient) may also cause concern. For instance, in one of my cases, the wife of an Orthodox Jewish man felt very uncomfortable about his need to perform daily religious rituals while in the CCU. She feared that her husband's rituals and use of a prayer shawl would be forbidden or ridiculed on the CCU. In this instance, worries over the spouse's religious beliefs added stress, albeit unnecessarily, and this required further exploration during the assessment. Discussion of religious beliefs can clarify the spouse's view of death and dying and may indicate a desire for spiritual guidance from a minister, rabbi, or priest.

INTERVENTION

Essential to any treatment is the establishment of a positive relationship. The social worker should be perceived by the spouse as a nonjudgmental, supportive member of the CCU team. An atmosphere of trust and support will enhance the spouse's ability to discuss previously denied or unarticulated feelings. Assurance must be conveyed to the spouse that intense feelings and out-of-character behavior are understood, even expected, within the context of a major medical crisis. Such assurance may open a window to cathartic release, which, although initially therapeutic, must lead to a more focused exploration of feelings, attitudes, and concerns.

When treating the cardiac spouse, the social worker must place emphasis on the present and assume an active, often directive role. On the basis of prior assessment, interventions may include problem clarification, goal setting, promotion of effective coping, concrete assistance, advocacy, and mobilization of social support. Group intervention and grief work are treatment paradigms that may also prove useful.

Problem Clarification

Problem clarification, in general terms, refers to the process by which the source of a crisis is brought into conscious awareness. In the presence of cardiac illness, the precipitant of the crisis is obvious, but its significance to the spouse may be less so. Clarification can put the features of the crisis into a realistic perspective and promote awareness of not simply external factors but also some of the internal dynamics causing distress. For instance, while assessing one spouse's marital relationship, I discovered that the patient had been emotionally abusive throughout the marriage. Further exploration revealed the wife's feelings of dependency, victimization, and anger, which had resulted in years of revenge fantasies focusing on his death. As a consequence, the wife felt responsible for his myocardial infarction. Her guilt created an impediment to focusing on the current crisis, until she was helped to recognize that the fantasies had served as a passive resolution to her marital problems. She was then able to cope with her husband's medical crisis.

Goal Setting

As noted, intervention must match specific needs. Goals must be realistic, attainable, and effective if they are to reduce stress. Although frequently initiated by the social worker, goal setting should involve the spouse. If a spouse is unable to perform the tasks necessary to achieve the set goals, then the social worker, as an active participant in treatment, should offer assistance. The spouse is encouraged to participate to the degree possible. For some spouses, dependence on the patient may be transferred to the social worker. Active assistance to the spouse must be balanced by steps taken to promote autonomous, effective coping. For example, one woman who was experiencing lightheadedness and chest tightness accepted the social worker's suggestion that she seek medical advice. Clearly distraught, the woman asked the social worker to arrange an appointment with a physician. Instead of doing this, the social worker provided several referrals and encouraged the spouse to make the appointment herself, with the social worker present for support.

Promotion of Effective Coping

The absence of effective coping mechanisms in a spouse requires an exploration of previous coping patterns. Prior assessment of a spouse's defensive style is also useful because it may be linked to coping choices. The spouse in denial about the severity of the patient's illness may, for example, rely on emotion-focused coping strategies, such as distancing and keeping emotions in check. Defenses such as denial, intellectualization, and displacement may be initially adaptive and should not be directly challenged or undermined. It is generally better to focus on previously effective coping strategies and current impediments to their use. Suggesting and encouraging alternative coping measures is part of this process.

Concrete Assistance

Impairment of day-to-day functioning will increase the spouse's feelings of helplessness and disorganization and may warrant immediate attention if further progress is to be realized. Concrete assistance may be offered in such areas as medical and psychiatric referrals; referrals to clergy; or help with medical insurance, lodging, and funeral arrangements. Information and education regarding "do not resuscitate" orders, health care proxies, and power of attorney privileges may also be required.

Advocacy

Advocacy is a valuable element of intervention. The social worker frequently acts as an intermediary between spouse and staff, particularly when the needs of these two parties diverge. Clashes do occur repeatedly over the structure of visiting hours. Despite recommendations for open visiting times (e.g., see Stillwell, 1984; Woellner, 1988), CCU hours are often fixed and limited. Some spouses simply view such visiting rules as too restrictive; for others, this issue may become the catalyst for a power struggle. Exploration of control and dependency needs, separation issues, feelings of entitlement, and displaced anger will help redirect emphasis from the external situation to the psychodynamic sources of the problem. For some spouses, concentration on concrete issues like visiting hours helps to fend off a host of uncomfortable feelings about the patient, the illness, and their relationship to both. Although compliance with unit regulations is the goal, such compliance may be deemed less therapeutic than the acceptance of a compromise. The social worker may thus advocate on the spouse's behalf for more flexible or extended visits. Collaboration with the nurse manager and staff nurses will provide understanding of the spouse's needs and assist in the formulation of special visiting allowances when appropriate.

Mobilization of Support

Activating support is an important feature of crisis intervention. Ideally, the spouse will be encouraged to recognize and seek out available supports from within his or her network. However, doctors, nurses, and other hospital staff are valuable sources of support as well (Hodovanic, Reardon, Reese, & Hedges, 1984; Mayou, Foster, & Williamson, 1978). Staff can provide instructional support in the form of orientation to the unit and explanation of the functions of bedside equipment, thereby reducing the spouse's confusion and sense of alienation. An adjunctive goal to gathering support is enabling the spouse to solicit and retain medical information by forming an alliance with the medical staff and attending physician. This is achieved by helping a spouse overcome the tentative and anxious feelings sometimes experienced in the presence of a medical professional. Effective strategies include writing down questions and answers or arranging to have another person present during a discussion with a doctor or nurse. For those displaying an insatiable need for informational input, an exploration of the underlying issues is called for.

Anticipatory Grief Work

Lindemann (1965) noted that grief reactions to death "are just one form of separation reaction" (p. 19). Another such reaction is anticipatory grief, a response to the anticipated death of a loved one. The sense of pending loss that often accompanies the spouse of a critically ill patient may manifest itself in such anticipatory grief reactions as depression, excessive thoughts about the partner, and increased reflection about expected adjustments to one's lifestyle.

The value of empathy and support cannot be overstated, particularly if a spouse is alone. A social worker should be available for a spouse's catharsis as well as to help provide emotional containment. Additional support, where it exists, should be garnered early, because a social or familial network will be valuable at the time of actual grief and can assist with the rituals of death. If the spouse is unprepared at the time of the patient's death, the social worker should offer referrals for such things as funeral directors or burial services.

Prior assessment—particularly of social supports, physiological and psychological functioning, cultural differences, and spiritual needs—will help identify those at high risk for complicated mourning. Such spouses should be offered access to bereavement groups or follow-up counseling with the social worker or another practitioner.

Some spouses, whether through denial or incomplete communication, are unprepared for a partner's death, even when it is imminent. It is imperative that the spouse be informed of the patient's medical status and prognosis throughout the course of hospitalization. This is best accomplished through arranged meetings with the attending physician or members of the CCU team.

Group Intervention

Group intervention with whoever is in the CCU waiting room is a highly recommended form of treatment for the families of CCU patients (Brown, Glazer, & Higgins, 1983; Fournet & Schaubhut, 1986; Halm, 1990). Groups can address the needs of many in a short period of time and provide a backdrop for identification of those spouses requiring individual intervention. Membership is often facilitated when the group's focus includes education as well as support. Time spent in a group helps a spouse recognize that he or she is not alone and may reduce inhibitions about sharing feelings. Indeed, it has been noted that female spouses of cardiac patients "seem to share with each other differently when they are not in their husband's presence" (Anderson, 1983, p. 128). Spouses are often freer to express themselves when they need not remain stoic for the patient's benefit. Additionally, groups may offer informal support, the acquisition of new coping skills, and a forum for the dissemination of information.

Providing Services in an Era of Health Care Reform

A commitment to provide psychological intervention to the cardiac spouse is threatened by the prevailing climate in many medical centers where cost-effectiveness has become a central measure of value. Downsizing and the elimination of services are survival tactics of hospitals struggling to remain financially solvent. Within this framework, the social worker's presence has become seriously threatened. To continue to deliver comprehensive care to the cardiac patient and his or her spouse, those who provide health care in a CCU setting must argue convincingly that social work services are cost-effective and valued.

CONCLUSION

A crisis is a transitional state from which one may emerge with new coping skills and an improved capacity for adaptation. The CCU social worker and staff are in a position to assist the spouse of a cardiac patient in crisis in a variety of ways. Such a commitment to the spouse can also benefit the patient and may enhance unit functioning.

REFERENCES

Anderson, M. P. (1983). Psychological disorders: Goals, treatments and outcomes. In L. H. Peterson (Ed.), *Cardiovascular rehabilitation: A comprehensive approach* (pp. 118–146). New York: Macmillan.

Bedsworth, J. A., & Molen, M. T. (1982). Psychological stress in spouses of patients with myocardial infarction. *Heart and Lung, 11,* 450–456.

Bohachick, P., & Anton, B. B. (1990). Psychosocial adjustment of patients and spouses to severe cardiomyopathy. *Research in Nursing and Health, 13,* 385–392.

Brown, D. G., Glazer, H., & Higgins, M. (1983). Group intervention: A psychosocial and educational approach to open heart surgery patients and their families. *Social Work in Health Care, 9*(2), 47–59.

Chatham, M. A. (1978). The effect of family involvement on patient's manifestations of postcardiotomy psychosis. *Heart and Lung, 7,* 995–999.

Chavez, C. W., & Faber, L. (1987). Effect of an education-orientation program on family members who visit their significant other in the intensive care unit. *Heart and Lung, 16,* 92–99.

Craven, R. F., & Sharp, B. H. (1972). The effect of illness on family functions. *Nursing Forum, 11*(2), 187–193.

Crawshaw, J. (1974). Community rehabilitation after acute myocardial infarction. *Heart and Lung, 3,* 258–262.

Davis, L. V. (1986). Role theory. In F. Turner (Ed.), *Social work treatment: Interlocking theoretical approaches* (3rd ed., pp. 541–563). New York: Free Press.

Fournet, K., & Schaubhut, R. M. (1986). What about spouses? *Focus on Critical Care, 13*(1), 14–18.

Halm, M. A. (1990). Effects of support groups on anxiety of family members during critical illness. *Heart and Lung, 19,* 62–71.

Hampe, S. O. (1975). Needs of the grieving spouse in a hospital setting. *Nursing Research, 24*(2), 113–120.

Hodovanic, B. H., Reardon, D., Reese, W., & Hedges, B. (1984). Family crisis intervention program in the medical intensive care unit. *Heart and Lung, 13,* 243–249.

Klein, R. F., Dean, A., & Bogdonoff, M. D. (1967). The impact of illness upon the spouse. *Journal of Chronic Disease, 20,* 241–248.

Lazarus, R., & Folkman, S. (1984). *Stress, appraisal and coping.* New York: Springer.

Lindemann, E. (1965). Symptomology and management in acute grief. In H. J. Parad (Ed.), *Crisis intervention: Selected readings* (4th ed., pp. 7–21). New York: Family Service Association of America.

Mayou, R., Foster, A., & Williamson, B. (1978). The psychological and social effects of myocardial infarction on wives. *British Medical Journal, 1,* 699–701.

Nyamathi, A. M. (1987). The coping responses of female spouses of patients with myocardial infarction. *Heart and Lung, 16,* 86–92.

Skelton, M., & Dominian, J. (1973). Psychological stress in wives of patients with myocardial infarction. *British Medical Journal, 2,* 101–103.

Speedling, E. J. (1980). Social structure and social behavior in an intensive care unit: Patient–family perspectives. *Social Work in Health Care, 6*(2), 1–22.

Stillwell, S. B. (1984). Importance of visiting needs as perceived by family members of patients in the intensive care unit. *Heart and Lung, 13,* 238–242.

Woellner, D. S. (1988). Flexible visiting hours in the adult critical care unit. *Focus on Critical Care, 15*(2), 66–69.

IV

CARDIAC PSYCHOLOGY IN PRACTICE

18

GETTING STARTED: ON BECOMING A CARDIAC PSYCHOTHERAPIST

PETER HALPERIN

This chapter is an overview for psychotherapists interested in treating cardiac patients, perhaps arising from the excitement imparted by reading this book, on how to prepare for and embark in the rewarding and much needed clinical specialty of cardiac psychology. I regard this as an informal consultation to the reader, as if we were discussing the issue over coffee. I am assuming that you have read this book and, therefore, are well educated about the wealth of scientific evidence supporting the need for psychological treatment of cardiac patients as well as about the many specific techniques for treating such patients, so I base my discussion on the "how to put it all together" point of view.

WHAT YOU NEED BEFORE YOU START

Existential Thought

First and foremost, be yourself. Why start with such a trite generality? Because I feel that what is essentially lacking in health care, and certainly for cardiac patients, is a genuine relationship with caring caregivers who are willing to authentically enter into the patient's deepest areas of fear and share their own humanity, because they must ultimately share the fear

435

of death that underlies the "problem" facing the cardiac patient. One way of not being yourself is to lose your unique identity by overidentification with the role of psychotherapist, to the exclusion of being a person. This, in fact, is one of the most important psychological issues for cardiac patients, who, having experienced a brush with death, want and need to live their lives more fully in accordance with personal values and desires that many have repressed in pursuit of professional goals. As therapists, we are tempted to subjugate our personal selves to our professional identities, certainly to obtain competence, prestige, and economic success. But, in addition, these choices are a means of dealing with the fear of death, because the roles we play—whether psychotherapist or amateur tennis player—are abstractions and thus do not die. When we lose ourselves in these roles we are in some measure acting on our existential fears. To be oneself, a unique person, is to be aware of the transience of this reality. It also means that we can bring to each moment, clinical and personal, a clarity of vision, purpose, and emotional connection available only to those who live with death, who live authentically. This synopsis of existential philosophy and psychotherapy is my starting point because it ultimately represents the goal of psychotherapy with the cardiac patient: to use the perspective gained by knowing that one is mortal and to reprioritize one's life, live it more fully, and, paradoxically, improve the quality of life as well as its quantity. It is beyond the scope of this chapter to explore how to cultivate such an existential awareness, but I cannot overemphasize the benefit of reading such texts as Yalom's (1980) classic *Existential Psychotherapy* and works by existential philosophers while trying to live life in accordance with these principles, seeking personal avenues, such as psychotherapy, that prepare you to live and therefore practice psychology in a humane, genuine, and giving fashion.

Professional Training

Indispensable areas of professional training include developing expertise in individual, couples, family, and, especially, group psychotherapy. Group training is highlighted because of the mounting evidence, as discussed in this book, that group psychotherapy for cardiac patients reduces their clinical risk. Other important reasons to look to this modality are the cost-effectiveness of groups, which will be an increasing issue in the new age of health care cost control, and the unique clinical aspects of groups. These include the provision of support (itself known to be of use with cardiac patients) as well as the importance of discovering that one is not alone with the frequent emotional consequences of cardiac disease (e.g., fear and depression) or isolated with a defense mechanism that, although helping to deal with the fear, often becomes the acute clinical problem: denial of the illness in general and of acute symptoms in particular. This is one of the most pressing of the behavioral issues for cardiac patients. By denying symptoms of a heart attack and thus delaying going to the hospital, millions of patients greatly increase their chance of dying from heart attacks every year. By denying their vulnerabilities, millions more partake in acutely risky behaviors, such as excess overexertion in inclement weather or indulging in extremes of rage and hostility. This issue is uniquely treatable in a group setting because patients struggle with a sense of shame that they alone could be "stupid" enough to deny symptoms or engage in high-risk activities and are greatly relieved to discover the near universality of denial, allowing them to focus on the problem. Although a thorough discussion of group therapy technique is beyond the scope of this chapter, I emphasize this very important clinical point of treating denial because of its fundamental role in helping cardiac patients and because treatment of denial is often left out of discussions that focus on treating hostility, depression, anxiety, or other psychological variables in heart disease.

Because major depression and panic disorder are known to be significant risk factors for cardiac patients and because these are often treated most effectively when medications are at least part of the treatment (Carney et al., 1988; Goldberg et al., 1990), it is essential that clinicians have the skills to diagnose these disorders as well as access to a psychiatrist for consultation regarding psychotropic medications.

Gaining Medical Knowledge

Perhaps most important, it is very helpful, if not essential, to become familiar with the realities that patients and their families confront when dealing with critical illness, recovery, or death within a medical setting. Learning the language of cardiology is fundamental to both understanding what patients are talking about when relating the experience of their illness, tests, and treatments and being able to help translate some of these words. Knowledge is power, and ignorance breeds increased anxiety and denial. The vast majority of cardiac patients have very little understanding of their illness. How could they, considering that most of what they know was taught to them at a time when their anxiety simply made learning impossible (e.g., in the cardiac care unit or some other overwhelmingly frightening setting)? One of the best services psychologists can provide is to teach patients with cardiac disease, in an atmosphere that minimizes anxiety and maximizes caring and support, to understand the essentials of their heart and coronary arteries and what happens in illness and in healing. Equally important is experiencing the range of emotions that patients, loved ones, and their caregivers go through in a hospital setting. This is the "music" of heart disease that accompanies the "words" of cardiology.

The best way to obtain this information and experience is to arrange for an apprenticeship with a hospital-based cardiologist over at least a 6-

month period, as did Robert Allan, coeditor of this book. A request for an opportunity to observe a cardiologist will likely be readily accepted by whomever you approach, especially because your psychological expertise will be of interest and can help the cardiologist in various settings. From a practical perspective, in addition to preparing you for your work, the personal relationships established with physicians and nurses can only help when it comes time for referrals to be made. It is also essential to read about cardiac physiology and pathophysiology in standard texts, such as Braunwald's (1992) *Heart Disease*.

STARTING A PRACTICE

Starting a psychotherapy practice focusing on clients with cardiac disease should be easy. Given the overwhelming evidence that psychological factors play a major role in cardiac pathology, that treating these factors significantly reduces cardiac risk, and that such treatment is so cost-effective, people should be knocking down the doors of psychologists to refer themselves or their patients to psychological care. Alas, this is not the case. The reasons for this resistance are both interesting and informative in terms of developing a strategy for building your practice. Below, I outline my understanding of this resistance.

Paradigm Issues

Americans still live with a medical worldview that understands illness and health in mechanical terms that, furthermore, tend to look only at the particular system that is ill. That is, heart disease is thought to exist only in the heart muscle and its coronary arteries, with a "little nod" toward the liver in terms of cholesterol metabolism. Because believing is seeing, and not the other way around, when a cardiologist reads in a cardiology journal that group psychotherapy greatly reduces the risk of repeated myocardial infarction, he or she simply does not "see" it. Unfortunately, then, all of the exciting evidence linking stress and psychological factors with heart disease (and the even more compelling evidence collected in this volume) regarding the effectiveness of treating coronary patients' stress has not penetrated the consciousness of mainstream cardiology. We are all, I believe, in the last days of this paradigm, and, as if living in Copernican times, we cardiac psychotherapists are trying to earn a living drawing charts of the heavens—depicting the earth revolving around the sun and getting very few takers. It is good to remember that patience is not only a virtue but also good for one's heart.

Socioeconomic Factors

Even if medical colleagues see the truth of the psychologist's position, they are moved by strong factors to, consciously or unconsciously, ignore it. Only very recently has the health care system come to realize that physicians are rewarded too much for what they do to patients and too little for what they do with them (i.e., talking with them). Mental health providers may grapple with similar problems: For example, as a psychotherapist, social worker, or allied mental health provider, would you give the same attention to new research on an antidepressant (which you cannot prescribe) that you would if it were a traditional part of your profession? Until more physicians earn a living by talking with patients, this socioeconomic reality will remain an important factor.

Countertransference

The average cardiologist lives a life that is more stressful than the vast majority of his or her patients. Cardiologists work harder and longer, have spent inhuman numbers of hours in rigorous and often dehumanizing training, and are constantly exposed to the threat of a "beep" from a patient's monitors that can transform a calm moment into full out sympathetic discharge. It can be somewhat frightening, and even unfair, for them to have to recognize that they put themselves at medical risk from this stress. A very good reason, then, to ignore risky behavior in their patients is that they can ignore it in themselves.

The Stigma of Psychotherapy

Unfortunately, for many potential psychotherapy clients, being referred for psychological evaluation or treatment is still akin to being called "crazy" or "unable to cope." Likewise, there is much discomfort among potential referring professionals, either because of their own similar misconceptions or because they do not want to engage their patients' resistance. This issue often results in caregivers neglecting to refer even those patients with severe, life-threatening depression or other major mental illnesses for psychological treatment, let alone relatively psychologically healthy cardiac patients for psychotherapy.

Overcoming Resistance

Being aware of the problems discussed above suggests a strategy that both avoids some of the pitfalls and establishes a framework to manage others. If you attempt to build your practice by appealing to cardiologists to refer clients to you or even by advertising directly to potential clients, then it will be most difficult to succeed. The cardiologists may tend to suffer from the "paradigmatic blindness" discussed above or may avoid bringing up the idea of psychotherapy with their patients, and patients may suffer from fear of the psychological process and denial of the need.

The best solution of which I am aware for psychologists to make contact with potential clients is to work within an existing cardiac rehabilitation program. Such programs can be found in most academic and community hospitals throughout the country. Patients who have documented coronary disease are referred to these rehabilitation programs by their doctors for exercise, dietary education, and—whether they realize it or not—stress reduction. Very few of these programs have psychiatrists or psychologists on staff. Instead, psychosocial issues are typically addressed by the nurses, who have the greatest amount of patient contact in these programs. These nurses, unlike most cardiologists, are all too aware of the prominent roles that depression, anxiety, hostility, and stress play in their patients' lives. Rather than having to persuade staff to refer patients, a psychologist might need only to make himself or herself available, and the usual response will be most positive and appreciative. This strategy essentially manages the issues of paradigm blindness, socioeconomic disincentives, and countertransference resistance.

Still to be solved is the problem of patients' aversion to psychological referral and the consequent problems that this makes for the rehabilitation staff in making referrals. Who should be referred? Who should be strongly urged to accept the referral? As long as these questions are individualized, the problem will exist and your psychological services will be underutilized, to both your and the patients' detriment. The last finesse is to, if at all possible, convince program coordinators to make a psychosocial evaluation and basic teaching about mind–body issues with regard to heart disease essential core components of the program, emphasizing that these are just as important as education about dietary factors and exercise. This is no less than the relative risk imposed by psychosocial factors warrants. If such components are successfully implemented, then the problem of triage for referral disappears. Seeing the psychologist becomes an automatic process; patients will not feel that they are being singled out but, rather, will tend to welcome the opportunity to talk with a "stress expert," which is a good thing to be known as these days. Furthermore, this level of integration means that the psychologist will be a true part of the staff and in a position to educate staff and participate in program development. After working in one rehabilitation program where my services were optional (not truly integrated into the program), I was fortunate to be able to codirect another program and to fully integrate the psychological component with all other treatment elements. I found the latter to be a far superior situation, for all the reasons mentioned above.

Intervention

Although all of the large-scale intervention trials described in this book involved the use of group therapy, there is also a clear need for individual, couples, and family treatment, which has encompassed much of my work. Some individuals prefer relating on a one-to-one basis, whereas others have joined a group after a course of individual treatment. It has seemed wise to begin treatment intensively, and I have often seen patients once or even twice weekly, in addition to group therapy, but generally for only a few months, or at least until clear behavioral change is in place. The majority of these patients have been quite different from the individuals who generally seek out the services of a psychotherapist. Most pride themselves in their self-sufficiency, and few admit to psychological problems or pain. To keep patients engaged, it has been necessary to maintain a lively dialogue. To ensure that the patient returns, each session should produce a sense that something concrete has been gained, such as new information or a "homework assignment" that may improve quality of life or reduce coronary risk. Humor is also a very helpful tool. A more passive, psychoanalytic approach would be doomed with many cardiac patients because they would quickly lose interest. Most important, although many forms of psychotherapy promote insight, cardiac psychology does not have the luxury of stopping there: Behavioral change, rather than just understanding, is necessary to reduce the very real risk factors associated with coronary heart disease.

Finally, I should mention two important practical considerations. Although psychological services are sometimes required for accredited cardiac rehabilitation programs, the standard insurance coverage for cardiac rehabilitation does not provide for such services. Instead, insurance coverage is reserved for exercise, dietary education, and general educational classes. Individual, family, and group therapy are reimbursable as mental health benefits, and patients are quite content as long as the bill is partly or entirely covered, regardless of the details of the insurance.

CONCLUSION

I have offered a brief description of skills needed to enter the field of cardiac psychology and practical advice about how to bring these skills to the care of cardiac patients. It is my hope and expectation that, as the medical paradigm continues to shift toward recognizing the importance of treating psychosocial factors contributing to cardiac disease, psychotherapists will more and more be found working with physicians in the care of these patients. The need for your services is great, and the deep satisfaction of the work is yours to experience.

REFERENCES

Braunwald, E. (Ed.). (1992). *Heart disease*. Philadelphia: W. B. Saunders.

Carney, R. M., Rich, M. W., Freedland, K. E., & Saini, J., et al. (1988). Major depressive disorder predicts cardiac events in patients with coronary artery disease. *Psychosomatic Medicine, 50,* 627–633.

Goldberg, R., Morris, P. L., Christian, F., & Badger, J., et al. (1990). Panic disorder in cardiac outpatients. *Psychosomatics, 31,* 168–173.

Yalom, I. D. (1980). *Existential psychotherapy*. New York: Basic Books.

19

CONCLUSIONS, TREATMENT GOALS, AND FUTURE DIRECTIONS

ROBERT ALLAN, STEPHEN SCHEIDT, and THOMAS G. PICKERING

The overriding conclusion that we draw from this volume is that cardiac psychology can, indeed, be "good medicine." There are substantial data supporting the relationship between modifiable psychosocial risk factors and coronary heart disease (CHD). More important, cardiac morbidity and, to a lesser extent, cardiac mortality have been reduced in three noteworthy clinical trials. Psychosocial intervention can improve quality of life and may save many millions of precious health care dollars in coming decades. Group psychotherapy is an inexpensive way to treat CHD, a lifestyle disorder for a substantial segment of the population, particularly when compared to the costs of hospitalization and invasive procedures in cardiology.

At this point in the evolution of cardiac psychology, then, what can be said about the strength of the relationship between the heart and mind? It appears to us that there is a clear and consistent relationship between a number of psychosocial factors and CHD risk, but one reason that the field has had such a checkered history is that this relationship is both modest and—given the enormous complexity and diversity of the human psyche—difficult to assess. The most compelling data relating stress and atherosclerosis come from animal studies (e.g., Kaplan, Botchin, & Manuck, 1994), where conditions can be controlled with far greater precision than in human study.

TREATMENT GOALS

Why does psychosocial intervention work with patients who have CHD? There are two general and quite distinct mechanisms that could explain the physiological link between heart and mind. First, such psychosocial factors as Type A behavior, cynical hostility, job strain, anxiety, and vital exhaustion could accelerate the chronic disease process. Each of these conditions or psychological characteristics has been postulated to elevate sympathetic nervous system activity and, hence, to promote coronary atherosclerosis, primarily as a result of excess secretion of catecholamines or other "stress hormones" (e.g., cortisol) over decades. Each of the three clinical trials presented in chapters 9 to 11 of this volume has made extensive efforts to reduce chronic sympathetic arousal by means of counseling, relaxation training, and improving anger and time-management skills. Although by no means a panacea for CHD, prevention programs should nonetheless promote calm, friendly, and relaxed living. Acute psychological stress as a trigger for cardiac events is the other potential leading mechanism linking heart and mind. Results from the ongoing Determinants of Time of Myocardial Infarction Onset Study have demonstrated an increased risk of myocardial infarction (MI) with strenuous physical exertion, particularly among people who do not regularly exercise. Episodes of anger have also been shown to increase risk of MI. Behavioral scientists have paid considerable attention to the cardiovascular reactivity hypothesis, and if increased reactivity does have a pathogenic role, then it seems most likely that it would influence the acute responses rather than the chronic disease process. Therefore, counseling patients to avoid such potential triggers is an important therapeutic intervention.

Thus, limiting both chronic and acute emotional arousability is a central goal of psychotherapy with patients who have CHD. It seems plausible that the treatments described in this volume have been sufficiently effective at reducing sympathetic arousal to reduce its effect on cardiac events, although it is certainly possible that some treatments have worked through other mechanisms. Given the relatively short duration of most intervention trials, it would seem reasonable to suppose that their benefits are attributable more to a damping effect on the acute response than on the chronic disease process.

Beyond this broad perspective, on the basis of currently available data, we suggest the following additional goals for treatment:

- Help patients reduce standard risk factors: cigarette smoking, hyperlipidemia, obesity, hypertension, and sedentary lifestyle. All of these risk factors have a lifestyle component for some patients. Support for lifestyle change, especially the more difficult task of sustaining such change once the threat from an acute event has subsided, should be central to any coronary risk reduction program.

- Provide emotional support. A cardiac event—particularly a life-threatening MI, coronary artery bypass graft (CABG) surgery, or resuscitation from cardiac arrest—is immensely unsettling. Many patients and their families have difficulty managing painful emotions surrounding these experiences, such as anxiety, fear, and anger. The opportunity to discuss these events in depth with a health professional can provide emotional support that can be valuable to the patient and family.
- Reduce cardiac denial: Teach and frequently reinforce the importance of early diagnosis and intervention for acute coronary events.
- Provide social support and reduce social isolation in the context of group therapy. Encourage and strengthen interpersonal relationships. Help patients work through blocks to intimacy.
- Reduce depression, with psychotherapy and, if needed, psychopharmacotherapy.
- Reduce anxiety: The relaxation response, or other forms of meditation, may be helpful in this regard. Psychopharmacological intervention may also be of benefit.
- Help patients deal with existential and spiritual issues by examining life values.

From the data currently available, a major, still unanswered question is, How extensive does a lifestyle program have to be for it to provide cardiologic benefit? Ornish's Lifestyle Heart Trial (see chap. 9) is an intensive program, requiring more than 14 hours per week and a stringent vegetarian diet with less than 10% fat. On the other hand, the Recurrent Coronary Prevention Project (chap. 10) and Project New Life (chap. 11) provided far less frequent involvement, with weekly meetings that were reduced to once a month or less after the first year of treatment (if not sooner). Thus, it appears that risk-reduction programs requiring a modest investment of time have produced significant benefits in treating CHD, whereas more intensive efforts have shown objective evidence of reversing coronary atherosclerosis and improving myocardial perfusion. Both kinds of programs should continue to be developed, because it is likely that different types of individuals will be attracted to programs of differing intensities.

FUTURE CLINICAL AND SCIENTIFIC INVESTIGATION

The following projects seem to us to be particularly fertile for investigation:

1. Investigate how social support works, and develop ways to enhance social support for those who otherwise might be vulnerable.
2. Attempt to develop interventions particularly useful for patients from lower socioeconomic backgrounds.
3. Screen patients routinely for depression, particularly before and after CABG surgery; investigate the mechanism and attempt preventive—perhaps even preoperative—psychological or other interventions.
4. Discover why so many patients do not return to work after CABG surgery.
5. Consider giving more attention to individuals with silent ischemia. Individuals who have silent ischemia are typically unaware of their physiological limitations and may represent a population particularly worthy of clinical trials for lifestyle intervention. It may be that either high-tech interventions (e.g., using some sort of ambulatory monitor and alarm) or low-tech interventions (taking one's own pulse) might reduce daily ischemia and possibly improve long-term outcome.
6. Look at psychosocial risk factors in men and in women, and determine how they are different.
7. Develop support groups for recipients of automatic implantable cardiac defibrillators, who have generally had one or more cardiac arrests. These "sudden death survivors" are often traumatized, and little work has been done in this area.

By far the most important task of cardiac psychology for the next few years is to better pinpoint physiological mechanisms linking psychosocial factors to CHD. The vast majority of studies done to date have invoked either increased sympathetic nervous system arousal or decreased parasympathetic arousal as the culprit mechanism, but this hypothesis is far from proven, and there are other likely candidates, such as the serotonergic system and the hypothalamus-pituitary-adrenal cortex axis. Far greater precision is needed to better direct behavioral and pharmacological interventions for reducing CHD. Indeed, the lack of rigorously proven mechanisms is probably the greatest single cause for the skepticism that is still common among both cardiologists and psychologists.

Once biological mechanisms are better understood, behavioral, physiological, and pharmacological interventions can be more precisely chosen, and the benefits of cardiac psychology should become clear to patients, families, and health professionals as well as to whatever health care system will be in place in the future.

REFERENCE

Kaplan, J. R., Botchin, M. B., & Manuck, S. B. (1994). Animal models of aggression and cardiovascular disease. In A. W. Siegman & T. W. Smith (Eds.), *Anger, hostility, and the heart* (pp. 127–148). Hillsdale, NJ: Erlbaum.

GLOSSARY

ABDOMINAL AORTIC ANEURYSM A bulge in the lower aorta, usually caused by weakening of its wall due to atherosclerosis. These aneurysms often expand slowly over years or decades, with increasing risk of rupture if they exceed a diameter of 5-6 cm. Their size can be monitored with noninvasive tests such as ultrasound or computerized tomography (CT) scans. Rupture is usually catastrophic, with well over a 50% death rate. Because the aneurysm can be repaired with reasonably low risk (usually by replacing that portion of the aorta with a synthetic graft), many patients have prophylactic repair done once aneurysms are discovered and are sufficiently large. Often referred to by the acronym AAA, or as *triple* A.

ACE (ANGIOTENSIN CONVERTING ENZYME) INHIBITOR A class of drugs that inhibit an enzyme called *angiotensin converting enzyme* that catalyzes the conversion of angiotensin-I, an inactive substance, into angiotensin-II, a very powerful vasoconstrictor. Blocking this enzyme blocks the formation of angiotensin-II and thus dilates blood vessels. ACE inhibitors are used widely in treating hypertension. They are also used widely in treating congestive heart failure, where they improve survival and reduce complications by reducing *afterload*: the pressure in the arteries that the heart has to pump against *after* the ventricle begins to contract and starts to eject blood.

ACUTE CORONARY SYNDROMES Sometimes used to refer to acute myocardial infarction, unstable angina, and sudden cardiac death—all of which appear to share a common mechanism of plaque rupture and thrombosis at the site of rupture, with varying clinical presentations.

449

ACUTE MYOCARDIAL INFARCTION   Death of a portion of heart muscle usually caused by sudden occlusion of a previously narrowed coronary artery. If the damage extends through the full thickness of the heart muscle wall, it is called a *transmural*, or *Q-wave infarct* (because the electrocardiogram develops a type of complex called a Q wave). Q-wave infarcts are almost always caused by a totally occlusive blood clot (thrombus) on top of the prior atherosclerotic plaque. The other type of infarct, non-Q-wave myocardial infarction (NQMI), affects only the inner part of the heart muscle wall and does not extend the full thickness to the outer wall. Such NQMIs often also have clots on top of plaques, but the clots do not totally obstruct the artery and some blood can still get through. *Heart attack* and *myocardial infarction* (MI) mean the same thing (i.e., death of heart muscle), but sometimes *heart attack* is used to describe other acute cardiac problems (e.g., hospitalization for acute angina or a major arrhythmia). Therefore, *MI* is the more correct term.

AFTERLOAD   The load on the heart after it begins to pump, opens the aortic valve, and starts to eject blood in systole. Determined by the state of the aortic valve and of the peripheral arteries. To be differentiated from *preload*, the load on the heart before ejection begins, which is determined by how much the ventricle is filled during diastole.

ALPHA-BLOCKERS   Drugs that block one branch of the sympathetic (adrenalin-related, or adrenergic) nervous system. Alpha sympathetic receptors are found mainly in the peripheral blood vessels and not in the heart (*see* BETA-BLOCKERS), so alpha-blockers are vasodilators and are used to treat hypertension. Examples include prazosin and terazosin.

ALVEOLI   The tiny air sacs of the lungs where oxygen and carbon dioxide exchange occurs between the inhaled air and the tiny blood vessels of the pulmonary circulation running in the walls of the alveoli.

AMBLYOPIA   Dimness of vision.

ANGINA PECTORIS   Transient chest discomfort (literally, "choking in the chest") that is a manifestation of coronary atherosclerotic disease. Angina tends to be precipitated by physical exertion or mental stress and is often worse in cold weather, after eating, or when patients are angry or under time pressure. It usually lasts 2–10 minutes and generally disappears on its own accord if the patient stops the precipitating activity. Although the classic complaint is discomfort and pain in the chest, many patients deny that the symptom is really pain and instead complain of "heaviness," "tightness," or a "constricting band" around the chest; shortness of breath; or sometimes symptoms located elsewhere, particularly in the jaw, the left shoulder, or the left arm or hand. Angina may also be experienced in the back and the right shoulder or arm and may resemble indigestion. However, this indigestion, or "heartburn," when associated with blocked arteries of the heart, occurs more often with physical activity or psychological stress than with eating. Angina is usually relieved by rest or, if severe, by the administration of sublingual nitroglycerin. Also referred to as *stable angina* or *chronic stable angina*.

ANGIOPLASTY   Literally, the "fixing of a blood vessel." The medical term used for angioplasty of a coronary artery is *percutaneous transluminal coronary angioplasty* (PTCA). PTCA uses specially designed catheters with a balloon at the tip that is deflated until the obstructive lesion in the coronary artery is reached. The balloon is placed next to the atherosclerotic lesion and inflated for 30–90 seconds at very high pressure, in hopes of "squashing" the atherosclerotic plaque and greatly reducing or eliminating the obstruction to blood flow. The technique is the same as for cardiac catheterization and is performed by interventional cardiologists in a catheterization laboratory (except that the operator needs more training and skill beyond diagnostic catheterization, and the hospital usually has cardiac surgery available for the rare case where a major complication necessitates emergency coronary artery bypass graft surgery). The current death rate with PTCA is about 0.5%, and the major complication rate (i.e., death, acute myocardial infarction, or emergency coronary artery bypass graft surgery) is about 3%. There are also other types of angioplasty, such as renal artery angioplasty or peripheral angioplasty of leg vessels.

ANTERIOR   The front of the body (e.g., the nose points anteriorly).

ANTICOAGULANT DRUGS   Drugs that interfere with the clotting system (the system that generates thrombin from prothrombin, and then fibrin—the actual material of a firm clot—from fibrinogen). Anticoagulant drugs interfere at several steps along the way of a complicated series of chemical reactions that produce blood clots. Warfarin is the most commonly used drug (in tablet form) for outpatients; heparin is active only intravenously or by injection and, so, is used for inpatients.

ANTILIPID DRUGS   Drugs that reduce elevated serum lipids. Most drugs on the market today either reduce low-density lipoprotein or increase high-density lipoprotein, but may do both. Examples are the "statin" drugs (lovastatin, simvastatin, or anything else with *statin* in its name), gemfibrozil, niacin, cholestyramine, and colestipol.

ANTIPLATELET DRUGS   Drugs that interfere with the action of platelets, whose usual function is to facilitate blood clotting, especially in areas of injury. This normal clotting function can become dangerous in patients who have atherosclerotic plaques, particularly if the plaques rupture. Interfering with platelet function may make totally occlusive clots less likely at such sites, and thus prevent myocardial infarctions. Aspirin is a powerful and long-lasting antiplatelet agent (i.e., several days benefit is obtained from one aspirin) and the most widely used drug of this class.

AORTIC INSUFFICIENCY (AI) OR AORTIC REGURGITATION (AR)   Leakage of the aortic valve, backward from the aorta into the left ventricle. Occurs as a result of rheumatic heart disease, severe hypertension, degenerative disease of the aortic valve, certain congenital conditions such as Marfan's disease, aortic dissection, and various diseases of the aortic root.

AORTIC ROOT   The first part of the aorta, which is the main blood vessel distributing blood to the entire body, as it leaves the heart and courses upward toward the neck before making a U-turn in the upper chest to descend down the entire trunk to the legs. The coronary arteries branch from the aorta in the root just above the aortic valve; any diseases of the root can affect the coronary arteries, the aortic valve itself, and the carotid arteries that feed the brain. Aortic dissection (*see* DISSECTING ANEURYSM) can sometimes cause major damage to the aortic root and is a surgical emergency; if the aorta is not repaired, then mortality is very high.

AORTIC STENOSIS   Narrowing of the aortic valve.

ARRHYTHMIA   A disturbance of the heart rhythm. Three major types: atrial arrhythmia, ventricular arrhythmia, and bradyarrhythmia. *Atrial arrhythmias* originate in the atria, the reservoir chambers of the heart, and are generally not life threatening. Examples include atrial tachycardia, atrial flutter, and atrial fibrillation; the last is very important because the uncoordinated quivering ("fibrillation") of the reservoir chambers without sufficient emptying of these chambers often leads to blood clots that can break loose (embolize) and are a frequent cause of strokes (this can be largely prevented by anticoagulation). *Ventricular arrhythmias*, originating in the ventricles—the pumping chambers—often are life threatening; sudden cardiac death is usually caused by ventricular fibrillation, in which all forward pumping activity of the heart ceases within a few seconds of onset of the arrhythmia. *Bradyarrhythmias* (*brady* = slow) are slow rhythms, including heart block and other slow rhythms, which can sometimes cause dizziness or syncope (fainting).

ATHERECTOMY   A specialized kind of angioplasty, in which rather than "squashing" an atherosclerotic plaque with a balloon, one cuts away the plaque with a blade. Performed in a cardiac catheterization laboratory in the same manner as percutaneous transluminal coronary angioplasty, with much the same indications and risks.

ATHEROSCLEROSIS   A pathologic process whereby plaques form on the inside of arteries, narrowing and sometimes blocking (occluding) them. The more general term *arteriosclerosis* refers to any sort of occlusive arterial disease; *atherosclerosis* refers to the most common etiology, which is related to fatty, especially cholesterol, deposits. Atherosclerosis can occur in many locations, but the places that are most common and cause the most clinical problems are in the heart (coronary atherosclerosis); in the brain (strokes and transient ischemic attacks); in the kidneys (some forms of hypertension mediated by renal artery atherosclerosis); in the distal aortic wall (abdominal aortic aneurysm); and in the peripheral arteries of the legs (leg pain with walking, known as *claudication*, or *peripheral vascular disease*).

ATRIAL FIBRILLATION   A very common type of atrial arrhythmia, found in several million people in the United States. *See* ARRHYTHMIA.

AUTOMATIC IMPLANTABLE CARDIOVERTER DEFIBRILLATOR (AICD)   An automated miniaturized electrical device that monitors the heartbeat, automatically detects a life-threatening rhythm such as ventricular tachycardia or ventricular fibrillation and then delivers a powerful electric shock to the heart to stop the arrhythmia; stopping the abnormal rhythm usually allows normal rhythm to resume. Surgery was previously required to install an AICD, but this can now often be done through intravenous catheters in an electrophysiologic laboratory. AICDs prevent sudden cardiac death in some patients.

BETA-BLOCKERS   A class of drugs that block the beta-adrenergic branch of the sympathetic nervous system. This branch controls heart rate, blood pressure, strength of cardiac contraction, and various other automatic functions, so that blockade of this portion of the autonomic nervous system causes heart rate, blood pressure, and strength of heart contraction to fall. The drugs are used to treat hypertension, angina, arrhythmias, and various other cardiac diseases. Examples include propranolol, metoprolol, atenolol, nadolol, and almost any other drug that ends in *lol*.

BRUCE PROTOCOL   The most widely used (but not the only) protocol for treadmill exercise testing. The first stage is walking at 1.7 mph (leisurely stroll) at a 10% grade; Stage 2 is 2.5 mph at 12% grade; Stage 3 is 3.4 mph (a bit faster than the usual city walking speed) with 14% grade; and Stage 4 is 4.2 mph at 16% grade (a workout for trained athletes). Each stage is 3-minutes long, and the intended end result is to increase the heart rate to ≥85% of a maximum predicted for the individual's age (approximately 220 − Age). If this endpoint is achieved, then the presence or absence of changes on the electrocardiogram recorded during and at the peak of the test are reasonably accurate in predicting presence or absence of significant coronary heart disease.

BYPASS SURGERY *See* CORONARY ARTERY BYPASS GRAFT SURGERY.

CALCIUM BLOCKERS A class of drugs that blocks entry of calcium into the smooth muscle cells in blood vessel walls, relaxes them, and thus dilates the vessels. Such drugs are used to treat hypertension and angina. Examples include nifedipine, nicardipine, amlodipine (and almost any other drug that ends in *pine*), diltiazem, and verapamil.

CARDIAC CATHETERIZATION A widely used diagnostic technique whereby catheters (long, flexible tubes a bit thicker than the cord of a lamp or telephone handset) are inserted through the skin into arteries or veins and passed into the heart and coronary arteries. Most common is a left heart catheterization, in which a catheter is inserted into an artery, usually the femoral artery in the groin, and passed backward through the aorta to the heart. Specially shaped catheters are inserted into the openings (ostia) of left and right coronary arteries, a radiopaque dye (substance that shows up on X ray) is injected first into one and then into the other coronary ostium, and motion pictures (cine films) are taken of the coronary artery system, usually in several projections (the camera is turned from side to side so that the arteries can be seen from several vantage points). A catheter is also usually passed backward through the aortic valve into the left ventricle to measure pressures, examine the aortic and mitral valves on the left side of the heart, and inject a large amount of the radiopaque dye quickly into the chamber of the left ventricle so that one gets a picture of the heart's shape, size, regional and overall pumping ability, and areas where it does not move properly (usually representing dead heart muscle); this last procedure is called a *ventriculogram*. In a right heart catheterization, the catheter is inserted in a vein, usually in the arm, and passed through the venous system into the right atrium, right ventricle, and pulmonary artery, usually for measurements of pressures and examination of the valves on the right side of the heart. A cardiac catheterization usually takes 60–90 minutes, can be done on an ambulatory basis if an elective procedure in a basically healthy patient, carries a miniscule risk of death (<1 per 1,000), and has a very small risk of major complications (a few per hundred) if candidates are chosen properly. It is the "gold standard" for assessing the presence and severity of coronary heart disease and the need for angioplasty or surgical correction of coronary artery or cardiac valve lesions.

CARDIOMYOPATHY A general term that simply means dysfunction of the heart muscle (*myo* = muscle). When used without a qualifying adjective, it usually denotes *idiopathic cardiomyopathy*, that is, dysfunction of the muscle without any other cardiac cause (i.e., no coronary heart disease and no valvular disease). Idiopathic cardiomyopathy, often called *dilated cardiomyopathy*, is a disease of unknown etiology, and the cardiac muscle dysfunction often causes congestive heart failure. Another cause of cardiomyopathy is a genetic disorder termed *hypertrophic cardiomyopathy*, whose older name was *idiopathic hypertrophic subaortic stenosis (IHSS)*. Finally, patients whose heart muscles have been severely damaged by one or more myocardial infarctions or who have much coronary heart disease are often said to have *ischemic cardiomyopathy*.

CAROTID ARTERY   The main blood vessels to the brain, one on either side of the neck, supplying most of the important motor and sensory areas of the brain. They are close to the surface in the neck, so the pulse can be felt there; firm pressure can be used as therapy to slow certain kinds of rapid arrhythmias. Noninvasive Doppler ultrasound can give a good picture of narrowings in the neck portion of these arteries. A certain proportion of strokes and transient ischemic attacks are caused by narrowings in the carotid arteries, and these can be cleaned out surgically with relatively low risk (*see* CAROTID ENDARTERECTOMY).

CAROTID ENDARTERECTOMY   A surgical procedure for cleaning out narrowed carotid arteries by opening the artery in the neck and surgically removing as much atherosclerotic plaque as possible. There is relatively low risk involved with the procedure, although when a complication occurs, it can be major (e.g., a stroke). Nevertheless, the small risk of stroke as a complication of the surgery is less than the risk of stroke if the surgery is not done on someone with symptoms (*see* TRANSIENT ISCHEMIC ATTACK) or a major carotid artery narrowing. *See also* CAROTID ARTERY.

CHOLESTEROL   A substance in many foods people eat, and one of the major fats carried in the bloodstream. A major risk factor for coronary heart disease is the level of cholesterol in the blood, termed *serum cholesterol*. This level, about 150–170 mg/dl in most vegetarian mammals (including strict vegetarian humans), is considered normal if below 200 mg/dl. The average in the United States is about 215 mg/dl, and many people with coronary heart disease have much higher levels. Two major components of the blood cholesterol level are low-density lipoprotein (LDL), which contributes to plaque buildup, and high-density lipoprotein (HDL), which protects against plaque buildup. The ratio of total serum cholesterol (TC) to HDL is referred to as the *TC:HDL ratio*, with 4.5 considered the upper limit of normal. TC:HDL ratios above 4.5 are unfavorable for development of atherosclerosis, whereas ratios below 4.5 are considered more favorable. *Dietary* cholesterol is found only in animal products. Saturated fat is considered more important for raising serum cholesterol levels than dietary cholesterol. However, many animal products have high levels of saturated fats as well as cholesterol. Average U.S. consumption of cholesterol is about 400 mg/day; most authorities recommend consumption of 300 mg/day or even 200 mg/day. A balance of dietary and genetic factors determines cholesterol levels, which is why some people, even with careful diets, still have high serum cholesterol.

CLAUDICATION   From the Latin *claudicare*, "to limp." Pain in the leg, usually a squeezing pain in the calf or thigh whenever the affected individual walks too far, too fast, or up hills. Caused by narrowing of arteries to the legs or peripheral vascular disease. Patients do not usually limp, but stop and stand still for 30–60 seconds, after which the pain disappears and they can resume walking. Also called *intermittent claudication*.

CONGESTIVE HEART FAILURE   A clinical syndrome in which the pumping ability of the heart is insufficient for the needs of the body. This can result from damage because of myocardial infarctions, from major valvular problems, increased stiffness of the muscle or pericardium, or from cardiomyopathy of any cause. When the heart cannot pump sufficiently, fluid accumulates in the lungs (causing shortness of breath, inability to lie flat, and other symptoms) and elsewhere in the body (causing leg edema, weight gain, and other symptoms).

CORONARY ARTERY BYPASS GRAFT (CABG) SURGERY   Surgical treatment of coronary artery blockages that cannot be treated with drugs or by angioplasty. The success of the surgery depends on the fact that coronary heart disease tends to be spotty: Areas of an artery may be badly diseased (narrowed or occluded), yet an inch or two farther down, the artery may be quite normal. Many years ago, attempts were made to open coronary arteries at the area of blockage and "clean out" the atherosclerotic plaques (called *coronary endarterectomy*, but with much higher risks than the carotid endarterectomy described above); this is now done only very rarely because it is simpler, quicker, and probably safer to ignore the diseased area of the artery and simply go around, or bypass, it. Bypass grafts can be either arteries or veins. One very common graft is usually done with the left internal mammary artery (LIMA), an artery running down the inside of the breastbone (the sternum) that is not needed in men or older women and can be cut loose from the sternum and attached to a coronary artery, which is almost always the left anterior descending (LAD) artery, lying on the front of the heart close to the sternum. Being an artery, the LIMA stays open better than vein grafts, but it is not usually long enough to reach any coronary artery other than the LAD.

Other coronary arteries are grafted by using pieces of vein taken from the legs, usually saphenous veins (there are many extra veins in the legs to take up the slack if some veins are removed). One end of the removed section of leg vein is sewn into the ascending aorta, and the other end is sewn into the coronary artery to be bypassed, beyond the area of obstruction. The average coronary bypass operation consists of one LIMA (arterial graft) to the LAD artery, and one, two, or three saphenous vein grafts (SVGs) to other arteries. (The sum total of grafts gives one boasting rights: e.g., "I had a double-vessel bypass or triple-vessel bypass," abbreviated as CABGx2 and CABGx3, respectively.) A CABG operation takes about 4 hours, in generally healthy patients under 80 years of age carries an operative mortality rate of about 2%–3%, and is 90%+ successful in curing angina, at least for 5–10 years.

CORONARY HEART DISEASE (CHD) OR CORONARY ARTERY DISEASE (CAD)   Disease of the arteries that supply blood to the heart itself. Three major coronary arteries run on the outside of the heart, with many smaller tributaries dipping down into the heart muscle. The major arteries are (a) the left anterior descending (LAD), which descends from the top of the heart (closer to the head) to the bottom (or apex, nearer to the feet) of the heart in front (anterior); (b) the left circumflex (LCx), which circles around to the left and supplies the left lateral and a bit of the posterior surface of the heart; and (c) the right coronary artery (RCA), which circles around the right border of the heart, supplies the right ventricle, and then supplies the very large bottom wall of the heart (that part facing the diaphragm). Both LAD and LCx originate from a common short trunk, the left main (LM) artery. Obstructive coronary heart disease is overwhelmingly caused by atherosclerotic plaques that form on the insides of the arteries, eventually interfere with blood flow, and may totally block the arteries. The four major clinical manifestations of coronary heart disease include angina pectoris, acute myocardial infarction, sudden cardiac death, and ischemic cardiomyopathy.

CREATINE KINASE (CK)   An enzyme in heart muscle cells that leaks out into the bloodstream if heart muscle cells die and, thus, is the most commonly used marker of a myocardial infarction. It takes several hours after an event for CK to leak out, so that three blood samples are generally drawn, immediately when the patient is first seen, and then 6 hours and 12–18 hours afterward. If all three samples are negative, then a myocardial infarct has been ruled out or excluded. Previously called *creatine phosphokinase*, or *CPK*.

CK-MB   One form of creatine kinase (CK), called an *isoenzyme* or *isozyme*, which is a subcategory of CK that is found almost exclusively in heart muscle (as opposed to other subcategories measured in the total CK, which are found in skeletal muscle all over the body, and in other organs). Thus, when trying to diagnose a myocardial infarction, one almost always measures total CK as well as the subcategory CK-MB. An elevation in the blood of total CK could come from many different places, whereas a rise in CK-MB, or even just a relatively larger amount of CK-MB as a percentage of the total amount of CK, indicates leakage from (and therefore damage to) heart muscle.

DIAPHORESIS   "Sweating."

DIASTOLIC PRESSURE   *See* SYSTOLIC PRESSURE.

DISSECTING ANEURYSM   Separation of the layers of the wall of the aorta, usually due to degenerative disease of the aortic wall. Because blood in the aorta is under very high pressure, if blood gets between the layers through a small tear in the aortic wall, it can "dissect" the layers from each other for long distances forward and backward from the initial opening, blocking blood flow to the arteries that branch from the aorta at many levels with resultant damage to the organs deprived of that blood flow, and sometimes even rupturing through the aorta's outer wall so that rapid exsanguination (bleeding to death) occurs. Also called *aortic dissection* and *dissecting hematoma.*

DIURETICS   Drugs that promote excretion of fluid (and salt, and often other substances, such as potassium) through the kidneys. Used to treat those who have had congestive heart failure, when the body retains excess salt and water, and for hypertension. There are several classes of diuretics, including the thiazides (e.g., hydrochlorothiazide) and the powerful so-called loop diuretics (because their action is primarily in a section of the kidney called the "loop of Henle"), such as furosemide (Lasix).

DOBUTAMINE   A drug that is similar to adrenaline (epinephrine) and similarly increases the force of contraction of the heart. Used for shock and after heart surgery to temporarily assist a failing heart by boosting its contractility. Also used in stress testing if a patient cannot do physical exercise (e.g., because of severe arthritis, neurological problems, or peripheral vascular disease): Instead of stressing the heart with physical exercise, examiners inject dobutamine, and the drug temporarily increases myocardial oxygen needs.

DYSPNEA   Shortness of breath, a common cardiovascular and cardiopulmonary symptom (dyspnea on exertion = DOE). This can be a symptom of heart disease, especially accumulation of fluid in the lungs as in congestive heart failure, but may be a symptom of angina pectoris, congenital heart disease, or lung disease.

ECHOCARDIOGRAPHY   A diagnostic technique using very high frequency sound, which penetrates body tissues and is reflected back by various body structures. A small handheld instrument called a *transducer* generates and broadcasts the sound waves and also receives and interprets their reflection back to the same spot. Computers then generate a picture of the moving structures of the heart that is displayed on a video screen or is printed. The "echo" is excellent at assessing presence and severity of disease of heart valves and gives a good idea of function of the heart muscle. It is increasingly used together with exercise ("exercise echo") for the diagnosis of coronary heart disease because it is capable of identifying regional abnormalities of ventricular wall motion that develop with exercise. An echocardiogram is noninvasive, painless, and totally without risk.

EDEMA   Fluid in tissues. Peripheral edema usually collects near the feet because of the effects of gravity (often best appreciated right over the shinbone, where there is usually little fat or joint tissue to confuse matters, and called *pretibial edema*). Peripheral edema is caused by increased pressure in veins, sometimes because of heart failure, but there are other causes. Pulmonary edema is fluid in the lungs; it too usually collects at the bases (bottom) of the lungs because of the effects of gravity, where it can be heard with a stethoscope as "rales" (a sound of air and fluid mixing that sounds like drawing air through a mouthful of spittle).

EJECTION FRACTION (EF)   The proportion of the total volume of blood in the heart at the beginning of contraction that is ejected with each beat. Normal left ventricular ejection fraction (LVEF) is 50% ± 5%. LVEF is a very powerful predictor of prognosis in many types of heart disease: After myocardial infarction or in cardiomyopathy, the lower the EF, the higher the mortality over the next few months or years.

ELECTROCARDIOGRAM (ECG)   A device that records the sum of electrical impulses from all the heart muscle cells by means of electrodes attached to the four limbs and the front of the chest. The ECG is a simple, rapid, noninvasive, and inexpensive test that is highly useful in diagnosing some cardiac diseases (e.g., a large acute myocardial infarction) but quite unhelpful and possibly even misleading in diagnosing others (e.g., chest pain attributable to coronary atherosclerosis may occur while a patient is exercising, yet the ECG taken while lying down at rest often shows nothing). (Also abbreviated EKG, from the German and Dutch inventors' spelling.)

ELECTROPHYSIOLOGIC STUDY (EPS)   Electrophysiology is a relatively new branch of cardiology that has had explosive growth of both diagnostic and therapeutic uses in the past few years. EPS usually refers to introduction of catheters into various chambers of the heart to both stimulate and possibly provoke an arrhythmia and record the electrical characteristics of the arrhythmia to determine how best to treat it. If the arrhythmia relies on an abnormal electrical pathway within the heart, then it is possible to destroy that pathway in many cases with radio-frequency ablation (RFA): delivery of a certain type of energy to a very small area next to the RFA catheter to ablate (destroy) the offending pathway.

EMBOLI   Blood clots that break loose and travel in the bloodstream to some faraway place, where they lodge and block a vessel, causing greater or lesser damage depending on what organ's blood supply has been obstructed. Emboli that form in veins, particularly leg veins, may break loose and travel in the direction of blood flow to and through the right side of the heart to the blood vessels in the lungs (called *pulmonary emboli*), where they can lodge and cause cough, hemoptysis (coughing up blood), pleuritic chest pain (pain with breathing), short-ness of breath, and various other signs and symptoms, death of a por-tion of lung tissue (pulmonary infarction), or even cardiovascular col-lapse and death if the clot obstructs enough blood flow to the lungs. Clots that form in the left side of the heart (on a valve, particularly an artificial mitral or aortic valve), in an area of endocarditis, in the pumping chamber of the heart near a recent infarct, or in a fibrillating left atrium, may break loose and travel anywhere in the body (called *systemic emboli*). By far the most critical destination for systemic emboli is the brain, because the carotid arteries are the first large arteries lo-cated straight ahead in the aorta after blood leaves the heart. Cerebral emboli are a very important and potentially preventable cause of strokes.

ENDOCARDITIS   The root *itis* means inflammation, so this literally means inflammation of the endocardium, the inner lining of the heart. How-ever, the vast majority of cases involve infection, not just inflamma-tion, most often caused by bacteria. Although occasional cases occur in people with normal hearts, there is usually some structural defect that predisposes someone to such an infection, most often some val-vular disease. There also needs to be a source of bacteria in the blood to lodge at the site of the structural defect; this is why one gives pro-phylactic antibiotics to patients with valvular disease before dental work (the mouth is a dirty place) or before surgery in areas like the bowels, which cannot be sterilized. This condition is also called *sub-acute bacterial endocarditis*, invariably referred to by the acronym SBE, even if onset may not involve the classic days to weeks of vague symp-toms before the patient becomes very ill.

ENDOTHELIUM   The innermost lining of blood vessels, one cell-layer thick. Ignored for years, considered akin to plastic wrap simply forming a barrier to keep liquid blood and blood components like red and white blood cells where they belong in the bloodstream, there has been an explosion of research interest in the endothelium in the past 5–10 years. It is now clear that endothelial cells have many functions, and it is quite likely that numerous types of endothelial dysfunction are highly important in the pathogenesis and clinical presentation of various diseases.

FIBROUS CAP   Fibrous (scar) tissue walling off an atherosclerotic plaque from the flowing blood. The material within a plaque—cholesterol and other fats, some within cells, some not; some lipids in their original form and some transformed by many different chemical reactions; cells that are attracted to the plaque and the products of some of these cells, alive and dead—can form a potent brew that seems irritating as well as highly capable of causing blood to clot. The body thus walls off plaques with fibrous tissue. The portion of the wall protruding into the lumen of the blood vessel is exposed to many forces: some mechanical from the sheer force of the flowing blood, some related to constituents of the blood that are attracted to or attach to the surface of the plaque, and some related to constituents of the plaque or the blood vessel wall itself. The precipitating event of the catastrophic clinical events of coronary heart disease (acute myocardial infarction and sudden cardiac death) is believed to be rupture of the fibrous cap overlying the long-standing atherosclerotic plaque. Why and how the fibrous cap ruptures when it does, and how this might be prevented, is one of the most important research areas in modern cardiology, with immense public health implications for prevention of clinical events.

GATED BLOOD POOL SCAN   *See* MUGA SCAN.

HIGH-DENSITY LIPOPROTEIN (HDL)   *See* LIPOPROTEIN.

HOLTER MONITOR   A small, portable device, named after inventor N. Holter, that is worn by the patient and records the electrocardiogram during daily activities, usually for 24 hours. The tape within the device is then returned to the hospital and scanned at about 200 times real time (so that the entire 24 hours can be scanned in 10 minutes or so), to look for abnormalities of cardiac rhythm. Also called a *24-hour monitor*.

HYPERTROPHY   Thickening, particularly of the heart muscle wall. Sometimes occurs in response to some other problem (e.g., long-standing hypertension, wherein the heart has to pump against constricted peripheral blood vessels and a higher blood pressure, and so the heart muscle wall thickens, or aortic stenosis, where the heart has to pump against a narrow aortic valve opening), sometimes for genetic reasons (hypertrophic cardiomyopathy), and sometimes for unknown reasons. Whatever the cause, cardiac hypertrophy is a major adverse prognostic factor in many epidemiological studies.

HYPOKALEMIA Low blood potassium. Very common in cardiac patients, because most diuretics cause a loss of potassium from the body along with the loss of water they are intended to produce. Prescribed supplemental potassium is often not taken by patients, because its taste is unpleasant, especially in liquid form. Such supplements are important, however, because hypokalemia predisposes patients to dangerous ventricular arrhythmias.

HYPONATREMIA Low blood sodium (<142 mg/dl). This is very infrequent as a clinical problem.

HYPOVOLEMIA, HYPOVOLEMIC SHOCK *Hypovolemia* means a loss of circulating blood volume, usually because of bleeding (e.g., gastrointestinal, such as a bleeding ulcer, or postoperatively, from a blood vessel that has not been tied off properly). It is manifested by low blood pressure. If the blood pressure goes so low that vital organs of the body can no longer be properly perfused (e.g., urine output falls below 30 cc/hr), confusion occurs because the brain is not receiving enough blood; the condition at this stage is called *hypovolemic shock*. It is highly important to diagnose hypovolemia, because it is easily treated by restoring the proper blood volume through transfusion of blood or other substances.

IDIOPATHIC CARDIOMYOPATHY OR IDIOPATHIC DILATED CARDIOMYOPATHY *See* CARDIOMYOPATHY.

IDIOPATHIC HYPERTROPHIC SUBAORTIC STENOSIS (IHSS) A genetic condition caused by mutations in genes controlling development of heart muscle fibers that results in abnormal shape and function of the heart muscle. In early stages, the muscle is often thicker and stronger than normal, sometimes contracting so vigorously that it clamps down on itself, almost totally obliterates the ventricular cavity, and obstructs its own outflow. Often the area of greatest hypertrophy is the septum between the left and right ventricle just below the aortic valve (called *asymmetric septal hypertrophy*, or ASH), so that when the ventricle clamps down supervigorously, its outflow is obstructed just below the aortic valve (thus the appelation "subaortic" stenosis). In late stages, the hypertrophied muscle sometimes dilates, loses strength, and resembles a dilated cardiomyopathy. This is important because it is not an uncommon condition, it occurs at all ages, it is associated with sudden cardiac death (especially after vigorous exercise), and it is a common cause of cardiomyopathy and congestive heart failure. IHSS is probably the most common cause of sudden cardiac death in young athletes. Also called *hypertrophic cardiomyopathy*, or HCM.

INTERMITTENT CLAUDICATION *See* CLAUDICATION.

INTERNAL MAMMARY ARTERY (IMA) *See* CORONARY ARTERY BYPASS GRAFT SURGERY.

ISCHEMIA Imbalance of oxygen and energy demand over supply. When applied to the heart, ischemia usually refers to myocardial oxygen demands that outstrip its blood supply because of atherosclerotic disease that limits the delivery of coronary blood flow.

ISCHEMIC CARDIOMYOPATHY *See* CARDIOMYOPATHY.

JEOPARDIZED MYOCARDIUM Heart muscle that is still alive, but in jeopardy of dying (infarcting) because of significant stenoses in the coronary arteries that supply that area. Often there are also problems elsewhere in the coronary tree, so the muscle in question has no alternative source of coronary blood supply. It is diagnosed by various tests that show the muscle to be alive (e.g., the area moving during systole or eventually taking up radioisotope tracers during the redistribution phase after a stress test) but not functioning properly (e.g., there are electrocardiogram, wall motion, or isotope-uptake abnormalities when a stress test requires more coronary flow to that area of muscle).

LIPID Fat. The main fats that circulate in the bloodstream are cholesterol and triglycerides. Circulating lipids are important for many purposes, including providing energy to various organs, building cell membranes, and providing raw materials for various hormones and other molecules, but excesses of certain lipids are associated with atherosclerotic disease. *See* LIPOPROTEINS.

LIPOPROTEINS Lipids, fatty substances, do not dissolve well in blood, a water-based substance ("oil and water don't mix"). Thus, for lipids to circulate in blood, they must be hooked to a special solubilizing protein called an *apoprotein*, and lipid + apoprotein = lipoprotein. Two common lipoproteins are measured to estimate risk of coronary heart disease: (a) low-density lipoprotein (LDL), which appears to carry cholesterol to places such as coronary arteries (with higher LDL levels indicating increased risk of coronary heart disease), and high-density lipoprotein (HDL), which seems to carry cholesterol from arteries to the liver, which metabolizes and then disposes of it (so that more of this so-called good cholesterol [HDL] decreases the risk of coronary heart disease).

LOW-DENSITY LIPOPROTEIN (LDL) *See* LIPOPROTEINS.

LUMEN The inner channel of a tubular organ (e.g., where the blood flows in a blood vessel).

MITRAL INSUFFICIENCY (MI) OR MITRAL REGURGITATION (MR) Leakage of blood backward through the mitral valve from the left ventricle to the left atrium. Usually caused by rheumatic heart disease, degenerative heart disease, congenital disease plus degeneration (e.g., an inherited tendency to mitral valve prolapse plus the passage of time), and occasionally due to ischemic heart disease (ischemia of the papillary muscle causing papillary muscle dysfunction and, thereby, mitral regurgitation).

MITRAL STENOSIS   Narrowing of the mitral valve: the valve between the left atrium and left ventricle. Essentially caused only by rheumatic heart disease.

MITRAL VALVE PROLAPSE (MVP)   A very common condition in which the structures of the mitral valve are longer (sometimes called *redundant*), looser (or *floppy*), and sometimes weaker (they do rupture occasionally). The tendency is for this to be an inherited (congenital) condition, but it takes years before clinical problems develop (if they do), so that the clinical manifestations are a blend of congenital plus degenerative disease. MVP occurs in all degrees of severity, starting with only a slight extra degree of "floppiness" of the valve leaflets, causing "prolapse" (abnormal protrusion of the valve backward into the left atrium as the left ventricle contracts). Ordinarily the papillary muscles and the valve chordae are supposed to tighten during contraction (systole) so that the valve is held taut and does not protrude backward into the atrium at all during systole. With a small amount of prolapse, sometimes a sound is made, a systolic click that is audible through a stethoscope. With more prolapse, sometimes a leak during systole develops and, so, a systolic murmur. In a very few cases, leaks can become very large; at times, one of the supporting structures can even rupture ("ruptured chordae") and massive mitral regurgitation can occur, requiring mitral valve surgery.

MUGA (MULTIPLE GATED ACQUISITION OF IMAGES) SCAN OR STRESS TEST   A type of stress test where the tracer dose of radioactivity (often technetium-99 bound to red blood cells) is injected and accumulates in the blood pool (thus, also called a *blood pool scan*) within the cavity of the left ventricle. Taking a picture of the radioactivity of the blood within the ventricle with a sophisticated sort of Geiger counter (the picture is called a scintigram) allows one to see the motion of the walls of the ventricle as they squeeze the imaged pool with each heartbeat. There is not enough radioactivity to get good images with a single beat, so radioactive emissions at exactly the same point during systole and diastole of several hundred consecutive beats are collected and compiled by a computer to form a composite set of images. The collection of images at exactly the same time during the pumping cycle, cycle after cycle, is managed by "gating": synchronizing the radioactivity collection to the electrocardiographic complex, which always starts off each mechanical pumping cycle. Also called *radionuclide ventricu-*

logram, but never called by its full name—only by the acronym MUGA.

NITRATES   A class of drugs derived from nitroglycerin (the same chemical as the explosive) that dilate blood vessels: coronary arteries, veins, and peripheral arteries (slightly). They are used mainly to treat angina. Nitroglycerin, the prototype, is only active through the skin (in patches) or mucous membranes (sublingual nitroglycerin is a pill taken under the tongue for acute attacks of angina). Other nitrate drugs have been developed that are longer acting and can be taken orally, including isosorbide dinitrate, isosorbide mononitrate, and several other drugs that usually contain *nitr* somewhere within their names.

NONINVASIVE   Used to refer to tests or therapies that do not "invade" the body, generally taken to mean not going inside of skin or body orifices (although a simple intravenous injection is usually ignored, and if that is the only breaking of the skin, the test is still usually referred to as *noninvasive*). Echocardiography and stress testing are noninvasive, whereas cardiac catheterization, angioplasty, and coronary artery bypass graft surgery are invasive.

NON-Q-WAVE INFARCT   *See* Q-WAVE INFARCT.

ORTHOPNEA   Shortness of breath when lying flat. Often a symptom of fluid in the lungs, as occurs with congestive heart failure.

ORTHOSTATIC HYPOTENSION   Fall in blood pressure when a person stands up. Normally, reflexes are activated so that blood pressure either stays nearly the same or rises a bit when people stand (because the head is now above the heart, and the effect of gravity needs to be counteracted to get blood to the brain). Some diseases, sometimes just the aging process, and a number of drugs (particularly alpha-blockers and central sympathetic blockers) cause orthostatic hypotension. The usual manifestation is dizziness and, in extreme cases, fainting when standing up.

OSTIUM   The first portion of a blood vessel (actually, just the opening where a vessel or other duct begins); in its plural form, *ostia*, most often refers to the coronary arteries. (Taken from "Ostium," the name of the ancient Mediterranean port near Rome that was Rome's "opening" to the sea.) Disease at an ostium, at the very beginning of a vessel, is particularly dangerous because the whole vessel is affected and, in the coronary arteries, is particularly hard to treat with angioplasty.

PALPITATIONS   Medical term for a number of complaints by patients that are variously described as "skipped beats," "extra heartbeats," or increased rate, awareness, or strength of heartbeat. Sometimes, but by no means always, a sign of cardiac arrhythmia.

PAPILLARY MUSCLE   Fingerlike protrusions of muscle on the inside of the ventricular walls that form the anchoring points for the chordae (the fibrous "struts" or "lines of the parachute") of the mitral and triscuspid valves. As the ventricles contract and eject blood, they obviously become much smaller; the job of the papillary muscles is to contract and "tighten up the lines" (hold the chordae taut), so that the valve leaflets stay in place and no blood leaks backward into the atria.

PERCUTANEOUS TRANSLUMINAL CORONARY ANGIOPLASTY See ANGIO-PLASTY.

PERFUSION STRESS TEST Several kinds of stress tests, including the thallium and sestamibi stress tests, use a radioactive isotope in the blood that is distributed through coronary arteries to all areas of the heart muscle that are well perfused. If there is obstruction in a particular coronary artery, there is less blood flow to the area of heart muscle served by that artery, less radioisotope reaches that area, and, thus, there are fewer scintillations or radioactivity "counts" in that spot. A map or picture is generated of the radioactive counts, using dots (darker or more dots mean more activity) or colors (various colors mean more or fewer counts); a "cold spot" (lack of activity) means less radioactivity and, thus, usually less blood flow in that area (i.e., a blockage in the coronary artery supplying the area of the cold spot).

PRELOAD See AFTERLOAD.

PRIAPISM Persistant, usually painful erection of the penis, caused by diseases and as a side effect of some drugs (e.g., trazodone [Desyrel]). A medical–surgical emergency, because clotting and permanent damage to the organ may occur if the condition is prolonged. (Named after Priapus, the Greek–Roman god of procreation, who was usually personified by an erect phallus.)

PRINZMETAL'S ANGINA A type of angina named after cardiologist Myron Prinzmetal, caused more by spasm of a coronary artery and acute interference with blood supply to the heart muscle than by atherosclerotic plaques. This vasospastic angina is quite rare, characterized by the lack of any relationship to physical exertion and a negative stress test, and recognized by an unusual electrocardiographic pattern: transient ST-segment elevation during pain (as opposed to usual, effort-related angina, which shows ST-segment depression during pain or during a stress test).

PTCA See ANGIOPLASTY.

PULMONARY EMBOLI Blood clots from the venous system that break loose and travel to the vessels of the lungs, where they lodge and can obstruct blood flow or even cause death of a portion of lung tissue. Their most common source is leg vein thrombosis, which in turn is very frequent with immobilization (e.g., bed rest after acute myocardial infarction or other cardiac problem or major surgery). Pulmonary emboli can be totally silent, may cause minor symptoms, or can kill suddenly with massive obstruction of the lung vessels; many postoperative deaths result from pulmonary emboli.

PULMONARY VALVE; PULMONIC STENOSIS OR PULMONIC INSUFFICIENCY   The outflow valve on the right side of the heart, between the right ventricle and the main pulmonary artery leading to the lungs. *Stenosis* refers to narrowing, and *insufficiency* refers to leaking. Diseases of this valve are infrequently seen in adults, except occasionally as a reaction to high pressures in the lungs from other causes or from congenital disease.

Q-WAVE INFARCT   An acute myocardial infarction associated with a Q wave: an electrocardiographic (ECG) pattern in which the initial deflection of the wave is downward in the lead facing the damaged area. This ECG pattern generally denotes myocardial damage through the entire thickness of the wall, from the inside to the outside surface of the heart muscle. Such infarcts are almost always associated with total occlusion by clot (thrombus) of the artery supplying the area that is damaged. Contrast with non-Q-wave infarction, where the damage is to the inside portion of the heart wall only and does not extend through to the outside surface. Non-Q infarcts are less likely to be associated with totally occlusive clots, although there is often a partially occlusive clot (thrombus) in the artery supplying the area of damage.

RADIO-FREQUENCY ABLATION (RFA)   A treatment for certain types of abnormal heart rhythms in which a catheter is introduced into the heart and a small area of heart muscle that is conducting electricity and causing the arrhythmia is destroyed by an intense burst of radio-frequency energy. *See* ELECTROPHYSIOLOGIC STUDY.

REFLEX TACHYCARDIA   Tachycardia (rapid heart rate) resulting from reflex stimulation of the sympathetic nervous system, usually because of major vasodilation and drop in blood pressure. Often caused by powerful vasodilating antihypertensive drugs (e.g., dihydropyridines).

RESTENOSIS   The return of a stenosis in a coronary artery after angioplasty or one of its variants, which is a major and unsolved problem. Restenosis has several different definitions, for example, return to greater than 50% stenosis or loss of more than half the improvement of the initial angioplasty. Restenosis occurs in 30%–40% or more of patients with initially successful angioplasty, often within 3–6 months of the initial procedure. The clinical picture of restenosis is amazingly variable: In many cases, there are no symptoms whatsoever, and the restenosis is discovered only if another catheterization is done; in other cases, recurrent angina suggests the diagnosis; and in only a very few cases (fortunately), a major acute problem occurs, such as myocardial infarction.

REVERSIBLE ISCHEMIA Ischemia (insufficiency of blood flow to a portion of the heart muscle) during exercise, which "reverses" (resolves) at rest. The normal perfusion at rest implies that the heart muscle in question is not dead, and, thus, revascularization (opening up the coronary artery supplying that area), either by angioplasty or coronary artery bypass graft surgery, might be beneficial. Reversible ischemia should be distinguished from "fixed defect," "scar," or "infarction"—all of which are used instead of "irreversible ischemia," the logical antonym. All of these connote lack of blood flow to an area of heart muscle both during exercise and during rest, implying that the tissue in question is dead and irreversibly damaged and so revascularization would be useless.

SAPHENOUS VEIN GRAFT (SVG) See CORONARY ARTERY BYPASS GRAFT SURGERY.

SCINTILLATION CAMERA A camera that senses emissions (scintillations) of a radioactive tracer substance that is injected into the body and (together with a computer when placed above the chest over the heart) can generate a map or picture of how much radioisotope has been taken up by various areas of the heart muscle. See PERFUSION STRESS TEST.

SESTAMIBI A relatively new radioisotope used for cardiac stress testing, a substance including the radioactive material technetium-99, which can be imaged initially in the blood pool within the left ventricle (and so can give an idea of the size and motion of the ventricle) and then distributed with coronary blood flow into the myocardium (so that it can be used to diagnose coronary heart disease). Often colloquially called *mibi*. See PERFUSION STRESS TEST.

SIGNAL-AVERAGED ELECTROCARDIOGRAM (SA-ECG) A test that searches for tiny abnormal electrical currents within the heart called *late potentials* that are a warning that the patient may be prone to serious ventricular arrhythmia. The test is simple, painless, and without risk, consisting of the standard ECG leads recorded for 5–10 minutes, running into a "black box" that manipulates the electrical activity to look for the late potentials that cannot be seen on the ordinary ECG. If the SA-ECG is positive, then patients will often be sent for an electrophysiologic study.

SILENT INFARCTION A myocardial infarction that occurs without chest pain or other clinical symptoms. This is surprisingly common and is often only discovered on routine electrocardiograms in many people; perhaps as many 25%–30% of all infarcts are silent. Silent infarction occurs more commonly in people with diabetes and those who are elderly.

SILENT ISCHEMIA Ischemia that is not perceived by the patient. Diagnosed either from an electrocardiogram (ECG) recorded while the patient is performing an exercise test (the ECG changes, but the patient feels no pain) or from a 24-hour Holter monitor worn during daily activities (the ECG changes, and the patient records no symptoms in his or her diary). Silent ischemia appears to be a reasonably good guide to the presence of coronary heart disease and carries the same adverse prognosis as perceived ischemia. Indeed, one might theorize that silent ischemia might be even worse than painful ischemia because the patient is not aware of the problem, and he or she does not stop the activity that might be the cause of the ischemia. (This remains only a hypothesis for now.)

STABLE ANGINA *See* ANGINA PECTORIS.

STENTS Small, tubular metal devices that fit inside a coronary artery, used to mechanically keep an artery open and prevent restenosis after angioplasty or one of its variants.

STREPTOKINASE *See* THROMBOLYTIC THERAPY.

SUDDEN CARDIAC DEATH Death occurring within a short time of the onset of symptoms in a person not otherwise expected to die. Various authors use different definitions, but the most common are witnessed collapse and death within 6 hours or unwitnessed death within the past 24 hours in a person not expected to die. Studies have shown that death occurring so quickly is overwhelmingly due to coronary heart disease, usually ventricular arrhythmia. In some cases, the ischemia is of acute onset, caused by a clot (thrombus) that suddenly blocks a coronary artery. Such acute coronary occlusions often are the cause of acute myocardial infarction, but in less fortunate persons, the occlusion precipitates an arrhythmia, usually ventricular fibrillation, that results in immediate cessation of cardiac pumping, unconsciousness within seconds, and death within 4–6 minutes if no resuscitation is undertaken. In other patients, the life-threatening arrhythmia stems from a more chronically damaged area, often in a patient with considerable scar tissue within the heart and less-than-excellent cardiac function. Note that the definition of sudden cardiac death does not exclude people who are known to have heart disease so long as death was not expected imminently (e.g., a person who had a myocardial infarction 6 months ago, but who was leading a normal life outside the hospital). The definition does exclude very sick people (e.g., those with terminal cancer whose final mode of death is stopping of the heart; this is not sudden cardiac death and not necessarily associated with the major atherosclerotic disease and acute or chronic ischemia that is almost invariable in sudden cardiac death). There are a few exceptions to the major role of coronary heart disease in sudden death. Cardiomyopathy, especially hypertrophic cardiomyopathy, is a cause of sudden cardiac death, also through the mechanism of ventricular arrhythmia; this is more commonly seen in young athletes who die suddenly.

SYNCOPE Fainting, a sudden loss of consciousness. (From the Greek root meaning "to cut"; i.e., to cut off consciousness.)

SYSTOLIC PRESSURE The period of time during which the heart pumps is *systole*, whereas the period of relaxation is *diastole*. Systolic pressure is the pressure measured in an artery when the heart pumps (the higher number of a blood pressure); diastolic pressure is the pressure when the heart relaxes (the lower number).

THALLIUM STRESS TEST A stress test using the radioisotope 201-thallium, a substance that is injected in a tracer dose and distributed wherever the blood goes. It is generally used to image coronary perfusion to the myocardium and, thus, diagnose coronary heart disease. *See* PERFUSION STRESS TEST.

THROMBOGENIC Likely to cause a thrombus (clot). Often applied to the material within an atherosclerotic plaque; if exposed to the flowing blood by rupture of the fibrous cap of a plaque, the contents of the plaque, being thrombogenic, are highly likely to cause a clot that may totally occlude the artery and cause a myocardial infarction or sudden cardiac death.

THROMBOLYTIC THERAPY Injection of substances that dissolve blood clots. Because most acute myocardial infarctions are caused by clots, dissolving the clot often makes a dramatic difference in the amount of muscle damage and, thus, in the short- and long-term death and complication rate. The earlier the thrombolytic agent is administered, the better the results. Four drugs available in the United States are tissue plasminogen activator (tPA), streptokinase (SK), urokinase (UK), and aniysolated plasminogen streptokinase activator complex (APSAC); the last two are used the least often.

THROMBOSIS Clotting.

tPA (TISSUE PLASMINOGEN ACTIVATOR) *See* THROMBOLYTIC THERAPY.

TRANSIENT ISCHEMIC ATTACK (TIA) Temporary interruption of blood supply to the brain, of short enough duration so that no brain cells actually die and no permanent damage results. Such attacks are accompanied by neurological symptoms just like a stroke, but unlike stroke, everything returns to normal within seconds to 10–20 minutes. TIAs are important warnings of future strokes; in some studies, one third or more of patients with TIAs suffered true strokes within a few months. A TIA usually prompts a search for a treatable cause of stroke, and then an anticlotting medication such as aspirin is often prescribed if nothing else can be done prophylactically.

TRICUSPID VALVE   The valve on the right side of the heart between the right atrium and right ventricle. *Tricuspid stenosis* is narrowing of this valve; this is almost never seen. *Tricuspid insufficiency* indicates a leak in this valve; this is seen as a result either of rheumatic disease or of any condition that greatly increases pressures within the pulmonary circulation and the right ventricle.

TRIGLYCERIDES   One of the circulating blood fats. The importance of elevated blood triglyceride has been hotly debated, with some experts suggesting this to be a very minor risk factor for coronary heart disease and others feeling it is quite important. The truth probably lies somewhere in-between, but triglycerides are certainly less important than high serum cholesterol or low-density lipoprotein or a very low high-density lipoprotein as a risk factor for coronary heart disease. Very high serum triglyceride levels may cause other medical problems (e.g., pancreatitis).

UNSTABLE ANGINA PECTORIS   A clinical syndrome in which angina occurs with increased frequency, severity, or duration in comparison with the usual "stable" anginal pattern, but particularly at rest or without obvious precipitating factors. This is in stark contrast to classic angina, which usually is precipitated by physical exertion, mental stress, cold, or some other factor that temporarily increases myocardial oxygen needs. Unstable angina is usually associated with a blood clot overlying an atherosclerotic plaque, but the clot does not totally block the artery as in an acute myocardial infarction.

VALVULAR HEART DISEASE   Disease of one of the four valves of the heart. The aortic and mitral valves are most commonly affected; the tricuspid and pulmonic valves on the right side of the heart, which are under much lower pressure, are much less commonly affected in adults. Valves can become diseased as a late result of rheumatic fever (rheumatic heart disease), as a result of degeneration with age (although in some patients, degenerative valvular disease occurs at a surprisingly early chronological age), in people with congenital abnormalities of valves (congenital valvular disease), and from other abnormalities. The disease is either a narrowing of a valve (stenosis) or leakage backward through a valve (insufficiency, or regurgitation), or both. If the valvular narrowing or leak is severe and prolonged enough, the heart muscle may be permanently damaged.

VASODILATOR   A drug that dilates blood vessels. *Arterial vasodilators* dilate arteries and are used to treat hypertension as well as congestive heart failure (*see* AFTERLOAD); *venous vasodilators* dilate veins, which pools blood in the periphery and reduces the amount of blood returned to the heart; *coronary vasodilators* dilate coronary arteries.

AUTHOR INDEX

Numbers in italics refer to listings in reference sections.

Hambrecht, R., *121, 176*
Hamburgen, M. E., *117*
Hampe, S. O., 422, *431*
Haney, T. L., 78–80, *110, 111, 112, 122, 195, 203, 212, 357*
Hanley, C., 391, *396*
Hanninen, O., 375, *383*
Harlan, E., 203, *217*
Harrell, F. E., *110, 122*
Harrington, D. P., *382*
Harris, M. I., 157, *172*
Harris, W. S., *173*
Harrison, D. G., 243, *252*
Harrison, M., *230*
Harshfield, G. A., *383*
Hartford, M., *111, 115*
Hartka, E., 399, *418*
Hartley, L. H., 365, *380*
Hartman, G. S., 226, *229*
Hartmann, G. W., *356*
Harvey, W., 6, *12, 363, 364, 381*
Haskell, W. L., 154, *173, 209, 214*
Hastings, J. E., 306, *308*
Hatano, S., 156, 166, *173*
Hauer, K., *121, 176*
Havel, R. J., *173*
Havik, O. E., 128, *144*
Hawkins, C. M., *54*
Hawkins, D. R., 369, *381*
Hawley, P. H., 282, *286*
Hayano, J., 374, *383*
Hayden, R., *395*
Hayes, J. G., *229, 230*
Hayes, V., 341, *356*
Haynes, C. T., *253, 356, 371, 383*
Haynes, S. G., 69, 70, *114, 180, 194, 276, 287*
Hazuda, H. P., 306, *309*
Heady, J. A., 385, *395*
Healy, R. W., 207, *218*
Hearn, M. D., 74, 75, *114, 181, 194*
Heath, G., 388, *395*
Heatherton, T. F., 377, *380, 381*
Heberden, W., *198*
Hebert, J. R., 3, *13*
Hecht, G M., *114*
Heckbert, S. R., *419*
Hecker, M., 203, *214*
Hecker, M. H., 78, 79, *114*
Hedges, B., 429, *431*
Hedges, S. M., *117, 355*
Heikkila, K., *116, 215*

Heinonen, O. P., *172, 417*
Heinsalmi, P., *172, 417*
Heistad, D. D., 243, *252*
Held, J., *173*
Heller, S. S., 69, 71, *112, 180, 193*
Hellerstein, H. K., 129, *143*
Helmer, D. C., 74, 75, *115*
Helmers, K. F., 77, 78, *115, 202, 214, 355*
Helo, P., *172, 417*
Helzer, J. E., *418*
Hennekens, C. H., 63n, *117, 161, 175, 217, 396*
Henry, J., 256, 272, *287*
Herbert, N., 90, *119*
Herd, J. A., *110, 113, 255, 287*
Herlitz, J. H., 102, *111, 115, 218*
Hershkowitz, B. D., 203, *212*
Hess, M. J., *12, 114, 252*
Hess, W. R., 364, 365, *382*
Hestrin, L., *120*
Heuser, R., *53*
Heyndrickx, G., *54*
Higgins, M., 198–201, *209, 214, 430, 431*
Higginson, L., *177*
Hill, D. R., 199, *213*
Hill, N. E., *117*
Hills, L. D., 16n, *53*
Hilton-Chalfen, S., *120*
Hinderliter, A., 334, *356*
Hinkle, L. E., 88, *115*
Hinton, R. B., *229*
HIPP investigators, *382*
Hirai, T., 366, *382*
Hirose, S., 398, *418*
Hirsch, L. J., *171*
Hirshfeld, J., *53*
Hjemdahl, P., 334, *356*
Hjortland, M. C., 152, *173*
Hlatky, M. A., 92, 93, *110, 115*
Hoberg, E., *176*
Hodis, H. N., *171*
Hodovanic, B. H., 429, *431*
Hoeg, J. M., 151, *173*
Hoffman, J. W., 376, *382*
Hofman, W. F., 379, *384*
Hollandsworth, J. G., Jr., 376, *383*
Hollingshead, A. B., 142, *143*
Hollman, J., *216*
Holloszy, J. O., 388, *395*
Holmberg, S., *111, 115*
Holme, I., *54, 60*
Holmes, D. R., 208, *214*

Holmes, O. W., 358
Holmes, T., 81, *115*
Holter, N. J., 24
Holubkov, A. L., *214*
Holubkov, R., *214, 215*
Home, E., 65–68, *115*
Höppener, P., 93, 94, *110, 204, 212*
Hopper, S., *173*
Horlock, P., *112*
Horwitz, R. I., 97, *111*
House, J. S., 95, 96, *115*
Houston, D., 333, *357*
Howard, B. V., 157, *172*
Howard, J. H., 283, *287*
Howell, R. H., *114, 115*
Hsieh, C. C., 392, *396*
Huang, T. N. C. S. W., 363, *382*
Huang Ti, 6
Hulley, S. B., 69, 70, 78, 107, *121, 195*
Hultgren, H. N., 291, *310*
Hunninghake, D. B., 166, 168, *173*
Hunter, J., 65–68, 86, *115*, 314
Hurley, J., 160, *173*
Hutter, A. M., 103, *120*
Huttunen, J. K., 152, 153, *172, 173, 417*
Hyde, R. T., 392, *396*

Ibrahim, M. A., 341, *355*
Ickovics, J. R., 199, 210, *216*
Imeson, J. D., 100, *114*
Innocent V, 314
Ironson, G., 80, *115, 380*
Isles, C. G., *12, 54, 176, 419*
Ismond, T., *116*
Isner, J. M., 104, *115*
Isom, O. W., *229*

Jacob, R. G., 379, *382*
Jacobs, B. H., 404, *418*
Jacobs, D. R., *121, 195*
Jacobs, G. D., 366, 369, *382*
Jacobs, J. C., *418*
Jacobs, S., 83, *115*
Jacobs, S. C., 9, *118, 206, 215, 216, 310, 326, 373, 381*
Jacobson, M. F., 160, *173*
Jaffe, A. S., *111, 204, 212*
Jain, D., 86, *115*
James, D., *110*

James, G. D., *383*
James, M., *215*
James, M. A., 104, *112*
James, S. A., 95, *111*
James, W., 280, 287, 349, *355, 359*
Jamieson, C. W., *172*
Jeffery, R. W., 201, *215*
Jenkins, C., 259, *287*
Jenkins, C. D., 69, *115, 120, 139, 143, 195, 256, 287, 292, 309*
Jenkins, R. A., 369, *384*
Jenkinson, C., 221, *230*
Jenkinson, C. M., 208, *215*
Jenner, E., 314
Jennings, C. A., *117*
Jennings, J. R., 88, *116, 140, 144*, 315, *316, 326*
Johansson, S., *218*
Johnson, C. A., 203, *217*
Johnson, C. L., *174, 176*
Johnson, J., *418*
Johnson, R. L., *11, 171*
Johnston, J. A., 410, *417, 418*
Johnstone, B., *418*
Johnstone, I. M., *173*
Jokela, V., 375, *383*
Jones, B. A., *216*
Jones, N. L., 391, *396*
Julius, S., 272, *286*
Just, H., 243, *253*

Kafka, H. P., 291, *309*
Kahn, M., *121*
Kaitaniemi, P., *172, 173, 417*
Kallio, V., *114*
Kalousdian, S., *172*
Kamarck, T., 88, *116, 140, 144*, 315, 316, *326*, 377, *380*
Kanchuger, M., *230*
Kane, J. P., 154, *173*
Kanglos, I., *118*
Kannel, W. B., 69, 70, 88, *112, 114, 116, 152, 172, 173, 180, 194, 203, 213*
Kaplan, B., 288, 334, *356*
Kaplan, B. H., 95, *111, 264, 283, 287, 330, 337, 340, 355*
Kaplan, C., *11, 171*
Kaplan, J. R., 90, 91, *112, 116, 122, 126, 143, 443, 447*
Kaplan, R. M., 291, *309*
Kaplinsky, E., *212*

Rossouw, J. E., 168, *176*
Roter, D., 141, *144*
Rothballer, K. B., *230*
Rouleau, J. L., *54*
Rozanski, A., 85, 86, *114, 115, 117, 120,*
355
Ruberman, W., 95, 97, *120, 126, 144,* 180,
195, 244, 253
Runyon, C. W., 283, *287*
Rusinek, H., *230*
Russell, B., *359*
Rutherford, J. D., *54, 118*
Rutsch, W., *54*
Ryan, T. J., 107, *117, 123*

Sacco, D. E., 154, *171*
Saini, J., *416, 442*
Sakakibara, M., 374, 376, *383*
Salem, D. N., 104, *115*
Sallis, J. F., 291, *309*
Saltz-Rennert, H., *172*
Salvia, L., *116*
Sanders, M., 63n, *117*
Sanmarco, M. E., 11, *171, 172*
Sanne, H., *396*
Sarna, S., *116, 215*
Saunders, R. D., *111*
Savage, M. P., *53*
Savageau, J. A., *143,* 292, *309*
SAVE Investigators, *54*
Savoia, M., 103, *120*
Scandinavian Simvastatin Survival Study
Group, 6, *12, 54, 58,* 168, 170,
176, 415, 419
Schaad, J. W., *383*
Schaefer, B. A., *11*
Schaefer, S. M., *171*
Schanberg, S. M., 357, *417*
Schatz, R. A., *53*
Schatzkin, A., 88, *116*
Schaubhut, R. M., 430, *431*
Scheidt, S., 10, 63n, 107, *110, 132,* 244,
252
Scheier, M. F., *120*
Scherwitz, L. W., *114, 119, 175, 233, 241,*
244, 252, 253, 258, 288, 289,
383, 396
Schlant, R. C., 16n, *54,* 155, *177*
Schleifer, S. J., 99, *121*
Schlierf, G., *121, 176*
Schlussel, Y., *121*

Schmidt, S., 160, *173*
Schnable, R., 369, *380*
Schnall, P. L., 93, *116, 121,* 333, *356*
Schneiderman, N., *380*
Schoenberger, J. A., *143*
Schouten, E. G. W., 93, *110, 205, 211,*
213, 305, *308*
Schroder, R., *122, 123*
Schroll, M., 76, 77, 99, *110, 111*
Schron, E. B., *110, 113, 143, 209, 217*
Schubert, F., *122, 123*
Schulenberg, W., *229*
Schuler, G., 105, *121,* 154, *176*
Schumaker, S., *143*
Schwartz, D., *116*
Schwartz, G., *117*
Schwartz, G. E., 316, *327*
Schwartz, J. E., *116, 121,* 333, *356*
Schwartz, S., *172*
Scklo, M., 95, *112*
Scotch, N., 69, *114*
Sears, R. R., 352, *354, 356*
Seeman, T. E., 96, *121,* 202, *212*
Segall, G. M., *115*
Seibel, M. M., 369, *381*
Selwyn, A. P., 90, *111, 112, 122, 123*
Selye, H., 6, *12*
Sempos, C. T., 158, *176*
Serruys, P. W., *54*
Shader, R. I., 411n1, *419*
Shaeffer, M. A., 394, *396*
Shaffi, A., *381*
Shaker, L. A., *216*
Shaknovich, A., *53*
Shapiro, A. P., *382*
Shapiro, D., 127, *145*
Shapiro, K., 272, *286*
Shapiro, P. A., *419*
Sharp, B. H., 423, *431*
Shaubhut, R. M., *431*
Shaw, L. J., 207, *217*
Shea, M., *112*
Shekelle, R. B., 69–71, 73–75, 78, 107,
121, 180, 181, *195, 203, 217,* 276,
290
Shelley, P. B., *359*
Shephard, R. J., 396, 398, *418*
Shepherd, J., 6, *12, 54, 58, 59,* 152, *176,*
415, 419
Sherwitz, L. W., *12, 356*
Sherwood, A., 333, 334, *355, 356*
Sherwood, J., *115, 118,* 207, *215–217*

SUBJECT INDEX

Bruce protocol, 22
Brush, Frederic, 128
Bumetanide (Bumex), 59
Bumex (bumetanide), 59
Bupropion (Wellbutrin), 409, 410
Burke Convalescence Home, 128
Buspar (buspirone), 411
Buspirone (Buspar), 411
Buss–Durkee Hostility Inventory, 77
Bypass graft surgery. *See* Coronary artery
bypass graft (CABG) surgery

CABG. *See* Coronary artery bypass graft
surgery
Calan (verapamil), 56, 413
Calcium blockers, 56
psychiatric side effects, 413
Calorie intake, calculating daily, 161–162
Canadian Cardiovascular Scale, 224
Capoten (captopril), 57, 414
Captopril (Capoten), 57, 414
Cardarone (amiodarone), 39, 61–62
Cardene (nicardipine), 56, 413
Cardiac Arrhythmia Pilot Study, 72, 89
Cardiac arrhythmias. *See* Arrhythmias
Cardiac Arrhythmia Suppression Trial,
209
Cardiac catheterization, 24, 36, 136
Cardiac clinics, 128
Cardiac denial, as risk factor for coronary
heart disease, 101–103
Cardiac drugs, side effects of, 411–416
ACE inhibitors, 414
adrenergic blockers, 414–415
anticoagulants, 415
antilipid agents, 415–416
beta-blockers, 411–412
calcium blockers, 413
nitrates, 413–414
Cardiac psychology, 5, 125–132, 443–446
applied, 127–128
benefits of, 126–127
clinical trials, 104–108
and communication with patient,
131–132
contributions of, 128–129
and coronary care unit, 130–131
definition of, 125
emergence of, as field, 7, 63

future research, directions for, 445–
446
goals of, 125
and individualization of medical
therapy, 139–140
and inpatient/outpatient care, 129–
130
mechanisms, physiological, 108, 109
origins of, 6, 127–128
and psyche–soma relationship, 127
treatment goals in, 444–445
of women with CHD. *See* Women
and coronary heart disease
Cardiac psychotherapy, as career, 435–441
existential considerations, 435–436
medical knowledge, gaining, 437–438
practice, starting, 438–441
and countertransference, 439
intervention, types of, 441
resistance, overcoming, 439–440
and social paradigm, 438
socioeconomic factors, 439
and stigma of psychotherapy, 439
professional training, 436–437
Cardiac reactivity. *See* Reactivity, cardiac
Cardiac rehabilitation. *See* Rehabilitation, cardiac
Cardiac surgery, 138–139
Cardiac transplantation, 50, 139
Cardiology, current state of, 6–7
Cardiomyopathy, 47–50
congestive heart failure (CHF), 48–50
etiology, 47–48
hypertrophic, 48
ischemic, 47
Cardiopulmonary resuscitation (CPR), 38
Cardiovascular disease. *See* Heart disease
Cardiovascular reactivity. *See* Reactivity,
cardiovascular
Cardiovascular reactivity hypothesis, 108
Cardizem. *See* Diltiazem
Cardura (doxazosin), 415
Carnivores, 150, 163
Casual conversation with patient, 132
Catapres (clonidine), 415
Catecholamine, 333
Catheterization, cardiac, 24, 36, 136
CCABOT. *See* Cornell Coronary Artery
Bypass Outcome Trials Group
CCPP (Coronary and Cancer Prevention
Project), 189–190

CCU. *See* Coronary Care Unit

Center for Epidemiological Studies—
Depression Scale (CES-D),
223–225

Central nervous system, and relaxation
response, 366, 369

Cerebrovascular accidents, fears related
to, 135–136

CES-D. *See* Center for Epidemiological
Studies—Depression Scale

CHD. *See* Coronary heart disease

Chest pain
coronary heart disease (CHD), due
to. *See* Angina pectoris
noncardiac, 103–104

CHF. *See* Congestive heart failure

Chlorthalidone (Hygroton), 59

Cholesterol, 19
control of levels of, 158–159
as primary cause of atherosclerosis,
150–155
women, levels in, 201

Cholesterol esters, 150

Cholestyramine (Questran), 58–59, 152,
169

Chordae, 40

Cigarette smoking, 95
as risk factor for atherosclerosis, 156

CK (creatine kinase), 34

Clonidine (Catapres), 415

Clots, with acute myocardial infarction,
35

Cocaine, 16

Cognitive appraisal, 423–424

Cognitive patterns
changing, in Project New Life, 302–
303
in Type A behavior pattern (TABP),
302

Cognitive restructuring, 371

Cognitive status, changes in, following
CABG surgery, 222–223

Cognitive therapy, in treatment of time
pathologies, 343–344

Colestid (colestipol), 59

Colestipol (Colestid), 59, 169

Communication with cardiac patient,
131–132

Compassion, expression of, in Lifestyle
Heart Trial group therapy, 248

Conditions, cardiovascular. *See* Heart disease

Congestive heart failure (CHF), 15, 16,
45, 135
and cardiomyopathy, 48–50

Conner, Lewis A., 128

Cook–Medley Hostility (Ho) Scale (of
MMPI), 74–78, 80, 99–100, 204

Corgard (nadolol), 55, 412

Cornell Coronary Artery Bypass Outcome Trials Group (CCABOT),
219, 221–228

Cornell Medical Index, 100

Coronary and Cancer Prevention Project
(CCPP), 189–190

Coronary arteries, 25–27

Coronary artery bypass graft (CABG)
surgery, 24, 26, 31–32, 99,
219–229
cognitive status changes following,
222–223
depression, postoperative, 223–225
female patients, 207–208
neurological changes following,
225–228
Project New Life for patients undergoing. *See* Project New Life
quality of life considerations,
220–222
rehabilitation, postoperative, 228
stroke as complication of, 225–226

Coronary artery disease. *See* Coronary
heart disease (CHD)

Coronary Artery Surgery Study, 220

Coronary atherosclerosis. *See* Atherosclerosis (coronary)

Coronary Care Unit (CCU), 125–126,
130–131
spouse of cardiac patient in. *See*
Spouse, in-hospital treatment of
cardiac

Coronary heart disease (CHD), 3–4,
16–40
acute syndromes, 32–40
arrhythmia, ventricular, 37–40
myocardial infarction (MI), acute,
33–36, 133–134, 147–150
non-Q MI, 36
sudden cardiac death (SCD),
38–40

White blood cells, 17
Women and coronary heart disease, 197–211
    prevalence, 198, 199
    prognosis/rehabilitation, 208–209
    Project New Life, 304–307
    recommendations, 210–211
    risk factors, 200–205
        depression, 204
        Framingham Heart Study, findings of, 201–202
        hostility, 202–204
        job strain, 202
        social support/isolation, 202

        Type A behavior, 203, 204
        vital exhaustion, 204–205
    stressful life events, role of, 205
    and Type A behavior pattern, 305, 306
    treatment, 207–208
    triggers of acute onset of coronary events, 205–207
Women's Health Initiative, 210
World Health Organization, 255

Zaroxolyn (metolazone), 60
Zestril (lisinopril), 57, 414
Zocor (simvastatin), 58, 415, 416
Zoloft (sertraline), 405, 406

ABOUT THE EDITORS

Robert Allan, PhD, is Clinical Assistant Professor of Psychology in Medicine and Psychiatry as well as Co-Founder and Co-Director of the Coronary Risk Reduction Program at The New York Hospital–Cornell Medical Center (NYH-CMC) in New York City. His practice specialty is the psychological treatment of cardiac patients and their families.

Allan earned his BA from Queens College, City University of New York, and his PhD in clinical psychology from New York University. After receiving his PhD, Allan took a position playing keyboards in a band at the Concord Hotel in the Catskill Mountains of New York. Subsequently, he studied music at the Juilliard School and spent 10 years performing popular music before returning to the fold of psychology.

Allan established the first stress reduction group program for cardiac patients in the New York metropolitan area in 1982 at the Nassau County chapter of the American Heart Association. He currently leads stress reduction support groups at NYH-CMC Cardiac Health Centers in Manhattan and Queens and at the 92nd Street YM-YWHA. In addition, he is site coordinator for the Determinants of Time of Myocardial Infarction Onset Study at NYH-CMC. Allan is also a member of the Board of Advisors of the National Institute for the Clinical Application of Behavioral Medicine.

Stephen Scheidt, MD, is Professor of Clinical Medicine, Director of the Cardiology Training Program at Cornell University Medical College, as well as Co-Founder and Co-Director of the Coronary Risk Reduction Program at The New York Hospital–Cornell Medical Center (NYH-CMC).

Scheidt earned a BA from Princeton University, was a Fulbright Fellow in Biochemistry at the University of Wurzburg, Germany, and received an MD from Columbia University College of Physicians and Surgeons. He has been a full-time faculty member at NYH-CMC for the past 26 years.

He has served as President of the New York Cardiological Society, as the New York Governor of the American College of Cardiology, and as Vice-President of the American Heart Association. He was also Principal Investigator for the Myocardial Infarction Research Unit at NYH-CMC. Scheidt has also held several administrative posts at Cornell University, including Associate Dean for Student Affairs and Assistant Dean for Continuing Medical Education from 1975 to 1994. He is a Fellow of the American College of Cardiology, the American College of Physicians, and the American Heart Association's Council on Clinical Cardiology.

Scheidt has authored more than 150 articles in cardiology and a book on basic electrocardiography with Dr. Frank Netter; he is also senior editor of *Cardiovascular Reviews & Reports* and the *American Journal of Geriatric Cardiology*. An internationally known cardiologist, since 1993 Scheidt has directed the Salzburg–Cornell Seminars: an annual collaborative program with the American–Austrian and Soros Foundations that brings state-of-the-art American medicine to Central and Eastern European physicians. He also serves on the Board of Directors of the New York State Peer Review Organization and Empire Blue Cross/Blue Shield of New York.